Why Do You Need This New Edition?

If you're wondering why you should buy this new edition of *Social Psychology*, here are 10 good reasons!

D1394607

1. Engaging online resources to help you succeed! The new MyPsychLab provides you with online study resources to help make your study time more effective, it includes: Pearson eText, Audio Text, a personalized study plan to help you succeed in the course, and more.

2. A brand new chapter: Chapter 12, "Social Psychology: A Guide to Dealing with Adversity and Achieving a Happy Life." This new chapter explores research by social psychologists that offers insights into the causes and effects of personal adversity and suggests means to overcoming it for a rich and meaningful life.

3. New feature essay: "EMOTIONS and . . . ." Appearing in every chapter, these new essays emphasize recent research on emotion, ensuring that coverage of this important topic is integrated into every chapter. Some examples include: "Cultural Differences in Inferring Others' Emotions," "Emotional Contagion," and "Mood, Feelings of Elevation, and Helping."

4. New feature essay: "SOCIAL LIFE in a CONNECTED WORLD." Appearing in every chapter, these new essays show how the discipline of social psychology is working to understand the nature and scope of the recent dramatic changes we are facing in our social world brought about by the Internet and a vast array of electronic devices that connect people to each other in many new ways. Some examples include: "Breaking Up Is Hard to Do, But Help Is Available," "Working with Others via Computer-Mediated Communication," and "Electronic Word-of-Mouth: Marketing and Persuasion."

5. Every chapter is updated with new research, new findings, and new theoretical perspectives; instructors will include this information on your exams.

6. Chapter 3, "Social Perception," includes: A new section on scent as a nonverbal clues a new discussion of fate attributions (concluding that negative events were somehow "meant to be"); and a new section on the accuracy of first impressions.

7. Chapter 4, "The Self," includes: New research which addresses the question of whether or not others close to us can predict our behavior better than we can; new research on why introspection fails (why we apparently don't know that spending our money on others makes us happier than spending it on ourselves); and a new section on how people can successfully engage in self control.

8. Chapter 7, "Interpersonal Attraction, Close Relationships, and Love" includes: A new section examining recent findings on the attractive properties of the color red; a new discussion of what we seek in romantic partners; and new data on the use of cooperative strategies in mate selection and attraction.

9. Chapter 8, "Social Influence," includes: New information on "facades" of conformity (instances in which people pretend to conform in order to make a good impression); a new section on "How much do we conform?"; and an entirely new section on why we choose, sometimes, not to go along with others.

10. Chapter 10, "Aggression," includes: New research on the effects of social exclusion as a cause of aggression; recent findings on the effects of exposure to media violence and playing violent video games; and new research on sexual jealousy and its foundations in evolutionary processes.

PEARSON

REGENTS UNIVERSITY LONDON WITHDRAWN

REGENTS COLLEGE LIBRARY

61000613

THIRTEENTH EDITION

Social **Psychology**

Robert A. Baron

Oklahoma State University

Nyla R. Branscombe

University of Kansas

PEARSON

Boston · Columbus · Indianapolis · New York · San Francisco · Upper Saddle River
Amsterdam · Cape Town · Dubai · London · Madrid · Milan · Munich · Paris · Montreal · Toronto
Delhi · Mexico City · Sao Paulo · Sydney · Hong Kong · Seoul · Singapore · Taipei · Tokyo

Editorial Director: Craig Campanella
Editor in Chief: Jessica Mosher
Executive Editor: Jeff Marshall
Senior Sponsoring Editor: Amber Mackey
Editorial Assistant: Samantha Solano
VP, Director of Marketing: Brandy Dawson
Executive Marketing Manager: Jeanette Koskinas
Marketing Manager: Nicole Kunzmann
Managing Editor: Maureen Richardson
Project Manager, Production: Shelly Kupperman
Operations Supervisor: Mary Fischer
Operations Specialist: Diane Peirano
Director: Blair Brown
Art Director: Jodi Notowitz
Interior Designer: Ilze Lemesis
Director, Digital Media: Brian Hyland
Senior Digital Media Editor: Michael Halas
Full-Service Project Management and Composition: Amy L. Saucier, Laserwords
Printer/Binder: R.R. Donnelley & Sons
Cover Printer: R.R. Donnelley & Sons
Text Font: Janson Text 9.75/12

Credits and acknowledgments borrowed from other sources and reproduced, with permission,
in this textbook appear on page 483.

"If you purchased this book within the United States or Canada you should be aware that it has been
imported without the approval of the Publisher or the Author".

Copyright © 2012, 2008, 2006 by Pearson Education, Inc.
All rights reserved. Printed in the United States of America. This publication is protected
by Copyright and permission should be obtained from the publisher prior to any prohibited
reproduction, storage in a retrieval system, or transmission in any form or by any means, electronic,
mechanical, photocopying, recording, or likewise. To obtain permission(s) to use material from
this work, please submit a written request to Pearson Education, Inc., Permissions Department,
One Lake Street, Upper Saddle River, New Jersey 07458 or you may fax your request to 201-236-3290.

10 9 8 7 6 5 4 3 2 1

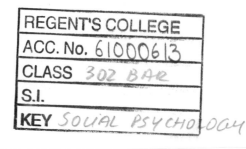
REGENT'S COLLEGE
ACC. No. 61000613
CLASS 302 BAR
S.I.
KEY SOCIAL PSYCHOLOGY

PEARSON

P.I.E. ISBN-10:   0-205-23199-3
P.I.E. ISBN-13:   978-0-205-23199-7

Dedication

To Donn Byrne, my truest lifelong friend;
Rebecca, the essential ingredient in my happiness,
And Jessica, Ted, Samantha, and Melissa, the heart of my small family

—Robert A. Baron

To Rose Croxall, Howard Branscombe, Marlene Boyd, and Elaine Haase—
all of whom have known and cared about me the longest. Here's to surviving
and overcoming the hardships!

—Nyla R. Branscombe

Brief **Contents**

Contents

3 Social Perception
Perceiving and Understanding Others   68

4 # The Self
Answering the Question "Who Am I?"   **102**

7 # Interpersonal Attraction, Close Relationships, and Love   214

8 Social Influence
Changing Others' Behavior   252

9 Prosocial Behavior
Helping Others   288

10 Aggression
Its Nature, Causes, and Control   **320**

11 Groups and Individuals
The Consequences of Belonging   **358**

12 Social Psychology
A Guide to Dealing with Adversity and Achieving a Happy Life   **396**

Special **Features**

EMOTIONS *and* . . .

SOCIAL LIFE *in a* CONNECTED WORLD

Preface

Social Life
(and Social Psychology) in the
Connected World

"The thing that we are trying to do at facebook is just help people connect and communicate more efficiently."
—*Mark Zuckerberg, founder of Facebook.*

"I want to put a ding in the universe."
—*Steve Jobs, Apple Computer*

"As we go forward, I hope we're going to continue…
to make really big differences in how people live and work."
—*Sergey Brin, co-founder of Google.*

*T*he goals stated in these quotations are truly impressive ones—producing basic changes in the ways people live, work, and relate to others—or, as Steve Jobs put it, *in everything* (the universe!). And, as you know, these goals have indeed been met—to "google" something has become a verb in everyday language and Facebook use is almost as common as cell phone use. In fact, just try to imagine life without your iPod, computer, wireless internet access, GPS in your car and on your phone, or the many forms of social media we use practically every day. Probably you cannot, because this technology has become woven into the very fabric of our lives so that we take our electronic gadgets for granted and use them as if they are extensions of ourselves. So the founders of Google, Facebook, Apple Computers, and many other high-tech companies have in fact attained their ambitious goals of changing how people live—all over the globe.

Clearly, then, the world—and the social world that is the primary focus of this book—have changed tremendously in recent years, perhaps more quickly and dramatically than at any time in the past. Further—and a key point we'll emphasize throughout the book—these changes have important implications for the social side of life, and for *social psychology*, the branch of psychology that studies all aspects of our behavior with and toward others, our feelings and thoughts about them, and the relationships we develop with them. The central message for social psychology as a field, and for any book that seeks to represent it, is simple: **Keep up with these social and technological changes or become irrelevant—or even worse—an obstacle to continued change.**

We're happy to report that as we move deeper into the 21st century, social psychology is in *no* danger of becoming obsolete or a barrier to continued social change. On the contrary, it continues to be the vibrant, adaptable field it has always been and, we predict, always will be. The scope of social psychological research (and knowledge) has expanded rapidly in the past few years (even, in fact, since publication of the previous edition of this book), and our field, far from blocking or resisting the many change now occurring all over the world, continues to embrace it fully. This commitment to change, and to an optimistic view of human nature, is reflected in comments by Donn Byrne (a well-known social psychologist and a former co-author of the first twelve editions of this textbook). When we asked him to explain why he was attracted to social psychology in the first place, here's how he replied:

> *"When I was a child, I wanted to become a physician . . . but two months before classes as medical school were to begin, my father had a heart attack and I had to change my plans. I . . . decided to pursue graduate studies in psychology . . . Like many psychology majors, I was attracted to the idea of becoming a clinical psychologist, but once I was a student, and began working on research, I found that my interests clearly involved social rather than clinical psychology. My first research project dealt with the way in which friendships are formed in a college classroom. I found that the primary variable was physical proximity and not race, religion, college major, or other seemingly important factors. When seats are assigned randomly (or alphabetically), any two students who sit side-by-side are likely to become acquainted—and subsequently friends. I found it both interesting and surprising that a student's social life could be determined in part by an instructor's seating chart.*
>
> *This first attempt at research (and my first publication) should have provided a clue that my future would not be as a clinician, but I stuck to my original plan and earned a Ph.D. degree in clinical psychology. Over the next few years, though, I slowly realized that my true interests, which focused mainly on interpersonal attraction, were in social psychology.*
>
> *What fascinated me then—and still does—is the fact that social psychology uses scientific methods to investigate such topics as friendship formation, prejudice, sexual behavior, aggression, and attitude formation. Further, it offers the possibility of new discoveries that challenge long-held beliefs. Do opposites attract? Research findings answer "Probably not," but they do confirm that birds of a feather tend to flock together (similarity is the basis for attraction and friendship). So scientific methods can greatly increase our understanding of the social side of life, just as, in other fields, they have revealed that the sun doesn't revolve around the earth and that malaria isn't caused by breathing "bad night air" but by a microbe carried by mosquitoes buzzing through the air. In any event, I hope that this brief sampling of my personal experiences will persuade you to consider two things:*
>
> 1. *You do not need to be overly concerned about choosing a major or agonizing about what you want to be "when you grow up." Unpredictable and unexpected events can prove to be much more important in determining your future than your best laid plans.*
> 2. *Try to sample many different fields when you sign up for college courses and sample as many job possibilities as you can by means of internships and volunteer work. You might surprise yourself by pursuing an unexpected career that you find both interesting and fulfilling. I know that I did."*

Now, back to our goals for this new edition. In essence, what we tried to accomplish is this: illustrate just how well our field has—and does—adjust to and reflect the changing social world. And changing it truly *is!* Who, even ten years ago, would have imagined an iPod? Kindles? That your cell phone could become your airline boarding pass? That 700,000,000 people world-wide would be active on Facebook? Or that "smart phones" would be able to do everything from finding a nearby restaurant to taking and sending photos almost instantaneously? And considering the "downside" of this technological revolution, who would have imagined that sending text messages would become so popular that many drivers do it even in heavy traffic, thus putting themselves and other drivers at great risk? Or, that persons jilted by their lovers would seek to "punish" them by sending damaging information or even sexually explicit photos of them, over the Internet? Truly, few, if any would have predicted these trends, because the rate at which technology is currently changing is staggering to behold, and every year brings a new array of innovative products, services, and high-tech "toys." But technology is not simply changing the way we carry out certain tasks: it is also changing the way we live and—most importantly—the nature of the social side of life. Yes, *love, aggression, persuasion,* and other basic aspects of social life remain, in essence, unchanged. But the ways in which they are *expressed* and *experienced*, have changed drastically.

So, how, precisely, did we set out to reflect these major trends while, at the same time, fully and accurately reflecting the core of our field—the knowledge and insights that social psychologists have gathered through decades of systematic research? Below is a summary of the major steps we took to accomplish these important goals.

Changes in Content: An Entirely New Chapter

Social Psychology: A Guide to Dealing with Adversity and Achieving a Happy Life (Chapter 12)

This is an ambitious-sounding title—one suggesting that social psychology can help *you* to deal with the "downside" of life and move toward personal happiness. That's a tall order, but we believe that our field can indeed offer a great deal in this respect. Here's how we introduce this new chapter (Chapter 12):

> "*. . . most people seek and expect to be happy: they want to overcome the adversities they experience and go on to enjoy a life that is not only happy, but meaningful, too. The journey to that goal is never easy, and along the way, most of us do encounter problems and obstacles. Can social psychology help us to handle these setbacks and to become what are often described as flourishing, happy people? We believe that it can. In fact, we believe that the knowledge acquired by social psychologists is invaluable in this respect: if carefully applied, it can help us turn adversity into strength, achievement, and contentment . . . *"

Why do we hold this view? Because, and again, in our own words:

> "*. . . research by social psychologists offers important insights into the causes and effects of personal adversity, and suggests important means for overcoming it on the way to a rich, fulfilling life. In this chapter, we'll summarize some of these contributions. In other words, we'll provide an overview of some of the important ways in which social psychology—with its scientific approach to the social side of life—can help us attain key personal goals. . . . *"

This new chapter then goes on to describe what we know about major causes of *social adversity* (e.g., loneliness, the devastating effects of social relationships that "go bad," social causes of obesity). We then examine how, based on social psychology's findings, the legal system can be made more fair and effective. Perhaps most important of all—in this chapter we examine the nature and causes of *happiness*. In discussing each of these topics, we describe what social psychologists, with their scientific approach and methods, have discovered, and how each of us can put this knowledge to use in our own lives so that we can move toward the happiness and satisfaction we desire. We believe that this is an important addition to the text, and is fully consistent with the optimistic, flexible, open-minded credo social psychology, as a field, has always embraced.

Changes in Content Within Each of the Other Chapters

Continuing a long tradition in which each edition of this textbook has included literally dozens of new topics, this 13th edition is indeed "new". In every chapter we present new lines of research, new findings, and new theoretical perspectives. Here is a partial list of the new topics included:

CHAPTER 1

- Vastly increased attention to the "connected world" in which we live throughout—especially, in a new section entitled: "The Search for Basic Principles in a Changing Social World."
- Many new examples throughout, several of which focus on the "connected world" such as "Facebook," humiliating others via e-mail and web, etc.

CHAPTER 2

- New research on the role of availability in self and other judgments was added, as is new research on cross-cultural differences in use of the representativeness heuristic. An entirely new section on the status quo bias—judging choices and objects that have been around longer as better—was added.
- A new section on reasoning by metaphor and its implications for social thought and behavior is included. A new table summarizes the many effects that metaphor priming can have.
- New research on optimism and overconfidence has been added and that whole section has been substantially updated. The counter factual thinking section was also updated.

CHAPTER 3

- A new section on scent as a nonverbal cue.
- A new discussion of fate attributions—concluding that negative events were somehow "meant to be."
- A new section on the accuracy of first impressions.

CHAPTER 4

- New research addresses the question of whether others close to you can predict our behavior better than we can.
- New research on why introspection fails, and particularly why we apparently don't know that spending our money on others makes us happier than spending it on ourselves.
- New section concerning how people can successfully engage in self-control, and the consequences of the depletion of self-control.

CHAPTER 5

- New research concerning attitude formation based on consumer-generated product reviews of online purchases—how electronic word-of-mouth works.
- New research addresses how parents' form attitudes toward new vaccines and the decision processes they go through in deciding whether to have their children vaccinated.
- New research considers how going to college and entering new social networks affects political attitudes.

CHAPTER 6

- New coverage of the growth of hate groups on the Web and the reasons why this is so.
- New research concerning the "glass cliff" and when women are especially likely to make it to the top.
- New research concerning how people manage to maintain an image of themselves as unprejudiced at the same time that they act in a prejudiced manner.

CHAPTER 7

- A new section examines recent findings concerning the attractive properties of the color red.
- New discussion of what we seek in romantic partners, and especially, how this is influenced by the social roles we expect to play (provider, homemaker).
- New data on the use of cooperative strategies in mate selection and attraction.
- A new discussion of the nature and impact of secret romances has been added.

CHAPTER 8

- New information on when people pretend to conform in order to make a good impression, and how much do we conform is now included.
- An entirely new section on why we choose, sometimes, *not* to go along—the effects of power, basic motives, and the desire for uniqueness.
- A discussion of a recent replication of Milgram's classic research on obedience is now included.

CHAPTER 9

- A new section examines factors that reduce the tendency to help others (e.g., social exclusion, darkness, or thinking about our time in economic terms, as attorneys often do).
- A new section on *defensive helping* has been added to the discussion of motives underlying prosocial behavior.
- A new section examines factors that increase or reduce the tendency to help others. This includes discussion of the effects of playing prosocial video games, and gratitude.

CHAPTER 10

- New research on the effects of *social exclusion* as a cause of aggression.
- Recent findings on the effects of exposure to media violence and playing violent video games has been included.
- New research on sexual jealousy, and its foundations in evolutionary processes, is now presented.
- A new discussion of the male gender role ("precarious manhood") and its effects on aggression.

CHAPTER 11

- A new section on "emotion norms" in different groups is now included.
- New research on cohesion in groups has been added.
- New research on "feeling misunderstood" by others during conflicts among different ethnic groups.
- A whole new section on leadership in groups.

CHAPTER 12

- This is an entirely new chapter. The primary emphasis is on how social psychological research can help people achieve a happy and meaningful life.

New Special Features

To fully reflect current trends in social psychological research and the field's responsiveness to social change, we now include two new kinds of special sections—ones that were **not** present in the previous edition. These are as follows:

EMOTIONS *and ...*

These new sections emphasize recent work on emotion and assure that this important topic is present in *every* chapter. We think this is much better than including a special chapter on emotion, as other texts about social psychology have done, because it integrates this important topic with all of social psychology. Some examples:

- A new **EMOTIONS** section on cultural differences in inferring others' emotions.
- A new **EMOTIONS** section on the role of emotion in attraction.
- A new **EMOTIONS** section concerning the stress that can occur when groups merge (i.e., corporate mergers).
- A new **EMOTIONS** section on when people are willing to die and kill for their group.
- A new **EMOTIONS** section on when advertisements that use emotions to sell are effective and when they are not.
- A new **EMOTIONS** section on whether positive self-talk improves mood and happiness with the self.

EMOTIONS *and* **SOCIAL PERCEPTION**

Why We Can't Always Predict Our Responses to Tragedy

Would you feel worse if you learned that one person was killed in a forest fire, or if you learned that 1,000 people were? Most people believe that they would feel worse upon learning about the large-scale tragedy compared to the smaller-scale one. Yet, much research indicates that our **affective forecasts**—predictions about how we would feel about an event we have not experienced—are often inaccurate (Dunn & Laham, 2006). To the extent that our cognition (affective forecasts) is based on a different way of processing information compared to actual emotional experience, these two types of responses—forecasting and experiencing—should differ. Because rational cognition is responsive to abstract symbols, including numbers, forecasting should vary depending on the scale of the tragedy being considered. Emotions, in contrast, which are based on concrete images and immediate experiences, may be relatively insensitive to the actual numbers of people killed, or more generally the scope of a tragedy.

To test this idea—that affective forecasting will be responsive to numbers, but that people who are actually experiencing the images from a tragedy will show an "emotional flatline" as the death toll increases, Dunn and Ashton-James (2008) conducted a number of studies. In one experiment, one group of participants was placed in the "experiencer role"; they were given a news article

about a deadly forest fire in Spain and were asked to report their actual emotions while reading about the tragedy. Another group of participants was placed in the "forecaster role" and they were simply asked to predict how they would feel "if they read about a deadly forest fire in Spain." The scope of the tragedy of the fire was also varied. Some participants were told that five people had been killed, while other participants were told that 10,000 people had been killed by the fire.

Did the size of the tragedy affect how bad participants actually reported feeling in the experience condition or they expected to feel in the forecasting condition? Yes, the size of the tragedy did affect how forecasters expected to feel, but the number of people killed in the fire did *not* affect how people actually reported feeling. Not only did forecasters overestimate how bad they would feel overall, but they believed they would be responsive to the magnitude of the tragedy whereas those who were actually exposed to the tragic loss information showed a "flatline" response and did not differentiate their emotional response according to numbers.

In a subsequent study, these researchers brought the tragedy closer to home—the victims were members of their own group. Students were told that either 15 or 500 American college students had been killed in the war in Iraq, and pictures of the sort shown in Figure 2.15 were presented to

FIGURE 2.15 Emotional Responses to the Tragedy of One or Many
People who are asked to forecast how they would feel about the tragic deaths of others believed they would feel worse as the number of people killed increased. However, people who were actually given the detailed information to read or view felt about the same regardless of how many people had died. This research is consistent with the idea that rational information processing, which occurs in forecasting, differs from actual emotional

- A new **EMOTIONS** section on emotional contagion.
- A new **EMOTIONS** section focuses on the effects of mood on willingness to help others
- A new **EMOTIONS** section on happiness that considers the question "Can people be too happy?

SOCIAL LIFE *in a* **CONNECTED WORLD**

The Use of Social Influence Tactics by Scammers on the Web—Internet Daters, Beware!

Ads for Internet dating services often show happy couples who started wonderful long-term relationships through their service (see Figure 8.15). Such couples certainly do exist and in fact, many people believe that Internet dating services fill important needs. But *watch out!*—they are also a place where ruthless people who seek to prey upon unsuspecting victims through the use of various tactics of social influence sometimes operate (Joinson, McKenna, Postmes, & Reips, 2007). Consider, for instance, the true case of Annette, one young woman who sought her perfect mate through Eharmony.com, a well-known and widely used dating service (this story was reported on eIAMB.org, a web page that specializes in unmasking scams on the Internet). Annette soon found someone who seemed just right: a 41-year-old Christian engineer named John from California who was working in Nigeria, accompanied by his daughter Hailey (eIAMB.org, June 27, 2010). Over several months, Annette communicated frequently with John and gradually built up what was, for her, a very appealing online relationship. The only problem was that just as he was about to return to the United States for a happy meeting with Annette, John—who was supposedly quite wealthy—experienced a series of major setbacks. First, his luggage containing all his traveler's checks was impounded at the airport. This meant that he didn't have enough funds to pay for tickets for himself and his daughter. Could Annette wire him $1,300? Thinking "He must really need the money—it's not a large amount," she did. But that was just the start. John then learned that he'd have to bribe the customs officials to release his luggage; that would cost several thousands more. And then the worst thing of all happened: his daughter Hailey was kidnapped and held for ransom. Could Annette help again? The upshot was that ultimately Annette sent "John" more than $40,000. She only stopped when she had nothing

left to send. Her family was shocked because Annette had always been a level-headed and stable person; how did she fall victim to this confidence artist who, of course, never existed—his identity and everything about him was manufactured by the person seeking to work this swindle.

The answer is complex, involving many principles of compliance. John started with a small request and only after it was granted, moved to larger ones later—the foot-in-the-door tactic. He also used guilt against Annette, writing, "If you don't give me the money, it means you don't love me." And he put pressure on his victim by indicating that if she didn't help immediately, he'd be unable to get out of Nigeria and come to see her. There's more, too, but as you can see, swindlers like this use effective compliance tactics when seeking victims through Internet dating services.

Annette's case is a real one, but it is only one of many because scams involving Internet dating appear to use basic techniques for gaining compliance from the victims that are well known to social psychologists. This means that you should always be cautious when using such services.

FIGURE 8.15   Internet Dating Services: Potential Benefits, Real Risks
Internet dating services often run ads like this one, showing happy couples who met and formed long-term relationships on their network. Such happy outcomes certainly occur, but watch out! There are unprincipled criminals out there just waiting to lure into a situation where you trust them enough to send them money. You'll never meet them—and in fact, they don't exist as described in their profiles, but you'll also never see your money again, either.

SOCIAL LIFE *in a* CONNECTED WORLD

These special sections emphasize the basic theme in the title of this Preface, and the fact that the social world *has* changed greatly in recent years, and they illustrate how social psychology is attempting to understand the nature and scope of these effects. Some examples:

- A new **SOCIAL LIFE** *in a* **CONNECTED WORLD** section focuses on the use of technology to end romantic relationships (e-mail, text messages, Internet break-up services).
- A new **SOCIAL LIFE** *in a* **CONNECTED WORLD** section on attribution and computer-mediated communication.
- A new **SOCIAL LIFE** *in a* **CONNECTED WORLD** section on working with people over the Internet that you have never met in real life.
- A new **SOCIAL LIFE** *in a* **CONNECTED WORLD** section on how gender is portrayed and enacted in video games.
- A new **SOCIAL LIFE** *in a* **CONNECTED WORLD** feature on the effects of social networking experience for offline social interaction.
- A new **SOCIAL LIFE** *in a* **CONNECTED WORLD** section on the use of social influence tactics by scammers on the Web, in the context of Internet dating.
- A new **SOCIAL LIFE** *in a* **THE CONNECTED WORLD** section that focuses on helping through the Internet—by providing small loans in developing countries.
- A new **SOCIAL LIFE** *in a* **CONNECTED WORLD** addressing how the Internet can help people lose weight

Features to Help You Learn About Social Psychology

Any textbook is good only to the extent that it is both useful and interesting to the students using it. To make this edition even better for students, we have included several student aids—features designed to enhance the book's appeal and usefulness. Included among these features are the following:

Chapter Openings Linked to Important Trends and Events in Society

All chapters begin with examples or events reflecting current trends and events in society—and in many cases, reflecting technological changes. A few examples:

- Facebook as a medium for presenting ourselves to others (Chapter 4)

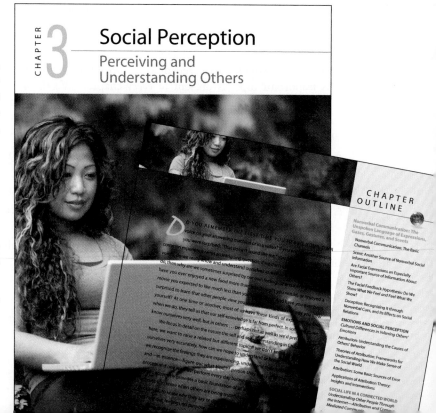

CHAPTER **3**

Social Perception
Perceiving and Understanding Others

CHAPTER OUTLINE

- Proposing marriage over the Internet (Chapter 7)
- Persuasion and scams on the Internet (Chapter 8)
- Aggression via the Web (e.g., sending damaging information to others) (Chapter 10)
- The role of decision-making groups in recent disasters (e.g., the oil spill of 2010 in the Gulf of Mexico) (Chapter 11)

Key Points

Every major section ends with a brief review of the key points covered.

End-of-Chapter Summaries

Each chapter ends with a summary that recaps the key points covered.

Special Labels on All Graphs and Charts

To make these easy to understand, we have continued to use the "special labels" that are a unique feature of this book.

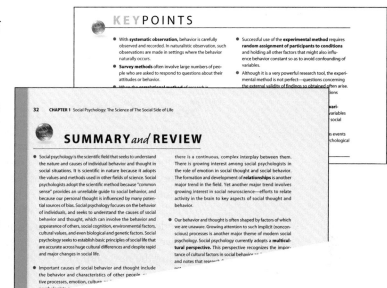

Supplementary Materials

All excellent texts are supported by a complete package of supplementary material, both for the students and the instructor. This text offers a full array of such aids including:

MyPsychLab

MyPsychLab (*www.mypsychlab.com*) combines proven learning applications with powerful online assessment to engage students, assess their learning, and help them succeed. *MyPsychLab* provides engaging experiences that personalize, stimulate, and measure learning for each student. And, it comes from a trusted partner with educational expertise and a deep commitment to helping students, instructors, and departments achieve their goals. *MyPsychLab* can be used by itself or linked to any learning management system.

Instructor's Manual (ISBN 0-205-20630-1)

The *Instructor's Manual* has been updated and improved to accompany the 13th edition. It includes chapter learning objectives, key terms, detailed chapter outlines, both classic and innovative lecture launchers, and out-of-class assignments and handouts. Each lecture and activity idea is linked to a specific learning objective.

Test Item File (ISBN 0-205-22690-6) and MyTest (ISBN 0-205-22691-4)

The *Test Item File* is composed of approximately 2,000 fully referenced multiple-choice, completion (fill-in-the-blank), short answer, and essay questions. Each question can be viewed by level of difficulty and skill types. The *Test Item File* is also available with *MyTest* software, a web-based test-generating software program which provides instructors "best-in-class" features in an easy to use program. Create tests and easily select questions with drag-and-drop or point-and-click functionality. Add or modify test questions using the built-in *Question Editor* and print tests in a variety of formats. The program comes with technical support.

PowerPoint Presentation (ISBN 0-205-20631-X)

The *PowerPoint* slides provide an active format for presenting concepts from each chapter and incorporating relevant figures and tables.

Classroom Response System (ISBN 0-205-86715-4)

The *Classroom Response System (CRS)* facilitates class participation in lectures and provides a method of measuring student comprehension with activities like student polling and in-class quizzes. *CRS* allows instructors to pose question to their students by using text-specific *PowerPoint* slides. Students reply using handheld transmitters called "clickers" which capture and immediately display student responses. These responses are saved in the system grade book and can be exported to learning management systems.

Some Concluding Words

Looking back over the changes we've made for this 13th edition, we truly believe we have done everything possible to make this edition the best one yet! We sought to create a textbook that fully captures the extent to which modern social psychology reflects, and embraces, the major changes now occurring in the social side of life. But, only *you* our colleagues and the students who use this textbook can tell us to what extent we have succeeded. So please do send us your comments, reactions, and suggestions. As in the past, we will listen to them very carefully, and do our best to use them constructively in planning the next edition.

Our warm regards and thanks!

Nyla R. Branscombe
nyla@ku.edu

Robert A. Baron
robert.baron@okstate.edu

Acknowledgments

WORDS OF THANKS

Now that the hard work of preparing a new edition is mostly behind us, we want to take this opportunity to thank the many talented and dedicated people whose help throughout the process has been truly invaluable.

First, our sincere thanks to the colleagues listed below who reviewed the 12th edition, and offered their suggestions for ways in which it could be improved. Their input was invaluable to us in planning this new edition: Greg Nichols, University of Kansas; William Goggin, University of Southern Mississippi; Michelle LaBrie, College of the Canyons; Badrinath Rao, Kettering University; Peter Spiegel, California State University, San Bernardino; Jennifer Zimmerman, DePaul University; Sarah Wood, University of Wisconsin - Stout; Maya Aloni, University at Buffalo, SUNY.

Second, we wish to offer our personal thanks to our editors at Pearson. It has been a true pleasure to work with Susan Hartman, Jeff Marshall, and Amber Mackey. Their helpful suggestions and good judgment were matched only by their enthusiasm and support for the book. We look forward to working with them for many years to come.

Third, our thanks to Peggy Flanagan, and Shelly Kupperman for handling production management. Special thanks are due to Amy Saucier who handled an incredible array of details and tasks with tremendous skill—and lots of patience for the authors! In addition, we wish to thank Naomi Kornhauser for an outstanding job in photo research, and to Ilze Lemesis and Leslie Osher for an excellent interior design and a very attractive cover.

We also wish to offer our thanks to the many colleagues who provided reprints and preprints of their work, and to the many students who kindly shared their thoughts about the prior edition of this textbook with us. These individuals are too numerous to list here, but their input is gratefully acknowledged.

Finally, our sincere thanks to everyone who worked on the supplements, for outstanding work on the Instructor's Manual, for the help in preparing the Study Guide, and for the help in preparing the Test Bank. To all of these truly outstanding people, and to many others too, our warmest personal regards and thanks.

—Robert A. Baron & Nyla R. Branscombe

About the **Authors**

Robert A. Baron is the Spears Professor of Entrepreneurship at Oklahoma State University. He received his Ph.D. in social psychology from the University of Iowa (1968). Professor Baron has held faculty appointments at Rensselaer Polytechnic Institute, Purdue, the Universities of Minnesota, Texas, South Carolina, Washington, Princeton University, and Oxford University. From 1979–1981 he was the Program Director for Social and Developmental Psychology at NSF. In 2001 he was appointed as a Visiting Senior Research Fellow by the French Ministry of Research (Universite de Toulouse & LIRHE). Professor Baron is a Fellow of APA and a Charter Fellow of APS. He has published more than 120 articles and 45 chapters, and is the author or co-author of 49 books in psychology and management. He serves on the boards of several major journals, and has received numerous awards for his research (e.g., "Thought Leader" award, Entrepreneurship Division, Academy of Management, 2009). He holds three U.S. patents and was founder and CEO of IEP, Inc. (1993–2000). His current research interests focus on applying the findings and principles of social psychology to the field of entrepreneurship, where he has studied such topics as the role of perception in opportunity recognition, how entrepreneurs' social skills influence their success, and the role of positive affect in entrepreneurship.

Nyla R. Branscombe is Professor of Psychology at University of Kansas. She received her B.A. from York University in Toronto, M.A. from the University of Western Ontario, and Ph.D. from Purdue University. She has served as Associate Editor for *Personality and Social Psychology Bulletin*, *British Journal of Social Psychology*, and *Group Processes and Intergroup Relations*.

Professor Branscombe has published more than 120 articles and chapters, has been co-recipient of the Otto Kleinberg prize for research on Intercultural and International Relations, and the 1996 and 2001 *Society of Personality and Social Psychology Publication Award*. She co-edited the 2004 volume "*Collective Guilt: International Perspectives*," published by Cambridge University Press, the 2007 volume "*Commemorating Brown: The Social Psychology of Racism and Discrimination*," published by the American Psychological Association, and the 2010 volume "*Rediscovering Social Identity*," published by Psychology Press.

Professor Branscombe's current research focuses on two main issues: the psychology of historically privileged groups—when and why they may feel collective guilt, and the psychology of disadvantaged groups—particularly how they cope with discrimination. She gratefully acknowledges ongoing research support from the *Canadian Institute for Advanced Research: Social Interactions, Identity, and Well-Being Program*.

Social
Psychology

CHAPTER 1

Social Psychology

The Science of the Social Side of Life

"LIFE," NOBEL PRIZE–WINNING AUTHOR ERNEST HEMINGWAY OFTEN SAID, "is a moveable feast." What he meant by these words (which he also used as the title of his memoirs) is this: life, like a feast, offers something for everyone, all tastes and preferences. And, like a feast, life presents many options, spreading an ever-shifting mixture of experiences before us—some filled with delight and joy, whereas others entail loss and sorrow.

Now, please take a small step back from the "moveable feast" that is *your* life, and consider the following question: "What is the most important or central aspect of it—the part most intimately linked to your hopes, plans, dreams, and happiness?" Is it your work, either in school or in a job? Your hobbies? Your religious or political beliefs? All these are important parts of our lives, but we believe that if you think about this question more deeply, you will conclude that in fact, the most important aspect of your life is other people: your family, friends, boyfriend, girlfriend, roommates, class-mates, professors, boss, coworkers, sports teammates—all the people you care about and with whom you interact. Do you still have lingering doubts on this score? Then try, for a moment, to imagine life in total isolation from others, as shown in movies such as *WALL-E*—the story of an intelligent robot left entirely alone on a deserted planet Earth (Figure 1.1). Would such a life, lived in total isolation, with no attachments to other people, no love, and no groups to which you belong, have any meaning? Would it even be worth living? While there are no firm answers to such questions, we do know that many people find the thought of such an isolated existence to be disturbing. Still have doubts? Then try to remember the last time your cell phone wasn't working or you lost access to Facebook, Twitter, or other social networks. How did it feel to be out of contact? Not pleasant, we're sure; and that's why it isn't surprising when we walk across campus and see many people texting and talking into their cell phones. Social contact *is* a central aspect of our lives, and in a very basic sense, defines who we are and the quality of our existence.

So now, get ready for an exciting journey, because the social side of life is the focus of this entire book. And we promise that the scope of this journey will be very broad indeed. But what precisely *is* social psychology? Basically, it's the branch of psychology that studies all aspects of our social existence—everything from attrac-tion, love, and helping on the one hand, to prejudice, exclusion, and violence on the other—plus everything in between. In addition, of course, social psychologists also investigate how groups influence us, as well as the nature and role of social

FIGURE 1.1 Would Life in Isolation Be Worth Living?
Can you imagine what it would be like to live entirely alone, having no contact with others? In the film "WALL-E," an intelligent (and very human) robot faced this situation—and clearly, he didn't like it.

thought—how we think about other people, and how this affects every aspect of our relations with them. Have you ever asked yourself questions such as:

Why do people fall in—and out—of love?

How can we get others to do what we want—to influence them in the ways we desire?

How do we know ourselves—our greatest strengths, our weaknesses, our deepest desires, and our strongest needs?

Why do we sometimes sacrifice our own interests or even welfare in order to help others? And why do we sometimes withhold such help, even when it is strongly needed?

Why do we sometimes lose our tempers and say or do things we later regret? And more generally, why are anger, aggression, and even violence so common between individuals, groups, or even entire countries?

If you have ever considered questions like these—and many others relating to the social side of life—you have come to the right place, because they are the ones addressed by social psychology, and ones we examine in this book. Now, though, you may be thinking, "That's a pretty big territory; does the field of social psychology really cover *all* this?" As you will soon see, it does, so we are not exaggerating: social psychology truly does investigate the entire span of social existence—a true rainbow of human social experience—but with the individual as the focus.

At this point, we hope we have whetted your appetite for the "moveable feast" that will follow, so we'd like to plunge right in and begin addressing topics and questions like the ones mentioned above. Before doing so, though, we feel it's important to provide you with some background information about the scope, nature, and methods of our field. This information will be useful to you in reading the entire book (as well as in your course), and in understanding how social psychologists go about answering fascinating questions about the social side of life, so it is crucial that we provide it here. To be efficient and hold these tasks to a minimum, we'll proceed as follows.

First, we present a more formal definition of social psychology—what it is and what it seeks to accomplish. Second, we'll describe several current trends in social psychology. These are reflected throughout this book, so knowing about them at the start will help you recognize them and understand why they are important. Third, we examine some of the methods used by social psychologists to answer questions about the social side of life. A working knowledge of these basic methods will help you to understand how social psychologists add to our understanding of social thought and social behavior, and will also be useful to you outside the context of this course. Then, we provide you with an overview of some of the special features in this book—features we think you will find helpful in many ways.

Social Psychology: An Overview

Providing a definition of almost any field is a complex task. In the case of social psychology, this difficulty is increased by two factors: the field's broad scope and its rapid rate of change. As you will see in every chapter of this book, social psychologists truly have a wide range of interests. Yet, despite this fact, most focus mainly on the following task: understanding how and why individuals behave, think, and feel as they do in social situations—ones involving the actual presence of other people, or their symbolic presence. Accordingly, we define social psychology *as the scientific field that seeks to understand the nature and causes of individual behavior, feelings, and thought in social situations.* Another way to put this is to say that *social psychology investigates the ways in which our thoughts, feelings, and actions are influenced by the social environments in which we live—by other people or our thoughts about them* (e.g., we imagine how they would react to actions we might perform). We'll now clarify this definition by taking a closer look at several of its key aspects.

Social Psychology Is Scientific in Nature

What is *science?* Many people seem to believe that this term refers only to fields such as chemistry, physics, and biology—ones that use the kind of equipment shown in Figure 1.2. If you share that view, you may find our suggestion that social psychology is a scientific discipline somewhat puzzling. How can a field that seeks to study the nature of love, the causes of aggression, and everything in between be scientific in the same sense as chemistry, physics, or computer science? The answer is surprisingly simple.

In reality, the term *science* does not refer to a special group of highly advanced fields. Rather, it refers to two things: (1) a set of values and (2) several methods that can be used to study a wide range of topics. In deciding whether a given field is or is not scientific, therefore, the critical question is, Does it adopt these values and methods? To the extent it does, it is scientific in nature. To the extent it does not, it falls outside the realm of science. We examine the procedures used by social psychologists in their research in detail in a later section, so here we focus on the core values that all fields must adopt to

FIGURE 1.2   What Is Science, Really?
Many people seem to believe that only fields that use sophisticated equipment like that shown (left) can be viewed as scientific. In fact, though, the term science *simply refers to adherence to a set of basic values (e.g., accuracy, objectivity) and use of a set of basic methods that can be applied to almost any aspect of the world around us—including the social side of life. In contrast, fields that are not scientific in nature (right) do not accept these values or use these methods.*

be considered scientific in nature. Four of these are most important:

Accuracy: A commitment to gathering and evaluating information about the world (including social behavior and thought) in as careful, precise, and error-free a manner as possible.

Objectivity: A commitment to obtaining and evaluating such information in a manner that is as free from bias as humanly possible.

Skepticism: A commitment to accepting findings as accurate only to the extent they have been verified over and over again.

Open-mindedness: A commitment to changing one's views—even views that are strongly held—if existing evidence suggests that these views are inaccurate.

Social psychology, as a field, is deeply committed to these values and applies them in its efforts to understand the nature of social behavior and social thought. For this reason, it makes sense to describe it as scientific in orientation. In contrast, fields that are not scientific make assertions about the world, and about people, that are not put to the careful test and analysis required by the values listed above. In such fields—ones like astrology and aromatherapy—intuition, faith, and unobservable forces are considered to be sufficient (see Figure 1.2) for reaching conclusions—the opposite of what is true in social psychology.

"But why adopt the scientific approach? Isn't social psychology just common sense?" Having taught for many years, we can almost hear you asking this question. And we understand why you might feel this way; after all, each of us has spent our entire lives interacting with other people and thinking about them, so in a sense, we are all amateur social psychologists. So, why don't we just rely on our own experience and intuition as a basis for understanding the social side of life? Our answer is straightforward: Because such sources provide an inconsistent and unreliable guide to understanding social behavior and social thought. Why? In part because our own experiences are unique and may not provide a solid foundation for answering general questions such as "Why do we sometimes go along 'with the group' even if we disagree with what it is doing?" "How can we know what other people are thinking or feeling at any given time?" In addition, common sense often provides inconsistent and contradictory ideas about various aspects of social life. For instance, consider the statement "Absence makes the heart grow fonder." Do you agree? Is it true that when people are separated from those they love, they miss them and so experience increased longing for them? Many people would agree. They would answer "Yes, that's right. Let me tell you about the time I was separated from..." But now consider the statement "Out of sight, out of mind." How about this one? Is it true? When people are separated from those they love, do they quickly find another romantic interest? (Many popular songs suggest that this so—for instance, in the song "Love the One You're With" written and recorded by Stephen Stills, he suggests that if you can't be with the person you love, you should love the person you are with.) As you can see, these two views—both suggested by common sense and popular culture—are contradictory. The same is true for many other informal observations about human behavior—they seem plausible, but often the opposite conclusion seems equally possible. How about these: "Two heads are better than one" and "Too many cooks spoil the broth." One suggests that when people work together, they perform better (e.g., make better decisions). The other suggests that when they work together, they may get in each other's way so that performance is actually reduced. Here's one more: Is it "Familiarity breeds content" (as we come to know others better, we tend to like them more—we feel more comfortable with them), or is it "Familiarity breeds contempt" (as we come to know others better, we tend to like them less). Common sense suggests that "more is more" where liking is concerned—the more familiar we are with others, the more we tend to like them, and there is some support for this view (see Chapter 7). On the other hand, though, research findings indicate that sometimes, the more we know about others (the better we come to know them), the less we like them (Norton, Frost, & Ariely, 2006). Why? Because as we learn more about others we recognize more ways in which we are dissimilar to them, and this growing awareness of dissimilarity causes us to notice yet more ways in which we are dissimilar, which leads to disliking.

We could continue, but by now, the main point should be clear: Common sense often suggests a confusing and inconsistent picture of human behavior. This doesn't mean that it is necessarily wrong; in fact, it often does offer intriguing clues and insights. But it doesn't tell us when various principles or generalizations hold—when, for instance, "Absence makes the heart grow fonder" and when it leads to "Out of sight, out of mind." Only a scientific approach that examines social behavior and thought in differing contexts can provide that kind of information, and this is one basic reason why social psychologists put their faith in the scientific method: it yields much more conclusive evidence. In fact, as we'll soon see, it is designed to help us determine not just which of the opposite sets of predictions mentioned above is correct, but also when and why one or the other might apply.

But this is not the only reason for being suspicious of common sense. Another one relates to the fact that unlike Mr. Spock of *Star Trek* fame, we are not perfect information-processing machines. On the contrary, as we'll note over and over again (e.g., Chapters 2, 3, 4, and 6), our thinking is subject to several types of biases that can lead us badly astray. Here's one example: Think back over major projects on which you have worked in the past (writing term papers, cooking a complicated dish, painting your room). Now, try to remember two things: (1) your initial estimates about how long it would take you to complete these jobs and (2) how long it actually took. Is there a gap between these two numbers? In all likelihood there is because most of us fall victim to the *planning fallacy*—a strong tendency to believe that projects will take less time than they actually do or, alternatively, that we can accomplish more in a given period of time than is really true. Moreover, we fall victim to this bias in our thought over and over again, despite repeated experiences that tell us "everything takes longer than we think it will." Why are we subject to this kind of error? Research by social psychologists indicates that part of the answer involves a tendency to think about the future when we are estimating how long a job will take. This prevents us from remembering how long similar tasks took in the past and that, in turn, leads us to underestimate the time we will need now (e.g., Buehler, Griffin, & Ross, 1994). This is just one of the many ways in which we can—and often do—make errors in thinking about other people (and ourselves); we'll consider many others in Chapter 3. Because we are prone to such errors in our informal thinking about the social world, we cannot rely on it—or on common sense—to solve the mysteries of social behavior. Rather, we need scientific evidence; and providing such evidence is, in essence, what social psychology is all about.

Social Psychology Focuses on the Behavior of Individuals

Societies differ greatly in terms of their views concerning courtship and marriage, yet it is still individuals who fall in love. Similarly, societies vary greatly in terms of their overall levels of violence, yet it is still individuals who perform aggressive actions or refrain from doing so. The same argument applies to virtually all other aspects of social behavior, from prejudice to helping: the actions are performed by, and the thoughts occur in, the minds of individuals, although they may, of course, be strongly influenced by other people. Because of this basic fact, the focus in social psychology is strongly on individuals. Social psychologists realize, of course, that we do not exist in isolation from social and cultural influences—far from it. As we will see throughout the book, much social behavior occurs in group settings, and these can exert powerful effects on us. But the field's major interest lies in understanding the factors that shape the actions and thoughts of individuals in social settings.

Social Psychology Seeks to Understand the Causes of Social Behavior and Thought

In a key sense, the heading of this section states the most central aspect of our definition. What it means is that social psychologists are primarily interested in understanding the many factors and conditions that shape the social behavior and thought of individuals—their actions, feelings, beliefs, memories, and inferences concerning other people. Obviously, a huge number of variables play a role in this regard. Most, though, fall under the four major headings described below.

THE ACTIONS AND CHARACTERISTICS OF OTHER PEOPLE   Imagine the following events:

> *You are at a party when you notice that a very attractive person is looking at you and smiling. In fact, this person is looking at you in a way that leaves little room for interpretation: that person is sending a clear signal saying, "Hey, let's get acquainted!"*

> *You are in a hurry and notice that you are driving faster than you usually do—above the speed limit, in fact. Suddenly, up ahead, you see the blinking lights of a state trooper who is in the process of pulling another driver over to the side of the road.*

Will these actions by other people have any effect on your behavior and thoughts?

Absolutely. Depending on your own personality, you may blush with pleasure when you see someone looking at you in a "let's get to know each other better" kind of way, and then, perhaps, go over and say "hello." And when you spot the state trooper's blinking light, you will almost certainly slow down—a lot! Instances like these, which occur hundreds of times each day, indicate that other people' behavior often has a powerful impact upon us (see Figure 1.3).

In addition, we are also often affected by others' appearance. Be honest: Don't you behave differently toward highly attractive people than toward less attractive ones? Toward very old people compared to young ones? Toward people who belong to racial and ethnic groups different from your own? And don't you sometimes form impressions of others' personalities and traits from their appearance? Your answer to these questions is probably yes because we do often react to the others' visible

FIGURE 1.3   Reacting to the Actions of Other People
As shown in these scenes, the behavior of other people often exerts powerful effects on our own behavior and thought.

characteristics, such as their appearance (e.g., McCall, 1997; Twenge & Manis, 1998). In fact, research findings (e.g., Hassin & Trope, 2000) indicate that we cannot ignore others' appearance even when we consciously try to do so and, as you probably already guess, it plays an important role in dating and romantic relationships (e.g., Burriss, Roberts, Welling, Puts, & Little, 2011). So despite warnings to avoid "judging books by their covers," we are often strongly affected by other people's appearance—even if we are unaware of such effects and might deny their existence (see Chapter 7). Interestingly, research findings indicate that relying on others' appearance as a guide to their characteristics is not always wrong; in fact, they can be relatively accurate, especially when we can observe others behaving spontaneously, rather than in posed photos (Nauman, Vazire, Rentfrow, & Gosling, 2009).

COGNITIVE PROCESSES   Suppose that you have arranged to meet a friend, and this person is late. In fact, after 30 minutes you begin to suspect that your friend will never arrive. Finally, she or he does appear and says, "Sorry…I forgot all about meeting you until a few minutes ago." How will you react? Probably with annoyance. Imagine that instead, however, your friend said, "I'm so sorry to be late. There was a big accident, and the traffic was tied up for miles." Now how will you react? Probably with less annoyance—but not necessarily. If your friend is often late and has used this excuse before, you may be suspicious about whether this explanation is true. In contrast, if this is the first time your friend has been late, or if your friend has never used such an excuse in the past, you may accept it as true. In other words, your reactions in this situation will depend strongly on your memories of your friend's past behavior and your inferences about whether her or his explanation is really true. Situations like this one call attention to the fact that cognitive processes play a crucial role in social behavior and social thought. We are always trying to make sense out of the social world, and this basic fact leads us to engage in lots of social cognition—to think long and hard about other people—what they are like, why they do what they do, how they might react to our behavior, and so on (e.g., Shah, 2003). Social psychologists are well aware of the importance of such processes and, in fact, social cognition is one of the most important areas of research in the field (e.g., Fiske, 2009; Killeya & Johnson, 1998; Swann & Gill, 1997).

ENVIRONMENTAL VARIABLES: IMPACT OF THE PHYSICAL WORLD   Are people more prone to wild impulsive behavior during the full moon than at other times (Rotton & Kelley, 1985)? Do we become more irritable and aggressive when the weather is hot and steamy than when it is cool and comfortable (Bell, Greene, Fisher, & Baum, 2001; Rotton & Cohn, 2000)? Does exposure to a pleasant smell in the air make people more helpful to others (Baron, 1997) and does that occur on baseball playing fields as well in crowded and largely unconditioned sections of cities (Larrick, Timmerman, Carton, & Abrevaya, 2011)? Research findings indicate that the physical environment does indeed influence our feelings, thoughts, and behavior, so these variables, too, certainly fall within the realm of modern social psychology.

BIOLOGICAL FACTORS   Is social behavior influenced by biological processes and genetic factors? In the past, most social psychologists would have answered no, at least to the genetic part of this question. Now, however, many have come to believe that our preferences, behaviors, emotions, and even attitudes are affected, to some extent, by our biological inheritance (Buss, 2008; Nisbett, 1990; Schmitt, 2004), although social experiences too have a powerful effect, and often interact with genetic factors in generating the complex patterns of our social lives (e.g., Gillath, Shaver, Baek, & Chun, 2008).

The view that biological factors play an important role in social behavior comes from the field of **evolutionary psychology** (e.g., Buss, 2004; Buss & Shackelford, 1997). This new branch of psychology suggests that our species, like all others on the planet, has been subject to the process of biological evolution throughout its history, and that as a result of this process, we now possess a large number of evolved psychological mechanisms that help (or once helped) us to deal with important problems relating to survival. How do these become

evolutionary psychology
A new branch of psychology that seeks to investigate the potential role of genetic factors in various aspects of human behavior.

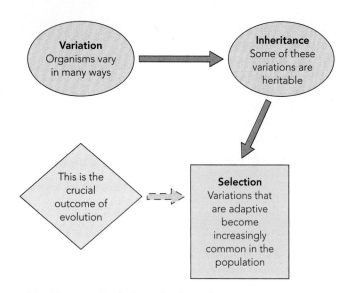

FIGURE 1.4   Evolution: An Overview

As shown here, evolution involves three major components: variation, inheritance, and selection.

part of our biological inheritance? Through the process of evolution, which, in turn, involves three basic components: *variation*, *inheritance*, and *selection*. Variation refers to the fact that organisms belonging to a given species vary in many different ways; indeed, such variation is a basic part of life on our planet. Human beings, as you already know, come in a wide variety of shapes and sizes, and vary on what sometimes seems to be an almost countless number of dimensions.

Inheritance refers to the fact that some of these variations can be passed from one generation to the next through complex mechanisms that we are only now beginning to fully understand. Selection refers to the fact that some variations give the individuals who possess them an "edge" in terms of reproduction: they are more likely to survive, find mates, and pass these variations on to succeeding generations. The result is that over time, more and more members of the species possess these variations. This change in the characteristics of a species over time—immensely long periods of time—is the concrete outcome of evolution. (See Figure 1.4 for a summary of this process.)

Social psychologists who adopt the evolutionary perspective suggest that this process applies to at least some aspects of social behavior. For instance, consider the question of mate preference. Why do we find some people attractive? According to the evolutionary perspective, because the characteristics they show—symmetrical facial features; well-toned, shapely bodies; clear skin; lustrous hair—are associated with "good genes"—they suggest that the people who possess them are likely to be healthy and vigorous, and therefore good mates (e.g., Schmitt & Buss, 2001; Tesser & Martin, 1996). For instance, these characteristics—the ones we find attractive—indicate that the people who show them have strong immune systems that protect them from many illnesses (e.g. Burriss et al., 2011; Li & Kenrick, 2006). Presumably, a preference for characteristics associated with good health and vigor among our ancestors increased the chances that they would reproduce successfully; this, in turn, contributed to our preference for people who possess these aspects of appearance.

Here's another example, and one that is perhaps a bit more surprising. When asked to indicate the characteristics in potential romantic partners that they find desirable, both genders—but especially women—rate a sense of humor high on the list (e.g., Buss, 2008). Why? From an evolutionary point of view, what is it about humor that makes it a desirable characteristic in others? One possibility is that a sense of humor signals high intelligence, and this tends to make humorous people attractive—after all, they have good genes (e.g., Griskevicius et al., in press). But another possibility is that a sense of humor signals something else: interest in forming new relationships. In other words, it is a sign that the humorous person is available—and interested. Research by Li et al. (2009) found that people are more likely to use humor and laugh at humor by others when they find these people attractive than when they do not, and that they perceived people who used humor during speed dating sessions as showing more romantic interest than ones who did not (see Figure 1.5).

Other topics have been studied from the evolutionary perspective (e.g., helping others; aggression; preferences for various ways of attracting people who are already in a relationship), and we'll describe this research in other chapters. Here, however, we wish to emphasize the fact that the evolutionary perspective does not suggest that we inherit specific patterns of social behavior; rather, it contends that we inherit tendencies or predispositions that may be apparent in our overt actions, depending on the environments in which we live. Similarly, this perspective does not suggest that we are "forced" or driven by our genes to act in specific ways. Rather, it merely suggests that because of our genetic inheritance, we have tendencies to behave in certain ways that, at least in the past, enhanced the chances that our ancestors would survive and pass their genes on to us. These tendencies can be—and often are—overridden by cognitive factors and the effects of experience (i.e., learning; Pettijohn & Jungeberg, 2004). For instance, what is viewed as attractive changes over time and is often very different in diverse cultures (e.g., overweight women are particularly desirable in Nigeria but less so in contemporary North America). So yes, genetic factors play some role in our behavior and thought, but they are clearly only one factor among many that influence how we think and act.

The Search for Basic Principles in a Changing Social World

One key goal of science is the development of basic principles that are accurate regardless of when or where they are applied or tested. For instance, in physics, Einstein's equation $e = mc^2$ is assumed to be true everywhere in the

FIGURE 1.5   Humor: An Important "Plus" in Dating
Research findings indicate that humor is viewed as a desirable charactersitic in potential romantic partners, partly because it is perceived as a sign that the person demonstrating it is interested in forming a new relationship. Such effects occur in many situations, including speed dating, as shown here. So, if you want romantic partners, keep on smiling and make jokes!

universe, and at all times—now, in the past, and in the future. Social psychologists, too, seek such basic principles. While they don't usually develop elegant mathematical expressions or equations, they do want to uncover the basic principles that govern social life. For instance, they'd like to determine what factors influence attraction, helping, prejudice, first impressions of other people, and so on. And the research they conduct is designed to yield such knowledge—basic principles that will be true across time and in different cultures.

On the other hand, they recognize the fact that cultures differ greatly and that the social world in which we live is constantly changing—in very important ways. For instance, even today, cultures vary greatly with respect to when and where people are expected to "dress up" rather than dress casually. While casual is acceptable in almost all contexts in the United States, more formal "dressy" attire is still expected in other cultures. This is a relatively trivial example, but the same point applies to more important aspects of social life, too: Should teenagers be allowed to date and meet without adult supervision? At what age should marriage occur? Are "gifts" to public officials acceptable or illegal bribes (see Figure 1.6)? At what age should people retire, and how should they be treated after they do? Cultures differ tremendously in these and countless other ways, and this complicates the task of establishing general principles of social behavior and social thought.

In addition, the social world is changing—and very rapidly, too. Because of social networks, cell phones, online dating, and many other changes, people now meet potential romantic partners in different ways than in the

FIGURE 1.6   Cultures Differ in Many Ways—Including Their Views About Bribes
In some cultures, it is considered acceptable—or even essential—to offer gifts (bribes?) to public officials. In others, such actions will land you in jail!

past when, typically, they were introduced by friends or met at dances arranged by their schools, churches, or other social organizations. Does this mean that the foundations of attraction are different today than in the past? Social psychologists believe that despite these changes, the same basic principles apply: Physical attractiveness is still a basic ingredient in romance, and although influence is now exerted in many ways not possible in the past (e.g., pop-ads on the Internet), the basic principles of persuasion, too, remain much the same (Goel, Mason, & Watts, 2010). In short, although the task of identifying basic, accurate principles of social behavior and social thought is complicated by the existence of huge cultural differences and rapid changes in social life, the goals of social psychological research remain within reach: uncovering basic, accurate facts about the social side of life that do apply in a wide range of contexts and situations.

KEYPOINTS

- Social psychology is the scientific field that seeks to understand the nature and causes of individual behavior and thought in social situations.

- It is scientific in nature because it adopts the values and methods used in other fields of science.

- Social psychologists adopt the scientific method because "common sense" provides an unreliable guide to social behavior, and because our personal thought is influenced by many potential sources of bias.

- Social psychology focuses on the behavior of individuals, and seeks to understand the causes of social behavior and thought, which can involve the behavior and appearance of others, social cognition, environmental

factors, cultural values, and even biological and genetic factors.

- Social psychology seeks to establish basic principles of social life that are accurate across huge cultural differences and despite rapid and major changes in social life.

- Important causes of social behavior and thought include the behavior and characteristics of other people, cognitive processes, emotions, cultures, and genetic factors.

Social Psychology: Summing Up

In sum, social psychology focuses mainly on understanding the causes of social behavior and social thought—on identifying factors that shape our feelings, behavior, and thought in social situations. It seeks to accomplish this goal through the use of scientific methods, and it takes careful note of the fact that social behavior and thought are influenced by a wide range of social, cognitive, environmental, cultural, and biological factors.

The remainder of this text is devoted to describing some of the key findings of social psychology. This information is truly fascinating, so we're certain that you will find it of interest—after all, it is about *us* and the social side of our lives! We're equally sure, however, that you will also find the outcomes of some research surprising, and that it will challenge many of your ideas about people and social relations. So please get ready for some new insights. We predict that after reading this book, you'll never think about the social side of life in quite the same way as before.

Social Psychology: Advances at the Boundaries

Textbooks, unlike fine wine, don't necessarily improve with age. So, to remain current, they must keep pace with changes in the fields they represent. Making certain that this book is current, in the best sense of this term, is one of our key goals, so you can be sure that what's presented in the chapters that follow provides a very contemporary summary of our current knowledge of the social side of life. Consistent with this belief, we now describe several major trends in modern social psychology—themes and ideas that represent what's newest and at the center of our field's attention. We do this primarily to emphasize the broad scope of social psychology, and also to alert you to topics we consider again in later chapters.

Cognition and Behavior: Two Sides of the Same Social Coin

In the past (actually, what's getting to be the dim and distant past!), social psychologists could be divided into two distinct groups: those who were primarily interested in social *behavior*—how people act in social situations—and those who were primarily interested in social *cognition*—how people attempt to make sense out of the social world and to understand themselves and others. This division has now totally disappeared. In modern social psychology, behavior and cognition are seen as intimately, and continuously, linked. In other words, there is virtually universal agreement in the field that we cannot hope to understand how and why people behave in certain ways in social situations without considering their thoughts, memory, intentions, emotions, attitudes, and beliefs. Similarly, virtually all social psychologists agree that there is a continuing and complex interplay between social thought and social behavior. What we think about others influences our actions toward them, and the consequences of these actions then affect our social thought. So, the loop is continuous and in trying to understand the social side of life, modern social psychology integrates both. That is be our approach throughout the book, and it is present in virtually every chapter.

The Role of Emotion in the Social Side of Life

Can you imagine life without feelings—emotions or moods? Probably not, because this, too, is a very central aspect of social life—and life more generally. Social psychologists have always been interested in emotions and moods, and with good reason: they play a key role in many aspects of social life. For instance, imagine that you want a favor from a friend or acquaintance—when would you ask for it, when this person is in a good mood or a bad one? Research findings indicate that you would do much better when that person is in a good mood, because positive moods (or *affect*, as social psychologists term such feelings) do increase our tendency to offer help to others (e.g., Isen & Levin, 1972). Similarly, suppose you are meeting someone for the first time. Do you think your current mood might influence your reactions to this person? If you answered "yes," you are in agreement with the results of systematic research, which indicates our impressions of others (and our thoughts about them) are strongly influenced by our current moods. More recently, social psychologists have been investigating the role of moods in a wider range of social behaviors and social thought (e.g., Forgas, Baumeister, & Tice, 2009). Overall, interest in this topic, including the impact of specific emotions, has increased. So, we include it here as another area in which rapid advances are being made at the boundaries of our current knowledge of social life. In addition, we represent this interest throughout the book in special sections within each chapter (e.g., "Emotion and Attitudes," "Emotion and Helping," "Emotion and Social Cognition"), so be on the lookout for these sections because they report some of the most fascinating research currently occurring in our field.

Relationships: How They Develop, Change, and Strengthen—or End

If the social side of life is as important as we suggested at the start of this chapter—and we firmly believe that it is—then **relationships** with others are its building blocks. When they are successful and satisfying, they add tremendously to our happiness, but when they go "wrong," they can disrupt every other aspect of our lives, and undermine our psychological health and well-being, and even our own self-concept (e.g., Slotter, Gardner, & Finkel,

relationships
Our social ties with other persons, ranging from casual acquaintance or passing friendships, to intense, long-term relationships such as marriage or lifetime friendships.

FIGURE 1.7 **The Warm Glow of Love**

When couples are in love, they often perceive each other in unreaslitically favorable ways. Is that good or bad for their future relationships? The answer is complex, but reaserch findings indicate that as long as they show some degree of reality or accuracy, it may be beneficial.

2010). Given these basic facts, social psychologists have long sought to understand the nature of social relationships—how they begin and change over time, and why, gradually, some strengthen and deepen, while others weaken and die—often, after causing tremendous pain to the people involved. In recent years, however, interest in these topics has increased greatly, and relationships are now receiving more research attention than ever before. The results of this research have been—and continue to be—remarkably revealing. We consider relationships in detail in Chapter 7, but here, to give you the flavor of this growing body of knowledge, we mention just a couple of lines of important and revealing research.

One such topic relates to the following question: "Is it better, in terms of building a strong relationship, to view one's partner (boyfriend, girlfriend, or spouse) realistically, or as we often do, through a 'golden, positive glow'?" Folklore suggests that "love is blind," and when in love, many people do tend to see only good in their partners (see Figure 1.7). Is that tendency good or bad for their relationships? Research findings suggest that in general, it is good, but only if it is restrained by a healthy degree of reality (i.e., accuracy; e.g., Fletcher, Simpson, & Boyes, 2006). For example, in one study on this issue (e.g., Luo & Snider, 2009), several hundred newlywed couples were asked to complete measures that revealed the extent to which they perceived their new spouses accurately, in a positive light, and as similar to themselves in many ways. Accuracy was measured by comparing each spouse's ratings of their partner on many dimensions with their partner's own self-ratings. The closer these scores, the higher the accuracy. Similarity bias was measured in a parallel way in terms of the extent to which each partner perceived his or her spouse as more similar to themselves than was actually the case. These measures of accuracy, positivity bias, and similarity bias were then related to marital satisfaction as expressed by both partners in each couple. Results revealed a clear picture: all three dimensions were important in predicting marital satisfaction. Positive and similarity bias contributed to such happiness, but accuracy did too. Overall, these findings indicate that it is indeed good to hold favorable perceptions of our romantic partners, but that these must be moderated by a dash of accuracy, too. We return to these questions in Chapter 7; here, we merely mention them to give you a basic idea of the kind of questions investigated in the context of relationships.

Another question concerning relationships that has received growing attention from social psychologists is this: What are the effects of a breakup? This is a case where common sense offers contradictory answers. On the one hand, it is widely believed that the breakup of a romantic relationship is traumatic, and may leave lasting psychological scars behind. On the other, the saying "What doesn't kill you makes you stronger" suggests that there are actual benefits from such painful experiences. Research on breakups suggests that there is some truth in both views. On the one hand, the breakup of romantic relationships *is* painful and distressing; in fact, it has been found to negatively affect individuals' self-concept, so that, for instance, they feel more vulnerable and less certain about who, precisely, they are (i.e., the clarity of their self-concept is reduced; Slotter et al., 2010). On the other hand, it appears that experiencing a breakup may increase the desire for another relationship, and encourage the people involved to actually form new ones—"on the rebound" (Spielmann, MacDonald, & Wilson, 2009). While there are real risks involved in rapidly forming new relationships, they do offer at least one major benefit: they help the people involved to let go of their former relationship and "move on" with their lives. These benefits are especially strong for people who are high in what social psychologists term *anxious attachment*—anxiety over the possibility of losing a partner and/or an inability to get as close to partners as one would prefer.

Overall, research on relationships has provided many important insights into this crucial part of our social lives, and offers helpful suggestions on how they can be strengthened and developed so that their beneficial effects are maximized and their potential costs reduced.

Social Neuroscience: Where Social Psychology and Brain Research Meet

In a basic sense, everything we do, feel, imagine, or create reflects activity within our brains. Are you understanding the words on this page? If so, it is the result of activity in your brain. Are you in a good mood? A bad one? Whatever you are feeling also reflects activity in your brain and biological systems. Can you remember what your third-grade teacher looked like? What your first ride on a roller coaster felt like? The smell of your favorite food? Do you have plans for the future—and do you think they can actually be achieved? All of these events and processes are the result of activity in various areas of your brain. In the past 20 years, powerful new tools for measuring activity in our brains as they function have been developed: functional magnetic resonance imaging (fMRI), positron emission tomography (PET) scans, and other techniques. Although they were initially developed for medical uses, and have generated major advances in surgery and other branches of medicine, they have also allowed psychologists and other scientists to peer into the human brain as people engage in various activities, and so to find out just what's happening at any given time. The result is that we now know much more about the complex relationships between neural events and psychological ones—feelings, thoughts, and overt actions.

Social psychologists, too, have begun to use these new tools to uncover the foundations of social thought and social behavior in our brains—to find out what portions of the brain and what complex systems within it are involved in key aspects of our social life—everything from prejudice and aggression, through underperforming on tasks due to "choking under pressure" (Mobbs et al., 2009), and empathy and helping (e.g., Van Berkum, Hollmean, Nieuwaland, Otten, & Murre, 2009). In conducting such research, social psychologists use the same basic tools as other scientists—they study events in the brain (through the use of fMRI and other kinds of brain scans), other neural activity, and even changes in the immune system (e.g., Taylor, Lerner, Sherman, Sage, & McDowell, 2003) in order to determine how these events are related to important social processes. The findings of this research have been truly fascinating. Here's one example of what we mean.

Attitudes and values are an important part of the social side of life; as we'll see in Chapter 5, they often shape our overt behavior and underlie powerful emotional reactions to events and people. But how are they represented in the brain, and how do they exert their powerful effects on our behavior, thought, and emotions? Social neuroscience research is providing intriguing answers. For example, consider a study by Van Berkum and colleagues (2009). This investigation was designed to determine what happens in the brain when people encounter statements that are consistent or inconsistent with their strongly held values and attitudes. To do this, they recruited two groups of participants known to hold opposite views on many social issues. One group (members of a strict Christian church) were known to be against euthanasia, growing equality of women in society, abortion, and the use of drugs. The other, self-described as "nonreligious," held opposite views on all these issues. Both groups were then exposed to statements relating to these attitudes on a computer screen, and while viewing them, electrical activity in their brains was carefully recorded. A key question asked by the researchers was, How quickly do people react, in terms of brain activity, to statements that disagree with their own attitudes or values? Do they react this way as soon as they encounter a single word inconsistent with their views (e.g., "acceptable" in the statement "I think euthanasia is acceptable..." if they are against this action) or only after reading the entire statement and considering it carefully. Previous research indicated that certain patterns of activity (N400, one kind of *event-related potential*—a kind of activity in the brain), occur very quickly when individuals encounter words inconsistent with their values—only 250 milliseconds after seeing them—and indicate that intensified processing of this word is occurring. Other patterns, in contrast, occur somewhat later, and reflect negative reactions to the value-inconsistent statement. It was predicted that each group would show stronger N400 reactions to words that were inconsistent with their values, so that, for instance, the Christian group would show stronger reactions to the word "acceptable" in connection with euthanasia, while the other group would express stronger reactions to the word "unacceptable" when linked to euthanasia. Results offered strong support for these predictions, and suggest that we do indeed process information that disagrees with our attitudes or values very quickly—long before we can put such reactions into words. So yes, attitudes and values do indeed exert powerful and far-reaching effects on activity within our brains—and on our overt actions.

Here's another example of how social psychologists are using the tools of neuroscience to study important aspects of social thought and behavior. Have you ever heard of *mirror neurons*? They are neurons in our brains that are activated during the observation and execution of actions, and it has been suggested that they play a key role in *empathy*— our capacity to experience, vicariously, the emotions and feelings of other people (e.g., Gazzola, Aziz-Zadeh, & Keysers, 2006). Mirror neurons are located in a portion of the brain known as the *frontal operculum* and in an intriguing study, Montgomery, Seeherman, and Haxby (2009) suggested that perhaps people who score high on a questionnaire measuring empathy would show more activity in this area of their brains when they viewed social facial expressions shown by others. To test this prediction, the researchers exposed two groups of individuals—ones who had scored high in a measure of empathy or low on this measure (an index of the capacity to take the perspective of other people) to video clips of others' facial expressions (e.g., smiling, frowning) or to faces that showed nonsocial movements (i.e., movements not associated with particular emotions). Activity in the brains of both groups of participants was recorded through fMRI scans as they watched the videos. Results were clear: as predicted, people high or moderate in empathy did indeed show higher activity in the frontal operculum (where mirror neurons are located) than people low in empathy (see Figure 1.8).

Research in the rapidly expanding field of social neuroscience is clearly at the forefront of advances in social psychology, and we represent it fully—and often—in this text. We should insert one warning, however. As noted by several experts in this field (e.g., Cacioppo et al., 2003), social neuroscience cannot provide the answer to every question we have about social thought or behavior. There are many aspects of social thought that cannot easily be related to activity in specific areas of the brain—aspects such as attitudes, attributions, group identities, and reciprocity (e.g., Willingham & Dunn, 2003). In principle, all of these components of social thought reflect activity in the brain, but this does not necessarily mean that it is best to try to study them in this way. In fact, the situation may be similar to that existing between chemistry and physics. All chemists agree that ultimately, every chemical reaction can be explained in terms of physics.

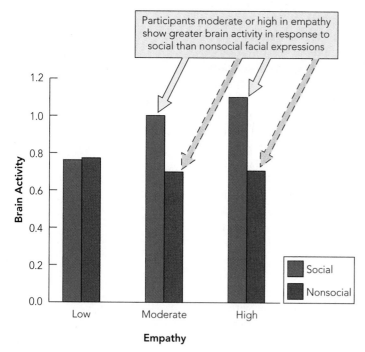

FIGURE 1.8 **The Neural Basis of Empathy**

Individuals high or moderate in a measure of empathy (the capacity to see the world through others' eyes) showed more activity in a portion of their brains (the frontal operculum) than persons low in empathy, when watching videos of other persons showing social facial expressions. In contrast, the groups did not differ in brain activity while watching videos showing nonsocial facial movements (i.e., ones unrelated to emotions). (Source: Based on data from Montgomery, Seeherman, & Haxby, 2009).

But the principles of chemistry are still so useful that chemists continue to use them in their research and do not all rush out and become physicists. The same may well be true for social psychology: it does not have to seek to understand all of its major topics in terms of activities in the brain or nervous system; other approaches, which we describe in later chapters, are still useful and can provide important new insights. Throughout this book, therefore, we describe research that uses a wide range of methods, from brain scans on the one hand, to direct observations of social behavior on the other. This reflects the current, eclectic nature of social psychology and is, therefore, the most appropriate content for this book.

The Role of Implicit (Nonconscious) Processes

Have you ever had the experience of meeting someone for the first time and taking an immediate liking—or disliking—to that person? Afterward, you may have wondered, "Why do I like (dislike) this person?" But probably, you didn't wonder for long because we are all experts at finding good reasons to explain our own actions or feelings. This speed in no way implies that we really do understand why we behave or think in certain ways. And in fact, a growing theme of recent research in social psychology has been just this: in many cases we really don't know why we think or behave as we do in social contexts. And, partly because of our errors in the way we process social information, and partly because we change greatly over time, we don't even know—with clarity—what would make us happy (Gilbert, 2006). So, for instance, people get a tattoo that they think will make them happy, only to realize, years later, that it is making them unhappy, not happy. In addition, our thoughts and actions are shaped by factors and processes of which we are only dimly aware, at best, and which often take place in an automatic manner, without any conscious thought or intentions on our part. This is one more reason why social psychologists are reluctant to trust "common sense" as a basis for reliable information about social behavior or social thought: We are unaware of many of the factors that influence how we think and how we behave and so cannot report on them accurately (e.g., Pelham, Mirenberg, & Jones, 2002). For example, consider first impressions: Recent findings indicate that we form these incredibly quickly—often within mere seconds of meeting other people (e.g., Gray, 2008). And, amazingly, sometimes these impressions appear to be accurate: We can form valid impressions of others' personalities even from a very brief exposure to them (e.g., Carney, Colvin, & Hall, 2007). But the picture is a mixed one: sometimes these first impressions are accurate and sometimes they are very wrong. This raises another question: Can we tell when our first impressions are likely to be useful and when they are not? In other words, can we tell whether to have confidence in them or mistrust them? Recent evidence reported by Ames, Kammrath, Suppes, and Bolger (2010) indicates that we cannot: We can't intuit when these impressions are likely to be accurate and when they are not. So, as these authors suggest (p. 273), "snap impression accuracy is sometimes above chance..." but we can't tell when that is the case. Clearly, nonconscious processes influence our judgments and actions in such cases, but perhaps they should not.

Research on the role of implicit (nonconscious) processes in our social behavior and thought has examined many other topics, such as the impact of our moods on what we tend to remember about other people or complex issues (e.g., Ruder & Bless, 2003), how negative attitudes toward members of social groups other than our own that we deny having can still influence our reactions toward them (e.g., Fazio & Hilden, 2001), and how we automatically evaluate people belonging to various social groups once we have concluded that they belong to that group (Castelli, Zobmaister, & Smith, 2004). In short, nonconscious factors and processing seem to play an important role in many aspects of social thought and social behavior. We examine such effects in several chapters since they continue to represent an important focus of current research (see, e.g., Chapters 2 and 6).

FIGURE 1.9   Diversity: A Fact of Life in Many Countries in the 21st Century
Populations in many countries—including the United States—are becoming increasingly ethnically diverse. Social psychologists take careful account of this fact by conducting research focused on understanding the role of cultural factors in social behavior and social thought.

Taking Full Account of Social Diversity

There can be no doubt that the United States—like many other countries—is undergoing a major social and cultural transformation. Recent figures indicate that 64 percent of the population identifies itself as White (of European heritage), while fully 36 percent identifies itself as belonging to some other group (13 percent African American, 4.5 percent American Indian, 14 percent Hispanic, 4.5 percent Asian/Pacific Islander, and 7 percent some other group). This represents a tremendous change from the 1960s, when approximately 90 percent of the population was of European descent. Indeed, in several states (e.g., California, New Mexico, Texas, Arizona), people of European heritage are now a minority (see Figure 1.9). In response to these tremendous shifts, psychologists have increasingly recognized the importance of taking cultural factors and differences into careful account in everything they do—teaching, research, counseling, and therapy; and social psychologists are certainly no exception to this rule. They have been increasingly sensitive to the fact that individuals' cultural, ethnic, and racial heritage often play a key role in their self-identity, and that this, in turn, can exert important effects on their behavior. This is in sharp contrast to the point of view that prevailed in the past, which suggested that cultural, ethnic, and gender differences are relatively unimportant. In contrast to that earlier perspective, social psychologists currently believe that such differences are very important, and must be taken carefully into account in our efforts to understand human behavior. As a result, psychology in general, and social psychology as well, now adopts a **multicultural perspective**—one that carefully and clearly recognizes the potential importance of gender, age, ethnicity, sexual orientation, disability, socioeconomic status, religious orientation, and many other social and cultural dimensions. This perspective has led to important changes in focus of social psychological research, which we cover in-depth in Chapters 4 and 6, and this trend seems likely to continue.

For instance, consider a study conducted in 10 different countries around the world, focused on what kind of body shape both men and women find most attractive in women (Swami et al., 2010). Participants were shown the drawings in Figure 1.10, and asked to choose the one they found most attractive; women were asked to select the one that they thought would be most attractive to men of their own age, and the one that most closely matched their current body. Results indicated that there were indeed cultural differences in the ratings provided by participants: raters in Oceania, south and west Asia, and Southeast Asia preferred heavier body types then those in North America and east Asia. However, larger differences occurred within cultures in terms of socioeconomic status: higher SES people (i.e., those higher in education and income) preferred slimmer body builds to those of lower SES status. This suggests that large differences exist with respect to this very basic aspect of social perception within cultures as well as between them. Clearly, increased recognition of diversity and cultural differences is a hallmark of

multicultural perspective
A focus on understanding the cultural and ethnic factors that influence social behavior.

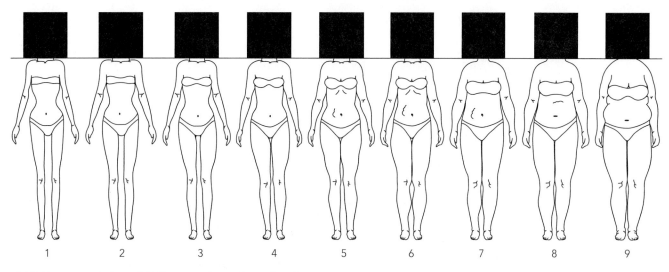

FIGURE 1.10   Cultural Differences in Preferred Body Types
Do people in different cultures prefer different body types or weights in women? Research conducted in 10 different countries indicates that they do, with people from cultures in some parts of Asia and Europe preferring rounder figures than people in North America. However, within each culture, differences between people high and low in socioeconomic status are even greater than those between different cultures. (Source: V. Swami, et.al, PERSONALITY AND SOCIAL PSYCHOLOGY BULLETIN, 36 (3) March 2010, p.17. © 2010 Sage Publications. Reprinted by permissions of SAGE Publications.).

modern social psychology, and we discuss research highlighting the importance of such factors at many points in this book.

 KEY POINTS

- Social psychologists currently recognize that social thought and social behavior are two sides of the same coin, and that there is a continuous, complex interplay between them.

- There is growing interest among social psychologists in the role of emotion in social thought and social behavior.

- The formation and development of **relationships** is another major trend in the field.

- Yet another major trend involves growing interest in social neuroscience—efforts to relate activity in the brain to key aspects of social thought and behavior.

- Our behavior and thought is often shaped by factors of which we are unaware. Growing attention to such implicit (nonconscious) processes is another major theme of modern social psychology.

- Social psychology currently adopts a **multicultural perspective.** This perspective recognizes the importance of cultural factors in social behavior and social thought, and notes that research findings obtained in one culture do not necessarily generalize to other cultures.

How Social Psychologists Answer the Questions They Ask: Research as the Route to Increased Knowledge

Now that we've provided you with an overview of some of the current trends in social psychology, we can turn to the third major task mentioned at the start of this chapter: explaining how social psychologists attempt to answer questions about social behavior and social thought. Since social psychology is scientific in orientation, they usually seek to accomplish this task through systematic research. To provide you with basic information about the specific techniques they use, we examine three related topics. First, we describe basic methods of research in social psychology. Next, we consider the role of theory in such research. Finally, we touch on some of the complex ethical issues relating to social psychological research.

Systematic Observation: Describing the World Around Us

One basic technique for studying social behavior involves **systematic observation**—carefully observing behavior as it occurs. Such observation is not the kind of informal observation we all practice from childhood on, such as people watching in an airport; rather, in a scientific field such as social psychology it is observation accompanied by careful, accurate measurement of a particular behavior across people. For example, suppose that a social psychologist wanted to find out how frequently people touch each other in different settings. The researcher could study this topic by going to shopping malls, restaurants and bars, college campuses, and many other locations and observe, in those settings, who touches whom, how they touch, and with what frequency. Such research (which has actually been conducted; see Chapter 3), would be employing what is known as *naturalistic observation*—observation of people's behavior in natural settings (Linden, 1992). Note that in such observation, the researcher would simply record what is happening in each context; she or he would make no attempt to change the behavior of the people being observed. In fact, such observation requires that the researcher take great pains to avoid influencing the people observed in any way. Thus, the psychologist would try to remain as inconspicuous as possible, and might even try to hide behind natural barriers such as telephone poles, walls, or even bushes!

Another technique that is often included under the heading of systematic observation is known as the **survey method**. Here, researchers ask large numbers of people to respond to questions about their attitudes or behavior. Surveys are used for many purposes—to measure attitudes toward specific issues such as smoking, to find out how voters feel about various political candidates, to determine how people feel about members of different social groups, and even to assess student reactions to professors (your college or university probably uses a form on which you rate your professors each semester). Social psychologists often use this method to assess attitudes toward a variety of social issues—for instance, national health care reform or affirmative action programs. Scientists and practitioners in other fields use the survey method to measure everything from life satisfaction around the globe to consumer reactions to new products.

Surveys offer several advantages. Information can be gathered about thousands or even hundreds of thousands of people with relative ease. In fact, surveys are now often conducted online, through the Internet. For instance, recent research on personal happiness is being conducted this way. To see for yourself how it works, just visit www. authentichappiness.com. The surveys presented there have been prepared by famous psychologists, and your replies—which are entirely confidential—will become part of a huge data set that is being used to find out why people are happy or unhappy, and ways in which they can increase their personal satisfaction with life. The site has been visited by millions of people and currently has over 750,000 registered users! (We'll return to this topic in detail in Chapter 12). In addition, survey sites can be used for many other purposes—for instance, to see how students rate their professors (see Figure 1.11).

In order to be useful as a research tool, though, surveys must meet certain requirements. First, the people who participate must be representative of the larger population about which conclusions are to be drawn—which raises the issue of sampling. If this condition is not met, serious errors can result. For instance, suppose that the website shown in Figure 1.11 is visited only by people who are already very happy—perhaps because unhappy people don't want to report on their feelings. Any results obtained would be questionable for describing American levels of happiness, because they do not represent

systematic observation
A method of research in which behavior is systematically observed and recorded.

survey method
A method of research in which a large number of people answer questions about their attitudes or behavior.

the entire range of happiness in the population as a whole.

Yet another issue that must be carefully addressed with respect to surveys is this: The way in which the items are worded can exert strong effects on the outcomes obtained. For instance, continuing with the happiness example we have been using, suppose a survey asked people to rate, "How happy are you in your life right now?" (on a 7-point scale where 1 = very unhappy and 7 = very happy). Many people (most?) might well answer 4 or above because overall, most people do seem to be relatively happy much of the time. But suppose the question asked: "Compared to the happiest you have ever been, how happy are you right now in your life?" (1 = much less happy; 7 = just as happy). In the context of this comparison to your peak level of happiness, many people might provide numbers lower than 4, because they know they have been happier *sometime* in the past. Comparing the results from these questions could be misleading, if the differences between them were ignored.

FIGURE 1.11   Using the Internet to Conduct Research—Or Just to Find Out How Other Students Rate Your Professor
Social psychologists sometimes collect survey data from sites they establish on the Internet. Many of these are set up for a specific study, but others, like the one shown here, remain open permanently, and often provide data from hundreds of thousands of persons. In addition, survey sites can be used for many other purposes—for instance, to learn how other students rate your professors.

In sum, the survey method can be a useful approach for studying some aspects of social behavior, but the results obtained are accurate only to the extent that issues relating to sampling and wording are carefully addressed.

Correlation: The Search for Relationships

At various times, you have probably noticed that some events appear to be related to the occurrence of others: as one changes, the other changes, too. For example, perhaps you've noticed that people who drive new, expensive cars tend to be older than people who drive old, inexpensive ones, or that people using social networks such as Facebook tend to be relatively young (although this is changing somewhat now). When two events are related in this way, they are said to be correlated, or that a correlation exists between them. The term *correlation* refers to a tendency for one event to be associated with changes in the other. Social psychologists refer to such changeable aspects of the natural world as *variables*, since they can take different values.

From a scientific point of view, knowing that there is a correlation between two variables can be very useful. When a correlation exists, it is possible to predict one variable from information about one or more other variables. The ability to make such predictions is one important goal of all branches of science, including social psychology. Being able to make accurate predictions can be very helpful. For instance, imagine that a correlation is observed between certain attitudes on the part of individuals (one variable) and the likelihood that they will later be very difficult to work with, both for their coworkers and boss (another variable). This correlation could be very useful in identifying potentially dangerous people so that companies can avoid hiring them. Similarly, suppose that a correlation is observed between certain patterns of behavior in married couples (e.g., the tendency to criticize each other harshly) and the likelihood that they will later divorce. Again, this information might be helpful in counseling the people involved and perhaps, if this was what they desired, in saving their relationship (see Chapter 7 for a discussion of why long-term relationships sometimes fail).

How accurately can such predictions be made? The stronger the correlation between the variables in question, the more accurate the predictions. Correlations can range from 0 to −1.00 or +1.00; the greater the departure from 0, the stronger the correlation. Positive numbers mean that as one variable increases, the other increases too. Negative numbers indicate that as one variable increases, the other decreases. For instance, there is a negative correlation between age and the amount of hair on the heads of males: the older they are, the less hair they have.

These basic facts underlie an important method of research sometimes used by social psychologists: the **correlational method**. In this approach, social psychologists attempt to determine whether, and to what extent, different variables are related to each other. This involves carefully measuring each variable, and then performing appropriate statistical tests to determine whether and to what degree the variables are correlated. Perhaps a concrete example will help.

Imagine that a social psychologist wants to find out whether the information posted by users on Facebook is accurate—whether it portrays the users realistically, or presents them as they would like to be (an idealized self-image). Furthermore, imagine that on the basis of previous studies, the researcher hypothesizes that the information people post on Facebook is indeed relatively accurate. How could this idea be tested? One very basic approach, using the correlational method of research, is as follows. First, posters on Facebook would complete measures of their personality (e.g., these could include extraversion, conscientiousness, openness to experience—ones found to be very basic in past research). Then, raters would read the profiles on Facebook and from this information, rate the posters on the same personality dimensions. As a cross-check, other people who know the posters well could also rate them on the same personality dimensions. Next, these sets of information would be compared (i.e., correlated) to see how closely they align. The higher the correlation between these ratings—the ones provided by the posters themselves and people who know them very well (i.e., self and other personality ratings)—the more accurately users of Facebook present themselves. Why? Because the ratings posted by people on Facebook agree with those provided by others who know them personally. In addition, to test the alternative idea that posters try to present themselves in an idealized way, these individuals could be asked to describe their "ideal selves," and this information, too, could be correlated with ratings of their Facebook postings. These basic methods were actually used by Back et al. (2010) in a study designed to find out whether, and to what extent, Facebook postings are accurate with respect to posters' personality. Results offered clear support for the **hypothesis** that these profiles are indeed accurate: Posted profiles closely matched the posters' actual personalities, as measured by personality scales they themselves completed and ratings by friends and family members. In addition, there was little evidence for attempts at idealized self-presentation. On the basis of this research, we can tentatively conclude that Facebook information is accurate and informative about posters' personalities; their personality scores predict their postings, and their postings predict their personality scores. But please emphasize the word *tentatively*, for two important reasons.

First, the fact that two variables are correlated in no way guarantees that they are causally related—that changes in one *cause* changes in the other. On the contrary, the relationship between them may be due to the fact that both variables are related to a third variable, and not really to each other. For instance, in this case, it is possible that people who post on Facebook are simply good at self-presentation—presenting themselves to

correlational method
A method of research in which a scientist systematically observes two or more variables to determine whether changes in one are accompanied by changes in the other.

hypothesis
An as yet unverified prediction concerning some aspect of social behavior or social thought.

others so as to "look good." To the extent that's true, then the correlation between their postings on Facebook and scores on personality tests could reflect this variable. Since they are high in self-presentation skills, their postings and their answers to personality tests both tend to put them in a good light. But in fact the two measures are unrelated to each in any direct or causal way.

Second, it is also possible that posting on Facebook leads to changes in posters' personalities, in the direction of becoming more like the information on Facebook. That may sound a little far-fetched, but it is still possible, and correlational research cannot definitely rule out such possibilities: it can't establish the direction of relationships between variables, just their existence and strength.

Despite these major drawbacks, the correlational method of research is sometimes very useful to social psychologists. It can be used in natural settings where experiments might be very difficult to conduct, and it is often highly efficient: a large amount of information can be obtained in a relatively short period of time. However, the fact that it is generally not conclusive with respect to cause-and-effect relationships is a serious one that leads social psychologists to prefer another method in many instances. It is to this approach that we turn next.

The Experimental Method: Knowledge Through Systematic Intervention

As we have just seen, the correlational method of research is very useful from the point of view of one important goal of science: making accurate predictions. It is less useful, though, from the point of view of attaining another important goal: *explanation*. This is sometimes known as the "why" question because scientists do not merely wish to describe the world and relationships between variables in it: they want to be able to explain these relationships, too.

In order to attain the goal of explanation, social psychologists employ a method of research known as **experimentation** or the **experimental method**. As the heading of this section suggests, experimentation involves the following strategy: One variable is changed systematically, and the effects of these changes on one or more other variables are carefully measured. If systematic changes in one variable produce changes in another variable (and if two additional conditions we describe below are also met), it is possible to conclude with reasonable certainty that there is indeed a causal relationship between these variables: that changes in one do indeed cause changes in the other. Because the experimental method is so valuable in answering this kind of question, it is frequently the method of choice in social psychology. But please bear in mind that there is no single "best" method of research. Rather, social psychologists, like all other scientists, choose the method that is most appropriate for studying a particular topic.

EXPERIMENTATION: ITS BASIC NATURE In its most basic form, the experimental method involves two key steps: (1) the presence or strength of some variable believed to affect an aspect of social behavior or thought is systematically changed and (2) the effects of such changes (if any) are carefully measured. The factor systematically varied by the researcher is termed the **independent variable**, while the aspect of behavior studied is termed the **dependent variable**. In a simple experiment, then, different groups of participants are randomly assigned to be exposed to contrasting levels of the independent variable (such as low, moderate, and high). The researcher then carefully measures their behavior to determine whether it does in fact vary with these changes in the independent variable. If it does—and if two other conditions are also met—the researcher can tentatively conclude that the independent variable does indeed cause changes in the aspect of behavior being studied.

To illustrate the basic nature of experimentation in social psychology, we'll use the following example. Suppose that a social psychologist is interested in the question,

experimentation (experimental method)
A method of research in which one or more factors (the independent variables) are systematically changed to determine whether such variations affect one or more other factors (dependent variables).

independent variable
The variable that is systematically changed (i.e., varied) in an experiment.

dependent variable
The variable that is measured in an experiment.

Does exposure to violent video games increase the likelihood that people will aggress against others in various ways (e.g., verbally, physically, spreading false rumors, or posting embarrassing photos of them on the Internet; see Figure 1.12). How can this possibility be investigated by using the experimental method? Here is one possibility.

Participants in the experiment could be asked to play a violent or nonviolent video game. After these experiences in the research, they would be placed in a situation where they could, if they wished, aggress against another person. For instance, they could be told that the next part of the study is concerned with taste sensitivity and asked to add as much hot sauce as they wish to a glass of water that another person will drink. Participants would taste a sample in which only one drop of sauce has been placed in the glass, so they would know how hot the drink would be if they added more than one drop. Lots of sauce would make the drink so hot that it would truly hurt the person who consumed it.

If playing aggressive video games increases aggression against others, then participants who played such games would use more hot sauce—and so inflict more pain on another person—than participants who examined the puzzle. If results indicate that this is the case, then the researcher could conclude, at least tentatively, that playing aggressive video games does increase subsequent, overt aggression. The researcher can offer this conclusion because if the study was done correctly, the only difference between the experiences of the two groups during the study is that one played violent games and the other did not. As a result, any difference in their behavior (in their aggression) can be attributed to this factor. It is important to note that in experimentation, the independent variable—in this case, exposure to one or another type of video game—is systematically changed by the researcher. In the correlational method, in contrast, variables are not altered in this manner; rather, naturally occurring changes in them are simply observed and recorded. By the way, research findings reported over several

FIGURE 1.12   The Experimental Method: Using It to Study the Effects of Violent Video Games

Does playing violent video games such as the one shown here increase the tendency to aggress against others? Using the experimental method, social psychologists can gather data on this important issue—and in fact, have already done so!

decades do indicate that regular exposure to violence in the media or in video games does seem to increase aggression against others, and that this link is in fact a casual one: regular or frequent exposure to violent content reduces sensitivity to such materials, and enhances aggressive thoughts and emotions (e.g., Krahe, Moller, Huesmann, Kirwill, Felber, & Berger, 2011).

EXPERIMENTATION: TWO KEY REQUIREMENTS FOR ITS SUCCESS   Earlier, we referred to two conditions that must be met before a researcher can conclude that changes in an independent variable have caused changes in a dependent variable. Let's consider these conditions now. The first involves what is termed **random assignment of participants to experimental conditions**. This means that all participants in an experiment must have an equal chance of being exposed to each level of the independent variable. The reason for this rule is simple: If participants are not randomly assigned to each condition, it may later be impossible to determine if differences in their behavior stem from differences they brought with them to the study, from the impact of the independent variable, or both. For instance, imagine that in the study on video games, all the people assigned to the violent game come from a judo club—they practice martial arts regularly—while all those assigned to play the other game come from a singing club. If those who play the violent games show higher levels of aggression, what does this tell us? Not much! The difference between the two groups stem from the fact that individuals who already show strong tendencies toward aggression (they are taking a judo class) are more aggressive than those who prefer singing; playing violent video games during the study might be completely unrelated to this difference, which existed prior to the experiment. As result, we can't tell why any differences between them occurred; we have violated random assignment of people to experimental treatments, and that makes the results virtually meaningless.

The second condition essential for successful experimentation is as follows: Insofar as possible, all factors other than the independent variable that might also affect participants' behavior must be held constant. To see why this is so, consider what will happen if, in the study on video games, two assistants collect the data. One is kind and friendly, the other is rude and nasty. By bad luck, the rude assistant collects most of the data for the aggressive game condition and the polite one collects most of the data from the nonaggressive game condition. Again, suppose that participants in the first group are more aggressive toward another person. What do the findings tell us? Again, virtually nothing, because we can't tell whether it was playing the aggressive video game or the rude treatment they received from the assistant that produced higher aggression. In situations like this, the independent variable is said to be *confounded* with another variable—one that is not under systematic investigation in the study. When such confounding occurs, the findings of an experiment may be largely uninterpretable (see Figure 1.13).

In sum, experimentation is, in several respects, the most powerful of social psychology's methods. It certainly isn't perfect—for example, since it is often conducted in laboratory settings that are quite different from the locations in which social behavior actually occurs, the question of *external validity* often arises: To what extent can the findings of experiments be generalized to real-life social situations and perhaps people different from those who participated in the research? And there are situations where, because of ethical or legal considerations, it can't be used. For instance, it would clearly be unethical to expose couples to conditions designed to weaken their trust in one another, or to expose research participants to a kind of television programming that may cause them to harm themselves. But in situations where it is appropriate and is used with skill and care, however, the experimental method can yield results that help us to answer complex questions about social behavior and social thought. Overall, though, please keep the following basic point in mind: there is no single best method of conducting research in social psychology. Rather, all methods offer advantages and disadvantages, so the guiding principle is that the method that is most appropriate to answering the questions being investigated is the one that should be used.

random assignment of participants to experimental conditions
A basic requirement for conducting valid experiments. According to this principle, research participants must have an equal chance of being exposed to each level of the independent variable.

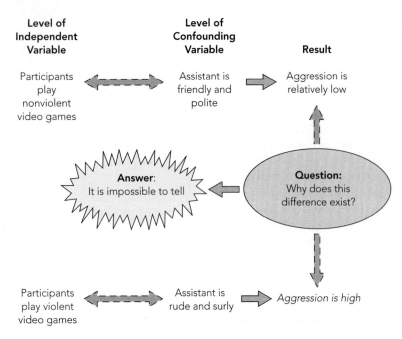

Level of Independent Variable	Level of Confounding Variable	Result

FIGURE 1.13 **Confounding of Variables: A Fatal Flaw in Experimentation**

In a hypothetical experiment designed to investigate the effects of playing violent video games on aggression, the independent variable is confounded with another variable, the behavior of the assistants conducting the study. One assistant is kind and polite and the other is rude and surly. The friendly assistant collects most of the data in nonviolent game condition, while the rude assistant collects most of the data in the violent game condition. Findings indicate that people who play the violent video games are more aggressive. But because of confounding of variables, we can't tell whether this is a result of playing these games or the assistant's rude treatment. The two variables are confounded, and the experiment doesn't provide useful information on the issue it is designed to study.

Further Thoughts on Causality: The Role of Mediating Variables

Earlier, we noted that social psychologists often use experimentation because it is helpful in answering questions about causality: Do changes in one variable produce (cause) changes in another? That is a very valuable kind of information to have because it helps us understand what events, thoughts, or situations lead to various outcomes—more or less helping, more or less aggression, more or less prejudice. Often, though, social psychologists take experimentation one step further in their efforts to answer the question of why—to understand why one variable produces changes in another. For instance, returning to the video game study described above, it is reasonable to ask, Why does playing such games increase aggression? Because it induces increased thoughts about harming others? Reminds people of real or imagined wrongs they have suffered at the hands of other people? Convinces them that aggression is okay since it leads to high scores in the game?

To get at this question of underlying processes, social psychologists often conduct studies in which they measure not just a single dependent variable, but other factors that they believe to be at work—factors that are influenced by the independent variable and then, in turn, affect the dependent measures. For instance, in this study, we could measure participants' thoughts about harming others and their beliefs about when and whether aggression is acceptable social behavior to see if these factors help explain why playing violent video games increases subsequent aggression. If they do, then they are termed **mediating variables**, ones that intervene between an independent variable (here, playing certain kinds of video games) and changes in social behavior or thought.

The Role of Theory in Social Psychology

There is one more aspect of social psychological research we should consider before concluding. As we noted earlier, in their research, social psychologists seek to do more than simply describe the world: they want to be able to *explain* it too. For instance, social psychologists are not interested in merely stating that racial prejudice is common in the United States (although, perhaps, decreasing); they want to be able to explain why some people are more prejudiced toward a particular group than are others. In social psychology, as in all branches of science, explanation involves the construction of theories—frameworks for explaining various events or processes. The procedure involved in building a theory goes something like this:

1. On the basis of existing evidence, a theory that reflects this evidence is proposed.
2. This theory, which consists of basic concepts and statements about how these concepts are related, helps to organize existing information and makes predictions about

mediating variable
A variable that is affected by an independent variable and then influences a dependent variable. Mediating variables help explain why or how specific variables influence social behavior or thought in certain ways.

observable events. For instance, the theory might predict the conditions under which individuals acquire racial prejudice.

3. These predictions, known as *hypotheses*, are then tested by actual research.

4. If results are consistent with the theory, confidence in its accuracy is increased. If they are not, the theory is modified and further tests are conducted.

5. Ultimately, the theory is either accepted as accurate or rejected as inaccurate. Even if it is accepted as accurate, however, the theory remains open to further refinement as improved methods of research are developed and additional evidence relevant to the theory's predictions is obtained.

This may sound a bit abstract, so let's turn to a concrete example. Suppose that a social psychologist formulates the following theory: When people believe that they hold a view that is in the minority, they will be slower to state it and this stems not from the strength of their views, but from reluctance to state minority opinions publicly where others will hear and perhaps disapprove of them for holding those views. This theory would lead to specific predictions—for instance, the minority slowness effect will be reduced if people can state their opinions privately (e.g., Bassili, 2003). If research findings are consistent with this prediction and with others derived from the theory, confidence in the theory is increased. If findings are not consistent with the theory, it will be modified or perhaps rejected, as noted above.

This process of formulating a theory, testing it, modifying the theory, testing it again, and so on lies close to the core of the scientific method, so it is an important aspect of social psychological research (see Figure 1.14). Thus, many different theories relating to important aspects of social behavior and social thought are presented in this book.

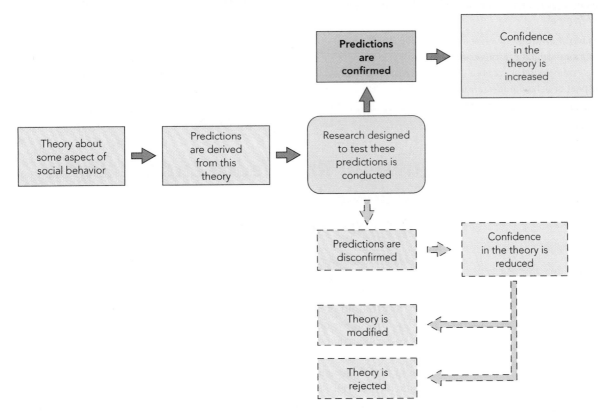

FIGURE 1.14   The Role of Theory in Social Psychological Research

Theories both organize existing knowledge and make predictions about how various events or processes will occur. Once a theory is formulated, hypotheses derived logically from it are tested through careful research. If results agree with the predictions, confidence in the theory is increased. If results disagree with such predictions, the theory may be modified or ultimately rejected as false.

Two final points. First, theories are never proven in any final, ultimate sense; rather, they are always open to test, and are accepted with more or less confidence depending on the weight of available evidence. Second, research is not undertaken to prove or verify a theory; it is performed to gather evidence relevant to the theory. If a researcher sets out to "prove" her or his pet theory, this is a serious violation of the principles of scientific skepticism, objectivity, and open-mindedness described on page 06.

KEY POINTS

- With **systematic observation,** behavior is carefully observed and recorded. In naturalistic observation, such observations are made in settings where the behavior naturally occurs.

- **Survey methods** often involve large numbers of people who are asked to respond to questions about their attitudes or behavior.

- When the **correlational method** of research is employed, two or more variables are measured to determine how they might be related to one another.

- The existence of even strong correlations between variables does not indicate that they are causally related to each other.

- **Experimentation** involves systematically altering one or more variables **(independent variables)** in order to determine whether changes in this variable affect some aspect of behavior **(dependent variables)**.

- Successful use of the **experimental method** requires **random assignment of participants to conditions** and holding all other factors that might also influence behavior constant so as to avoid confounding of variables.

- Although it is a very powerful research tool, the experimental method is not perfect—questions concerning the external validity of findings so obtained often arise. Furthermore, it cannot be used in some situations because of practical or ethical considerations.

- Research designed to investigate **mediating variables** adds to understanding of how specific variables influence certain aspects of social behavior or social thought.

- Theories are frameworks for explaining various events or processes. They play a key role in social psychological research.

The Quest for Knowledge and the Rights of Individuals: In Search of an Appropriate Balance

In their use of experimentation, correlation, and systematic observation, social psychologists do not differ from researchers in other fields. One technique, however, does seem to be unique to research in social psychology: **deception**. This technique involves efforts by researchers to withhold or conceal information about the purposes of a study from participants. The reason for doing so is simple: Many social psychologists believe that if participants know the true purposes of a study, their behavior in it will be changed by that knowledge. Thus, the research will not yield valid information about social behavior or social thought, unless deception is employed.

Some kinds of research do seem to require the use of temporary deception. For example, consider the video game study described above. If participants know that the purpose of a study is to investigate the impact of such games, isn't it likely that they might lean over backward to avoid showing it? Similarly, consider a study of the effects of physical appearance on attraction between strangers. Again, if participants know that the

deception
A technique whereby researchers withhold information about the purposes or procedures of a study from people participating in it.

researcher is interested in this topic, they might work hard to avoid being influenced by a stranger's appearance. In this and many other cases, social psychologists feel compelled to employ temporary deception in their research (Suls & Rosnow, 1988). However, the use of deception raises important ethical issues that cannot be ignored.

First, there is the chance, however slim, that deception may result in some kind of harm to the people exposed to it. They may be upset by the procedures used or by their own reactions to them. For example, in several studies concerned with helping in emergencies, participants were exposed to seemingly real emergency situations. For instance, they overheard what seemed to be a medical emergency—another person having an apparent seizure (e.g., Darley & Latané, 1968). Many participants were strongly upset by these staged events, and others were disturbed by the fact that although they recognized the need to help, they failed to do so. Clearly, the fact that participants experienced emotional upset raises complex ethical issues about just how far researchers can go when studying even very important topics such as this one.

We should hasten to emphasize that such research represents an extreme use of deception: generally, deception takes much milder forms. For example, participants may receive a request for help from a stranger who is actually an assistant of the researchers; or they may be informed that most other students in their university hold certain views when in fact they do not. Still, even in such cases, the potential for some kind of harmful effects to participants exists and this is a potentially serious drawback to the use of deception.

Second, there is the possibility that participants will resent being "fooled" during a study and, as a result, they will acquire negative attitudes toward social psychology and psychological research in general; for instance, they may become suspicious about information presented by researchers (Kelman, 1967). To the extent such reactions occur—and recent findings indicate that they do, at least to a degree (Epley & Huff, 1998)—they have disturbing implications for the future of social psychology, which places much emphasis on scientific research.

Because of such possibilities, the use of deception poses something of a dilemma to social psychologists. On the one hand, it seems essential to their research. On the other, its use raises serious problems. How can this issue be resolved? While opinion remains somewhat divided, most social psychologists agree on the following points. First, deception should never be used to persuade people to take part in a study; withholding information about what will happen in an experiment or providing misleading information in order to induce people to take part in it is definitely not acceptable (Sigall, 1997). Second, most social psychologists agree that temporary deception may sometimes be acceptable, provided two basic safeguards are employed. One of these is **informed consent**—giving participants as much information as possible about the procedures to be followed before they make their decision to participate. In short, this is the opposite of withholding information in order to persuade people to participate. The second is careful **debriefing**—providing participants with a full description of the purposes of a study after they have participated in it (see Figure 1.15). Such information should also include an explanation of deception, and why it was necessary to employ it.

Fortunately, existing evidence indicates that together, informed consent and thorough debriefing can substantially reduce the potential dangers of deception (Smith & Richardson, 1985). For example, most participants report that they view temporary deception as acceptable, provided that potential benefits outweigh potential costs and if there is no other means of obtaining the information sought (Rogers, 1980; Sharpe, Adair, & Roese, 1992). However, as we noted above, there is some indication that they do become somewhat more suspicious about what researchers tell them during an experiment; even worse, such increased suspiciousness seems to last over several months (Epley & Huff, 1998).

Overall, then, it appears that most research participants do not react negatively to temporary deception as long as its purpose and necessity are subsequently made clear. However, these findings do not mean that the safety or appropriateness of deception

informed consent
A procedure in which research participants are provided with as much information as possible about a research project before deciding whether to participate in it.

debriefing
Procedures at the conclusion of a research session in which participants are given full information about the nature of the research and the hypothesis or hypotheses under investigation.

FIGURE 1.15 Careful Debriefing: A Requirement in Studies Using Deception
After an experimental session is completed, participants should be provided with thorough debriefing—full information about the experiment's goals and the reasons why temporary deception is considered necessary.

should be taken for granted (Rubin, 1985). On the contrary, the guiding principles for all researchers planning to use this procedure should be: (1) Use deception only when it is absolutely essential to do so—when no other means for conducting the research exists; (2) always proceed with caution; and (3) make certain that every possible precaution is taken to protect the rights, safety, and well-being of research participants. In terms of the latter, all universities in the United States who receive federal funding must have an Institutional Review Board to review the ethics, including a cost–benefit analysis when deception is to be employed, for all proposed research involving human participants.

 # KEYPOINTS

- **Deception** involves efforts by social psychologists to withhold or conceal information about the purposes of a study from participants.
- Most social psychologists believe that temporary deception is often necessary in order to obtain valid research results.

- However, most social psychologists view deception as acceptable only when important safeguards are employed: **informed consent** and thorough **debriefing**.

Getting the Most Out of This Book: A User's Guide

A textbook that is hard to read or understand is like a dull tool: it really can't do what it is designed to do. We are fully aware of this fact, so we have tried our best to make this book as easy to read as possible, and have included a number of features designed to make it more enjoyable—and useful—for you. Here is a brief overview of the steps we've taken to make reading this book a pleasant and informative experience.

First, each chapter begins with an outline of the topics to be covered. This is followed by a chapter-opening story that "sets the stage," and explains how the topics to be covered are related to important aspects of our everyday lives. Within each chapter, key terms are printed in **boldface** type and are followed by a definition. These terms are also defined in the margins of the pages on which they are first mentioned, as well as in a glossary at the end of the book. To help you understand what you have read, each major section is followed by a list of Key Points—a brief summary of the major points. All figures and tables are clear and simple, and most contain special labels and notes designed to help you understand them (see Figure 1.8 for an example). Finally, each chapter ends with a Summary and Review. Reviewing this section can be an important aid to your studying.

Second, this book has an underlying theme, which we have already stated (see page 6), but want to emphasize again: Social psychology seeks basic principles concerning social thought and social behavior—principles that apply very generally, in all cultures and settings. But it recognizes that the context in which the social side of life occurs is very important. Because of the growing role of technology in our lives, the ways in which we interact with other people have changed and now often occur via cell phones, computers, and other electronic devices rather than in face-to-face encounters. We believe that the basic principles of social psychology apply to these new contexts too, but that their accuracy in the "cyber" or "electronic" world must be established by careful research. To take account of this major change in the settings and modes of expression of social behavior, we report research concerning social networks, the Internet, and related topics throughout the book. In addition, to call special attention to their growing importance, we include special sections with up-to-date research in each chapter, titled "Social Life in a Connected World." A few examples: Dating on the Internet; Humiliating Others Through the Web; Helping in Social Networks. We think that these sections will take account of important societal changes that are, indeed, strongly affecting the nature and form of the social side of life.

An additional theme in modern social psychology—and one we have already described—is growing interest in the role of emotion in our social thought and actions. To highlight recent advances in our knowledge of this topic, we will include another type of special section titled "Emotions and..." (for example, "Emotions and Attitudes," "Emotions and Aggression," "Emotions and Group Life"). These sections illustrate the powerful influence of the feeling side of social life, and are based on current and informative research in the field.

We think that together, these features will help you get the most out of this book, and from your first contact with social psychology. Good luck! And may your first encounter with our field prove to be a rich, informative, valuable, and enjoyable experience.

SUMMARY *and* REVIEW

- Social psychology is the scientific field that seeks to understand the nature and causes of individual behavior and thought in social situations. It is scientific in nature because it adopts the values and methods used in other fields of science. Social psychologists adopt the scientific method because "common sense" provides an unreliable guide to social behavior, and because our personal thought is influenced by many potential sources of bias. Social psychology focuses on the behavior of individuals, and seeks to understand the causes of social behavior and thought, which can involve the behavior and appearance of others, social cognition, environmental factors, cultural values, and even biological and genetic factors. Social psychology seeks to establish basic principles of social life that are accurate across huge cultural differences and despite rapid and major changes in social life.

- Important causes of social behavior and thought include the behavior and characteristics of other people, cognitive processes, emotion, culture, and genetic factors. Social psychologists currently recognize that social thought and social behavior are two sides of the same coin, and that there is a continuous, complex interplay between them. There is growing interest among social psychologists in the role of emotion in social thought and social behavior. The formation and development of **relationships** is another major trend in the field. Yet another major trend involves growing interest in social neuroscience—efforts to relate activity in the brain to key aspects of social thought and behavior.

- Our behavior and thought is often shaped by factors of which we are unaware. Growing attention to such implicit (nonconscious) processes is another major theme of modern social psychology. Social psychology currently adopts a **multicultural perspective.** This perspective recognizes the importance of cultural factors in social behavior and social thought, and notes that research findings obtained in one culture do not necessarily generalize to other cultures. With **systematic observation,** behavior is carefully observed and recorded. In naturalistic observation, such observations are made in settings where the behavior naturally occurs. **Survey methods** often involve large numbers of people who are asked to respond to questions about their attitudes or behavior. When the **correlational method** of research is employed, two or more variables are measured to determine how they might be related to one another. The existence of even strong correlations between variables does not indicate that they are causally related to each other.

● **Experimentation** involves systematically altering one or more variables **(independent variables)** in order to determine whether changes in this variable affect some aspect of behavior **(dependent variables)**. Successful use of the experimental method requires **random assignment of participants to conditions** and holding all other factors that might also influence behavior constant so as to avoid confounding of variables. Although it is a very powerful research tool, the experimental method is not perfect—questions concerning

the external validity of findings so obtained often arise. Furthermore, it cannot be used in some situations because of practical or ethical considerations. Research designed to investigate **mediating variables** adds to understanding of how specific variables influence certain aspects of social behavior or social thought. Theories are frameworks for explaining various events or processes. They play a key role in social psychological research.

● **Deception** involves efforts by social psychologists to withhold or conceal information about the purposes of a study from participants. Most social psychologists believe that temporary deception is often necessary in order to obtain valid research results. However, they view deception as acceptable only when important safeguards are employed: **informed consent** and thorough **debriefing.**

KEY TERMS

correlational method   (p. 22)

debriefing   (p. 29)

deception   (p. 28)

dependent variable   (p. 23)

evolutionary
   psychology   (p. 9)

experimentation (experimental
   method)   (p. 23)

hypothesis   (p. 22)

independent variable   (p. 23)

informed consent   (p. 29)

mediating variable   (p. 26)

multicultural perspective   (p. 18)

random assignment of participants to
   experimental conditions   (p. 25)

relationships   (p. 13)

survey method   (p. 20)

systematic observation   (p. 20)

CHAPTER 2

Social Cognition

How We Think About the Social World

T HE PROPOSAL TO BUILD A MOSQUE WITHIN AN ISLAMIC CULTURAL CENTER near Ground Zero in New York City created a lot of conflict. Those on the anti-mosque side are vehemently opposed to the mosque being built where the developers want to build it. These folks say that of course the mosque can be built anywhere that the law allows, but "sensitivities" call for it to be moved "further away."

On the other side, Mayor Michael Bloomberg has said that we cannot allow ourselves to be talked into the idea of moving the planned mosque's future location. He claims there is no justification for moving it—that the opposition has the wrong idea entirely. In his view, locating the mosque elsewhere means that the 9/11 terrorists have accomplished their goal of either cowing us into submission and/or making us fight among ourselves.

Perhaps a social psychological analysis of how people think about the social world can help us to deconstruct this conflict. As you will see in this chapter, people often use mental shortcuts or rules of thumb to arrive at judgments. One that people use a lot is called the *representativeness heuristic,* a rule of thumb wherein people judge a current event by considering how much it resembles another event or category. One of the key symptoms of judging by representativeness is called "ignoring the base rate." Let's see how this can help us understand the debate about the mosque placement in New York.

At the time of the 9/11 attack there were about 900 million peaceful Muslims in the world. We're talking about Arabs throughout the Middle East, but also Turkey, India, Indonesia, and parts of Africa. And, of course, that 900 million includes the 6 million Muslims living in the United States. As for Al-Qaeda's numbers, on ABC's "This Week" in June 2010, Leon Panetta (Director of the CIA) said that there are probably less than 50 Al-Qaeda members hiding out in Pakistan. But let's allow for the possibility of thousands more in Yemen, Somalia, Afghanistan, and other places in which Al-Qaeda could be hanging out. All told, let's speculate that our total complement of Al-Qaeda is 9,000 or less.

Given the overall population of Muslims in the world (900 million) and the Al-Qaeda number as 9,000, that would mean we have a ratio of 9 Al-Qaeda for every 900,000 Muslims, or, dividing by 9, about 1 Al-Qaeda member for every 100,000 peaceful Muslims. No matter how hard you try, it is quite ridiculous to make a judgment about 100,000 Muslims who have never attacked Americans based on the attitudes or actions of one member of Al-Qaeda. This is a clear example of ignoring the base rate.

FIGURE 2.1   Using the Representativeness Heuristic and Ignoring the Base Rate

As these protestors of building an Islamic Cultural Center including a mosque in New York imply on their signs, all Muslims are being judged in terms of their presumed resemblance to the 9/11 terrorism-perpetrators. Of course, the base rate of almost 1 billion Muslims in the world who live peacefully and do not commit nor support such crimes is ignored when the representativeness heuristic is employed.

But people might try anyway, so let's take up a second argument. Another aspect of the representative heuristic is the nature of that which is being represented. After 9/11, people's perceptions of Muslims changed. Before 9/11, Arab Muslims in particular were perhaps seen as backward desert-dwellers, but not as threatening or dangerous to Americans. But how representative is Al-Qaeda of the 900 million Muslims in the world? That is, if Al-Qaeda were the "army" of Muslims everywhere, then we might feel more justified in blaming all people of the Islamic faith for 9/11. But, in fact, across the Muslim world, Al-Qaeda is considered a deviant group. By deviant, we mean that the attitudes and beliefs, as well as the behaviors of Al-Qaeda, are markedly different from peaceful Muslims.

How so, you might ask? Well, for one thing, peaceful Muslims may get mad just as you and I do, but they do *not* believe that the Koran permits the indiscriminate killing of 3,000 innocent people, as was done on 9/11 by Al-Qaeda. Thus, the actions of Al-Qaeda are not representative of the general population of Muslims, and have almost nothing to do with the religion of Islam and the Koran as understood by ordinary Muslim devotees.

Of course, we use the representativeness heuristic every day as a shortcut to forming opinions about people in various groups and the probability that they will behave in particular ways. But, in the case of the so-called Ground Zero mosque, use of the representativeness heuristic as shown in Figure 2.1 alters people's perception of the blameworthiness of Islam with regard to 9/11, and that changes people's impressions of whether an Islamic place of worship should be built close to Ground Zero.

Building a mosque near Ground Zero . . . what, you may be wondering, does this have to do with the major focus of this chapter, **social cognition**—how we think about the social world, our attempts to understand it, and ourselves and our place in it (e.g., Fiske & Taylor, 2008; Higgins & Kruglanski, 1996)? The answer is simple: this conflict captures several key issues relating to social cognition that we examine in the rest of this chapter. First, it suggests very strongly that often our thinking about the social world proceeds on "automatic"—quickly, effortlessly, and without lots of careful reasoning. As we'll see later, such automatic thought or automatic processing offers important advantages—it requires

social cognition
The manner in which we interpret, analyze, remember, and use information about the social world.

little or no effort and can be very efficient. While such automatic processes, including heuristic use, can lead to satisfactory judgments, it can also lead to important errors in the conclusions we draw.

This incident also illustrates that although we do a lot of social thought on "automatic," we do sometimes stop and think much more carefully and logically about it (e.g., Should one Muslim's actions be taken as representative of 100,000 Muslims?). Such *controlled processing*, as social psychologists term it, tends to occur when something unexpected happens—something that jolts us out of automatic, effortless thought. For example, when New York's Mayor Bloomberg expressly questioned the validity of comparing "Muslims" to the 9/11 attackers, and argued that moving the mosque elsewhere would mean that the terrorists had won by making the United States a less free society, some people did indeed question their initial premise. As we'll see in later sections, unexpected events often trigger such careful, effortful thought.

In the remainder of this chapter, we examine the several types of **heuristics**—simple rules of thumb we often use to make inferences quickly, and with minimal effort—that people frequently use, and describe the research conducted by social psychologists addressing how they operate. Next, we consider in-depth the idea that often, social thought occurs in an automatic manner. In other words, it often unfolds in a quick and relatively effortless manner rather than in a careful, systematic, and effortful one. We consider how a basic component of social thought—*schemas*, or mental frameworks that allow us to organize large amounts of information in an efficient manner—can exert strong effects on social thought— effects that are not always beneficial from the point of view of accuracy. After considering how schema use can lead to judgment errors, we examine several specific tendencies or "tilts" in social thought—tendencies that can lead us to false conclusions about others or the social world. Finally, we focus on the complex interplay between **affect**—our current feelings or moods—and various aspects of social cognition (e.g., Forgas, 1995a, 2000).

heuristics
Simple rules for making complex decisions or drawing inferences in a rapid manner and seemingly effortless manner.

affect
Our current feelings and moods.

Heuristics: How We Reduce Our Effort in Social Cognition

Several states have passed or are considering adopting laws that ban talking on hand-held cell phones and texting while driving. Why? Because—as the cartoon in Figure 2.2 indicates—these are very dangerous practices, particularly texting. It has been found over and over again that when drivers are distracted, they are more likely to get into accidents, and talking or texting can certainly be highly distracting. What about global positioning systems (GPS), which show maps to drivers; do you think that they, too, can lead to distraction and cause accidents?

At any given time, we are capable of handling a certain amount of

FIGURE 2.2   Distraction: A Potential Cause of Accidents
Our capacity to process incoming information is definitely limited, and can easily be exceeded. This can happen when drivers are texting or talking on the phone while driving. As this cartoon suggests, fatal accidents can result.

information; additional input beyond this puts us into a state of **information overload** where the demands on our cognitive system are greater than its capacity. In addition, our processing capacity can be depleted by high levels of stress or other demands (e.g., Chajut & Algom, 2003). To deal with such situations, people adopt various strategies designed to "stretch" their cognitive resources—to let them do more, with less effort, than would otherwise be the case. This is one major reason why so much of our social thought occurs on "automatic"—in a quick and effortless way. We discuss the costs and potential benefits of such thought later. Here, however, we focus on techniques we use to deal quickly with large amounts of information, especially under **conditions of uncertainty**—where the "correct" answer is difficult to know or would take a great deal of effort to determine. While many strategies for making sense of complex information exist, one of the most useful tactics involves the use of *heuristics*—simple rules for making complex decisions or drawing inferences in a rapid and efficient manner.

Representativeness: Judging by Resemblance

Suppose that you have just met your next-door neighbor for the first time. While chatting with her, you notice that she is dressed conservatively, is neat in her personal habits, has a very large library in her home, and seems to be very gentle and a little shy. Later you realize that she never mentioned what she does for a living. Is she a business manager, a physician, a waitress, an artist, a dancer, or a librarian? One quick way of making a guess is to compare her with your **prototype**—consisting of the attributes possessed by other members of each of these occupations. How well does she resemble people you have met in each of these fields or, perhaps, the typical member of these fields (Shah & Oppenheimer, 2009)? If you proceed in this manner, you may quickly conclude that she is probably a librarian; her traits seem closer to those associated with this profession than they do to the traits associated with being a physician, dancer, or executive. If you made your judgment about your neighbor's occupation in this manner, you would be using the **representativeness heuristic.** In other words, you would make your judgment on the basis of a relatively simple rule: The more an individual seems to resemble or match a given group, the more likely she or he is to belong to that group.

Are such judgments accurate? Often they are, because belonging to certain groups does affect the behavior and style of people in them, and because people with certain traits are attracted to particular groups in the first place. But sometimes, judgments based on representativeness are wrong, mainly for the following reason: Decisions or judgments made on the basis of this rule tend to ignore *base rates*—the frequency with which given events or patterns (e.g., occupations) occur in the total population (Kahneman & Frederick, 2002; Kahneman & Tversky, 1973). In fact, there are many more business managers than librarians—perhaps 50 times as many. Thus, even though your neighbor seemed more similar to the prototype of librarians than managers in terms of her traits, the chances are actually higher that she is a manager than a librarian. Likewise, as we saw in the opening example, ignoring the base rate that consists of millions of Muslims who are nonviolent can lead to errors in our thinking about people.

The representativeness heuristic is used not only in judging the similarity of people to a category prototype, but also when judging whether specific causes resemble and are therefore likely to produce effects that are similar in terms of magnitude. That is, when people are asked to judge the likelihood that a particular effect (e.g., either many or a few people die of a disease) was produced by a particular cause (e.g., an unusually infectious bacteria or a standard strain), they are likely to expect the strength of the cause to match its effect. However, cultural groups differ in the extent to which they rely on the representative heuristic and expect "like to go with like" in terms of causes and effects. In particular, people from Asia tend to consider more potential causal factors when judging effects than do Americans (Choi, Dalal, Kim-Prieto, & Park, 2003). Because they consider more information and arrive at more complex attributions when judging an event,

information overload
Instances in which our ability to process information is exceeded.

conditions of uncertainty
Where the "correct" answer is difficult to know or would take a great deal of effort to determine.

prototype
Summary of the common attributes possessed by members of a category.

representativeness heuristic
A strategy for making judgments based on the extent to which current stimuli or events resemble other stimuli or categories.

Asians should show less evidence of thinking based on the representative heuristic—a judgment simplification strategy—compared to North Americans.

To test this reasoning, Spina et al. (2010) asked students in China and Canada to rate the likelihood that a high- or low-magnitude effect (few or many deaths) was caused by a virus that differed in magnitude (a strain that was treatment-resistant or a standard strain that could be controlled with medical treatment). While participants in both national groups showed evidence of expecting high-magnitude effects (many deaths) to be produced by high-magnitude causes (the treatment-resistant virus strain) and low-magnitude effects (few deaths) to be produced by low-magnitude causes (the standard strain of the virus), Canadian participants showed this effect much more strongly than the Chinese participants. Such reasoning differences could potentially result in difficulty when members of different groups seek to achieve agreement on how best to tackle problems affecting the world as a whole—such as climate change. Westerners may expect that "big causes" have to be tackled to reduce the likelihood of global warming, whereas Asians may be comfortable emphasizing more "minor causes" of substantial outcomes such as climate change.

Availability: "If I Can Retrieve Instances, They Must Be Frequent"

When estimating event frequencies or their likelihood, people may simply not know the "correct" answer—even for events in their own lives. So how do they arrive at a response? Ask yourself, how often have you talked on your cell phone while driving? Well, *I* can remember quite a few instances, so I'd have to guess it is quite often. This is an instance of judging frequency based on the ease with which instances can be brought to mind. Now consider another, non-self-related question: Are you safer driving in a huge SUV or in a smaller, lighter car? Many people would answer: "In the big SUV"—thinking, as shown in Figure 2.3, that if you are in an accident, you are less likely to get hurt in a big vehicle compared to a small one. While that might seem to be correct, actual data

indicate that death rates (number of deaths per 1 million vehicles on the road) are higher for SUVs than smaller cars (e.g., Gladwell, 2005). So why do so many people conclude, falsely, that they are safer in a bulky SUV? Like the cell phone–use question, the answer seems to involve what comes to mind when we think about this question. Most people can recall scenes in which a huge vehicle had literally crushed another smaller vehicle in an accident. Because such scenes are dramatic, we can readily bring them to mind. But this "ease of retrieval" effect may mislead us: We assume that because such scenes are readily available in memory, they accurately reflect the overall frequency, when, in fact, they don't. For instance, such recall does not remind us of the fact that SUVs are involved in accidents more often than smaller, lighter cars; that large SUVs tip over more easily than other vehicles; or

FIGURE 2.3   Availability Heuristic Use: Images Like These Come Readily to Mind

People believe they are safer and less likely to get into an accident with a larger SUV than a smaller car—in part, because images like these come readily to mind. But, actually, SUVs are involved in more accidents than smaller cars.

that SUVs are favored by less careful drivers who are more likely to be involved in accidents!

This and many similar judgment errors illustrate the operation of the **availability heuristic,** another cognitive "rule of thumb" suggesting that the easier it is to bring information to mind, the greater its impact on subsequent judgments or decisions. While use of this heuristic can make good sense much of the time—after all, the fact that we can bring some types of information to mind quite easily suggests that it may indeed be frequent or important so it *should* influence our judgments and decisions. But relying on availability in making social judgments can also lead to errors. Specifically, it can lead us to overestimate the likelihood of events that are dramatic but rare because they are easy to bring to mind. Consistent with this principle, many people fear travel in airplanes more than travel in automobiles, even though the chances of dying in an auto accident are hundreds of times higher. Likewise, people overestimate murder as a cause of death, and underestimate more mundane but much more frequent killers such as heart disease and stroke. The idea here is that because of the frequency that murder and other dramatic causes of death are presented in the mass media, instances are easier to retrieve from memory than are various natural causes of death that are rarely presented in the media. Here's another example: Physicians who examine the same patient often reach different diagnoses about the patient's illness. Why? One reason is that physicians have different experiences in their medical practices, and so find different kinds of diseases easier to bring to mind. Their diagnoses then reflect these differences in ease of retrieval—or, their reliance on the availability heuristic.

Interestingly, research suggests that there is more to the availability heuristic than merely the subjective ease with which relevant information comes to mind. In addition, the amount of information we can bring to mind seems to matter, too (e.g., Schwarz et al., 1991). The more information we can think of, the greater its impact on our judgments. Which of these two factors is more important? The answer appears to involve the kind of judgment we are making. If it is one involving emotions or feelings, we tend to rely on the "ease" rule, whereas if it is one involving facts or the task is inherently difficult, we tend to rely more on the "amount" rule (e.g., Rothman & Hardin, 1997; Ruder & Bless, 2003).

It is also the case that the ease of bringing instances to mind affects judgments that are self-relevant more readily than judgments about others. In fact, even judgments about objects that we are personally familiar with—say, consumer brands—are influenced by ease of retrieval more than judgments about brands that we are less familiar with (Tybout, Sternthal, Malaviya, Bakamitsos, & Park, 2005). This is because when we are aware that we have less information about others or unfamiliar objects, making judgments about them seems more difficult and ease of retrieval is given less weight. But when we think we are familiar with the task, know more about the task, or the task itself is easy, then ease of retrieval is particularly likely to be the basis of our judgment. Let's see how this plays out in judgments of risk.

Harvard University students were asked to make judgments about how safe their college town, Cambridge, Massachusetts, was after they had been asked to recall either two or six examples of when they or another student "had felt unsafe or feared for their safety around campus" (Caruso, 2008). Of course, it should be (and was for these participants) easier to recall two instances when they felt unsafe than to recall six instances, and it should be easier to retrieve instances when you felt a particular way than when another person did. Those students who had an easy job of recalling unsafe examples for themselves rated their town as more unsafe than when they had a difficult time retrieving more examples. Use of the perceived ease of recall, though, was not applied to judgments of the safety of one's own town when the examples brought to mind concerned someone else's experiences. Consider another example: Would you find it easier to generate two instances that are diagnostic of your creativity, or six instances? What about instances for an acquaintance? As shown in Figure 2.4, students did find it easier to generate

availability heuristic
A strategy for making judgments on the basis of how easily specific kinds of information can be brought to mind.

two examples of their own creativity compared to six examples, and this influenced their ratings of their own creativity. Ease of retrieving examples of creativity for an acquaintance did not affect ratings of creativity for that other because subjective ease of retrieval is given less weight.

Anchoring and Adjustment: Where You Begin Makes a Difference

When people attempt to sell something—whether it be a house on HGTV, or a car through an ad in a newspaper—they typically set the "asking" price higher than they really expect to get. Likewise, buyers often bid initially less than they expect to ultimately pay. This is mostly because buyers and sellers want to give themselves some room for bargaining. Often the selling price is the starting point for discussion; the buyer offers less, the seller counters, and the process continues until an agreement is reached, or one or the other gives up. It turns out that when a seller sets a starting price, this is an important advantage because of another heuristic that strongly influences our thinking: **anchoring and adjustment.** This heuristic involves the tendency to deal with uncertainty in many situations by using something we do know as a starting point, and then making adjustments to it. The seller's price provides such a starting point, to which buyers try to make adjustments in order to lower the price they pay. Such lowering makes the buyer feel that, by comparison to the original asking price, they are getting a very good deal. This too is how "sale pricing" and highly visible "reductions" work in retail stores—the original starting point sets the comparison so shoppers feel like they are then getting a bargain.

In a sense, the existence of the anchoring and adjustment heuristic is far from surprising. In uncertain situations we have to start somewhere. What is more surprising, however, is how powerful this effect is even in situations where, rationally, it should not operate. For instance, consider an unsettling study by Englich, Mussweiler, and Strack (2006), indicating that even court decisions and sentences can be strongly influenced by anchoring and adjustment and that, moreover, this occurs even for experienced judges!

In this research, the participants were highly experienced legal professionals in Germany. They were asked to read a very realistic court case and then learned of prison sentences recommended for the defendant. In one study, these recommendations were from a journalist—someone with no legal training. In another study, the recommended sentences were actually generated by throwing dice—randomly, and with no connection to the crime itself. Finally, in another, they were from an experienced prosecutor. Some of the recommendations were lenient (e.g., 1 month of probation) and others were harsh (e.g., 3 years in prison for the same crime). After receiving this information, the experienced legal participants made their own sentencing recommendations. The recommendations of these experts should *not* be influenced by the anchors they received, especially when the sources were either irrelevant or purely random in two conditions (lenient or

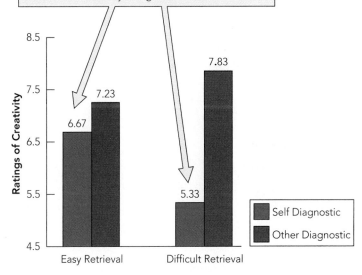

When easy to retrieve examples diagnostic of the self being creative, rated own creativity was higher than when it was difficult to retrieve creative examples for the self. Ease of retrieving examples for others had no effect on creativity ratings of the other

FIGURE 2.4   Availability Heuristic Use: Perceived Creativity of the Self Depends on Ease of Retrieval

Ratings of perceived self-creativity depended on ease of retrieval. When it was easy (vs. difficult) to generate diagnostic examples for the self, then perceived self-creativity increased. The ease or difficulty of generating creative instances for another person did not affect judgments of the other's creativity. (Source: Based on research by Caruso, 2008).

anchoring and adjustment heuristic
A heuristic that involves the tendency to use a number of value as a starting point to which we then make adjustments.

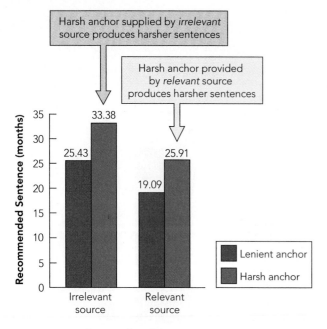

FIGURE 2.5   Anchoring and Adjustment in Legal Decisions

When experienced legal experts learned of the sentences recommended by an irrelevant source (someone with no legal training—a journalist, or even just a throw of a dice), their own recommendations were strongly influenced by these anchors. Harsher sentences were recommended when the anchors were harsh, and more lenient sentences when the anchors were lenient. The same anchoring effects were found when the source of the anchor was relevant—an experienced prosecutor. These findings indicate that anchoring often exerts powerful effects on social thought. (Source: Based on data from Englich, Mussweiler, & Strack, 2006).

harsh recommendations from a journalist or ones generated by the throw of dice). But, as you can see in Figure 2.5, these anchors did have significant effects: Sentences were harsher when participants were exposed to a harsh anchor but more lenient when they were exposed to a lenient anchor. Furthermore, it did *not* matter whether the source of the anchor was a journalist, an experienced prosecutor, or merely the throw of dice. These findings, while a compelling demonstration of the power of anchoring, are also quite disturbing. If even experienced and highly trained legal experts can be influenced by anchoring and adjustment, it seems clear that this is indeed a very powerful effect—and indicative of how shortcuts in social thought can have real consequences in important life contexts.

Why are the effects of the anchoring and adjustment heuristic so powerful? Research findings indicate that one reason is that although we do make adjustments to anchors, these adjustments are often not sufficient to overcome the initial impact of the anchors. In other words, we seem to stop as soon as a value we consider plausible is reached (Epley & Gilovich, 2006). In a sense, this is yet another example of the "save mental effort" principle that we tend to follow in many contexts and across many different aspects of social thought. Interestingly, the tendency to make insufficient judgments is greater when individuals are in a state in which they are less capable of engaging in effortful thought—for instance, after consuming alcohol or when people are busy doing other tasks (Epley & Gilovich, 2006). Overall, then, it appears that our tendency to let initial anchors influence our judgments—even in important situations—does stem, to an important degree, from a tendency to avoid the effortful work involved in making adjustments away from initial anchors.

Status Quo Heuristic: "What Is, Is Good"

When people are asked to make judgments and choices, they seem to act as though they believe the status quo is good. Similar to the availability heuristic, objects and options that are more easily retrieved from memory may be judged in a heuristic fashion as "good," as better than objects and options that are new, rarely encountered, or represent a change from the status quo. As with the other types of heuristics we've discussed, assuming that a product that has long been on the market is superior to a new version might seem to be logical because across time bad products tend to be removed from the market. But, it is also the case that old products stay on the market through inertia, and people may continue buying it partly out of habit. Indeed, many marketers seem to believe that people prefer new over the old—if their emphasis on "new and improved" on packaging is any indication!

In a series of studies, Eidelman, Pattershall and Crandall (2010) have put the issue of whether people heuristically favor "old" over "new," or the opposite, to the test. Participants in one study were given a piece of chocolate to taste. Before doing so, they were told either that the chocolate was first sold in its region of Europe in 1937 or in 2003. In the former case, the product was said to be on the market for 70 years and in the latter for only 3 years. Participants were then asked to rate how much they enjoyed the taste of the chocolate, whether they were impressed by it, and whether they would purchase it. They were then asked about the reasons for their evaluation of the chocolate. Overwhelmingly, participants rated the chocolate that was said to have been in existence longer as more delicious than the chocolate that represented a new brand. These participants seemed to be unaware that time on the market had influenced their evaluations of the chocolate—they uniformly rated that as the least important reason for their evaluation and, instead, rated "its taste" as the most important factor affecting their evaluation. But, it was exactly the same chocolate and only the supposed length of time on the market differed! These researchers also showed in another experiment that students favored a degree requirement proposal that was said to already be in existence over the same proposal when it was framed as representing a change from the present. Furthermore, when the length of time a practice (acupuncture) was said to be in existence was varied—250, 500, 1,000, or 2,000 years—its perceived effectiveness increased across the time intervals. Likewise, a painting whose aesthetic qualities were to be judged was rated more pleasing when it was said to have been painted in 1905 compared to when it was said to have been painted more recently, in 2005. So, people do seem to use heuristically the length of time a product or practice has been in existence as a cue to its goodness. Although judgments of all products are unlikely to be biased in favor of age, and occasionally novelty may win, tradition or longevity often does seem to imply heuristically that the "tried and true" is better than the new.

 # KEYPOINTS

- Because we have limited cognitive capacity, we often attempt to reduce the effort we expend on **social cognition**—how we think about other people and events. Given our limited capacity to process information, we often experience **information overload**. To deal with complex information, where the correct answer is not obvious (**conditions of uncertainty**), we make use of **heuristics**—simple rules for making decisions in a quick and relatively effortless manner.

- One such heuristic is **representativeness**, which suggests that the more similar an individual or subgroup of people is to typical members of a given group—the group's **prototype**—the more likely they will be seen as belonging to that group.

- Using the representativeness heuristic can lead to erroneous decisions when *base rates* are underused but are relevant.

- There are cultural differences in using representativeness to evaluate the likelihood that a particular cause

was responsible for an effect. Asians tend to expect that "like will go with like" less than Westerners do.

- Another heuristic is **availability**, which suggests that the easier it is to bring information to mind, the greater its impact on subsequent decisions or judgments. In some cases, availability may also involve the amount of information we bring to mind. We tend to apply the ease of retrieval rule to judgments about ourselves more than to judgments about others.

- A third heuristic is **anchoring and adjustment**, which leads us to use a number or value as a starting point from which we then make adjustments. These adjustments may not be sufficient to reflect actual social reality, perhaps because once we attain a plausible value, we stop the process.

- Objects and options that are more *easily retrieved from memory* may be judged in a heuristic fashion as "good," as better than objects and options that are new, rarely encountered, or represent a change from the status quo.

Schemas: Mental Frameworks for Organizing Social Information

What happens when you visit your doctor? We all know it goes something like this. You enter and give your health insurance information. Then you sit and wait! If you are lucky, the wait is not very long and a nurse takes you into an examining room. Once there, you wait some more. Eventually, the doctor enters and talks to you and perhaps examines you. Finally, you leave and perhaps pay some part of your bill (the co-pay) on the way out. It doesn't matter who your doctor is or where you live—this sequence of events,

FIGURE 2.6 Schemas: Mental Frameworks Concerning Routine Events

Through experience, we acquire schemas—mental frameworks for organizing, interpreting, and processing social information. For instance, you almost certainly have well-developed schemas for such events as boarding an airplane (top photo) and going to the dentist (bottom photo). In other words, you know what to expect in these and many other situations, and are prepared to behave in them in certain sequences.

schemas
Mental frameworks centering on a specific theme that help us to organize social information.

or something very much like it, will take place. None of this surprises you; in fact, you expect this sequence to occur—including the waiting. Why? Through past experience, you have built up a mental framework containing the essential features of this kind of situation—visiting a health professional. Similarly, you have formed other mental frameworks reflecting going to restaurants, getting a haircut, shopping for groceries, going to the movies, or boarding an airplane (see Figure 2.6).

Social psychologists term such frameworks **schemas,** and define them as mental frameworks that help us to organize social information, and that guide our actions and the processing of information relevant to those contexts. Since your personal experience in such situations is probably similar to that of others in your culture, everyone in a given society will tend to share many basic schemas. Once schemas are formed, they play a role in determining what we notice about the social world, what information we remember, and how we use and interpret such information. Let's take a closer look at these effects because as we'll soon see, they exert an important impact on our understanding of the social world and our relations with other people.

The Impact of Schemas on Social Cognition: Attention, Encoding, Retrieval

How do schemas influence social thought? Research findings suggest that they influence three basic processes: attention, encoding, and retrieval. *Attention* refers to what information we notice. *Encoding* refers to the processes through which information we notice gets stored in memory. Finally, *retrieval* refers to the processes through which we recover information from memory in order to use it in some manner—for example, in making judgments about other people.

Schemas have been found to influence all of these aspects of social cognition (Wyer & Srull, 1994). With respect to attention, schemas often act as a kind of filter: information consistent with them is more likely to be noticed and to enter our consciousness. Schemas are particularly likely to be relied on when we are experiencing *cognitive load*—when we are trying to handle a lot of information at one time (Kunda, 1999). In this case, we rely on our schemas because they help us process information efficiently.

Turning to encoding—the information that becomes the focus of our attention is much more likely to be stored in long-term memory. In general, it is information that is consistent with our schemas that is encoded. However, information that is sharply inconsistent with our schemas—information that does *not* agree with our expectations in a given situation—may be encoded into a separate memory location and marked with a unique "tag." Schema-inconsistent information is sometimes so unexpected that it literally seizes our attention and almost forces us to make a mental note of it (Stangor & McMillan, 1992). Here's an example: You have a well-developed schema for the role of "professor." You expect professors to come to class, to lecture, to answer questions, to give and grade exams, and so on. Suppose that one of your professors comes to class and instead of lecturing does magic tricks. You will certainly remember this experience because it is so inconsistent with your schema for professors—your mental framework for how professors behave in the classroom.

That leads us to the third process: retrieval from memory. What information is most readily remembered—information that is consistent with our schemas or information that is inconsistent with these mental frameworks? This is a complex question that has been investigated in many different studies (e.g., Stangor & McMillan, 1992; Tice, Bratslavky, & Baumeister, 2000). Overall, research suggests that people tend to report remembering information that is consistent with schemas more than information that is inconsistent. However, this could potentially stem from differences in actual memory or, alternatively, from simple response tendencies. In other words, information inconsistent with schemas might be present in memory as strongly as information consistent with schemas, but people simply report the information that is consistent with their schemas. In fact, the latter appears to be the case. When measures of memory are corrected for this response tendency, or when individuals are asked to actually *recall* information rather than indicate whether they recognize it, a strong tendency to remember information that is *incongruent* (i.e., does not fit) with schemas appears. So, the answer to the question, Which do we remember better—information consistent or inconsistent with our schemas?, *depends on the memory measure employed.* In general, people *report* information consistent with their schemas, but information inconsistent with schemas may be strongly present in memory, too.

Priming: Which Schemas Guide Our Thought?

We all develop a large array of schemas—cognitive frameworks that help us interpret and use social information. That raises an interesting question: Which of these frameworks influence our thought at any given point in time? One answer involves the strength of various schemas: the stronger and better-developed schemas are, the more likely they are to influence our thinking, and especially our memory for social information (e.g., Stangor & McMillan, 1992; Tice et al., 2000).

Second, schemas can be temporarily activated by what is known as **priming**—transitory increases in the ease with which specific schemas can be activated (Sparrow & Wegner, 2006). For instance, suppose you have just seen a violent movie. Now, you are looking for a parking spot and you notice one, but another driver turns in front of you and takes it first. Do you perceive her behavior as aggressive? Because the violent movie has activated your schema for "aggression," you may, in fact, be more likely to perceive her taking the parking spot as aggressive. This illustrates the effects of priming—recent experiences make some schemas active, and as a result, they exert effects on our current thinking.

Can priming be deactivated, or are we doomed to see the world in terms of the schema activated by our most recent experience? Social psychologists describe **unpriming** as a process by which thoughts or actions that have been primed by a recent experience dissipates once it finds expression. Unpriming effects are clearly demonstrated in a study by Sparrow and Wegner (2006). Participants were given a series of very easy "yes–no" questions (e.g., "Does a triangle have three sides?"). One group of participants was told to try to answer the questions randomly—*not* correctly. Another group responded to the questions twice; the first time, they were told to try to answer them correctly, while the second time, they were to try to answer them randomly. It was predicted that participants in the first group would not be able to answer the questions randomly; their schema for "answering correctly" would be activated, and lead them to provide the correct answers. In contrast, participants who answered the questions twice—first correctly and then randomly—would do better at responding randomly. Their first set of answers would provide expression for the schema "answer questions correctly," and so permit them to answer randomly the second time around. That's precisely what happened; those who only answered the question once and were told to do so randomly were actually correct 58 percent of the time—their activated schema prevented them from replying in a truly random manner. The participants who first answered the questions correctly and then randomly did much better: their answers the second time were correct only 49 percent of the time—they did show random performance. These findings indicate that once primed schemas are somehow expressed, unpriming occurs, and the influence of the primed schemas disappears. Figure 2.7 summarizes the nature of unpriming. If primed schemas are *not* expressed, however, their effects may persist for long periods of time—even years (Budson & Price, 2005; Mitchell, 2006).

priming
A situation that occurs when stimuli or events increase the availability in memory or consciousness of specific types of information held in memory.

unpriming
Refers to the fact that the effects of the schemas tend to persist until they are somehow expressed in thought or behavior and only then do their effects decrease.

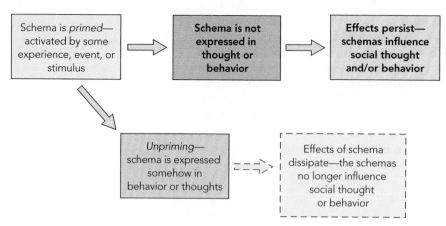

FIGURE 2.7   Unpriming of Schemas: Bringing the Effects of Priming to an End
When schemas are primed—activated by experiences, events, or stimuli, their effects tend to persist. In fact, they have been observed over years even. If the schema is somehow expressed in thought or behavior, however, unpriming may occur, and the impact of the schema may decrease or even disappear. (Source: Based on findings reported by Sparrow & Wegner, 2006).

Schema Persistence: Why Even Discredited Schemas Can Sometimes Influence Our Thought and Behavior

Although schemas are based on our past experience and are often helpful—they permit us to make sense out of a vast array of social information—they have an important "downside" too. By influencing what we notice, enter into memory, and later remember, schemas can produce distortions in our understanding of the social world. Unfortunately, schemas are often resistant to change—they show a strong **perseverance effect,** remaining unchanged even in the face of contradictory information (Kunda & Oleson, 1995). Perhaps even worse, schemas can sometimes be *self-fulfilling:* They influence our responses to the social world in ways that *make* it consistent with the schema!

Do our cognitive frameworks—our schemas—actually shape the social world as well as reflect it? A large body of evidence suggests that this is definitely so (e.g., Madon, Jussim, & Eccles, 1997; Smith, Jussim, & Eccles, 1999). Perhaps the most dramatic evidence that schemas can be self-fulfilling was provided by Rosenthal and Jacobson (1968), in a famous study of teachers and the unintended effects of their expectations on students. These researchers went to an elementary school and administered an IQ test to all students. Then they told the teachers that some of the students had scored very high and were about to "bloom" academically. The teachers were not given such information about other students, who constituted a control group. Although the researchers had chosen the names of the students for each group randomly, they predicted that this information would alter teachers' expectations about the children and their behavior toward them.

To find out if this was true, 8 months later the researchers tested both groups of children once again. Results were clear: those who had been described as "bloomers" to their teachers showed significantly larger gains on the IQ test than those in the control group. In short, teachers' beliefs about the students had operated in a *self-fulfilling manner:* The students whose teachers believed they would "bloom," actually did. So schemas can be a two-edged sword: They can help us make sense of the social world and process information efficiently, but they can also lock us into acting in ways that create the world that we expect.

Reasoning by Metaphor: How Social Attitudes and Behavior Are Affected by Figures of Speech

perseverance effect
The tendency for beliefs and schemas to remain unchanged even in the face of contradictory information.

metaphor
A linguistic device that relates or draws a comparison between one abstract concept and another dissimilar concept.

Might **metaphors**—linguistic devices that relate a typically abstract concept to another dissimilar concept—shape how we perceive and respond to the social world? Because metaphors can activate different kinds of social knowledge, they can influence how we interpret events (Landau, Meier, & Keefer, 2010). Consider just a few metaphors:

Her presentation bombed; everyone affiliated with her tried to run for cover.

He lifted the spirits of the audience; he received a warm reception.

Where is our relationship heading? Are we on the right track?

What you should notice first is that although you may not have heard any of those specific metaphors before, you can easily understand what is being communicated. In each of these examples, abstract concepts are being used to give a particular meaning to a concrete event. In the first sentence, people's knowledge of warfare is being used to structure our understanding of people's response to the contents of a talk. In the second example, both weight and temperature are used to guide our understanding of people's response to the contents of another talk. In the last example, the concept of a journey or travel is being applied to love and relationships.

Does such metaphor use have consequences for social judgment and behavior? New research is emerging that suggests this is so (Landau et al., 2010). Table 2.1 presents a selection of metaphors, which when primed, can influenced a number of different types of relevant social inferences and behavior. Let's just consider one example. In order to make the contamination metaphor available, Landau, Sullivan, and Greenberg (2009) had participants first read about the many airborne bacteria in the environment, which were described as either harmful to humans or not. Then, in a seemingly unrelated task about American domestic issues, statements relating to the United States were presented using the body metaphor ("After the Civil War, the United States experienced an unprecedented *growth spurt*") or without it ("After the Civil War, the United States experienced an unprecedented period of innovation"). In the third phase of the study, participants were asked to indicate their attitudes toward immigration. For those with a concern about "body contamination"—because they'd been told about how bacteria can harm humans—more negative attitudes toward immigration were expressed when the metaphor of the United States as a body had been made salient compared to when the United States had been described without this metaphor. So, how we talk—literally the pictures we paint with our words—can affect how we interpret and respond to the social world.

TABLE 2.1 Metaphors Can Affect Social Attitudes and Behavior

A variety of metaphors, when primed, have been shown to affect attitudes, memory, judgments, and physical perceptions.

METAPHOR PRIMING	EFFECT ON SOCIAL JUDGMENT
Nations are bodies (Landau, Sullivan & Greenberg, 2009)	Framing U.S. as body led to harsher attitudes toward immigration in those motivated to protect their body from contamination
Good is up; Bad is down (Crawford, Margolies, Drake, & Murphy, 2006)	Positive items presented in higher location and negative items in lower location recalled best
God is up (Chasteen, Burdzy, & Pratt, 2009)	Photos of people presented in a high (vs. low) position on screen were judged as having a stronger belief in God
Social exclusion is physical cold (Zhong & Leonardelli, 2008)	Recalling a time of social exclusion (vs. acceptance) resulted in the room being perceived as 5 degrees colder
Past is backward; Future is forward (Miles, Nind, & Macrae, 2010)	Backward postural sway was exhibited when thinking of the past and forward sway shown when thinking of the future

(*Source:* Based on research by Landau, Meier, & Keefer, 2010).

KEY POINTS

- A basic component of social cognition are **schemas**—mental frameworks developed through experience that, once formed, help us to organize and make sense of social information.

- Once formed schemas exert powerful effects on what we notice (attention), enter into memory (encoding), and later remember (retrieval). Individuals report remembering more information that is consistent with their schemas than information that is inconsistent with them, but in fact, inconsistent information, too, is strongly represented in memory.

- Schemas are often primed—activated by experiences, events, or stimuli. Once they are primed, the effects of the schemas tend to persist until they are somehow

expressed in thought or behavior; such expression (known as **unpriming**) then reduces the likelihood they will influence thought or behavior.

- Schemas help us to process information, but they show a strong **perseverance effect** even in the face of disconfirming information, thus distorting our understanding of the social world.

- Schemas can also exert self-fulfilling effects, causing us to behave in ways that create confirmation of our expectancies.

- **Metaphors**—linguistic devices that relate an abstract concept to another dissimilar concept—can shape how we perceive and respond to the social world.

Automatic and Controlled Processing: Two Basic Modes of Social Thought

Social thought can occur in either of two distinctly different ways: in a systematic, logical, and highly effortful manner known as *controlled processing*, or in a fast, relatively effortless, and intuitive manner known as **automatic processing.** This distinction has been confirmed in literally hundreds of different studies and it is now recognized as an important aspect of social thought. But this doesn't mean that these two kinds of thought are totally independent; in fact, recent evidence suggests that automatic and controlled processing may often occur together, especially in situations involving some uncertainty (Sherman et al., 2008). Still, the distinction between them is important and worth us considering very carefully.

While a great deal of evidence supports the existence of these two different modes of social thought, perhaps the most convincing support is provided by the kind of social neuroscience research described briefly in Chapter 1—research that examines activity in the human brain as an individual processes social information. The findings of such research suggest that people actually possess two different neural systems for processing social information—one that operates in an automatic manner and another that operates in a systematic and controlled manner. Moreover, the operation of these two systems is reflected by activation in different regions of the brain. For instance, consider research on *evaluative reactions*—a very basic kind of social judgment relating to whether we like or dislike something (a person, idea, or object). Such evaluations can occur in two distinct ways: simple good–bad judgments that occur in a rapid and seemingly automatic manner (Phelps et al., 2001) or through more effortful thought in which we think carefully and logically, weighing all the relevant points fully and systematically (e.g., Duncan & Owen, 2000). The first kind of reaction seems to occur primarily in the amygdala, while the second seems to involve portions of the prefrontal cortex (especially the medial prefrontal cortex and ventrolateral prefrontal cortex (e.g., Cunningham, Johnson, Gatenby, Gore, & Banaji, 2003). In addition, as we'll note in a later discussion of the relationship between cognition and affect (between thought and emotions or moods), we also seem to possess two distinct brain systems for processing these types of information, with controlled processing (reasoning, logic) occurring primarily in the prefrontal cortex areas of the brain, and emotion-related, automatic reactions occurring mainly in the limbic system, structures deep inside the brain (e.g., Cohen, 2005).

Overall, the results of social neuroscience studies, as well as more traditional methods of social psychological research, suggest that the distinction between automatic and controlled processing is indeed real—and very important. We'll be illustrating this fact in many places throughout this book, but here, we'll try to clarify why it is so important by examining two specific issues relating to automatic processing: the effects of automatic processing on social behavior, and the benefits provided by such processing.

Automatic Processing and Automatic Social Behavior

Once a concept is activated, it can exert important effects on social thought and behavior. Often, people act in ways that are consistent with their schemas, even if they do not intend to do so, and are unaware that they are acting in this manner. For example, in a well-known study by Bargh, Chen, and Burrows (1996), these researchers first activated either the schema for the trait of rudeness or the schema for the trait of politeness through priming. To do so, participants worked on unscrambling scrambled sentences containing words related either to rudeness (e.g., *bold, rude, impolitely, bluntly*) or words related to politeness (e.g., *cordially, patiently, polite, courteous*). People in a third (control) group unscrambled sentences containing words unrelated to either trait (e.g., *exercising, flawlessly, occasionally, rapidly*). After completing this task, participants in the study were asked to report back to the experimenter, who would give them additional tasks.

automatic processing
This occurs when, after extensive experience with a task or type of information, we reach the stage where we can perform the task or process the information in a seemingly effortless, automatic, and nonconscious manner.

When they approached the experimenter, he or she was engaged in a conversation with another person (an accomplice). The experimenter continued this conversation, ignoring the participant. The major dependent measure was whether the participant interrupted the conversation in order to receive further instructions. The researchers predicted that people for whom the trait rudeness had been primed would be more likely to interrupt than those for whom the trait politeness had been primed, and this is precisely what happened. Further findings indicated that these effects occurred despite the fact that participants' ratings of the experimenter in terms of politeness did not differ across the three experimental conditions. Thus, these differences in behavior seemed to occur in a nonconscious, automatic manner.

In a second study, Bargh et al. (1996) either primed the stereotype for *elderly* (again through exposure to words related to this schema) or did not prime it. Then they timed the number of seconds it took participants to walk down a hallway at the end of the study. As predicted, those for whom the stereotype elderly had been primed actually walked slower! Together, the results of these and other studies (e.g., Dijksterhuis & Bargh, 2001) indicate that activating stereotypes or schemas can exert seemingly automatic effects on behavior—effects that occur in the absence of intention or conscious awareness. Clearly, then, automatic processing is an important aspect of social thought—one that can affect overt behavior.

But additional research suggests that the effects of automatic processing may be even more general than that of triggering particular forms of behavior. Once automatic processing is initiated (e.g., through priming), individuals may—again unconsciously—begin to prepare for future interactions with the people or groups who are the focus of this automatic processing. As suggested by Cesario, Plaks, and Higgins (2006), activating a schema may not merely trigger behaviors consistent with this schema; it may also activate behaviors that, in a sense, "get the people involved ready" to actually interact with others.

A study conducted by Cesario et al. (2006) clearly illustrates such effects. Participants were primed with photos of men labeled "GAY" or "STRAIGHT." These photos were shown so quickly that participants could not actually see the images; but as in many other studies, it was expected that the photos would prime (activate) schemas for these two groups. Then, in what seemed to be unrelated procedures, the computer on which the study was being conducted locked up, and participants were instructed to get the experimenter to help get it started. When the experimenter entered, he acted in a hostile manner. The key question was: would participants whose negative stereotype (schemas) of gays had been primed behave more hostilely than those whose stereotypes of heterosexuals had been primed? If so, this would be directly *contrary* to the stereotype of gays, which generally suggests that such people are passive and nonaggressive. However, it would be *consistent* with the view that priming this schema motivates individuals to prepare to interact with members of the people or group who are the focus of the schema—in this case, a group they do not like. Results offered clear support for this prediction: when interacting with the experimenter, participants did in fact show greater hostility if they had been primed with faces labeled "GAY" than with faces labeled "STRAIGHT." Remember: this activation was automatic because participants could not consciously report seeing these photos; they were presented for only 11 msec. The different predictions of these two views—(1) schemas trigger behaviors consistent with the schemas or (2) schemas trigger motivated preparation to interact with the people or groups who are the subject of the schemas—are summarized in Figure 2.8.

Stereotypes (Schemas) Trigger Schema-Consistent Behaviors

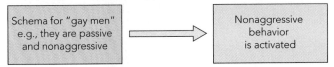

Stereotypes (Schemas) Trigger Preparation for Interacting with Persons or Groups Who are the Focus of the Schemas

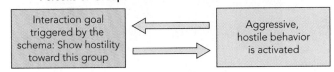

FIGURE 2.8   Automatic Processing Initiates Preparation for Future Interactions
Activation of schemas can trigger behaviors consistent with these cognitive frameworks. Recent research suggests that in addition, once activated, schemas may also trigger motivated efforts to prepare for interacting with the persons or groups who are the focus of these schemas. In the case of gay men, for instance, this enhances tendencies for heterosexuals to act in a hostile, aggressive manner. (Source: Based on suggestions by Cesario, Plaks, & Higgins, 2006).

The Benefits of Automatic Processing: Beyond Mere Efficiency

One kind of automatic processing with which most people are familiar occurs when we try to remember something (someone's name, a thought we previously had)—but don't succeed. When that happens, we often turn to doing something else while the search for the information we want goes on automatically, and without our conscious awareness. Often, this kind of memory search is successful, and the missing name or fact pops into mind. In such cases, we are dimly aware that *something* was happening, but can't really describe it. Research on this aspect of automatic processing confirms that we often attempt to deal with problems, and even complex decisions, while our attention is directed elsewhere (e.g., Dijksterhuis & Nordgren, 2007). Perhaps even more surprising, recent evidence indicates that sometimes it may be superior to careful, conscious thought in terms of making excellent decisions (Galdi, Arcuri, & Gawronski, 2008).

A clear illustration of these advantages is provided by research conducted by Dijksterhuis and van Olden (2006). These social psychologists asked students to look at various posters and indicate the one they liked most. In one condition (immediate decision), the posters were all shown on a computer screen simultaneously, and students made their decision immediately. In another condition (conscious thought), the posters were shown one at a time for 90 seconds, and after looking at them, the students were given paper and asked to list their thoughts and evaluations—to think carefully about the posters and their preferences for them. Finally, in a third condition (unconscious thought), participants worked on another task (solving anagrams) after seeing the posters, preventing them from consciously thinking about their preferences. Several minutes later, students indicated which poster they liked.

All the participants then received a surprise: they were given their favorite poster to take home. Three to five weeks later, they were phoned and asked how satisfied they were with the poster they had received and how much they would want (in Euros) if they sold their poster. The researchers predicted that participants would actually be most satisfied with their choice in the unconscious condition, where they made the choice without an opportunity to think consciously about it, and as you can see from Figure 2.9, this is precisely what happened. This suggests—surprisingly—that participants actually made better decisions, in terms of being satisfied with them, when they did so on "automatic" rather than when they had a chance to think about them carefully.

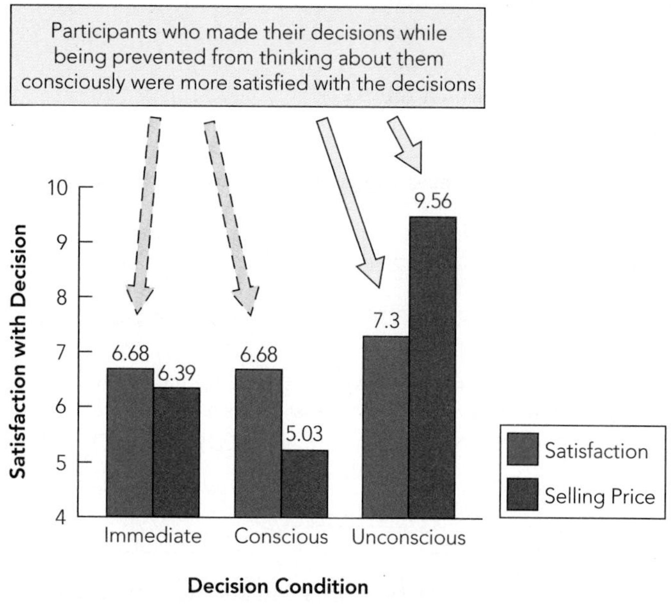

Why is this so? Perhaps because conscious thought has strict limits in terms of the amount of information it can handle, so when we think actively about decisions we may not be unable to take account of all available information. In contrast, unconscious, automatic thought has much greater capacity. Similarly, when we think about decisions consciously, we may fail to weight the various dimensions or elements accurately and thinking about these dimensions may get us confused about which were actually the most important. Unconscious, automatic processing may therefore reflect our real preferences more clearly. Whatever the precise reason, these findings, and those of many related studies (e.g., Ito, Chiao, Devine, Lorig, & Cacioppo, 2006), suggest that automatic processing offers important advantages beyond those of merely being quick and efficient. Certainly, there are real drawbacks to relying solely on conscious thought in making decisions, even though conscious thought is important in other ways, particularly in facilitating social

FIGURE 2.9 **The Benefits of Automatic (Unconscious) Thought**

Participants who were prevented from thinking consciously about their preferences for various posters (unconscious condition) were more satisfied with the choices they made than participants who could engage in careful, systematic thought (conscious) or participants who made their choice immediately after seeing the poster (immediate). These findings suggest that automatic processing offers more benefits than simply being quick and efficient. (Source: Based on data from Djiksterhuis & van Olden, 2006).

interaction (Baumeister & Masicampo, 2010). In our special feature "SOCIAL LIFE IN A CONNECTED WORLD: Dealing with Information Overload and Improving Choices," we consider the perils of relying on only conscious processes in environments that exceed our processing capacities.

SOCIAL LIFE *in a* CONNECTED WORLD

Dealing with Information Overload and Improving Choices

Get on almost any Internet site, and you're likely to be overloaded pretty quickly. As we have emphasized in this chapter, human beings are limited in the amount of information they can process and people routinely use heuristics to help them process all that incoming information. Information overload and the strategies people use to deal with it is similar to the problem of choice overload.

Barry Schwartz, in his 2004 book, *The Paradox of Choice,* talks about the negative consequences of having too many choices, a situation we can experience in both our online and bricks-and-mortar lives. Despite the negative reactions we can experience from having our choices restricted, as Schwartz points out, even when choosing a pair of jeans, the multiplicity of choices may give us a headache—both figuratively and literally! He isolates one factor as key: the whole idea of higher expectations. When we had only one type of jeans to pick from (Levi's 501s), and we had to break those ill-fitting jeans in, we could always blame the "world" for our discomfort. But when we have zillions of types of jeans to choose from, we can only blame ourselves if we don't end up with a perfect pair! After all, we made the choice, and there were so *many* to choose from!

While at first glance, it might seem wonderful that we have so many choices—for everything from health insurance plans to types of jeans to nail polish colors—but having so many choices can have a paralyzing effect. Not only that, even if the paralysis is overcome, we can end up less satisfied with our outcomes. What are some of the processes that lead to this negative effect? Well, the more options we have, the easier it is to imagine that another option than the one we chose would have been better than the one we actually did choose. Going back to the jeans example, even when we finally choose a pair of jeans, and it seems like an excellent choice, we still may be set up for an unexpected burden: long-term self-blame! We always feel that we could have done better, and so it is supremely easy to be disappointed when the options we have to choose from are abundant.

Turning to the online world, there is evidence that we might even be better off if we had fewer choices. Thaler and Sunstein (2008) take a stab at explaining how people might best deal with all the choices that Amazon, eBay, and other institutions offer us online. These researchers posit that we would be better off by limiting excessive choices by using "choice architecture," a method by which alternatives are crafted on the Web in order that people may more easily make better choices. Choice architecture simply means taking advantage of people's heuristic use in order to help them make the best choices. If we knew, for example, that people tend to choose the second option they see, these researchers suggest we should place the option that is likely to be best for most people in that position.

Take the potentially complicated issue of "school choice": only a tiny percentage of students actually switched schools when the choice was made available. In that situation, it was found that while many choices were offered, parents faced a very complex multistage process for getting their child transferred to another school.

In this case, parents used the "status quo" heuristic, as opposed to choosing a school that might be better equipped to help their child. Given that parents had to access a 100-page booklet with descriptions of 190 schools written by employees of the schools, where each school's positive features were given—most chose not to! Even if they had done so, the booklet did not include information on physical location, test scores, attendance rates, and racial composition, although that information was available on the district Website for those who searched around to find it. Thus, parents would have needed to combine very complex information from two sources in order to select a good school for their child. No wonder virtually every parent chose not to do so!

So school administrators tried a novel experiment to address this problem. In the past, low-income parents tended to put less weight than high-income parents on school quality. In effect, this allowed for higher-income parents to unwittingly "game the system." In their experiment, a random sample of parents received a list of schools giving the average test scores as well as acceptance rates at various schools for which any given student was actually eligible. With this newer simplified presentation of the crucial information, would low-income parents select better schools? Turns out that parents who received the information in a way that highlighted the crucial information in an accessible style did

(continued)

SOCIAL LIFE *in a* **CONNECTED WORLD** *(continued)*

place more emphasis on school quality and low-income parents' school choice decisions were similar to parents whose incomes were much higher. Thaler and Sunstein's (2008) research makes clear that choice-making by people of all backgrounds can be improved, leading them to better lives, if we allow simple forms of choice architecture to be utilized.

The problem of information overload and the resultant excessive choices to be made is a daunting one. In the online world, we are constantly marketed to. In a social media environment, we're faced with tons of choices. In interactions between ordinary people and government agencies, there is often the presence of complex materials. In general, information overload has the effect of narrowing people's thinking processes, just when they need to systematically evaluate far too many options. Understanding the heuristics people use when faced with complex information can help improve people's ability to cope with the many choices that must be made—and that's increasingly important in our overloaded "cyber-world."

KEYPOINTS

- A large amount of evidence indicates that the distinction between automatic and controlled processing is a very basic one. In fact, different regions of the brain appear to be involved in these two types of processing, especially with respect to evaluations of various aspects of the social world.

- When schemas or other cognitive frameworks are activated (even without our conscious awareness of such activation), they strongly influence our behavior, triggering actions consistent with the frameworks and also preparing us to interact with the people or groups who are the focus of these schemas.

- **Automatic processing** is clearly quick and efficient; in addition, however, it may also sometimes offer other advantages too—such as decisions with which we are more satisfied.

- Having available too many choices can be paralyzing, and encourages dissatisfaction with the choices we do make.

- Use of "choice architecture"—where the best alternative for most people is strategically placed so that people who are automatically processing are more likely to select that option—can improve decision making and satisfaction with the outcomes.

Potential Sources of Error in Social Cognition: Why Total Rationality Is Rarer Than You Think

Human beings are definitely not computers, and our thinking is not simply based on rational self-interest as economists have long assumed (Akerlof & Shiller, 2009). The judgments people make systematically deviate in a number of ways from perfect rationality; this is true for critical decisions such as what career path to pursue or whom to marry, as well as financial decisions such as picking stocks to invest in or credit card use—our actions often reflect overconfidence and optimism (Gärling, Kirchler, Lewis, & van Raaij, 2009). While we can *imagine* being able to reason in a perfectly logical way, we know from our own experience that often we fall short of this goal. In our efforts to understand others and make sense out of the social world, we are subject to a wide range of tendencies that, together, can lead us into serious error. We now consider several of these "tilts" in social cognition. Before doing so, however, we should emphasize the following point: While these aspects of social thought do sometimes result in errors, they can also be adaptive. They often reduce the effort required for navigating the social world. As we saw with heuristic use—they supply us with tangible benefits as well as exacting important costs.

As we'll soon see, there are many different ways in which our social thought departs from rationality. To acquaint you with a wide range of these effects, we start with a basic tendency that seems to occur in a wide range of situations and often produces important errors in our social thought: our tendency to be optimistic—often, overly so. After considering this far-reaching general tendency, we turn to several other ways in which social thought departs from rationality, ones that are also important but tend to occur in specific situations rather than generally like our tendency to be overly optimistic.

A Basic "Tilt" in Social Thought: Our Powerful Tendency to Be Overly Optimistic

If we were completely rational in the ways in which we think about the social world, we would simply gather information, process it, and then use it to make judgments and decisions. Instead, in many ways, most people tend to "see the world through rose-colored glasses," which is known as the **optimistic bias**—a powerful predisposition to overlook risks and expect things to turn out well. In fact, research findings indicate that most people believe that they are *more* likely than others to experience positive events, and *less* likely to experience negative events (Shepperd, Carroll, & Sweeny, 2008). Our strong leaning toward optimism can be seen in many specific judgments—most people believe that they are more likely than others to get a good job, have a happy marriage, and live to a ripe old age, but less likely to experience negative outcomes such as being fired, getting seriously ill, or getting divorced (Kruger & Burrus, 2004; Schwarzer, 1994).

Similarly, we often have greater confidence in our beliefs or judgments than is justified—an effect known as the **overconfidence barrier.** Vallone, Griffin, Lin, and Ross (1990) illustrated how overconfident people can be in their predictions about themselves by asking students to indicate early in the academic year whether they would perform a number of actions (e.g., drop a course, move on or off campus) and to indicate how confident they were in their predictions. The students were wrong a substantial proportion of the time, and even when they were 100 percent confident in their predictions they were wrong 15 percent of the time!

Ironically enough, people who are *least* competent in a domain are often the *most* likely to be overconfident of their judgments in that domain! Like many other types of judgments, we frequently have to assess our competence under conditions of uncertainty—where all the relevant information is not known. Consider just a few examples: have we picked the best health insurance plan to meet our future needs, are our retirement funds sufficiently diversified to weather even a rocky stock market, is our new kitchen design optimal, are the essays we write for class covering all the essential points on the topic? Caputo and Dunning (2005) have pointed out that one critical reason why we may be overly confident of our judgments and actions in all these cases is that we often are lacking critical information—that is, we do not know enough to know what we have missed. These researchers argue that for many tasks overconfidence stems from *errors of omission*. Suppose you were asked to come up with as many uses as possible for WD-40, an oil lubricant. You come up with what you think is an impressive list of 20 legitimate uses for it. Would you then see yourself as competent at this task? Based on the research conducted by Caputo and Dunning, people do confidently rate their abilities as high under these circumstances, but they should not because they have no way of knowing the other 1,980 legitimate uses for this product that they have missed! Indeed, when these researchers told their participants the possible solutions to their tasks that had been missed, people's confidence in their ability dropped and then more strongly correlated with objective measures of performance. So, one important reason we display overconfidence is that we lack the relevant feedback that would help moderate our confidence. As the cartoon in Figure 2.10 suggests, overconfidence may explain why entrepreneurs who start a new business believe that their chances of making it work are much higher than is actually true (Baron & Shane, 2007).

optimistic bias
Our predisposition to expect things to turn out well overall.

overconfidence barrier
The tendency to have more confidence in the accuracy of our own judgments than is reasonable.

"*You asked for a loan of $50 million so you could open 800 pizza restaurants. How about you start with one and build from there?*"

FIGURE 2.10 **Overconfidence in Action: Believing You'll Score Big Before You Have Started**

As research findings (Baron & Shane, 2007) indicate, business entrepreneurs frequently express greater confidence in their likelihood of succeeding than the objective odds would warrant.

THE ROCKY PAST VERSUS THE GOLDEN FUTURE: OPTIMISM AT WORK Think back over your life. Did it have peaks—times when things were going great for you, and valleys—times when things were not good? Now, in contrast, try to imagine your future: How do you think it will unfold? If you are like most people, you may notice a difference in these descriptions. While most of us recognize that our past has been mixed in terms of "highs" and "lows," we tend to forecast a very rosy or golden future—one in which we will be quite happy and in which few negative events happen to us. In fact, research by Newby-Clark and Ross (2003) indicates that this tendency is so strong that it occurs even when people have just recalled negative episodes from their own pasts. What accounts for this difference? One possibility is that when we think about the past, we can recall failures, unpleasant events, and other disappointments, whereas these unexpected possibilities are not salient when we think about our future. When we think about the future, in contrast, we tend to concentrate on desirable goals, personal happiness, and doing things we have always wanted to do—such as traveling to exotic places. Since our thinking is dominated by these positive thoughts, we make highly optimistic predictions about the future, and tend to perceive it as indeed golden, at least in its promise or potential for us. In short, the optimistic bias seems to occur not just for specific tasks or situations, but for projections of our entire future as well.

Perhaps people also feel optimistic about the future—because it just feels good to do so! But, still, might there be hidden costs of being optimistic about ourselves and our future—particularly if we get there and find that optimism was misplaced? New research by Sweeny and Shepperd (2010) has addressed these questions. Students in a psychology class were asked to estimate the grade they would receive on their first exam and their emotional state was measured. Then, the students received their grade and their emotions were again measured. First of all, those students who were more optimistic about the grade they would receive reported more positive emotions, suggesting that optimism does feel good. But what happens when the students learned whether their optimism was warranted or not (i.e., they learned their exam grade)? For those optimistic students who overestimated their exam scores, when they learned their actual score, they felt much worse than the realists or pessimists who did not do so. The good news is, however, 24 hours later, the negative emotions the optimists felt had dissipated. This means that while being optimistic about our future outcomes can make us feel good, if the basis for it is disconfirmed, we may feel bad—but fortunately only temporarily!

WHEN OPTIMISM AFFECTS OUR ABILITY TO PLAN EFFECTIVELY Yet another illustration of optimism at work is the **planning fallacy**—our tendency to believe that we can get more done in a given period of time than we actually can, or that a given job will take less time than it really will. We can see this aspect of the optimistic bias in announced schedules for public works (e.g., new roads, airports, bridges, stadiums) that have no chance of being met. Individuals, too, adopt unrealistically optimistic schedules for their own work (see Figure 2.11). If you have ever estimated that a project would take you

planning fallacy
The tendency to make optimistic predictions concerning how long a given task will take for completion.

a certain amount of time but then found that it took considerably longer, you are already familiar with this effect, and with the planning fallacy.

Why do we (repeatedly) fall prey to this particular kind of optimism? According to Buehler et al. (1994), social psychologists who have studied this tendency in detail, several factors play a role. One is that when individuals make predictions about how long it will take them to complete a given task, they enter a *planning* or *narrative* mode of thought in which they focus primarily on the future and how they will perform the task. This, in turn, prevents them from looking backward in time and remembering how long similar tasks took them in the past. As a result, one important "reality check" that might help them avoid being overly optimistic is removed. In addition, when individuals *do* consider past experiences in which tasks took longer than expected, they tend to attribute such outcomes to factors outside their control. The result: they tend to overlook important potential obstacles that can't be easily foreseen

FIGURE 2.11   The Planning Fallacy
The tendency to believe that the plans we construct are doable, that we can accomplish more than we actually can in a given period of time, or that nothing will interfere with the achievement of our goals reflects the planning fallacy in action. Few projects are actually completed as originally planned, or on schedule!

when predicting how long a task will take, and fall prey to the planning fallacy. These predictions have been confirmed in several studies (e.g., Buehler et al., 1994), and they provide important insights into the origins of the tendency to make optimistic predictions about task completion.

These cognitive factors are not the entire story, though. Additional findings suggest that another factor, *motivation* to complete a task, also plays an important role in the planning fallacy. When predicting what will happen, individuals often guess that what will happen is what they *want* to happen (Johnson & Sherman, 1990). In cases where they are strongly motivated to complete a task, people make overoptimistic predictions about when they will attain this desired state of affairs (Buehler, Griffin, & MacDonald, 1997). It appears, then, that our estimates of when we will complete a task are indeed influenced by our hopes and desires: we want to finish early or on time, so we predict that we will.

Are some people more prone to the planning fallacy than others? As we just discussed, when people are focused on the goal of completing a task, rather than the steps involved in doing so, they are likely to make overly optimistic predictions for how much time it will take to do so. Weick and Guinote (2010) proposed that people in powerful positions are more likely to fall prey to the planning fallacy because they are focused on the goal of getting the task done, whereas people who occupy less powerful positions are more likely to be focused on the *how* or the steps needed to be taken to get the job done. These researchers tested this idea by having some participants think about an episode in their past when they occupied a position of relative power, or an episode in which they were in a position of relative powerlessness. Subsequently, both groups of participants were asked to format a document using software that was complicated, but before actually doing so they were asked to estimate how long it would take them to do

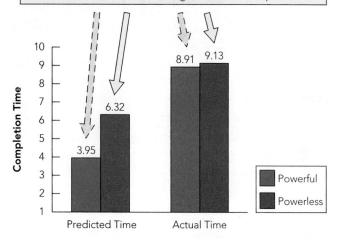

Those who thought of themselves in a powerful position underestimated how long it would take them to complete the task more than those thinking of themselves as powerless

FIGURE 2.12 Power and the Planning Fallacy

Both powerful and powerless people seriously underestimated how long it would take them to complete a complex word processing task, but those who thought of themselves occupying a powerful position mispredicted the time that would be needed most. These results are consistent with the idea that power leads us to focus too narrowly on task completion, rather than the steps involved in getting there, which can lead us to seriously underestimate how long it will take us to finish a task. (Source: Based on research by Weick & Guinote, 2010).

so. As shown in Figure 2.12, both groups of participants showed the planning fallacy—that is, both groups seriously underestimated the number of minutes they would need to complete the editing task. However, as the researchers predicted, although there was no difference in actual performance time, those who first thought of themselves as occupying a position of power underestimated how long it would take them much more than did participants who thought of themselves as occupying a position of powerlessness. These results are consistent with the idea that power leads us to focus too narrowly on task completion, rather than the steps involved in getting there, which can lead us to seriously underestimate how long it will take to finish tasks.

Situation-Specific Sources of Error in Social Cognition: Counterfactual Thinking and Magical Thinking

The optimistic bias is very general in nature; as we've seen, it can be found in a wide range of social situations. Other important forms of bias in our social thought are more restricted in the sense that they tend to occur only in certain kinds of situations. We now examine two of these—*counterfactual thinking* and what is sometimes termed *magical thinking*.

COUNTERFACTUAL THINKING: IMAGINING "WHAT MIGHT HAVE BEEN"   Suppose that you take an important exam; when you receive your score, it is a C−, a much lower grade than you had hoped. What thoughts will enter your mind as you consider your grade? If you are like most people, you may quickly begin to imagine "what might have been"—receiving a higher grade—along with thoughts about how you could have obtained that better outcome. "If only I had studied more, or come to class more often," you may think to yourself. And then, perhaps you may begin to formulate plans for actually *doing* better on the next test.

Such thoughts about "what might have been"—known in social psychology as **counterfactual thinking**—occur in a wide range of situations, not just ones in which we experience disappointments. For instance, suppose you read an article in the newspaper about someone who left work at the normal time and was injured in an automobile accident in which another driver ran a stop sign. Certainly, you would feel sympathy for this person and would probably recommend some form of compensation. But now imagine the same story with a slight difference: the same person was injured in the same kind of accident, but in this case, he had left work early to run an errand. Since the accident is the same, you should rationally feel the same amount of sympathy for the victim. But in fact, you may not because given that he left work earlier than usual, it is easy to imagine him *not* being in the accident. Or, suppose he took an unusual route home instead of his normal one. Would that make a difference in the sympathy you would feel? Research indicates that the answer is yes—emotional responses differ depending on how easy it is to mentally undo the circumstances that preceded it. Because it is easier to undo in our minds taking the unusual route than the normal one, sympathy for the accident will also differ. In other words, counterfactual thoughts about what might have happened instead of what did happen can influence your sympathy—as well as your recommendations concerning compensation for the victim (e.g., Miller & McFarland, 1987). This difference in the intensity of the sympathy evoked has been observed even for highly tragic events, including cases of rape and the loss of a child in an auto accident (Branscombe,

counterfactual thinking
The tendency to imagine other outcomes in a situation than the ones that actually occurred ("What might have been").

Owen, Garstka, & Coleman, 1996; Davis, Lehman, Wortman, Silver, & Thompson, 1995; Wolf, 2010).

Counterfactual thoughts seem to occur automatically in many situations—we simply can't help imagining that things might have turned out differently. To overcome these automatic tendencies, therefore, we must try to correct for their influence, and this requires both active processing in which we suppress the counterfactual thoughts or discount them. Consistent with this idea, studies have demonstrated that anything that reduces our information-processing capacity actually *strengthens* the impact of counterfactual thoughts on our judgments and behavior (Goldinger, Kleider, Azuma, & Beike, 2003). Together, this research indicates that counterfactual thinking—imagining what did not actually happen—can influence our social thought.

When counterfactual thinking does occur, a wide range of effects can follow—some of which are beneficial and some of which are costly to the people involved (Kray, Galinsky, & Wong, 2006; Nario-Redmond & Branscombe, 1996). Depending on its focus, imagining counterfactuals for outcomes we receive can yield either boosts to, or reductions in, our current moods. If individuals imagine *upward counterfactuals*, comparing their current outcomes with more favorable ones than they experienced, the result may be strong feelings of dissatisfaction or envy, especially when people do not feel capable of obtaining better outcomes in the future (Sanna, 1997). Olympic athletes who win a silver medal but who can easily imagine winning a gold one experience such reactions (Medvec, Madey, & Gilovich, 1995). Alternatively, if individuals compare their current outcomes with less favorable ones—it might have been worse—they may experience positive feelings of satisfaction or hopefulness. Such reactions have been found among Olympic athletes who win bronze medals, and who can easily imagine what it would be like to have not won any medal whatsoever. In sum, engaging in counterfactual thought can strongly influence current affective states, and willingness to gamble on obtaining those outcomes in the future (Petrocelli & Sherman, 2010).

In addition, it appears that we often use counterfactual thinking to mitigate the bitterness of disappointments. After tragic events such as the death of a loved one, people often find solace in thinking: "Nothing more could be done; the death was inevitable." In other words, they adjust their view concerning the inevitability of the death so as to make it seem more certain and therefore unavoidable. In contrast, if they have different counterfactual thoughts—"If only the illness had been diagnosed sooner . . ." or "If only we had gotten him to the hospital quicker . . ."—their suffering may be increased. So by assuming that negative events or disappointments were inevitable, it tends to make these events more bearable (Tykocinski, 2001).

Finally, we should note that counterfactual thinking can sometimes help us to perform better—to do a better job at various tasks. Why? Because by imagining how we might have done better, we may come up with improved strategies and ways of using our effort more effectively. So, sometimes—for instance, when we expect to repeat various tasks—engaging in counterfactual thought can enhance performance on important tasks (Kray et al., 2006). Our tendency to think not only about what is, but also about what might have been, therefore, can have far-reaching effects on many aspects of our social thought and social behavior.

MAGICAL THINKING, TERROR MANAGEMENT, AND BELIEF IN THE SUPERNATURAL

Please answer truthfully:

If you are in class and don't want the professor to call on you, do you try to avoid thinking about being called on?

If you were given an opportunity to buy travel insurance, would you feel you were "tempting fate" and inviting calamity by not purchasing it?

If someone offered you a piece of chocolate shaped like a cockroach—would you eat it?

FIGURE 2.13 **Magical Thinking: An Example**
Would you eat the candy shown here? Many people would not, even though they realize that the shape of the candy has nothing to do with its taste. This illustrates the law of similarity—one aspect of what social psychologists term magical thinking.

On the basis of purely rational considerations, you know that your answers should be "no," "no," and "yes." But are those the answers you actually gave? Probably not. In fact, research findings indicate that human beings are quite susceptible to what has been termed **magical thinking** (Rozin & Nemeroff, 1990). Such thinking makes assumptions that don't hold up to rational scrutiny but that are compelling nonetheless (Risen & Gilovich, 2007). One principle of such magical thinking assumes that one's thoughts can influence the physical world in a manner not governed by the laws of physics; if you think about being called on by your professor, it does not change the probability that you actually will be! Likewise, simply sticking pins in a doll and thinking about it as hurting your enemy does not mean such "voodoo" really can result in harm to another person. But, based on the *law of similarity*, which suggests that things that resemble one another share basic properties, it might be easy to think that sticking a doll that looks like an enemy can cause the same kind of harm to the real person. For the same reason, people won't eat a chocolate shaped like a cockroach even though they know, rationally, that its shape has nothing to do with its taste (see Figure 2.13). People also seem to believe that they are "buying peace of mind" when they purchase insurance; that is, not only will they be covered if something does go wrong, but that the very act of buying the insurance will ensure it does not go wrong! Research indicates that by turning down an insurance opportunity, people believe they are "tempting fate" and increasing the likelihood that disaster will strike (Tykocinski, 2008).

Surprising as it may seem, our thinking about many situations is frequently influenced by such magical thinking. So, what is the basis of such seemingly nonrational thinking? Some theorists have suggested that because human beings are uniquely aware of the fact that we will certainly die, this, in turn, causes us to engage in what is known as **terror management**—efforts to come to terms with this certainty and its unsettling implications (Greenberg et al., 2003). One kind of thinking that helps is belief in the supernatural—powers outside our understanding and control—that can influence our lives. Recent research indicates that when we are reminded of our own mortality, such beliefs are strengthened (Norenzayan & Hansen, 2006). In short, when we come face to face with the certainty of our own deaths, we try to manage the strong reactions this produces, and one way of doing this is to engage in thinking that is largely outside of what we consider to be rational thought.

So, the next time you are tempted to make fun of someone's superstitious belief (e.g., fear of the number 13 or of a black cat crossing one's path), don't be too quick to laugh: Your own thinking is almost certainly *not* totally free from the kind of "magical" (i.e., nonrational) assumptions that seem to underlie a considerable portion of our social thought.

magical thinking
Thinking involving assumptions that don't hold up to rational scrutiny—for example, the belief that things that resemble one another share fundamental properties.

terror management
Our efforts to come to terms with certainty of our own death and its unsettling implications.

KEYPOINTS

- Social thought departs from rationality in a number of ways. People show a strong optimistic bias, expecting that we are more likely than others to experience positive outcomes but less likely than others to experience negative ones.

- In addition, people tend to exhibit **overconfidence** in their predictions, and those who have the least competence in a domain are most likely to be overly confident of their judgments in that domain. This seems to be due to *errors of omission,* where we lack comparison information that would help moderate our confidence.

- People make more **optimistic** judgments about their future than their past. Optimism that is not born out in reality can result in negative emotions.

- People make overly optimistic predictions about how long it will take them to complete a given task, an effect known as the **planning fallacy.** This occurs repeatedly both because we fail to consider obstacles we may encounter when predicting how long a task will take and because we are motivated to complete a task so fail to consider all the time-consuming steps necessary to do so.

- In many situations, individuals imagine "what might have been"—they engage in **counterfactual thinking.** Such thought can affect our sympathy for people who have experienced negative outcomes. But upward counterfactuals can also motivate us to perform better in the future in hope of avoiding the outcome that did occur.

- There are important limits on our ability to think rationally about the social world. One involves magical thinking—assuming our thoughts can influence the physical world or that our actions (e.g., not buying insurance) may "tempt fate" and increase the likelihood of negative events. Based on similarity of two objects, we seem to believe that the properties of one can pass to the other.

- One form of such thinking—belief in the supernatural—stems, at least in part, from **terror management**—our efforts to cope with the knowledge that we will die. Reminders of our own mortality strengthen supernatural beliefs.

Affect and Cognition: How Feelings Shape Thought and Thought Shapes Feelings

Think of a time in your own life when you were in a very good mood—something good had happened and you were feeling very happy. Now, in contrast, remember a time when you were in a very bad mood—something negative had occurred and you were feeling down and blue. Was your thinking about the world different at these two times? In other words, did you remember different kinds of events or experiences, reason differently, and perhaps think about other people in contrasting ways? In all likelihood you did, because a large body of research findings indicate that there is a continuous and complex interplay between *affect*—our current moods or emotions—and *cognition*—various aspects of the ways in which we think, process, store, remember, and use information (e.g., Forgas, 2000; Isen & Labroo, 2003). We don't use the word *interplay* lightly because, in fact, existing evidence strongly suggests that the relationship between affect and cognition is very much a two-way street: Our emotions and moods strongly influence several aspects of cognition, and cognition, in turn, exerts strong effects on our emotions and moods (e.g., Baron, 2008; McDonald & Hirt, 1997; Seta, Hayes, & Seta, 1994). We now take a closer look at the nature of these effects.

The Influence of Affect on Cognition

First, and perhaps most obviously, our current moods can influence our perceptions of the world around us. When we are in a good mood (experiencing positive affect), we tend to perceive almost everything—situations, other people, ideas, even new inventions—in more positive terms than we do when we are in a negative mood (Blanchette & Richards, 2010; Clore, Schwarz, & Conway, 1993). Indeed, this effect is so strong and so pervasive that we are even more likely to judge statements as true if we encounter them while in a positive mood than if we read or hear them while in a neutral or negative mood (Garcia-Marques, Mackie, Claypool, & Garcia-Marques, 2004). Positive moods can also encourage people to feel they understand the world better (e.g., Hicks, Cicero, Trent, Burton, & King, 2010). When these researchers presented stimuli that have inherent ambiguity—such Zen koans as "If a placebo has an effect, is it any less real than the real thing?" or abstract art pictures—to participants, those in positive moods consistently reported greater understanding had been derived from the stimuli, particularly among participants that had first reported that they tend to use heuristics when making judgments (e.g., agree with statements such as "I rely on my intuitive impressions").

Such effects have important practical implications. For instance, consider their impact on job interviews—a context in which interviewers meet many people for the first time. A growing body of evidence indicates that even experienced interviewers cannot avoid being influenced by their current moods: They assign higher ratings to the people they interview when they are in a good mood than when they are in a bad mood (e.g., Baron, 1993a; Robbins & DeNisi, 1994). While positive moods can increase our confidence about our interpretation given to actions performed by other people, they can also result in less accuracy (Forgas, Vargas, & Laham, 2005).

Another way in which affect influences cognition involves its impact on memory. Here, two different, but related, kinds of effects seem to occur. One is known as **mood congruence effects.** This refers to the fact that current moods strongly determine which information in a given situation is noticed and entered into memory. In other words, current moods serve as a kind of filter, permitting primarily information consistent with these moods to enter into long-term storage. Second, affect also influences what specific information is *retrieved* from memory, an effect known as **mood dependent memory** (e.g., Baddeley, 1990; Eich, 1995). When experiencing a particular mood, individuals are more likely to remember information they acquired in the past while in a similar mood than information they acquired while in a different mood. Current moods, in other words, serve as a kind of *retrieval cue*, prompting recall of information consistent with these moods. Here's an illustration of the difference between these two effects. Suppose that you meet two people for the first time. You meet one when you are in a very good mood but meet the other one when you are in a very bad mood (e.g., you just learned that you did poorly on an important exam). Because of mood congruence effects, you will probably notice and store in memory mainly positive information about the first person, but you are more likely to notice and store in memory mainly negative information about the second person. Your mood when you meet these people determines what you notice and remember about them.

Now, imagine that at a later time, you are in a good mood. Which person comes to mind? Probably, the one you met while in a similar (good) mood. Here, your current mood serves to trigger memories of information you acquired (and stored in memory) when you were in a similar mood in the past. Together, mood congruence and mood-dependent memory strongly influence the information we store in memory. Since this is the information we can later remember, the impact of affect on memory has important implications for many aspects of social thought and social behavior. Figure 2.14 summarizes these points concerning mood and memory.

Our current moods also influence another important component of cognition: creativity. The results of several studies suggest that being in a happy mood can increase creativity—perhaps because being in a happy mood activates a wider range of ideas or associations than being in a negative mood, and creativity consists, in part, of combining such associations into new patterns (Estrada, Isen, & Young, 1995; Isen, 2000). A recent meta-analysis combining all the studies investigating the relationship between mood and creativity (Baas, De Dreu, & Nijstad, 2008) indicates that positive moods facilitate creativity most when they are relatively high in arousal (e.g., happiness) rather than low in arousal (e.g., relaxation).

mood congruence effects
The fact that we are more likely to store or remember positive information when in a positive mood and negative information when in a negative mood.

mood dependent memory
The fact that what we remember while in a given mood may be determined, in part, by what we learned when previously in that mood.

A third way in which affect influences cognition involves the tendency to engage in *heuristic processing*, thinking that relies heavily on mental "shortcuts" (heuristics) and knowledge acquired through past experience. This, in turn, has important implications for decision making and problem solving—activities we all perform frequently. Research findings indicate that people experiencing positive affect are more likely than people experiencing negative affect to engage in heuristic thought (i.e., to rely on previously acquired "rules of thumb" and previously gathered information) in dealing with current problems or decisions (Mackie & Worth, 1989; Park & Banaji, 2000; Wegner & Petty, 1994). If these are applicable to the new situation, they can be helpful. If not, they can get in the way of both effective decision making and performance.

Finally, we should mention that our current moods often influence our interpretations of the motives behind people's behavior. Positive affect tends to promote attributions of positive motives, while negative affect tends to encourage attributions of negative motives (Forgas, 2000). As we note in Chapter 3, our thoughts about the cause of others' behavior play an important role in many situations, so this is another way in which the interplay between affect and cognition can have important effects.

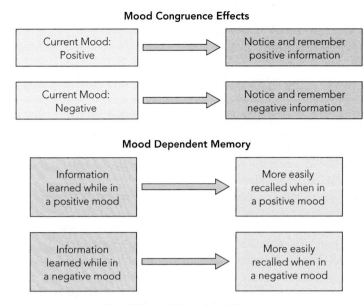

FIGURE 2.14   **The Effects of Mood on Memory**
Our moods influence what we remember through two mechanisms: mood congruence effects, which refer to the fact that we are more likely to store or remember information consistent with our current mood, and mood dependent memory, which refers to the fact that we tend to remember information consistent with our current moods.

The Influence of Cognition on Affect

Most research on the relationship between affect and cognition has focused on how feelings influence thought. However, there is also strong evidence for the reverse: the impact of cognition on affect. One aspect of this relationship is described in what is known as the *two-factor theory* of emotion (Schachter, 1964). This theory suggests that often, we don't know our own feelings or attitudes directly. Rather, since these internal reactions are often somewhat ambiguous, we infer their nature from the external world—from the kinds of situations in which we experience these reactions. For example, if we experience increased arousal in the presence of an attractive person, we may conclude that we are in love. In contrast, if we experience increased arousal after being cut off in traffic by another driver, we may conclude that what we feel is anger.

A second way in which cognition can influence emotions is by activating schemas containing a strong affective component. For example, if we categorize an individual as belonging to a group different than our own, we may experience a different emotional response than if we categorized that same individual as a member of our own group. Let's consider a case of watching a person receive a seemingly painful needle injection in the hand. When the picture was of an African hand, Caucasian participants exhibited lower empathic reactions as indicated by reduced brain activity in the pain areas of the brain relative to when the picture of the hand receiving the injection was also Caucasian (Avenanti, Sirigu, & Aglioti, 2010). The same results—in reverse—were observed for participants of African descent; greater empathic pain reactions in the brain were observed when the hand was Black compared to when it was White. These results indicate that how we think about others—and who we think those others are—tells us how we feel about such people, and whether we "feel" their pain or not. But, do we always know how we will feel about the suffering of others? For detailed information on this important issue, please see our special section, "EMOTIONS AND SOCIAL COGNITION: Why We Can't Always Predict Our Responses to Tragedy."

EMOTIONS *and* SOCIAL COGNITION

Why We Can't Always Predict Our Responses to Tragedy

Would you feel worse if you learned that one person was killed in a forest fire, or if you learned that 1,000 people were? Most people believe that they would feel worse upon learning about the large-scale tragedy compared to the smaller-scale one. Yet, much research indicates that our **affective forecasts**—predictions about how we would feel about an event we have not experienced—are often inaccurate (Dunn & Laham, 2006). To the extent that our cognition (affective forecasts) is based on a different way of processing information compared to actual emotional experience, these two types of responses—forecasting and experiencing—should differ. Because rational cognition is responsive to abstract symbols, including numbers, forecasting should vary depending on the scale of the tragedy being considered. Emotions, in contrast, which are based on concrete images and immediate experiences, may be relatively insensitive to the actual numbers of people killed, or more generally the scope of a tragedy.

To test this idea—that affective forecasting will be responsive to numbers, but that people who are actually experiencing the images from a tragedy will show an "emotional flatline" as the death toll increases, Dunn and Ashton-James (2008) conducted a number of studies. In one experiment, one group of participants was placed in the "experiencer role"; they were given a news article

about a deadly forest fire in Spain and were asked to report their actual emotions while reading about the tragedy. Another group of participants was placed in the "forecaster role" and they were simply asked to predict how they would feel "if they read about a deadly forest fire in Spain." The scope of the tragedy of the fire was also varied. Some participants were told that five people had been killed, while other participants were told that 10,000 people had been killed by the fire.

Did the size of the tragedy affect how bad participants actually reported feeling in the experience condition or they expected to feel in the forecasting condition? Yes, the size of the tragedy did affect how forecasters expected to feel, but the number of people killed in the fire did *not* affect how people actually reported feeling. Not only did forecasters overestimate how bad they would feel overall, but they believed they would be responsive to the magnitude of the tragedy whereas those who were actually exposed to the tragic loss information showed a "flatline" response and did not differentiate their emotional response according to numbers.

In a subsequent study, these researchers brought the tragedy closer to home—the victims were members of their own group. Students were told that either 15 or 500 American college students had been killed in the war in Iraq, and pictures of the sort shown in Figure 2.15 were presented to

FIGURE 2.15   Emotional Responses to the Tragegy of One or Many
People who are asked to forecast how they would feel about the tragic deaths of others believed they would feel worse as the number of people killed increased. However, people who were actually given the detailed information to read or view felt about the same regardless of how many people had died. This research is consistent with the idea that rational information processing, which occurs in forecasting, differs from actual emotional experience.

the *experiencers* on a website prepared for the study. The *forecaster* participants were not shown the actual pictures or website, but were asked to imagine how they would feel if they viewed one of the website versions. Again, participants who were only forecasting how they would feel overestimated their negative affect compared to the experiencers, and the forecasters were sensitive to the number of deaths while the experiencers were not.

Forecasting affective responses to tragedy may not only lead to inaccuracies in general (overestimates of how distressed people will be). Forecasting appears to also result in specific errors: expecting greater mobilization on the part of others as the scope of the tragedy increases, although those who are actually exposed to and consuming images of the tragedy do not respond differentially according to the numbers of people who have suffered.

A third way in which our thoughts can influence our affective states involves our efforts to regulate our own emotions and feelings. This topic has important practical implications, so we'll examine it carefully.

affective forecasts
Predictions about how we would feel about events we have not actually experienced.

COGNITION AND THE REGULATION OF AFFECTIVE STATES   Learning to regulate our emotions is an important task; negative events and outcomes are an unavoidable part of life, so learning to cope with the negative feelings these events generate is crucial for personal adjustment—and for good social relations with others. Among the most important techniques we use for regulating our moods and emotions are ones involving cognitive mechanisms. In other words, we use our thoughts to regulate our feelings. Many techniques for accomplishing this goal exist, but here, we'll consider one that is especially common—giving in to temptation as a means of improving our current mood.

When we feel "down" or distressed, we often engage in activities that we know might be bad for us in the long run, but that make us feel better, at least temporarily (e.g., engage in some "retail therapy" by going shopping, eat fattening snacks, drink alcohol; see Figure 2.16). These actions make us feel better, but we know full well that they have an important "downside." Why, then, do we choose to do them? In the past it was assumed that people engage in such actions because the emotional distress we are experiencing reduces either our capacity or motivation to control our impulses to do things that are enjoyable but potentially bad for us. However, Tice et al. (2000) argue that cognitive factors in fact play a role in such behavior; we yield to such temptations because it helps us deal with strong negative feelings.

To test this prediction, Tice et al. (2000) conducted a study in which participants were first put into a good or bad mood (by reading stories in which they either saved a child's life or ran a red light and caused the death of a child). Then, participants were either told that their moods could change over time or their moods were "frozen" and could not change much. Participants then were led to believe they would work on an intelligence test on which they would receive feedback. Before doing the test, though, they would have a 15-minute practice session to prepare for it. The experimenter then left them in a room containing materials for practicing for the test *and* distracters—other tasks on which they could work. For half the participants these tasks were attractive and tempting (e.g., a challenging puzzle, a video game, popular magazines). For the others, they were less attractive (a preschool-level plastic puzzle, out-of-date technical journals). The main question was this: would people in a bad mood spend more of the practice time than people in a good mood playing with the distracters (procrastinating)? More importantly, would this occur only in the condition where participants believed they could change their own moods? After all, there would be no use in playing with the distracters if participants believed that their moods were "frozen" and could not be altered. Tice et al. predicted that people in a bad mood would procrastinate more, but only when they

FIGURE 2.16 Consciously Regulating Our Negative Moods
When people are feeling down, many engage in activities designed to make them feel better—they go shopping, consume alcohol, and so on. Research findings suggest that engaging in such actions is the result of conscious strategy for regulating our emotions.

believed doing so would enhance their moods—and the results offered clear support for the prediction. These findings indicate that the tendency to yield to temptation is a conscious choice, not a simple lapse in the ability to control our own impulses.

Affect and Cognition: Social Neuroscience Evidence for Two Separate Systems

So far we have argued that affect and cognition are intimately linked, and in fact, existing evidence suggests that this is certainly the case. However, we should also note that recent findings using neuroscience techniques (e.g., scanning of human brains as individuals perform various activities) indicate that actually two distinct systems for processing social information may exist within the human brain (e.g., Cohen, 2005). One system is concerned with what might be termed "reason"—logical thought—whereas the other deals primarily with affect or emotion. These two systems, although distinct in certain respects, interact in many ways during problem solving, decision making, and other important forms of cognition. For instance, consider research employing what is known as an "ultimatum" paradigm.

In such research, two people are told that they can divide a given sum (e.g., $10) between them. One person can suggest an initial division and the second can accept or reject it. Since any division provides the second person with positive payoffs, total rationality (and classic economic theory) suggests that acceptance of any division offered is the most rational (and best) course of action. In fact, however, most people reject divisions that give them less than $3, and many reject divisions that offer them less than $5. Magnetic resonance imaging (MRI) scans of the brains of people performing this task reveal that when they receive offers they view as unfair, brain regions related both to reasoning (e.g., the dorsolateral prefrontal cortex) and to emotion (e.g., the limbic system) are active. However, the greater the amount of activity in the emotion-processing regions, the greater the likelihood that individuals will reject the offers—and act in ways that are, in a sense, contrary to their own economic interests (e.g., Sanfey, Rilling, Aronson, Nystrum, & Cohen, 2003). These findings, and those of many other studies, provide concrete evidence for the existence of two distinct systems (reason and emotion) that interact in complex ways during decision making and other cognitive processes (e.g., Gabaix & Laibson, 2006; Naqvi, Shiv, & Bechara, 2006).

Additional research indicates that the neural system for emotion tends to be impulsive, preferring immediate rewards, whereas the system for reason is more forward-looking and accepting of delays that ultimately yield larger rewards. For instance, when offered the choice between an immediate gain (a $15 Amazon.com gift now) and a larger one in 2 weeks (a $20 gift voucher), increased activity occurs in both emotion-related and reason-processing regions of the brain. The immediate option, however, induces greater activity in the emotion-related areas (e.g., the limbic system; McClure, Laibson, Loewenstein, & Cohen, 2004).

Overall, then, evidence from research using modern techniques for scanning brain activity during cognitive processes suggests that affect plays a fundamental role in human thought, and that if we wish to fully understand the complex ways in which we think about the social world and our place in it, we must take this fact into careful account because certain aspects of our thought can also influence our feelings. Affect and cognition are not one-way streets; they are a divided highway, with the potential of one influencing the other.

KEY POINTS

- Affect influences cognition in several ways. Our current moods can cause us to react positively or negatively to new stimuli, including other people, the extent to which we think systematically or heuristically, and can influence memory through **mood dependent memory and mood congruence effects**.

- When we are in a positive mood, we tend to think heuristically to a greater extent than when we are a negative mood. Specifically, we show increased reliance on stereotypes and other mental shortcuts.

- Cognition influences affect through our interpretation of emotion-provoking events and through the activation of schemas containing a strong affective component. Brain activity reflective of empathy in response to pain experienced by another person depends on how we categorize the other person.

- **Affective forecasts**—predictions about how we would feel about an event we have not experienced—are often inaccurate because cognition and affect are based in different systems. Those in a forecasting role are sensitive to the numbers of people harmed, whereas those in an experience role are not differentially responsive to the magnitude of the tragedy.

- We employ several cognitive techniques to regulate our emotions or feelings. For instance, when distressed, we can consciously choose to engage in activities that, while damaging in the long run, make us feel better in the short run.

- Research in social neuroscience indicates that we may actually possess two distinct systems for processing social information—one concerned with logical thought and the other with affect or emotion.

SUMMARY *and* REVIEW

● Because we have limited cognitive capacity, we often attempt to reduce the effort we expend on **social cognition**—how we think about other people and the social world. Given our limited capacity to process information, we often experience **information overload.** To cope with this, we make use of **heuristics**—simple rules of thumb—for making decisions in a quick and relatively effortless manner. One such heuristic is **representativeness,** which suggests that the more similar an individual is to typical members of a given group, the more likely she or he is to belong to that group. When using the representativeness heuristic, people tend to ignore base rates—frequencies of events or patterns in the total population. Another heuristic is **availability,** which suggests that the easier it is to bring information to mind, the greater its impact on subsequent decisions or judgments. Use of availability can lead us astray to the extent that vivid events are easier to bring to mind, but as not necessarily more frequent in occurrence. A third heuristic is **anchoring and adjustment,** which leads us to use a number or value as a starting point from which we then make adjustments. These adjustments may not be sufficient to reflect actual social reality, perhaps because once we attain a plausible value, we stop the process. A fourth heuristic, status quo, leads us to favor "old" over "new."

● One basic component of social cognition is **schemas**—mental frameworks developed through experience that, once formed, help us to organize social information. Once-formed schemas exert powerful effects on what we notice (attention), enter into memory (encoding), and later remember (retrieval). Individuals report remembering more information consistent with their schemas than information inconsistent with them, but in fact, inconsistent information too is strongly represented in memory. Schemas are often *primed*—activated by experiences, events, or stimuli. Once they are primed, the effects of the schemas tend to persist until they are somehow expressed in thought or behavior; such expression (known as **unpriming**) then reduces their effects. Schemas help us to process information, but they often persist even in the face of disconfirming information. Schemas can also exert self-fulfilling effects, causing us to behave in ways that confirm them. **Metaphors,** which relate an abstract concept to another dissimilar one, can shape how we respond to the social world.

● A large amount of evidence indicates that the distinction between automatic and controlled processing is a very basic one. In fact, different regions of the brain appear to be involved in these two types of processing, especially with respect to evaluations of various aspects of the social world. When schemas or other cognitive frameworks are activated (even without our conscious awareness of such activation), they can influence our behavior, triggering actions consistent with the frameworks and also preparing us to interact with the people or groups who are the focus of these schemas. Automatic processing is quick and efficient; in addition, however, it may also sometimes offer other advantages too—such as increased satisfaction with decisions. Decisions we must make under **conditions of uncertainty** can be improved with "choice architecture," which involves identifying the heuristics people use and placing the options in the order and format where most people are likely to select the option that will benefit them.

- People show a strong **optimistic bias,** expecting positive events and outcomes and fewer negatives in many contexts. In addition, people tend to be overconfident in their judgments and predictions about themselves. This occurs because people make errors of omission; they lack the comparison information that would allow them to know what factors they have not considered. One example of our optimism at work is the **planning fallacy**—our tendency to believe that a task will take less time than it really will. In many situations, individuals imagine "what might have been"—they engage in **counterfactual thinking.** Such thought can affect our sympathy for people who have experienced negative outcomes. Counterfactual thinking seems to occur automatically in many situations, and adding cognitive load strengthens its impact on judgments.

- There are important limits on our ability to think rationally about the social world. One involves **magical thinking**—thinking based on assumptions that don't hold up to rational scrutiny. For instance, we may believe that if two objects are in contact, properties can pass from one to the other. One form of such thinking—belief in the supernatural—stems, at least in part, from **terror management**—our efforts to cope with the knowledge that we will die.

- Affect influences cognition in several ways. Our current moods influence our perceptions of the world around us, the extent to which we think systematically or heuristically, and influence memory through mood-congruence effects and mood-dependent memory. Affect can also influence creativity and our interpretations of others' behavior. Cognition influences affect through our interpretation of emotion-provoking events and through the activation of schemas containing a strong affective component. In addition, we employ several cognitive techniques to regulate our emotions or feelings (e.g., consciously giving in to temptation to reduce negative feelings). Although affect and cognition are closely related, social neuroscience research indicates that they involve distinct systems within the brain. People make **affective forecasts**—predictions about how they would feel about an event they have not experienced—using the cognitive system, but respond with the emotional system when confronted with those events.

KEY TERMS

affect (p. 37)

affective forecasts (p. 63)

anchoring and adjustment heuristic (p. 41)

automatic processing (p. 48)

availability heuristic (p. 40)

counterfactual thinking (p. 56)

conditions of uncertainty (p. 38)

heuristics (p. 37)

information overload (p. 38)

magical thinking (p. 58)

metaphor (p. 46)

mood congruence effects (p. 60)

mood dependent memory (p. 60)

optimistic bias (p. 53)

overconfidence barrier (p. 53)

perseverance effect (p. 46)

planning fallacy (p. 54)

priming (p. 45)

prototype (p. 38)

representativeness heuristic (p. 38)

schemas (p. 44)

social cognition (p. 36)

terror management (p. 58)

unpriming (p. 45)

CHAPTER 3

Social Perception

Perceiving and Understanding Others

*D*O YOU REMEMBER THE FIRST TIME YOU HEARD YOUR OWN voice on your answering machine or in a video? If you are like most people, you were surprised: "That doesn't sound like me," you probably thought. This common experience raises an intriguing question: If we don't even recognize our own voices, do we really know and understand ourselves as well as we think we do? If we do, then why are we sometimes surprised by our own feelings or actions? For instance, have you ever enjoyed a new food more than you thought you would, or enjoyed a movie you expected to like much less than you anticipated? And have you ever been surprised to learn that other people view you very differently than the way you view yourself? At one time or another, most of us have these kinds of experiences, and when we do, they tell us that our self-knowledge is far from perfect. In some ways, we know ourselves very well, but in others . . . perhaps not as well as we'd prefer.

We focus in detail on the nature the self and self-understanding in Chapter 4, but here, we want to raise a related but different topic: If we don't know or understand ourselves very accurately, how can we hope to understand or know *others?* How can we recognize the feelings they are experiencing, understand their motives and goals, and—in essence—figure out what kind of person they really are? This is a crucial process and one we must perform every day because perceiving and understanding others accurately provides a basic foundation of all social life. For instance, it's often important to know when others are being truthful and when they are attempting to deceive us, to know *why* they say or do certain things (e.g., did they make a remark that hurt our feelings on purpose, or by accident), and whether the outward face they show really reflects their true inner selves. Accomplishing these tasks is crucial because to the extent we perform them well, we can predict others' future feelings and actions accurately; to the extent we remain "clueless" about them, we have very little chance of achieving that important goal, and very little likelihood of getting along well with them. So, how do we do it? How do we manage to perform the task of **social perception**—the process through which we seek to know and understand other people? That's the focus of the present chapter.

In this chapter, we describe the ways in which we attempt to understand other people, why it is often so difficult to perform this task well, and when we are most likely to get it right—or wrong! (See Figure 3.1.) Obtaining van accurate

"*Even just sitting here, I'm receiving a tremendous amount of information from you.*"

FIGURE 3.1 **Are We Good at Understanding Others?**
As shown here, we use many different sources of information in our efforts to understand others. This complex task seems effortless for the woman in this cartoon, but in fact, attaining accurate understanding of others is often difficult.

social perception
The process through which we seek to know and understand other people.

nonverbal communication
Communication between individuals that does not involve the content of spoken language. It relies instead on an unspoken language of facial expressions, eye contact, and body language.

attribution
The process through which we seek to identify the causes of others' behavior and so gain knowledge of their stable traits and dispositions.

impression formation
The process through which we form impressions of others.

impression management (self-presentation)
Efforts by individuals to produce favorable first impressions on others.

understanding of others is very important because they play such a central role in our lives, but in fact, it actually involves many different tasks. We focus on some of the most important here.

First, we consider the ways in which we learn about others from **nonverbal communication**—information provided not by their words, but by their facial expressions, eye contact, body movements, postures, and even changes in their body chemistry, which are communicated through tiny amounts of substances released into the air (e.g., Ekman, 2003; Miller & Maner, 2010). Next, we examine **attribution,** the process through which we attempt to understand the reasons behind others' behavior—why they have acted as they have in a given situation, what goals they are seeking, and what intentions they have (e.g., Burrus & Roese, 2006). This a crucial process because, as we'll soon see, the conclusions we reach about why others behave as they do can strongly influence our reactions to what they say and do. Third, we examine the nature of **impression formation**—how we form first impressions of others, and **impression management** (or **self-presentation**)—how we try to ensure that these impressions are favorable ones.

Nonverbal Communication: The Unspoken Language of Expressions, Gazes, Gestures, and Scents

When are other people more likely to do favors for you—when they are in a good mood or a bad one? And when are they more likely to lose their temper and lash out at you; when they are feeling happy and content, or when they are feeling tense and irritable? Careful research reveals that often, social actions—our own and those of other people—are affected by temporary factors or causes. Changing moods, shifting emotions, fatigue, illness, drugs—even hidden biological processes such as the menstrual cycle—can all influence the ways in which we think and behave.

Because such temporary factors exert important effects on social behavior and thought, information about them is both important and useful. Thus, we often try to find out how others are feeling *right now*. Sometimes, doing so is quite straightforward—we ask other people how they are feeling or what kind of mood they are in, and they tell us. Sometimes, though, other people are unwilling to reveal their inner feelings (e.g., DePaulo et al., 2003; Forrest & Feldman, 2000). For example, negotiators often hide their reactions from their opponents; and salespeople frequently show more liking and friendliness toward potential customers than they really feel. And on other occasions, they aren't sure, themselves, just what these feelings or other reactions are!

In situations like these, and in ones in which we can't ask others how they are feeling, we pay careful attention to *nonverbal cues* provided by changes in their facial expressions, eye contact, posture, body movements, and other expressive actions. As noted by De Paulo et al. (2003), such behavior is relatively *irrepressible*—difficult to control—so that even when others try to conceal their inner feelings from us, these often "leak out" in many ways through nonverbal cues. The information conveyed by such cues, and our efforts to interpret this input, are often described by the term nonverbal communication (Ko, Judd, & Blair, 2006), and we now take a close look at this intriguing aspect of our efforts to understand others.

Nonverbal Communication: The Basic Channels

Think for a moment: Do you act differently when you are feeling very happy than when you are feeling really sad? Most likely, you do. People tend to behave differently when experiencing different emotional states. But precisely how do differences in your inner states—your emotions, feelings, and moods—show up in your behavior? This question relates to the *basic channels* through which such communication takes place. Research findings indicate that five of these channels exist: *facial expressions*, *eye contact*, *body movements*, *posture*, and *touching*.

FACIAL EXPRESSIONS AS CLUES TO OTHERS' EMOTIONS   More than 2,000 years ago, the Roman orator Cicero stated: "The face is the image of the soul." By this he meant that human feelings and emotions are often reflected in the face and can be read there in specific expressions. Modern research suggests that Cicero was correct: It is possible to learn much about others' current moods and feelings from their facial expressions. In fact, it appears that five different basic emotions are represented clearly, and from a very early age, on the human face: anger, fear, happiness, sadness, and disgust (Izard, 1991; Rozin, Lowery, & Ebert, 1994). (*Surprise*, has also been suggested as a basic emotion reflected clearly in facial expressions, but recent evidence concerning this suggestion is mixed, so it may not be as basic or as clearly represented in facial expressions as other emotions; Reisenzein, Bordgen, Holtbernd, & Matz, 2006).

It's important to realize that the fact that only five different emotions are represented on our faces does *not* imply that human beings can show only a small number of facial expressions. On the contrary, emotions occur in many combinations (e.g., joy together with sorrow, fear combined with anger) and each of these reactions can vary greatly in strength. Thus, while there may be only a small number of basic themes in facial expressions, the number of variations on these themes is immense (see Figure 3.2).

Now for another important question: Are facial expressions universal? In other words, if you traveled to a remote part of the world and visited a group of people who had never before met an outsider, would their facial expressions in various situations resemble your own? Would they smile in reaction to events that made them happy, frown when exposed to conditions that made then angry, and so on? Furthermore, would you

FIGURE 3.2   Facial Expressions: The Range Is Huge
Although only five basic emotions are represented in distinct facial expressions that can be recognized across various cultures, these emotions can occur in many combinations and be shown to varying degrees. The result? The number of unique facial expressions any one person can show is truly immense.

be able to recognize these distinct expressions as readily as the ones shown by people belonging to your own culture? Early research on this question seemed to suggest that facial expressions are universal in both respects (e.g., Ekman & Friesen, 1975) and with few exceptions, these results have been confirmed in more recent research (Effenbin & Ambady, 2002). In fact, it has been found that certain facial expressions—smiles, frowns, and other signs of sadness) occur, and are recognized as representing basic underlying emotions (e.g., happiness, anger, sadness) in many different cultures (e.g., Shaver, Murdaya, & Fraley, 2001). While the overall pattern of findings is not entirely consistent (e.g., Russell, 1994; Carroll & Russell, 1996), it seems reasonable to conclude that some facial expressions provide clear signals of underlying emotional states, and are recognized as doing so all over the world. Cultural differences certainly do exist with respect to the precise meaning of facial expressions, but unlike spoken languages, they do not seem to require much in the way of translation.

While many different studies provide clear evidence for these conclusions, research conducted with athletes competing in the Olympics are especially interesting in this respect. When photos of the faces of these athletic stars are taken at various times (on winning or losing their matches, when receiving their medals, while posing for photographers), clear evidence of recognizable facial expressions—ones reflecting the athletes' underlying emotional states—is obtained (Matsumoto & Willingham, 2006). For instance, almost all gold medal winners smile clearly and openly when they win their matches, and also when they receive their medals. Most bronze medalists, too, smile—although not as high a percentage as among gold medal winners. In contrast, very few silver medal winners smile. Why does this difference between bronze and silver medal winners exist? As we noted in Chapter 2, it is because the bronze medal winners are happy to have won *any* medal—and their facial expressions show this. In contrast, silver medalists torture themselves with (counterfactual) thoughts about how they could have received "the gold" if only . . . (see Figure 3.3).

Additional findings indicate that when posing for photographers, gold and bronze medal winners show true (real) smiles; silver medal winners, in contrast, show the kind of "social smiling" everyone can show when a smile is required—but does not reflect underlying happiness. These findings, and those of many other studies, indicate that others' facial expressions are often a very useful guide to their feelings. Thus, it is not at all surprising that we rely on such information as a basis for forming accurate perceptions of others—or at least, perceptions of how they are feeling right now. Interestingly—and as you might expect—when people know each other very well (e.g., they are very close friends), they are better at "reading" each other's nonverbal cues—especially subtle ones—than when they are strangers or casual acquaintances (Zhang & Parmley, 2011). So clearly, becoming familiar with another person's range and form of facial expression can be helpful in terms of knowing what they are really feeling.

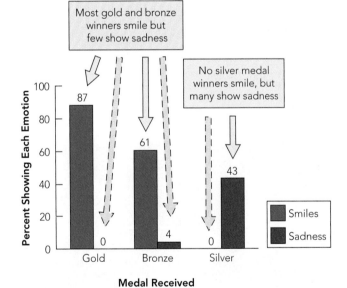

FIGURE 3.3 Facial Expressions Among Gold, Silver, and Bronze Medal Olympic Medal Winners

As shown here, gold medal winners and bronze medal winners smiled frequently (at the conclusion of their matches and when receiving their medals). In contrast, silver medal winners did not smile; they showed sadness instead. These findings reflect the underlying emotions of these athletes: gold and bronze medal winners are happy with their results; silver medal winners, in contrast, are unhappy because they imagine "getting the gold." (Source: Based on data from Matsumoto & Willingham, 2006).

GAZES AND STARES: EYE CONTACT AS A NONVERBAL CUE Have you ever had a conversation with someone wearing vary dark or mirrored sunglasses? If so, you realize that this can be an uncomfortable situation. Since you can't see the other person's eyes, you are uncertain about how he or she is reacting. Taking note of the importance of cues provided by others' eyes, ancient poets often described the eyes as "windows to the soul." In one important sense, they were correct: We do often learn much about others' feelings from their eyes. For example, we interpret a high level of gazing from another as a sign of liking or friendliness (Kleinke, 1986). In contrast, if others avoid eye contact with us, we may conclude that they are unfriendly, don't like us, or are simply shy.

While a high level of eye contact with others is usually interpreted as a sign of liking or positive feelings, there is one exception to this general rule. If another person gazes at us continuously and maintains such contact regardless of what we do, he or she can be said to be **staring.** A stare is often interpreted as a sign of anger or hostility—as in *cold stare*—and most people find this particular nonverbal cue disturbing (Ellsworth & Carlsmith, 1973). In fact, we may quickly terminate social interaction with someone who stares at us and may even leave the scene (Greenbaum & Rosenfield, 1978). This is one reason why experts on "road rage"—highly aggressive driving by motorists, sometimes followed by actual assaults—recommend that drivers avoid eye contact with people who are disobeying traffic laws and rules of the road (e.g., Bushman, 1998). Apparently, such people, who are already in a highly excitable state, interpret anything approaching a stare from another driver as an aggressive act, and react accordingly.

BODY LANGUAGE: GESTURES, POSTURE, AND MOVEMENTS　　Try this simple demonstration for yourself:

> *First, remember some incident that made you angry—the angrier the better. Think about it for a minute.*
>
> *Now, try to remember another incident, one that made you feel sad—again, the sadder the better.*

Compare your behavior in the two contexts. Did you change your posture or move your hands, arms, or legs as your thoughts shifted from the first event to the second? There is a good chance that you did, for our current moods or emotions are often reflected in the position, posture, and movement of our bodies. Together, such nonverbal behaviors are termed **body language,** and they, too, can provide useful information about others.

First, body language often reveals others' emotional states. Large numbers of movements—especially ones in which one part of the body does something to another part (touching, rubbing, scratching)—suggest emotional arousal. The greater the frequency of such behavior, the higher the level of arousal or nervousness.

Larger patterns of movements, involving the whole body, can also be informative. Such phrases as "she adopted a threatening posture," and "he greeted her with open arms" suggest that different body orientations or postures indicate contrasting emotional states. In fact, research by Aronoff, Woike, and Hyman (1992) confirms this possibility. These researchers first identified two groups of characters in classical ballet: ones who played a dangerous or threatening role (e.g., Macbeth, the Angel of Death, Lizzie Borden) and ones who played warm, sympathetic roles (Juliet, Romeo). Then they examined examples of dancing by these characters in actual ballets to see if they adopted different kinds of postures. Aronoff and his colleagues predicted that the dangerous, threatening characters would show more diagonal or angular postures, whereas the warm, sympathetic characters would show more rounded postures, and results strongly confirmed this hypothesis. These and related findings indicate that large-scale body movements or postures can sometimes provide important information about others' emotions, and even about their apparent traits.

More specific information about others' feelings is often provided by gestures. These fall into several categories, but perhaps the most important are emblems—body movements carrying specific meanings in a given culture. Do you recognize the gestures shown

staring
A form of eye contact in which one person continues to gaze steadily at another regardless of what the recipient does.

body language
Cues provided by the position, posture, and movement of others' bodies or body parts.

FIGURE 3.4   Gestures: One Form of Nonverbal Communication
Do you recognize the gestures shown here? Can you tell what they mean? In the United States and other Western cultures, each of these gestures has a clear meaning. However, they might well have no meaning or entirely different meanings, in other cultures.

in Figure 3.4? In the United States and several other countries, these movements have clear and definite meanings. However, in other cultures, they might have no meaning, or even a different meaning. For this reason, it is wise to be careful about using gestures while traveling in cultures different from your own: you may offend the people around you without meaning to do so!

TOUCHING: WHAT DOES IT CONVEY?   Suppose that during a brief conversation with another person, he or she touched you briefly. How would you react? What information would this behavior convey? The answer to both questions is, it depends. And what it depends on is several factors relating to who does the touching (a friend, a stranger, a member of your own or the other gender); the nature of this physical contact (brief or prolonged, gentle or rough, what part of the body is touched); and the context in which the touching takes place (a business or social setting, a doctor's office). Depending on such factors, touch can suggest affection, sexual interest, dominance, caring, or even aggression. Despite such complexities, existing evidence indicates that when touching is considered appropriate, it often produces positive reactions in the person being touched (e.g., Alagna, Whitcher, & Fisher, 1979; Levav & Argo, 2010). But remember, it must be viewed as appropriate to produce such reactions!

One acceptable way in which people in many different cultures touch strangers is through handshaking. "Pop psychology" and even books on etiquette (e.g., Vanderbilt, 1957) suggest that handshakes reveal much about other people—for instance, their personalities—and that a firm handshake is a good way to make a favorable first impression on others. Are such observations true? Is this form of nonverbal communication actually revealing? Research findings (e.g., Chaplin, Phillips, Brown, Clanton, & Stein, 2000) suggest that it is. The firmer, longer, and more vigorous others' handshakes are, the higher we tend to rate them in terms of extraversion and openness to experience, and the more favorable our first impressions of them tend to be.

Other forms of touching, too, can sometimes be appropriate. For instance, Levav and Argo (2010) found that a light, comforting pat on the arm can induce feelings of security among both women and men—but only if the touching is performed by a woman. Such feelings of security, in turn, influence actual behavior: individuals touched on the shoulder by a female experimenter actually showed greater risk taking in an investment task than those not touched, or ones who were touched only through handshakes.

In sum, touching can serve as another source of nonverbal communication, and when it is appropriate (as, for example, in handshakes in cultures that view this as an appropriate means of greeting others), it can induce positive reactions. If it is viewed as inappropriate, however, it can encourage negative perceptions of the person doing the touching.

Scent: Another Source of Nonverbal Social Information

Although facial expressions, body movements, gestures, eye contact, and touching are basic and important sources of nonverbal information, they are not the only ones. Much can also be learned from what are termed *paralinguistic cues*—changes in the tone or inflection of others' voices (quite apart from the meaning of their words). And recent research indicates that even subtle cues relating to others' body chemistry can be revealing. For instance, research by Miller and Maner (2010) indicates that changes in women's internal chemistry occurring during the menstrual cycle can be transmitted to others (especially, perhaps, men) through subtle olfactory cues—changes in the aromas emitted by their bodies.

In this research, a large number of women were asked to wear clean T-shirts several nights during the month—either right around the time they were ovulating (days 13–15 of their menstrual cycles), and when ovulation had passed (days 20–22). The T-shirts were then sealed in plastic bags and presented to men who opened the bags slightly and smelled the shirts. The men did not know anything about the women involved or their menstrual cycles, but when their testosterone was measured, clear results emerged: Men who smelled the T-shirts worn by ovulating women showed higher testosterone levels than those who sniffed the T-shirts worn by nonovulating women, or who sniffed clean T-shirts not worn by anyone; see Figure 3.5). Interestingly, the men couldn't report detecting differences in the scents of the shirts worn during ovulation and after it was over, but their testosterone levels still differed. Overall, these findings indicate that shifts in body chemistry, too, can provide nonverbal cues about other people—at least in the case of women and their menstrual cycle. So truly, we do have many sources of information about other people' internal states, and not all of it is revealed by facial expressions, eye contact, or other basic channels of nonverbal communication.

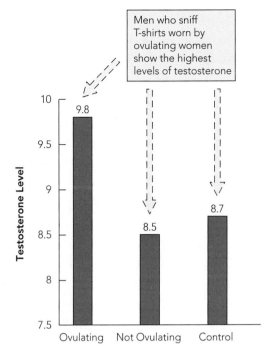

FIGURE 3.5   Body Scent as a Subtle Nonverbal Cue

Men's own testosterone was higher when they sniffed T-shirts worn by ovulating women than when they sniffed T-shirts worn by women who were not longer ovulating, or clean T-shirts not worn by anyone. These findings indicate that changes in body chemistry, reflected in subtle changes in body odor, can serve as an informational nonverbal cue. (Source: Based on data from Miller & Maner, 2010).

Are Facial Expressions an Especially Important Source of Information About Others?

Having pointed out that there are many sources of nonverbal information about others, we next want to emphasize that although this is certainly true, growing evidence suggests that facial expressions are especially important in this respect (e.g., Tsao & Livingstone, 2008). In a sense, this is not surprising because we direct lots of attention to others' faces as we interact with them. In support of this basic fact, several different research findings combine to suggest that facial expressions are indeed a uniquely crucial source of information about others.

First, it is almost impossible to ignore such information. For instance, many studies indicate that having an opportunity to view visual stimuli on one occasion often reduces attention to these stimuli on subsequent occasions. This is not true for facial expressions, however. Even after viewing them once, they still grip our attention the next time they are presented (e.g., Blagrove & Watson, 2010). Moreover, this is especially true for negative facial expressions. Even if such expressions are seen on one occasion, they are still easier to notice than other stimuli on later occasions. For example, individuals can spot an angry face in an array of faces more quickly than neutral or smiling faces.

Second, to the extent a person's neutral facial expression resembles a particular emotional expression, they are seen as showing this emotion, even when in fact they are not experiencing any strong emotion (Zebrowitz, Kikuchi, & Fellous, 2007, in press). Male faces, for example, are seen as resembling angry expressions to a greater extent than female faces, and black and Korean faces are seen as resembling expressions of happiness or surprise to a greater extent than white faces, even when the people whose faces shown are not actually experiencing any emotion. In short, we tend to perceive more in others' faces than is really there, interpreting the basic appearance of their faces as suggestive of specific emotions, even if these aren't really present. This, too, suggests that facial expressions are an especially important source of nonverbal information—although, in fact, the conclusions we reach in this respect may be far from accurate.

Finally and perhaps most interesting, facial expressions not only serve as a source of information for observers, who use them to understand what the people showing such expressions are feeling, but also play a role in generating such emotions or feelings. In other words, as William James (1894), one of the first prominent American psychologists, suggested, facial expressions are not only external signs of internal states, they can also trigger or influence internal emotional experiences. The view that facial expressions can actually trigger emotions is known as the *facial feedback hypothesis*, and is so interesting that we now consider it closely.

The Facial Feedback Hypothesis: Do We Show What We Feel *and* Feel What We Show?

In essence, the facial feedback hypothesis (Laird, 1984) suggests that there is a close link between the facial expressions we show and our internal feelings, and that this relationship works both ways: yes, the expressions we show reflect our internal feelings or emotions, but in addition, these expressions also feed back into our brains and influence our subjective experiences of emotion. In short, we don't only show what we feel inside on our faces—we also sometimes feel, inside, what we show!

Many studies offer support for this view. For instance, McCanne and Anderson (1987) asked female participants to imagine positive and negative events (e.g., "You inherit a million dollars," "You lose a really close friendship"). While imagining these events, they were told to either enhance or suppress tension in certain facial muscles. One of these muscles is active when we smile or view happy scenes. The other is active when we frown or view unhappy scenes. Measurements of electrical activity of both muscles indicated that after a few practice trials, most people could carry out this task quite successfully. They could enhance or suppress muscle tension when told to do so, and could do this without any visible change in their facial expressions.

After imagining each scene, participants rated their emotional experiences in terms of enjoyment or distress. If the facial feedback hypothesis is correct, these ratings should be affected by participants' efforts to enhance or suppress muscle tension. If they enhanced activity in muscles associated with smiling, they would report more enjoyment of the positive events. If they suppressed such activity, they would report less enjoyment. Results offered clear support for these predictions. Participants reported less enjoyment of the positive events when they suppressed activity in the appropriate muscle and a slight tendency to report less distress to the negative events when they suppressed the muscle involved in frowning. In addition—and of special interest—participants also reported less ability to imagine and experience scenes of both types when suppressing activity in their facial muscles.

Convincing as these findings are, there is an important problem in interpreting them: perhaps instructions to tense or inhibit certain muscles could have influenced participants' reports of their own emotional experiences. To get around such problems, more recent research (Davis, Senghas, Brandt, & Ochsner, 2010) has used a very ingenious solution: They compared the emotional reactions to positive and negative video clips of two groups of people who received injections of anti-wrinkle drugs. One group received injections of Botox, a drug that paralyzes muscles involved in facial expressions, while another received Restylane, a drug that simply fills in wrinkles without paralyzing facial muscles. The injections were given by a licensed physician, and participants in both groups rated how they felt after viewing each video clip on a scale of very negative to very positive. They did this twice—8 days before the injections, and again, 14–24 days after receiving them. If the facial feedback hypothesis is correct, then people receiving Botox should report weaker emotional reactions to the video clips. That is, they should report weaker negative feelings to the negative clips, and weaker positive feelings to the positive clips. In fact, that's precisely what occurred (see Figure 3.6). These findings suggest that feedback from our facial muscles does indeed play a role in shaping our emotional experiences. So it does seem to be the case that what we show on our faces influences what we experience "inside," and the words of one old song that suggests that we "Let a smile be our umbrella on a rainy, rainy day" appears to contain a sizeable grain of truth.

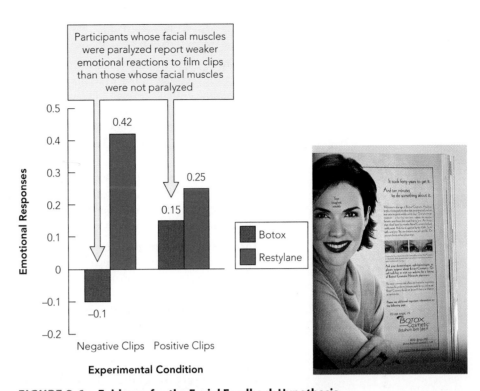

FIGURE 3.6   Evidence for the Facial Feedback Hypothesis
Participants who received injections of Botox, which paralyzes facial muscles, reported less negative reactions to negative film clips and less positive reactions to mildly positive film clips, than participants who received Restylane, a drug that does not paralyze muscles.

Deception: Recognizing It Through Nonverbal Cues, and Its Effects on Social Relations

Be honest: how often do you tell lies? This includes very small "white lies" designed to avoid hurting others' feelings or accomplish other positive social purposes to ones designed to get us out of trouble or further our own goals ("I'm sorry, Professor—I missed the exam because of an unexpected death in my family . . ."). In fact, research findings indicate that most people tell at least one lie every day (DePaulo & Kashy, 1998) and use deception in almost 20 percent of their social interactions. Experiments confirming these findings indicate that a majority of strangers lie to each other at least once during a brief first encounter (Feldman, Forrest, & Happ, 2002; Tyler & Feldman, 2004). Why do people lie? As we've already suggested, for many reasons: to avoid hurting others' feelings, to conceal their real feelings or reactions, to avoid punishment for misdeeds. In short, lying is an all-too-common part of social life. This fact raises two important questions: (1) How good are we at recognizing deception by others? (2) How can we do a better job at this task? The answer to the first question is somewhat discouraging. In general, we do only a little better than chance in determining whether others are lying or telling the truth (e.g., Ekman, 2001; Malone & DePaulo, 2001). There are many reasons why this so, including the fact that we tend to perceive others as truthful and so don't search for clues to deception (Ekman, 2001); our desire to be polite, which makes us reluctant to discover or report deception by others; and our lack of attention to nonverbal cues that might reveal deception (e.g., Etcoff, Ekman, Magee, & Frank, 2000). Recently, another explanation—and a very compelling one—has been added to this list: we tend to assume that if people are truthful in one situation or context, they will be truthful in others, and this can prevent us from realizing that they might indeed lie on some occasions (e.g., O'Sullivan, 2003). We return to this possibility in more detail in our later discussion of attribution.

Given the fact that nearly everyone engages in deception at least occasionally, how can we recognize such actions? The answer seems to involve careful attention to both nonverbal and verbal cues that can reveal the fact that others are trying to deceive us. With respect to nonverbal cues, the following information has been found to be very helpful (e.g., DePaulo et al., 2003):

1. **Microexpressions:** These are fleeting facial expressions lasting only a few tenths of a second. Such reactions appear on the face very quickly after an emotion-provoking event and are difficult to suppress. As a result, they can be very revealing about others' true feelings or emotions.

2. **Interchannel discrepancies:** A second nonverbal cue revealing of deception is known as interchannel discrepancies. (The term *channel* refers to type of nonverbal cues; for instance, facial expressions are one channel, body movements are another.) These are inconsistencies between nonverbal cues from different basic channels. These result from the fact that people who are lying often find it difficult to control all these channels at once. For instance, they may manage their facial expressions well, but may have difficulty looking you in the eye as they tell their lie.

3. **Eye contact:** Efforts at deception are often revealed by certain aspects of eye contact. People who are lying often blink more often and show pupils that are more dilated than people who are telling the truth. They may also show an unusually low level of eye contact or—surprisingly—an unusually high one as they attempt to fake being honest by looking others right in the eye.

4. **Exaggerated facial expressions:** Finally, people who are lying sometimes show exaggerated facial expressions. They may smile more—or more broadly—than usual or may show greater sorrow than is typical in a given situation. A prime example: someone says no to a request you've made and then shows exaggerated regret. This is a good sign that the reasons the person has supplied for saying "no" may not be true.

In addition to these nonverbal cues, other signs of deception are sometimes present in nonverbal aspects of what people actually say, or in the words they choose. When people are lying, the pitch of their voices often rises—especially when they are highly motivated to lie. Similarly, they often take longer to begin—to respond to a question or describe events. And they may show a greater tendency to start sentences, stop them, and begin again. In other words, certain aspects of people's **linguistic style** can be revealing of deception.

In sum, through careful attention to nonverbal cues and to various aspects of the way people speak (e.g., the pitch of their voices), we can often tell when others are lying—or merely trying to hide their feelings from us. Success in detecting deception is far from certain; some people are very skillful liars. But if you pay careful attention to the cues described above, you will make their task of "pulling the wool over your eyes" much more difficult, and may become as successful at this task as a group of people identified by Paul Ekman—a leading expert on facial expressions—who can reliably distinguish lies from the truth more than 80 percent of the time (Coniff, 2004). (These people, by the way, did not belong to a particular profession—they were simply a heterogeneous group of individuals who were exceptionally good at detecting deception.) Is this a useful skill? Absolutely; imagine the benefits if we could hire—or train—such people to work at airports or other locations, identifying terrorists. Clearly, then, understanding how we can learn to recognize deception has important implications not just for individuals, but also for society as a whole.

microexpressions
Fleeting facial expressions lasting only a few tenths of a second.

linguistic style
Aspects of speech apart from the meaning of the words employed.

THE EFFECTS OF DECEPTION ON SOCIAL RELATIONS   Assuming that deception is an all-too-common aspect of social life, what are its effects? As you might guess, they are largely negative. First, recent findings (e.g., Tyler, Feldman, & Reichert, 2006), indicate that when people find themselves on the receiving end of lies, they react with mistrust of, and disliking toward, the liar. In fact, the more lies a stranger tells, the more these people are disliked and the less they are trusted. Furthermore, and perhaps of even greater interest, after being exposed to someone who has lied, most people are more willing to engage in such behavior themselves. Evidence for such effects is provided by research conducted by Tyler et al. (2006), which found that when people had information suggesting clearly that another person had lied to them, they were more likely to lie themselves, and not just to the person who has lied to them; they are also more willing to lie to others.

Together, these findings indicate that lying undermines the quality of social relations. Once it begins in a relationship or group, it is difficult to reverse, and the result may be a serious decline in mutual trust and faith. (Often, we use nonverbal cues to obtain information on others' emotions. This assumes that emotions are "inside" each person, but sometimes spill out onto their faces or their eye contact and body movements. Is that a valid model of emotion? Or do emotions sometimes reside in relations between people? For information on this issue, please see the "EMOTIONS AND SOCIAL PERCEPTION: Cultural Differences in Inferring Others' Emotions" section below.)

EMOTIONS *and* SOCIAL PERCEPTION

Cultural Differences in Inferring Others' Emotions

Where do your emotions come from? If you are a White American or a member of many other individualistic cultures, your answer is almost certainly "from inside me." In other words, you believe that events occur, and you experience emotions in response to them; your emotions, in other words, are uniquely yours. But if you are Japanese, or a member of many other collectivist cultures, you may have a different answer: "Emotions come from my relations with others." In other words, they don't occur in isolation, inside you, but rather involve other people, too. So, if you win a prize, as an American you might say, "I'm happy because of my accomplishment." If you are Japanese, you might say, "I'm happy because my parents and friends will be proud of me."

If that's true, then perhaps people belonging to different cultures infer others' emotions in somewhat different ways. Americans, for instance, would look at their facial expressions, body posture, and other nonverbal cues. Japanese, in contrast, might consider not only such cues, but also their relations with other people: Even if you are smiling, you can't really be happy unless other important people in your life are also experiencing positive reactions.

Evidence for precisely this kind of cultural difference has been reported in many studies (e.g., Mesquita & Leu, 2007), but an especially revealing set of findings have been reported by Uchida, Townsend, Markus, and Berksieker (2009).

In a series of related studies, they examined the emotional reactions of American and Japanese athletes who had participated in the Olympics. In one study, for instance, the number of emotion words used by the athletes during interviews by the media were recorded. Results indicated that Japanese athletes used more emotion words when questions asked were related to their relationships with others (e.g., "What kind of support has your family given you?"). In a follow-up experiment, American and Japanese students were shown photos of American and Japanese athletes who had won medals at the Olympics. The photos showed the athletes standing alone or with their teammates (see Figure 3.7). Participants were asked to describe how the athletes felt when receiving their medals. It was predicted that the Japanese students would use more emotion words when the athletes were shown with teammates, while Americans would use more emotion words when they

(continued)

EMOTIONS *and* **SOCIAL PERCEPTION** *(continued)*

FIGURE 3.7   Are Emotions Inside People or Between Them?
Whether emotions are seen as something inside individuals or reactions that involve relationships between people depends on cultural factors. In recent research, Japanese students perceived more emotions in athletes who won medals at the Olympics when they were shown with teammates than when they were shown alone. Americans showed the opposite pattern.

were shown alone. Results offered strong support for this prediction.

In short, although nonverbal cues are an important source of information about others' emotions in all cultures, the extent to which they are used to infer others' feelings varies across cultures. In individualistic cultures such as the United States, facial expressions, body movements, eye contact, and other nonverbal cues are a primary source of such information. In collectivist cultures, in contrast, relationships between people play a major role. So where do emotions reside, inside people or between them? The answer seems to depend, to an important extent, on the culture in which you live.

KEYPOINTS

- **Social perception** involves the processes through which we seek to understand other people. It plays a key role in social behavior and social thought.

- In order to understand others' emotional states, we often rely on **nonverbal communication**—an unspoken language of facial expressions, eye contact, and body movements and postures.

- While facial expressions for all basic emotions may not be as universal as once believed, they do often provide useful information about others' emotional states. Useful information on this issue is also provided by eye contact, body language, touching, and even scent.

- Growing evidence indicates that facial expressions are an especially important source of nonverbal information about others.

- Recent findings indicate that handshaking provides useful nonverbal cues about others' personality, and can influence first impressions of strangers.

- Scent also serves as a nonverbal cue, and subtle cues concerning women's menstrual cycle can be transmitted in this way.

- The *facial feedback hypothesis* suggests that we not only show what we feel in our facial expressions, but these expressions influence our emotional states.

- If we pay careful attention to certain nonverbal cues, we can recognize efforts at deception by others—even if these people are from a culture other than our own.

- Whether emotions are perceived as "inside" people or largely between them seems to depend on cultural factors.

Attribution: Understanding the Causes of Others' Behavior

You meet a very attractive person at a party. You'd like to see him or her again, so you ask, "Would you like to get together for a movie next week?" Your dreams of a wonderful romance are shattered when this person answers, "No, sorry . . . I can't do it next week." Now, you are left wondering why they refused your invitation. Because they don't like you as much as you like them? Because they are currently in a serious relationship and don't want to date anyone else? Because they are so busy with other commitments that they have no spare time? The conclusion you reach will be important to your self-esteem (you'd like to believe that this person wants to see you again, but is just too busy right now) and it will also strongly influence what you do next. If you conclude that, in fact, they don't like you or are involved in a serious relationship, the chances are lower that you'll try to arrange another meeting than if you decide that they are just too busy now.

This simple example illustrates an important fact about social perception: Often, we want to know more than simply how they are feeling right now. In addition, we want to know why they have said or done various things, and further, what kind of person they really are—what lasting traits, interests, motives, and goals they have. For instance, to mention just one of countless possibilities, we want to know if other people are high or low in self-control: to what extent can they regulate their own actions effectively (e.g., control their tempers, do what's required even if it is not what they prefer). If they are high in self-control we tend to view them as trustworthy, while if they are low on this aspect of self-regulation, we may conclude that they are unpredictable and not someone we can rely on (Righetti & Finkenauer, 2011). Social psychologists believe that our inter-est in such questions stems, in large part, from our basic desire to understand cause-and-effect relationships in the social world (Pittman, 1993; Van Overwalle, 1998). We don't simply want to know *how* others have acted—that's something we can readily observe. We also want to understand *why* they have done so, too, because this knowledge can help us to understand them better and also can help us to better predict their future actions. The process through which we seek such information and draw inferences is known as attri-bution. More formally, attribution refers to our efforts to understand the causes behind others' behavior and, on some occasions, the causes behind our behavior, too. Let's now take a closer look at what social psychologists have learned about this important aspect of social perception (e.g., Graham & Folkes, 1990; Heider, 1958; Read & Miller, 1998).

Theories of Attribution: Frameworks for Understanding How We Make Sense of the Social World

Because attribution is complex, many theories have been proposed to explain its opera-tion. Here, we focus on two classic views that continue to be especially influential.

FROM ACTS TO DISPOSITIONS: USING OTHERS' BEHAVIOR AS A GUIDE TO THEIR LASTING TRAITS   The first of these theories—Jones and Davis's (1965) theory of **correspondent inference**—asks how we use information about others' behavior as a basis for inferring their traits. In other words, the theory is concerned with how we decide, on the basis of others' overt actions, whether they possess specific traits or dispositions likely to remain fairly stable over time.

At first glance, this might seem to be a simple task. Others' behavior provides us with a rich source on which to draw, so if we observe it carefully, we should be able to learn a lot about them. Up to a point, this is true. The task is complicated, however, by the following fact: Often, individuals act in certain ways not because doing so reflects their own preferences or traits, but rather because external factors leave them little choice. For

correspondent inference
A theory describing how we use others' behavior as a basis for inferring their stable dispositions.

example, suppose you go to a restaurant and the young woman who greets you at the "Please Wait to Be Seated" sign smiles and acts in a friendly manner. Does this mean that she is a friendly person who simply "likes people"? It's possible, but perhaps she is acting in this way because that is what her job requires; she has no choice. Her boss has told her, "We are always friendly to our customers; I won't tolerate anything else." Situations like this are common, and in them, using others' behavior as a guide to their lasting traits or motives can be very misleading.

How do we cope with such complications? According to Jones and Davis's theory (Jones & Davis, 1965; Jones & McGillis, 1976), we accomplish this task by focusing our attention on certain types of actions—those most likely to prove informative.

First, we consider only behavior that seems to have been freely chosen, while largely ignoring ones that were somehow forced on the person in question. Second, we pay careful attention to actions that show what Jones and Davis term **noncommon effects**—effects that can be caused by one specific factor, but not by others. (Don't confuse this word with uncommon, which simply means infrequent.) Why are actions that produce noncommon effects informative? Because they allow us to zero in on the causes of others' behavior. For example, imagine that one of your friends has just gotten engaged. His future spouse is very attractive, has a great personality, is wildly in love with your friend, and is very rich. What can you learn about your friend from his decision to marry this woman? Not much. There are so many good reasons that you can't choose among them. In contrast, imagine that your friend's fiancé is very attractive, but that she treats him with indifference and is known to be extremely boring; also, she is deeply in debt and known to be someone who usually lives far beyond her means. Does the fact that your friend is marrying this woman tell you anything about him under these conditions? Definitely. You can probably conclude that he cares more about physical beauty than about personality or wealth. As you can see from this example, then, we can usually learn more about others from actions on their part that yield noncommon effects than from ones that do not.

Finally, Jones and Davis suggest that we also pay greater attention to actions by others that are low in *social desirability* than to actions that are high on this dimension. In other words, we learn more about others' traits from actions they perform that are somehow out of the ordinary than from actions that are very much like those of most other people.

In sum, according to the theory proposed by Jones and Davis, we are most likely to conclude that others' behavior reflects their stable traits (i.e., we are likely to reach correspondent inferences about them), when that behavior (1) is freely chosen; (2) yields distinctive, noncommon effects; and (3) is low in social desirability.

KELLEY'S THEORY OF CAUSAL ATTRIBUTIONS: HOW WE ANSWER THE QUESTION "WHY?" Consider the following events:

> *You arrange to meet someone at a restaurant, but she doesn't show up, so after waiting 20 minutes, you leave.*
>
> *You leave several text messages for a friend, but he doesn't return them.*
>
> *You expect a promotion in your job, but don't receive it.*

In all these situations, you would probably wonder why these events occurred: Why didn't your acquaintance show up at the restaurant—did she forget? Did this person do it on purpose? Why has your friend failed to return your messages—is he angry with you or is his cell phone not working? Why didn't you get the promotion—is your boss disappointed in your performance? Were you the victim of some kind of discrimination? In many situations, this is the central attributional task we face. We want to know why other people have acted as they have or why events have turned out in a specific way. Such knowledge is crucial, for only if we understand the causes behind others' actions or events that occur can we hope to make sense out of the social world (and potentially prevent those bad outcomes from coming our way again in the future). Obviously, the number of specific causes behind others' behavior is very large. To make the task more

noncommon effects
Effects produced by a particular cause that could not be produced by any other apparent cause.

manageable, therefore, we often begin with a preliminary question: Did others' behavior stem mainly from internal causes (their own traits, motives, intentions), mainly from external causes (some aspect of the social or physical world); or from a combination of the two? For example, you might wonder whether you didn't receive the promotion because you really haven't worked very hard (an internal cause), because your boss is unfair and biased against you (an external cause), or perhaps because of both factors. How do we attempt to answer this question? A theory proposed by Kelley (Kelley, 1972; Kelley & Michela, 1980) provides important insights into this process.

According to Kelley, in our attempts to answer the why question about others' behavior, we focus on three major types of information. First, we consider **consensus**—the extent to which other people react to a given stimulus or event in the same manner as the person we are considering. The higher the proportion of people who react in the same way, the higher the consensus. Second, we consider **consistency**—the extent to which the person in question reacts to the stimulus or event in the same way on other occasions, over time. And third, we examine **distinctiveness**—the extent to which this person reacts in the same manner to other, different stimuli or events.

According to Kelley's theory, we are most likely to attribute another's behavior to internal causes under conditions in which consensus and distinctiveness are low but consistency is high. In contrast, we are most likely to attribute another's behavior to external causes when consensus, consistency, and distinctiveness are all high. Finally, we usually attribute another's behavior to a combination of internal and external factors when consensus is low but consistency and distinctiveness are high. Perhaps a concrete example will help illustrate the very reasonable nature of these ideas.

Imagine that you see a server in a restaurant flirt with a customer. This behavior raises an interesting question: Why does the server act this way? Because of internal causes or external causes? Is he simply someone who likes to flirt (an internal cause)? Or is the customer extremely attractive—someone with whom many people flirt (an external cause)? According to Kelley's theory, your decision (as an observer of this scene) would depend on information relating to the three factors mentioned above. First, assume that the following conditions prevail: (1) You observe other servers flirting with this customer (consensus is high); (2) you have seen this server flirt with the same customer on other occasions (consistency is high); and (3) you have not seen this server flirt with other customers (distinctiveness is high). Under these conditions—high consensus, consistency, and distinctiveness—you would probably attribute the clerk's behavior to external causes—this customer is very attractive and that's why the server flirts with her.

Now, in contrast, assume these conditions exist: (1) No other servers flirt with the customer (consensus is low); (2) you have seen this server flirt with the same customer on other occasions (consistency is high); and (3) you have seen this server flirt with many other customers, too (distinctiveness is low). In this case, Kelley's theory suggests that you would attribute the server's behavior to internal causes: the server is simply a person who likes to flirt (see Figure 3.8).

The basic assumptions of Kelley's theory have been confirmed in a wide range of social situations, so it seems to provide important insights into the nature of causal attributions. However, research on the theory also suggests the need for certain modifications or extensions, as described below.

OTHER DIMENSIONS OF CAUSAL ATTRIBUTION   While we are often very interested in knowing whether others' behavior stemmed mainly from internal or external causes, this is not the entire story. In addition, we are also concerned with two other questions: (1) Are the causal factors that influenced their behavior likely to be stable over time or likely to change? (2) Are these factors controllable—can the individual change or influence them if he or she wishes to do so (Weiner, 1993, 1995)? These dimensions are independent of the internal–external dimension we have just considered. For instance, some internal causes of behavior tend to be quite stable over time, such as personality traits or temperament (e.g., Miles & Carey, 1997). In contrast, other internal causes can, and

consensus
The extent to which other people react to some stimulus or even in the same manner as the person we are considering.

consistency
The extent to which an individual responds to a given stimulus or situation in the same way on different occasions (i.e., across time).

distinctiveness
The extent to which an individual responds in the same manner to different stimuli or events.

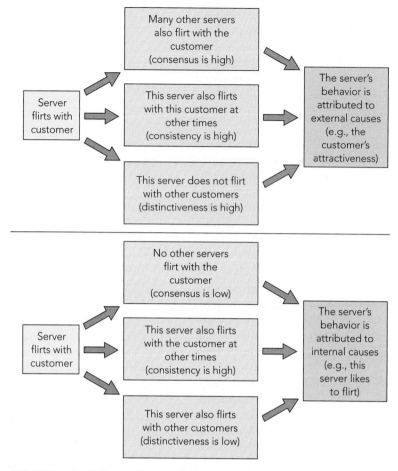

FIGURE 3.8   Kelley's Theory of Causal Attribution: An Example

Under the conditions shown in the top part of this figure, we would attribute the server's behavior to external causes—for example, the attractiveness of this customer. Under the conditions shown in the bottom part, however, we would attribute the server's behavior to internal causes—for instance, this person likes to flirt.

often do, change greatly—for instance, motives, health, and fatigue. Similarly, some internal causes are controllable—individuals can, if they wish, learn to hold their tempers in check; other internal causes, such as chronic illnesses or disabilities, are not. The same is true for external causes of behavior: some are stable over time (e.g., laws or social norms telling how we should behave in various situations) whereas others are not (e.g., bad luck). A large body of evidence indicates that in trying to understand the causes behind others' behavior, we do take note of all three of these dimensions—internal–external, stable–unstable, controllable–uncontrollable (Weiner, 1985, 1995).

ARE THE EVENTS IN OUR LIVES "MEANT TO BE," OR DO WE MAKE THEM HAPPEN?: FATE ATTRIBUTIONS VERSUS PERSONAL CHOICE   Suppose something unexpected but important happens in your life: you suddenly win the lottery or you are planning to take a vacation and then, just before leaving, break your leg and can't go. How do we account for such events? One interpretation is that they are due to our own actions: you broke your leg because you foolishly tried to reach something on a very high shelf while standing on a rickety chair. Another is attributing such events to *fate*—forces outside our understanding and control. To the extent this is so, then such events occur because they were "simply meant to be."

Both interpretations are possible, so what factors lead us to prefer one over the other? This intriguing question has been investigated in many studies (e.g., Burrus & Roese, 2006; Trope & Liberman, 2003), but some of the most interesting answers are provided by research conducted by Norenzayan and Lee (2010). These social psychologists suggested that belief in fate is related to two more basic beliefs: religious convictions concerning the existence of God, and a belief in *complex causality*—the idea that many causes influence such events, and that no one cause is essential. This, too, leads to the conclusion that unlikely events that occur are "meant to be," since so many factors combine to lead to their occurrence that the presence or absence of one makes little difference—the events are "overdetermined."

To test these predictions, Norenzayan and Lee (2010) asked participants who identified themselves as Christians or as nonreligious, and who were either of European heritage or East Asian heritage, to read brief stories describing unexpected and improbable events, and then indicated the extent to which these were due to fate or to chance. Here's an example: "*It was 8:00 a.m. in the morning and the street was busy as usual. Kelly, on her way to school, stopped and reached down for her shoelace. While bent over she found a little diamond ring lying right in front of her, which couldn't have been spotted otherwise.*" The researchers predicted that people with strong religious beliefs would be more likely to attribute unlikely events such as this to the fact that they were "meant to be," and that East Asians would be more likely to do this too, since they have strong cultural beliefs concerning complex causality. As you can see from Figure 3.9, this is precisely what was found. In further studies, Norenazyan and Lee found that belief in fate (that events were "meant to be") was mediated by belief in God for the Christians and by a belief in causal complexity for the East Asians.

ACTION IDENTIFICATION AND THE ATTRIBUTION PROCESS   When we see other people perform some action, and try to understand it—why they are doing it, what they want to accomplish—we have a wide range of interpretations open to us. For instance, suppose you saw someone putting loose change into a jar. You could conclude: "She wants to avoid losing the change so she puts it into the jar." Alternatively, you could conclude: "She is trying to save so that she can contribute to her own education." The first is a low-level interpretation that focuses on the action itself and involves little in the way of planning or long-range goals to the person involved; the second, in contrast, attributes such plans, intentions, and goals to this person. The action is the same (putting changes into a jar) but our interpretation of it—and of why it occurs—is very different. The level of interpretation we use is known as **action identification.**

Research findings indicate that this is a basic aspect of attribution. When we view others' actions as involving little more than the actions themselves, we also tend to make few attributions about their intentions, goals, or higher-order cognition. When, instead, we view others' actions as having greater meaning, we attribute much greater mental activity to them. We see their actions not simply as produced by the present situation, but as reflecting much more—the person's goals, characteristics, intentions—their *mind*, if you will. Research conducted by Kozak, Marsh, and Wegner (2006) provides strong support for this reasoning. Across several studies, they found that the more others' actions are interpreted at higher levels (as reflecting more than the action itself), the actors are also seen as possessing more complex motives, goals, and thought processes. So, where attribution is concerned, it is not simply what other people do that counts; our interpretations of these actions is crucial too, and can shape our perceptions of the people in question.

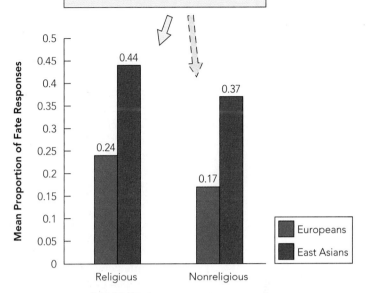

Religious persons attribute improbable events to fate more than nonreligious persons; this was true for both Europeans and East Asians

FIGURE 3.9   Are Improbable Events "Meant to Be"—Caused by Fate—or By Our Own Actions?
Research findings indicate that improbable but important events are often attributed to fate rather than to personal actions. Recently, it has been found that religious persons who have strong beliefs in God and persons from cultures with strong beliefs in causal complexity (i.e., many factors combine to produce unlikely events) are more likely to make such attributions than other persons. (Source: Based on data from Norenzayan & Lee, 2010).

Attribution: Some Basic Sources of Error

A basic theme we develop throughout this book is that although we generally do a good job of thinking about the social world, we are far from perfect in this respect. In fact, our efforts to understand other people—and ourselves—are subject to several types of errors that can lead us to false conclusions about why others have acted as they have and how they will act in the future. We now describe several of these errors.

THE CORRESPONDENCE BIAS: OVERESTIMATING THE ROLE OF DISPOSITIONAL CAUSES   Imagine that you witness the following scene. A man arrives at a meeting 1 hour late. Upon entering, he drops his notes on the floor. While trying to pick them up, his glasses fall off and break. Later, he spills coffee all over his tie. How would you explain these events? The chances are good that you would reach conclusions such as "This person is disorganized and clumsy." Are such attributions accurate? Perhaps, but it is also

action identification
The level of interpretation we place on an action; low-level interpretations focus on the action itself, while higher-level interpretations focus on its ultimate goals.

possible that the man was late because of unavoidable delays at the airport, he dropped his notes because they were printed on slick paper, and he spilled his coffee because the cup was too hot to hold. The fact that you would be less likely to consider such potential external causes of his behavior illustrates what Jones (1979) labeled **correspondence bias**—the tendency to explain others' actions as stemming from (corresponding to) dispositions even in the presence of clear situational causes (e.g., Gilbert & Malone, 1995). This bias seems to be so general in scope that many social psychologists refer to it as the **fundamental attribution error.** In short, we tend to perceive others as acting as they do because they are "that kind of person," rather than because of the many external factors that may influence their behavior. This tendency occurs in a wide range of contexts but appears to be strongest in situations where both consensus and distinctiveness are low, as predicted by Kelley's theory, and when we are trying to predict others' behavior in the far-off future rather than the immediate future (Nussbaum, Trope, & Liberman, 2003; Van Overwalle, 1997). Why? Because when we think of the far-off future we tend to do so in abstract terms and this leads us to think about others in terms of global traits; as a result, we tend to overlook potential external causes of their behavior. While this fundamental attribution error has been demonstrated in many studies, it was first reported by Jones and Harris (1967) and then, a few years later, by Nisbett, Caputo, Legbant, and Marecek (1973). This research had such a strong effect on subsequent efforts to understand attribution that we now describe it in some detail.

THE CORRESPONDENCE BIAS: STRONGER THAN YOU MIGHT GUESS! Suppose that you read a short essay written by another person—an essay dealing with an important topic. On the basis of this essay, you would get an idea of where the writer stands with respect to this issue—is she "pro" or "anti"? So far, so good. But now assume that before reading the essay, you learned that the author had been instructed to write it so as to support a particular position—again, "pro" or "anti." From a purely rational perspective, you should realize that in this case, the essay tells you nothing about the writer's true views; after all, she (or he) is merely following instructions. But two social psychologists—Jones and Harris (1967)—reasoned that in fact, the fundamental attribution error is so strong that even in the second case, we would assume that we can determine the writer's views from the essay—even though this person was told to write it in a particular way.

To test this reasoning, they asked research participants to read a short essay that either supported or opposed Fidel Castro's rule in Cuba (remember, the research was conducted in 1967). In one condition, participants were told that the essay-writer had free choice as to what position to take. In another, they were told that he or she was instructed to write the essay in a pro-Castro or anti-Castro manner. After reading the essay, participants were asked to estimate the essay-writer's true beliefs. Results were clear: even in the condition where the writer had been instructed to take one position or the other, research participants assumed that they could tell the writer's real views from the essay. In other words, they attributed the essay-writer's actions to internal factors (his or her true beliefs), even though they knew that this was not the case! Clearly, this was a dramatic demonstration of the fundamental attribution error in action.

Subsequent research that can also be viewed as "classic" in the field reached the same conclusions. For instance, in a revealing study by Nisbett et al. (1973), participants were shown a series of 20 paired traits (e.g., quiet–talkative, lenient–firm) and were asked to decide which of these traits were true of themselves, their best friend, their father, a casual acquaintance—or Walter Cronkite (a famous newscaster at the time). The participants were also offered a third choice: They could choose "depends on the situation." Results again offered strong evidence for the fundamental attribution error: the participants in the study chose "depends on the situation" much more often for

correspondence bias (fundamental attribution error)
The tendency to explain others' actions as stemming from dispositions even in the presence of clear situational causes.

fundamental attribution error (correspondence bias)
The tendency to overestimate the impact of dispositional cues on others' behavior.

themselves than for the other people. In other words, they reported that their own behavior varied from situation to situation, whereas that of other people (their best friend, father, or even a famous news anchor) reflected primarily personal traits (see Figure 3.10).

Together, early studies like these provided powerful evidence for the fact that our efforts to understand others' behavior—and our own actions—are not totally rational. On the contrary, they are influenced by a number of "tilts" or biases; and among these, the fundamental attribution error is one of the strongest.

THE CORRESPONDENCE BIAS AND GENDER: "SHE'S EMOTIONAL, BUT HE'S JUST HAVING A BAD DAY"

Be honest: do you believe, in your heart of hearts, that women are more emotional than men—that they are more likely to have strong emotions and to let these feelings influence their judgments and behavior? If so, you have a lot of company because even today, after truly major changes in beliefs about women and men, many people still hold the view that women are more emotional than men. In fact, research designed to find out if this idea is correct has generally yielded negative findings (e.g., Feldman Barrett, Robin, Pietromonaco, & Russell, 1998). But the belief persists anyway. Why? The correspondence bias offers one explanation: Perhaps when people behave emotionally, we are more likely to attribute this to stable characteristics for women than for men. In other words, when both a man and a woman demonstrate equal levels of emotionality, we attribute the woman's reactions to her personality but the man's reactions to external factors in the situation. In short, the correspondence bias operates more strongly with respect to attributions about women than men, at least in this context.

Clear evidence for this reasoning has been reported by Barrett and Bliss-Moreau (2009). They showed photos of males and females exhibiting specific emotions on their faces: anger, fear, sadness, disgust. Each photo was accompanied by a sentence explaining the emotion shown (see Figure 3.11 for photos similar to the ones used in the research). For instance, a sad face was accompanied by the following words: "Was disappointed by a lover." An angry face was linked to "Was cut off by another driver." In short, participants were given clear situational explanations for why the people shown were experiencing their emotions.

After viewing the faces and sentences, participants saw the same faces once again, but this time they were told to make a "snap decision" about whether each person shown was emotional or having a bad day; they did this by pressing two different keys on a keyboard. It was predicted that despite the situational explanations offered for the target person's emotional expressions, participants would be more likely to label the women as emotional and the men as simply having a bad day. That's precisely what happened, and these findings suggest that one reason for persistence of beliefs that women are more emotional than men involves the fact that the correspondence bias operates more strongly for women.

WHY DOES THE FUNDAMENTAL ATTRIBUTION ERROR OCCUR?

Social psychologists have conducted many studies in order to find out why this bias occurs (e.g., Robins, Spranca, & Mendelsohn, 1996), but the issue is still somewhat in doubt. One possibility is

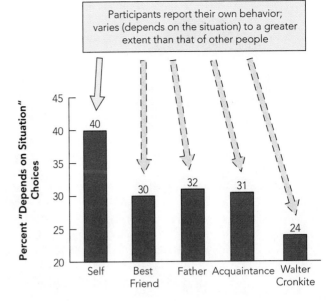

FIGURE 3.10 The Fundamental Attribution Error in Action: Classic Evidence

Participants in the study shown here were asked to indicate which of the traits in 20 pairs of traits were true of themselves and several other people (their best friend, fathers, etc.). They also had the option of choosing another response: "Depends on the situation." They were much more likely to do this with respect to their own behavior than that of other persons. In other words, they recognized that their own actions were strongly influenced by external causes, but assumed that the actions of other persons stem primarily from internal causes, such as their own traits. (Source: Based on data from Nisbett et al., 1973).

FIGURE 3.11 **The Correspondence Bias and Gender**
When shown photos of persons experiencing strong emotions, along with explanations for why they were having these emotions, research participants still attributed women's emotional reactions to dispositional characteristics (they are "emotional"), but men's reactions to situational (external) causes (they are just having a "bad day").

that when we observe another person's behavior, we tend to focus on his or her actions and the context in which the person behaves; hence potential situational causes of his or her behavior often fade into the background. As a result, dispositional causes (internal causes) are easier to notice (they are more salient) than situational ones. In other words, from our perspective, the person we are observing is high in perceptual salience and is the focus of our attention, whereas situational factors that might also have influenced this person's behavior are less salient and so seem less important to us. Another explanation is that we notice such situational causes but give them insufficient weight in our attributions. Still another explanation is when we focus on others' behavior, we tend to begin by assuming that their actions reflect their underlying characteristics. Then, we attempt to correct for any possible effects of the external world—the current situation—by taking these into account. (This involves the mental shortcut known as *anchoring and adjustment*, which we discussed in Chapter 2.) This correction, however, is often insufficient—we don't make enough allowance for the impact of external factors. We don't give enough weight to the possibility of delays at the airport or a slippery floor when reaching our conclusions (Gilbert & Malone, 1995).

Evidence for this two-step process—a quick, automatic reaction followed by a slower, more controlled corrections—has been obtained in many studies (e.g., Chaiken & Trope, 1999; Gilbert, 2002), so it seems to offer a compelling explanation for the correspondence bias (i.e., fundamental attribution error). In fact, it appears that most people are aware of this process, or at least aware of the fact they start by assuming that other people behave as they do because of internal causes (e.g., their personality, their true beliefs), but then correct this assumption, at least to a degree, by taking account of situational constraints.   Perhaps even more interesting, we tend to assume that we adjust our attributions to take account of situational constraints more than other people do. In other words, we perceive that we are less likely to fall victim to the correspondence bias than others.

THE ACTOR–OBSERVER EFFECT: "YOU FELL; I WAS PUSHED" The fundamental attribution error, powerful as it is, applies mainly to attributions we make about others—we don't tend to "overattribute" our own actions to external causes. This fact helps explain another and closely related type of attributional bias known as the **actor–observer effect** (Jones & Nisbett, 1971), the tendency to attribute our own behavior to situational (external) causes but that of others to dispositional (internal) ones. Thus, when we see another person trip and fall, we tend to attribute this event to his or her clumsiness. If we trip, however, we are more likely to attribute this event to situational causes, such as ice on the sidewalk.

Why does the actor–observer effect occur? In part because we are quite aware of the many external factors affecting our own actions but are less aware of such factors when we turn our attention to the actions of other people. Thus, we tend to perceive our own

actor-observer effect
The tendency to attribute our own behavior mainly to situational causes but the behavior of others mainly to internal (dispositional) causes.

behavior as arising largely from situational causes, but that of others as deriving mainly from their traits or dispositions.

THE SELF-SERVING BIAS: "I'M GOOD; YOU ARE LUCKY" Suppose that you write a paper and when you get it back, you find the following comment on the first page: "An outstanding paper—one of the best I've seen in years. A+." To what will you attribute this success? Probably, you will explain it in terms of internal causes—your high level of talent, the effort you invested in writing the paper, and so on.

Now, in contrast, imagine that when you get the paper back, these comments are written on it. "Unsatisfactory paper—one of the worst I've seen in years. D−." How will you interpret this outcome? The chances are good that you will be tempted to focus mainly on external (situational factors)—the difficulty of the task, your professor's unfairly harsh grading standards, the fact that you didn't have enough time to do a good job, and so on.

This tendency to attribute our own positive outcomes to internal causes but negative ones to external factors is known as the **self-serving bias,** and it appears to be both general in scope and powerful in its effects (Brown & Rogers, 1991; Miller & Ross, 1975).

Why does this tilt in our attributions occur? Several possibilities have been suggested, but most of these fall into two categories: cognitive and motivational explanations. The cognitive model suggests that the self-serving bias stems mainly from certain tendencies in the way we process social information (Ross, 1977; see also Chapter 2). Specifically, it suggests that we attribute positive outcomes to internal causes, but negative ones to external causes because we expect to succeed and have a tendency to attribute expected outcomes to internal causes more than to external causes. In contrast, the motivational explanation suggests that the self-serving bias stems from our need to protect and enhance our self-esteem or the related desire to look good to others (Greenberg, Pyszczynski, & Solomon, 1986). While both cognitive and motivational factors may well play a role in this kind of attributional error, research evidence seems to offer more support for the motivational view (e.g., Brown & Rogers, 1991).

Regardless of the origins of the self-serving bias, it can be the cause of much interpersonal friction. It often leads people working with others on a joint task to perceive that they, not their partners, have made the major contributions, and to blame others in the group for negative outcomes.

Interestingly, the results of several studies indicate that the strength of the self-serving bias varies across cultures (e.g., Oettingen, 1995; Oettingen & Seligman, 1990). In particular, it is weaker in cultures, such as those in Asia, that place a greater emphasis on group outcomes and group harmony, than it is in Western cultures, where individual accomplishments are emphasized and it is considered appropriate for winners to gloat (at least a little!) over their victories. For example, Lee and Seligman (1997) found that Americans of European descent showed a larger self-serving bias than either Chinese Americans or mainland Chinese. Once again, therefore, we see that cultural factors often play an important role even in very basic aspects of social behavior and social thought.

THE SELF-SERVING BIAS AND EXPLANATIONS FOR UNEXPECTED, NEGATIVE EVENTS Everyone experiences unexpected negative events: your computer "eats" important files that can no longer be found; your school's team loses even though it was strongly favored to win. How do we explain such events? Often, it appears, we attribute them to external agencies: our computer was "out to get us," our school's team was robbed by biased referees, and so on. But when positive events occur—we find the missing files, our team wins—we tend to attribute these events to internal causes—our competence in handling our computer, our team's skills and talents. In other words, we tend to attribute negative events to external causes, but positive ones to internal causes just as the self-serving bias suggests. In a sense, though, this is an extension of the self-serving bias because it focuses on agents—intentional agents that initiate and cause the negative events (our computer, evil referees). That we do tend to show this negativity

self-serving bias
The tendency to attribute positive outcomes to internal causes (e.g., one's own traits or characteristics) but negative outcomes or events to external causes (e.g., chance, task difficulty).

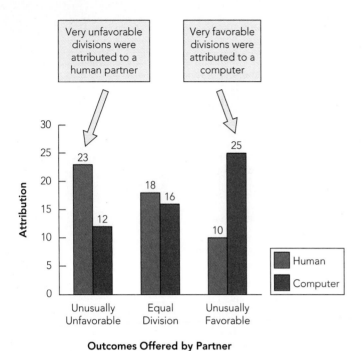

FIGURE 3.12 Attributing Negative Events to External Agents

As shown here, when individuals were offered a very unfavorable division in an ultimatum game, they tended to attribute this outcome to a human agent—a real partner. When they were offered a very favorable outcome, though, they tended to attribute it to a computer. These findings suggest that we tend to attribute negative outcomes or events to external agents who cause them to happen. (Source: Based on data from Morewedge, 2009).

bias in explaining unfavorable outcomes is illustrated by research conducted by Morewedge (2009).

Participants in the study conducted by Morewedge (2009) played an "ultimatum game" in which a partner was given $3.00 and could divide it in any way the partner wished. Participants could then decide to accept or decline these divisions. In one condition, the partner offered very favorable divisions: $2.25 to the participant, only $0.75 to the partner. In another the partner offered an equal division—$1.50 to each player. And in a very unfavorable condition, the partner's division was $0.75 to the participant, and $2.25 to the partner. After playing the game several times, participants were asked whether they thought that the partner was a real person or a computer. It was predicted that they would be more likely to believe that the partner was human in the very unfavorable condition, and most likely to be a computer in the very favorable condition. Why? Because the tendency to attribute negative events to external agents would lead participants to perceive the unfair division as the work of another person, not a mere machine. As you can see from Figure 3.12, that is precisely what happened. So, clearly, the tendency to attribute negative events to external causes is a strong and general one that strongly influences our understanding of the social world.

Before concluding this discussion of the many ways in which our attributions depart from the original "perfectly logical person" described by Kelley (1972), we should note that despite all the errors described here, social perception is still often quite accurate—we do, in many cases, reach useful and valid conclusions about others' traits and motives from observing their behavior. We examine some of the evidence pointing to this conclusion as part of our later discussion of the process of impression formation.

Applications of Attribution Theory: Insights and Interventions

Kurt Lewin, one of the founders of modern social psychology, often remarked, "There's nothing as practical as a good theory." By this he meant that once we obtain scientific understanding of some aspect of social behavior or social thought, we can, potentially, put this knowledge to practical use. Where attribution theory is concerned, this has definitely been the case. As basic knowledge about attribution has grown, so too has the range of practical problems to which such information has been applied (Graham & Folkes, 1990; Miller & Rempel, 2004). As an example of such research, we examine how attribution theory has been applied to understanding one key aspect of mental health: depression.

ATTRIBUTION AND DEPRESSION Depression is the most common psychological disorder. In fact, it has been estimated that almost half of all human beings experience such problems at some time during their lives (e.g., Blazer, Kessler, McGonagle, & Swartz, 1994). Although many factors play a role in depression, one that has received increasing attention is what might be termed a *self-defeating* pattern of attributions. In contrast to most people, who show the self-serving bias described above, depressed individuals tend to adopt an opposite pattern. They attribute negative outcomes to lasting, internal causes such as their own traits or lack of ability, but attribute positive outcomes to temporary, external causes such as good luck or special favors from others. As a result, such people perceive that they have little or no control over what happens to them—they are simply being blown about by the winds of unpredictable fate. Little wonder that they become depressed and tend to give up on life! And once they are depressed, the tendency to engage in this self-defeating pattern is strengthened, and a vicious cycle is often initiated.

Fortunately, several forms of therapy that focus on changing such attributions have been developed, and appear to be quite successful (e.g., Bruder et al., 1997; Robinson, Berman, & Neimeyer, 1990). These new forms of therapy focus on getting depressed people to change their attributions—to take personal credit for successful outcomes, to stop blaming themselves for negative outcomes (especially ones that can't be avoided), and to view at least some failures as the result of external factors beyond their control. Since attribution theory provides the basis for these new forms of treatment, it has certainly proven very useful in this respect. (Does attribution also play a role in our reactions to other people when we interact with them on the Internet rather than in face-to-face situations? For information on this important topic, please see the "SOCIAL LIFE IN A CONNECTED WORLD: Understanding Other People Through the Internet—Attribution and Computer-Mediated Communication" section below.)

SOCIAL LIFE *in a* CONNECTED WORLD

Understanding Other People Through the Internet—Attribution and Computer-Mediated Communication

Do you use e-mail? Most people do, and in today's business world, it has become a truly essential tool (see Figure 3.13). One real advantage it offers is that it provides instantaneous communication between people, even if they live on opposite sides of the world. Another is that it is essentially free, so people can communicate as often with as many different people as they wish, with no, or minimal, economic costs. These points suggest that e-mail is an unmixed blessing, but is that true? Although it is fast, free, and readily available, it does reduce communication between people to words appearing on a computer screen. Gone are other sources of information provided by others' appearance, facial expressions, tone of voice, and other verbal and nonverbal cues. In a

FIGURE 3.13   E-Mail and the Correspondence Bias
E-mail is now an essential part of life and work, and it certainly offers incredible speed and convenience. But it also eliminates much information that we receive when we interact with people face-to-face. Research findings indicate that this permits the correspondence bias to operate very strongly.

(continued)

sense, e-mail substitutes speed and ease for the rich array of information offered by face-to-face contact with others (e.g., Junemann & Lloyd, 2003). That can certainly be an advantage because sometimes, personal cues (e.g., whether others are attractive or unattractive, young or old, fit or overweight, and so on) are distracting and can get in the way of clear and effective communication. But elimination of these cues may also make the task of forming accurate perceptions of others more difficult.

Suppose, for instance, that you receive an e-mail message and it is short to the point of being abrupt or even rude. Why did the sender transmit such a message? Because they are an unpleasant person, in a big hurry, or—perhaps—because they are from another culture and don't know the proper forms of politeness in your culture? Similarly, suppose their message has lots of spelling and grammatical errors. Is this because they are a careless or lazy person, or could it be because they are from another culture and don't know English very well? Clearly, the attributions we form in such situations can strongly affect our impressions of the senders of e-mail messages, and this, in turn, can influence our future interactions with them.

Growing evidence suggests that, in fact, e-mail does leave lots of room for interpretation and errors concerning other people. And please remember the powerful influence of the correspondence bias: We tend to interpret others' actions as stemming from their personalities or stable traits rather than situational factors unless we have strong evidence to the contrary. To see if this kind of bias operates in e-mail, Vignovic and Thompson (2010) conducted a study in which several hundred employees of an organization received e-mail messages from a stranger. The messages either indicated that the sender was from another culture or did not provide such information, and were of three types: they had no spelling or grammatical errors and were polite, contained spelling or grammatical errors but were polite, or contained no spelling and grammatical errors but were not

polite (i.e., too terse and lacking in conversational tone). After receiving the messages, participants rated the senders on a number of dimensions—their personality (conscientiousness, extraversion, agreeableness), intelligence, cognitive trustworthiness, and affective trustworthiness. In addition, cross-cutting these variables, participants learned that the sender was from their own culture or another culture.

The authors hypothesized that knowing an e-mail sender was from a different culture would reduce negative reactions to both spelling and grammatical errors and a lack of politeness in the message. That is, when they learned that the sender was from another culture, they would make more favorable attributions about this person, assuming that these errors stemmed from the sender's lack of knowledge of English or what's polite in American culture. Results offered support for the first of these predictions: When participants learned that the sender was from another culture, they did not down-rate this person in terms of conscientiousness, intelligence, and other characteristics. However, learning that the sender was from a different culture did *not* reduce the negative effects of a lack of politeness. The authors suggest that this may be due to the fact politeness is a more ambiguous aspect of behavior than spelling or grammar and that consequently, it requires more cognitive effort to adjust initial negative reactions to take account of additional information (i.e., that the sender is from a different culture). Whatever the reason, the practical implications are clear: The correspondence bias operates in attributions about others based on e-mail just as it does in attributions based on face-to-face contacts with them, and although its impact can be reduced, it can continue to strongly influence perceptions of others even if we know about possible external causes of their actions.

In short, e-mail is a wonderful tool, but like every other tool, it has a potential downside too, especially if used without full consideration of cultural differences with respect to what constitutes politeness.

KEYPOINTS

- In order to obtain information about others' lasting traits, motives, and intentions, we often engage in **attribution**—efforts to understand why they have acted as they have. According to Jones and Davis's theory of **correspondent inference,** we attempt to infer others' traits from observing certain aspects of their behavior—especially behavior that is freely chosen, produces noncommon effects, and is low in social desirability.

- According to another theory, Kelley's theory of causal attribution, we are interested in the question of whether others' behavior stemmed from internal or external causes. To answer this question, we focus on information relating to **consensus, consistency,** and **distinctiveness**.

- Two other important dimensions of causal attribution relate to whether specific causes of behavior are stable over time and controllable or not controllable.

- Another issue relating to attribution concerns the extent to which we attribute events in our lives to fate—what was "meant to be"—or to personal causes. Individuals who believe strongly in the existence of God are more likely to attribute improbable but important events to "what was meant to be"; this is also true of people whose cultural heritage accepts complex causality for important events.

- Attribution is subject to many potential sources of bias. One of the most important of these is the **correspondence bias**—the tendency to explain others' actions as stemming from dispositions even in the presence of situational causes.

- Despite major changes in gender roles in recent decades, many people continue to attribute emotional displays by women to dispositional factors ("they are emotional") whereas attributing the same levels of emotion among men to external causes.

- Two other attributional errors are the **actor–observer effect**—the tendency to attribute our own behavior to external (situational causes) but that of others to internal causes—and the **self-serving bias**—the tendency to attribute positive outcomes to internal causes but negative ones to external causes. The self-serving bias is especially strong for negative events, which are often attributed to external agents who cause them.

- Attribution has been applied to many practical problems, often with great success. For instance, it has been applied to understanding the causes of depression, and to treating this important mental disorder.

- Attribution also appears to operate in electronic communication over the Internet (e.g., through e-mail).

Impression Formation and Impression Management: Combining Information About Others

When we meet another person for the first time, we are—quite literally—flooded with information. We can see, at a glance, how they look and dress, how they speak, and how they behave. Although the amount of information reaching us is large, we somehow manage to combine it into an initial *first impression* of this person—a mental representation that is the basis for our reactions to him or her. Clearly, then, impression formation is an important aspect of social perception. This fact raises several important questions: What, exactly, are first impressions? How are they formed—and how quickly? Are they accurate? We now examine what social psychologists have discovered about these and related issues. To do so, we first begin with some famous and classic research in the field, and then move on to more recent research and its findings.

The Beginnings of Research on First Impressions: Asch's Research on Central and Peripheral Traits

As we have already seen, some aspects of social perception, such as attribution, require lots of hard mental work: It's not always easy to draw inferences about others' motives or traits from their behavior. In contrast, forming first impressions seems to be relatively effortless. As Solomon Asch, one of the founders of experimental social psychology, put it, "We look at a person and immediately a certain impression of his character forms itself in us. A glance, a few spoken words are sufficient to tell us a story about a highly complex matter . . ." (1946, p. 258). How do we manage to do this? How, in short, do we form unified impressions of others in the quick and seemingly effortless way that we often do? This is the question Asch set out to study.

At the time Asch conducted his research, social psychologists were heavily influenced by the work of *Gestalt psychologists*, specialists in the field of perception. A basic principle of Gestalt psychology was this: "The whole is often greater than the sum of its parts." This means that what we perceive is often more than the sum of individual sensations. To illustrate this point for yourself, simply look at any painting (except a very modern one!). What you see is not individual splotches of paint on the canvas; rather, you perceive an integrated whole—a portrait, a landscape, a bowl of fruit—whatever the artist intended. So as Gestalt psychologists suggested, each part of the world around us is interpreted, and understood, in terms of its relationships to other parts or stimuli—in effect, as a totality.

Asch applied these ideas to understanding impression formation, suggesting that we do not form impressions simply by adding together all of the traits we observe in other people. Rather, we perceive these traits in relation to one another, so that the traits cease to exist individually and become, instead, part of an integrated, dynamic whole. How could these ideas be tested? Asch came up with an ingenious answer. He gave individuals lists of traits supposedly possessed by a stranger, and then asked them to indicate their impressions of this person by putting check marks next to traits (on a much longer list) that they felt fit their overall impression of the stranger.

For example, in one study, participants read one of the following two lists:

intelligent—skillful—industrious—warm—determined—practical—cautious
intelligent—skillful—industrious—cold—determined—practical—cautious

As you can see, the lists differ only with respect to two words: *warm* and *cold*. Thus, if people form impressions merely by adding together individual traits, the impressions formed by people exposed to these two lists shouldn't differ very much. However, this was not the case. People who read the list containing *warm* were much more likely to view the stranger as generous, happy, good-natured, sociable, popular, and altruistic than were people who read the list containing *cold*. The words *warm* and *cold*, Asch concluded, were *central traits*—ones that strongly shaped overall impressions of the stranger and colored the other adjectives in the lists. Asch obtained additional support for this view by substituting the words *polite* and *blunt* for *warm* and *cold*. When he did this, the two lists yielded highly similar impressions of the stranger. So, *polite* and *blunt* it appeared were not central traits that colored the entire impressions of the stranger.

On the basis of many studies such as this one, Asch concluded that forming impressions of others involves more than simply combining individual traits. As he put it: "There is an attempt to form an impression of the *entire* person . . . . As soon as two or more traits are understood to belong to one person they cease to exist as isolated traits, and come into immediate . . . interaction . . . . The subject perceives not this *and* that quality, but the two entering into a particular relation . . ." (1946, p. 284). While research on impression formation has become far more sophisticated since Asch's early work, many of his basic ideas about impression formation have withstood the test of time. Thus, his research exerted a lasting impact and is still worthy of careful attention even today.

How Quickly Are First Impressions Formed— and Are They Accurate?

Until quite recently, one general conclusion from social psychological research on first impressions was this: They are formed quickly but are often inaccurate. In the past few years, however, a growing body of research evidence suggests that these conclusions should be modified: Many studies have reported that even working with what are known as **thin slices** of information about others—for instance, photos or short videos of them—perceivers' first impressions are reasonably accurate (e.g., Borkenau, Mauer, Riemann, Spinath, & Angleitner, 2004). People do better in forming first impressions of some characteristics than others (e.g., Gray, 2008), but overall, they can accomplish this task fairly well—very quickly and with better-than-chance accuracy. How quickly? In one study on this topic (Willis & Todorov, 2006), participants viewed faces of strangers for very brief periods of time: one-tenth of a second, half a second, or a second. Then, they rated these people on several traits—trustworthiness, competence, likeability, aggressiveness, attractiveness—and indicated their confidence in these ratings. These ratings were compared with ratings provided by another group of people who examined photos of the same actors without any time constraints—they could examine them as long as they wished. If we really do form first impressions very quickly, then the ratings of the two groups should be very similar (i.e., they should be highly correlated). This is exactly what occurred; in fact, correlations between the two sets of ratings (the ones done without any time limits and the ones completed at short exposure times) ranged from about .60 to about .75, indicating that we do indeed form impressions of others very quickly. So, first impressions can be formed very quickly and are at least slightly better than chance in terms of accuracy.

But what factors, specifically, determine the accuracy of first impressions? No clear answers to this question yet exist, but several recent studies provide some clues about what these factors may be (Gray, 2008). One possibility is that their level of confidence in their judgments plays a role. The greater their confidence, the more accurate the impressions. Research by Arnes, Kammrath, Suppes, and Bolger (2010) was designed to test this possibility. To do so, they asked university students to observe short videotapes showing other students (MBA students) in a simulated job interview. After viewing the videos, they rated these people on several aspects of personality (extraversion, agreeableness, conscientiousness, emotional stability), and also rated their confidence in these judgments. The MBA students completed a standard personality scale, which provided information on each of the dimensions of personality rated by participants, so accuracy could be readily assessed. Results indicated that the perceivers did slightly better than chance—their first impressions of the MBA students were somewhat in line with the actual personality scores of these individuals. However, their degree of confidence in these judgments was not related to this accuracy, so in general, they could not tell how accurate their first impressions were.

In further studies, Ames and colleagues (2010) found that the relationship between perceivers' confidence in their own first impressions and the accuracy of these impressions was curvilinear: when confidence was very low, their first impressions were in fact inaccurate. As confidence rose, however, accuracy, too, increased, but only up to a point. Then it leveled off or even declined (see Figure 3.14). In addition, perceivers who used a gut-level "intuitive" approach to forming first impressions did better than ones who used a more analytical approach.

Overall, these findings indicate that people can indeed form first impressions of others on the basis of small amounts of information and that these impressions show better than chance-level accuracy. Further, when individuals believe that their impressions of others are accurate, they often are—at least, to a greater extent than is the case when they believe that these impressions are not accurate (Biesanz, Human, Paquin, Chan, Parisotto, Sarrachino, & Gillis, 2011). In other words, people are reasonably good at recognizing when their impressions of others are, and when they are not, valid. We should add that in general, most people are quite

thin slices
Refers to small amounts of information about others we use to form first impressions of them.

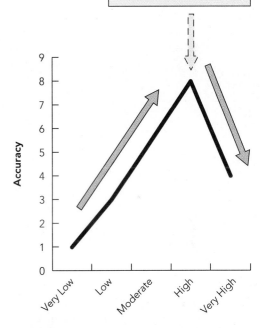

FIGURE 3.14   First Impressions: Is Confidence in Them Related to Their Accuracy?
Research findings indicate that although first impressions formed on the basis of a "thin slice" of information can be somewhat accurate, such accuracy is not closely related to confidence in the impressions. In fact, the relationship between rated confidence and actual accuracy appears to be curvilinear in nature. At very low levels of confidence, accuracy is also low, but as confidence rises, so, too, does accuracy— but only up to a point, beyond which even if confidence continues to increase, accuracy declines. So we should not trust our confidence in our first impressions as a good guide to their accuracy. (Source: Based on suggestions by Ames, Kammrath, Suppes & Bolger, 2010).

confident about the validity of their first impressions, a and although such confidence and actual accuracy are related, the link is not as strong as we might wish—or as most people believe it is. So, should we trust our first impressions of others? The best answer seems to be "To some extent—but always remembering that they are far from completely accurate, and we can't judge their accuracy very well." The bottom line then appears to be to approach first impressions with caution.

Implicit Personality Theories: Schemas That Shape First Impressions

Suppose one of your friends described someone they had just met as helpful and kind. Would you now assume that this person is also sincere? Probably. And what if your friend described this stranger as practical and intelligent; would you now assume that he or she is also ambitious? Again, the chances are good that you might. But why, in the absence of information on these specific traits, would you assume that this person possesses them? In part because we all possess what social psychologists describe as **implicit personality theories**—beliefs about what traits or characteristics tend to go together (e.g., Sedikes & Anderson, 1994). These theories, which can be viewed as a specific kind of schema, suggest that when individuals possess some traits, they are likely to possess others, too. Such expectations are strongly shaped by the cultures in which we live. For instance, in many societies—but not all—it is assumed that "what is beautiful is good"—that people who are attractive also possess other positive traits, such as good social skills and an interest in enjoying the good things in life (e.g., Wheeler & Kim, 1997). Similarly, in some cultures—but again, not in all—there is a schema for "the jock"—a young male who loves sports, prefers beer to wine, and can, on occasion (e.g., during an important game), be loud and coarse. Again, once an individual is seen as having one of these traits, he or she is seen as possessing others because typically, we expect them to covary (to go together).

These tendencies to assume that certain traits or characteristics go together are very common and can be observed in many contexts. For instance, you may well have implicit beliefs about the characteristics related to birth order. A large body of research findings indicates that we expect first-borns to be high achievers who are aggressive, ambitious, dominant, and independent, while we expect middle-borns to be caring, friendly, outgoing, and thoughtful. Only children, in contrast, are expected to be independent, self-centered, selfish, and spoiled (e.g., Nyman, 1995).

The strength and generality of these implicit beliefs about the effects of birth order are illustrated very clearly in research conducted recently by Herrera, Zajonc, Wieczorkowska, and Cichomski (2003). These researchers asked participants to rate firstborns, only children, middle-borns, last-borns, and themselves on various trait dimensions: agreeable–disagreeable, bold–timid, creative–uncreative, emotional–unemotional, extraverted–introverted, responsible–irresponsible, and several others. Results indicated clear differences in expectations about the traits supposedly shown by each group. Firstborns were seen as being more intelligent, responsible, obedient, stable, and unemotional; only children were seen as being the most disagreeable; middle-borns were expected to be envious and the least bold; and last-borns were seen as the most creative, emotional, disobedient, and irresponsible. So clearly, implicit beliefs about links between birth order and important traits exist.

Perhaps more surprising, additional findings indicated that birth order was actually related to important life outcomes: In a large sample of people living in Poland, the earlier individuals' position in their families' birth order, the higher their occupational status and the more education they completed. This illustrates an important point we made in Chapter 2: beliefs and expectations are often self-fulfilling, at least to a degree. More generally, the findings reported by Herrera et al. (2003) and many other researchers indicate that our beliefs about birth order can be viewed as one important kind of implicit

implicit personality theories
Beliefs about what traits or characteristics tend to go together.

personality theory: We do strongly believe that an individual's place in his or her family's birth order is related to many different traits.

In sum, our impressions of others are often strongly shaped by our beliefs about what traits or characteristics go together. Indeed, these beliefs are often so strong that we will sometimes bend our perceptions of other people to be consistent with them. The result? We can form impressions of others that reflect our implicit beliefs more than their actual traits (e.g., Gawronski, 2003).

Impression Management: Tactics for "Looking Good" to Others

The desire to make a favorable impression on others is a strong one, so most of us do our best to "look good" to others when we meet them for the first time. Social psychologists use the term impression management (or *self-presentation*) to describe these efforts to make a good impression on others, and the results of their research on this process suggest that it is well worth the effort: People who perform impression management successfully do often gain important advantages in many situations (e.g., Sharp & Getz, 1996; Wayne & Liden, 1995). What tactics do people use to create favorable impressions on others? Which work best? And is impression management related to subsequent behavior in social or work situations? Let's see what careful research has revealed about these intriguing issues.

TACTICS OF IMPRESSION MANAGEMENT While individuals use many different techniques for boosting their image, most of these fall into two major categories: *self-enhancement*—efforts to increase their appeal to others—and *other-enhancement*—efforts to make the target person feel good in various ways.

With respect to self-enhancement, specific strategies include efforts to boost one's appearance—either physical or professional. Physical appearance relates to the attractiveness and physical appeal of the individual, while professional appearance relates to personal grooming, appropriate dress, and personal hygiene (Hosada et al., 2003). The existence of huge beauty aids and clothing industries suggests ways in which people attempt to improve both aspects of their appearance (see Figure 3.15).

Additional tactics of self-enhancement involving efforts to appear competent and accomplished through such steps as describing past achievements, describing positive qualities one possesses ("I'm very easygoing," "I'm organized and get things done on time"), taking responsibility for positive events in one's life that occurred in the past ("I graduated early because I really worked hard . . ."), or explaining how they (the person engaging in impression management) overcame daunting obstacles (Stevens & Kristoff, 1995). Several of these tactics are readily visible in online dating services (e.g., Match.com) and in information people post about themselves on Facebook or other social networks, where people attempt to "look good" to others (potential romantic partners, old friends and new ones).

Another major group of impression management tactics are known as *other-enhancement*. In these strategies, individuals basically seek to induce positive moods and reactions in others through the use of a variety of tactics (Byrne, 1992). Perhaps the most commonly used tactic of this type is *ingratiation*—flattering others in various ways (Kilduff & Day, 1994). Additional tactics of other-enhancement involve expressing agreement with the target person's views, showing a high degree of interest in this person, doing small favors for them, asking for their advice and feedback in some manner (Morrison & Bies, 1991), or expressing liking for them nonverbally (e.g., through high levels of eye contact, nodding in agreement, and smiling; Wayne & Ferris, 1990).

FIGURE 3.15 Efforts to Boost Our Own Apperance Are Truly Big Business!
One common tactic of impression management involves efforts to boost our personal or professional appearance. Such efforts support huge cosmetics, clothing, and retail industries.

Does Impression Management Work? Does It Really Boost Impressions of the People Using It?

That individuals often employ such tactics is obvious: You can probably recall many instances in which you either used, or were the target of, such strategies. A key question, however, is this: *Do they work?* Do these tactics of impression management succeed in generating positive feelings and reactions on the part of the people toward whom they are directed? The answer provided by a growing body of literature is clear: *yes*, provided they are used with skill and care. For example, in one recent meta-analysis, Barrick, Shaffer, and DeGrassi (2009) examined the results of dozens of studies concerned with the tactics and success of impression management. These studies were primarily concerned with the use of impression management tactics in job interviews, and results indicated that in this respect, impression management is often very successful. The greater the extent to which job applicants used various tactics of impression management, the higher the ratings they received from interviewers—and so, the more likely they were to be hired. This was especially true when interviews were open-ended rather than carefully structured, but overall, there was clear evidence that using both self-enhancement and other-enhancement tactics was beneficial to job applicants; these tactics did succeed in raising their evaluations in the interviews.

In addition, this meta-analysis examined another important question: What happens after people who use impression management successfully are hired? Do they actually turn out to be excellent employees? There are some grounds for predicting that this would be true. People who use impression management tactics successfully may be higher in social skills than people who don't. As a result, after they are hired, they may get along better with others, and this can help them succeed in their new jobs. On the other hand, many other factors aside from being effective in making a good first impression on others play a role in job performance, so the relationship between these two factors—use of impression management tactics and job performance—may be relatively weak. That's exactly what Barrick and colleagues (2009) found: While effective use of impression management tactics did increase ratings by interviewers, they were only weakly related to later ratings of actual job performance. So, as the authors note, "what you see (in an interview) may not always be what you get" in terms of excellent job performance later on.

Many other studies report similar findings and conclusions (Wayne, Liden, Graf, & Ferris, 1997; Witt & Ferris, 2003). But—and this is an important "but"—the use of these tactics also involves potential pitfalls: If they are overused, or used ineffectively, they can backfire and produce negative rather than positive reactions from others. For instance, in one interesting study, Vonk (1998) found strong evidence for what she terms the *slime effect*—a tendency to form very negative impressions of others who play up to their superiors, but treat subordinates with disdain and contempt. And in other research (e.g., Baron, 1986), it has been reported that the use of too many different tactics of impression management (especially, too much flattery of others), can lead to suspicion and mistrust rather than increased liking and higher evaluations. The moral of these findings is clear: While tactics of impression management often succeed, this is not always the case, and sometimes they can boomerang, adversely affecting reactions to the people who use them.

WHY DO PEOPLE ENGAGE IN IMPRESSION MANAGEMENT?   So far, we have assumed that people engage in impression management for one straightforward reason: to enhance others' reactions to them. This is certainly the primary reason for such behavior. But research findings indicate that there many others, too. For instance, efforts at impression management (often termed *self-presentation*) may serve to boost the moods of people who engage in it. This might be the case because efforts to appear cheerful, happy, and pleasant might—through the kind of mechanisms suggested by the facial feedback hypothesis—generate actual increases in such feelings. In other words, by attempting to appear happy and positive, people may actually encourage such feelings (Tyler & Rosier, 2009). In fact, research by Dunn, Biesanz, Human, and Finn (2009) suggests that this is really the case. They had dating couples rate their moods both before and after interacting with an opposite-sex stranger or their own dating partner. Although the participants predicted that they would feel happier after interacting with their own dating partners, they actually showed a bigger boost in mood after interacting with a stranger. Why? Perhaps because they engaged in more impression management with a stranger than their own partners. In a sense, this is not surprising: Almost everyone has had the experience of feeling happier and more positive after special efforts to enhance their own appearance (e.g., before a prom or other special event) (Figure 3.16).

In short, although we generally engage in impression management in order to increase others' evaluations of us, there may be some extra benefits to such tactics for the people who use them: Attempting to "look good" to others can often make us feel better in very basic ways.

FIGURE 3.16   Impression Management: Does It Make Us Feel Better?
Research findings indicate that when people engage in efforts to improve their own appearance (one tactic of impression management), this actually boosts their current moods.

KEY POINTS

- Most people are concerned with making good first impressions on others because they believe that these impressions will exert lasting effects.

- Research on *impression formation*—the process through which we form impressions of others—suggests that this is true. Asch's classic research on impression formation indicated that impressions of others involve more than simple summaries of their traits and that some traits (central traits) can influence the interpretation of other traits.

- First impressions are formed very quickly and even if based on limited information, can be somewhat accurate. However, confidence in the accuracy of such impressions is not closely related to their actual accuracy.

- In order to make a good impression on others, individuals often engage in *impression management* (self-presentation).

- Many techniques are used for this purpose, but most fall under two major headings: *self-enhancement*—efforts to boost one's appeal to others, and *other-enhancement*—efforts to induce positive moods or reactions in others.

- Existing evidence indicates that impression management works; it often succeeds in generating positive first impressions of the people using it.

- The use of such tactics is not closely related to behavior at later times, however. For instance, the people hired for jobs because they use impression management effectively don't necessarily become high-performing employees.

SUMMARY *and* REVIEW

- **Social perception** involves the processes through which we seek to understand other people. It plays a key role in social behavior and social thought. In order to understand others' emotional states, we often rely on **nonverbal communication**—an unspoken language of facial expressions, eye contact, and body movements and postures. While facial expressions for all basic emotions may not be as universal as once believed, they do often provide useful information about others' emotional states. Useful information on this issue is also provided by eye contact, **body language,** touching, and even scent. Growing evidence indicates that facial expressions are an especially important source of nonverbal information about others. Recent findings indicate that handshaking provides useful nonverbal cues about others' personalities, and can influence first impressions of strangers. Scent also serves as a nonverbal cue, and subtle cues concerning women's menstrual cycle can be transmitted in this way.

- The *facial feedback hypothesis* suggests that we not only show what we feel in our facial expressions, these expressions influence our emotional states. If we pay careful attention to certain nonverbal cues, we can recognize efforts at deception by others—even if these people are from a culture other than our own. Whether emotions are perceived as "inside" people or largely between them seems to depend on cultural factors.

- In order to obtain information about others' lasting traits, motives, and intentions, we often engage in **attribution**—efforts to understand why they have acted as they have. According to Jones and Davis's theory of **correspondent inference,** we attempt to infer others' traits from observing certain aspects of their behavior—especially behavior that is freely chosen, produces **noncommon effects,** and is low in social desirability. According to another theory, Kelley's theory of causal attribution, we are interested in the question of whether others' behavior stemmed from internal or external causes. To answer this question, we focus on information relating to **consensus, consistency,** and **distinctiveness.** Two other important dimensions of causal attribution relate to whether specific causes of behavior are stable over time and controllable or not controllable.

- Another issue relating to attribution concerns the extent to which we attribute events in our lives to fate—what was "meant to be"—or to personal causes. Individuals who believe strongly in the existence of God are more likely to attribute improbable but important events to "what was meant to be"; this is also true of people whose cultural heritage accepts complex causality for important events. Attribution is subject to many potential sources of bias. One of the most important of these is the **correspondence bias**—the tendency to explain others' actions as stemming from dispositions even in the presence of situational causes. Despite major changes in gender roles in recent decades, many people continue to attribute emotional displays by women to dispositional factors ("they are emotional") while attributing the same levels of emotion among men to external causes.

● Two other attributional errors are the **actor–observer effect**—the tendency to attribute our own behavior to external (situational causes) but that of others to internal causes—and the **self-serving bias**—the tendency to attribute our positive outcomes to internal causes but negative ones to external causes. The self-serving bias is especially strong for negative events, which are often attributed to external agents who cause them. Attribution has been applied to many practical problems, often with great success. For instance, it has been applied to understanding the causes of depression, and to treating this important mental disorder. Attribution also appears to operate in electronic communication over the Internet (e.g., through e-mail).

● Most people are concerned with making good first impressions on others because they believe that these impressions will exert lasting effects. Research on **impression formation**—the process through which we form impressions of others—suggests that this is true. Asch's classic research on impression formation indicated that impressions of others involve more than simple summaries of their traits and that some traits (central traits) can influence the interpretation of other traits. First impressions are formed very quickly and even if based on limited information, can be somewhat accurate. However, confidence in the accuracy of such impressions is not closely related to their actual accuracy. In order to make a good impression on others, individuals often engage in **impression management** (self-presentation). Many techniques are used for this purpose, but most fall under two major headings: *self-enhancement*—efforts to boost one's appeal to others—and *other-enhancement*—efforts to induce positive moods or reactions in others. Existing evidence indicates that impression management works; it often succeeds in generating positive first impressions of the people using it. The use of such tactics is not closely related to behavior at later times, however. For instance, the people hired for jobs because they use impression management effectively don't necessarily become high-performing employees.

KEY TERMS

action identification (p. 85)

actor-observer effect (p. 88)

attribution (p. 70)

body language (p. 73)

consensus (p. 83)

consistency (p. 83)

correspondence bias (fundamental attribution error) (p. 86)

correspondent inference (p. 81)

distinctiveness (p. 83)

fundamental attribution error (correspondence bias) (p. 86)

implicit personality theories (p. 96)

impression formation (p. 70)

impression management (self-presentation) (p. 70)

linguistic style (p. 78)

microexpressions (p. 78)

noncommon effects (p. 82)

nonverbal communication (p. 70)

self-serving bias (p. 89)

social perception (p. 70)

staring (p. 73)

thin slices (p. 95)

The Self

Answering the Question "Who Am I?"

*I*n the movie *To Die For,* Nicole Kidman, who plays the generally clueless main character, comments somewhat insightfully about the impact of television on the perception of ourselves: "You're not anybody in America unless you're on TV. On TV is where we learn about who we really are." Being on the Internet today, like being on TV then, may be thought of, in a philosophical sense, as providing a similar public forum for validating the personal self. So, in a sense, a person might "come alive" because they exist in a profile on Facebook; indeed, for some, *not* being on Facebook could be like being excluded from an important social group—and represent a kind of social death.

Is the converse also true? Does being on Facebook provide a way for people to extend their personal existence and that of their loved ones? Perhaps it is worth considering whether, when a person dies, if their self continues to be represented on Facebook—if you can still find their profile there—is something crucial about that person still here with us? Jack Brehm, a great social psychologist who spent most of his career at the University of Kansas, died in 2009 at the age of 81. After his death, a memorial page was set up for him on Facebook. Since then, it has been rather amazing to see over 150 people become "friends" of his online, and several hundred people visit Jack's Facebook page every month. Perhaps people "check in" at his Facebook page to enhance their memories of him by seeing photos from his life; it is possible too that writing comments about their experiences with him is a means of "keeping him alive." Do you think it is possible to claim that Jack and others live on in any real sense by their continued existence on Facebook? According to *Newsweek's* (Miller, 2010) coverage of this growing trend of people creating tributes for friends using Facebook, and the high number of requests to maintain the Facebook pages of people who are deceased ("R.I.P. on Facebook"), this year Facebook changed its policy to allow people's pages to remain active in perpetuity.

By providing this sort of cradle-to-grave social existence of the self, Facebook may be regarded as a new and important social environment. Although Facebook is a constructed environment, we argue that it is one in which many interesting aspects of self and identity can be readily observed. Like the social environment of your family, your school, work, or 'other' social life, the Facebook environment is one where you can expect to have friends, carry on conversations with others, and express yourself and your preferences (e.g., indicate your favorite books and movies). You may even use Facebook as a place where you document your personal growth—many people post photos of themselves at different stages throughout their lifespan.

FIGURE 4.1   Online Interaction or Live Interaction: The Same or Different?
Perhaps the self-presentational aspects of Facebook differs in a number of respcets from self-presentation IRL (in real life)? IRL, friends for this fellow might be considerable harder to come by than they are on Facebook.

As the largest social networking site, Facebook meets the criteria for a genuine social environment. It is a social network in that it makes your friends available to connect with—regardless of whether they are actually online at the time you post or not. As suggested in Figure 4.1, Facebook allows people to become friends with others they may otherwise have never met in real life. So the question is, Is a "friend" on Facebook, whom you've never met in real life, an actual friend?

To answer that, let's take a quick look backward. Once upon a time, many people had "pen pals." A pen pal was a friend with whom one communicated by letter, without ever having met that person. In some ways, you may think of the pen-pal idea as being ahead of its time, a precursor to the Internet. No one thought they had an obligation to meet a pen pal, but they were nevertheless a real social connection.

On the other hand, no one would have thought that their privacy could be massively compromised with a pen-pal letter. Sharing of information is a significant way in which Facebook (and other social networking sites) has created a different kind of social environment. On Facebook, unlike in real life, your privacy may be compromised in ways that allow marketers to target you. Whether you see this as a big problem or a minor inconvenience is determined by how much you value your privacy. Older people seem to want to guard their privacy more than younger ones, who don't seem to care as much. But, when you put yourself out there in today's online world, you can expect to be directly marketed to, often with the ads being based on the information you provided online about yourself!

The nature of the self and how we think and feel about ourselves have been central topics of research in social psychology. While examining a number of important issues that have been investigated concerning the nature of self, we'll also consider the impact of Internet technology on how we experience and present ourselves to others. As the cartoon in Figure 4.2 suggests, we can choose to withhold some crucial information about ourselves when communicating over the Internet. So, how does our ability to control what others learn about us via social networking sites and other Internet venues affect how we see ourselves and, importantly, how others see us? Who is more accurate in predicting our behavior—ourselves or others who know us well? In this chapter we examine research that has examined these questions.

After we consider the issue of whether people present themselves online differently from how they present themselves to others offline, and whether we ourselves change as a result of Internet use, we turn to the larger question of the methods that people use to gain self-knowledge. We also consider whether people have just one self or many selves and, if each of us has many selves, then a critical issue is whether one aspect of the self is more *true* or predictive of behavior than another. Do people experience themselves the same way all the time, or does their experience of themselves depend on the context and the nature of the social comparison it evokes? What role does social comparison play in how we evaluate ourselves?

After considering these questions, we turn to several important issues related to self-esteem: What is it, how do we get it, and how do we lose it? Is there a downside to having high self-esteem? Are there group differences in average level of self-esteem? Specifically, do men and women differ in their levels of self-esteem? Finally, we look in depth at how people manage when their self is a target of prejudice. What are the consequences of feeling excluded or devalued based on group membership for a number of self-related processes, including the emotional and performance consequences of such potential rejection of the self by others.

"On the Internet, nobody knows you're a dog."

FIGURE 4.2   Not All Aspects of Ourselves Are Equally Available When We Communicate Over the Internet

As shown in this cartoon, it may be easier to conceal important information about ourselves on the internet than in face-to-face encounters. (Source: Peter Steiner, The New Yorker, page 61 of July 5, 1993).

Self-Presentation: Managing the Self in Different Social Contexts

William Shakespeare said long ago in his play *As You Like It*, "All the world's a stage, and all the men and women merely players." In social psychological terms, this means that all of us are faced with the task of presenting ourselves to a variety of audiences, and we may play different roles (be different selves) in different contexts (act in different plays). Nowhere is the *choice* of how to present ourselves more obvious than on social networking sites such as Facebook. We can choose to reveal a lot about who we think we are—including photographic evidence of our behavior on Facebook—or we can, to some extent, limit who can have access to such information (e.g., by setting the privacy controls so that only official "friends" can access our wall postings and photo albums). But, how much can we really control what others learn about us and the inferences they draw based on that information? In fact, is it possible that others might know more about us—and be better at predicting our behavior—than we are ourselves?

Self–Other Accuracy in Predicting Our Behavior

There are many reasons to think people really do know themselves better than anyone else does. After all, each of us has access to our internal mental states (e.g., feelings, thoughts, aspirations, and intentions), which others do not (Pronin & Kruger, 2007; Wilson & Dunn, 2004). For this reason alone, it seems intuitively obvious that it *must* be the case that we must know ourselves best—but is it true? Indeed, research evidence suggests that having access to our intentions, which observers do not have, is one reason why we are sometimes inaccurate about ourselves (Chambers, Epley, Savitsky, & Windschitl, 2008). Consider the following example. My friend Shirley is chronically late for *everything*. Frequently, she's more than a half hour late; I simply cannot count on her to be ready when I arrive to pick her up or for her to arrive on time if we are meeting somewhere. You probably know someone like this too. But, would she characterize herself that way? Probably not. But, you might ask, how could she *not* know this about herself? Well, it could be that precisely because she knows her intentions—that she means to be on time and has access to how much effort she puts into trying to achieve that goal—that this information could lead her to believe she *actually* is mostly on time! So, at least in this regard, might I fairly claim that I know her better than she knows herself—because I certainly can more accurately predict her behavior, at least in this domain?

Despite such examples, many people strongly believe that they know themselves better than others know them, although, ironically enough, those same people claim that they know some *others* better than those others know themselves (Pronin, Kruger, Savitsky, & Ross, 2001). In deciding who is most accurate—ourselves or close others—part of the problem for research on this question has been that people provide both their own self ratings and they also report on their behavior. As I'm sure you can see, such behavioral self-reports are hardly an *objective* criterion for determining accuracy! Continuing with our example of Shirley, she'd be likely to say she might be occasionally late, but that she tries hard to always be on time—and she might even recall a few instances where that was true. But, still, might we have some basis for being suspicious of those behavioral self-reports?

So is the self–other accuracy problem simply impossible to address? New research has found a clever way to at least deal with the problem of collecting both self perceptions and behavior frequencies from the same source. To develop a more objective index of how a person actually behaves on a daily basis, Vazire and Mehl (2008) had participants wear a digital audio recorder with a microphone that recorded the ambient sounds of people's lives during waking hours, coming on approximately every 12.5 minutes for 4 days. Research assistants later coded the sounds recorded according to the categories shown in Table 4.1. Before the participants' actual behaviors were assessed in this way, they provided self-ratings concerning the extent to which they perform each behavior (more or less than

TABLE 4.1   Who Is More Accurate About Our Behavior: Self or Others?

Relationships between the frequency of behaviors and the participant's self-ratings was sometimes higher (e.g., talking to same sex) than any one close others' ratings of the participant or the aggregated ratings of the three close others. But, often, a close other's ratings of the participants' behavioral frequencies (e.g., attending class) was more strongly related to actual behavioral frequencies. So, sometimes we can predict ourselves better than others can, but not always!

BEHAVIOR	SELF	AGGREGATED INFORMANTS	SINGLE INFORMANT
With other people	.14	.36**	.30**
On the phone	.37**	.40**	.32**
Talking one-on-one	−.06	.25*	.22*
Talking in a group	.25*	.20*	.25*
Talking to same sex	.34**	.25*	.13
Talking to opposite sex	.31**	.32**	.18
Laughing	.23*	.25*	.13
Singing	.34**	.29**	.34**
Crying	.18	.16	.19
Arguing	.28**	−.05	.09
Listening to music	.40**	.34**	.26*
Watching TV	.55**	.39**	.36**
On the computer	.29**	.31**	.20
At work	.25*	.35**	.22*
Attending class	.07	.33**	.26*
Socializing	.18	.30**	.27*
Indoors	.16	.16	.20
Outdoors	.11	.05	.10
Commuting	.27**	.16	.14
At a coffee shop/bar/ restaurant	.27**	.15	.24*

Source: Based on research by Vazire & Mehl, 2008.

the average person) on a daily basis. These researchers also recruited three informants who knew each participant well (e.g., friends, parents, romantic partners) to provide the same ratings concerning the frequency that the participant engages in each behavior, using the same average person as a comparison. As you can see in Table 4.1, sometimes the participant's own rating was more strongly related to the frequency of their actual behavior, but sometimes others' ratings of the participant was more strongly related to actual behavior. So, at times, other people do seem to "know" us better (can predict our behavior) better than we ourselves can.

Some people may put information about themselves on the Web (e.g., myspace. com) because they believe such information better reflects who they are than does the "live" impression they leave in the "real world." Marcus, Machilek, and Schütz (2006) confirmed that the "self and other" agreement about what a person is like was higher for Web-based social interactions than for real-world interactions. That is, when interacting with another person via their self-constructed Web page, viewers infer attributes that agree with the self-image of the person who constructed the page. Of course, this might just mean that people who present themselves on the Web can more easily manage others' impressions of them than they can when the interaction is face to face because they have total control over what information is being conveyed on the Internet. (To learn more about how our behavior can change by interacting with other people over the Internet, please see our special section "SOCIAL LIFE IN A CONNECTED WORLD: Does Facebook Use Change Our Offline Behavior?".)

SOCIAL LIFE *in a* CONNECTED WORLD

Does Facebook Use Change Our Offline Behavior?

Cyber-optimists and cyber-pessimists are locked in an ongoing intellectual skirmish about the effects of Facebook, the most popular social networking site. Some argue that such Internet communication is ruining the brains of young people, whereas others claim that it represents an entirely new and creative way of interacting. One way to assess the validity of these positions is to examine people's motivations for joining a social networking site. If some people actually seek to interact on the Internet for different reasons than other people, then it might well be that some could be negatively affected whereas others might be positively affected.

So why do people join Facebook? Zywicka and Danowski (2008) conducted a study to examine this question and test two competing hypotheses. The first, "The Social Compensation" hypothesis, argues that introverts and socially anxious adolescents who have difficulty developing friendships are likely to use Facebook because they seek to substitute online contacts for an undesirable offline social life. An investigation into Internet use by Caplan (2005) had previously suggested that individuals who lack self-presentational skills are more likely to be attracted to online social interaction relative to

face-to-face communication, a view that is amusingly illustrated in Figure 4.3. The second, "The Social Enhancement" hypothesis, in contrast, suggests that extroverted and outgoing adolescents are motivated to add online contacts to their already large network of offline friends to create an image of themselves that reflects their existing positive self-view (Valkenburg, Schouten, & Peter,

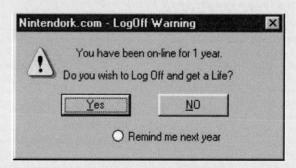

FIGURE 4.3   Is Online Living Equivalent to Having a Satisfying "Real-Life"?
To what extent are our "virtual selves" different or the same as our "real-life" selves?

(continued)

SOCIAL LIFE *in a* **CONNECTED WORLD** *(continued)*

2005). Some evidence emerged to support both of these hypotheses. That is, less socially skilled people find that online interaction welcomes them more than their "real life." On the other hand, socially skilled individuals are motivated to add friends to enhance their already positive self-view.

In studying the **social capital**—the number of social ties each person has among other Facebook users—Ellison, Steinfield, and Lampe (2007) found stronger evidence in support of the Social Compensation hypothesis than the Social Enhancement hypothesis. Those who were lower in life satisfaction and lower in self-esteem developed more social capital by using Facebook—they related to more diverse others and developed a variety of useful relationships on Facebook. In addition, Joinson (2003) points out that anxious teens may ask for a date using Facebook, instant messaging, or e-mail because it disguises their nervousness! So, this research revealed that socially skilled users maintain their high self-esteem by high use of Facebook, while users with initially poor skills increased their self-esteem as their Facebook usage increased. These results may explain why users with both high and low self-esteem find the Facebook culture desirable.

Based on research conducted by Bargh, McKenna, and Fitzsimons (2002), it appears that people who are shy and less socially skilled are able to express what they perceive to be their "true selves" more accurately over the Internet than in face-to-face interaction. So, perhaps some Facebook users may not be trying to manage their image so much as they are attempting to express their true selves, which they find difficult to do in other formats. Consistent with this idea, after involvement in a chat session, introverted individuals reported finding their "true self" online, while extroverts typically find it in face-to-face interactions (Amichai-Hamburger, Wainapel, & Fox, 2002). This suggests that introverts may have a significant motivation for joining Facebook.

Is there any possibility that people may capitalize on their Facebook experience subsequently in the offline world? Joinson (2003)

suggests that as users are accepted on Facebook and they make some friends, they may activate a hoped-for, "possible self" as a popular, socially skilled person. In turn, this may cause them to interpret their offline experiences differently. Thus, those who receive validation for their hoped-for or possible self may want to experience that same self in real life as well, fostering higher offline self-esteem and, possibly, increased offline social success (Bargh et al., 2002).

Sheeks and Birchmeier (2007) tested this idea and concluded that shy, socially anxious people were able to gain some social skills and social success by going online. As can be seen in Figure 4.4, some social skills gained by online interaction were transferred to "real life," and this was primarily among those who were initially shy, nonskilled people.

So, who's right—cyber-optimists or cyber-pessimists? Cyber-optimists predict increased social success following online activities, compared with their offline interactions before the online experience. That is, in the offline environment, there may be a wider disparity between people lacking social skills on the one hand, and the socially skilled on the other, but that this is less true following Internet experience. It would seem, then, based on this research, that cyber-optimists are right.

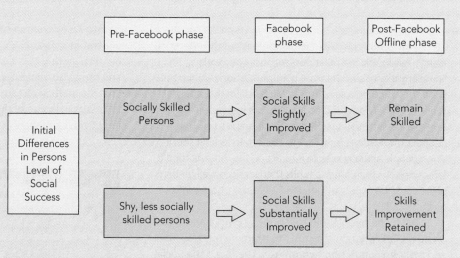

FIGURE 4.4 **Less Socially Skilled People Do Benefit from Facebook Social Interactions**

In a longitudinal study of teens who initially differed in their levels of social skills, during the Facebook phase of the study the shy and socially anxious individuals gained confidence and online friends. Importantly, these teens were able to transfer their new skills to their "real life" in the post-Facebook phase, although they still remained somewhat less socially skilled than the socially skilled group. (Source: Based on research by Sheeks & Birchmeier, 2007).

Self-Presentation Tactics

What do people do when they are trying to affect the impression that others form of them? (Recall that we discussed this topic in Chapter 3, "Social Perception.") First of all, people can try to ensure that others form impressions based on their most favorable self-aspects; that is, they can engage in **self-promotion.** If we want others to think we're smart, we can emphasize our intelligence "credentials"—grades obtained, awards won, and degrees sought. If we want others to conclude we are fun, we can choose to tell them about the great parties we attend or those we've hosted. Sometimes this works. If we say we're really good at something, people will often believe us, and saying so may even help convince ourselves that it's true!

Considerable research from a **self-verification perspective**—the processes we use to lead others to agree with our own self-views—suggests that negotiation occurs with others to ensure they agree with our self-claims (Swann, 2005). For example, while trading self-relevant information with a potential roommate, you might stress the student part of your self-concept—emphasize your good study habits and pride in your good grades—and underplay your fun qualities. This potential roommate might even note that "You don't sound like you're very interested in having fun here at college." To gain that person's agreement with your most central self-perception—serious student—you may even be willing to entertain a negative assessment of your fun quotient, as long as the other person is willing to go along with your self-assessment of the dimension most critical to you. Indeed, in this interaction, the potential roommate might wish to emphasize his or her party side. In this instance, it may be especially useful for you to downplay your own partying skills so that the other can achieve distinctiveness on this dimension. Through this sort of self-presentational exchange process, you may "buy" the roommate's self-assessment as a party type, to the extent that it helps you to "sell" your own self-assessment as an excellent student.

So, according to the self-verification view, even if it means potentially receiving information that is negative about ourselves, we may still wish to have other people—particularly those closest to us—see us as we see ourselves (Swann & Bosson, 2010). Suppose you are certain that you lack athletic ability, are shy, or that you lack math skills. Even though these attributes might be seen as relatively negative compared to their alternatives—athletic star, extroverted, or math whiz—you might prefer to have people see you consistent with how you see yourself. Research has revealed that, when given a choice, we prefer to be with other people who verify our views about ourselves rather than with those who fail to verify our dearly held self-views—even if those are not so flattering (Chen, Chen, & Shaw, 2004). However, there are real limits to this effect. As Swann and Bosson (2010) note, people who fear they are low in physical attractiveness do not appreciate close others who verify this self-view!

We can also choose to create a favorable self-presentation by conveying our positive regard for others. It is most assuredly true that we like to feel that others respect us, and we really like those who convey this to us (Tyler & Blader, 2000). To achieve this end, you can present yourself to others as someone who particularly values or respects them. In general, as we discussed in Chapter 3, when we want to make a good impression on others, it can be useful to employ **ingratiation** tactics. That is, we can make others like us by praising them. This is generally quite effective, unless we overdo it and then people will suspect we are not sincere (Vonk, 1999). To achieve the same end, sometimes we can be **self-deprecating**—imply that we are not as good as someone else—to communicate admiration or to simply lower the audience's expectations of our abilities.

Are our self-presentations always honest? Or are they at times strategic and occasionally less than straightforward? Research indicates that college students report telling lies to other people about twice a day (Kashy & DePaulo, 1996), frequently to advance their own interests but sometimes to help protect the other

social capital
The number of social ties each person has to others; typically these are connections people can draw on for knowledge, assistance, or other social goods.

self-promotion
Attempting to present ourselves to others as having positive attributes.

self-verification perspective
Theory that addresses the processes by which we lead others to agree with our views of ourselves; wanting others to agree with how we see ourselves.

ingratiation
When we try to make others like us by conveying that we like them; praising others to flatter them.

self-deprecating
Putting ourselves down or implying that we are not as good as someone else.

"You are guilty of fraudulent advertising! You really don't like Mozart, long walks in the country, or candlelit dinners! You are not a nonsmoker! And you are neither sensitive nor caring!"

FIGURE 4.5   To Be Honest or Be Popular, That Is the Question!
As this cartoon suggests, when we try to present ourselves in the most socially desirable light to be popular, those little 'fibs' may be found out rather quickly.

person. Consistent with the latter possibility, those people who tell more lies are more popular. For an amusing take on this issue, see Figure 4.5. In a study addressing how honest self-presentations on the Internet are, Ellison, Heino, and Gibbs (2006) conclude that it seems people often attempt to balance the desire to present an authentic sense of self with some "self-deceptive white lies." That is, people's profiles online typically reflect their "ideal self" rather than their "actual self." Thus, there seems to be some variations in how "honesty" is enacted online and common sense may be correct in claiming that "you can't believe everything you read online."

KEYPOINTS

- Facebook may be a medium through which we "come alive" and continue to exist even after death.

- Do we really know ourselves better than even our close others do? Even though we have access to information (intentions, goals) that others do not, that information itself may bias our own behavioral self-reports. Research that independently recorded people's actual behavior has revealed that sometimes we can predict our own behavior better than others can, but sometimes the reverse is true.

- Research has revealed that socially skilled users maintain their high skills by use of Facebook, whereas users with initially poor skills increased their skills and maintained those in the offline interactions.

- These results may explain why users with both high and low social skills find the Facebook culture desirable. Differences between shy and nonshy people are reduced when interactions take place over the Internet.

- We can choose various self-presentational strategies, including **self-promotion** and **ingratiation** tactics. We can also agree with others' preferred self-presentations so that they will concur with our own attempts to self-verify.

- Sometimes we are less than honest with other people, and this is often rewarded with greater popularity. Online we may present ourselves in terms of our "ideal" rather than "actual" self.

Self-Knowledge: Determining Who We Are

We now turn to some of the ways in which we seek to gain self-knowledge. One straightforward method is to try to directly analyze ourselves. Another method is to try to see ourselves as we think others see us—to take an observer's perspective on the self. We consider the consequences of both of these approaches for judgments of the self, and then we consider what social psychological research says about how we can get to know ourselves better.

Introspection: Looking Inward to Discover the Causes of Our Own Behavior

One important method that people often assume to be useful for learning about the self is to engage in **introspection**—to privately think about the factors that made us who we are. In a whole host of self-help books that sell millions of copies per year, we are told time and again that the best way to get to know ourselves is by looking inwardly. Indeed, many people in our society believe that the more we introspect about ourselves—particularly the more we examine the reasons for why we act as we do—the greater the self-understanding we will achieve. The many such introspection-oriented books, as shown in Figure 4.6, that are on the market tell us that the road to self-knowledge runs through self-inspection. Is this really the best way to learn about and arrive at an accurate understanding of ourselves?

First of all, considerable social psychological research has revealed that we do not always know or have conscious access to the reasons for our actions, although we can certainly generate—after the fact—what might seem to be logical theories of why we acted as we did (Nisbett & Wilson, 1977). Because we often genuinely don't know why we feel a particular way, generating reasons (which might well be inaccurate) could cause us to arrive at false conclusions. Wilson and Kraft (1993) illustrated how this can happen in a series of studies concerning introspection on topics ranging from "why I feel as I do about my romantic partner" to "why I like one type of jam over another." They found that, after introspecting about the reasons for their feelings, people changed their attitudes, at least temporarily, to match their stated reasons. As you might imagine, this can lead to regrettable inferences and choices because the original feelings—based on other factors entirely—are still there. So, thinking about reasons for our actions can misdirect our quest for self-knowledge when our behavior is really driven by our feelings.

Another way in which introspection might be rather misleading to us is when we attempt to predict our future feelings in response to some event. Try imagining how you would feel living in a new city, being fired from your job, or living with another person for many years. When we are not in these specific circumstances, we might not be able to accurately predict how we would respond when we are in them, and this applies to both positive and negative future circumstances.

Why is it we have so much difficulty predicting our future responses? When we think about something terrible happening to us and try to predict how we would feel 1 year after the event, we are likely to focus exclusively on the awfulness of that event and neglect all the other factors that will almost certainly contribute to our happiness level as the year progresses (Gilbert & Wilson, 2000). Consequently, people predict that they would feel much worse than they actually would when the future arrives. Likewise, for positive events, if we focus on only that great future event, we will mispredict our happiness as being considerably higher than the actual moderate feelings that are likely 1 year later. In the case of predicting our responses to such positive events in the future, miscalculation would occur because we are unlikely to consider the daily hassles we are also likely to experience in the future, and those would most definitely moderate how we actually feel.

Let's consider another important way in which introspection can lead us astray. Think now about whether spending money on a gift for someone else or spending that same amount of money on something for yourself would make you happier. If you are like most people, you are likely to think that buying something cool for yourself would make you happier than using your money to buy something for someone else. But, yet, recent research has revealed exactly the opposite—that spending money on others makes us happier than spending money on ourselves! In a nationally representative sample of Americans, Dunn, Aknin, and Norton (2008) asked respondents to rate how happy they

FIGURE 4.6 Self-Help Books Recommend Introspection
These pop psychology books imply that the route to self-knowledge lies in introspection, but recent research reveals that such self-reflection can be misleading. Depending on the nature of the factors that are actually driving our behavior, introspection may misdirect us about why we respond as we do.

introspection
To privately contemplate "who we are." It is a method for attempting to gain self knowledge.

were and to indicate how much of their monthly income they spend on expenses and gifts for themselves versus gifts for others and donations to charity. Overall, of course, people spent more on themselves than on others, but the important question is which actually predicts respondents' happiness? These researchers found that personal spending was unrelated to happiness, but that spending on others predicted greater happiness. This was true regardless of people's level of annual income—so whether you are rich or poor, there seems to be a happiness bonus for giving to others!

But, you might say, this was a correlational study and therefore we can't be sure that spending on others causally drove respondents' happiness. So, Dunn et al. (2008) performed a simple but telling experiment. They had psychology students rate their happiness in the morning and then they were given either $5 or $20 that they had to spend by 5:00 P.M. that same day. Half of the participants were told to spend that money on a personal bill or gift for themselves, while the other half were told to spend the money on a charitable donation or gift for someone else. Which group was happier at the end of the day? Regardless of the amount of money they were given to spend, participants reported significantly greater happiness when they spent their windfall on others compared to those who spent it on themselves. This experiment provides clear evidence that how we choose to spend our money is more important for our happiness—and in a counterintuitive direction—than is how much money we make (see Chapter 12 for more information on this issue). However, new participants who were asked to simply estimate which condition would bring them greater happiness overwhelmingly thought that spending the money on themselves would make them happier than would spending it on others. And, those who simply estimated how they would feel reported that receiving $20 would bring greater happiness than receiving $5. But neither of these self-predictions turned out to be true! What this means is that we often don't know how events will affect us and simply introspecting about it will not help us learn how events actually do affect our emotions and behavior.

The Self from the Other's Standpoint

As we saw in an earlier section of this chapter, sometimes other people are more accurate in predicting our behavior than we are. So, one way that we can attempt to learn about ourselves is by taking an "observer" perspective on own past. Because actors and observers differ in their focus of attention, and observers are less likely to be swayed by knowing our intentions and so forth, they could potentially have greater insight into when we will behave as we have done in the past. In contrast, as actors, we direct our attention outwardly, and tend to attribute more situational causes for their behavior (e.g., it was the traffic that made me late, the phone rang just as I was going out, etc.). Observers, though, focus their attention directly on the actor, and they tend to attribute more dispositional causes for the same behavior (see Chapter 3 for more on actor–observer differences). Therefore, if we take an observer's perspective on ourselves, we should be more likely to characterize ourselves in dispositional or trait terms. Pronin and Ross (2006) found this to be true when people were asked to describe themselves as they were 5 years ago or as they are today. The self in the present was seen as varying with different situations and was characterized less frequently in terms of general dispositions or traits than was the past self. As shown in Figure 4.7, this was the case regardless of the actual age of the participants (and therefore the length of their pasts). Both middle-aged and college-aged participants saw themselves in terms of consistent traits (as observers

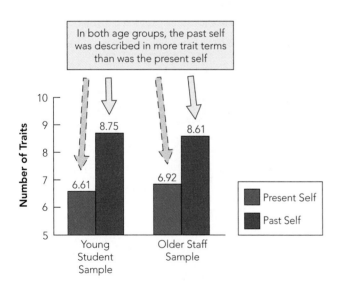

FIGURE 4.7   Selves Across Time: Taking an Observer's Perspective on One's Past Self

In both college students and middle-aged staff members, the past self was described in more trait terms—as observers do—than was the present self.   (Source: Based on data from Pronin & Ross, 2006).

tend to) when they were describing themselves in the past compared to when they were describing their present selves.

GAINING ACCURATE SELF KNOWLEDGE How might considering ourselves from an observer's perspective change the way we characterize ourselves and therefore provide self-insight? Pronin and Ross (2006) used different types of acting techniques as a method for examining how considering ourselves from an observer's perspective changes how we characterize ourselves. The participants were divided into two groups and were given "acting" instructions using one of two methods. In the "method-acting" condition, they were told that the goal was to "feel as if you *are* this other person." In the "standard-acting" condition, they were told that the goal was to "put on a performance so that you *appear* to others as though you are this person." After practicing various scenes using their assigned method, the participants were then told to enact a family dinner when they were 14 years old. In this case, everyone played their past self from one of two perspectives: One group was told to play their past self from the perspective of someone experiencing it, and the other group was told to play their past self as if they were an outside observer. Again, the number of consistent dispositions or traits used to describe their 14-year-old self was the central measure of interest: Did taking an observer stance on the self lead to greater trait consistency perceptions of the self? The answer was a clear yes. Those who performed with the method-actor technique were more actor-like and saw themselves in terms of few consistent traits, whereas those who played themselves from a more "observer-acting" perspective saw themselves in terms of consistent traits. So, when we try to learn about the self from the vantage point of another, we are more likely to see ourselves as observers do—in terms of consistent behavioral tendencies. So, one way to gain self-insight is to try to see ourselves as others do, and consider the possibility that they are more right than we are!

But is all introspection inevitably misleading? No. It depends on *what* we introspect about. When the behavior in question is actually based on a conscious decision-making process—and is not based on unconscious emotional factors—thinking about those reasons might well lead to accurate self-judgments. On the other hand, when we fail to take into account factors that really do influence how we feel (e.g., giving to others can make us happy), introspection is unlikely to lead to accurate self-inferences. So, while looking inward can be helpful, it may lead us astray under plenty of circumstances. When asked, people can easily generate reasons for why they do what they do, but those reasons may be based on self-theories about the causes of behavior and, as we saw with the effects of spending money on ourselves versus others, those theories may not be correct! By relying on such theories, we may remain unaware of the real reasons—for example, emotional factors—that cause our behavior. It is also the case that most of us may not have very good theories about how thinking about emotional events will affect us. For example, recent research (Koo, Algoe, Wilson, & Gilbert, 2008) has revealed that rather than thinking about positive outcomes that have happened to us, if instead we think about how those same positive outcomes might not have happened to us at all, we will feel happier. So, it is fair to say that gaining insight into one's own emotions, motivations, and behaviors can be tricky indeed.

KEYPOINTS

- One common method by which we attempt to gain self-knowledge is through **introspection**—looking inwardly to assess and understand why we do what we do.

- When it comes to self-queries about why we acted as we did, mistaken results can occur if we do not have conscious access to the factors that actually influenced

our responses, although after the fact we can and do construct explanations that seem plausible to us.

- When it comes to predicting how we might feel in the future, we fail to take into account other events that will moderate how we will feel besides the extreme and isolated event being judged.

- Most people believe that spending money on themselves will make them happier than spending the same amount on others. But research demonstrates that the opposite is true. What this means is we often don't know how our actions will affect us and introspecting about it won't help.

- One way self-reflection can be helpful is to take an observer's standpoint on our behavior. Doing so leads us to see ourselves in more trait-like consistent terms.

Who Am I?: Personal versus Social Identity

According to **social identity theory** (Tajfel & Turner, 1986), we can perceive ourselves differently at any given moment in time, depending on where we are on the **personal-versus-social identity continuum.** At the personal end of this continuum, we think of ourselves primarily as individuals. At the social end, we think of ourselves as members of specific social groups. We do not experience all aspects of our self-concept simultaneously; where we place ourselves on this continuum at any given moment will influence how we think about ourselves. This momentary **salience**—the part of our identity that is the focus of our attention—can affect much in terms of how we perceive ourselves and respond to others.

When our personal identity is salient and we think of ourselves as unique individuals, this results in self-descriptions that emphasize how we differ from other individuals. For example, you might describe yourself as fun when thinking of yourself at the personal identity level—to emphasize your self-perception as having more of this attribute than other individuals you are using as the comparison. Personal identity self-description can be thought of as an **intragroup comparison**—involving comparisons with other individuals who share our group membership. For this reason, when describing the personal self, which group is the referent can affect the content of our self-descriptions (Oakes, Haslam, & Turner, 1994; Reynolds et al., 2010). Consider how you might characterize yourself if you were asked to describe how you are different from others. You could describe yourself as particularly liberal if you were comparing yourself to your parents, but if you were indicating how you are different from other college students you might say that you are rather conservative. The point is that even for personal identity, the content we generate to describe ourselves depends on some comparison, and this can result in us thinking about and describing ourselves differently—in this example as either liberal or conservative—depending on the comparative context.

At the social identity end of the continuum, perceiving ourselves as members of a group means we emphasize what we share with other group members. We describe ourselves in terms of the attributes that differentiate our group from another comparison group. Descriptions of the self at the social identity level are **intergroup comparisons** in nature—they involve contrasts between groups. For example, when your social identity as a fraternity or sorority group member is salient, you may ascribe traits to yourself that you share with other members of your group. Attributes of athleticism and self-motivation might, for example, differentiate your group from other fraternities or sororities that you see as being more studious and scholarly than your group. For many people, their gender group is another important social identity and, when salient, can affect self-perceptions. So, if you are female and your gender is salient, you might perceive the attributes that you believe you share with other women (e.g., warm and caring) and that you perceive as differentiating women from men as self-descriptive. Likewise, if you are male, when gender is salient, you might think of yourself (i.e., self-stereotype) in terms of attributes that are believed to characterize men and that differentiate them from women (e.g., independent, strong).

social identity theory
Addresses how we respond when our group identity is salient. Suggests that we will move closer to positive others with whom we share an identity but distance from other ingroup members who perform poorly or otherwise make our social identity negative.

personal-versus-social identity continuum
At the personal level, the self is thought of as a unique individual, whereas at the social identity level, the self is seen as a member of a group

salience
When someone or some object stands out from its background or is the focus of attention.

intragroup comparisons
Judgments that result from comparisons between individuals who are members of the same group.

intergroup comparisons
Judgments that result from comparisons between our group and another group.

What's important to note here is that when you think of yourself as an individual, the content of your self-description is likely to differ from when you are thinking of yourself as a member of a category that you share with others. Of course, as these examples indicate, most of us are members of a variety of different groups (e.g., gender group, occupation, age group, sexual orientation, nationality, sports team), but all of these will not be salient at the same time and they may differ considerably in how important they are to us. But when a particular social identity is salient, people are likely to act in ways that reflect that aspect of their self-concept. Thus there may be a number of situational factors that will alter how we define ourselves, and the actions that stem from those self-definitions will differ accordingly. Figure 4.8 summarizes the processes involved and consequences of experiencing the self in personal rather than social identity terms.

So, at any given time we can define ourselves differently, thus creating many "selves." Can we say that one of these is the "true" self—either the personal self or any one of a person's potential social identities? Not really. All of these could be correct portraits of the self and accurately predict behavior, depending on the context and comparison dimension (Oakes & Reynolds, 1997; Reynolds et al., 2010). Note, too, how some ways of thinking about ourselves could even imply behaviors that are opposite to those that would result from other self-descriptions (e.g., fun vs. scholarly; liberal vs. conservative).

Despite such potential variability in self-definition, most of us manage to maintain a coherent image of ourselves, while recognizing that we may define ourselves and behave differently in different situations. This can occur either because the domains in which we see ourselves as inconsistent are deemed to be relatively unimportant, or they simply are not salient when we think of ourselves in terms of any particular identity (Patrick, Neighbors, & Knee, 2004). We have more to say below on how people manage conflict among the different aspects of the self.

Who I Think I Am Depends on the Social Context

People do describe themselves differently depending on whether the question they are asked implies a specific situation or is more open-ended. This effect was illustrated by Mendoza-Denton, Ayduk, Mischel, Shoda, and Testa (2001). In their study, participants were given one of two different types of sentence completion tasks. When the prompt was open-ended, such as "I am a (an) . . . person," self-definition as an individual is implied. In this condition, participants' responses were primarily trait-like and global (e.g., "I am an ambitious person"). When, however, the prompt implied particular settings, "I am a (an) . . . when . . ." then the responses were more contingent on the situation considered by the participant (e.g., "I am an ambitious person when a professor provides me with a challenge").

People also differ across time and place in the extent to which they emphasize the personal self and its uniqueness from others. For example, a recent analysis of the names given to the 325 million American babies born between 1880 and 2007 indicates that

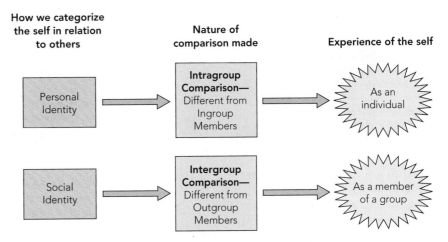

FIGURE 4.8 **The Personal versus Social Identity Continuum**
Depending on how we define ourselves—in terms of our personal or a social identity— the self will be defined in terms of the content that results from either an intragroup or intergroup comparison. The resulting salient identity experience will be either as an individual or as a member of a social group. (Source: Based on Oakes, Haslam, & Turner, 1994).

parents have increasingly, across time, given their children less common names, with this trend escalating particularly after 1980 (Twenge, Abebe, & Campbell, 2010). Presumably, it is easier to—and there's a greater expectancy that you will—differentiate yourself from others when you have a unique name that you do not share with them. This massive shift away from common given names, which was observed across all ethnic groups, has been reflected in an increasing emphasis on individualism across this century, with Americans increasingly endorsing individualistic traits for themselves (Twenge, Konrath, Foster, Campbell, & Bushman, 2008).

How might the social context serve to cue social identities that differentially emphasize the personal self and individualism? Research has revealed that bilingual Asian students living in Hong Kong answer the question, "Who am I?" when it is asked in English in terms of personal traits that differentiate them from others, reflecting an individualistic self-construal. However, when they are asked the same question in Chinese, these bilingual students describe themselves in terms of group memberships that they share with others, reflecting a more interdependent self-construal (Trafimow, Silverman, Fan, & Law, 1997). Thus, important differences in self-descriptions emerge primarily when a particular group identity is activated, as it was in this example, when thinking of the self in English versus Chinese.

Such context shifts in self-definition can influence how we categorize ourselves in relation to other people, and this in turn, can affect how we respond to others (Ryan, David, & Reynolds, 2004). When participants categorize a person in need as a fellow university student—so that person is seen as a member of the same category as the participant—then men and women were equally likely to display high levels of care-oriented responses toward that person. In contrast, when participants categorized themselves in terms of their gender, then women displayed significantly more care-oriented responses than did men. In fact, men reduced their care-oriented responses to the person in need in the gender salient condition compared to the shared university-identity condition. Thus gender differences in caring responses toward another individual depend on gender being a salient category. Of course, gender is a powerful social category that is likely to be activated a great deal of the time (Fiske & Stevens, 1993). This means it is likely to influence perceptions of the self and our responses to others with some frequency.

Not only must gender be salient for gender differences in **self-construal** or how we characterize ourselves to emerge, but research (Guimond et al., 2007) has also revealed that how we perceive ourselves depends on which gender group serves as the comparison. In a five-nation study, these investigators found that only when men and women were asked to compare themselves to members of the other gender group (an intergroup comparison was made) did they display the expected gender difference in rated self-insecurity. That is, when women compared themselves to men they said they were insecure, and when men compared themselves to women they said they were not insecure. In this case, people saw themselves as consistent with their own gender group's stereotype. However, as shown in Figure 4.9, when the same self-judgments were made in an intragroup context—where women compared their standing to other women and men compared their standing to other men—no reliable gender differences in perceived insecurity of the self were found. So, how we see ourselves—in terms of what traits we have—depends on the comparison we use when assessing ourselves.

self-construal

How we characterize ourselves, which can vary depending on what identity is salient at any given moment.

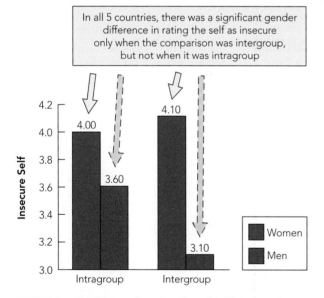

FIGURE 4.9 Measuring Gendered Self-Perceptions Around the World

In a cross-cultural study of 950 participants from five nations (France, Belgium, Malaysia, The Netherlands, and USA), gender differences in perceiving the self as anxious, fearful, and insecure were present only when people compared themselves to members of the other gender group, but no significant gender difference was found when the self was compared to members of their own gender group. *(Source: Based on data from Guimond et al., 2007).*

WHEN AND WHY ARE SOME ASPECTS OF THE SELF MORE SALIENT THAN OTHERS?
What determines which aspect of the self will be most influential at any given moment? This is an important question precisely because the self aspect that is salient can have a major impact on our self-perceptions and behavior.

First, one aspect of the self might be especially relevant to a particular context (e.g., thinking of ourselves as fun when at a party but as hard working when we are at work). Second, features of the context can make one aspect of the self highly distinctive, with that aspect of identity forming the basis of self-perception. For example, suppose an office is composed of only one woman among several men. In this context, the woman's gender distinguishes her from her colleagues and is therefore likely to be frequently salient. Thus the lone woman is particularly likely to feel "like a woman," and she may be treated based on the stereotype of that group (Fuegen & Biernat, 2002; Yoder & Berendsen, 2001). Similarly, African American students at predominantly white universities where other minority group members are rare are likely to think of themselves in terms of their race (Pollak & Niemann, 1998; Postmes & Branscombe, 2002).

Third, some people may be more ready to categorize themselves in terms of a particular personal trait (e.g., intelligence) or social identity (e.g., gender) because of its importance to the self. People who are highly identified with their national group (e.g., Americans) are more reactive to threat to that identity than are people who are less identified (Branscombe & Wann, 1994). Fourth, other people, including how they refer to us linguistically, can cue us to think of ourselves in personal versus social identity terms. Aspects of the self-concept that are referred to as nouns (e.g., *woman*, *student*) are particularly likely to activate social identities (Simon, 2004). Nouns suggest discrete categories, which trigger perceptions of members of those categories as sharing a fundamental nature or essence that is different from members of other categories (Lickel, Hamilton, & Sherman, 2001). In contrast, aspects of the self that are referred to with either adjectives or verbs (e.g., *athletic*, *taller*, *extremely supportive*) reference perceived differences between people within a category (Turner & Onorato, 1999) and are especially likely to elicit self-perceptions at the personal identity level.

EMOTIONAL CONSEQUENCES WHEN CHOICES ARE MADE BY DIFFERENT SELVES
Have you ever had the experience of buying something new and later, after getting it home, you think, "What on earth was I thinking when I selected that?" Well, you are not alone! Recent research by LeBoeuf, Shafir, and Bayuk (2010) has illuminated this post-consumer regret process, explaining it in terms of different salient selves at the time the purchase is made and when you later experience it. Let's see how this process could play out with your student identity.

While most students come to college to develop their intellectual skills, this stage of life also involves developing the social side of oneself. To test whether the salience of these differing aspects of an identity affects the choices we make, LeBoeuf et al. (2010) first made one of these aspects of the student identity salient by asking participants to take a survey about world issues (the "Scholar" identity condition) or about campus socializing (the "Socialite" condition). Participants were then given an opportunity to choose from different consumer items—magazines in this study. When the scholar aspect of their identity was salient, the students chose more scholarly publications (e.g., *The Economist*, *The Wall Street Journal*), but selected more social publications (e.g., *Cosmopolitan*, *Sports Illustrated*) in the Socialite condition. In a subsequent study, the same pattern of results was obtained when Chinese Americans first thought of themselves in terms of their Chinese identity ("think of your favorite Chinese holiday") or their American identity ("think of your favorite American holiday"). In this case, those whose American self aspect was salient chose cars that were more unique in color, whereas those whose Chinese self aspect was salient chose more traditional car colors. These studies illustrate that the aspect of ourselves that is salient can affect our consumer choices.

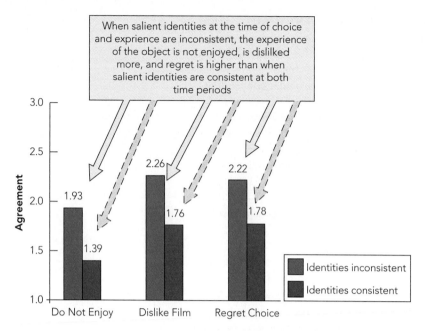

When salient identities at the time of choice and exprience are inconsistent, the experience of the object is not enjoyed, is dislilked more, and regret is higher than when salient identities are consistent at both time periods

FIGURE 4.10 **When Choices Are Made by Different Salient Selves**
When participants made film choices while one aspect of their identity was salient (Student as Scholar or Student as Socializer) but another aspect of their identity was salient at the time they experienced the film, the experience was less positive than when the identities matched at both time periods. Because identity salience can fluctuate, this is one reason why we can come to regret choices that looked good to us earlier. (*Source: Based on research by LeBoeuf, Shafir, & Bayuk, 2010*).

But, what about the issue of satisfaction (or regret) over the choices we have already made? Does the degree of satisfaction we experience depend on there being a match between the self aspect that is salient when the choice is made and the self aspect that is salient when the choice is experienced or evaluated? To answer this question, LeBoeuf et al. (2010) again made their participants' student identity—either the scholarly or socializing aspect—salient. This was again done simply by giving participants a survey about "world issues" to activate the scholarly self, or a survey about "campus life" to activate the socialite self. At this point, participants were simply asked to choose a film to watch. Once the film choice was made, but before watching the film clip, their original or the other self aspect was made salient—students were reminded of their scholarly self by asking about their interest in attending graduate school or their socialite self by asking about their interest in various university sports teams.

As can be seen in Figure 4.10, participants who watched the film that they chose when the same identity aspect was salient enjoyed the experience, liked the film, and did not regret their choice, whereas those whose identities in each time period were inconsistent with each other did not enjoy the experience, disliked the film more, and regretted their choice. These findings indicate that our choices and experiences stemming from them can depend on which aspect of our selves is salient, and they go some way toward explaining that question we have to occasionally ask ourselves, "What was I thinking when I selected that option?"

Who I Am Depends on Others' Treatment

How others treat us, and how we believe they will treat us in the future, have important implications for how we think about ourselves. When it comes to the self, no one is truly an island. If we expect that others will reject us because of some aspect of ourselves, there are a few response options available to us (Tajfel, 1978). To the extent that it is possible to change an aspect of ourselves and avoid being rejected, we could potentially choose to do that. In fact, we could choose to only change that particular feature when we anticipate being in the presence of others who will reject us because of it. In other words, for some aspects of ourselves, we can attempt to hide them from disapproving others. For example, the current U.S. military policy of "don't ask, don't tell" implies there are group identities we can choose to reveal or not. However, this option will be practically impossible for some social identities. We can't easily hide or change our race, gender, or age. In some cases, even if we could alter the part of the self that brings rejection, we may rebel against those rejecting us by making that feature even more self-defining. That is, we may emphasize that feature as a method of contrasting ourselves from those who reject us—in effect, we can publicly communicate that we value something different than those who might judge us negatively because of it.

This point was illustrated in research conducted by Jetten, Branscombe, Schmitt, and Spears (2001). These researchers studied young people who elect to get body piercings in visible parts of the body other than earlobes (e.g., navel, tongue, eyebrow), a practice that has gained in popularity. How we dress and alter our bodies can be conceptualized as important identity markers—ways of communicating to the world who we are. Although some identity markers may bring acceptance into peer groups, they may be perceived by other groups as weird or antinormative. Today, getting body piercings and tattoos may be comparable to the wearing of blue jeans and men having long hair in the 1960s. These identity markers were the visible indicator of a "hippie" identity, reflecting a self-perception as a rebel against the establishment. Like their 1960s counterparts, today's young people who opt for visible body piercings and tattoos appear to be engaged in a similar form of rebel identity construction.

FIGURE 4.11   Claiming an Identity That Is "Non-Mainstream"
Many forms of body adornment and body modification are visual indicators of how we see ourselves—our identities. These young women may be conveying to the "mainstream" that they are not one of them, and that they want to "fit in" with their peer group.

People who get such visible markings often know that they are likely to be discriminated against because of them. This expectation can lead to stronger self-definition in terms of a social identity that is actively rejecting the dominant culture's standards of beauty. An expectation of rejection and devaluation on the part of the culture as a whole can result in increasingly strong identification with a newly forming cultural group. Those with body piercings who were led to expect rejection from the mainstream identified more strongly with other people who have body piercings than did those who were led to expect acceptance from the mainstream (Jetten et al., 2001). As Figure 4.11 illustrates, people with body piercings and tattoos seem to be communicating that "we are different from the mainstream." If the practice of getting body piercings ultimately becomes diffused throughout the culture—as happened when everyone started wearing blue jeans—then those who are attempting to convey their collective difference from the mainstream may be compelled to become increasingly more extreme to achieve the same identity end.

The Self Across Time: Past and Future Selves

Sometimes people think about the ways they have developed and changed across time. Studies of **autobiographical memory** (Wilson & Ross, 2001) have revealed that by comparing our present selves with our past selves, we feel good about ourselves to the extent that we perceive improvement over time. Ross and Wilson (2003) performed a series of studies in which they asked people to describe a past self—either a self that was perceived to be far in the past or one that was more recent. Criticism of the "distant" past self was greater than the self that was perceived as "nearer" to the present. These researchers argued that derogating our distant past selves allows us to feel good because then we can feel like we have really grown (i.e., are better now). In contrast, when people feel close in time to some self-failure, the current self is seen less positively than when that same failure is seen as far in the distant past. Consistent with this self-protective idea,

autobiographical memory
Concerned with memory of the ourselves in the past, sometimes over the life course as a whole.

FIGURE 4.12   Will You Be Celebrating Your New College Graduate Self Soon?

Achieving some possible selves can be hard work, but well worth the effort!

when people are asked to write about two memorable life experiences—one in which they were blameworthy and one in which they were praiseworthy—people generated more recent praiseworthy events but described blameworthy events that are further in their past (Escobedo & Adolphs, 2010).

What about self comparisons in the other direction—are there emotional consequences of thinking about future **possible selves?** Thinking about a positively valued possible self can inspire people to forego current activities that are enjoyable but will not help, or might even hinder, bringing about this improved future self (Markus & Nurius, 1986). In this instance, we may forego immediately enjoyable activities to achieve the goal of becoming our desired possible self.

Think about what may be required to attain a valued future self or add a new identity. You may have to give up fun time in order to attain the status of being a college graduate, complete years of schooling and long internships to become a doctor, or put in many grueling hours in law school and study for state bar exams to become a lawyer. Lockwood and Kunda (1999) found that *role models*—other people we wish to imitate or be like—can inspire us to invest in such long-term achievements, but we must see the possible self that the role model represents as being potentially attainable. The image of a possible future self has been found to influence people's motivation to study harder, give up smoking, or invest in parenting classes when a new and improved self is imagined as likely to result from such changes. We may suffer in the present as long as we believe a more desired future possible self is achievable. The photo in Figure 4.12 shows the joy that can be experienced when a new identity—as a college graduate—is attained.

People also consider how to avoid negative and feared future possible selves, for example, when we are making New Year's resolutions. Polivy and Herman (2000) suggest that envisioning the self-changes required to avoid these outcomes can induce feelings of control and optimism, but failing to keep those resolutions is a common experience and repeated failures can lead to unhappiness. When people feel they want to change but cannot succeed in doing so, they may be tempted to reduce this uncomfortable state of self-awareness by distracting themselves—either in mundane ways such as getting lost in a novel or in more damaging ways such as consuming heavy amounts of alcohol (Baumeister, 1991).

Self-Control: Why It Can Be Difficult to Do

People often want to change themselves by, for example, quitting smoking, going on a diet, studying more effectively, and so on—but they may find it difficult to stick with such long-range goals. Instead, people often succumb to the lure of an immediate reward and break with their prior commitment. In other words, we fail to control ourselves in some meaningful way.

How does the way we think about ourselves affect our success in endeavors that require **self-control**—refraining from actions we like, but performing actions we prefer not to? How difficult is it to stick to long-term goals, even though short-term outcomes might be more immediately gratifying? Some researchers have suggested that the act of controlling ourselves is taxing and makes exercising subsequent self-control more difficult. Vohs and Heatherton (2000) have claimed that we have a limited ability to regulate ourselves, and if we use our control resources on unimportant tasks, there will be less available for the important ones. People who are first required to control themselves in

possible selves
Image of how we might be in the future—either a "dreaded" potential to be avoided or "desired" potential that can be strived for.

self-control
Achieved by refraining from actions we like and instead performing actions we prefer not to do as a means of achieving a long-term goal.

some way (e.g., not think about a particular topic, engage in two tasks simultaneously, or control their emotional expression) do less well on later self-control tasks than those who have not had to recently control themselves. Consider Vohs and Heatherton's study of chronic dieters who have a long history of attempting to resist temptation in the interests of achieving long-term weight loss. When these participants were first placed close to a dish of appealing candy, their ability to self-regulate on a second task was reduced—so they ate more ice cream than those who did not have to first control themselves. So, not only is controlling ourselves sometimes difficult to do in the first place, but after doing so successfully, it can impair our ability to do so again.

To the extent that self-control is a finite resource, **ego-depletion**—the diminished capacity to exert subsequent self-control after previously doing so—might be expected in many domains requiring self-regulation. A recent meta-analysis of studies in which ego-depletion has occurred (due to effort to exert self-control on a prior task) reports effects on a wide variety of outcomes (Hagger, Wood, Stiff, & Chatzisarantis, 2010). Prior efforts to exert self-control had negative consequences for subsequent self-control efforts, including greater subjective fatigue, perceived difficulty of achieving self-control, and lowered blood glucose levels. Ego-depletion was least likely to impair subsequent self-control when the initial control effort was shorter rather than longer, when participants had received training in self-regulation, and a rest period occurs between the initial and subsequent self-control tasks. Self-control can also be increased by thinking abstractly about our goals (Fujita & Han, 2009); that is, we have to remind ourselves of our overall goals and plan (e.g., desire to lose weight) rather than the details of what we are doing right now (e.g., not diving into that chocolate cake). To sum up, the ability to control ourselves—either to avoid doing what we no longer want to do or staying focused and doing more of what we do want—can be increased, but it appears to take practice, and many factors can undermine development of this skill!

ego-depletion
The lowered capacity to exert subsequent self-control following earlier efforts to exert self-control. Performance decrements are typically observed when people's ego strength has been depleted by prior efforts at self-control.

KEY POINTS

- How we think about ourselves can vary in terms of whether the personal self or the social self is salient, with our behavior based on **intragroup** (contrasts with other ingroup members) or **intergroup** comparisons (contrasts with the outgroup). People have multiple social identities, each of which could have rather different implications for behavior, depending on which is activated in a particular context.

- The context that we find ourselves in can alter the aspect of the self that is salient. Gender differences will be exhibited most when our gender group identity is salient, and they may be absent entirely when another group identity is salient. For example, gender differences in perceived insecurity of the self across five different nations are observed when the self is compared to members of the other gender group but not when the self is compared to members of one's own gender group.

- Several different factors can influence what aspect of the self is salient and influential for our behavior: when the context makes one aspect particularly relevant,

when the context makes one distinct from others, when one is of greater importance to us, and others' treatment of us or language use.

- We can regret or be unsatisfied with choices we make when a different self aspect is salient when we consume the goods compared to when they were selected.

- One response to perceived rejection by others is to emphasize the aspect of one's identity that differentiates the self from those rejecting us. To create a self-perception as a rebel one can take on a feature that differentiates members of one's peer group from the mainstream.

- Images of future **possible selves** can inspire us to make difficult changes in the present to achieve this more desirable self.

- **Self-control** has been conceptualized as a limited resource and **ego-depletion** following efforts to self-regulate can make it more difficult to exert self-control subsequently. Self-control is most likely to be achieved when we focus on our abstract goals rather than the details of what we are doing right now.

1. I feel that I am a person of worth, at least on an equal basis with others.
2. I feel that I have a number of good qualities.
3. All in all, I am inclined to feel that I am a failure.*
4. I am able to do things as well as most other people.
5. I feel I do not have much to be proud of.*
6. I take a positive attitude toward myself.
7. On the whole, I am satisfied with myself.
8. I wish I could have more respect for myself.*
9. I certainly feel useless at times.*
10. At times I think I am no good at all.*

FIGURE 4.13   Measurement: The Rosenberg Self-Esteem Scale
Each of the items with an asterisk is reverse-scored, and then an average of all ten items is computed so that higher numbers indicate greater self-esteem.   (Source: Rosenberg, Morris. 1989. Society and the Adolescent Self-Image. Revised editions. Middletown, CT: Wesleyan University Press.).

Self-Esteem: Attitudes Toward Ourselves

For the most part, **self-esteem** has been conceptualized by social psychologists as the overall attitude people hold toward themselves. What kind of attitude do you have toward yourself—is it positive or negative? Is your attitude toward yourself stable, or do you think your self-esteem varies across time and contexts? New evidence has emerged showing that the average level of self-esteem in American high school students has been gradually increasing over time (Twenge & Campbell, 2008). Relative to students in the 1970s, students in 2006 report on average liking themselves considerably more.

The Measurement of Self-Esteem

The most common method of measuring personal self-esteem as an overall trait-like self-evaluation is with the 10-item Rosenberg (1965) scale. As shown in Figure 4.13, the items on this scale are quite transparent. On this measure, people are asked to provide their own explicit attitude toward themselves. Given that most people can guess what is being assessed with these items, it is not surprising that scores on this scale correlate very highly with responses to the single item, "I have high self-esteem" (Robins, Hendin, & Trzesniewski, 2001). There are also more specific measures of self-esteem that are used to assess self-esteem in particular domains, such as academics, personal relationships, appearance, and athletics, with scores on these more specific types of self-esteem being predicted by performance indicators in those domains (Swann, Chang-Schneider, & McClarty, 2007).

As Figure 4.14 illustrates, people's self-esteem seems to be responsive to life events. When we reflect on our achievements, self-esteem increases (Sedikides, Wildschut, Arndt, & Routledge, 2008). Likewise, considering our failures harms self-esteem. For example, when people are reminded of the ways they fall short of their ideals, self-esteem decreases (Eisenstadt & Leippe, 1994). When people with low self-esteem experience negative feedback, their self-esteem suffers further declines (DeHart & Pelham, 2007). Being ostracized, excluded, or ignored by other people can be psychologically painful and cause reductions in self-esteem (DeWall et al., 2010; Williams, 2001).

Researchers have recently attempted to measure self-esteem with greater subtlety (Greenwald & Farnham, 2000). Self-esteem scores based on explicit measures such as the Rosenberg scale could be biased by self-presentation concerns. Responses might be guided by norms—for example, people may report high levels of self-esteem because they think that is "normal" and what others do. To bypass such normative and conscious strategic concerns, researchers have developed a number of ways of assessing self-esteem implicitly by assessing automatic associations between the self and positive or negative concepts. The most common of the **implicit self-esteem** measures assessing self feelings of which we are not consciously aware is the Implicit Associations Test (Greenwald & Nosek, 2008; Ranganath, Smith, & Nosek, 2008). Responses on these two types of measures of self-esteem—implicit and explicit—are often not correlated, which is consistent with the assumption that these two types of measures are capturing different processes.

self-esteem
The degree to which we perceive ourselves positively or negatively; our overall attitude toward ourselves. It can be measured explicitly or implicitly.

implicit self-esteem
Feelings about the self of which we are not consciously aware.

FIGURE 4.14   Self-Esteem: Attitudes toward the Self
One's self-esteem, or attitude about oneself, can range from very positive to very negative. At least temporarily, the individuals shown here would seem to be expressing very negative and very positive attitudes about themselves.

An important question is whether implicit self-esteem changes with the circumstances, as we know explicit self-esteem does. To test this idea, Dijksterhuis (2004) used the logic of classical conditioning procedures to test whether implicit self-esteem can be improved without the participant's conscious awareness. After repeatedly pairing representations of the self (I or me) with positive trait terms (e.g., nice, smart, warm) that were presented subliminally (too quickly for participants to consciously recognize them), implicit self-esteem was found to be significantly higher for these participants than for those in a control group who were not exposed to such self-positive trait pairings. Furthermore, this subliminal conditioning procedure prevented participants from suffering a self-esteem reduction when they were later given negative false feedback about their intelligence. Therefore, and consistent with research on explicit self-esteem (such as studies using the Rosenberg scale) that shows people with high self-esteem are less vulnerable to threat following a failure experience, this subliminal training procedure appears to provide similar self-protection at the implicit level when faced with a threat to the self.

Consistent with this analysis concerning nonconscious influences on self-esteem, DeHart, Pelham, and Tennen (2006) found that young adults whose parents were consistently nurturing of them reported higher implicit self-esteem than those whose parents were less nurturing. Conversely, young adults whose parents were overprotective of them showed lower implicit self-esteem than those whose parents displayed trust in them during their teenage years. Such implicit messages—based on our experiences with our parents—may lay the foundation for implicit associations between the self and positive attributes or the self and negative attributes. (For more information on one strategy for improving self-esteem, see our special feature below, "EMOTIONS AND THE SELF: Does Talking Positively to Ourselves Really Work?".)

EMOTIONS *and* THE SELF

Does Talking Positively to Ourselves Really Work?

When you are facing a big challenge, do you follow the advice that Norman Vincent Peale offered the world in his (1952) book, *The Power of Positive Thinking* (see Figure 4.15)? His advice was simple enough: "Tell yourself that you can do anything, and you will"; "tell yourself that you're great, and you will be." Who practices this advice? And does doing so really work?

To address these questions, Wood, Perunovic, and Lee (2009) first simply asked college students when and how often they use positive self-talk (e.g., "I will win," "I will beat this illness"). Only 3 percent of their sample said they "never"

do this, while 8 percent said they do so "almost daily," with the majority somewhere in between. As might be expected, their participants were most likely to say they use positive self-talk before undertaking a challenge (e.g., before an exam or before giving a presentation).

But, these researchers' real interest was in the *consequences* of engaging in such self-talk for people's mood and happiness. In other words, does such positive self-talk work—that is, does make us feel better? Wood et al. (2009) suggested that such positive self-talk, for some people, could be useful, but for other people, it might backfire and make them feel even worse about themselves. How could that be? Well, for people who already have low self-esteem, such positive self-talk might cause them to recognize the sizeable discrepancy between what they'd like to be and the way they actually are. For those with high self-esteem, in contrast, it represents a confirmation of their already positive self-views. In fact, for low self-esteem people, positive self-talk might simply serve to remind them that they are not measuring up to important standards—particularly the "American standard" that we should think only positive thoughts (Ehrenreich, 2009). Indeed, such reminders of not meeting important standards might have greater psychological consequences than negative thoughts themselves.

To test these ideas, Wood et al. (2009) first selected participants who scored high or low on an explicit measure of self-esteem. All participants were asked to think about the statement "I am a lovable person," but what they were to focus on when they did so was varied. In the "Positive focus" condition participants were asked to "focus *only* on the ways and times this statement is *true*," whereas in the "Neutral focus" condition they were asked to focus on how this statement "may be true of you *or* ways in which it may not be true of you." After this task, participants' moods were assessed, as were their ratings of happiness with themselves. As shown in Figure 4.16, the task focus had no effect on people with high self-esteem; regardless of condition they were happier with themselves than were people with low self-esteem. What's of particular interest is the effect of focusing only on how it is true that "I am a lovable person" has on low self-esteem people. In this case, happiness with the self was actually lower than when the same self-statement was considered more neutrally—in terms of whether it might or it might not be true. So, overall, this study provides evidence that positive self-talk may not be as beneficial as once believed. In fact, the very people such positive self-talk is designed to help—those with low self-esteem—can be harmed by doing so!

FIGURE 4.15   Classic Advice: You Can Do Anything Through Positive Thinking!

This book by Norman Vincent Peale has been a big-seller for more than 50 years, but perhaps the effects of practicing such positive self-talk are more complex than originally supposed.

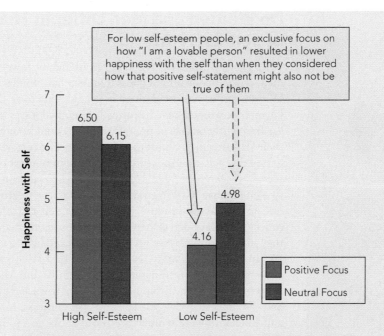

For low self-esteem people, an exclusive focus on how "I am a lovable person" resulted in lower happiness with the self than when they considered how that positive self-statement might also not be true of them

FIGURE 4.16   Effects of Positive Self-Talk Depend on Level of Self-Esteem

For people with low self-esteem, focusing on how a positive self-statement is true of themselves lowered happiness with the self relative to when they are able to consider more neutrally that the statement might or might not be true of them. Positive self-talk had no effect on people who were already high in self-esteem. So, positive self-talk can have either no effect or, worse, backfire and effects opposite to what was intended   (Source: Based on research by Wood, Perunovic, & Lee, 2009).

Is High Self-Esteem Always Beneficial?

Given the many techniques that have been developed for raising people's self-esteem, it is reasonable to ask whether high self-esteem is a crucial goal for which we should all strive. A variety of social scientists have suggested that the lack of high self-esteem (or the presence of low self-esteem) is the root of many social ills, including drug abuse, poor school performance, depression, and eating disorders. In fact, some have argued that low self-esteem might be an important cause of aggression and general negativity toward others. However, strong evidence has now accumulated in favor of the opposite conclusion—that high self-esteem is associated with bullying, narcissism, exhibitionism, self-aggrandizing, and interpersonal aggression (Baumeister, Campbell, Krueger, & Vohs, 2005). For example, it is men with high self-esteem, not those with low self-esteem, who are most likely to commit violent acts when someone disputes their favorable view of themselves.

Why might this be the case? To the extent that high self-esteem implies superiority to others, that view of the self may need to be defended with some frequency—whenever the individual's pride is threatened. It may even be that high self-esteem when it is coupled with instability (making for greater volatility) results in the most hostility and defensive responding (Kernis, Cornell, Sun, Berry, & Harlow, 1993). When unstable high self-esteem people experience failure, their underlying self-doubt is reflected in physiological responses indicative of threat (Seery, Blascovich, Weisbuch, & Vick, 2004). Thus, while there are clear benefits in terms of self-confidence, persistence at tasks following failure, and willingness to take on new challenges for individuals who have a favorable view of themselves (Baumeister, Campbell, Krueger, & Vohs, 2003), there also appears to be a potential downside.

FIGURE 4.17   Struggling to Achieve Self-Esteem When You Feel You Don't Measure Up

Research indicates that many socially disadvantaged groups do have, on average, somewhat lower self-esteem than groups that are socially advantaged. To the extent that self-esteem reflects how we believe others appraise us, high self-esteem can be difficult to achieve for those who are excluded from valued social roles.

Do Women and Men Differ in Their Levels of Self-Esteem?

Who do you think, on average, has higher or lower self-esteem—women or men? Many people might guess that men have higher self-esteem than women. Why might social psychologists predict this too? Because, as we discuss in Chapter 6, women have historically occupied lower status social positions and are frequently targets of prejudice, these could have negative consequences for their self-esteem. Beginning with George Herbert Mead (1934), who first suggested that self-esteem is affected by how important others in our environment see us, women have been expected to have lower self-esteem overall compared to men because self-esteem is responsive to the treatment we receive from others. As the photo in Figure 4.17 suggests, self-esteem in girls and women may reflect their devalued status in the larger society; many can end up feeling that they just do not measure up to societal standards.

In a 14-nation study, Williams and Best (1990) assessed the self-concepts of women and men. In nations, such as India and Malaysia, where women are expected to remain in the home in their roles as wives and mothers, women had the most negative self-concepts. In contrast, in nations, such as England and Finland, where women are more active in the labor force and the status difference between women and men is less, members of each gender tend to perceive themselves equally favorably. This research suggests that when women are excluded from important life arenas, they will have worse self-concepts than men. Longitudinal research with employed women in the United States finds that women in jobs in which gender discrimination is most frequent exhibit increasingly poorer emotional and physical health over time (Pavalko, Mossakowski, & Hamilton, 2003). Harm to women—as a function of employment in a discriminatory work environment—can be observed in comparison to their health status before such employment began.

A meta-analysis comparing the global self-esteem of women and men in 226 samples collected in the United States and Canada from 1982 to 1992 likewise found that men have reliably higher self-esteem than women (Major, Barr, Zubek, & Babey, 1999). Although the size of the effect obtained across all these studies was not large, as Prentice and Miller (1992) point out, sometimes small differences between groups can be quite impressive. Precisely because there are substantial differences within each gender group in level of self-esteem, being able to detect reliable group differences in self-esteem both within and across nations is remarkable. Major et al. (1999) found that the self-esteem difference between men and women was less among those in the professional class and greatest among those in the middle and lower classes. Again, those women who have attained culturally desirable positions suffer less self-esteem loss than those who are more likely to experience the greatest devaluation. In fact, higher education is associated with better self-esteem in women across the lifespan (Orth, Trzesniewski, & Robins, 2010).

Consistent with the idea that the degree of gender discrimination matters for self-esteem, there was no reliable gender difference in self-esteem among preadolescents, but beginning in puberty when discrimination experiences are more likely, a reliable self-esteem difference emerges that continues through adulthood, with women's self-esteem levels being lower than men's. However, recent longitudinal research has noted that the substantial gender difference in self-esteem that they observed during the adult working years begins to decline at about 65 years of age, with the gender groups converging in old age (Orth et al., 2010).

So, is the commonsense notion correct after all—does overall self-esteem suffer for groups that are devalued in a given society? The research findings offer a straightforward answer for gender: yes. Likewise, for many other devalued groups, perceiving and experiencing discrimination has a significant negative effect on a variety of indicators of physical and psychological well-being (Pascoe & Smart Richman, 2009). How badly self-esteem suffers depends on how much discrimination and devaluation the group that is the subject of such treatment experiences (Hansen & Sassenberg, 2006).

KEYPOINTS

- **Self-esteem** is our overall attitude toward ourselves. Self-esteem is most frequently measured with explicit items that directly assess our perceived level of self-esteem. Other more implicit measures assess the strength of the positive or negative association between ourselves and stimuli associated with us, including trait terms such as warm and honest. People may not be aware of these implicit self-feelings.

- Self-esteem is responsive to life experiences, and more specific forms of self-esteem depend on how we perform in those domains. Even **implicit self-esteem** can change with circumstances.

- People often engage in positive self-talk, especially when preparing for a challenge. Recent research has found that such positive self-talk in low self-esteem

people can backfire and make them feel less happy about themselves.

- Low self-esteem may not be predictive of the social ills many had thought. In fact, high self-esteem—especially when it is unstable—is associated with violent reactions when that superior view of the self is threatened.

- There is a small but reliable gender difference in self-esteem. Women's self-esteem is worse than men's to the extent that they live in a nation with more exclusion of women from public life compared to women who live in a nation with higher labor-force participation by women. Among those U.S. women who work in occupations in which discrimination is frequent and pervasive, lower self-esteem is more prevalent than among women in occupations in which discrimination is encountered less often.

Social Comparison: How We Evaluate Ourselves

How do we evaluate ourselves and decide whether we're good or bad in various domains, what our best and worst traits are, and how likable we are to others? Social psychologists believe that all human judgment is relative to some comparison standard (Kahneman & Miller, 1986). So, how we think and feel about ourselves will depend on the standard of comparison we use. To take a simple example, if you compare your ability to complete a puzzle to a child's ability to solve it, you'll probably feel pretty good about your ability. This would represent a **downward social comparison**—where your own performance is compared with someone who is less capable than yourself. On the other hand, if you compare your performance on the same task to a puzzle expert, you might not fare so well and not feel so good about yourself. This is the nature of **upward social comparisons,** which tend to be threatening to our self-image. Clearly, being able to evaluate ourselves positively depends on choosing the right standard of comparison!

You might be wondering why we compare ourselves to other people at all. Festinger's (1954) **social comparison theory** suggests that we compare ourselves to others because for many domains and attributes, there is no objective yardstick to evaluate ourselves against; other people are therefore highly informative. Are we brilliant or average? Charming or not charming? We can't tell by looking into a mirror or introspecting, but perhaps we can acquire useful information about these and many other questions by comparing ourselves with others. Indeed, feeling uncertain about ourselves is one of the central conditions that leads people to engage in social comparison and otherwise assess the extent to which we are meeting cultural norms (van den Bos, 2009; Wood, 1989).

downward social comparison
A comparison of the self to another who does less well than or is inferior to us.

upward social comparison
A comparison of the self to another who does better than or is superior to us.

social comparison theory
Festinger (1954) suggested that people compare themselves to others because for many domains and attributes there is no objective yardstick to evaluate ourselves against, and other people are therefore highly informative.

To whom do we compare ourselves, or how do we decide what standard of comparison to use? It depends on our motive for the comparison. Do we want an accurate assessment of ourselves, or do we want to simply feel good about ourselves? In general, the desire to see ourselves positively appears to be more powerful than either the desire to accurately assess ourselves or to verify strongly held beliefs about ourselves (Sedikides & Gregg, 2003). But, suppose, for the moment, that we really do want an accurate assessment. Festinger (1954) originally suggested we can gauge our abilities most accurately by comparing our performance with someone who is similar to us. But what determines similarity? Do we base it on age, gender, nationality, occupation, year in school, or something else entirely? In general, similarity tends to be based on broad social categories, such as gender, race, or experience in a particular task domain (Goethals & Darley, 1977; Wood, 1989).

Often, by using comparisons with others who share a social category with us, we can judge ourselves more positively than when we compare ourselves with others who are members of a different social category (especially if members of that category are more advantaged than our own). This is partly because there are different performance expectations for members of different categories in particular domains (e.g., children vs. adults, men vs. women). To the extent that the context encourages us to categorize ourselves as a member of a category with relatively low expectations in a particular domain, we will be able to conclude that we measure up rather well. For example, a woman could console herself by thinking that her salary is "pretty good for a woman," while she would feel considerably worse if she made the same comparison to men, who on average are paid more (Reskin & Padavic, 1994; Vasquez, 2001). Self-judgments are often less negative when the standards of our ingroup are used (Biernat, Eidelman, & Fuegan, 2002). Indeed, such ingroup comparisons may protect members of disadvantaged groups from painful social comparisons with members of more advantaged groups (Crocker & Major, 1989; Major, 1994).

Some suggest that the goal of perceiving the self positively is the "master motive" of human beings (Baumeister, 1998). How we achieve the generally positive self-perception that most of us have of ourselves depends on how we categorize ourselves in relation to comparison others (Wood & Wilson, 2003). Such self-categorization influences how particular comparisons affect us by influencing the *meaning* of the comparison. Two influential perspectives on the self—the **self-evaluation maintenance model** and social identity theory—both build on Festinger's (1954) original social comparison theory to describe the consequences of social comparison in different contexts.

Self-evaluation maintenance (Tesser, 1988) applies when we categorize the self at the personal level and we compare ourselves as an individual to another individual. Social identity theory (Tajfel & Turner, 1986) applies when we categorize ourselves at the group level (e.g., as a woman), and the comparison other is categorized as sharing the same category as ourselves (e.g., another woman). When the context encourages comparison at the group level, the same other person will be responded to differently than when the context suggests a comparison between individuals. For example, another member of our gender group who performs poorly might be embarrassing to our gender identity when we categorize ourselves as also belonging to that group. In contrast, that same poor-performing ingroup member could be flattering if we were to compare ourselves personally to that other individual.

Let's consider first what happens in an interpersonal comparison context. When someone with whom you compare yourself outperforms you in an area that is important to you, you will be motivated to distance yourself from the person because this information evokes a relatively painful interpersonal comparison. After all, this other person has done better than you have on something that matters to you. Conversely, when you compare yourself to another person who performs even worse than you, then you will be more likely to align yourself with that other person because the comparison is positive. By performing worse than you, this person makes you look good by comparison. Such

self-evaluation maintenance model
This perspective suggests that to maintain a positive view of ourselves, we distance ourselves from others who perform better than we do on valued dimensions and move closer to others who perform worse than us. This view suggests that doing so will protect our self-esteem.

psychological movement toward and away from a comparison other who performs better or worse than us illustrates an important means by which positive self-evaluations are maintained when our personal identities are salient.

So, will we always dislike others who do better than us? No—it depends on how we categorize ourselves in relation to the other. According to social identity theory, we are motivated to perceive our groups positively, and this should especially be the case for those who most strongly value a particular social identity. Other people, when categorized as a member of the same group as ourselves, can help make our group more positive when they perform well. Therefore when we think of ourselves at the social identity level, say in terms of a sports team, then a strong-performing teammate will enhance our group's identity instead of threatening it.

Therefore, either disliking or liking of the same high-performing other person can occur, depending on whether you think of that person as another individual or as someone who shares your group identity. The other's excellent performance has negative implications for you when you compare yourself to him or her as an individual, but positive implications for you when you compare members of your group to those of another group.

To test this idea that different responses to the same person can occur, Schmitt, Silvia, and Branscombe (2000) first selected participants for whom the performance dimension was relevant to the self; they said that being creative was important to them. Responses to another person who performs better or equally poorly as the self will depend on how you categorize yourself—at the individual level or at the social identity level. As shown in Figure 4.18, when participants believed their performance as an individual would be compared to the other person, they liked the poor-performing target more than the high-performing target who represented a threat to their positive personal self-image. In contrast, when participants categorized themselves in terms of the gender group that they shared with that person and the expected comparison was intergroup in nature (between women and men), then the high-performing other woman was evaluated more positively than the similar-to-self poor-performing other. Why? Because this talented person made the participants' group—women—look good. Because different contexts can induce us to categorize ourselves as an individual or as a member of a group, it has important implications for the effects that upward and downward social comparisons will have on self-evaluation.

above average effect
The tendency for people to rate themselves as above the average on most positive social attributes.

Self-Serving Biases and Unrealistic Optimism

Most people want to feel positively about themselves, and there are a number of strategies that can be used to ensure we see ourselves favorably much of the time. Many of us show the **above average effect**—we think we are better than the average person on almost every dimension imaginable (Alicke, Vredenburg, Hiatt, & Govorun, 2001; Klar, 2002). Indeed, people's tendency to see themselves as better than their peers (in terms of both their traits and abilities) predicts increases in self-esteem across time (Zuckerman & O'Loughlin, 2006).

Even when we are directly provided with negative social feedback that contradicts our typically rosy view of

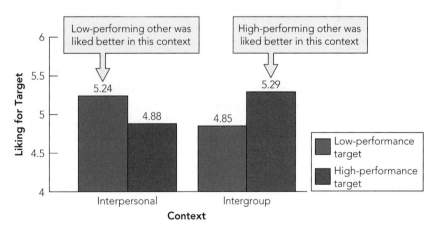

FIGURE 4.18 How Do We Evaluate Another Who Performs Better or Worse Than Us?
Research findings indicate that it depends on whether the context is interpersonal, where the personal self is at stake, or intergroup, with the social self at stake. As illustrated here, the low performing target is liked best in an interpersonal context. The high-performing target is liked best in an intergroup context. (Source: Based on data from Schmitt, Silvia, & Branscombe, 2000).

ourselves, we show evidence of forgetting such instances and emphasizing information that supports our favored positive self-perceptions (Sanitioso & Wlodarski, 2004). Likewise, information that might imply we are responsible for negative outcomes is assessed critically, and our ability to refute such arguments appears to be rather remarkable (Greenwald, 2002).

In contrast to our resistance to accepting responsibility for negative outcomes, we easily accept information that suggests we are responsible for our successes. Not only do people show self-serving biases for their personal outcomes, but they do so also for their group's achievements. Fans of sports teams often believe that their presence and cheering was responsible for their team's success (Wann & Branscombe, 1993).

People's positive self-assessments are particularly important as they relate to our capacity for getting things done. It turns out that, on the whole, we are unrealistically optimistic, and this has implications for our mental and physical health. A classic paper by Taylor and Brown (1988) documented the many forms of positive illusions that people hold. By illusion, we do not mean grandiose beliefs about the self—as might be found in some forms of psychopathology. Rather, "unrealistic optimism," for example, involves seeing our own chances for success in life as *slightly higher* than our peers' chances. Of course, it can't be true that all of us have higher likelihoods of successful life outcomes than our peers—we are not living in Garrison Keillor's Lake Wobegon, so we can't all be above average.

Sorrentino and colleagues (2005) showed such optimism was not limited to North Americans, but is also found among the Japanese. Indeed, such optimism is on the rise among Americans. For example, expectations among high school students that they will obtain a graduate degree rose to 50 percent by 2006, a number that is dramatically higher than the actual percentage that will do so (Twenge & Campbell, 2008). In a more mundane realm, Taylor (1989) notes that people's daily things-to-do lists are a "poignant example" of the unrealistic optimism phenomenon. We routinely fail to get even half of what's on our list accomplished (that's certainly true for my life!), but we repeat the same behavior day after day, oblivious to how unrealistic our plans are and continuing to expect to get everything on our list done.

Taylor and Brown (1988) documented the connection between positive illusions and contentment, confidence, and feelings of personal control. People who believe they can finish their to-do lists are more likely to proceed with feelings of self-efficacy and higher motivation than people who are more realistic. Thus higher motivation and greater persistence are associated with unrealistic optimism—and these lead to higher levels of performance on average and greater feelings of satisfaction.

But surely, you might wonder, isn't there a downside? Poor decisions must end up producing bad consequences when reality doesn't match up to those expectations. Despite the many reasons you might generate for why unrealistic optimism could be dangerous or unwise, the most disconcerting one concerns the question of physical health (Armor & Taylor, 2002). However, this line of research has consistently failed to obtain a significant relationship between optimistic expectations and risky health-related behavior. So, unrealistic optimism would appear to be generally adaptive. Yet, recent research (Hmieleski & Baron, 2009) in an important context in which there is considerable risk of failure—that of starting a new business—has revealed that *very* high levels of optimism in management is associated with poorer business outcomes (e.g., venture revenue and growth).

KEY POINTS

- Social comparison is a central means by which we evaluate ourselves. **Downward social comparison** refers to instances in which we compare to someone of lesser ability than ourselves. Such comparisons can be flattering.

- **Upward social comparisons,** in contrast, refer to instances in which we compare to someone who outperforms us in areas central to the self. People often compare their abilities to others who are similar to them in terms of broad social categories such as gender, race, or experience with a task.

- We often find people who outperform us to be threatening when we compare ourselves to them as individuals, but they are experienced more positively when we categorize ourselves and them together as members of the same group.

- Social comparison theory spawned two perspectives on the consequences of negative or upward social comparisons for the self: the **self-evaluation maintenance model** and **social identity theory.** When we are categorized at the individual level, we distance from a better-performing other, but when we are categorized at the social identity level, we distance from the poor-performing other.

- Most people show unrealistic optimism when it comes to their outcomes relative to others. Such positive illusions have been linked with various adaptive outcomes.

The Self as Target of Prejudice

Although the experience of not getting what you want is generally negative, how such undesirable outcomes is explained has important consequences for how people feel about themselves, and by extension, how people cope. As you saw in Chapter 3, attributions affect the meaning derived from events; as a result, some attributions for a negative outcome are more psychologically harmful than others, for example, they can cause depression and undermine self-esteem (Weiner, 1985). We now consider the emotional and behavioral consequences of perceiving the self as a target of prejudice.

Emotional Consequences: How Well-Being Can Suffer

Suppose you receive negative feedback about your performance on some task, or you receive some other type of undesirable outcome from another person. As illustrated in Figure 4.19, it is possible to make several different attributions for that unfavorable event, and different types of attributions have different emotional consequences. The worst possible attribution for psychological well-being is when the outcome is attributed to an aspect of yourself that you perceive as unchangeable—it is an internal and stable attribute that affects outcomes in many situations (e.g., you conclude your performance on this task means you're uniquely unintelligent for a college student). The next, slightly better attribution that can be made for that same outcome is an attribution to prejudice (e.g., you received a poor grade on the task because the grader is biased against your group). While prejudice can affect outcomes in quite a few situations, it is unlikely to be applicable across as many situations as being unintelligent. For this reason, making an attribution to prejudice is better for psychological well-being when such prejudice is thought to be rare compared to when prejudice may be encountered frequently (Schmitt, Branscombe, & Postmes, 2003). What is fundamentally important for whether psychological well-being will be harmed is how likely it is that you can expect to encounter discriminatory treatment in the future. True external attributions, which could reflect both stable (e.g., the other person is a jerk to everyone) and unstable (e.g., the other person is having a bad day, I had bad luck this time) causes

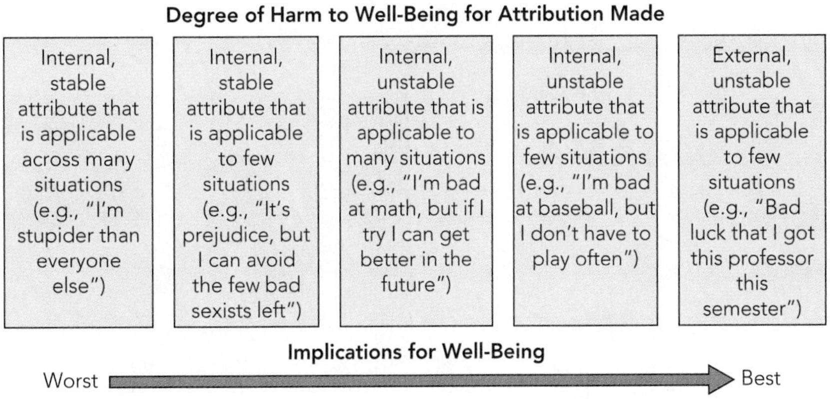

Degree of Harm to Well-Being for Attribution Made

| Internal, stable attribute that is applicable across many situations (e.g., "I'm stupider than everyone else") | Internal, stable attribute that is applicable to few situations (e.g., "It's prejudice, but I can avoid the few bad sexists left") | Internal, unstable attribute that is applicable to many situations (e.g., "I'm bad at math, but if I try I can get better in the future") | Internal, unstable attribute that is applicable to few situations (e.g., "I'm bad at baseball, but I don't have to play often") | External, unstable attribute that is applicable to few situations (e.g., "Bad luck that I got this professor this semester") |

Implications for Well-Being

Worst ➤ Best

FIGURE 4.19   Attributions for a Negative Outcome Differ in How Harmful They Are for Well-Being
As this figure illustrates, the worst attribution a person can make for a bad performance for well-being is that there is something unique about themselves that is stable and applicable to many situations. The best attribution—for well-being—will be that the outcome is due entirely to something external, is unstable, and is unlikely to be encountered again.

are the most likely to protect the attributor's self and well-being. All attributions for a negative outcome are not "equal" in terms of their implications for well-being.

Behavioral Consequences: Stereotype Threat Effects on Performance

Perceived prejudice not only affects psychological well-being; it can also interfere with our ability to acquire new skills. Several studies have found that when people fear that others will discover their devalued group membership, as might be the case for concealable stigmas (think of gays and lesbians in the military), such fear can negatively affect people's ability to learn and can affect performance (Frable, Blackstone, & Scherbaum, 1990; Lord & Saenz, 1985; Schmader, 2010).

How might these performance deficits in those with a stigmatized self be prevented? Research suggests that a critical issue is the extent to which people can affirm themselves in other ways. Martens, Johns, Greenberg, and Schimel (2006) examined whether first having people affirm their most valued attribute, perhaps a talent for art or another accomplishment, would eliminate cognitive deficits in those who were later reminded of their stigmatized group membership; this was exactly what they found. Thus, it is the extent to which a negative stereotype may define a person's entire worth that leads to underperformance, and reaffirming the individual's worth can provide protection.

Another important way that underperformance effects may be overcome is by making salient the stereotype-defying accomplishments of an important role model who shares one's stigmatized group membership. In a test of whether the Democratic nomination convention speech and subsequent election to the Presidency of Barack Obama could have a beneficial effect on African Americans' verbal test performance, Marx, Ko, and Friedman (2009) gave a random selection of Americans a difficult verbal test before and immediately after exposure to these accomplishments. While the test performance of whites and African Americans before the Democratic convention differed (with African Americans scoring less well than whites), after exposure to the achievements of a fellow famous ingroup member, African Americans' performance on this difficult verbal test improved; in fact, following Barack Obama's election, no racial difference in test performance was observed. So, making salient the stereotype-defying accomplishments of another person who shares one's stigmatized group, as shown in Figure 4.20, can powerfully counter vulnerability to performance deficits.

Stereotype threat, which is a particular kind of social identity threat, occurs when people believe they might be judged in light of a

stereotype threat
Can occur when people believe that they might be judged in light of a negative stereotype about their group or that, because of their performance, they may in some way confirm a negative stereotype of their group.

FIGURE 4.20 **The Stereotype-Defying Accomplishment of Another Who Shares One's Stigmatized Identity Improves Test Performance**
Research by Marx et al. (2009) found that making salient the achievements of a famous fellow ingroup member improved verbal test scores in a random sample of African Americans.

negative stereotype about their social identity or that they may inadvertently act in some way to confirm a negative stereotype of their group (Logel et al., 2009; Steele, 1997; Steele, Spencer, & Aronson, 2002). When people value their ability in a certain domain (e.g., math), but it is one in which their group is stereotyped as performing poorly (e.g., women), stereotype threat can occur. When those who are vulnerable to this threat are reminded in either an overt or subtle way that the stereotype might apply to them, then performance in that domain can be undermined. Consider the experience of the women engineering students studied by Logel et al. (2009). When these women were exposed to a sexist man, their subsequent performance on a math test was undermined, although their performance on an English test was unaffected. Interacting with the sexist man made their identity as women salient, and while trying to counteract this threat by suppressing thoughts of gender stereotypes, they inadvertently confirmed the stereotype about women's poor math ability.

Such stereotype threat effects are fairly difficult to control. For example, simply telling women before they take a math test that men do better on math than women do (Spencer, Steele, & Quinn, 1999) or having African Americans indicate their race before taking a difficult verbal test (Steele & Aronson, 1995) is sufficient to evoke stereotype threat and hurt their performance. Indeed, because women are negatively stereotyped as being worse at math than men, women tend to perform more poorly when they simply take a difficult math test in the presence of men, whereas they tend to perform better when the same test is taken only in the presence of other women (Inzlicht & Ben-Zeev, 2000).

Consider the dilemma of women who have taken a lot of math classes and who perceive math to be an important aspect of their self-concept. What if they also value their identity as women? When they find themselves exposed to information that suggests there are reliable sex differences in math ability, with men doing better than women, these women are likely to experience threat. How then do they manage to cope with such threat, without simultaneously distancing from either the domain or their group as a whole? Pronin, Steele, and Ross (2004) found that high math-identified women distanced themselves only from gender-stereotypic dimensions that are deemed to be incompatible with math success (e.g., leaving work to raise children, being flirtatious) but they did not do so for gender-stereotypic dimensions deemed to be irrelevant to math success (e.g., being empathic, being fashion conscious). Disidentification from aspects of their gender group occurred only in the stereotype threat condition but not when it was absent, suggesting it was a motivated process designed to alleviate the threat experienced.

Why do stereotype threat–based performance decrements occur? Some researchers suggest that anxiety is evoked in women, African Americans, and Latinos when their group membership is portrayed as predictive of poor performance (Osborne, 2001). As a result of such anxiety, their actual performance on the relevant test is disrupted. Some studies have, however, failed to find increased self-reported anxiety among stigmatized group members experiencing stereotype threat (Aronson et al., 1999). This could be because members of stigmatized groups are reluctant to admit their feelings of anxiety, or it may be that they do not actually realize they are feeling anxious so they cannot accurately report those feelings.

Research that has examined nonverbal measures of anxiety illustrates how anxiety does play a crucial role in stereotype threat effects. In a clever test of the hypothesis that anxiety causes stereotype threat performance deficits, Bosson, Haymovitz, and Pinel (2004) first either reminded or did not remind gay and straight participants of their category membership before videotaping their interactions with young children in a nursery school. Participants were first asked to indicate their sexual orientation on a form just before they interacted with the children. After this subtle reminder that their sexual orientation group is stereotyped as one that is dangerous to children, the gay participants' childcare skills (as rated by judges unaware of the hypotheses and procedure) suffered compared to when they were not so reminded of their category membership and its associated stereotype. This same group membership reminder had no effect on the straight participants because there is no associated stereotype of danger to children. Consequently, straight participants were not at risk of potentially confirming a negative stereotype in the performance situation they faced.

Was increased anxiety in the gay men the cause of the reduction in their rated childcare skills? On standard self-report measures of anxiety and evaluation apprehension, the answer would seem to be no—Bosson et al. (2004) did not obtain differences in these self-reports as a function of either sexual orientation or stereotype threat condition. Importantly, however, independent judges' ratings of nonverbal anxiety—as indicated by various behaviors indicating discomfort during the interaction with the children—were affected by sexual orientation and stereotype threat. Among the gay men who were reminded of their category membership, their anxiety was discernible in their nonverbal behavior compared to the gay men who were not experiencing stereotype threat. That is, although the gay men experiencing stereotype threat did not rate themselves as more anxious, they were visibly more fidgety, they averted their eyes more, and otherwise exhibited signs of discomfort more than gay men not experiencing stereotype threat. And, this nonverbal anxiety disrupted their interactions with the children. However, among heterosexual men, reminders of their category membership tended to result in fewer nonverbal symptoms of anxiety compared to when their category was not made relevant.

Is it only for groups that are historically devalued in the culture as a whole that stereotype threat effects have been observed? No. Such effects occur with men, who are not a devalued group as a whole but who are stereotyped as being less emotional than women (Leyens, Desert, Croizet, & Darcis, 2000). When men were reminded of the stereotype concerning their emotional deficits, their performance on a task requiring them to identify emotions suffered. In an even more dramatic way, Stone, Lynch, Sjomeling, and Darley (1999) illustrated a similar point. They found that stereotype threat effects can occur among dominant group members as long as their group is expected to perform less favorably than the comparison group. In their research, white men who expected to be compared to African American men performed more poorly on an athletic performance task when they believed it reflected "natural athletic ability." The reverse occurred when white men believed the exact same task reflected "sports intelligence," which is a dimension on which they expect to excel as compared with African American men. Likewise, although there is no stereotype that whites perform poorly on math, when they are threatened by a potentially negative comparison to Asians who are stereotyped as performing better than whites, then they show math performance deficiencies (Aronson et al., 1999). Thus expecting to do poorly in comparison to another group can undermine performance, even in members of historically advantaged groups. While we examine related issues on the effects of stereotyping on its targets in Chapter 6, the research we have reviewed here on stereotype threat effects illustrates the importance of group membership for the experience of threat to the self, and how such threat can easily disrupt performance.

KEYPOINTS

- Emotional responses to a negative outcome received by the self depend on the attribution made for it. Some attributions have more negative implications for well-being than others.

- When outcomes are attributed to unchanging aspects of the self that have implications for outcomes in many

situations, well-being will be worse than when attributions are made to something external to the self that is unstable. When prejudice is seen as pervasive, then well-being will be harmed more than if it is seen as isolated or rare.

- The fear of being found out by others in terms of having a negatively valued group identity can disrupt performance. Affirming another aspect of the self or exposure to a stereotype-defying role model who shares one's stigma can result in improved performance.

- **Stereotype threat** effects occur in capable people in a domain they value. They have been observed in historically devalued group members (African Americans, women) and in dominant groups (whites, men) when they believe they might negatively compare on an important dimension with members of another group.

- Stereotype threat effects are difficult to control, and they can be induced easily. Simply requiring people to

indicate their group membership before taking a test in a domain in which they are vulnerable is enough to undermine performance.

- When people experience stereotype threat, they can distance themselves from the negative part of the stereotype about one's group.

- Anxiety appears to be one mechanism by which stereotype threat effects occur. However, self-report measures of anxiety often fail to reveal its importance, although nonverbal indicators of anxiety do predict performance disruption.

SUMMARY *and* REVIEW

- Sometimes close others can be better at predicting our behavior than we ourselves are. That is because observers and actors attend to different behavioral features. Sometimes people put information about themselves on the Web that observers see as accurate. People who are initially shy and low in social skills prefer interacting via Facebook and other social networking sites. Such experience can improve social skills, and this improvement transfers to their subsequent offline social interactions.

- We face many audiences and how we present ourselves to others can vary. We might attempt to engage in **self-promotion**—present our most favorable self-aspects—on some occasions and on others we may be motivated to present ourselves in ways that induce others to agree with our own self-views. That is, we may engage in **self-verification,** even if it means having others agree with the negative qualities we believe we possess. We may also create a favorable self-presentation by using **ingratiation** tactics that convey respect for others.

- Self-knowledge is sought through two primary methods: **introspection** and considering ourselves from others' vantage point. Introspection is tricky because we often don't have conscious access to the emotional factors that affect our behavioral choices, or to what actually brings happiness. We also may have difficulty predicting how we will feel in the future because we neglect to consider other events that will also occur besides the focal ones considered. When we think of ourselves by taking an observer's perspective, we see the self in more trait terms and less responsive to situations, as observers do.

- How we think about ourselves varies depending on where we are on a **personal-versus-social identity continuum** at any given moment in time. At the personal identity level we can think of ourselves in terms of attributes that differentiate ourselves from other individuals, and therefore will be based on **intragroup comparison.** At the **social identity** level, perceptions of ourselves are based on attributes that are shared with other group members; perception of the self at the social identity level stems from **intergroup comparison** processes.

- Self-definitions can vary across situations, with each being valid predictors of behavior in those settings. How we conceptualize ourselves can also depend on how others expect us to be and how we believe they will treat us. Across time, Americans have increasingly come to define themselves in terms of individualistic traits. Context shifts that change whether or not we define ourselves in terms of our gender can result in gender differences in **self-construal** appearing or disappearing. What aspect of the self is influential at any moment in time depends on context, distinctiveness of the attribute, importance of the identity, and how others refer to us.

- Different aspects of the self may be salient when a selection is made and when it is experienced or consumed. Dissatisfaction and regret are higher when the self aspects are inconsistent with each other when the choice is made and when it is experienced.

- When other people reject us because of some aspect of our identity, people often rebel against those doing the rejecting and make that feature even more self-defining. Today, people who get body piercings and tattoos are attempting to communicate their difference from the "mainstream."

- Other future **possible selves,** besides who we are currently, can motivate us to attempt self-change. Role models can represent future possible selves that we can attain. When people compare their present self to their past self, the further in the past that self is, the more we downgrade it relative to our present self. This approach to **autobiographical memory** allows us to feel good about our current self. Dreaded possible selves can lead us to give up certain behaviors (e.g., smoking), while desired possible selves can lead us to work long hours to attain them.

- **Self-control** is necessary if we are to forego immediate pleasures in exchange for long-term goals. How the self is construed affects our ability to resist temptation. Self-control may be a resource that can be temporarily used up—**ego-depletion**—which makes it more difficult to self-regulate. Subsequent self-control can be more difficult when the initial control effort was longer, when no rest period is given, or when people lack training in self-regulation.

- How we feel about ourselves can be assessed directly and explicitly, as well as with more implicit or indirect methods. Both explicit and implicit measures of **self-esteem** are responsive to life events. Positive self-talk (thinking about how "I'm a lovable person") can backfire and reduce mood and happiness with the self in low self-esteem people.

- High self-esteem comes with risks. It is correlated with an increased likelihood of interpersonal aggression, which appears to be in response to the greater need to defend one's superior self-view. Thus, while there are clear benefits to high self-esteem, there appears to be also a downside.

- Women do, on average, have lower self-esteem than men. This is particularly the case in nations where women do not participate in the labor force, and in the United States among middle-class and lower-class women who work in environments in which gender-based devaluation is most frequent.

- **Social comparison** is a vital means by which we judge ourselves. **Upward social comparisons** at the personal level can be painful, and **downward social comparisons** at this level of identity can be comforting. The reverse is true when one's social identity is salient—we dislike another ingroup member who performs poorly but respond positively to an ingroup member who performs better than us because that person makes our group look good.

- Most people show self-serving biases, such as the **above-average effect,** where we see ourselves more positively (and less negatively) than we see most other people. We consistently hold positive illusions about ourselves and are unrealistically optimistic about our ability to avoid negative outcomes. Americans' optimistic expectations for themselves have been rising. Such unrealistic optimism is, however, predictive of positive mental and physical health.

- Attributions for negative outcomes can differ in their implications for psychological well-being. When the self is seen as a target of pervasive discrimination, it is more harmful for self-esteem than when it is seen as reflecting an isolated outcome.

- **Stereotype threat** effects can occur in historically devalued groups when they are simply reminded of their group membership and fear they might confirm negative stereotypes about their group. Stereotype threat can undermine performance in dominant group members as well, when they fear a negative comparison with members of another group that is expected to outperform them. This undermining of performance only occurs on dimensions relevant to the stereotype. Stereotype threat performance decrements can be prevented by (1) affirming the self in another way, (2) exposure to a stereotype-defying role model, and (3) distancing from aspects of the stereotype that are incompatible with high performance. Anxiety, at least nonverbal indicators of it, appears to play a role in the emergence of stereotype threat–based performance deficits.

- Members of any group can be vulnerable to performing less favorably when a salient comparison group is expected to perform better at a task. Stereotype threat research reveals how our group memberships can affect our self-concepts and performance on tasks we care deeply about.

KEY TERMS

above average effect (p. 129)

autobiographical memory (p. 119)

downward social comparison (p. 127)

ego-depletion (p. 121)

implicit self-esteem (p. 122)

ingratiation (p. 109)

intergroup comparisons (p. 114)

intragroup comparisons (p. 114)

introspection (p. 111)

personal-versus-social identity continuum (p. 114)

possible selves (p. 120)

salience (p. 114)

self-construal (p. 116)

self-control (p. 120)

self-deprecating (p. 109)

self-esteem (p. 122)

self-evaluation maintenance model (p. 128)

self-promotion (p. 109)

self-verification perspective (p. 109)

social capital (p. 108)

social comparison theory (p. 127)

social identity theory (p. 114)

stereotype threat (p. 132)

upward social comparison (p. 127)

CHAPTER 5

Attitudes

Evaluating and Responding to the Social World

W HAT IS THE BASIS OF PEOPLE'S ATTITUDES TOWARD President Barack Obama? Might how people feel about him affect what they believe about him? What if an attitude is formed based on beliefs that are "disproven"? Let's consider these questions in terms of an issue we hear about frequently in the blogs, as well as legitimate news outlets—is President Obama a Muslim? In analyzing attitudes toward President Obama, the Pew Research Center reports that, as of August 2010, 18 percent of the U.S. population believes that Obama is a Muslim, a new high. How does such a belief get formed? And why does that belief, despite attempts to deny or correct it, apparently have such staying power?

First of all, Obama's well-known personal history has some unusual features. He was born in 1961 in Hawaii to a white American mother, but his biological father was a Muslim from Kenya. Although Obama had little contact with his father during his childhood, the young Barack lived for 4 years with his mother and stepfather in Indonesia, which is the largest Muslim country in the world. For these reasons, people might expect that Obama was introduced early on to the teachings of Islam. On the other hand, when Barack was 10 years old he returned to Hawaii to live with his Christian grandparents, and after that he attended universities on the mainland. As an adult, Obama and his wife went to church and had a close relationship for 20 years with Jeremiah Wright, a Christian preacher in Chicago, although amazingly some say he did this while simultaneously (and secretly) attending a mosque!

The idea that beliefs persist, and continue to be held onto by people—even when strong disconfirmation is provided—is not a new issue to social psychologists. Leon Festinger and colleagues, in their 1956 book, *When Prophecy Fails,* provides us with an inside look at this seeming mystery. In this early investigation of attitudes, Festinger describes a certain Mrs. Keech, a Utah woman of deep faith, who believed that the world was going to end on the morning of December 21, 1954. Festinger details his realization that there was very little that could displace either the woman's or her followers' ardent belief that, indeed, the end of the world was nigh.

This early research revealed several characteristics that are likely to cause people to ignore disconfirming evidence (factual evidence that proves a strongly held belief to be wrong). One such characteristic illustrates our true believer situation rather

139

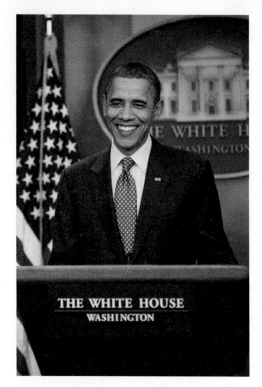

FIGURE 5.1   How Are Attitudes Toward President Barack Obama Formed?

Do our beliefs (cognitions) shape our attitudes (feelings)? Or, is it the other way around—do our feelings shape our beliefs? Do attitudes change when we are confronted with information that disconfirms our beliefs, or are those beliefs likely to be maintained to the extent that we can find others who share those beliefs?

perfectly: If Mrs. Keech could convince others of her basic premise, then the magnitude of her discomfort following disconfirmation of her belief would be reduced. Indeed, these researchers found that the inevitable disconfirmation of the belief that the world would end was followed by an enthusiastic effort at proselytizing others to join her group. If true believers can find others who provide social support by sharing their beliefs, then the pain of exposure to disconfirming evidence is lessened. As we discuss in this chapter, there is considerable evidence that people hold beliefs that help them make sense of their emotions, even in the face of evidence that strongly disconfirms those beliefs (Boden & Berenbaum, 2010).

Nowadays, with the aid of the Internet, attitude formation can be facilitated from the beginning by the knowledge that other people share one's beliefs. People on the Internet can find each other and begin to build up a store of "evidence" such as Obama's father's religion or his early years in Indonesia, which they collectively agree points to Obama's Muslim identity, even if that evidence is circumstantial at best. And, when additional facts point to Obama's Christian faith, true believers are likely to embrace their belief in his Muslim identity even more strongly! That is, disconfirming evidence can fuel true believers' adherence to their belief, and sharing it with others can further cement that belief in place (see Figure 5.1).

In this chapter we explore the factors that shape the attitudes we hold, and address the key question of whether our attitudes are simply a product of rational thought. We consider how other people affect the attitudes we form, and what happens when we react against their attempts to influence us. How people respond to explicit attempts to persuade them is a complicated issue involving several different processes. We consider when, for example, people closely scrutinize the arguments presented in a message and when communicator credibility is not closely examined (see Figure 5.2 for an amusing take on this issue). We also address the important issue of when and how we manage to persuade ourselves—why our behavior can lead us to change our own attitudes. Along the way we consider whether all attitudes are equal, or if some attitudes are more strongly linked to behavior than others. Lastly, we examine the process by which our attitudes guide our behavior.

Social psychologists use the term **attitude** to refer to people's *evaluation* of almost any aspect of the world (e.g., Olson & Kendrick, 2008; Petty, Wheeler, & Tormala, 2003). People can have favorable or unfavorable reactions to issues, ideas, objects, actions (do you like white water rafting), a specific person (such as Barack Obama) or entire social groups (Muslims). Some attitudes are quite stable and resistant to change, whereas others may be unstable and show considerable variability depending on the situation (Schwarz & Bohner, 2001). We may hold some attitudes with great certainty, while our attitudes toward other objects or issues may be relatively unclear or uncertain (Tormala & Rucker, 2007).

What is *your* attitude toward the legalization of marijuana, an issue currently on the agenda of many state legislatures—(see Figure 5.3)? Is your attitude toward marijuana

attitude
Evaluation of various aspects of the social world

likely to depend on whether you have used it or not? Later in this chapter we consider how our own actions can influence our attitudes (Maio & Thomas, 2007). Does it matter whether you think other people see its use as acceptable or not? What role does consensus—the extent to which we see others as sharing our attitudes—have on the attitudes we hold? Does the fact that this is an issue undergoing social change (see the map of U.S. states that have already or are currently considering legalizing marijuana in Figure 5.3) mean that many people's attitudes are likely to be unstable and subject to change? Does the purpose or how marijuana legalization messages are framed—for the treatment of medical problems or recreational use—matter for the attitudes people hold?

The study of attitudes is central to the field of social psychology because attitudes are capable of coloring virtually every aspect of our

FIGURE 5.2   Why Do So Many People Seem to Agree with This Erroneous Belief?
Public opinion polls in 2010 indicate that 18 percent of the U.S. population agrees with the belief that "President Obama is a Muslim." As this cartoon suggests, perhaps the credibility of the people who support this view should be more closely examined!

experience. Even when we do not have strong attitudes toward a specific issue such as the legalization of marijuana, related values can influence what attitudes we form. Let's consider public attitudes toward various scientific issues, specifically the use of human embryonic stem cells. Research findings indicate that attitudes toward such novel issues are shaped by long-term values—religious beliefs predict the formation of these new attitudes—rather than the extent to which the public possesses scientific knowledge on the topic (Ho, Brossard, & Scheufele, 2008). As we saw in Chapter 2, the tendency to evaluate stimuli as positive or negative—something we favor or are against—appears to be an initial step in our efforts to make sense out of the world. In fact, such reactions occur almost immediately, even before we can fully integrate a new stimulus into our previous experience. Responding to a stimulus in terms of our attitudes—on an immediately evaluative basis—produces different brain wave activity than when a response is made on a nonevaluative basis (Crites & Cacioppo, 1996). Our brains operate differently depending on whether we are engaged in rapid evaluative perception or a more thoughtful examination of our world.

In addition, attitudes can influence our thoughts, even if they are not always reflected in our overt behavior. Moreover, while many of our attitudes are **explicit attitudes**—conscious and reportable—other attitudes may be **implicit attitudes**—uncontrollable and perhaps not consciously accessible to us. Consider this explicit versus implicit attitudes distinction as it applies to racial attitudes. Many "color-blind" or self-perceived egalitarian Americans will report positive explicit attitudes toward African Americans. However, they may also display negative involuntary evaluative reactions toward African Americans—implicit attitudes—because it is almost impossible to grow up in the United States without acquiring such negative racial associations (Fazio & Olson, 2003). Furthermore, such implicit attitudes have consequences for important outcomes such as juror decision making when the defendant is African American (Goff, Eberhardt, Williams, & Jackson, 2008).

While social psychologists can learn people's attitudes about many objects from their conscious reports of the thoughts and feelings they have about them, another approach is required if we want to learn someone's implicit attitudes—that is, attitudes they may be either unwilling or unable to report. A method for assessing these is the *Implicit Association Test* (IAT; Greenwald, McGhee, & Schwarz, 1998). The IAT is based on the fact that we

explicit attitudes
Consciously accessible attitudes that are controllable and easy to report.

implicit attitudes
Unconscious associations between objects and evaluative responses.

may associate various social objects more or less readily with positive or negative descriptive words. When there is a close association between a social group—say, Canadians—and some evaluative word such as "polite," one's reaction in identifying this connection is faster than if the social object was paired with a word that one did not readily associate with Canadians, perhaps "rude." Quicker reactions to positive objects and one social group over another can reflect differential valuing of that group. Consider the gender gap in wages that continues to exist today. Might it be that this is due, in part, to the valued attribute of "money" being automatically associated with men versus women? Recent research by Williams, Paluck, and Spencer-Rodgers (2010) using the IAT obtained evidence that male references (e.g., man, son, husband) were automatically associated with wealth-related terms (e.g., rich, cash, paycheck) as indicated by faster response latencies to those pairings than with female references (e.g., mother, aunt, daughter). If you dare, the website http://implicit.harvard.edu/implicit offers a wide-ranging set of IATs about groups that you can take to learn your implicit attitudes about those groups.

Before doing so, though, consider one warning: Although the IAT is viewed by some investigators as an important way to "get inside your head," a criticism that has been leveled at this test is that it really assesses commonly known connections between social groups and various adjectives, even though the respondent might not actually endorse the validity of those connections. That is, one might be fully aware of a common negative stereotype regarding a particular social group, but not personally concur with that negative belief. Consider the possibility raised by Arkes and Tetlock (2004). Because well-known African American leader Jesse Jackson is likely to have knowledge of the negative stereotypic attributes associated with African Americans—he might

Legalized states   States considering legalized medical marijuana   Non-legalized states

FIGURE 5.3   Marijuana Attitudes: To Support Legalization or Not

As of 2010, 15 U.S. states have legalized the use of marijuana for medical purposes, and another 15 states are considering legislation to do so. What factors influence people's attitudes toward this substance?

"fail" the IAT! That is, this measure might indicate that he holds negative attitudes toward his own group, African Americans. This implies that such implicit measures may be assessing familiarity with the culture rather than an individual's *actual* attitudes. Moreover, research has revealed that the IAT is susceptible to deliberate faking (Fiedler, Messner, & Bluemke, 2006) and that it becomes easier to do so as people gain experience with the IAT (Blair, 2002). Thus, the meaning of IAT scores remains controversial (Gawronski, LeBel, & Peters, 2007). Taken together, though, it is clear from a meta-analytic review of research on implicit and explicit attitudes that they reflect distinct evaluations of the world around us, and implicit attitudes can predict some behaviors better than explicit attitude measures (Greenwald, Poehlman, Uhlmann, & Banaji, 2009).

Another reason that social psychologists view attitudes as important is that they *do* often affect our behavior. This is especially likely to be true when attitudes are strong and accessible (Ajzen, 2001; Bizer, Tormala, Rucker, & Petty, 2006; Fazio, 2000). What is your attitude toward Bristol Palin and Paris Hilton? If positive, you may enjoy hearing about events in their lives on *Entertainment Tonight* as shown in Figure 5.4. Do you like reality TV? If so, we might safely predict that you will probably choose to watch *Survivor*, *Sarah Palin's Alaska*, *Dancing with the Stars*, or *The Apprentice*.

FIGURE 5.4   Attitudes Toward Celebrities Predict Behaviors Reflecting Interest in Their Lives
When people hold positive attitudes toward particular celebrities (from left to right: Bristol Palin and Paris Hilton), they are likely to enjoy hearing about events in their lives, follow their postings on twitter, and generally attend to information about them.

Because attitudes can also affect important behavioral choices that have long-term consequences, it is important to understand how thought processes influence attitude-based decision making. Suppose you receive an e-mail from your student health services office encouraging you to get the flu shot this fall in order to ward off potentially catching the flu in the future? What factors are likely to influence your choice to do so or not? Because people differ in the extent to which they give weight to future consequences when they make such decisions, this might affect how information about getting vaccinated is processed and therefore attitude-based decisions. Morison, Cozzolino, and Orbell (2010) proposed the model shown in Figure 5.5 where considering future consequences should lead to more positive thoughts about a message concerning the vaccine's benefits and risks, and these thoughts should predict attitudes toward the vaccine. To test their model, these investigators first assessed parents' tendencies to consider future consequences of their decisions, and then gave them

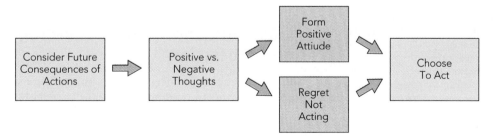

FIGURE 5.5   Factors That Influence Attitudes and Medical Decision-Making
People who consider the future consequences of their actions reported more positive than negative thoughts about a vaccine after reading balanced information about its potential benefits and risks, and this predicted their attitudes about the vaccine and the extent to which regret for not acting was anticipated—which then predicted the decision to have their daughter vaccinated for the human papilloma virus (an important cause of cervical cancer in adult women). (Source: Based on research by Morison, Cozzolino, & Orbell, 2010).

balanced information concerning the benefits and risks of agreeing to have their daughters vaccinated for the human papilloma virus (which causes cervical cancer in women). After reading the information about the virus and vaccine, parents listed their thoughts about it, which were later coded as positive or negative. Then, attitudes toward the vaccine were measured, as was anticipated regret if they did not have their daughter vaccinated and she gets the virus in the future. Finally, the parents' agreement to have their daughter vaccinated was assessed. Results supported the model: Parents who think more about future consequences of their actions generated more positive thoughts (relative to negative thoughts) about the vaccination, which in turn predicted more positive attitudes toward the vaccine and greater anticipated regret of not doing so—and these both fed into choosing to have their daughter vaccinated within the next year. So, sometimes attitudes are formed on the basis of careful consideration of the information and, once those attitudes are formed, they can predict behavior in important domains such as medical decision making.

In this chapter, we consider many influences on *attitude formation*. After doing so, we consider in-depth a question we have already raised: When do attitudes influence behavior and when do they not? Then, we turn to the important question of how attitudes are changed—the process of *persuasion*. We also examine some reasons *why* attitudes are often resistant to change. Finally, we consider the intriguing fact that on some occasions our own actions shape our attitudes rather than vice versa. The process that underlies such effects is known as *cognitive dissonance*, and it has fascinating implications not just for attitude change, but for many aspects of social behavior as well.

Attitude Formation: How Attitudes Develop

How do you feel about each of the following: people who cover their bodies in tattoos, telemarketers, the TV programs *Modern Family*, *Lost*, and *Lie to Me*, sushi, the police, dancing, cats, and people who talk on their cell phones while driving? Most people have attitudes about these issues and objects. But where, precisely, did these views come from? Did you acquire them as a result of your own experiences with each, from other people with whom you have had personal contact, or through exposure via the media? Are your attitudes toward these objects constant across time, or are they flexible and likely to change as conditions do? One important means by which our attitudes develop is through the process of **social learning.** In other words, many of our views are acquired in situations where we interact with others, or simply observe their behavior. Such learning occurs through several processes, which are outlined below.

Classical Conditioning: Learning Based on Association

It is a basic principle of psychology that when a stimulus that is capable of evoking a response—the **unconditioned stimulus**—regularly precedes another neutral stimulus, the one that occurs first can become a signal for the second—the **conditioned stimulus.** Advertisers and other persuasion agents have considerable expertise in using this principle to create positive attitudes toward their products. Although tricky in the details, it is actually a fairly straightforward method for creating attitudes. First, you need to know what your potential audience already responds positively toward (what to use as the unconditioned stimulus). If you are marketing a new beer, and your target audience is young adult males, you might safely assume that attractive young women will produce a positive response. Second, you need to pair your product repeatedly (the formerly neutral or conditioned stimulus—say, your beer logo) with images of beautiful women and,

social learning
The process through which we acquire new information, forms of behavior, or attitudes from other people.

classical conditioning
A basic form of learning in which one stimulus, initially neutral, acquires the capacity to evoke reactions through repeated pairing with another stimulus. In a sense, one stimulus becomes a signal for the presentation or occurrence of the other.

unconditioned stimulus
A stimulus that evokes a positive or negative response without substantial learning.

conditioned stimulus
The stimulus that comes to stand for or signal a prior unconditioned stimulus.

before long, positive attitudes will be formed toward your new beer! As shown in Figure 5.6, many alcohol manufacturers have used this principle to beneficially affect sales of its product.

Such classical conditioning can affect attitudes via two pathways: the direct and indirect route (Sweldens, van Osselaer, & Janiszewski, 2010). The more generally effective and typical method used—*the direct route*—can be seen in the advertisement. That is, positive stimuli (e.g., lots of *different* women) are repeatedly paired with the product, with the aim being to directly transfer the affect felt toward them to the brand. However, by pairing a *specific* celebrity endorser who is already liked by the target audience with the new brand, a memory link between the two can be established. In this case—the indirect route—the idea is that following repeatedly presenting that specific celebrity with the product, then whenever that celebrity is thought of, the product too will come to mind. Think here of Michael Jordan; does Nike come to mind more rapidly for you? For this indirect conditioning process to work, people need not be aware that this memory link is being formed, but they do need to feel positively toward the uncon-ditioned stimulus—that is, that particular celebrity (Stahl, Unkelbach, & Corneille, 2009). Figure 5.7 presents a recent example of this indirect conditioning approach and advertising.

FIGURE 5.6   Classical Conditioning of Attitudes—The Direct Route
Initially people may be neutral toward this brand's label. However after repeatedly pairing this product's logo with an "unconditioned stimulus" of various women who are attractive to the targeted group of young males, seeing the beer logo may come to elicit positive attitudes on its own.

Not only can classical conditioning contribute to shaping our atti-tudes—it can do so even though we are not aware of the stimuli that serve as the basis for this kind of conditioning. For instance, in one experiment (Krosnick, Betz, Jussim, & Lynn, 1992), students saw photos of a stranger engaged in routine daily activities such as shopping in a grocery store or walking into her apartment. While these photos were shown, other pho-tos known to induce either positive or negative feelings were exposed for very brief periods of time—so brief that participants were not aware of their presence. Participants who were nonconsciously exposed to photos that induced positive feelings (e.g., a newlywed couple, people playing cards and laughing) liked the stranger better than participants who had been exposed to photos that nonconsciously induce negative feelings (e.g., open-heart surgery, a werewolf). Even though participants were not aware that they had been exposed to the second group of photos because they were presented very briefly, the photos did significantly influence the attitudes that were formed toward the stranger. Those exposed to the positive photos reported more favorable attitudes toward this person than those exposed to the negative photos. These findings suggest that atti-tudes can be influenced by **subliminal conditioning**—classical conditioning that occurs in the absence of conscious awareness of the stimuli involved.

Indeed, **mere exposure**—having seen an object before, but too rapidly to remember having seen it—can result in attitude formation (Bornstein & D'Agostino, 1992). We know that this is a case of subliminal con-ditioning because patients with advanced Alzheimer's disease—who therefore cannot remember seeing the stimuli—show evidence of having formed new attitudes as a result of mere exposure (Winograd, Goldstein, Monarch, Peluso, & Goldman, 1999). It is also the case that even when we can remember being exposed to information, its mere repetition creates

FIGURE 5.7   Classical Conditioning of Attitudes—The Indirect Route
The manufacturers of these watches hope that by repeatedly pairing Tiger Woods with their product, a memory link between that celebrity and the product will be created. If the link formed in memory is sufficiently strong, then whenever consumers think of that celebrity, their watch brand name will come to mind.

a sense of familiarity and results in more positive attitudes. Moons, Mackie, and Garcia-Marques (2009) refer to this as the **illusion of truth effect.** The studies by these researchers revealed that more positive attitudes developed following exposure to *either* weak or strong arguments—as long as little detailed message processing occurred. Although this has substantial implications for the likely impact of advertising on the attitudes we form—as a result of merely hearing the message repeated—it is good to know that this effect *can* be overcome when people are motivated to and able to process extensively the message.

Once formed, such attitudes can influence behavior—even when those attitudes are inconsistent with how we are explicitly expected to behave. Consider the child whose attitudes toward an ethnic or religious group such as Arabs or Muslims have been classically conditioned to be negative, and who later are placed in a classroom where such negative attitudes are non-normative (i.e., they are deemed unacceptable). Research conducted in Switzerland by Falomir-Pichastor, Munoz-Rojas, Invernizzi, and Mugny (2004) has revealed that, as shown in Figure 5.8, when the norms are anti-discriminatory, if feelings of threat from that "outsider" group are low, then the expression of prejudice can be reduced. When, however, feelings of threat are high, then the child is likely to continue to show prejudice even when the norms are anti-discriminatory. This research illustrates that only when threat is absent are attempts to change negative responses effective using explicit norms.

Instrumental Conditioning: Rewards for the "Right" Views

When we asked you earlier to think about your attitudes toward marijuana, some of you may have thought immediately "Oh, that's wrong!" This is because most children have been repeatedly praised or rewarded by their parents and teachers ("just say no" programs) for stating such views. As a result, individuals learn which views are seen as the "correct" attitudes to hold—because of the rewards received for voicing those attitudes by the people they identify with and want to be accepted by. Attitudes that are followed by positive outcomes tend to be strengthened and are likely to be repeated, whereas attitudes that are followed by negative outcomes are weakened so their likelihood of being expressed again is reduced. Thus, another way in which attitudes are acquired is through the process of **instrumental conditioning**—differential rewards and punishments. Sometimes the conditioning process is rather subtle, with the reward being psychological acceptance—by rewarding children with smiles, approval, or hugs for stating the "right" views. Because of this form of conditioning, until the teen years—when peer influences become especially strong—most children express political, religious, and social views that are highly similar to those of their parents and other family members (Oskamp & Schultz, 2005).

What happens when we find ourselves in a new context where our prior attitudes may or may not be supported? Part of the college experience involves leaving behind our families and high school friends and entering new **social networks**—sets of individuals with whom we interact on a regular basis (Eaton, Majka, & Visser, 2008). The new networks (e.g., new sorority or fraternity) we find ourselves in may contain individuals who share our attitudes toward important social issues, or they may be composed of individuals holding diverse and diverging attitudes toward

subliminal conditioning
Classical conditioning of attitudes by exposure to stimuli that are below individuals' threshold of conscious awareness.

mere exposure
By having seen before, but not necessarily remembering having done so, attitudes toward an object can be formed.

illusion of truth effect
The mere repetition of information creates a sense of familiarity and more positive attitudes.

instrumental conditioning
A basic form of learning in which responses that lead to positive outcomes or which permit avoidance of negative outcomes are strengthened.

social networks
Composed of individuals with whom we have interpersonal relationships and interact with on a regular basis.

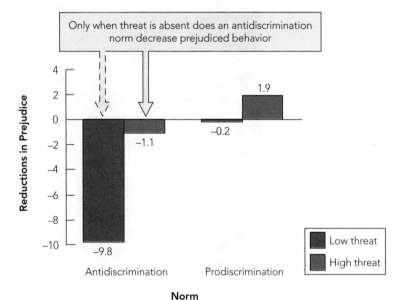

FIGURE 5.8   Feelings of Threat Can Result in Prejudiced Action, Even When Norms Are Anti-Discriminatory

In this study, an anti-discrimination norm against showing prejudice toward foreigners was only effective at reducing favoritism toward members of their own group when people were feeling little threat. But, if a pro-discrimination norm is present, people discriminate by showing favoritism toward their own group members regardless of feelings of threat. (Source: Based on research by Falomir-Pichastor, Munoz-Rojas, Invernizzi, & Mugny, 2004).

those issues. Do new attitudes form as we enter new networks in order to garner rewards from agreeing with others who are newly important to us? To investigate this issue, Levitan and Visser (2009) assessed the political attitudes of students at the University of Chicago when they arrived on campus and determined over the course of the next 2 months the networks the students became part of, and how close the students felt toward each new network member. This allowed the researchers to determine the effect of attitude diversity among these new peers on students' political attitudes. Those students who entered networks with more diverse attitudes toward affirmative action exhibited greater change in their attitudes over the 2-month period. These results suggest that new social networks can be quite influential—particularly when they introduce new strong arguments not previously encountered (Levitan & Visser, 2008). The desire to fit in with others and be rewarded for holding the same attitudes can be a powerful motivator of attitude formation and change.

It is also the case that people may be consciously aware that different groups they are members of will reward (or punish) them for expressing support for particular attitude positions. Rather than being influenced to change our attitudes, we may find ourselves expressing one view on a topic to one audience and another view to a different audience. Indeed, as the cartoon in Figure 5.9 suggests, elections are sometimes won or lost on a candidate's success at delivering the right view to the right audience! Fortunately, for most of us, not only is our every word not recorded, with the possibility of those words being replayed to another audience with a different view, but our potentially incompatible audiences tend to remain physically separated. What this means is that we are less likely than politicians to be caught expressing different attitudes to different audiences!

One way that social psychologists assess the extent to which people's reported attitudes depend on the expected audience is by varying who might learn of their attitude position. For example, people seeking membership in a fraternity or sorority (e.g., pledges) express different attitudes about other fraternities and sororities depending on whether they believe their attitudes will remain private or they think that the powerful members of their group who will be controlling their admittance will learn of the attitude position they advocated (Noel, Wann, & Branscombe, 1995). When those who are attempting to gain membership in an organization believe that other members will learn of "their attitudes," they derogate other fraternities or sororities as a means of communicating to decision makers that the particular organization they want to be admitted to is seen as the most desirable. Yet, when they believe their attitude responses will be private, they do not derogate other fraternities or sororities. Thus, both the attitudes we form and our attitude expression can depend on the rewards we have received in the past and those we expect to receive in the future for expressing particular attitudes.

"Good God! He's giving the white-collar voters' speech to the blue collars."

FIGURE 5.9   Expressing Different Attitudes to Different Audiences
To gain rewards, politicians often tailor their message to match those of their audience. Disaster can strike when the wrong audience gets the wrong message!

Observational Learning: Learning by Exposure to Others

A third means by which attitudes are formed can operate even when direct rewards for acquiring or expressing those attitudes are absent. This process is **observational learning,** and it occurs when individuals acquire attitudes or behaviors simply by observing others (Bandura, 1997). For example, people acquire attitudes toward many topics and objects by exposure to advertising—where we see "people like us" or "people like we want to become" acting positively or negatively toward different kinds of objects or issues. Just think how much observational learning most of us are doing as we watch television!

Why do people often adopt the attitudes that they hear others express, or acquire the behaviors they observe in others? One answer involves the mechanism of **social comparison**—our tendency to compare ourselves with others in order to determine whether our view of social reality is correct or not (Festinger, 1954). That is, to the extent that our views agree with those of others, we tend to conclude that our ideas and attitudes are accurate; after all, if others hold the same views, these views *must* be right! But are we equally likely to adopt all others' attitudes, or does it depend on our relationship to those others?

People often adjust their attitudes so as to hold views closer to those of others who they value and identify with—their **reference groups.** For example, Terry and Hogg (1996) found that the adoption of favorable attitudes toward wearing sunscreen depended on the extent to which the respondents identified with the group advocating this change. As a result of observing the attitudes held by others who we identify with, new attitudes can be formed.

Consider how this could affect the attitudes you form toward a new social group with whom you have personally had no contact. Imagine that you heard someone you like and respect expressing negative views toward this group. Would this influence your attitudes? While it might be tempting to say "Absolutely not!", research findings indicate that hearing others whom we see as similar to ourselves state negative views about a group can lead us to adopt similar attitudes—without ever meeting any members of that group (e.g., Maio, Esses, & Bell, 1994; Terry, Hogg, & Duck, 1999). In such cases, attitudes are being shaped by our own desire to be similar to people we like. Now imagine that you heard someone you dislike and see as dissimilar to yourself expressing negative views toward this group. In this case, you might be less influenced by this person's attitude position. People are not troubled by disagreement with, and in fact expect to hold different attitudes from, people whom they categorize as different from themselves; it is, however, uncomfortable to differ on important attitudes from people who we see as similar to ourselves and therefore with whom we expect to agree (Turner, 1991).

Not only are people differentially influenced by others' attitude positions depending on how much they identify with those others, they also *expect* to be influenced by other people's attitude positions differentially depending on how much they identify with those others. When a message concerning safe sex and AIDS prevention was created for university students, those who identified with their university's student group believed that they would be personally influenced by the position advocated in the message, whereas those who were low in identification with their university's student group did not expect to be personally influenced by the message (Duck, Hogg, & Terry, 1999). Thus, when we identify with a

observational learning
A basic form of learning in which individuals acquire new forms of behavior as a result of observing others.

social comparison
The process through which we compare ourselves to others to determine whether our view of social reality is, or is not, correct.

reference groups
Groups of people with whom we identify and whose opinions we value.

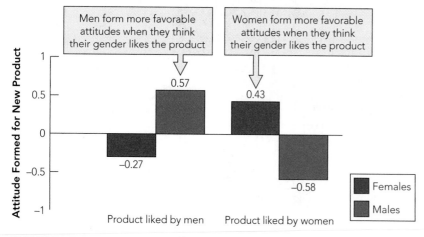

FIGURE 5.10   Attitude Formation Among Those Who Are Highly Identified with Their Gender Group
Men formed more positive attitudes toward the new product when they thought other men liked it, but women formed more positive attitudes toward the product when they thought other women liked it.   (Source: Based on data in Fleming & Petty, 2000).

group, we expect to be influenced by those others and, in fact, are likely to take on the attitudes that are perceived to be normative for that group.

To see this process in action, suppose you were exposed to a new product you have never encountered before. How might the identity relevance of the message influence the attitude you form? To address this question, Fleming and Petty (2000) first selected students to participate in the study who were either high or low in identification with their gender group. Then, they introduced a new snack product ("Snickerdoodles") to men and women as either "women's favorite snack food" or "men's favorite snack food." As Figure 5.10 illustrates, among those who were highly identified with their gender group, a more favorable attitude toward this product was formed when the message was framed in terms of their own group liking that food. In contrast, among those low in identification with their gender group, no differences in the attitudes they formed toward the new food was found as a function of which group was said to favor that food. These findings indicate that the attitudes we form are indeed strongly influenced by our identification with various groups and our perception of what attitudes are held by members of those groups.

KEYPOINTS

- **Attitudes** can reflect evaluations of any aspect of the world. Attitudes help us understand people's responses to new stimuli. Attitudes toward new topics can be shaped by long-term values, including religious beliefs.

- Attitudes can be **explicit**—conscious and easy to report—or **implicit**—which implies they are uncontrollable and potentially not consciously accessible. The *Implicit Association Test* is often used to assess whether the associations people have between a group or object are positive or negative.

- Attitudes are acquired from other people through **social learning** processes. Such learning can involve **classical conditioning, instrumental conditioning,** or **observational learning.**

- Attitudes can be classically conditioned even without our awareness—via **subliminal conditioning** and **mere exposure.**

- Attitudes that are acquired through instrumental conditioning stem from differential rewards and punishments for adopting particular views. Attitudes shift as people enter new **social networks** composed of individuals who hold diverging attitudes.

- Because we compare ourselves with others to determine whether our view of social reality is correct or not, we often adopt the attitudes that others hold. As a result of the process of **social comparison,** we tend to adopt the attitude position of those we see as similar to ourselves but not of those we see as dissimilar.

- When we identify with a group, we expect to be influenced by messages that are aimed at our group. We do not expect to be influenced when we do not identify with the group to which the attitude-relevant message is aimed.

When and Why Do Attitudes Influence Behavior?

So far we have considered the processes responsible for the attitudes we form. But we haven't addressed another important question: Do attitudes predict behavior? This question was first addressed more than 70 years ago in a classic study by LaPiere (1934). To determine whether people with negative attitudes toward a specific social group would in fact act in line with their attitudes, he spent 2 years traveling around the United States with a young Chinese couple. Along the way, they stopped at 184 restaurants and 66 hotels and motels. In the majority of the cases, they were treated courteously; in fact, they were refused service only once. After their travels were completed, LaPiere wrote to all the businesses where he and the Chinese couple had stayed or dined, asking whether they would or would not offer service to Chinese visitors. The results were startling: 92 percent of the restaurants and 91 percent of the hotels that responded said no to Chinese customers!

These results seemed to indicate that there is often a sizeable gap between attitudes and behavior—that is, what a person says and what that person actually does when confronted with the object of that attitude may be quite different. Does this mean that attitudes don't predict behavior? Not necessarily. To understand why attitudes might not straightforwardly predict behavior, we need to recognize that there are various norms that can affect the likelihood of discriminatory behavior. So even the most prejudiced people will not always act on their attitudes—when there are strong situational pressures to do otherwise. Likewise, there are social conditions under which people who do not think of themselves as prejudiced may find themselves discriminating against others based on their group membership. Let's consider now how the social context can affect the link between attitudes and behavior.

Role of the Social Context in the Link Between Attitudes and Behavior

You have probably experienced a gap between your own attitudes and behavior on many occasions—this is because the social context can directly affect the attitude–behavior connection. For instance, what would you say if one of your friends shows you a new tattoo of which he or she is proud and asks for your opinion? Would you state that you do *not* like it, if that was your view? The chances are quite good that you would try to avoid hurting your friend's feelings so you might even say you *like* it even though your attitude is negative. In such cases, we are clearly aware of our conscious choice not to act on our "true" attitude. As this example illustrates, depending on the degree to which the action has social consequences or not, attitudes may be differentially related to behavior. In contrast to your attitude–behavior inconsistency in responding to your friend's tattoo, your attitude might be a very good predictor of whether *you* would get a tattoo or not.

Because of the important role that the social context plays in determining when attitudes and behavior will be related, recent research has focused on the factors that determine *when* consistency can be expected, as well as the issue of *how* attitudes influence behavior. Several factors determine the extent to which attitudes and behavior correspond, with aspects of the situation influencing the extent to which attitudes determine behavior. In addition, features of the attitudes themselves are also important—for example, how *certain* you are of your own attitude. Attitudes that we hold with greater certainty are more strongly linked to behavior (Tormala & Petty, 2004) compared to attitudes about which we feel some uncertainty. Indeed, when people are induced to think that their attitudes are stable across time, they feel more certain about those attitudes and are more likely to act on them (Petrocelli, Clarkson, Tormala, & Hendrix, 2010). It is well known that older people are often more certain of their attitudes than are young people. Recent research suggests that this is partly due to older people placing greater value on "standing firm" or being resolute in the attitude positions they adopt, and for this reason they tend to show greater attitude–behavior consistency compared to younger people (Eaton, Visser, Krosnick, & Anand, 2009).

Have you ever been worried about what others would think of you if you expressed your "true" attitude toward an issue? If so, you will understand the dilemma that Stanford University students experienced in a study conducted by Miller and Morrison (2009). The private attitudes of those students toward heavy alcohol consumption were relatively negative. But, they believed that other students' attitudes toward heavy alcohol consumption were more positive than their own (an instance of **pluralistic ignorance,** where we erroneously believe others have attitudes different than ourselves). When these students were randomly assigned to receive information about other Stanford students' alcohol attitudes—that they held either more positive or more negative attitudes than their own—the students differed in how comfortable they felt expressing their attitude about alcohol use with another Stanford student and their likelihood of choosing alcohol policies as a topic for discussion. The students expressed greater comfort discussing campus drinking and chose that topic for

pluralistic ignorance
When we collectively misunderstand what attitudes others hold and believe erroneously that others have different attitudes than us.

discussion more often when they thought other students' attitudes were more pro-alcohol than their own, but they were less willing to do so when they learned other students' attitudes were more negative than their own. This pattern of wanting to express attitudes in the direction of the perceived campus norm but not when our attitudes go against the norm was especially strong for students who identified highly with their student group.

Strength of Attitudes

Consider the following situation: a large company markets a dangerous product to the public for decades, while internally sharing memos about the addictiveness of the product and how to manipulate that addictiveness. Along the way, an executive of the company has serious moral qualms about the rightness of these actions. Eventually, the concerned employee tips off the news media about these practices and an investigation is begun. The "whistle-blower" is eventually found out and is even sued by his former employer (although the lawsuit that was initiated against him is ultimately dropped).

You may recognize the person and company being described here because these events were ultimately made into a movie, *The Insider*. It was Jeffrey Wigand who blew the whistle on the practices of the tobacco industry in general and his former employer in particular—Brown & Williamson. Why might people take such drastic and potentially risky action (i.e., informing on their employer)? The answer is clear: Such people are passionately committed to the notion that corporations must be honest, especially when there is the potential for damage to the public. Attitudes like these—that are based on moral convictions—can give rise to intense emotion and strongly predict behavior (Mullen & Skitka, 2006). In other words, whether attitudes will predict sustained and potentially costly behavior depends on the strength of the attitudes. Let's consider why attitude strength has this effect.

The term *strength* captures the *extremity* of an attitude (how strong the emotional reaction is), the degree of *certainty* with which an attitude is held (the sense that you know what your attitude is and the feeling that it is the correct position to hold), as well as the extent to which the attitude is based on *personal experience* with the attitude object. These three factors can affect attitude *accessibility* (how easily the attitude comes to mind in various situations), which ultimately determines the extent to which attitudes drive our behavior (Fazio, Ledbetter, & Towles-Schwen, 2000). As shown in Figure 5.11, all of these components of attitude strength are interrelated, and each plays a role in the likelihood that attitudes will be accessible and affect behavior (Petty & Krosnick, 1995). We now take a closer look at each of these important factors.

Attitude Extremity: Role of Vested Interests

Let's consider first attitude *extremity*—the extent to which an individual feels strongly—in one direction or the other—about an issue (Visser, Bizer, & Krosnick, 2006). One of the key determinants of this is what social psychologists term vested interest—the extent to which the attitude is relevant to the concerns of the individual who holds it. This typically amounts to whether the object or issue might have important consequences for this person. The results of many studies indicate that the greater such vested interest, the stronger the impact of the attitude on behavior (Crano, 1995; Visser, Krosnick, & Simmons, 2003). For example, when students

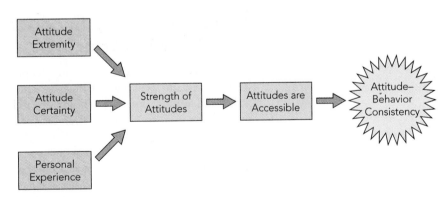

FIGURE 5.11   How Attitude Strength Influences Attitude–Behavior Consistency
Attitudes that are extreme, certain, and formed on the basis of personal experience with the attitude object tend to be strong attitudes, which are more likely to be accessible when a behavioral response is made. Greater attitude–behavior consistency is found when attitudes are strong rather than weak. (Sources: Based on research by Clarkson, Tormala, DeSensi, & Wheeler, 2009; Petrocelli, Tormala, & Rucker, 2007).

at a large university were telephoned and asked if they would participate in a campaign *against* increasing the legal age for drinking alcohol from 18 to 21, their responses depended on whether they would be affected by the policy change or not (Sivacek & Crano, 1982). Students who would be affected by this new law—those younger than 21—have a stronger stake in this issue than those who would not be affected by the law because they were already 21 or would reach this age before the law took effect. Thus, it was predicted that those in the first group—whose interests were at stake—would be much more likely to join a rally against the proposed policy change than those in the second group. This is exactly what happened: While more than 47 percent of those with high vested interest agreed to take part in the campaign, only 12 percent of those in the low vested interest group did so.

Not only do people with a vested interest behave in a way that supports their cause, they are likely to elaborate on arguments that favor their position. By doing so, attitude-consistent thoughts come to mind when an issue is made salient. For example, Haugtvedt and Wegener (1994) found that when participants were asked to consider a nuclear power plant being built in their own state (high personal relevance) they developed more counterarguments against the plan than when the power plant might be potentially built in a distant state (low personal relevance). Thus, attitudes based on vested interest are more likely to be thought about carefully, be resistant to change, and be an accessible guide for behavior.

Recent research findings indicate that vested interests are particularly likely to affect judgments and behavior in the immediate context, whereas abstract values do so when the judgment or behavior is in the distant future (Hunt, Kim, Borgida, & Chaiken, 2010). The issue these researchers tackled was one that has long puzzled those interested in voting, and that Frank (2004) addressed in his book, *What's the Matter with Kansas?* That is, when do people vote their economic self-interests and when do they "apparently act against their economic self-interests" and instead vote in favor of value-based proposals? To test when vested interests are paramount and when they may play a lesser role in behavior, students' material interests were pitted against their egalitarian values. White American students were given a proposal that would be enacted at their university either immediately or in the distant future. It would involve raising tuition by 10 percent in order to restore funds used for recruiting minority students that had been cut. Participants in the immediate condition who would experience the increase *opposed* the proposal, particularly when their own financial strain was high. In effect, they acted on their economic self-interests. In contrast, participants in the distant condition *favored* the proposal to the extent that they had egalitarian social attitudes. This research suggests that vested material interests do affect attitudes and voting when the policy is framed as having an immediate impact, but that for policies framed as having an impact only in the future, people favored and voted based on their values.

Attitude Certainty: Importance of Clarity and Correctness

Research has identified two important components of attitude certainty: attitude clarity—being clear about what one's attitude is—and attitude correctness—feeling one's attitude is the valid or the proper one to hold. Research by Petrocelli, Tormala, and Rucker (2007) provides evidence for the distinction between these two components of attitude certainty by showing how different factors affect them.

To accomplish this task, Petrocelli and colleagues (2007) first determined that their participants felt negatively about a specific attitude issue: requiring students to carry identification cards with them at all times. Then, in order to manipulate the perception of *consensus* concerning their attitude position, half of the participants were given feedback that most other students (89 percent) agreed with their attitude toward the identification card issue, while the other half were told that most other students disagreed (only 11 percent) with them. Although attitude clarity was equivalent in both the high and low consensus conditions, perceived correctness was greater when consensus was high (the 89 percent condition) rather than low (11 percent). When a person learns that others share one's attitudes, it acts as justification for that attitude and thereby increases certainty.

Clarity, the other component of attitude certainty, reflects a lack of ambivalence about an attitude issue. The more often you are asked to report on your attitude, the more it will facilitate clarity and thereby certainty. Repeatedly stating your attitude appears to "work" by increasing your subjective sense that you really *do* know how you feel about an object or issue. When Petrocelli et al. (2007) had their participants express their attitudes toward gun control either several times or only once, attitude certainty differed. Those in the "more expressions" condition had greater certainty about their attitudes toward gun control than those in the "single expression" condition.

What happens when both the clarity and correctness components are varied simultaneously? Returning to the identity card example, Petrocelli et al. (2007) gave students with negative attitudes toward the policy manipulations that were designed to affect both correctness (consensus) and clarity (repeated expression). The students were then given a persuasive message with strong arguments in favor of the policy but against their initial attitudes—why the policy would enhance student safety. More attitude change resulted in the low-clarity case than the high-clarity condition (single vs. repeated expression), and more attitude change occurred in the low-correctness versus the high-correctness condition (low vs. high consensus). Both components of attitude certainty, when they are high, can increase resistance to a persuasive message—each independently contributed to resistance to persuasion.

The social context too is important in assessing the relative effects of attitude clarity and correctness. High clarity will be more predictive of behavior in private but not public contexts—where correctness concerns are likely to be greater. Moreover, when people's attitudes are attacked, successfully resisting those attacks may well increase perceptions of attitude certainty because mounting and expressing counterarguments will increase perceptions of attitude correctness. In terms of attitude–behavior consistency, an attitude that is high on *both* clarity and correctness is most likely to reliably predict behavior in public and in private.

Role of Personal Experience

Depending on how attitudes are formed initially, the link between attitudes and behavior can differ. Considerable evidence indicates that attitudes formed on the basis of direct experience with the object about which we hold a particular attitude can exert stronger effects on behavior than ones formed indirectly. This is because attitudes formed on the basis of direct experience are likely to be stronger and be more likely to come to mind when in the presence of the attitude object (Tormala, Petty, & Brinol, 2002). Similarly, attitudes based on personal relevance are more likely to be elaborated on in terms of supporting arguments, and this makes them resistant to change (Wegener, Petty, Smoak, & Fabrigar, 2004). Consider the difference between having a friend tell you that a particular car model, "Brand X," is a lemon versus having experienced some failures with this brand yourself. When looking at new models of "Brand X," would your friend's opinion even come to mind? Maybe not. Would your own experiences come to mind? Probably. Thus, when you have direct experience with an attitude object it is likely to be quite personally relevant and strong, and your attitude toward it is likely to predict your behavior toward it in the future.

Personal experience is one way to create involvement with an issue, and people who are more involved with an issue and whose values are linked with that issue are more likely to act on their attitudes (Blankenship & Wegener, 2008). For example, when students were asked to consider a novel issue—whether a fictitious country, Tashkentistan, should be allowed to join the European Union—in light of a value of importance to them (e.g., freedom) or in light of a value of little importance (e.g., unity), they spent more time thinking about and elaborating on the message when it involved important values compared to when it did not. This elaboration resulted in stronger attitudes, which in turn guides behavior even in contexts where those attitudes are under attack.

In sum, existing evidence suggests that attitudes really *do* affect behavior (Eagly & Chaiken, 1993; Petty & Krosnick, 1995). However, the strength of this link is strongly determined by a number of different factors. First of all, situational constraints may not permit us to overtly express our attitudes. Second, attitude extremity, which is a function of whether we have a vested interest in the issue or not, influences whether our attitudes translate into behavior, and this is particularly likely when a message is framed as having an immediate impact rather than one far in the future. Third, attitudes that are clear and experienced as correct are more likely to affect behavior than are those that lack clarity or that we are uncertain about their correctness. Fourth, whether we have personal experience with the attitude object or perceive it as relevant to our important values can affect the accessibility of the attitude, and attitudes that are more accessible are more likely to determine behavior compared to those that are not accessible. For more information on how emotions can influence the attitudes we form about a product, see our special feature, "EMOTIONS AND ATTITUDE FORMATION: When What the Ad Promises Matches How We Feel."

EMOTIONS *and* ATTITUDE FORMATION

When What the Ad Promises Matches How We Feel

How do different emotions affect the attitudes we form toward products that make particular claims about the emotions they will bring? Consider the two advertising photos shown in Figure 5.12. Some vacation ads promise that we will experience much excitement—sailing, playing sports, diving, meeting new people, and so on. We might call these high-arousal positive promises. Other ads for similar locations (i.e., sandy beaches, a warm sea) promise relaxation and peace and quiet—essentially, they offer an opportunity to get "away from it all." We can refer to those as low-arousal positive promise ads. You, no doubt, have had to consider this question when deciding what kind of "spring break" to have—one filled with work, helping people in need in a far-off place, one filled with fun

with your student friends in Florida, or one relaxing, catching up on sleep, and reading a good book. Which will it be this year? Perhaps the choice depends on how you are feeling at the time you are forming an opinion about the options and making the decision.

The question that Kim, Park, and Schwarz (2010) asked in their research on this issue was, What are the consequences of experiencing incidental positive feelings that differ in level of arousal at the time we are forming our attitudes toward these vacation products? Of course, we know from much research that people who are in a good mood evaluate all sorts of consumer products more positively than people in bad moods (Schwarz & Clore, 2007). But, positive emotions come in different levels of arousal: high

FIGURE 5.12 **Role of Current Emotions in Attitude Formation: When the Ad Promises Excitement and You Want Peace or Vice Versa**
When an ad promised either an adventurous or a serene vacation in Japan, participants rated the adventurous product more positively when they were first induced to feel excited rather than peaceful and, conversely, they rated the serene vacation product more positively when they were induced to feel peaceful rather than excited. This was the case when participants' attention was not drawn to their current feelings, which permitted their current feelings to serve as information when forming attitudes toward the vacation products.

(excitement) and low (peaceful). If people use their current emotions as information when forming an attitude toward a new stimulus, then as long as attention is not drawn to their current emotional state, which would discredit its validity for judging the new stimulus, responses to these different vacation products should be affected. However, when attention is drawn to the incidental nature of their current emotional state, it should eliminate use of that emotion as information, and undermine its effect on attitude formation (Schwarz & Clore, 1983).

To test these ideas, participants were first induced to feel either excited or peaceful by describing in detail a life event they had experienced reflecting one of those emotions. After that, as seemingly part of another study entirely, they were given one of two ads for a trip to Japan to evaluate. In one version, the trip was described as "Full of Adventure," with exciting and stimulating activities. In the other version, the trip to Japan was described as "Full of Serenity," featuring peaceful and tranquil activities. After the ad for one of the trip versions was examined, half of the participants were alerted to the potential effect of their own mood on their judgments, or no such awareness cue was provided. Participants were then asked to indicate how much they would like to visit Japan—the advertised destination, and whether taking a trip to this location would be a good decision.

First of all, participants reported feeling equally positive across conditions, but they reported feeling more excited in the excitement writing task condition and more serenity in the serene writing task condition. As predicted, in the absence of an awareness cue reminding participants of the true source of their current feelings and its potential effect on their judgments, the adventurous vacation was rated more favorably when participants felt excited rather than peaceful and the serene vacation was rated more favorably when participants felt peaceful rather than excited. However, when the awareness cue was present, the emotion participants were feeling no longer had an effect on the attitude formed about the vacation options. In a subsequent study, these researchers found the same pattern of effects on participants' expectations that the vacation product they viewed would in fact deliver on its emotional claims were they to actually go on that trip. When current feelings were not discredited as information, then participants believed that the trip to Japan would in fact deliver adventure or serenity, depending on how the participants were feeling (excited or peaceful). So, when you are trying to decide whether "an action will be good for you to do or not," those products that promise to make you feel the specific positive emotion you are currently experiencing may often have an advantage.

KEYPOINTS

- Attitudes toward a group, issue, or object do not always directly predict behavior. Rather, there are situational constraints and norms that affect our willingness to express our true attitudes. Concerns about what others, especially those with whom we identify, may think of us can limit the extent to which our attitudes and behavior are consistent.

- People often show **pluralistic ignorance**—erroneously believing that others have different attitudes than themselves. This can limit the extent to which we express our attitudes in public.

- Strong attitudes are ones we are committed to, and we typically have moral values to support them. For this

reason, they are more likely to be accessible at the time we take action and are particularly likely to influence behavior.

- Attitude strength subsumes several factors: *extremity, certainty*, and *degree of personal experience*. Those attitudes that are more extreme, certain (both in terms of clarity and perceived correctness), and based on personal experience or important values are more likely to be accessible and guide behavior than are less extreme, unclear, and indirectly formed attitudes.

- Attitude formation can be affected by the specific emotion we are currently feeling when exposed to the object.

How Do Attitudes Guide Behavior?

When it comes to the question of how attitudes guide behavior, it should come as no surprise that researchers have found that there is more than one basic mechanism through which attitudes can shape behavior. We first consider behaviors that are driven by attitudes based on reasoned thought, and then examine the role of attitudes in more spontaneous behavioral responses.

Attitudes Arrived at Through Reasoned Thought

In some situations we give careful, deliberate thought to our attitudes and their implications for our behavior. Insight into the nature of this process is provided by the **theory of reasoned action,** which was later refined and termed the **theory of planned behavior** (Ajzen & Fishbein, 1980). This theoretical view starts with the notion that the decision to engage in a particular behavior is the result of a rational process. Various behavioral options are considered, the consequences or outcomes of each are evaluated, and a decision is reached to act or not to act. That decision is then reflected in *behavioral intentions,* which are often good predictors of whether we will act on our attitudes in a given situation (Ajzen, 1987). Indeed, for a number of behavioral domains—from condom use to engaging in regular exercise—intentions *are* moderately correlated with behavior (Albarracin, Johnson, Fishbein, & Muellerleile, 2001).

Recent research has made it clear that the intention–behavior relationship is even stronger when people have formed a plan for how and when they will translate their intentions into behavior (Frye & Lord, 2009; Webb & Sheeran, 2007). Suppose, for example, that you form the intention to go to the gym to work out. If you develop a plan for *how* you will translate your intention into actual behavior—beginning with setting your alarm, preparing your exercise clothes, and so forth—you will be more likely to succeed at doing so. In my own case, because I formed the intention to walk three mornings a week, I made a commitment to do so with my next-door neighbor. The reason why this is a particularly effective **implementation plan** is that I no longer have to assess whether I *really* want to go out today—in the cold, rain, or whatever, or rely on having my attitude toward getting more exercise be accessible at that time of the morning. As Gollwitzer (1999) has noted, such a plan to implement our intentions is very effective because it involves delegating control of one's behavior to the situation—in my case, my alarm clock beeping and, if that hasn't worked, my neighbor ringing my doorbell!

But, how do you form an intention to change some aspect of your behavior? According to the theory, intentions are determined by two factors: *Attitudes toward the behavior*—people's positive or negative evaluations of performing the behavior (whether they think it will yield positive or negative consequences), and *subjective norms*—people's perceptions of whether others will approve or disapprove of this behavior. A third factor, *perceived behavioral control*—people's appraisals of their ability to perform the behavior—was subsequently added to the theory (Ajzen, 1991). Perhaps a specific example will help illustrate the nature of these ideas.

Suppose an adolescent male is considering joining Facebook. Will he actually take action, find the website, and go through the process of joining up? First, the answer will depend on his intentions, which will be strongly influenced by his attitude toward Facebook. His decision of whether to join or not will also be based on perceived norms and the extent to which he feels able to execute the decision. If the teen believes that becoming a member will be relatively painless and it will make him look more sociable (he has positive attitudes toward the behavior), he also believes that people whose opinions he values will approve of this action (subjective norms), and that he can readily do it (he knows how to access Facebook, upload some photos, and he believes he can control how much of his private data is exposed), his intentions to carry out this action may be quite strong. On the other hand, if he believes that joining Facebook might be dangerous because of the exposure of private data, joining might not really lead to more interaction with friends, or his friends will disapprove of his joining, then his intention to join will be relatively weak. His intentions are more likely to translate into behavior if he formulates a plan for when and how to join (e.g., "On Friday when I get done with school, I'll access the Facebook website and join up"). Of course, even the best of intentions can be thwarted by situational factors (e.g., an emergency that he has to attend to comes up on Friday), but, in general, intentions are an important predictor of behavior.

Reasoned action and planned behavior ideas have been used to predict behavior in many settings, with considerable success. Indeed, research suggests that these theories are useful for predicting such divergent behaviors as soldiers' conduct on the battlefront (Ajzen & Fishbein, 2005) and whether individuals drive a vehicle after they have

theory of reasoned action
A theory suggesting that the decision to engage in a particular behavior is the result of a rational process in which behavioral options are considered, consequences or outcomes of each are evaluated, and a decision is reached to act or not to act. That decision is then reflected in behavioral intentions, which strongly influence overt behavior.

theory of planned behavior
An extension of the theory of reasoned action, suggesting that in addition to attitudes toward a given behavior and subjective norms about it, individuals also consider their ability to perform the behavior.

implementation plan
A plan for how to implement our intentions to carry out some action.

consumed alcohol (MacDonald, Zanna, & Fong, 1995). Other behaviors, including use of the recreational drug *ecstasy*, can be predicted with careful measurement of the components suggested by these theories. For example, Orbell, Blair, Sherlock, and Conner (2001) found that having a positive attitude toward ecstasy, seeing its use as normatively accepted by one's peer group, and having perceived control over using it were all significant predictors of intentions to use this drug. In fact, attitudes, subjective norms, and intentions were all significant predictors of actual ecstasy use 2 months later.

Attitudes and Spontaneous Behavioral Reactions

Our ability to predict behavior in situations where people have the time and opportunity to reflect carefully on various possible actions that they might undertake is quite good. However, in many situations, people have to act quickly and their reactions are more spontaneous. Suppose another driver cuts in front of you on the highway without signaling. In such cases, attitudes seem to influence behavior in a more direct and seemingly automatic manner, with intentions playing a less important role. According to one theoretical view—Fazio's **attitude-to-behavior process model** (Fazio, 1990; Fazio & Roskos-Ewoldsen, 1994)—the process works as follows. Some event activates an attitude; that attitude, once activated, influences how we perceive the attitude object. At the same time, our knowledge about what's appropriate in a given situation (our knowledge of various social norms) is also activated. Together, the attitude and the previously stored information about what's appropriate or expected shape our *definition* of the event. This perception, in turn, influences our behavior. Let's consider a concrete example.

Imagine that someone cuts into your traffic lane as you are driving (see Figure 5.13). This event triggers your attitude toward people who engage in such dangerous and discourteous behavior and, at the same time, your understanding of how people are expected to behave on expressways. As a result, you perceive this behavior as non-normative, which influences your

attitude-to-behavior process model
A model of how attitudes guide behavior that emphasizes the influence of attitudes and stored knowledge of what is appropriate in a given situation on an individual's definition of the present situation. This definition, in turn, influences overt behavior.

definition of and your response to that event. You might think, "Who does this person think he/she is? What nerve!" or, perhaps your response is more situational, "Gee, this person must be in a big hurry." Whichever of these interpretations of the event is given, it will shape the individual's behavior. Several studies provide support for this perspective on how attitudes can influence behavior by affecting the interpretation given to the situation.

In short, attitudes affect our behavior through at least two mechanisms, and these operate under somewhat contrasting conditions. When we have time to engage in careful, reasoned thought, we can weigh all the alternatives and decide how we will act. Under the hectic conditions of everyday life, however, we often don't have time for this kind of deliberate weighing of alternatives, and often people's responses appear to be much faster than such deliberate thought processes can account for. In such cases, our attitudes seem to spontaneously shape our perceptions of various events—often with very little conscious cognitive processing—and

FIGURE 5.13   Spontaneous Attitude-to-Behavior Process Effects
According to the attitude-to-behavior process view, events trigger our attitudes and, simultaneously, the appropriate norms for how people should or typically do behave in a given situation. In this case, being cut off in traffic by another driver triggers our attitudes toward such persons and our knowledge that this action is atypical. This interpretation, in turn, determines how we behave. Thus, attitudes are an important factor in shaping our overt behavior.

habit
Repeatedly performing a specific behavior so responses become relatively automatic whenever that situation is encountered.

thereby shapes our immediate behavioral reactions (e.g., Bargh & Chartrand, 2000; Dovidio, Brigham, Johnson, & Gaertner, 1996). To the extent that a person repeatedly performs a specific behavior—and a **habit** is formed—that person's responses may become relatively automatic whenever that same situation is encountered (Wood, Quinn, & Kashy, 2002).

KEY POINTS

- Several factors affect the strength of the relationship between attitudes and behavior; some of these relate to the situation in which the attitudes are activated, and some to aspects of the attitudes themselves.

- Attitudes seem to influence behavior through two different mechanisms. When we can give careful thought to our attitudes, *intentions* derived from our attitudes, *norms,* and *perceived control over the behavior* all predict behavior. In situations where we do not engage in such deliberate thought, attitudes may be automatically activated and influence behavior by shaping perceptions of the situation, which in turn dictate behavior.

The Fine Art of Persuasion: How Attitudes Are Changed

persuasion
Efforts to change others' attitudes through the use of various kinds of messages.

How many times in the last few days has someone tried to change your attitudes about something or other? If you stop and think for a moment, you may be surprised at the answer, for it is clear that each day we are literally bombarded with such attempts, some of which are illustrated in Figure 5.14. Billboards, television commercials, magazine ads, telemarketers, pop-up ads on your computer, and even our friends—the list of potential "would-be persuaders" seems almost endless. To what extent are such attempts at **persuasion**—efforts to change our attitudes through the use of various kinds of messages—successful? And what factors determine if they succeed or fail? Social psychologists have studied these issues for decades, and as we'll soon see, their efforts have yielded important insights into the cognitive processes that play a role in persuasion (e.g., Petty et al., 2003; Wegener & Carlston, 2005).

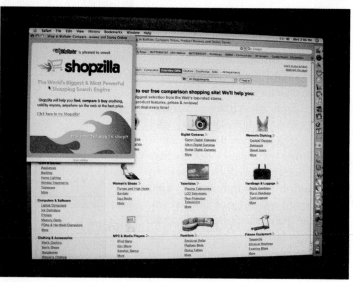

FIGURE 5.14 Persuasion: A Part of Daily Life
Each day we are bombarded with dozens of messages designed to change our attitudes or our behavior. Clearly, if they weren't effective some of the time, advertisers would not pay the sums that they do for these opportunities to try and persuade us to buy what they are promoting.

Persuasion: Communicators, Messages, and Audiences

Early research efforts aimed at understanding persuasion involved the study of the following elements: some *source* directs some type of *message* to some person or group of people (the *audience*). Persuasion research conducted by Hovland, Janis, and Kelley (1953) focused on these key elements, asking: "*Who* says *what* to *whom* with what effect?" This approach yielded a number of important findings, with the following being the most consistently obtained.

- Communicators who are *credible*—who seem to know what they are talking about or who are expert with respect to the topics or issues they are presenting—are more persuasive than those who are seen as lacking expertise. For instance, in a famous study on this topic, Hovland and Weiss (1951) asked participants to read communications dealing with various issues (e.g., atomic submarines, the future of movie theaters—remember, this was back in 1950!). The supposed source of these messages was varied so as to be high or low in credibility. For instance, for atomic submarines, a highly credible source was the famous scientist Robert J. Oppenheimer, while the low-credibility source was *Pravda*, the newspaper of the Communist party in the Soviet Union (notice how the credible source was an ingroup member, but the low-redibility source for these American participants was an outgroup source). Participants expressed their attitudes toward these issues a week before the experiment, and then immediately after receiving the communications. Those who were told that the source of the messages they read was a highly credible ingroup member showed significantly greater attitude change than those who thought the message was from the outgroup, which lacked trustworthiness and credibility. Indeed, members of our own group are typically seen as more credible and therefore are likely to influence us more than those with whom we do not share a group membership and with whom we might even *expect* to disagree (Turner, 1991).

  Communicators can, though, lose their credibility and therefore their ability to persuade. One means by which credibility can be undermined is if you learn that a communicator has a personal stake (financial or otherwise) in persuading you to adopt a particular position. Consequently, communicators are seen as most credible and therefore persuasive when they are perceived as arguing against their self-interests (Eagly, Chaiken, & Wood, 1981).

- Communicators who are physically attractive are more persuasive than communicators who are not attractive (Hovland & Weiss, 1951). Frequently, as shown in Figure 5.15, advertisers who use attractive models are attempting to suggest to us that if we buy their product, we too will be perceived as attractive. Another way that communicators can be seen as attractive is via their perceived likeability (Eagly & Chaiken, 1993). We are more likely to be persuaded by a communicator we like than one we dislike. This is one reason why famous sports figures such as Kobe Bryant, musicians such as Beyoncé

FIGURE 5.15   Role of Attractiveness in Persuasion: Can the Same Person Persuade Us to Buy Different Kinds of Products?

Research reveals that we are more persuaded by someone we view as attractive and like. In fact, actresses such as Catherine Zeta-Jones shown here are selected to be spokesperson for many different products—both those that are beauty-relevant (cosmetics, jewelry) and those that are not (cell phones).

Knowles, and actresses such as Catherine Zeta-Jones are selected as spokespeople for various products—we already like them so are more readily persuaded by them.

- Messages that do not appear to be designed to change our attitudes are often more successful than those that seem to be designed to achieve this goal (Walster & Festinger, 1962). Indeed, a meta-analysis of the existing research on this issue indicates that forewarning does typically lessen the extent to which attitude change occurs (Benoit, 1998). So, simply knowing that a sales pitch is coming your way undermines its persuasiveness.

- One approach to persuasion that has received considerable research attention is the effect of **fear appeals**—messages that are intended to arouse fear in the recipient. For example, Janis and Feshbach (1953) gave people one of three messages about the tooth decay that can result from not brushing one's teeth. They found that the mild fear-inducing message resulted in the greatest subsequent tooth brushing, while the most fear-inducing message resulted in the least increase in brushing. When the message is sufficiently fear arousing that people genuinely feel threatened, they are likely to argue against the threat, or else dismiss its applicability to themselves (Liberman & Chaiken, 1992; Taylor & Shepperd, 1998). Figure 5.16 illustrates some of the gruesome fear-based ads that have been used in an attempt to frighten people about the consequences if they fail to change their behavior. Despite the long-standing use of such fear-based messages, a recent meta-analysis of studies examining the role of fear in persuasion finds that they are not generally effective at changing people's health-related behaviors (de Hoog, Stroebe, & de Wit, 2007).

fear appeals
Attempting to change people's behaviors by use of a message that induces fear.

Might inducing more moderate levels of fear work better? There is some evidence that this is the case—but it needs to be paired with specific methods of behavioral change that will allow the negative consequences to be avoided (Petty, 1995). If people do not know how to change, or do not believe that they can succeed in doing so, fear will do little except induce avoidance and defensive responses.

Research findings (Broemer, 2004) suggest that health messages

FIGURE 5.16   **Using Fear to Encourage Change**

Many messages use frightening images in an attempt to "scare people" into changing their attitudes and behavior, including the sorts of warnings illustrated here that are aimed at getting people to stop smoking and behave in environmentally friendly ways to mitigate climate change.

of various sorts can be more effective if they are framed in a positive manner (e.g., how to attain good health) rather than in a negative manner (e.g., risks and the undesirable consequences that can follow from a particular behavior). For example, any health message can be framed positively as "Do this and you will feel better." Negative framing of the same message might be "If you don't do this, you will shorten your life." The point is that the same health information can be framed in terms of potential benefits of taking a particular action or in terms of the negative consequences that will ensue if you don't take that action.

Positively framed messages are often *more* effective persuasion devices than fear appeals. Consider how message framing and perceived risk of having a serious outcome befall the self can affect persuasion following exposure to a message designed to encourage low-income ethnic minority women to be tested for HIV (Apanovitch, McCarthy, & Salovey, 2003). Those women who perceived themselves as unlikely to test positive for HIV were more likely to be persuaded to be tested (and they actually got tested) when the message was framed in terms of the gains to be had by doing so (e.g., "The peace of mind you'll get or you won't have to worry that you could spread the virus") than when the message was framed in terms of potential losses they would otherwise experience (e.g., "You won't have peace of mind or you could spread the virus unknowingly to those you care about"). Positive framing can be effective in inducing change—especially when individuals fail to perceive themselves as especially at risk.

Early research on persuasion certainly provided important insights into the factors that influence persuasion. What such work did *not* do, however, was offer a comprehensive account of *how* persuasion occurs. For instance, why, precisely, are highly credible or attractive communicators more effective in changing attitudes than less credible or attractive ones? Why might positive message framing (rather than negative, fear-based) produce more attitude change? In recent years, social psychologists have recognized that to answer such questions, it is necessary to carefully examine the cognitive processes that underlie persuasion—in other words, what goes on in people's minds while they listen to a persuasive message. It is to this highly sophisticated work that we turn next.

The Cognitive Processes Underlying Persuasion

What happens when you are exposed to a persuasive message—for instance, when you watch a television commercial or see ads pop up on your screen as you surf the Internet? Your first answer might be something like, "I think about what's being said," and in a sense, that's correct. But as we saw in Chapter 2 people often do the least amount of cognitive work that they can in a given situation. Indeed, people may *want* to avoid listening to such commercial messages (and thanks to DVDs and TiVo, people can sometimes skip commercials entirely!). But when you are subjected to a message, the central issue—the one that seems to provide the key to understanding the entire process of persuasion—is really, "How do we process (absorb, interpret, evaluate) the information contained in such messages?" The answer that has emerged from hundreds of separate studies is that basically, we can process persuasive messages in two distinct ways.

SYSTEMATIC VERSUS HEURISTIC PROCESSING   The first type of processing we can employ is known as **systematic processing** or the **central route to persuasion,** and it involves careful consideration of message content and the ideas it contains. Such processing requires effort, and it absorbs much of our information-processing capacity. The second approach, known as **heuristic processing** or the **peripheral route to persuasion,** involves the use of mental shortcuts such as the belief that "experts' statements can be trusted," or the idea that "if it makes me feel good, I'm in favor of it." This kind of processing requires less effort and allows us to react to persuasive messages in an automatic manner. It occurs in response to cues in the message or situation that evoke various mental shortcuts (e.g., beautiful models evoke the "What's beautiful is good and worth listening to" heuristic).

When do we engage in each of these two distinct modes of thought? Modern theories of persuasion such as the **elaboration-likelihood model** (ELM; e.g., Petty & Cacioppo,

systematic processing
Processing of information in a persuasive message that involves careful consideration of message content and ideas.

central route to persuasion
Attitude change resulting from systematic processing of information presented in persuasive messages.

heuristic processing
Processing of information in a peruasive message that involves the use of simple rules of thumb or mental shortcuts.

peripheral route to persuasion
Attitude change that occurs in response to peripheral persuasion cues, which is often based on information concerning the expertise or status of would-be persuaders.

elaboration-likelihood model (ELM)
A theory suggesting that persuasion can occur in either of two distinct ways, differing in the amount of cognitive effort or elaboration the message receives.

1986; Petty et al., 2005) and the heuristic-systematic model (e.g., Chaiken, Liberman, & Eagly, 1989; Eagly & Chaiken, 1998) provide the following answer. We engage in the most effortful and systematic processing when our motivation and capacity to process information relating to the persuasive message is high. This type of processing occurs if we have a lot of knowledge about the topic, we have a lot of time to engage in careful thought, or the issue is sufficiently important to us and we believe it is essential to form an accurate view (Maheswaran & Chaiken, 1991; Petty & Cacioppo, 1990).

In contrast, we engage in the type of processing that requires less effort (heuristic processing) when we lack the ability or capacity to process more carefully (we must make up our minds very quickly or we have little knowledge about the issue) or when our motivation to perform such cognitive work is low (the issue is unimportant to us or has little potential effect on us). Advertisers, politicians, salespeople, and others wishing to change our attitudes prefer to push us into the heuristic mode of processing because, for reasons we describe later, it is often easier to change our attitudes when we think in this mode than when we engage in more careful and systematic processing. Strong arguments in favor of the position being advocated aren't needed when people do not process those arguments very carefully! The two routes to persuasion suggested by the ELM model are shown in Figure 5.17.

What role might consuming a drug like caffeine have on persuasion? The central route to persuasion works when people attend to a message and systematically process its contents. Given that caffeine intake should increase people's ability to systematically process the contents of a message, if people have the opportunity to focus on a persuasive message without being distracted, they should be persuaded more after consuming caffeine than after not consuming it. In contrast, when people are highly distracted, it should prevent them from systematically processing the message and, if caffeine works via the central route, distraction should lessen the extent to which they are persuaded. Research findings have supported these ideas: in low-distraction conditions, those who have consumed caffeine agree more with the message (they are persuaded away from their original opinion) than those who received a caffeine-free placebo. In contrast, when people are distracted and systematic processing of the message content is impossible, there is no difference in the attitudes of those who consumed caffeine and those who did not (Martin, Hamilton,

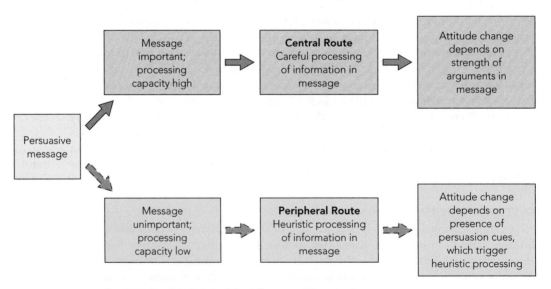

FIGURE 5.17   The ELM Model: A Cognitive Theory of Persuasion

According to the elaboration likelihood model (ELM), persuasion can occur in one of two ways. First, we can be persuaded by systematically processing the information contained in the persuasive messages (the central route), or second, by use of heuristics or mental one word shortcuts (the peripheral route). Systematic processing occurs when the message is important to us and we have the cognitive resources available to think about it carefully. Heuristic processing is most likely when the message is not important to us or we do not have the cognitive resources (or time) to engage in careful thought. (Source: Based on suggestions by Petty & Cacioppo, 1986).

McKimmie, Terry, & Martin, 2007). It is the increased thinking about the message when people are not distracted that can result in increased persuasion in caffeine drinkers. So, as shown in Figure 5.18, be prepared to think carefully about the messages you are exposed to when you get your next "caffeine fix"!

The discovery of these two contrasting modes of processing—systematic versus heuristic—has provided an important key to understanding when and how persuasion occurs. For instance, when persuasive messages are not interesting or relevant to individuals, the degree of persuasion they produce is *not* strongly influenced by the strength of the arguments these messages contain. When such messages are highly relevant to individuals, however, they are much more successful in inducing persuasion when the arguments they contain *are* strong and convincing. Can you

FIGURE 5.18 **Drinking Beverages Containing Caffeine Can Increase Persuasion**
Are these people, after getting a "dose" of caffeine, more likely to be persuaded by the messages they receive—than people who have not consumed caffeine? Yes, to the extent that the message is systematically processed.

see why this so? According to modern theories such as the ELM that consider these dual pathways, when relevance is low, individuals tend to process messages through the heuristic mode, using various mental shortcuts. Thus, argument strength has little impact. In contrast, when relevance is high, they process persuasive messages more systematically and in this mode, argument strength *is* important (e.g., Petty & Cacioppo, 1990).

Similarly, the systematic versus heuristic distinction helps explain why people can be more easily persuaded when they are distracted than when they are not. Under these conditions, the capacity to process the information in a persuasive message is limited, so people adopt the heuristic mode of thought. If the message contains the "right" cues that will induce heuristic processing (e.g., communicators who are attractive or seemingly expert), persuasion may occur because people respond to these cues and *not* to the arguments being presented. In sum, the modern cognitive approach really does seem to provide the crucial key to understanding many aspects of persuasion. In the following section, "SOCIAL LIFE IN A CONNECTED WORLD: Electronic Word-of-Mouth Marketing and Persuasion," we illustrate ways that persuasion can occur over the Internet.

SOCIAL LIFE *in a* CONNECTED WORLD

Electronic Word-of-Mouth Marketing and Persuasion

Word-of-mouth marketing has been around for a long time—it simply involves providing opinions, including recommendations and general product information, in an informal, person-to-person manner (Katz & Lazarsfeld, 1955). If you have ever told someone about a good restaurant, book, movie, or made some other type of product recommendation, you've been engaged in word-of-mouth marketing. In what has come to be called eWOM (electronic word-of-mouth), Facebook, Twitter, and the many other Internet forums shown in Figure 5.19 have become means by which the transmission of word-of-mouth communications are electronically accomplished. With the increasing use of the Internet, eWOM has become a powerful and useful resource for consumers.

(continued)

FIGURE 5.19   Electronic Word-of-Mouth Marketing Forums

All of these are channels by which word-of-mouth marketing and persuasion occurs. "Friends" on Facebook, for example, comment on new products and create a "buzz" within their own social network.

I know that before I lay out $10 to see a movie, I check out what other people have to say about it on *Rotten Tomatoes* or another movie review website. But, how do we make sense of the reviews that people provide on such sites? According to Lee and Youn (2009), the more the consumer attributes a communicator's review about a product to that product's actual features, the more the consumer will perceive that communicator as credible. This leads to greater confidence in the accuracy of the review and increases the likelihood of consumer persuasion.

In the eWOM situation, there is generally less control over the flow of "advertising" in the traditional sense (Chen & Lee, 2008). Typically, in what we will call the "buzz" situation, one is tracking a conversation on Facebook or receiving tweets on Twitter, all of which involve some sort of textual material in a conversational format. We know that eWOM connects diverse individual consumers to enable conversation. This helps people utilize information from the eWOM network to make purchase decisions. But the consumer must evaluate the credibility of those who are making recommendations. In eWOM, people's questioning of the credibility of online reviews can be a real problem for marketers.

Cheung, Luo, Sia, and Chen (2009) conducted a study to investigate factors that influence credibility judgments of online consumer recommendations. Informational determinants include argument strength, source credibility, and confirmation with prior beliefs. Normative determinants include recommendation consistency and recommendation rating. Because the reader does not typically know the person who is making the recommendation, a positive response to an informational message is likely to be based on the sheer number of positive recommendations one is exposed to. Cheung et al. (2009) found that credibility is a major concern for information receivers. So recommendation ratings and recommendation consistency, the two normative components, are particularly important determinants of whether consumers are influenced.

Some information-based determinants—argument strength, source credibility, and confirmation of prior beliefs—significantly influence perceived eWOM credibility (Cheung et al., 2009). A contributor's reputation as being credible is an indicator that readers use to evaluate the eWOM message. Argument quality is also important. Readers do not simply follow comments blindly. If an online recommendation is inconsistent with the receiver's prior beliefs, the receiver will tend to suspect its credibility.

The large numbers of participants in online discussion forums allow consumers to assess consistency in eWOM messages. If a similar experience is repeatedly reported by different forum users, readers are likely to believe it. In addition, the combined rating of past readers helps users understand how other readers tend to judge an online recommendation. This increases confidence in posted reviews.

Most online retailers (e.g., Amazon.com, Zappos.com, Overstock.com, ColdwaterCreek.com) provide an opportunity for consumers to contribute after-purchase reviews. These are intended to influence consumers' online purchase intentions. Of course, consumers seek quality information and believe that at least some reviews by other consumers provide useful information. However, Zhu and Zhang (2010) found it is mostly extremely satisfied and extremely dissatisfied users who write reviews, so the consumer tends to be exposed to extreme views. Mere popularity, by itself, can be informational to buyers, and they respond to this. But these researchers found that low-selling items, or niche market products, benefited more by reviews, although they were hurt by even one bad review. Reviews are more influential when those who write them have more Internet experience. In general, retailers believe that their online reviews are very helpful to consumers.

Many consumers use the Internet to evaluate, in an informal manner, product information in what has come to be called eWOM. Facebook, Twitter, MySpace, and others are all ways in which people gain access to others' opinions. In the online environment, some consumers become inadvertent marketers and influence other consumers.

KEY POINTS

- Early research on **persuasion**—efforts to change attitudes through the use of messages—focused primarily on characteristics of the *communicator* (e.g., expertise, attractiveness), *message* (e.g., fear appeals, one-sided vs. two-sided arguments), and *audience*.

- Communicators who are deemed credible, physically attractive, and offer messages that seem not to be designed to persuade us tend to be most persuasive.

- **Fear appeals**—messages that are intended to arouse fear—if too frightening tend not to be effective. Positively framed messages are often more effective persuasion devices.

- Modern theories of persuasion include the **elaboration-likelihood model** (ELM) and the *heuristic-systematic model.* Research based on these models has sought to understand the cognitive processes that play a role in persuasion.

- Persuasive messages can be processed in two distinct ways: through **systematic processing** or **central route to persuasion,** which involves careful attention to message content, or through **heuristic processing** or **peripheral route to persuasion,** which involves the use of mental shortcuts (e.g., "experts are usually right").

- Argument strength only affects persuasion when more systematic processing is engaged, whereas peripheral cues such as features of the communicator's attractiveness or expertise only affect persuasion when more heuristic processing occurs.

- Substances such as caffeine can affect persuasion because of their effects on systematic processing of the information in a message.

- *Electronic word-of-mouth* persuasion depends on communicator credibility, consistency among reviewer recommendations, and consistency of the message with prior beliefs.

Resisting Persuasion Attempts

As we have been discussing, people can be persuaded to change their attitudes and behavior—either because they think systematically about a compelling message, or because they are influenced by more peripheral cues. Why then might people sometimes be a "tough sell" where efforts to change attitudes are concerned? The answer involves several factors that, together, enhance our ability to resist even highly skilled efforts at persuasion.

Reactance: Protecting Our Personal Freedom

Few of us like being told what to do, but in a sense that is precisely what advertisers and other would-be persuaders do. You have probably experienced another individual who increasingly pressures you to get you to change your attitude on some issue. In both of these instances, whether "public" persuaders or private ones, you are on the receiving end of threats to your freedom to decide for yourself. As a result, you may experience a growing level of annoyance and resentment. The final outcome: Not only do you resist their persuasion attempts, but you may actually lean over backward to adopt views *opposite* to those the would-be persuader wants you to adopt. Such behavior is an example of what social psychologists call **reactance**—a negative reaction to efforts by others to reduce our freedom by getting us to believe or do what *they* want (Brehm, 1966). Research indicates that in such situations, we do often change our attitudes and behavior in the opposite direction from what we are being urged to believe or to do. Indeed, when we are feeling reactance, strong arguments in favor of attitude change can increase opposition compared to moderate or weak arguments (Fuegen & Brehm, 2004). The existence of reactance is one reason why hard-sell attempts at persuasion often fail. When individuals perceive such appeals as direct threats to their

reactance
Negative reactions to threats to one's personal freedom. Reactance often increases resistance to persuasion and can even produce negative attitude change or opposite to what was intended.

personal freedom (or their image of being an independent person), they are strongly motivated to resist.

Forewarning: Prior Knowledge of Persuasive Intent

When we watch television, we fully expect there to be commercials, and we know full well that these messages are designed to persuade us to purchase various products. Similarly, we know that when we listen to a political speech that the person delivering it is attempting to persuade us to vote for him or her. Does the fact that we know in advance about the persuasive intent behind such messages help us to resist them? Research on the effects of such advance knowledge—known as **forewarning**—indicates that it does (e.g., Cialdini & Petty, 1979; Johnson, 1994). When we know that a speech or written appeal is designed to alter our views, we are often less likely to be affected by it than when we do not possess such knowledge. Why? Because forewarning influences several cognitive processes that play an important role in persuasion.

First, forewarning provides us with more opportunity to formulate *counterarguments*—those that refute the message—and that can lessen the message's impact. In addition, forewarning provides us with more time to recall relevant information that may prove useful in refuting the persuasive message. Wood and Quinn (2003) found that forewarning was generally effective at increasing resistance, and that simply *expecting* to receive a persuasive message (without actually even receiving it) can influence attitudes in a resistant direction. In many cases, then, forewarned is indeed forearmed where persuasion is concerned. But what if you are distracted between the time of the warning and receipt of the message—to such an extent that it prevents you from forming counterarguments? Research has revealed that forewarning does not prevent persuasion when people are distracted; in this case, people are no more likely to resist the message than those not forewarned of the upcoming persuasive appeal.

There are instances where forewarnings can encourage attitude shifts toward the position being advocated in a message, but this effect appears to be a temporary response to people's desire to defend their view of themselves as not gullible or easily influenced (Quinn & Wood, 2004). In this case, because people make the attitude shift before they receive the persuasive appeal, they can convince themselves that they were not in fact influenced at all! Furthermore, in such cases, distraction after forewarning has been received—which presumably would inhibit thought—has no effect on the extent to which attitudes are changed in the direction of the expected message. In this type of forewarning situation, people appear to be using a simple heuristic (e.g., I'll look stupid if I don't agree with what this expert says) and change their attitudes before they even receive the message.

Selective Avoidance of Persuasion Attempts

Still another way in which we resist attempts at persuasion is through **selective avoidance,** a tendency to direct our attention away from information that challenges our existing attitudes. Television viewing provides a clear illustration of the effects of selective avoidance. People do not simply sit in front of the television passively absorbing whatever the media decides to dish out. Instead, they channel-surf, mute the commercials, tape their favorite programs, or simply cognitively "tune out" when confronted with information contrary to their views. The opposite effect occurs as well. When we encounter information that *supports* our views, we tend to give it our full attention. Such tendencies to ignore information that contradicts our attitudes, while actively attending to information consistent with them, constitute two sides of what social psychologists term *selective exposure*. Such selectivity in what we make the focus of our attention helps ensure that many of our attitudes remain largely intact for long periods of time.

forewarning
Advance knowledge that one is about to become the target of an attempt at persuasion. Forewarning often increases resistance to the persuasion that follows.

selective avoidance
A tendency to direct attention away from information that challenges existing attitudes. Such avoidance increases resistance to persuasion.

Actively Defending Our Attitudes: Counterarguing Against the Competition

Ignoring or screening out information incongruent with our current views is certainly one way of resisting persuasion. But growing evidence suggests that in addition to this kind of passive defense of our attitudes, we also use a more active strategy as well: We actively counterargue against views that are contrary to our own (Eagly, Chen, Chaiken, & Shaw-Barnes, 1999). By doing so, it makes the opposing views more memorable than they would be otherwise, but it reduces their impact on our attitudes.

Eagly, Kulesa, Brannon, Shaw, and Hutson-Comeaux (2000) identified students as either "pro-choice" or "pro-life" in their attitudes toward abortion. These students were then exposed to persuasive messages that were either consistent with their attitudes or were contrary to their views. After hearing the messages, participants reported their attitudes toward abortion, the strength of their attitudes, and listed all the arguments in the message they could recall (a measure of memory). In addition, they listed the thoughts they had while listening to the message; this provided information on the extent to which they counterargued against the message when it was contrary to their own views.

The results indicated that the counterattitudinal message and the proattitudinal message were equally memorable. However, participants reported thinking more systematically about the counterattitudinal message, and reported having more oppositional thoughts about it—a clear sign that they were indeed counterarguing against this message. In contrast, they reported more supportive thoughts in response to the proattitudinal message. Therefore, one reason we are so good at resisting persuasion is that we not only ignore information that is inconsistent with our current views, but we also carefully process counterattitudinal input and argue actively against it. In this way, exposure to arguments opposed to our attitudes can serve to strengthen the views we already hold, making us more resistant to subsequent efforts to change them.

Individual Differences in Resistance to Persuasion

People differ in their vulnerability to persuasion (Brinol, Rucker, Tormala, & Petty, 2004). Some people may be resistant because they are motivated to engage in counterarguing; they therefore would agree with items such as "When someone challenges my beliefs, I enjoy disputing what they have to say" and "I take pleasure in arguing with those who have opinions that differ from my own." On the other hand, some people are relatively resistant to persuasion because they attempt to bolster their own beliefs when they encounter counterattitudinal messages. Those individuals would be likely to agree with items such as "When someone has a different perspective on an issue, I like to make a mental list of the reasons in support of my perspective" and "When someone gives me a point of view that conflicts with my attitudes, I like to think about why my views are right for me." To determine whether scores on these two measures of resistance to persuasion were in fact predictive of attitude change in a persuasion situation, Brinol et al. (2004) measured these self-beliefs and then gave participants an advertisement for "Brown's Department Store." These researchers found that scores on both these measures assessing different approaches to resisting persuasion predicted successful resistance to the message in the advertisement. Furthermore, the types of thoughts people have when they are confronted with a counterattitudinal message are predicted by their preference for resisting persuasion by either counterarguing or bolstering their initial attitude position. So, apparently people do know something about how they deal with attempts to persuade them, and they use their favored techniques quite effectively!

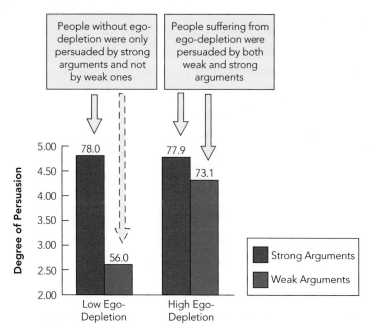

FIGURE 5.20   Evidence That Ego-Depletion Can Make Weak Ideas Persuasive

People who were not ego-depleted differentiated between weak and strong arguments, and were only persuaded by strong arguments. In contrast, people suffering from ego-depletion failed to differentiate between strong and weak arguments, and were therefore persuaded by both. (Source: Based on data from Wheeler, Brinol, & Hermann, 2007).

Ego-Depletion Can Undermine Resistance

As we just described, your ability to resist persuasion can result from successful counterarguing against a persuasive message or consciously considering why your initial attitude is better than the position you are being asked to adopt. Factors that make either of these strategies more difficult—because they undermine our ability to engage in **self-regulation**—could certainly undermine our ability to resist persuasion. To the extent that people have a limited capacity to self-regulate (i.e., to engage their will power in controlling their own thinking), prior expenditure of these limited resources could leave us vulnerable to persuasion. For example, when people are tired, have failed to self-regulate on a prior task, or otherwise are in a state of **ego-depletion,** they may simply acquiesce when confronted with a counterattitudinal message—that is, they will show attitude change.

To test this possibility, Wheeler, Brinol, and Hermann (2007) gave participants an easy or difficult first task, with the difficult task being designed to deplete their self-regulation resources. Subsequently, participants were given a weak or strong message arguing in favor of mandatory comprehensive examinations for graduation—a topic these students were initially strongly against. Did ego-depletion result in people being more persuaded by bad (weak) arguments? The answer, as shown in Figure 5.20, was a resounding yes. The weak arguments were unpersuasive to the non-ego-depleted people, but they were just as persuasive to those who were ego-depleted as were the strong arguments. For participants in the low depletion condition, strong arguments were more persuasive than weak ones, as you might expect. Examination of the participants' thoughts in response to the message verified that the low depletion participants had more favorable thoughts about the message when the arguments were strong compared to when they were weak. In contrast, the thoughts of the ego-depleted participants were equally as favorable in the strong and weak arguments case.

Recent research has confirmed too that those who have resisted a persuasive message have less ability to subsequently exert self-control (Burkley, 2008; Vohs et al., 2008; Wang, Novemsky, Dhar, & Baumeister, 2010). So not only does prior resistance deplete our self-control, which results in greater vulnerability to persuasion, but when we're depleted, we may find it more difficult to resist would-be persuaders' weak messages! Furthermore, when we are in the position of attempting to persuade others, we are more likely to be dishonest when our capacity to exert control has been depleted (Mead, Baumeister, Gino, Schweitzer, & Ariely, 2009). Participants in this research were first given a resource depleting essay to write—without using words that contained the letters A and N, or an easy one where the letters X and Z were not used. Then, participants had to find numbers in a matrix that summed to 10. Participants' performance on this task was scored by the experimenter in one condition (where cheating was not possible), or was self-scored in the other condition (where cheating was possible). Those in the resource-depleted condition and who self-scored their own performance showed the greatest cheating in reporting their performance. This research suggests that we need to beware of communicators who are the most tired when they

self-regulation
Limited capacity to engage our willpower and control our own thinking and emotions.

ego-depletion
When our capacity to self-regulate has been reduced because of prior expenditures of limited resources.

are attempting to persuade us—for they may be the most tempted to color the truth in ways that favor them over us!

KEYPOINTS

- Several factors contribute to our ability to *resist persuasion*. One such factor is **reactance**—negative reactions to efforts by others to reduce or limit our personal freedom, which can produce greater overall opposition to the message content.

- Resistance to persuasion is often increased by **forewarning**—the knowledge that someone will be trying to change our attitudes—and by **selective avoidance**—the tendency to avoid exposure to information that contradicts our views.

- When we are exposed to persuasive messages that are contrary to our existing views, we actively

- counterargue against them. This is a critical means by which our resistance to persuasion is increased.

- There are also individual differences in the ability to resist persuasion. Those include consciously counterarguing messages we receive, and bolstering our initial attitude position when confronted with a counterattitudinal message.

- **Ego-depletion** from exerting effort on another task can undermine our ability to **self-regulate** and resist persuasion. When ego-depleted, people are equally likely to be persuaded by both strong and weak messages. As persuaders, the ego-depleted are also less likely to be honest.

Cognitive Dissonance: What Is It and How Do We Manage It?

When we first introduced the question of whether, and to what extent, attitudes and behavior are linked, we noted that in many situations, there is a sizable gap between what we feel on the inside (positive or negative reactions to some object or issue) and what we show on the outside. For instance, I have a neighbor who recently purchased a huge SUV. I have strong negative attitudes toward such giant vehicles because they get very low gas mileage, add to pollution, and block my view while driving. But when my neighbor asked how I liked her new vehicle, I hesitated and then said "Nice, very nice," with as much enthusiasm as I could muster. She is a very good neighbor who looks after my cats when I'm away, and I did not want to offend her. But I certainly felt uncomfortable when I uttered those words. Why? Because in this situation I was aware that my behavior was *not* consistent with my attitudes and this is an uncomfortable state to be in. Social psychologists term my negative reaction **cognitive dissonance** —an unpleasant state that occurs when we notice that our attitudes and our behavior are inconsistent. As you will see, when we cannot justify our attitude-inconsistent behavior (but note that I tried to do so by saying how important it was to not offend my neighbor) we may end up changing our own attitudes.

Any time you become aware of saying what you don't really believe (e.g., praise something you don't actually like "just to be polite"), make a difficult decision that requires you to reject an alternative you find attractive, or discover that something you've invested effort or money in is not as good as you expected, you are likely to experience dissonance. In all these situations, there is a gap between your attitudes and your actions, and such gaps tend to make us uncomfortable. Recent research has revealed that the discomfort associated with dissonance is reflected in elevated activity in the left front regions of our brain (Harmon-Jones, Harmon-Jones, Fearn, Sigelman, & Johnson, 2008). Most important from the present perspective, cognitive dissonance can sometimes lead us to change our own attitudes—to shift them so that they *are* consistent with our overt behavior, even in the absence of any strong external pressure to do so.

cognitive dissonance
An internal state that results when individuals notice inconsistency between two or more attitudes or between their attitudes and their behavior.

Dissonance and Attitude Change: The Effects of Induced Compliance

We can engage in attitude-discrepant behavior for many reasons, and some of these are more compelling than others. When will our attitudes change more: When there are "good" reasons for engaging in attitude-discrepant behavior or when there is little justification for doing so? As we already noted, cognitive dissonance theory argues that dissonance will be stronger when we have *few* reasons for engaging in attitude-discrepant behavior. This is so because when we have little justification and therefore cannot explain away our actions to ourselves, dissonance will be quite intense.

In the first test of this idea, participants were first asked to engage in an extremely boring series of tasks—turning pegs in a board full of holes (Festinger & Carlsmith, 1959). After the task was over, the experimenter made an unusual request: he told participants that his research assistant had not shown up that day and he asked if the participant would "fill in" by greeting the next participant, and telling that person that the task to be performed was an *interesting* one. Half of these participants were told that they would be paid $20 if they would tell this fib to the waiting participant, and the other half were told that they would receive $1 for doing so. After doing the "favor" of telling the person waiting this fib about the experiment, the participants were asked to report their own attitudes toward the boring task (i.e., rate how interesting the task was).

The participants who were paid $20 rated the task as *less* interesting than participants who were paid $1. When you were paid $20, you would have had a justification for lying, but not if you were paid $1 to tell that same lie! So, if given *insufficient justification* for your behavior, a situation that was more true in the $1 (than the $20) condition of the experiment, there is a greater need to reduce your dissonance. So, what do people do to reduce their greater dissonance in the $1 condition? They change the cognition that is causing the problem! Since, in this example, you can't change the lie you told (i.e., deny your behavior), you can decide it wasn't really a lie at all by "making" the boring task more interesting and reporting your attitude as being more positive in the $1 condition than in the $20 condition.

As Figure 5.21 illustrates, cognitive dissonance theory predicts that it will be easier to change individuals' attitudes by offering them *just enough* to get them to engage in attitude-discrepant behavior. Social psychologists sometimes refer to this surprising prediction as the **less-leads-to-more effect**—less reasons or rewards for an action often leads to greater attitude change—and it has been confirmed in many studies (Harmon-Jones, 2000; Leippe & Eisenstadt, 1994). Indeed, the more money or other rewards that are offered to people for them to behave in an attitude-discrepant way provides a justification for their actions and can undermine the likelihood that attitude change will occur. Thus, coercion will serve to undermine dissonance. In addition, small rewards lead to greater attitude change primarily when people believe that they were personally responsible for both the chosen course of action and any negative effects it produced. For instance, when ordered by an authority to do a particular

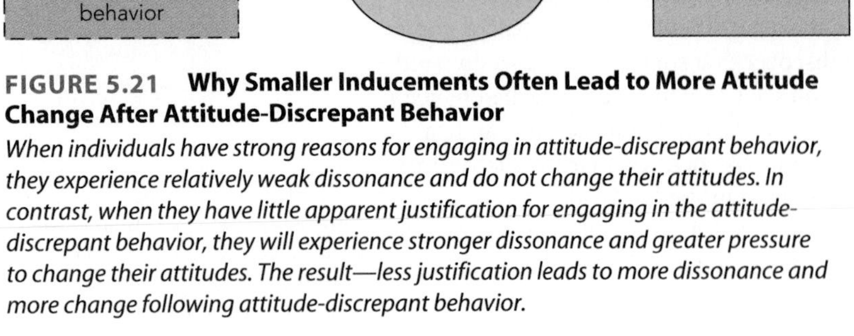

less-leads-to-more effect
The fact that offering individuals small rewards for engaging in counterattitudinal behavior often produces more dissonance, and so more attitude change, than offering them larger rewards.

FIGURE 5.21   Why Smaller Inducements Often Lead to More Attitude Change After Attitude-Discrepant Behavior
When individuals have strong reasons for engaging in attitude-discrepant behavior, they experience relatively weak dissonance and do not change their attitudes. In contrast, when they have little apparent justification for engaging in the attitude-discrepant behavior, they will experience stronger dissonance and greater pressure to change their attitudes. The result—less justification leads to more dissonance and more change following attitude-discrepant behavior.

behavior that is inconsistent with our personal attitudes, we may not feel responsible for our actions and therefore not experience dissonance.

Alternative Strategies for Resolving Dissonance

As we have described, dissonance theory began with a very reasonable idea: People find inconsistency between their attitudes and actions uncomfortable. But is changing our attitudes the only method by which we can resolve dissonance? No, we can also alter our behavior so it is more consistent with our attitudes—for example, we could resolve to only buy organic products *in the future* and not change our "green environmental attitudes" after we've made some nonenvironmentally friendly purchase.

We can also reduce cognitive dissonance by acquiring new information (justifications) that supports our behavior. Recall our chapter opening: How might Mrs. Keech and her followers deal with their dissonance when the prophecy failed and the world did not end on the specified date? They were faced with two dissonant cognitions: "we predicted the end of the world on a certain date" and "that date has undeniably passed, and the world has not ended." After disconfirmation of the prophecy, they did *not* conclude their belief in the prophecy had been wrong, but instead the group sought to add followers in order to *reaffirm* the rightness of their beliefs. Adding followers to the group adds a consonant cognition: *great numbers* of faithful believers couldn't be wrong! Indeed, when the "end of the world" date had passed, the group reported that Earth had been spared *because* of their strong faith. By adding this belief that their faith saved Earth, these believers were able to resolve their dissonance, without changing their attitudes or behavior.

Another option for managing dissonance when inconsistency is salient involves deciding that the inconsistency actually doesn't matter! In other words, we can engage in *trivialization*—concluding that either the attitudes or behaviors in question are not important so any inconsistency between them is of no importance (Simon, Greenberg, & Brehm, 1995).

All of these strategies can be viewed as *direct* methods of dissonance reduction: They focus on the attitude–behavior discrepancy that is causing the dissonance. Research by Steele and his colleagues (e.g., Steele, 1988; Steele & Lui, 1983) indicates that dissonance can be reduced via *indirect* means. That is, although the basic discrepancy between the attitude and behavior are left intact, the unpleasant or negative feelings generated by dissonance can still be reduced by, for example, consuming alcohol. Adoption of indirect tactics to reduce dissonance is most likely when the attitude–behavior discrepancy involves *important* attitudes or self-beliefs (so trivialization isn't feasible). Under these conditions, individuals experiencing dissonance may not focus so much on reducing the gap between their attitudes and behavior, but instead on other methods that will allow them to feel good about themselves despite the gap (Steele, Spencer, & Lynch, 1993).

Specifically, people will engage in *self-affirmation*—restoring positive self-evaluations that are threatened by the dissonance (Elliot & Devine, 1994; Tesser, Martin, & Cornell, 1996). This can be accomplished by focusing on positive self-attributes—good things about oneself. For instance, when I experienced dissonance as a result of saying nice things about my neighbor's giant new SUV, even though I am strongly against such vehicles, I could remind myself that I am a considerate person. By contemplating positive aspects of the self, it can help to reduce the discomfort produced by my failure to act in a way that was consistent with my pro-environmental (and anti-SUV) attitudes. However we choose to reduce dissonance—through indirect tactics or direct strategies that are aimed at reducing the attitude–behavior discrepancy—we all find strategies to help us deal with the discomfort that comes from being aware of discrepancies between our attitudes and behavior.

When Dissonance Is a Tool for Beneficial Changes in Behavior

- People who don't wear seat belts are much more likely to die in accidents than those who do . . .
- People who smoke are much more likely to suffer from lung cancer and heart disease than those who don't . . .
- People who engage in unprotected sex are much more likely than those who engage in safe sex to contract dangerous diseases, including AIDS, as well as have unplanned pregnancies . . .

Most of us know these statements are true, and our attitudes are generally favorable toward using seat belts, quitting smoking, and engaging in safe sex (Carey, Morrison-Beedy, & Johnson, 1997). Despite having positive attitudes, they are often not translated into overt actions: Some people continue to drive without seatbelts, to smoke, and to have unprotected sex. To address these major social problems, perhaps what's needed is not so much a change in attitudes as shifts in overt behavior. Can dissonance be used to promote beneficial behavioral changes? A growing body of evidence suggests that it can (Batson, Kobrynowicz, Dinnerstein, Kampf, & Wilson, 1997; Gibbons, Eggleston, & Benthin, 1997), especially when it is used to generate feelings of **hypocrisy**—publicly advocating some attitude, and then making salient to the person that they have acted in a way that is inconsistent with their own attitudes. Such feelings might be sufficiently intense that only actions that reduce dissonance directly, by inducing behavioral change, may be effective. These predictions concerning the possibility of dissonance-induced behavior change have been tested in several studies.

hypocrisy
Publicly advocating some attitudes or behavior and then acting in a way that is inconsistent with these attitudes or behavior.

Stone, Wiegand, Cooper, and Aronson (1997) asked participants to prepare a videotape advocating the use of condoms (safe sex) to avoid contracting AIDS. Next, participants were asked to think about reasons why they themselves hadn't used condoms in the past (*personal reasons*) or reasons why people in general sometimes fail to use condoms (*normative reasons* that didn't center on their own behavior). The researchers predicted that dissonance would be maximized in the personal reasons condition, where participants had to come face-to-face with their own hypocrisy. Then, all people in the study were given a choice between a direct means of reducing dissonance—purchasing condoms at a reduced price—or an indirect means of reducing dissonance—making a donation to a program designed to aid homeless people (see Figure 5.22). The results indicated that when participants had been asked to focus on the reasons why they didn't engage in safe sex in the past, an overwhelming majority chose to purchase condoms, suggesting that their behavior in the future will be different—the direct route to dissonance reduction. In contrast, when asked to think about reasons why people in general didn't engage in safe sex, more actually chose the indirect route to dissonance reduction—a donation to the aid-the-homeless project—and didn't change their behavior.

FIGURE 5.22 **Indirect Route to Dissonance Reduction**

When individuals are made to confront their own hypocrisy, most choose to reduce their dissonance through direct means (by changing their behavior). However, when individuals are asked to think about reasons why people in general do not act according to their beliefs, many choose to reduce dissonance via an indirect route such as donating to charity. Doing so allows people to feel better about themselves, even though their own behavior does not change.

These findings suggest that using dissonance to make our own hypocrisy salient can indeed be a powerful tool for changing our behavior in desirable ways. For maximum effectiveness, however, such procedures must involve several elements: People must publicly advocate the desired behaviors (e.g., using condoms), they need to be induced to think about their own behavioral failures in the past, and they must be given access to direct means for reducing their dissonance (i.e., a method for changing their behavior). When these conditions are met, dissonance can bring about beneficial changes in behavior.

KEY POINTS

- **Cognitive dissonance** is an aversive state that occurs when we notice discrepancies between our attitudes and our behavior. Experiencing dissonance does indeed produce increased left frontal cortical activity and attitude change.

- Dissonance often occurs in situations involving *forced compliance,* in which we are minimally induced by external factors to say or do things that are inconsistent with our attitudes.

- Dissonance can lead to attitude change when we have reasons that are barely sufficient to get us to engage in attitude–discrepant behavior. Stronger reasons (or larger rewards) produce *less* attitude change; this

- is sometimes referred to as the **less-leads-to-more effect.**

- Dissonance can be reduced directly (e.g., changing our attitudes) or by adding cognitions that justify our behavior.

- Other methods for dealing with dissonance include *trivialization* and *indirect* methods such as *self-affirmation* on some other dimension.

- Dissonance induced through **hypocrisy**—inducing individuals to advocate certain attitudes or behaviors and then reminding them that their own behavior has not always been consistent with these attitudes—can be a powerful tool for inducing beneficial changes in behavior.

SUMMARY *and* REVIEW

- **Attitudes** are evaluations that can color our experience of virtually any aspect of the world. Often, attitudes are **explicit**—consciously accessible and easy to report. But attitudes can also be **implicit,** and therefore not consciously accessible or controllable. Attitudes are often acquired from other people through **social learning.** Such learning can involve *classical* **conditioning, instrumental conditioning, or observational learning.** In fact, attitudes can be formed via **subliminal conditioning**—which occurs in the absence of conscious awareness of the stimuli involved—and **mere exposure.** Attitudes are also formed on the basis of **social comparison**—our tendency to compare ourselves with others to determine whether our view of social reality is or is not correct. In order to be similar to others we like, we accept the attitudes that they hold, to the extent that we identify with that group. As we move into new **social networks,** attitudes can shift rapidly as a means of fitting in when those networks consist of people holding diverging attitudes.

- Several factors affect the strength of the relationship between attitudes and behavior. *Situational constraints* may prevent us from expressing our attitudes overtly—including concerns about what others may think of us. People often show **pluralistic ignorance**—erroneously believing that others have different attitudes than we do, which can limit our willingness to express our attitudes in public. Several aspects of attitudes themselves also moderate the attitude–behavior link. These include factors related to attitude strength, including the *extremity* of our attitude position, the *certainty* with which

our attitudes are held, and whether we have *personal experience* with the attitude object. All of these factors can make our attitudes more accessible, and therefore likely to guide our behavior.

- Attitudes can influence behavior through two different mechanisms. According to the **theory of reasoned action** and **theory of planned behavior,** when we can give careful thought to our attitudes, intentions derived from our attitudes strongly predict behavior. According to the **attitude-to-behavior process model,** in situations where our behavior is more spontaneous and we don't engage in such deliberate thought, attitudes influence behavior by shaping our perception and interpretation of the situation.

- Early research on **persuasion**—efforts to change attitudes through the use of messages—focused primarily on the *source,* the *message,* and the *audience.* **Fear appeals** are limited in their ability to produce health behavior change. More recent research has sought to understand the cognitive processes that play a role in persuasion. Such research suggests that we process persuasive messages in two distinct ways: through **systematic processing,** which involves careful attention to message content, or through **heuristic processing,** which involves the use of mental shortcuts (e.g., "experts are usually right"). Consuming caffeine increases the extent to which people are persuaded by increasing their ability to systematically process the message contents. Normative and informational cues affect the extent to which we are persuaded by *electronic word-of-mouth* communications.

- Several factors contribute to such people's ability to resist persuasion. One factor is **reactance**—negative reactions to efforts by others to reduce or limit our personal freedom. When people feel reactance, they often change their attitudes in the *opposite* direction from that advocated. This is one reason why the "hard-sell" can be counterproductive. Resistance to persuasion is often increased by **forewarning**—the knowledge that someone is trying to change our attitudes. This typically gives us a chance to counterargue against the expected persuasive appeal, and thereby resist the message content when it is presented. Forewarning does not prevent persuasion though when people are distracted and therefore unable to expend effort refuting the message in advance.

- People also maintain their current attitudes by **selective avoidance**—the tendency to overlook or disregard information that contradicts our existing views. Likewise, people give close attention to information that supports their views, and by means of *selective exposure* will actively seek out information that is consistent with their existing attitudes.

- When exposed to information that is inconsistent with our views, we can actively counterargue against them. The more people have oppositional thoughts when exposed to a counterattitudinal message, the more they are able to resist being persuaded by it. In a sense, people provide their own defense against persuasion attempts. People also differ in their vulnerability to persuasion. Some people are aware that they use counterarguing and others know they attempt to bolster their original views when they are in persuasion situations.

- Our ability to resist persuasion can depend on our own psychological state—whether we are **ego-depleted** or not. When ego-depleted, people experience greater difficulty **self-regulating,** which can undermine our ability to resist persuasion. Research has revealed that when people are ego-depleted, they do not differentiate between messages with strong and weak arguments and are equally persuaded by both. In contrast, when ego-depletion is low, people are not persuaded by weak arguments, only by strong arguments.

- **Cognitive dissonance** is an unpleasant state that occurs when we notice discrepancies between our attitudes and our behavior. Dissonance is aversive and attempts to resolve it are reflected in increased cortical activity. Festinger and Carlsmith's (1959) classic study illustrated that dissonance is stronger when we have little justification for our attitude-inconsistent behavior. In contrast, stronger reasons (or larger rewards) can produce *less* attitude change—the **less-leads-to-more effect**—because the person feels justified in their attitude–inconsistent behavior in that case.

● Dissonance often occurs in situations involving *forced compliance*—ones in which we are induced by external factors to say or do things that are inconsistent with our true attitudes. In such situations, attitude change is maximal when we have reasons that are barely sufficient to get us to engage in attitude–discrepant behavior. Other means of coping with dissonance, besides changing our attitudes, include adding justifications, trivialization, or concluding that the inconsistency doesn't matter. Dissonance can also be dealt with by use of indirect strategies; that is, to the extent that the self can be affirmed by focusing on some other positive feature of the self, then dissonance can be reduced without changing one's attitudes. Dissonance that is induced by making us aware of our own **hypocrisy** can result in behavioral changes.

KEY TERMS

attitude (p. 140)

attitude-to-behavior process model (p. 157)

central route to persuasion (p. 161)

classical conditioning (p. 144)

cognitive dissonance (p. 169)

conditioned stimulus (p. 144)

ego-depletion (p. 168)

elaboration-likelihood model (ELM) (p. 161)

explicit attitudes (p. 141)

fear appeals (p. 160)

forewarning (p. 166)

habit (p. 158)

heuristic processing (p. 161)

hypocrisy (p. 172)

illusion of truth effect (p. 146)

implicit attitudes (p. 141)

implementation plan (p. 156)

instrumental conditioning (p. 146)

less-leads-to-more effect (p. 170)

mere exposure (p. 145)

observational learning (p. 148)

peripheral route to persuasion (p. 161)

persuasion (p. 158)

pluralistic ignorance (p. 150)

reactance (p. 165)

reference groups (p. 148)

selective avoidance (p. 166)

self-regulation (p. 168)

social comparison (p. 148)

social learning (p. 144)

social networks (p. 146)

subliminal conditioning (p. 145)

systematic processing (p. 161)

theory of planned behavior (p. 156)

theory of reasoned action (p. 156)

unconditioned stimulus (p. 144)

CHAPTER 6

The Causes, Effects, and Cures of Stereotyping, Prejudice, and Discrimination

*I*n many countries around the world, same-sex marriage is accepted. Indeed, in Argentina, Belgium, Canada, Germany, Iceland, the Netherlands, Norway, Portugal, South Africa, Spain, and Sweden, same-sex marriage is now legal. So why is the United States—where same-sex marriage continues to be a hotly contested social and legal issue—one of the major holdouts in legalizing same-sex marriage? Given that in the United States individual freedom is a guiding value, shouldn't we expect that it would lead the world in ensuring that people are free to marry whomever they want?

Not according to the citizens of California, a majority of whom in 2008 voted in favor of Proposition 8—a state constitutional amendment that banned same-sex marriage. In May 2009, a legal challenge was mounted against Proposition 8 in a federal court. Despite the fact that individual states (now at least 30) continue to pass laws barring gays and lesbians from marrying, in August 2010 the court legalized same-sex marriages in California. Throughout the year-long battle of public opinion leading up to U.S. District Judge Vaughn Walker's decision in this case, opponents strenuously resisted legalizing same-sex marriage. Judge Walker's federal court ruling was extremely clear, based on two simple arguments: There was no compelling state interest for banning gay marriage and no evidence was presented that allowing same-sex marriage would hurt heterosexuals.

Before addressing the issue of why resistance to same-sex marriage continues in the United States, let's look at some national opinion poll numbers. In August 2009, an Associated Press poll asked respondents, "Should the federal government give legal recognition to *marriages* between couples of the same sex?" The results: yes, 46 percent; no, 53 percent; and unsure, 1 percent.

In that same month, in another national survey, the Pew Research Center asked people a slightly different question: "Do you favor or oppose allowing gay and lesbian couples to enter into *legal agreements* with each other that would give them many of the same rights as married couples?" In this case, results showed 57 percent favored, whereas only 37 percent were opposed, and 6 percent were unsure.

What's clear from these opinion surveys is that at any given time there are fewer Americans objecting to civil unions than to same-sex marriages. It appears that, rather than objecting to providing the specific rights that marriage would grant to gays and lesbians, it is the word *marriage* itself that rankles many. If you leave out the "M word," Americans are more willing to accept the legal joining of two gays or lesbians.

But the gay and lesbian community has been reluctant to accept the second-class citizenship that acceptance of civil unions seems to imply. Their opposition appears to be based on gays and lesbians knowing that, just like heterosexual people, a formal marriage "seals the deal," by providing a ceremonial legitimacy that a civil union does not provide. The gay community seems to recognize that a civil union is not marriage—rather, it's a diminished status that relegates them to a separate and superficially equal position.

Indeed, it may be in the subtle distinction between "marriage" and "civil unions" that we can find the answer to our question, Why do so many Americans seem to oppose "same-sex marriage"? What is it about the difference between these two concepts—marriage and civil unions—that upsets so many people?

The social identity approach to prejudice helps us answer this question. As you'll learn in this chapter, people are motivated to protect the value and distinctiveness of their own group, and that may be a critical component of what is going on with heterosexuals' opposition to same-sex marriage.

Schmitt, Lehmiller, and Walsh (2007) proposed that the label applied to same-sex partnerships would determine the level of support received, with "civil unions" being accepted more than "marriages." More specifically, they suggested that same-sex marriage represents a threat to the positive distinctiveness of heterosexual identity in a way that civil unions do not. Merely sharing the same label—marriage—for same-sex relationships increases heterosexuals' negative feelings toward gays and lesbians.

Such perceived threat in heterosexuals may help to explain why the U.S. public is more supportive of same-sex civil unions than same-sex marriages—civil unions are less threatening to heterosexual identity, reflecting what has been observed in national opinion polls with questions using these labels. So, prejudice toward gays and lesbians seems to stem, in part, from a fear for one's own group identity. As shown in Figure 6.1, concern about the fate of marriage for heterosexuals is often the basis for opposition to same-sex marriage.

So while many believe that Americans have moved away from blatant expressions of prejudice and contend that American society has made considerable strides toward being more tolerant, perhaps some features of prejudice are built into most cultures—including the desire to protect one's own group—and are therefore still with us. While the content of

FIGURE 6.1   Does Perceiving Threat to Heterosexuals Increase Prejudice Toward Gays and Lesbians?
As these images suggest, those who support same-sex marriage perceive it as a human right and opposition as aimed at protecting heterosexual privilege, whereas those who oppose same-sex marriage perceive it as a threat to traditional marriage and family values.

stereotypes and the targets of prejudice may change, the underpinnings of these psychological phenomena may not be so different at all.

At some time or other, everyone comes face to face with **prejudice**—negative emotional responses or dislike based on group membership. Such experience with prejudice can come about either because we are the target of it, we observe others' prejudicial treatment of members of another group such as gays and lesbians as we discussed in the opening example, or when we recognize prejudice in ourselves and realize our actions toward some groups are less positive compared to how we respond to members of our own group. As you will see in this chapter, the *roots* of prejudice can be found in the cognitive and emotional processes that social psychologists have measured with reference to a variety of different social groups.

As we discussed in Chapter 4, prejudice based on group memberships such as marital status, gender, religion, age, language spoken, sexual orientation, occupation, or body weight, to name just a few, can have important consequences for its victims. Prejudice may be perceived by its perpetrators or its victims as legitimate and justified (Crandall, Eshleman, & O'Brien, 2002; Jetten, Schmitt, Branscombe, Garza, & Mewse, 2010) or it can be seen as entirely illegitimate and something that individuals should actively strive to eliminate (Maddux, Barden, Brewer, & Petty, 2005; Monteith, Ashburn-Nardo, Voils, & Czopp, 2002). Furthermore, prejudice and discriminatory treatment can be blatant or it can be relatively subtle (Barreto & Ellemers, 2005; Dovidio, Gaertner, & Kawakami, 2010). Indeed, all forms of **discrimination**—*differential treatment based on group membership*—are not necessarily perceived by its perpetrators, and responded to by its targets, in the same way.

In this chapter we begin by considering how our own group membership affects perceptions of social events. As you saw in the opening, heterosexuals are likely to respond to issues such as same-sex marriage differently than gays and lesbians. Likewise, when we examine the nature of *stereotyping*—beliefs about what members of a social group are like—and consider how it is related to discrimination, we need to consider the role of the perceiver's group membership. In this section, we particularly emphasize gender stereotyping, in part because its role in our own lives is easy to recognize—we all have a stake in gender relations. Although there is a high degree of interpersonal contact between men and women, which tends to be absent in many other cases including racial and religious groups (Jackman, 1994), gender-based discrimination continues to affect a substantial proportion of the population, particularly in the workplace. We next turn to perspectives on the origins and nature of prejudice, and address why it so persistent across time and social groups. Lastly, we explore various strategies that have been used to successfully change stereotypes and reduce prejudice.

How Members of Different Groups Perceive Inequality

There are substantial group differences in the perceived legitimacy of prejudice and discrimination, and in how much progress is thought to have been made toward their reduction, depending on whether one is a member of the group targeted or the group perpetrating the unequal treatment. For example, white and black Americans show substantial differences in how much discrimination and racial inequality they perceive to be present in employment wages (Miron, Warner, & Branscombe, in press). Furthermore, whites perceive less

prejudice
Negative emotional responses based on group membership.

discrimination
Differential (usually negative) behaviors directed toward members of different social groups.

racism in many everyday events than do blacks (Johnson, Simmons, Trawalter, Ferguson, & Reed, 2003). This pattern is presently found in many groups that differ in status—with high-status groups perceiving the status differential that favors them as less than members of lower-status groups (Exline & Lobel, 1999). In terms of perceptions of how much progress has been made in moving toward equality, national surveys consistently find that white respondents perceive there to have been "a lot of progress," whereas black respondents are more likely to perceive that there has been "not much progress" toward equality. In this sense, in the United States, there continues to be a "racial divide." Is one group correct and one group incorrect in their perceptions? How are we to account for such different subjective perceptions and evaluations of the *same* events and outcomes?

An important step in accounting for these differing perceptions involves consideration of the different meanings and implications derived from any potential change in the status relations between the groups. According to Kahneman and Tversky's (1984) prospect theory (for which the 2002 Nobel Prize in economics was awarded), people are **risk averse**—they tend to weigh possible losses more heavily than equivalent potential gains. To take a monetary example, the possibility of losing a dollar is subjectively more negative than the possibility of gaining a dollar is positive.

How might this idea apply to racial perceptions of social changes that could result in greater racial equality? Let's assume that whites will perceive greater equality from the standpoint of a potential "loss" for their group—compared to their historically privileged position. Whites will therefore respond to additional movement toward equality more negatively, and suppose that more change has already occurred, than will blacks. In contrast, if we assume that blacks are likely to see greater equality as a potential "gain" for them—compared to their historically disadvantaged position—then change toward increased equality will be experienced as a positive. But, if a "possible loss" evokes more intense emotion than a "possible gain" does, then increased equality should be more negative for whites than the same increased equality is positive for blacks. Research has revealed that white Americans who are highly identified with their racial group, when their race-based privileges are questioned, do respond negatively—with increased racism (Branscombe, Schmitt, & Schiffhauer, 2007) and greater support for tokenism, which ensures that the number of African Americans employed is limited (Richard & Wright, 2010).

Indeed, even a cursory look at racist websites, such as those shown in Figure 6.2—of which there are a disturbingly large number—reveals that such hate groups often frame the

risk averse
We weigh possible losses more heavily than equivalent potential gains. As a result, we respond more negatively to changes that are framed as potential losses than positively to changes that are framed as potential gains.

FIGURE 6.2 **Hate Groups on the Internet**
Hate groups incite concerns about their own group by claiming they are "losing ground" and that the targeted group is illegitimately gaining. Hate is then seen as justified in order to protect their own group.

state of existing race relations as "white people are losing ground." This is, of course, not unlike how the Nazis and other anti-Semitic groups (again, all too easily found on the Internet) framed German, and more recently Christian, losses (and Jewish gains). There is both historical and contemporary evidence that hate crimes increase as minorities are perceived as gaining political power (Dancygier & Green, 2010).

Although hate group members are *not* typical white Americans, perhaps this tendency to see social change as a zero-sum outcome in which "we are losing" plays a role in explaining the consistent discrepancies that are observed between minority and majority perceptions of inequality. To test this explanation, Eibach and Keegan (2006) had white and non-white participants create a graph—in one of three forms—depicting change in the racial composition of students in U.S. universities from 1960 to the present. In the "Minority gains and white losses" case, the percentages they were asked to insert showed the percent of whites going down and the exact same percentage increase in favor of minorities. In a "white losses only" case, the graphs the students were asked to draw simply showed a reduction in the percentage of whites, and in the "Minorities gain only" case they simply showed an increase in the percentage of minorities at American universities.

In both conditions where "white losses" were included, white participants saw race relations in a more "zero-sum" fashion than when "Minority gains" alone were considered. What impact did this have on judged progress toward equality? As shown in Figure 6.3, in the two conditions where participants focused on "white losses," there were racial group differences in judged progress—mirroring the consistently obtained national survey findings. white participants perceived greater progress toward equality for minorities than did non-white participants. However, when only "Minority gains" were considered, whites perceived less progress toward equality; in fact, in that case, their perceptions were no different than the non-white participants. So, the "racial divide" in

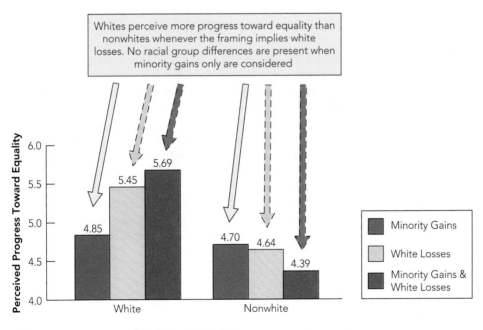

FIGURE 6.3   Opportunities in American Society Can Be Framed As Gains or Losses

When admissions to United States universities were framed as minorities' gains, white participants judged overall progress toward equality in the United States as less than when those same changes were framed as white losses. Only in the minorities' gains condition, did white and nonwhite participants not differ from each other in perceptions of progress toward equality. For the minority participants, the framing had no effect on judged progress. (Source: Based on data from Eibach & Keegan, 2006).

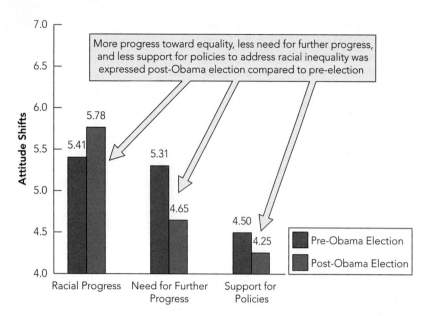

FIGURE 6.4 **Perceptions of Racial Progress and Need for Future Progress Was Affected by the Election of Barack Obama**
Ironically, the election of Barack Obama reduced the perceived need for further progress toward racial equality and support for policies to achieve that goal. In fact, the election of the first African American as U.S. President seems to have implied to white Americans that substantial racial progress has already been made. (Source: Based on data from Kaiser, Drury, Spalding, Cheryan, & O'Brien, 2009).

public perceptions of events would appear to stem in part from whites' framing social change as involving losses in status and outcomes for their own group.

It is worth considering whether a similar tendency to frame affirmative action as a loss of white privilege or as a gain for minorities can account for racial differences in support for that social change policy too (Crosby, 2004). Recent research reveals that when whites expect that affirmative action procedures will negatively affect white Americans' chances to obtain jobs and promotions—by focusing on possible losses their own racial group could experience—whites oppose affirmative action policies, regardless of what impact it might have on minority groups (Lowery, Unzueta, Goff, & Knowles, 2006). Similarly, among white South Africans, support for affirmative action for black South Africans depends on the extent to which they are perceived as a threat to white South Africans' high-status jobs and access to good housing (Durrheim et al., 2009). Likewise, when immigrants are perceived as a threat to the dominant group's economic position, opposition to the naturalization of immigrants increases; such increased legitimization of discrimination against immigrants has been observed in response to perceived threat in 21 European nations (Pereira, Vala, & Costa-Lopes, 2009).

Has the election of Barack Obama to the U.S. Presidency changed these racial dynamics in perceptions of progress and support for policies that are aimed at addressing racial inequality such as affirmative action? Yes, but ironically, as shown in Figure 6.4, recent research has revealed that pre- to post-election white Americans came to believe that there is *less* need for further racial progress and *less* support for social policies aimed at increasing equality is expressed (Kaiser, Drury, Spalding, Cheryan, & O'Brien, 2009). Clearly, the election of Barack Obama is but one dramatic example of how much race relations in the United States have changed since the 1954 U.S. Supreme Court decision, *Brown v. Topeka Board of Education*, which made racial segregation in public institutions such as schools illegal. However, as we discuss later, the presence of "token" (numerically infrequent) minorities or women in highly visible positions can lead majority group members to believe that not only has substantial change occurred, but that there is less need for further social change.

KEYPOINTS

- Discriminatory treatment can be based on many different category memberships including age, race, marital status, occupation, gender, religion, language spoken, sexual orientation, and body weight.

- All forms of differential treatment based on group membership are not perceived and responded to in the same way. Some forms are perceived as legitimate, while others people actively strive to eliminate in themselves and others.

- Prospect theory argues that people are **risk averse**—and they therefore weigh possible losses more heavily than equivalent potential gains.

- When change is seen as a potential loss, those who are privileged respond more negatively to further change and suppose that more change has already occurred compared to those who do not see it as a loss for them.

- Social groups differ in the value they accord "equality." When equality is framed as a loss for whites, they perceive that more progress has already occurred and they are less supportive of affirmative action. Perceived threat

to the dominant group's economic well-being lowers support for affirmative action in white South Africans and for immigration among Europeans.

- The election of Barack Obama, which was indeed unimaginable only a few decades earlier, had the effect of increasing white Americans' perceptions that substantial racial progress has been made, and also decreased the perceived need for policies aimed at creating greater racial equality.

The Nature and Origins of Stereotyping

In everyday conversation, the terms *stereotyping*, *prejudice*, and *discrimination* are often used interchangeably. However, social psychologists have traditionally drawn a distinction between them by building on the more general attitude concept (see Chapter 5). That is, **stereotypes** are considered the cognitive component of attitudes toward a social group—specifically, beliefs about what a particular group is like. Prejudice is considered the affective component, or the feelings we have about a particular group. Discrimination concerns the behavioral component, or differential actions taken toward members of specific social groups.

According to this attitude approach, some groups are characterized by negative stereotypes and this leads to a general feeling of hostility (although, as we'll see, there might actually be other types of emotions underlying prejudice toward different groups), which then results in a *conscious intention* to discriminate against members of the targeted group. As we describe recent research in this chapter, ask yourself the following question, which researchers are increasingly raising: "How well does the prevailing attitude approach to stereotyping, prejudice, and discrimination capture the phenomena of interest?" (Adams, Biernat, Branscombe, Crandall, & Wrightsman, 2008). Are there questions and findings the attitude approach cannot address or account for? Are stereotypes about social groups always negative beliefs—for example, do we typically stereotype groups of which we are members in negative terms? Is prejudice always reflected in exclusion and hostility? Could there be such a thing as "benevolent prejudice"? Can discrimination occur without any conscious intention to do so? These are all issues that we consider in this chapter.

stereotypes
Beliefs about social groups in terms of the traits or characteristics that they are believed to share. Stereotypes are cognitive frameworks that influence the processing of social information.

gender stereotypes
Stereotypes concerning the traits possessed by females and males and that distinguish the two genders from each other.

Stereotyping: Beliefs About Social Groups

Stereotypes about groups are the beliefs and expectations that we have concerning what members of those groups are like. Stereotypes can include more than just traits; physical appearance, abilities, and behaviors are all common components of stereotypic expectancies (Biernat & Thompson, 2002; Deaux & LaFrance, 1998; Zhang, Schmader, & Forbes, 2009). The traits thought to distinguish between one group and another can be either positive or negative, they can be accurate or inaccurate, and may be either agreed with or rejected by members of the stereotyped group.

Gender stereotypes—beliefs concerning the characteristics of women and men—contain both positive and negative traits (see Table 6.1). Stereotypes of each gender are typically the converse of one another. For instance, on the positive side of the gender stereotype for women, they are viewed as being kind, nurturant, and considerate. On the negative side, they are viewed as being dependent, weak, and overly emotional. Thus, our collective portrait of women is that they are high on warmth but low on competence (Fiske, Cuddy, Glick, & Xu, 2002). Indeed, perceptions of

TABLE 6.1 Common Traits Stereotypically Associated with Women and Men

As this list of stereotypic traits implies, women are seen as "nicer and warm," whereas men are seen as more "competent and independent."

FEMALE TRAITS	MALE TRAITS
Warm	Competent
Emotional	Stable
Kind/polite	Tough/coarse
Sensitive	Self-confident
Follower	Leader
Weak	Strong
Friendly	Accomplished
Fashionable	Nonconformist
Gentle	Aggressive

Source: Compiled based on Deaux & Kite, 1993; Eagly & Mladinic, 1994; Fiske, Cuddy, Glick, & Xu, 2002.

women are similar on these two dimensions to other groups (e.g., the elderly) who are seen as relatively low in status and nonthreatening (Eagly, 1987; Stewart, Vassar, Sanchez, & David, 2000).

Men too are assumed to have both positive and negative stereotypic traits (e.g., they are viewed as decisive, assertive, and accomplished, but also as aggressive, insensitive, and arrogant). Such a portrait—being perceived as high on competence but low on communal attributes—reflects men's relatively high status (e.g., the category "rich people" is perceived similarly on these two dimensions; Cikara & Fiske, 2009). Interestingly, because of the strong emphasis on warmth in the stereotype for women, people tend to feel somewhat more positively about women on the whole compared to men—a finding described by Eagly and Mladinic (1994) as the "women are wonderful" effect.

Despite this greater perceived likeability, women face a key problem: the traits they supposedly possess tend to be viewed as less appropriate for high-status positions than the traits presumed to be possessed by men. Women's traits make them seem appropriate for "support roles" rather than "leadership roles" (Eagly & Sczesny, 2009). Although dramatic change has occurred in the extent to which women participate in the labor force—from 20 percent in 1900 to 59 percent in 2005 (U.S. Census Bureau, 2007)—the vast majority of working women in the United States and other nations are in occupations that bring less status and monetary compensation than comparably skilled male-dominated occupations (Peterson & Runyan, 1993; Tomaskovic-Devey et al., 2006).

STEREOTYPES AND THE "GLASS CEILING"   Women are particularly underrepresented in the corporate world; only 16 percent of corporate officers in the United States are women and only about 1 percent of CEO positions in Fortune 500 companies are occupied by women (Catalyst, 2010; U.S. Bureau of Labor Statistics, 2006). In other ways, although the political power structure remains heavily male dominated (Center for American Women and Politics, 2005), women have been seeking elected office in record numbers (Center for Women and Politics, 2010). For example, in the 2010 U.S. elections, 36 women ran for the Senate (19 Democrats, 17 Republicans), 262 women sought election to Congress (134 Democrats, 128 Republicans), and 26 women sought to win their state's Governor's office (12 Democrats, 14 Republicans). In addition to Ruth Bader Ginsburg, with the appointment of Sonia Sotomayor in 2009 and Elena Kagan in 2010, the U.S. Supreme Court now has its highest representation of women—33 percent.

Despite the gains for women in these important institutions, in corporate settings women are primarily making it into middle management but not the higher echelons. This situation, where women find it difficult to advance, may be indicative of a **glass ceiling**—a final barrier that prevents women, as a group, from reaching top positions in the workplace. Several studies have confirmed that a "think manager—think male" bias exists and can help explain how the glass ceiling is maintained (Bruckmüller & Branscombe, 2010; Schein, 2001). Because the stereotypic attributes of a "typical manager" overlap considerably with the "typical man" and share fewer attributes with the "typical woman," this leads to a perceived "lack of fit" of women for positions of organizational leadership (Eagly & Sczesny, 2009; Heilman, 2001). The cartoon in Figure 6.5 provides an amusing illustration of how the perceived lack of fit of those newly entering the field and the group membership of typical leaders of the past may be perceived.

Despite the remaining hurdles, evidence is emerging that such gender stereotyping in workplace contexts is weakening. Duehr and Bono (2006) report that the inconsistency between the stereotype of women and the stereotype of leaders in terms of agentic traits has decreased over the past 10 years, particularly among women. Furthermore, women are increasingly being perceived as just as competent as men in political leadership roles, with representative samples from many nations reporting reductions in explicit agreement with ideas such as "men make better political leaders than women" (Eagly & Sczesny, 2009).

So is it just a matter of being perceived as "leadership material"—will such change mean that gender discrimination in the workplace is a thing of the past? Even when women do break through the glass ceiling, they experience less favorable outcomes in

glass ceiling
Barriers based on attitudinal or organizational bias that prevent qualified females from advancing to top-level positions.

their careers because of their gender than do men (Heilman & Okimoto, 2007; Stroh, Langlands, & Simpson, 2004). For example, when women serve as leaders, they tend to receive lower evaluations from subordinates than males, even when they act similarly (Eagly, Makijani, & Klonsky, 1992; Lyness & Heilman, 2006). Indeed, those women who have been successful in competitive, male-dominated work environments are most likely to report experiencing gender discrimination compared to those in gender stereotypic occupations (Redersdorff, Martinot, & Branscombe, 2004), and they are especially likely to be evaluated negatively when their leadership style is task-focused or authoritarian (Eagly & Karau, 2002).

In other words, when women violate stereotypic expectancies concerning warmth and nurturance, and instead act according to the prototype of a leader, particularly in masculine domains, they are likely to face hostility and rejection (Glick & Rudman, 2010). Violations of stereotype-based expectancies by women in the workplace appear to evoke threat in some men, particularly among those inclined to sexually harass (Maass, Cadinu, Guarnieri, & Grasselli, 2003). Indeed, both women and men seem to be aware of the consequences of appearing to violate gender-stereotypic expectancies. Because of fear of the social punishments that are likely following such violations, when told that they were highly successful on a knowledge test typical of the other gender group, participants were more likely to lie about which test they performed well on and to hide their success from others (Rudman & Fairchild, 2004). These results suggest that it takes a lot of courage to attempt to defy gender stereotypes! (For more information on the effects of gender stereotyping in video games, please see our special section "SOCIAL LIFE IN A CONNECTED WORLD: Representations of Female and Male Figures in Video Games.")

"To begin with, I would like to express my sincere thanks and deep appreciation for the opportunity to meet with you. While there are still profound differences between us, I think the very fact of my presence here today is a major breakthrough."

FIGURE 6.5   Progress Toward Gender Equality in Management Remains a Worthy but Ongoing Process

As this cartoon illustrates, women's (or the dragon's) presence in male-dominated professions (the knights' domain) represents a "good start," but there might seem to be some fit issues between the old membership and the new leadership. (Source: The New Yorker, 1983).

GENDER STEREOTYPES AND THE "GLASS CLIFF"   When, then, are women most likely to gain access to high-status positions—or break through the glass ceiling? Michelle Ryan and Alex Haslam offered the intriguing hypothesis that times of crisis may be "prime time" for women's advancement. There are a host of individual examples that might seem to confirm the idea that women achieve leadership positions when "things are going downhill." Here's a few examples. Shortly after Sunoco Oil's shares fell by 52 percent in 2008, Lynn Laverty Elsenhans was appointed CEO. Kate Swann was appointed CEO of the bookseller W.H. Smith following a substantial share price drop that required massive job cuts. And, not to leave out the political leadership realm, Johanna Siguroardottir was appointed the first female Prime Minister of Iceland shortly after that country's economy collapsed. To investigate whether these examples are merely coincidental or represent a real phenomena, in an intriguing series of studies, Ryan and Haslam (2005, 2007) provided evidence that women are indeed more likely to gain admittance to valued leadership positions when a crisis has occurred, the leadership position is more precarious, and there is greater risk of failure—what they refer to as the **glass cliff effect.**

glass cliff effect
Choosing women for leadership positions that are risky, precarious, or when the outcome is more likely to result in failure.

SOCIAL LIFE *in a* CONNECTED WORLD

Representations of Female and Male Figures in Video Games

You may have thought that the **objectification of females**—regarding them as mere bodies that exist for the pleasure of others—was over and done with. In schools and workplaces all over America, existing legislation is aimed at guarding against sexual misconduct, harassment, and mistreatment of females. The 1964 Civil Rights Act, Title IX, which was signed into law in 1975, and the Equal Employment Opportunity Commission are both aimed at guaranteeing females equal rights.

How then could it be that we have created an important new venue where, for all practical purposes, people of all ages can engage in violent and misogynistic behaviors with impunity? But such a place does exist. You can call it the "video game place," a place where literally thousands of people engage in online and offline gaming, much of which is loaded with pretty offensive sexism.

Who *Is* in the Video Gaming Community?

Many people believe that video games are primarily played by pale, socially inept, teenage males and, historically, there was some truth to that—young men did perceive game play more positively than women. However, Behm-Morawitz and Mastro (2009) report that the video game market is now $10 billion a year in the United States alone, and while the average devotee is a male who is about 34 years of age, a wide variety of consumers play video games today. Indeed, 40 percent of all game players in the United States are female, and 80 percent of girls grades 4–12 report playing video games. Thus, the image that many hold of the lone adolescent male playing video games is not really accurate, as girls and women are playing too, in ever-growing numbers.

For this reason, concern has been raised about the availability of "playable" female characters in video games. The percentage of games with female characters differs widely across the many video games that are available, but more female characters are being offered every day. According to Behm-Morawitz and Mastro (2009), 80 percent of role playing games (e.g., Second Life) now have some female characters.

Gender Content of Video Games

Dill and Thill (2007) found that video games offer the most blatant sex-role stereotyping of any type of mass media. For example, 83 percent of male video game characters exhibit violent and hypermasculine attributes, and when female characters do appear in video games, they mostly serve as *victims* or *prizes* to be won. That is, they are portrayed as either the "damsel in distress" awaiting male rescue or the alluring

sex object. In the gaming world though, such stereotypes of women are generally thought of as harmless fun. Is it true?

In one study, Fox and Bailenson (2009) tested the effects of sexualized (suggestively clad) and nonsexualized (conservatively clad) virtual representations of women who exhibited high-responsive gaze or low-responsive gaze behavior. Thus, avatar behavior (high or low gaze) and dress (suggestive or conservative) were manipulated. The avatars shown in the game were "embodied agents," that is, avatars who look like humans but whose responses are controlled by computer algorithms. Such computer-aided figures allow the experimenters to be sure that only the dress and gaze of the avatars varied (the face and figure remained the same). After viewing the avatar in the condition to which they were assigned, male and female undergraduates completed measures of hostile and benevolent sexism, as well as Burt's (1980) rape myth acceptance measure, which assesses beliefs such as, "In the majority of rapes, the victim is promiscuous or has a bad reputation."

The findings revealed that avatars with suggestive dress in the high-gaze condition and avatars in the conservative dress low-gaze condition produced the highest ratings on the rape myth acceptance measure. The high-gaze, suggestive-dress condition also resulted in more hostile sexism, but the low-gaze, conservative-dress condition generated more benevolent sexism. The fact that the avatar with suggestive dress and the come-hither stare is perceived as highly sexualized should come as no surprise, and both male and female participants viewing her showed higher levels of rape myth acceptance. The gaze-avoidant, conservatively dressed avatar apparently projected a submissive nature, which is consistent with a common stereotypic depiction of women as virgins that is prevalent all across the gaming world.

As troubling as the above results might be, it is worth inquiring what effect exposure to such gaming content has on subsequent behavior. To find out, Dill, Brown, and Collins (2008) conducted a study to determine changes in behavior that result from exposure to these different images of women. Participants were exposed to one of the two female images shown in Figure 6.6—either an objectified female video game character or a female politician. Males who were exposed to the objectified images showed *increased* tolerance for sexual harassment when judging a real-life case of sexual harassment between a female college student and a male professor. In contrast, female participants who were exposed to the objectified image of women showed *decreased* tolerance for sexual harassment. This may be because when women see that they are being objectified and demeaned compared to men—they are energized to advocate for the just treatment of women.

Despite a lot of progress in terms of laws aimed at protecting girls and women in educational and workplace environments, we are still fighting the same battles in the gaming world. Video game makers continue to place stereotypically drawn avatars in their products. Yet, it is no longer in doubt that exposure to stereotypically drawn characters produces real change in attitudes, which are then transformed into changes in real-life behavior. Unfortunately, so far, the creators of most computer games have simply ignored this fact.

FIGURE 6.6 **Does Exposure to Objectified Images of Women Affect Behavior?**
Males who were exposed to the objectified female image, similar to the one on the left, later showed increased tolerance when judging a case of sexual harassment compared to males exposed to the non-objectified female image (Senator Mary Landrieu of Louisiana), similar to the one on the right.

In their first archival studies, they analyzed large companies on the London Stock Exchange, assessing their performance before new members were appointed to the boards of directors. Ryan and Haslam (2005) found that companies that had experienced consistently poor stock performance in the months preceding the appointment were more likely to appoint a woman to their boards, whereas those that were performing well in the period before the appointment were unlikely to do so.

To ensure that the "bad corporate performance history" was the cause of women being selected for these positions, in a series of experiments using different respondent populations (e.g., students, managers), these researchers found that when people were presented with an equally qualified male and female candidate, the female was selected significantly more often when the position was risky and the male candidate was selected more often when the situation was not risky (Ryan, Haslam, Hersby, Kulich, & Wilson-Kovacs, 2009). Table 6.2 provides a summary of the contexts studied and findings obtained. What these findings imply is that when men's stereotypic leadership attributes appear not to be working because the organization that has been historically led by men is on a downhill trend, then, and only then, are women with their presumed stereotypic communal attributes seen as suitable for leadership (Bruckmüller & Branscombe, 2010).

objectification of females
Regarding them as mere bodies that exist for the pleasure of others.

TABLE 6.2 Are Women Most Likely to Be Appointed to Leadership Positions Under Risky Conditions?

As shown in this table, research reveals that women are consistently more likely to be selected compared to men for precarious leadership positions, whereas men are more likely to be selected when there are "good prospects" of success.

Conditions under which women have been found to be placed on "the glass cliff": respondents were provided with information about two equally qualified candidates and they favor selecting the woman over the man when:

- The organizational unit to be managed is in crisis, rather than when it is running smoothly
- Financial director for large company is to be hired when the company is on a downward trajectory versus an upward trajectory
- An attorney is appointed to a legal case that is doomed to fail, rather than when it has a good chance of success
- A director for a music festival is selected when it is declining in popularity, rather than when it is increasing in popularity
- A political candidate is selected to run when the election is unwinnable versus certain to win
- CEO hired for a supermarket chain that is losing money and closing stores versus making money and opening new stores

Source: Based on research summarize in Ryan, Haslam, Hersby, Kulich, & Wilson-Kovacs, 2009.

CONSEQUENCES OF TOKEN WOMEN IN HIGH PLACES Does the success of those individual women who do manage to break through the glass ceiling in business or politics (see Figure 6.7 for examples) make discrimination seem less plausible as an explanation for other women's relative lack of success? To the extent that the success of such numerically infrequent high-status women is taken as evidence that gender no longer matters, people may infer that the relative absence of women in high places is due to their lacking the necessary qualities or motivation to succeed. For this reason, the success of a few women may obscure the structural nature of the disadvantages that women on the whole still face. Thus, the presence of a few successful women can lead those who do not achieve similar success to believe that they only have themselves to blame (Schmitt, Ellemers, & Branscombe, 2003). A number of laboratory experiments have confirmed that tokenism, where only a few members of a previously excluded group are admitted, can be a highly effective strategy for deterring collective protest in disadvantaged groups. For instance, allowing even a small percentage (e.g., 2 percent) of low-status group members to advance into a higher-status group deters collective resistance and leads disadvantaged group members to favor individual attempts to overcome barriers (Lalonde & Silverman, 1994; Wright, Taylor, & Moghaddam, 1990).

What effect does exposure to visible tokens have on women and men who are observers? Might it make ordinary women and men complacent with regard to the ongoing barriers that women as a group face, and result in beliefs that help to maintain the status quo? Recent research has explored the consequences of exposure to token practices within an organization (Danaher & Branscombe, 2010). In one experiment, university women were first told that Boards of Regents govern universities in the United States. They were then told that the composition of the board at their university had been stable over the past 10 years and they were given a list of 10 fictitious names of people on the board. In the "open" condition, five of the names were female; in the "token" condition, only one name was female; in the "closed" condition, no female names were present, so all 10 board member names were male. The women were then asked to imagine that a seat on their Board of Regents had been vacated and that they were offered the newly opened seat. From this perspective, participants were asked to indicate the extent to which they would identify with the organization, and they completed a measure assessing their beliefs about meritocracy (e.g., "All people have equal opportunity to succeed").

In both the open and token conditions, women reported believing in meritocracy more than in the closed condition. Likewise, in both the open and token conditions, the participants reported greater identification with the organization than in the closed condition. This means that token conditions—to the same degree as when there is equal gender representation—encourages women to maintain their faith that they can move up and engenders allegiance to organizations where they are substantially underrepresented. In a subsequent experiment, both men and women were asked to imagine serving as an employee in an organization whose hiring policies resulted in 50 percent of employees being women (open), 10 percent were women (token), or only 2 percent were women (virtually closed). The open condition was seen as more fair to women and the closed condition was seen as more fair to men, but the token condition was perceived by both genders as *equally fair for women and men.* Token practices therefore appear to serve to maintain the status quo by making women's token representation in organizational settings appear fair.

There are other negative consequences of tokenism, especially when the subsequent performance and well-being of the people occupying those positions are considered. First, people who are hired as token representatives of their groups are perceived quite negatively by other members of the organization (Fuegen & Biernat, 2002; Yoder & Berendsen,

FIGURE 6.7 **Do Visible and High Status Women Lead Us to Believe That Discrimination Is a Thing of the Past?**
Hillary Clinton, U.S. Secretary of State, and Mary Fallin, Governor of Oklahoma, are both visible women who occupy important political positions. Does their presence suggest to ordinary women and men that group membership is no longer an important impediment for getting ahead?

2001). In a sense, then, such tokens are "set up" to be marginalized by their coworkers. Job applicants who are identified as "affirmative action hirees" are perceived as less competent by people reviewing their files than applicants who are not identified in this manner (Heilman, Block, & Lucas, 1992). Second, as shown in Figure 6.8, when Brown, Charnsangavej, Keough, Newman, and Rentfrow (2000) told some women that they were selected to lead a group because "there was a quota for their gender," the women's performance in that role was undermined compared to when the women were led to believe that their qualifications as well as their gender played a role in their selection.

Hiring people as token members of their group is just one form of **tokenism;** it can be manifested in other ways as well. Performing trivial positive actions for the targets of prejudice can serve as an excuse or justification for later discriminatory treatment (Wright, 2001). For perpetrators of this form of tokenism, prior positive actions serve as a *credential* that indicates their "nonprejudiced" identity (Monin & Miller, 2001), which in turn frees them to later discriminate. In whatever form it occurs, research indicates that tokenism can have at least two negative effects. First, it lets prejudiced people off the hook; they can point to the token as public proof that they aren't really bigoted, and the presence of a token helps to maintain perceptions that the existing system is legitimate and fair—even among members of the disadvantaged group. Second, it can be damaging to the self-esteem and confidence of the targets of prejudice, including those few people who are selected as tokens.

RESPONSES TO THOSE WHO SPEAK OUT ABOUT DISCRIMINA-TION What happens when tokens or other targets of discrimination complain about their treatment? Complaining about unjust circumstances can serve a useful function (Kowalski, 1996). It draws people's attention to undesirable conditions and can ultimately bring about improved future outcomes. However, complaining can also be

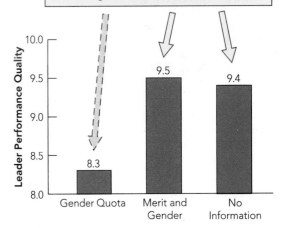

FIGURE 6.8 **Believing You Are Selected Strictly Based on Group Membership Leads to Underperformance as a Leader**
When women were told that they were selected because of a quota, their leadership performance was reduced compared to when they believed their qualifications also played a role in their selection, or when no information was given about why they were made leader. (Source: Based on data from Brown, Charnsangavej, Keough, Newman, & Rentfrow, 2000).

construed as attempting to escape personal responsibility, and that is one reason why observers might be suspicious of it.

To test this idea, Kaiser and Miller (2001) told participants about an African American student who attributed his negative grade on an essay to racial discrimination (the "complaint" condition), or that he accepted responsibility for his bad outcome (the "I'm responsible" condition). Regardless of whether the white perceivers in the study thought the bad grade was due to discrimination or not, they evaluated the student more negatively in the "complaint" condition than in the "I'm responsible" condition. Thus, even when we as observers think that another person's negative outcome is not that person's fault, we have a negative impression when that individual does not accept responsibility for the outcome and instead attributes it (accurately) to discrimination!

Moreover, members of the complainer's own ingroup may disapprove of discrimination claimers, when they believe it could suggest to outgroup members that the ingroup is given to unjustified griping (Garcia, Horstman Reser, Amo, Redersdorff, & Branscombe, 2005). Only when the complainer's ingroup believes that the complaint is appropriate because the discrimination is serious and that complaining is likely to improve the situation of the group as a whole are they likely to support a fellow ingroup member who complains about discriminatory treatment (Garcia, Schmitt, Branscombe, & Ellemers, 2010).

Is Stereotyping Absent If Members of Different Groups Are Rated the Same?

Most of us would be quick to answer this question with a definite yes, but we would be wrong! Biernat's (2005) work on **shifting standards** indicates that, although the same evaluation ratings can be given to members of different groups, stereotypes may have, nevertheless, influenced those ratings. Furthermore, those identical evaluation ratings given to members of different groups will not necessarily translate into the same behavioral expectations for the people rated—suggesting that stereotyping has occurred.

How does this work? People can use different standards—but the same words—to describe different objects. For example, I may say that I have a large cat and a small car, but I don't mean that my large cat is anywhere near the size of my small car! When I use the word *large* to describe both a car and a cat, I am using different comparisons ("large as cats go" and "small compared to other cars").

Likewise, for judgments of people, I may use the same sort of language to describe two basketball players whom I believe will actually perform quite differently. Consider the two basketball players shown in Figure 6.9. I might refer to the 10-year-old basketball player as "great," but that does not mean the same thing as when I say my favorite NBA player is "great." The 10-year-old is excellent *in comparison to other child players*, whereas the NBA player is excellent *in comparison to other professional players*. Terms such as good–bad and small–large can mask our use of different standards or category memberships—in this case, age. But other standards are available—standards that will always mean the same thing no matter what is being referred to. That is, when rating a basketball player, I might use a standard such as "percentage of free throws made over the course of a season"; such a standard is the same no matter who (the 10-year-old or the NBA player) is attempting to sink those shots from the free-throw line. These standards are referred to as **objective scales** because the meaning is the same no matter who they are applied to, whereas standards that can take on different meanings, depending on who they are applied to, are called **subjective scales.** Because people shift the meaning with subjective standards and language, it allows for real stereotyping effects to be present, *even when the same rating is given to two quite different targets.*

Let's see how this would play out when a person has to evaluate a male and a female and decide which should be appointed to a management position. If the evaluator believes that males have more competence in management than females, although both the female and male candidates are rated "good" on their likelihood of business success, that "good" rating will translate into different things on measures whose meaning is the same no

tokenism

Tokenism can refer to hiring based on group membership. It can concern a numerically infrequent presence of members of a particular category or it can refer to instances where individuals perform trivial positive actions for members of out-groups that are later used as an excuse for refusing more meaningful beneficial actions for members of these groups.

shifting standards

When we use one group as the standard but shift to use another group as the comparison standard when judging members of a different group.

objective scales

Those with measurement units that are tied to external reality so that they mean the same thing regardless of category membership (e.g., dollars earned, feet and inches, chosen or rejected).

subjective scales

Response scales that are open to interpretation and lack an externally grounded referent, including scales labeled from good to bad or weak to strong. They are said to be subjective because they can take on different meanings depending on the group membership of the person being evaluated.

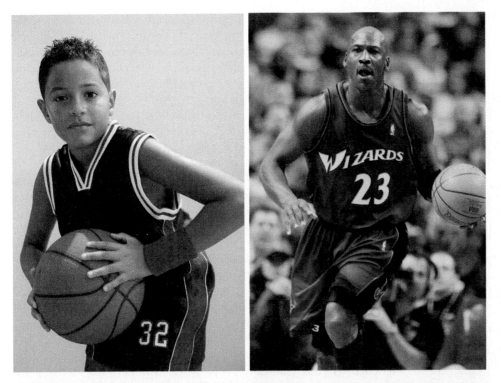

FIGURE 6.9 **Does It Mean the Same Thing When We Give Different People the Same Ratings?**

We might give both the 10-year-old player on the left and Michael Jordan the player on the right a "6" on a 1 to 6 ("very poor to very good") subjective rating scale. But the "6" rating for the boy might translate into low expectations for his ability to consistently sink baskets, whereas the "6" for the professional player would translate into high expectations for sinking baskets (% of shots sunk being an objective scale with a constant meaning no matter who it is applied to).

matter who is rated. So when asked to rate the male and female applicants on their potential sales capabilities in dollars they will sell per year, the male may be rated higher on this objective measure than the female applicant. Thus, the use of subjective rating scales can conceal the presence of stereotypical judgments, whereas use of objective scales tends to expose them. Numerous studies have supported the process where "same" ratings on subjective scales do not mean "equal" on objective scales, or the absence of stereotyping. In fact, the more people show evidence of using shifting race-based standards, the more they behaviorally discriminate against black job candidates and organizations (Biernat, Collins, Katzarska-Miller, & Thompson, 2009).

Can We Be Victims of Stereotyping and Not Even Recognize It?: The Case of Single People

Do people always recognize when they stereotype themselves and others? Or are there circumstances in which we might largely concur with widely held stereotypes—even ones that reflect poorly on ourselves? DePaulo (2006) points out one intriguing instance of this in her research on **singlism**—the negative stereotyping and discrimination that is directed toward people who are single. In a study of over 1,000 undergraduates, DePaulo and Morris (2006) measured how single and married people are characterized. As shown in Table 6.3, the attributes these primarily single participants used to describe "singles" are fairly negative, particularly in contrast to how they described

singlism
Negative stereotyping and discrimination directed toward people who are single.

TABLE 6.3 Traits Stereotypically Associated with Single and Married People

As this list of stereotypic traits illustrates, single people are stereotyped in largely negative terms, whereas those who are married are characterized in terms of more positive attributes.

TRAITS OF SINGLE PEOPLE	TRAITS OF MARRIED PEOPLE
Immature	Mature
Insecure	Stable
Self-centered	Kind
Unhappy	Happy
Ugly	Honest
Lonely	Loving
Independent	Giving

Source: Compiled based on DePaulo & Morris, 2006.

"married" people. And the differences in the descriptions spontaneously used to describe these groups was often quite substantial: 50 percent of the time, married people were described as kind, giving, and caring, but those attributes were applied to single people only 2 percent of the time. Furthermore, this difference in how married and single people are stereotyped is even greater when the targets are described as over 40 years old compared to when they were said to be 25 years of age.

Although single people currently represent more than 40 percent of American adults (U.S. Census Bureau, 2007), there is no shortage of evidence of discrimination against them (DePaulo & Morris, 2006). When asked to indicate who they would prefer to rent property to, undergraduates overwhelmingly chose a married couple (70 percent) over a single man (12 percent) or single woman (18 percent). There are also a variety of legal privileges that come with married status: employer-subsidized health benefits for spouses, discounts on auto insurance, club memberships, and travel, as well as tax and Social Security benefits. So, why is this inequality not salient (and protested) by its victims? One reason seems to be that it isn't even noticed by single people. When singles are asked if they are members of any groups that might be targets of discrimination, DePaulo and Morris (2006) found that only 4 percent spontaneously mention "single" as such a category. When asked directly if singles might be stigmatized, only 30 percent of singles say that could be the case! In contrast, almost *all* members of other stigmatized groups, including those based on race, weight, and sexual orientation, agree they could be discriminated against.

So a lack of awareness of the negative stereotyping and discrimination they face does appear to be part of the explanation for why singles themselves fail to acknowledge singlism. But might it also be a case in which people (even its victims) feel that such discrimination is warranted and therefore legitimate? When Morris, Sinclair, and DePaulo (2007) asked whether a landlord who refused to rent a property to various categories of people—an African American, woman, elderly, homosexual, or obese person—had used stereotypes and engaged in discrimination, participants agreed that was the case, but not when the person who was refused the rental was single. These results support the idea that discrimination against single people is seen—by both single and married people—as more legitimate than any of these other forms of discrimination. As we discuss in the next section on prejudice, there are groups who we seem to feel it is justified to feel prejudice toward (although it is not typical for members of those groups to agree!).

DePaulo and Morris (2006) suggest that negative stereotyping and discrimination against singles serve to protect and glorify an important social institution—marriage—and this is a central reason why it is so widespread and heavily legitimized. Singles, by definition, challenge the existing belief system that finding and marrying one's soulmate is crucial to having a meaningful life. By derogating those who challenge that idea, we can all believe in vital cultural "myths." Consider how just knowing that the people shown in Figure 6.10 have chosen to be single or are part of a couple can change what inferences we might make about what they are likely to be like.

Why Do People Form and Use Stereotypes?

Stereotypes often function as *schemas*, which as we saw in Chapter 2 are cognitive frameworks for organizing, interpreting, and recalling information (Fiske & Taylor, 2008). So categorizing people according to their group membership can be efficient for human beings who often act like "cognitive misers" and invest the least amount of cognitive effort possible in many situations. Thus, one important reason people hold stereotypes is that doing so can conserve the cognitive effort that may be used for other tasks (Bodenhausen, 1993; Macrae, Milne, & Bodenhausen, 1994). According to this view, we can simply rely on our stereotypes when responding to others and making behavioral choices.

But which stereotype are we most likely to use if people can be categorized in terms of several different group memberships? Consider the person shown in Figure 6.11. Are we most likely to stereotype her as a woman, African American, or waitress? Both race and

FIGURE 6.10   How Does Being Single or Being Part of a Couple Influence Our Perception of People?
Do the single people in Panels A and B seem more self-centered and less well-adjusted compared to when we see them as part of a couple as shown in Panel C? Research by DePaulo (2006) suggests this is the case.

gender are dominant categories that people frequently employ, but given the restaurant context and the likely interaction with her as a customer, research suggests that people would be most likely to stereotype her in terms of her occupation (Yzerbyt & Demoulin, 2010). Indeed, as you'll see below, stereotypes can serve important motivational purposes; in addition to providing us with a sense that we can predict others' behavior, they can help us feel positive about our own group identity in comparison to other social groups. For now though, let's consider what the cognitive miser perspective has illustrated in terms of how stereotypes are used.

STEREOTYPES: HOW THEY OPERATE   Consider the following groups: homosexuals, U.S. soldiers, Asian Americans, homeless people, Russians, professors, and dog lovers. Suppose you were asked to list the traits most characteristic of each. You would probably not find this a difficult task. Most people can easily construct a list for each group and they could probably do so even for groups with whom they have had limited contact. Stereotypes provide us with information about the typical traits possessed by people belonging to these groups and, once activated, these traits seem to come automatically to mind (Bodenhausen & Hugenberg, 2009). It is this fact that explains the ease with which you can construct such lists, even though you may not have had much direct experience with those groups.

Stereotypes act as theories, guiding what we attend to and exerting strong effects on how we process social information (Yzerbyt, Rocher, & Schradron, 1997). Information relevant to an activated stereotype is often processed more quickly, and remembered better, than information unrelated to it (Dovidio, Evans, & Tyler, 1986; Macrae, Bodenhausen, Milne, & Ford, 1997). Similarly, stereotypes lead us to pay attention to specific types of information—usually, information consistent with our stereotypes.

FIGURE 6.11   What Stereotype Is Most Likely to Be Activated and Applied to Predict This Person's Behavior?
Even though race and gender are basic categories that are readily employed, given the context, we are particularly likely to perceive this person in terms of her occupational role.

When we encounter someone who belongs to a group about whom we have a stereotype, and this person does not seem to fit the stereotype (e.g., a highly intelligent and cultivated person who is also a member of a low-status occupational group), we do not necessarily alter our stereotype about what is typical of members of that group. Rather, we place such people into a special category or **subtype** consisting of people who do not confirm the schema or stereotype (Queller & Smith, 2002; Richards & Hewstone, 2001). Subtyping acts to protect the stereotype of the group as a whole (Park, Wolsko, & Judd, 2001). When the disconfirming target is seen as not typical of the group as a whole, stereotypes are not revised.

DO STEREOTYPES EVER CHANGE?   If stereotypes are automatically activated and we interpret information in ways that allow us to maintain our stereotypes, this raises the question, Do stereotypes ever change? Many theorists have suggested that stereotyping will be stable as long as the nature of the intergroup relationship that exists between those groups is stable (e.g., Eagly, 1987; Oakes et al., 1994; Pettigrew, 1981; Tajfel, 1981). That is, because we construct stereotypes that reflect how we see members of different groups actually behaving, stereotype change should occur when the relations between the groups change (so the behaviors we observe change accordingly).

In an interesting demonstration of this process, Dasgupta and Asgari (2004) assessed women students' gender stereotypes in their first year and again in their second year in college. The students in this study were attending either a women's college where by their second year they would have had more repeated exposure to women faculty behaving in nontraditional ways or they were attending a coeducational college where they would have had considerably less exposure to women faculty. As expected, agreement with gender stereotypes was significantly reduced among the students attending a women's college compared to those attending a coeducational college, and the extent of the stereotype reduction effect that occurred was predicted by the number of women faculty the students had exposure to in a classroom setting.

subtype
A subset of a group that is not consistent with the stereotype of the group as a whole.

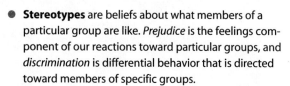

KEYPOINTS

- **Stereotypes** are beliefs about what members of a particular group are like. *Prejudice* is the feelings component of our reactions toward particular groups, and *discrimination* is differential behavior that is directed toward members of specific groups.

- **Gender stereotypes**—beliefs about the different attributes that males and females possess—play an important role in the differential outcomes that men and women receive. Women are stereotyped as high on warmth but low on competence, while men are stereotyped as low on warmth but high on competence.

- A **glass ceiling** exists such that women encounter more barriers than men in their careers, and as a result find it difficult to move into top positions. Women are especially likely to be affected in the workplace by the "think manager–think male" bias.

- Women who violate stereotypic expectancies, especially on the warmth dimension, are likely to face hostility. Defying gender stereotypes is difficult for both women and men.

- Some of the most blatant stereotyping of girls and women today can be found in video games. Exposure to sexist video game content elevates tolerance of sexual harassment in males.

- Women are most likely to be appointed to leadership positions when a crisis has occurred, the position is more precarious, and there is a greater risk of failure, which has been referred to as the **glass cliff effect.** When men's stereotypic attributes appear to have led the organization downhill, then women's presumed stereotypic communal attributes are seen as suitable in a new leader.

- **Tokenism**—the hiring or acceptance of only a few members of a particular group—has two effects: it maintains perceptions that the system is not discriminatory and it harms how tokens are perceived by others and can undermine performance when they believe their appointment to leadership positions was without regard to their merit. Exposure to token conditions can maintain people's perceptions of fairness and their belief in meritocracy.

- Publicly claiming discrimination as a cause of one's outcomes can produce negative responses in both outgroup and ingroup members, albeit for different reasons.

- Stereotypes can influence behavior even in the absence of different **subjective scale** ratings. When **objective scale** measures are employed, where **shifting standards** cannot occur and the meaning of the response is constant, the effect of stereotypes can be observed.

- In the case of **singlism**—negative stereotyping and discrimination directed toward people who are single— both single and married people show the effect. Singlism may stem from the targets being unaware of the

discrimination they face, or because they too see it as legitimate to be biased against their group.

- Stereotypes lead us to attend to information that is consistent with them, and to construe inconsistent information in ways that allow us to maintain our stereotypes. When a person's actions are strongly stereotype-discrepant, we **subtype** that person as a special case that proves the rule and do not change our stereotypes.

- Stereotypes change as the relations between the groups are altered. Those who are exposed to women in nontraditional roles show reductions in gender stereotyping.

Prejudice: Feelings Toward Social Groups

Prejudice has been traditionally considered the feeling component of attitudes toward social groups. It reflects a negative response to another person based solely on that person's membership in a particular group—which Gordon Allport, in his 1954 book *The Nature of Prejudice*, referred to as "antipathy" that is generalized to the group as a whole. In that sense, prejudice is *not* personal—it is an affective reaction toward the category (Turner, Hogg, Oakes, Reicher, & Wetherell, 1987). In other words, a person who is prejudiced toward some social group is predisposed to evaluate its members negatively because they belong to that group. Discrimination has been traditionally defined as less favorable treatment or negative actions directed toward members of disliked groups (Pettigrew, 2007). Whether prejudice will be expressed in overt discrimination or not will depend on the perceived norms or acceptability of doing so (Crandall et al., 2002; Jetten, Spears, & Manstead, 1997). Indeed, as you will see in the final section of this chapter, changing the perceived norms for treatment of a particular group is sufficient to alter prejudice expression.

Research has illustrated that individuals who score higher on measures of prejudice toward a particular group do tend to process information about that group differently than individuals who score lower on measures of prejudice. For example, information relating to the targets of the prejudice is given more attention than information not relating to them (Hugenberg & Bodenhausen, 2003). Indeed, those who are high in prejudice toward a particular social group are very concerned with learning the group membership of a person (when that is ambiguous). This is because they believe the groups have underlying **essences**—often some biologically based feature that distinguishes that group from other groups, which can serve as justification for their differential treatment (Yzerbyt, Corneille, & Estrada, 2001). As a result of consistently categorizing people in terms of their group membership, one's feelings about that group are legitimized, which results in discrimination (Talaska, Fiske, & Chaiken, 2008).

As an attitude, prejudice is the negative feelings experienced on the part of the prejudiced when they are in the presence of, or merely think about, members of the groups they dislike (Brewer & Brown, 1998). However, some theorists have suggested that all prejudices are not the same—or at least they are not based on the same type of negative feelings. According to this view, we may not be able to speak of "prejudice" as a *generic* negative emotional response at all. Instead, we may need to distinguish between prejudices that are associated with specific intergroup emotions including fear, anger, envy, guilt, or disgust (Glick, 2002; Mackie & Smith, 2002). As depicted in Figure 6.12, even when the level of prejudice toward different groups (i.e., overall negative feelings

essence
Typically some biologically based feature that is used to distinguish one group and another; frequently can serve as justification for the differential treatment of those groups.

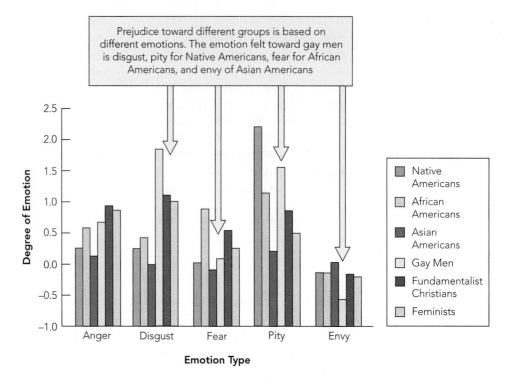

FIGURE 6.12   Different Social Groups Evoke Different Emotional Responses
Even when overall prejudice level is similar toward different groups, quite different emotional profiles—relative to the participants' own ingroup—may be evoked. This has important implications for how prejudice toward different groups might best be changed.   (Source: Based on data from Cottrell & Neuberg, 2005).

toward that group) is similar, distinct emotions can form the primary basis of prejudicial responses. For example, these respondents' primary emotional response toward Native Americans was pity, but their primary emotional response toward gay men was disgust (Cottrell & Neuberg, 2005).

Depending on what emotion underlies prejudice toward a particular group, the discriminatory actions that might be expected could be rather different. For example, when people's prejudice primarily reflects anger, then they may attempt to directly harm the outgroup (Mackie, Devos, & Smith, 2000). In contrast, prejudice based on pity or guilt might lead to avoidance of the outgroup because of the distress their plight evokes (Miron, Branscombe, & Schmitt, 2006). According to this perspective, prejudice reduction efforts may need to tackle the specific intergroup emotion on which prejudice toward a group is based. For example, to the extent that fear is reduced when prejudice is based on that emotion, then discrimination can also be reduced (Miller, Smith, & Mackie, 2004).

Research also suggests that inducing some negative emotions can directly lead to discrimination (DeSteno, Dasgupta, Bartlett, & Cajdric, 2004). In two experiments, these researchers found that after experiencing anger, but not sadness or a neutral state, more negative attitudes toward an outgroup was expressed. In these studies, participants were first assigned to **minimal groups**—they were falsely told that they *belong* to a social group that was created in the context of the study. Specifically, participants were told there were members of the group "overestimaters" or "underestimaters" of event frequencies. Once participants were categorized in this way, they were given an emotion-inducing writing task (e.g., to write in detail about when they felt very angry, very sad, or neutral in the past). Finally, participants were asked to evaluate other members of their ingroup (e.g., those wearing the same colored wristband) or the outgroup (e.g., those wearing a different-colored wristband).

minimal groups
When we are categorized into different groups based on some "minimal" criteria we tend to favor others who are categorized in the same group as ourselves compared to those categorized as members of a different group.

As shown in Figure 6.13, reaction times to associate positive or negative evaluation words with the ingroup and outgroup differed depending on the type of negative emotion participants experienced. When feeling angry, they more rapidly associated the outgroup with negative evaluations and the ingroup with positive evaluations, whereas it took considerably longer to learn to associate the outgroup with positive evaluations and the ingroup with negative evaluations. When either feeling sad or neutral, in contrast, no difference in time to associate the ingroup and outgroup with positive or negative evaluations was obtained. This suggests that even **incidental feelings** of anger—those caused by factors other than the outgroup per se (in this case, the writing task)—can generate automatic prejudice toward members of groups to which we do not belong.

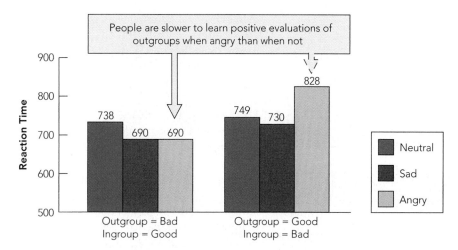

FIGURE 6.13 Prejudice Can Develop from Incidental Feelings of Anger
When feeling angry, people take longer to learn to associate positive evaluations about members of an outgroup than to learn to associate positive evaluations with members of their ingroup. Likewise, it takes longer to develop negative associations between the ingroup when angry, although negative associations about the outgroup develop rapidly. These differences in time to develop associations were only present when anger was induced and not when sadness or a neutral mood preceded the evaluation pairing task. (Source: Based on data from DeSteno et al., 2004).

As you can see, such **implicit associations**—links between group membership and evaluative responses—can be triggered in a seemingly automatic manner as a result of ingroup and outgroup categorization. As we discussed in Chapter 5, implicit attitudes can influence behavior (Fazio & Hilden, 2001; Greenwald et al., 2002). The important point about such implicit prejudice is this: we may not be aware of it, although our judgments and decisions about other people and how we interact with them can be influenced. Consider the decisions made by white participants in a simple video game about whether to shoot or not shoot either black or white targets who were armed or unarmed (Correll, Urland, & Ito, 2006). Overall, participants were quicker in deciding to shoot armed black targets than armed white targets, and they were faster in deciding not to shoot unarmed whites compared to unarmed blacks. Those who had stronger implicit associations between blacks and violence were especially likely to show these decision biases. Such automatic prejudice effects are particularly difficult to inhibit following alcohol consumption (Bartholow, Dickter, & Sestir, 2006). In these studies, participants' ability to stop responding in a stereotype-consistent fashion was lower when they drank alcohol compared to when no alcohol was consumed.

Before turning to a discussion of the many ways that prejudice can be expressed in overt behavior, we first address two important questions: What motives might affect the extent to which prejudice is felt? What psychological benefits might people get from expressing prejudice toward particular groups?

The Origins of Prejudice: Contrasting Perspectives

Several important perspectives have been developed to answer the question, Where does prejudice come from, and why does it persist? The most general response to this question has focused on perceived **threat**—be it either material or symbolic—to a valued ingroup (Esses, Jackson, & Bennett-AbuyAyyash, 2010). We consider first how perceptions of threat to self-esteem and group interests are critical for prejudice. Then we contemplate how competition for scarce resources can increase prejudice. At the end of this section, we consider whether categorizing the self as a member of a group, and others as

incidental feelings
Those feelings induced separately or before a target is encountered; as a result, those feelings are irrelevant to the group being judged but can still affect judgments of the target.

implicit associations
Links between group membership and trait associations or evaluations that the perceiver may be unaware of. They can be activated automatically based on the group membership of a target.

threat
It primarily concerns fear that our group interests will be undermined or our self-esteem is in jeopardy.

members of a different group, is a sufficient condition for prejudice to occur. Based on a cross-cultural study of 186 different societies, it is clear that the more important loyalty to one's own ingroup is, the greater the support there is for prejudice toward outgroups (Cohen, Montoya, & Insko, 2006). So feelings about one's own group are related to feelings about outgroups.

THREATS TO SELF-ESTEEM   It is certainly true that prejudice cannot be understood unless *threat* and how it affects people is taken into account. People want to see their own group positively (Tajfel & Turner, 1986), which in practice means more positively than some other group. When an event threatens people's perceptions of their group's value, they may retaliate by derogating the source of the threat. It is also the case that perceiving a threat to our group can lead us to identify more with our ingroup. Several studies, using reminders of the terrorist attacks of September 11, 2001, as the threatening event, have found increases in identification with the nation and representatives of it such as former President George W. Bush (Landau et al., 2004).

Does the event that threatens one's group identity need to involve possible death, or is it sufficient that it simply implies your group is not as positive as you would like to see it, for prejudice responses to occur? To test this idea, American college students, who differed in the extent to which they placed value on their identity as Americans, were shown one of two 6-minute videos based on the movie *Rocky IV* (Branscombe & Wann, 1994). In one clip, Rocky (an American boxer played by Sylvester Stallone) won the match against Ivan (a supposedly Russian contender). This version was not threatening, for it supports Americans' positive views of their group as winners. In the other clip, Rocky loses the fight to Ivan, the Russian. This version was threatening, particularly to those who highly value their identity as Americans, and it lowered feelings of self-esteem based on group membership. The question is, Can exposure to such a minor threat to identity in the laboratory result in prejudice? The answer obtained was yes—those who were highly identified as Americans and who saw the threatening Rocky "as loser" film clip showed increased prejudice toward Russians and advocated they be kept out of the United States in the future. In fact, the more these participants negatively evaluated Russians, the more their self-esteem based on their group membership subsequently increased.

This research suggests that holding prejudiced views of an outgroup allows group members to bolster their own group's image, particularly when it has been threatened. By "putting down" members of another group, we can affirm our own group's comparative value—and such prejudice is most strongly expressed when threat is experienced. The important role of such perceived threat to one's group has been demonstrated in a wide variety of group contexts: Whites' prejudice toward black Americans (Stephan et al., 2002), prejudice toward various immigrant groups (Esses, Jackson, Nolan, & Armstrong, 1999; Stephan, Renfro, Esses, Stephan, & Martin, 2005), Catholics and Protestants in Northern Ireland (Tausch, Hewstone, Kenworthy, & Cairns, 2007), and men's prejudice and sabotaging actions toward women they perceive as "moving in" on males' traditional territory (Rudman & Fairchild, 2004). Evidence for this process, illustrated in Figure 6.14, has been obtained in numerous studies.

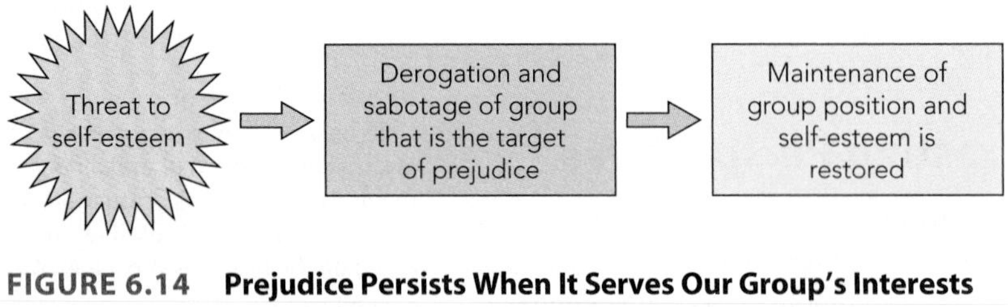

Overall, then, advantaged groups exhibit prejudice toward outgroups most strongly when they are experiencing a threat to their group's image and interests. Because of the critical role that perceived threat can play in maintaining and escalating prejudice, recent research has addressed how such threat may be reduced (Riek, Mania, Gaertner, McDonald, & Lamoreaux, 2010). They found that simply reminding people who value their ingroup identity—as Democrats or Republicans—that

FIGURE 6.14   Prejudice Persists When It Serves Our Group's Interests
When self-esteem is threatened, people are most likely to derogate the groups representing the threat. Indeed, doing so helps to boost or restore threatened self-esteem. Via this mechanism, groups can maintain their dominant positions. (Source: Based on data from Branscombe & Wann, 1994; Rudman & Fairchild, 2004).

they shared a more inclusive identity (American) with the other group lowered perceived threat and prejudice. We return to this technique, known as recategorization, in our discussion of procedures for reducing prejudice.

COMPETITION FOR RESOURCES AS A SOURCE OF PREJUDICE   It is sad but true that the things people want most—good jobs, nice homes—are in short supply. Quite frequently, these are **zero-sum outcomes**—if one group gets them, the other group can't. Consider the conflict between the Israelis and Palestinians, which has been ongoing since the creation of the state of Israel in 1948. Both want to control Jerusalem. This sort of conflict over desirable territory has been considered within **realistic conflict theory** to be a major cause of prejudice (Bobo, 1983). The theory further suggests that as competition escalates, the members of the groups involved will come to view each other in increasingly negative terms. They may label each other as "enemies," view their own group as morally superior, draw the boundaries between themselves and their opponents more firmly, and, under extreme conditions, may come to see the opposing group as not even human (Bar-Tal, 2003). From this perspective, what starts out as simple competition can escalate into full-scale prejudice (see Figure 6.15).

A classic study by Sherif, Harvey, White, Hood, and Sherif (1961) confirms that competition can intensify conflict, although as you will see, it may not be the *most basic cause* of conflict between groups. Well-adjusted middle-class boys were brought to a summer camp called Robber's Cave, located in rural Oklahoma. The boys were randomly assigned to two different groups and placed in well-separated cabins so they were unaware of the existence of the other group. Initially, the boys in each cabin enjoyed hiking, swimming, and other sports, and the boys rapidly developed strong attachments to their group—choosing names for themselves (Rattlers and Eagles) and making up flags with their groups' symbols on them. In the second phase of the study, the groups were brought together and they began a series of competitions. They were told that the winning team would receive a trophy and various desirable prizes; since the boys wanted the prizes badly, the stage was set for intense competition.

As the boys competed, the tension between the groups rose. At first it was limited to verbal taunts, but soon escalated into direct acts—such as when the Rattlers broke into the Eagles' cabin, overturning beds and generally wreaking havoc. The two groups voiced

zero-sum outcomes
Those that only one person or group can have. So, if one group gets them, the other group can't.

realistic conflict theory
The view that prejudice stems from direct competition between various social groups over scarce and valued resources.

FIGURE 6.15   Intergroup Competition as a Source of Prejudice
When groups compete with each other for valued resources (e.g., land), they may come to view each other in increasingly hostile terms. The way to Jerusalem is shown in the language of the Israelis (Hebrew) and the Palestinians (Arabic), the two groups in competition for this territory, which some claim actually belongs to members of all the world's great religions.

increasingly negative views of each other, while heaping praise on their own group. In short, strong prejudice developed.

In the final phase, competition was eliminated, but that alone did not reduce the negative reactions toward the other group. Only when conditions were altered so that the groups found it necessary to work together to reach **superordinate goals**—ones they both desired but neither group could achieve alone—did dramatic change occur. The boys worked cooperatively together to restore their water supply (secretly sabotaged by the researchers), combined funds to rent a movie, and jointly repaired a broken-down truck so they could all go into town to get ice cream. The tensions between the groups gradually decreased, and many cross-group friendships developed.

Despite what Sherif's research showed about factors that can elevate and reduce intergroup conflict, what he did not show is whether competition is *necessary* for prejudice to develop. In fact, prior to the introduction of the competition, the *mere knowledge* of the other group was sufficient to generate name-calling between the two groups of boys. Perhaps simply being a member of a group and identifying with it is sufficient for prejudice to emerge. This is the idea that Tajfel and Turner (1986) developed further in their social identity theory, which we turn to next.

ROLE OF SOCIAL CATEGORIZATION: THE US-VERSUS-THEM EFFECT "How is genocide possible?" This was a question that preoccupied Henri Tajfel throughout his life, in part because he was a Jew who had lived through the Nazi Holocaust. Unlike some who believed that the source of such intergroup violence lay in irrationality, Tajfel (1982) believed that there were important cognitive processes involved. He argued that a history of conflict, personal animosity, individual self-interest, or competition were not *necessary* to create group behavior. Perhaps, as with boys in Sherif's study, if people were merely categorized into different groups, then you would see the beginnings of ingroup loyalty and outgroup discrimination. Indeed, he was searching for a "baseline" condition where prejudice would be lacking when he stumbled onto the most basic condition needed to create discrimination.

superordinate goals
Those that can only be achieved by cooperation between groups.

Tajfel, Billig, Bundy, and Flament (1971) originated a paradigm for studying intergroup behavior in which participants were categorized into groups on some trivial basis. He had participants view a set of pictures—as shown in Figure 6.16—by the artists Klee and Kandinsky. In all instances, participants were assigned to one group or the other randomly, but were told that it was based on whether they had shared a preference for Klee or Kandinsky paintings. Each group that was so created had no purpose, no history, no contact among its members, no leader—that is, nothing whatsoever that would cause it to be a real "group."

The task of the participants was simply to allocate points or money between two other participants—one of whom was an

FIGURE 6.16   Social Categorization: InGroups and OutGroups
Which painting do you prefer? In Panel A, the artist Paul Klee's work is shown, and a Kandinsky painting is shown in Panel B. A "minimal" categorization can be created by telling participants that they share a preference for one artist over the other.

ingroup member and one of whom was an outgroup member. Participants on average awarded members of their own group more money than members of the other group. Furthermore, when participants could choose to allocate more money in *absolute terms* to members of their own group, they chose to allocate smaller absolute amounts *if* that would also mean allocating *relatively* less to members of the other group, suggesting that the participants were attempting to maximize the difference between the rewards given to the two groups. The results of these experiments were shocking at the time because they illustrated how people could be divided into distinct categories on almost any basis, and doing so could result in different perceptions of, and actions toward, *us* (members of their own group) versus *them* (members of the other group).

Once the social world is divided into "us" and "them," it takes on emotional significance. Some differences are granted social importance and have meaning for our identities (Oakes et al., 1994). People in the "us" category are viewed in more favorable terms, whereas those in the "them" category are perceived more negatively. Indeed, it may be widely *expected* that some groups should be disliked, whereas prejudice toward other groups is seen as not justified (Crandall et al., 2002). For example, college students who were asked to rate the extent to which it was appropriate or legitimate to express prejudice toward 105 different social groups did so easily. The top 10 groups it is acceptable to display prejudice toward, and the 10 for whom it is least legitimate to express prejudice against, are shown in Table 6.4.

How, precisely, does social categorization result in prejudice? **Social identity theory** suggests that individuals seek to feel positively about the groups to which they belong, and part of our self-esteem is derived from our social group memberships. Since people who are identified with their group are most likely to express favoritism toward their own group and a corresponding bias against outgroups, valuing our own group will have predictable consequences for prejudice. (For more information on how feeling "fused with our group" can affect willingness to engage in extreme actions to benefit and protect it, please see our special feature, "EMOTIONS AND PREJUDICE: When Are People Willing to Die and Kill for Their Group?".)

TABLE 6.4   Who Do We Believe It Is OK or Not OK to Express Prejudice Toward?

The "top 10" list on the left indicates what groups college students perceive it to be acceptable and legitimate to feel prejudice toward. The "top 10" list on the right indicates what groups they perceive it to be unacceptable and illegitimate to feel prejudice toward. How do you think these lists would differ for people living in other regions of the United States besides the Midwest? How might they differ for people who are members of different ethnic groups?

PREJUDICE LEGITIMIZED	PREJUDICE SEEN AS ILLEGITIMATE
Rapists	Blind people
Child abusers	Women homemakers
Child molesters	People who are deaf
Wife beaters	People who are mentally impaired
Terrorists	Family men
Racists	Farmers
Ku Klux Klan members	Male nurses
Drunk drivers	Librarians
Nazi party members	Bowling league members
Pregnant women who drink alcohol	Dog owners

Source: Based on data provided by Crandall, Eshleman, & O'Brien, 2002.

social identity theory
A theory concerned with the consequences of perceiving ourselves as a member of a social group and identifying with it.

EMOTIONS *and* PREJUDICE

When Are People Willing to Die and Kill for Their Group?

Would you be willing to sacrifice your own life to save other members of your ingroup? Would you be willing to kill terrorists who represent a threat to your ingroup? Of course, soldiers have always been expected to answer yes to such questions—to be willing to lay down their lives for their country. But new research has asked these questions of ordinary citizens in Spain (Swann, Gómez, Dovidio, Hart, & Jetten, 2010).

The measure these researchers used to assess "identity fusion"—the extent to which you see yourself and your group as overlapping—is shown at the top of Figure 6.17. If the group is your nation, which graphic image would you pick to reflect your relationship to your group? People who select option E are said to be "fused" with their group, while those who select options A–D are said to be "nonfused." The idea is that people who see themselves as fused with their

(continued)

EMOTIONS *and* **PREJUDICE** *(continued)*

nation yoke their individual agency to the group and see the group's outcomes as like their own. Therefore, when given an opportunity to defend and protect their group, they will be more willing to do so than those who do not yoke themselves to their group.

In a series of experiments, fused and nonfused students at a university in Madrid were asked how they would respond to a moral dilemma. The dilemma they were confronted with has been referred to as the "trolley problem." First, the students were asked to imagine a runaway trolley

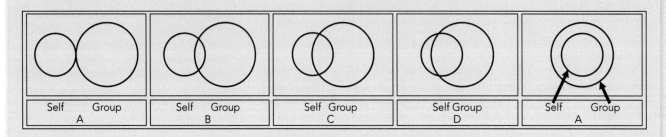

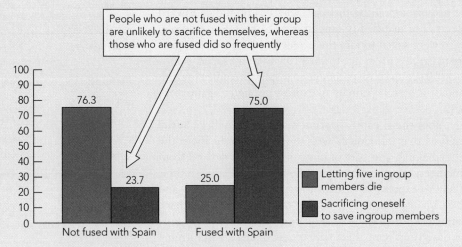

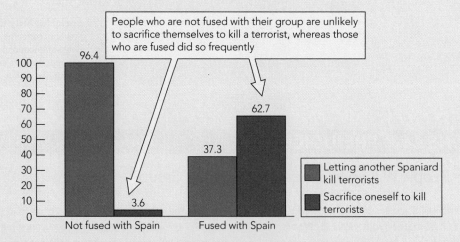

FIGURE 6.17   Identity Fusion: Dying and Killing for One's Group

People who are "fused" see themselves as completely overlapping with their group—indicated by their endorsement of a pictorial representation that places the self completely inside the group (response option "E"). A greater percentage of those who were fused with their national group, Spain, were willing to sacrifice themselves to save ingroup members (graph A) and to kill a terrorist who represented a threat to their ingroup (graph B) than were people who were not fused. (Source: Based on research by Swann, Gómez, Dovidio, Hart, & Jetten, 2010).

that was about to kill five of their ingroup members, unless the participant jumped from a bridge onto the trolley's path, thereby redirecting the trolley away from the others. Participants had to choose between letting the trolley crush five of their fellow ingroup members or sacrificing themselves to save the five other Spaniards (who were strangers to them). As you can see in the top graph in Figure 6.17, 75 percent of those who were fused with Spain chose to sacrifice themselves to save five others, whereas only 24 percent who were not fused chose to do so. This study suggests that fused individuals believe they would act morally in ways aimed at benefiting the ingroup, even at their own personal expense. And it isn't just that fused people are more altruistic than nonfused people. In a subsequent study, when these Spanish students were led to consider Europeans their ingroup, they were more willing to sacrifice their lives to save five other Europeans than were nonfused Spaniards, but they were not willing to do so to save outgroup members—in this case, Americans. Their emotional responses depended on *who* they believed were at risk of being run over by the trolley.

So, while fused people may be more willing to die to protect their ingroup than those who are not fused, are they also willing to kill others who represent a threat to their group? To investigate this possibility, the researchers first asked Spanish students to imagine that it was March 11, 2004, the day Al-Qaeda terrorists set off bombs in the Madrid railway system. Participants were to imagine themselves standing on a footbridge in the station where the attacks occurred, when they see the terrorists who set off the bombs running on the tracks below. Although another Spaniard was preparing to jump into the path of an approaching train so that it would veer onto the tracks where the terrorists were and kill them, participants were asked to decide whether they would allow the other Spaniard to jump and cause the train to change tracks and kill the terrorists or if they would push the other Spaniard aside and jump to their own death in order to be the one who killed the terrorists.

As the second graph in Figure 6.17 illustrates, 62 percent of the fused participants said they would sacrifice themselves to kill the terrorists, whereas only 4 percent of the nonfused participants did so. Indeed, virtually all of the nonfused with Spain students said they would let someone else die to kill the terrorists, whereas only about one-third of the fused participants were willing to let someone else, who was prepared to do so, potentially have the glory of killing those who had harmed the ingroup. When people's identities are fused with a group, they appear willing to undertake extreme forms of self-sacrifice and do mortal harm to outgroups that represent a threat to their group. This research provides us with insight into how emotional responses to others and extreme behavior can be influenced by people's relationship to their group (fused or not fused) and how we categorize those who have been put at risk ("us" or "them").

KEY POINTS

- *Prejudice* is the feelings component of attitudes toward members of a group as a whole.

- *Discrimination* refers to the unfavorable treatment or negative actions directed toward members of disliked groups. Whether discrimination will be expressed or not depends on the perceived norms or acceptability of doing so.

- Research indicates that prejudice may reflect more specific underlying emotional responses toward different outgroups, including fear, anger, guilt, pity, and disgust. Different behaviors are likely, depending on the emotional basis of the prejudice.

- **Implicit associations**—links between group membership and evaluations—can be triggered automatically from categorizing others as ingroup or outgroup members.

- Prejudice persists because derogating outgroups can protect our self-esteem. **Threat** to our group's interests can motivate prejudice, and perceived competition between groups for resources can escalate conflict.

- The Robber's Cave study of two groups of boys at a summer camp who had been in conflict showed that **superordinate goals**—where desired outcomes can only be obtained if the groups work together—can help to reduce conflict.

- According to **social identity theory,** prejudice is derived from our tendency to divide the world into "us" and "them" and to view our own group more favorably than various outgroups. This is true even when the groups are formed on a trivial basis.

- People may feel it is legitimate to display prejudice toward some groups, but see it as highly illegitimate to express prejudice toward other groups.

- People who are fused with their group are particularly likely to sacrifice their own lives to save other ingroup members. People fused with Spain, when reminded of the terrorist attacks on their nation, expressed a greater willingness to shove aside another Spaniard and kill themselves in order to kill the terrorists compared to people not fused with Spain.

Discrimination: Prejudice in Action

Attitudes, as we noted in Chapter 5, are not always reflected in overt actions, and prejudice is no exception to this. In many cases, people with negative attitudes toward various groups cannot express their views directly. Laws, social pressure, fear of retaliation—all serve to deter them from putting their prejudiced views into practice. For these reasons, blatant forms of discrimination—negative actions toward the objects of racial, ethnic, and gender prejudice—have decreased in recent years in the United States and many other countries (Devine, Plant, & Blair, 2001; Swim & Campbell, 2001). Thus, actions such as restricting members of various groups to certain seats on buses or in movie theaters, barring them from public schools—all common in the past—have vanished. This is not to suggest that extreme expressions of prejudice do not occur. On the contrary, dramatic instances of "hate crimes"—crimes based on racial, ethnic, and other types of prejudice—do occur. For instance, Matthew Shepard, a college student, was murdered in Wyoming in 1998 because of his sexual preference (he was homosexual), and in 2010 several gay students committed suicide in response to the bullying they experienced because of their sexual orientation. Despite these extreme incidents, prejudice, in general, often finds expression in much more subtle forms of behavior. We turn now to these *subtle* or *disguised* forms of discrimination.

Modern Racism: More Subtle, But Just as Deadly

At one time, many people felt no qualms about expressing openly racist beliefs (Sears, 2007). Now, few Americans agree with such anti-black sentiments. Does this mean that racism is on the wane? Many social psychologists believe that "old-fashioned racism," encompassing blatant feelings of superiority, has been replaced by more subtle forms, which they term **modern racism** (McConahay, 1986; Swim Aikin, Hall, & Hunter, 1995).

What is such racism like? It can involve concealing prejudice from others in public settings, but expressing bigoted attitudes when it is safe to do so, for instance, in the company of friends known to share these views. Indeed, peers' prejudiced attitudes are one of the best predictors of one's own prejudiced attitudes (Poteat & Spanierman, 2010). It might also involve attributing various bigoted views to sources other than prejudice, whenever another explanation for potentially biased behavior is feasible. It could also involve attempting to appear "color blind" and refusing to acknowledge race as a means of suggesting one isn't racist.

In an interesting demonstration of this strategy (Norton, Sommers, Apfelbaum, Pura, & Ariely, 2006), white participants who were concerned about appearing racist were placed in a setting where they had to describe other individuals to either a black partner or a white partner. When their partner in this game was black, participants were reluctant to use race as a descriptive term—even when highly diagnostic of the people they were asked to describe (e.g., the only black person in a group of whites). In contrast, when their partner was white, the same people the participant was to describe were referred to in terms of their race. Precisely because many people want to conceal their racist attitudes—both from others as well as from themselves—and "failing to even notice race" might seem to be one way of doing so, social psychologists have had to develop unobtrusive means of studying such attitudes. Let's take a look at how such attitudes can be detected.

MEASURING IMPLICIT RACIAL ATTITUDES: FINDING A "BONA FIDE PIPELINE"   The most straightforward approach to measuring prejudice is to simply ask people to express their views toward various racial or ethnic groups. But many people are not willing to admit to holding prejudiced views, so alternative ways of assessing their actual views have been developed. In recent years, as we discussed in Chapter 5, social psychologists have recognized that many attitudes people hold are *implicit*—they exist and can influence behavior, but the people holding them may not be aware of their impact. In fact, in some cases, they might vigorously deny that they have such views, and instead proclaim their "color blindness"

modern racism
More subtle beliefs than blatant feelings of superiority. It consists primarily of thinking minorities are seeking and receiving more benefits than they deserve and a denial that discrimination affects their outcomes.

(Dovidio & Gaertner, 1999; Greenwald & Banaji, 1995). How then can such subtle forms of prejudice be measured? Several different methods have been developed (Kawakami & Dovidio, 2001), but most are based on *priming*—where exposure to certain stimuli or events "prime" information held in memory, making it easier to bring to mind, or more available to influence our current reactions.

One technique that makes use of priming to study implicit or automatically activated racial attitudes is known as the **bona fide pipeline** (Banaji & Hardin, 1996; Towles-Schwen & Fazio, 2001). With this procedure, participants see various adjectives and are asked to indicate whether they have a "good" or "bad" meaning by pushing one of two buttons. Before seeing each adjective, however, they are briefly exposed to faces of people belonging to various racial groups (blacks, whites, Asians, Latinos). It is reasoned that implicit racial attitudes will be revealed by how quickly participants respond to the words that have a negative meaning. In contrast, participants will respond more slowly to words with a positive meaning after being primed with the faces of those same minority group members because the positive meaning is inconsistent with the negative attitude elicited by the priming stimulus.

Research findings using this procedure indicate that people do indeed have implicit racial attitudes that are automatically elicited, and that such automatically elicited attitudes, in turn, can influence important forms of behavior such as decisions concerning others and the degree of friendliness that is expressed in interactions with them (Fazio & Hilden, 2001; Towles-Schwen & Fazio, 2001). The important point to note is this: Despite the fact that blatant forms of racism and sexism have decreased, automatic prejudice is very much alive, and, through more subtle kinds of reactions, continues to affect behavior.

HOW PREJUDICED PEOPLE MAINTAIN AN "UNPREJUDICED" SELF-IMAGE Despite the evidence of ongoing racial inequality, as well as widespread existence of subtle and implicit prejudice, many white Americans believe they are unprejudiced (Feagin & Vera, 1995; Saucier, 2002). So, given the strong evidence that racial prejudice is still with us (Dovidio et al., 2010), how do people who harbor prejudice come to perceive themselves as unprejudiced?

Recent research suggests that it is through social comparison with extreme images of bigots that many people who are prejudiced can perceive themselves as not matching that prototype (O'Brien et al., 2010). In a series of studies, these researchers exposed participants to words or images reflecting extreme bigotry such as those shown in Figure 6.18. In each case, participants exposed to the bigotry primes rated themselves as more unprejudiced than participants exposed to race-neutral materials. In fact, when the possibility that they might be revealed as harboring racism was suggested, participants expressed greater interest in viewing extreme racist materials than participants who were not threatened with the possibility that their own racism might be revealed.

WHEN WE CONFRONT WHAT OUR GROUP HAS DONE TO ANOTHER GROUP People want to think of the groups that they belong to and identify with as being good and moral. In recent years, particularly with the release of photographs of American soldiers humiliating Muslim detainees and torturing them at Abu Ghraib prison in Iraq and elsewhere, research has considered the question of how people respond when they learn about the prejudicial actions of their own group. Do we perceive such harmful actions as torture, or as justifiable? In a representative sample of American adults, Crandall, Eidelman, Skitka, and Morgan (2009) described such practices of torture against detainees as either part of the status quo, having been used for more than 40 years, or as new and something their group had never done previously. They found that torture was seen as more justifiable when described as a long-standing practice compared to when it was described as something new.

Exposure to how one's group has acted in a prejudiced fashion toward other groups can evoke defenses in order to avoid the aversive feelings of **collective guilt**—an emotional response that people can experience when they perceive their group as responsible for illegitimate wrongdoings (Branscombe & Miron, 2004). When the ingroup's responsibility

bona fide pipeline
A technique that uses priming to measure implicit racial attitudes.

collective guilt
The emotion that can be experienced when we are confronted with the harmful actions done by our ingroup against an outgroup. It is most likely to be experienced when the harmful actions are seen as illegitimate.

FIGURE 6.18 **Extreme Representations of Racists Help Many Maintain the View That They are Unprejudiced**

Exposure to extreme images or even just the labels of these groups (e.g., KKK) relative to a control condition in which these images are absent increases white American students' perception that they are unprejudiced. This is because these racist groups set an extreme comparison, which college students do not match.

for the harmful actions cannot be denied, people can "blame the victims" for its occurrence by suggesting that they deserved the outcomes they received. Derogation of victims helps perpetrators to be "less burdened" when faced with their harm doing (Bandura, 1990). At its most extreme, the victims can even be excluded from the category "human" entirely so they are seen as not deserving humane treatment at all, which will permit any harm done to them to be seen as justified (Bar-Tal, 1990). As Aquino, Reed, Thau, and Freeman (2006) illustrate in their research, dehumanization of the victims helps to justify our group's actions as having served a "righteous purpose"—that of retaliating against our enemy's "evil." **Moral disengagement**—no longer seeing sanctioning as necessary for perpetrating harm—makes it "okay" for our military personnel to mistreat prisoners in Abu Ghraib or at Guantanamo Bay, if doing so can be seen as somehow protecting the ingroup (Bandura, 1999).

There are other ways that people can deal with their group's harm-doing—such as motivated forgetting. Sahdra and Ross (2007) have shown that people's memory for harmful behaviors committed by their ingroup is not equivalent to their memory of instances where their ingroup was victimized by another group. In their research, Sikh and Hindu Canadians were asked about their memories concerning events that were committed in India by Sikhs and Hindus, in which each group had targeted innocent and unarmed members of the other group for violent acts. When asked to recall three incidents from the 1980s (a period of heavy intergroup violence), incidents where their own group had been perpetrators of violence were less likely to be remembered compared to incidents in which their group members were the victims of violence. Those who were more highly identified with their ingroup recalled the fewest instances of ingroup harm-doing to others. Members of both the groups involved in this religious conflict tailored their memories so that events in which their group perpetrated harm to others were more difficult to bring to mind than events in which the other group victimized their group. Thus, people have available to them a variety of motivated mental strategies that help them maintain a favorable view of their ingroup, despite its prejudicial treatment of others.

moral disengagement
No longer seeing sanctioning as necessary for perpetrating harm that has been legitimized.

KEYPOINTS

- Blatant racial discrimination has decreased, but more subtle forms such as **modern racism** persist.
- Those high in modern racism may want to hide their prejudice. The **bona fide pipeline** is based on the assumption that people are unaware of their prejudices, but they can be revealed with *implicit* measures where priming a category to which the individual has negative attitudes will result in faster responses to words with negative meanings.
- People can maintain the view that they are unprejudiced by comparing themselves to extreme bigots.

- When we are exposed to instances in which members of our own group have behaved in a prejudicial fashion, we can avoid feeling **collective guilt** to the extent that we can conclude the harmful acts were legitimate because it is a long-standing practice, the people harmed do not warrant concern, or because doing so serves the ingroup's higher goals. People also show evidence of motivated forgetting of their own group's harm-doing.

Why Prejudice Is Not Inevitable: Techniques for Countering Its Effects

Prejudice, in some form, appears to be an all-too-common aspect of life in most, if not all, societies (Sidanius & Pratto, 1999). Does this mean that it is inevitable? As we explained throughout this chapter, prejudice certainly has some clear properties (e.g., it will escalate under competition, when others are categorized as the outgroup). Yet, under the right conditions, prejudice toward particular groups can be reduced. We now turn to some of the techniques that social psychologists have developed in their attempts to reduce prejudice.

On Learning Not to Hate

According to the **social learning view,** children acquire negative attitudes toward various social groups because they hear such views expressed by significant others, and because they are directly rewarded (with love, praise, and approval) for adopting these views. In addition, people's own direct experience with people belonging to other groups also shapes attitudes. Evidence for the strong impact of both these types of childhood experiences on several aspects of racial prejudice has been reported (Towles-Schwen & Fazio, 2003). That is, the more white participants' parents are prejudiced, and the less positive participants' own interactions with minority group people were, the more discriminatory their behavior when interacting with African Americans.

Perhaps the degree to which parents' racial attitudes and their childrens' are related depends on the extent to which children identify with their parents (Sinclair, Dunn, & Lowery, 2005). Children who care about making their parents proud of them should show the greatest parental influence. In a sample of fourth and fifth graders, it was found that parental and children's racial attitudes were positively related *only* among children with relatively high identification with their parents.

However, people continue to be socialized in terms of ethnic attitudes well beyond childhood. What are the consequences of joining institutions that subtly support either diversity or prejudice toward particular outgroups? Guimond (2000) investigated this issue among Canadian military personnel. He found that English Canadians became significantly more prejudiced toward specific outgroups (e.g., French Canadians, immigrants, and civilians) and internalized justifications for the economic gap between their own group and these outgroups as they progressed through the 4-year officer training program. Furthermore, he found that the more they identified with the military, the more they showed increases in prejudice over time. It would seem therefore that institutions,

social learning view (of prejudice)
The view that prejudice is acquired through direct and vicarious experiences in much the same manner as other attitudes.

which can be molded to value diversity or prejudice, can exert considerable influence on the adults who identify with them.

The Potential Benefits of Contact

Can racial prejudice be reduced by increasing the degree of contact between different groups? The idea that it can do so is known as the **contact hypothesis** and there are several good reasons for predicting that such a strategy can be effective (Pettigrew, 1997). Increased contact among people from different groups can lead to a growing recognition of similarities between them—which can change the categorizations that people employ. As we saw earlier, those who are categorized as "us" are responded to more positively than those categorized as "them." Increased contact, or merely having knowledge that other members of our group have such contact with outgroup members, can signal that the norms of the group are not so "anti-outgroup" as individuals might initially have believed. The existence of cross-group friendships suggests that members of the outgroup do not necessarily dislike members of our ingroup, and this knowledge can reduce intergroup anxiety.

Consider, for example, the situation of Catholics and Protestants in Northern Ireland. Members of these groups live in highly segregated housing districts, and contact between the members of the two groups is often perceived negatively. Social psychologists there (Paolini, Hewstone, Cairns, & Voci, 2004) have, however, found that direct contact between members of these two religious groups, as well as indirect contact (via knowledge of other ingroup members' friendships with outgroup members) can reduce prejudice by reducing anxiety about future encounters with outgroup members.

Other research has likewise suggested that among linguistic groups throughout Europe, positive contact that is seen as reflective of increased cooperation between the groups can change norms so that group equality is favored and, thereby, reduce prejudice (Van Dick et al., 2004). Moreover, the beneficial effects of such cross-group friendships can readily spread to other people who have not themselves experienced such contacts: simply knowing about them can be enough.

In a series of studies involving heterosexuals who were friends with a gay man, Vonofakou, Hewstone, and Voci (2007) found that degree of perceived closeness with the friend and the extent to which the gay friend was seen as typical of that group predicted lower prejudice toward gay men as a whole. Perceived closeness lessened anxiety about interacting with gay people, and perceiving the friend as typical ensured that the friend was not subtyped as different from other members of the group—optimal conditions for generalization of contact and stereotype change.

Recategorization: Changing the Boundaries

Think back to your high school days. Imagine that your school's basketball team was playing an important game against a rival school from a nearby town. In this case, you would certainly view your own school as "us" and the other school as "them." But now imagine that the other school's team won, and went on to play against a team from another state in a national tournament. *Now* how would you view them? The chances are good that under these conditions, you would view the other school's team (the team you lost to) as "us"; after all, they now represent *your* state. And of course, if a team from a state other than your own was playing against teams from other countries, you might then view them as "us" relative to the "foreign team."

Situations like this, in which we shift the boundary between "us" and "them," are quite common in everyday life, and they raise an interesting question: Can such shifts—or **recategorizations** as they are termed by social psychologists—be used to reduce prejudice? The **common ingroup identity model** suggests that it can (Gaertner, Rust, Dovidio, Bachman, & Anastasio, 1994; Riek et al., 2010). To the extent that individuals who belong to different social groups come to view themselves as members of a *single social entity*, their attitudes toward each other become more positive. So, while "us and them" categorical

contact hypothesis
The view that increased contact between members of various social groups can be effective in reducing prejudice between them.

recategorization
Shifts in the boundaries between our ingroup ("us") and some outgroup ("them"). As a result of such recategorization, people formerly viewed as outgroup members may now be viewed as belonging to the ingroup and consequently are viewed more positively.

common ingroup identity model
A theory suggesting that to the extent individuals in different groups view themselves as members of a single social entity, intergroup bias will be reduced.

distinctions can produce prejudice, as we learned earlier in this chapter, when "them" becomes "us," prejudice should be eliminated.

How can we induce people who belong to different groups to perceive themselves as members of a single group? As Sherif et al. (1961) observed at the Robber's Cave boys camp discussed earlier, when individuals belonging to initially distinct groups work together toward shared or superordinate goals, they come to perceive themselves as a single social entity. Then, feelings of hostility toward the former outgroup—toward "them"—seem to fade away. Such effects have been demonstrated in several studies (Gaertner, Mann, Dovidio, Murrell, & Pomare, 1990; Gaertner, Mann, Murrell, & Dovidio, 1989), both in the laboratory and the field. When recategorization is successfully induced, it has proven to be a useful technique for reducing prejudice toward those who were previously categorized as outgroup members.

The power of shifting to a more inclusive category for reductions in negative feelings toward an outgroup has been shown even among groups with a long history, including one group's brutality toward another. Consider how Jews in the present are likely to feel about Germans, given the Holocaust history. Although that conflict has long been terminated, to the extent that the victim group continues to categorize Jews and Germans as separate and distinct groups, contemporary Germans are likely to be responded to with prejudice—even though they were not alive during the time of the Nazi atrocities against the Jews. In a strong test of the recategorization hypothesis, Jewish Americans were induced to either think about Jews and Germans as separate groups, or to categorize them as members of a single and maximally inclusive group—that of humans (Wohl & Branscombe, 2005). Following this manipulation, Jewish participants were asked to indicate the extent to which they were willing to forgive Germans for the past. In the condition, where Germans and Jews were thought about as separate groups, participants reported less forgiveness of Germans compared to when the two groups were included in one social category—that of humans. Including members of an outgroup in the same category as the ingroup has important consequences for prejudice reduction and willingness to have social contact—even with members of an "old enemy" group.

The Benefits of Guilt for Prejudice Reduction

When people are confronted with instances in which they have personally behaved in a prejudiced fashion, it can lead to feelings of guilt for having violated one's personal standards (Monteith, Devine, & Zuwerink, 1993; Plant & Devine, 1998). But what about when a person is a member of a group that has a history of being prejudiced toward another group—might that person feel "guilt by association," even if that person has not personally behaved in a prejudiced fashion? Considerable research has now revealed that people can feel collective guilt based on the actions of other members of their group (Branscombe, 2004). Can such feelings of collective guilt be used as a means of reducing racism?

In a set of studies, Powell, Branscombe, and Schmitt (2005) found evidence that feeling collective guilt can reduce racism. First, these researchers recognized that the difference between two groups can be framed either in terms of the disadvantages experienced by one group *or* the advantages experienced by the other. Therefore, in one condition, white participants were asked to write down all the advantages they receive because of their race. In the other condition, participants were asked to write down all the disadvantages that blacks receive because of their race. This simply varied how the existing racial inequality was framed. As expected, the white advantage framing resulted in significantly more collective guilt than did the black disadvantage framing. Furthermore, as shown in Figure 6.19, the more collective guilt was experienced in the white advantage condition, the lower subsequent racism, whereas the black disadvantage framing did not have this effect. Reflecting on racial inequality can be an effective means of lowering racism, to the extent that the problem is seen as one involving the ingroup as beneficiary. Indeed, when perceptions of inequality as stemming from white advantage are combined with a sense of efficacy to bring about social change, feeling collective guilt can lead to anti-discrimination behavior (Stewart, Latu, Branscombe, & Denney, 2010).

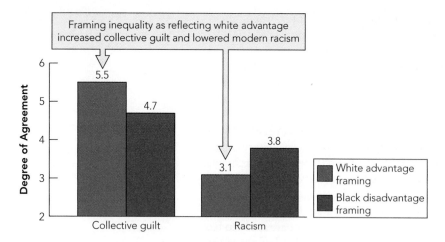

FIGURE 6.19 Collective Guilt Can Reduce Racism

The same inequality between groups can be framed as either reflecting the advantages of one group or the disadvantages of the other. Having white Americans think about inequality as white advantage led to increased feelings of collective guilt and this, in turn, resulted in lowered racism. A little collective guilt then may have social benefits. (Source: *Based on data from Powell, Branscombe, & Schmitt, 2005*).

Can We Learn to "Just Say No" to Stereotyping and Biased Attributions?

Throughout this chapter, we have noted that the tendency to think about others in terms of their group membership is a key factor in the occurrence of prejudice. As described earlier, individuals acquire stereotypes by learning to associate certain characteristics (e.g., negative traits such as "hostile" or "dangerous") with various racial or ethnic groups; once such automatic associations are formed, members of these groups can serve as primes for racial or ethnic stereotypes, which are then automatically activated. Can individuals actively break the "stereotype habit" by saying no to the stereotypic traits they associate with a specific group? Kawakami, Dovidio, Moll, Hermsen, and Russn (2000) reasoned that people can learn not to rely on stereotypes they already possess.

To test this idea, the researchers conducted several studies where participants' stereotypic associations were first assessed. After this, participants were divided into two groups. In one group—those in the stereotype maintaining condition—participants were instructed to respond "yes" when they were presented with a photograph of a white person and a white stereotype word (e.g., *ambitious* or *uptight*) or a photograph of a black person and a black stereotype word (e.g., *athletic* or *poor*). They were told to respond "no" to stereotype-inconsistent word–picture pairings (e.g., a word consistent with the stereotype for whites, but paired with a photo of a black individual). Those in a second group, the *stereotype negation* condition, were told to respond "no" when presented with a photo of a white person and a word consistent with this stereotype or a photo of a black person and a word consistent with the stereotype for blacks. On the other hand, they were told to respond "yes" to stereotype-inconsistent pairings of words and pictures. In other words, they practiced negating their own implicit racial stereotypes. Participants in both groups performed these procedures several hundred times.

The results were clear. Reliance on stereotypes can be reduced through the process of repeatedly saying no to them. Prior to negation training, participants categorized white faces more quickly than black faces after seeing white stereotype words, but black faces more quickly after seeing black stereotype words. After negation training designed to weaken these implicit stereotypes, however, these differences disappeared. Although we do not yet know how reduced stereotype activation influences actual interactions with group members, the possibility that people can learn to say no to racial and ethnic stereotypes, with practice in doing so, is encouraging.

Can the same practice in making nonstereotypic attributions for negative outgroup behavior be taught and thereby reduce stereotyping? As we discussed in Chapter 3, people display the *fundamental attribution bias*, and when applied to groups we see negative behaviors on the part of outgroup members as due to their internal qualities and positive behaviors by outgroup members as situationally (i.e., externally) caused. Recent research by Stewart, Latu, Kawakami, and Myers (2010) indicates that by repeatedly pairing external attributions for negative behavior with black faces, as shown in Figure 6.20(a) compared to trials with the neutral task as shown in Figure 6.20(b), implicit racial stereotyping can be reduced. Following such attributional training, the speed of responding to black faces with negative attributes did not differ from the speed of responding to white faces paired with those negative attributes.

Social Influence as a Means of Reducing Prejudice

Providing people with evidence that members of their own group like members of another group that is typically the target of prejudice can sometimes serve to weaken such negative reactions (Pettigrew, 1997; Wright, Aron, McLaughlin-Volpe, & Ropp, 1997). In contrast, when stereotypic beliefs are said to be endorsed by the individual's ingroup and that individual's membership in that group is salient, then the ingroup's beliefs are more predictive of prejudice than are the individual's personal beliefs about the outgroup (Haslam & Wilson, 2000; Poteat & Spanierman, 2010). This suggests that stereotypes that we believe to be widely shared within our own group play a critical role in the expression of prejudice.

Evidence that social influence processes can be used to reduce prejudice was reported by Stanger, Sechrist, and Jost (2001). White students were first asked to estimate the percentage of African Americans possessing various stereotypical traits. After completing these estimates, participants were given information suggesting that other students in their university disagreed with their ratings. In one condition (favorable feedback), they learned that other students held more favorable views of African Americans than they did (i.e., the other students estimated a higher incidence of positive traits and a lower incidence of negative traits than they did). In another condition (unfavorable feedback), they learned that other students held less favorable views of African Americans than they did (i.e., these people estimated a higher incidence of negative traits and a lower incidence of positive traits). After receiving this information, participants again estimated the percentage of African Americans possessing positive and negative traits. Participants' racial attitudes were indeed affected by social influence. Endorsement of negative stereotypes increased in the unfavorable feedback condition, while endorsement of such stereotypes decreased in the favorable feedback condition.

Together, these findings indicate that racial attitudes certainly do not exist in a social vacuum; on the contrary, the attitudes that individuals hold are influenced not only by their early experience but also by current peer members of their group. The moral is clear: If people can be induced to believe that their prejudiced views are "out of line" with those of most other people—especially those they respect—they may well change those views toward a less prejudiced position.

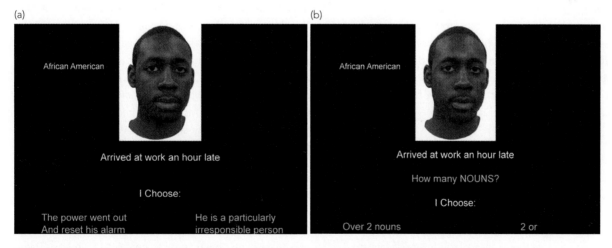

FIGURE 6.20 **Consider the Situation: Combatting Prejudice with Attributional Training**
Without the training to make situational attributions for negative behavior by black men—as was the case in the control condition in Figure b, white participants associated negative traits with black faces more quickly than they associated those traits with white faces. However, following repeated training to make situational/external attributions for those same negative behaviors, as shown in Figure a (e.g., "his power went out and reset his alarm"), implicit negative stereotyping disappeared. (Source: Based on research by Stewart, Latu, Kawakami, & Myers, 2010).

KEYPOINTS

- Social psychologists believe that stereotyping and prejudice are not inevitable; a variety of reduction techniques have been successfully employed.

- Children acquire prejudiced attitudes from their parents, and this is especially the case for children who strongly identify with their parents. Participating in institutions and having peers that justify discrimination help to maintain prejudiced attitudes.

- The **contact hypothesis** suggests that bringing previously segregated groups into contact can reduce prejudice; especially when the contact is with outgroup members who are seen as typical of their group, the contact is seen as important, results in cross-group friendships, and anxiety about interacting with outgroup members is reduced.

- As suggested by the **common ingroup identity model,** prejudice can also be reduced through *recategorization*— shifting the boundary between "us" and "them" to include former outgroups in the "us" category. This is the case even for long-standing enemy groups when the maximal category—humans—is used.

- Emotional techniques for reducing prejudice are also effective. People with egalitarian standards can feel guilty when they violate those beliefs and personally behave in a prejudicial fashion. People can also feel *collective guilt* for their group's prejudiced actions. By framing inequality as due to the ingroup's advantages, collective guilt can be induced and this in turn can reduce racism and increase anti-discrimination behavior when people feel able to make a difference.

- Reductions in prejudiced responses can also be accomplished by training individuals to say no to associations between stereotypes and specific social groups or by training them to make situational attributions for negative outgroup behavior.

- Social influence plays an important role in both the maintenance and reduction of prejudice. We want to hold beliefs that we see as normative of our group; providing individuals with evidence suggesting that members of their group hold less prejudiced views than they previously believed can reduce prejudice.

SUMMARY *and* REVIEW

- Discriminatory treatment can be based on many different types of category memberships—from those that are temporary and based on "minimal" criteria, to long-term group memberships such as ethnicity, gender, religion, sexual orientation, and age. Discrimination based on all these types of group memberships are not perceived and responded to in the same way; some forms of discrimination are seen as legitimate, whereas others are seen as illegitimate.

- Members of different groups are likely to perceive discrimination and the relations between those groups rather differently. When changes to the existing relations between racial groups are assessed, whites see more progress toward equality than do blacks. Research suggests that this is partly due to whites perceiving change and equality as a potential loss for them, whereas blacks perceive the same increases in egalitarianism as gains. People are **risk averse,** with potential losses having greater psychological impact than potential gains.

- **Gender stereotypes** are beliefs about the different attributes that males and females possess. Women are stereotyped as

high on warmth dimensions but low on competence, while men are viewed as possessing the reverse combination of traits. The **glass ceiling** effect is when qualified women have disproportionate difficulty attaining high-level positions. Women are most likely to be sabotaged when men are experiencing threat and women behave in a stereotype-inconsistent manner. Stereotypes lead us to attend to information that is consistent with them, and to construe inconsistent information in ways that allow us to maintain our stereotypes. Women are more likely to be appointed to leadership positions following a crisis and when there is greater risk of failure—the **glass cliff effect.**

- **Tokenism**—the hiring or acceptance of only a few members of a particular group—has two effects: it maintains perceptions that the system is not discriminatory (belief in meritocracy) and it can harm how tokens are perceived by others. Those who complain about discrimination risk negative evaluations.

- Stereotypes can influence behavior even in the absence of different **subjective scale** evaluations of men and women. When **objective scale** measures are employed, where **shifting**

standards cannot be used and the meaning of the response is constant, women are likely to receive worse outcomes than men.

- **Singlism** is negative stereotyping and discrimination directed toward people who are single. Both those who are single and those who are married show this bias, which may arise either because it is seen by them as legitimate or because they lack an awareness of the bias.

- **Stereotypes** are resistant to change, but they are revised as the relations between the groups are altered. Women who are repeatedly exposed to women faculty behaving in nontraditional roles show less agreement with gender stereotypes.

- **Prejudice** can be considered an attitude (usually negative) toward members of a social group. It can be triggered in a seemingly automatic manner and can be implicit in nature. Prejudice may reflect more specific underlying emotional responses to different outgroups including fear, anger, guilt, pity, envy, and disgust.

- According to **social identity theory,** prejudice is derived from our tendency to divide the world into "us" and "them" and to view our own group more favorably than various outgroups. Prejudice persists because disparaging outgroups can protect our self-esteem. **Threat** to our group's interests can motivate prejudice, and perceived competition between groups for resources can escalate conflict.

- While blatant **discrimination** has clearly decreased, more subtle forms such as **modern racism** persist. The **bona fide pipeline** uses implicit measures to assess prejudices that people may be unaware they have. People can maintain an unprejudiced self-image by comparing themselves to those with extremely bigoted attitudes.

- When we are exposed to instances where members of our own group have behaved in a prejudicial fashion, we can feel **collective guilt** to the extent that we do not engage in strategies that allow us to conclude our group's harmful acts were legitimate. People also show evidence of "motivated forgetting," where instances of our group's harm doing toward others are more difficult to recall than are instances in which our group was harmed by an enemy outgroup.

- Social psychologists believe that prejudice can be reduced by several techniques. One technique involves *direct contact* between members of different groups. Particularly when an outgroup member is seen as typical of their group, the contact is viewed as important, and it results in cross-group friendships, then intergroup anxiety can be lessened and prejudice reduced. Simply knowing that members of one's own group have formed friendships with members of an outgroup may be sufficient to reduce prejudice.

- As suggested by the **common ingroup identity model,** prejudice can also be reduced through *recategorization*—shifting the boundary between "us" and "them" so as to include former outgroups in the "us" category. This is the case even for long-standing enemy groups when the more inclusive category is that of "human." Prejudice reduction can also be accomplished by training individuals to say no to associations between stereotypes and specific social groups, and to make situational attributions for negative outgroup behaviors. Emotions can be used to motivate others to be nonprejudiced; feeling collective guilt can result in reductions in racism when the ingroup is focused on as a cause of existing racial inequality. Providing individuals with evidence suggesting that one's ingroup has less prejudiced views than oneself can be used to effectively reduce prejudice.

KEY TERMS

bona fide pipeline (p. 205)

collective guilt (p. 205)

common ingroup identity model (p. 208)

contact hypothesis (p. 208)

discrimination (p. 179)

essence (p. 195)

gender stereotypes (p. 183)

glass ceiling (p. 184)

glass cliff effect (p. 185)

implicit associations (p. 197)

incidental feelings (p. 197)

minimal groups (p. 196)

modern racism (p. 204)

moral disengagement (p. 206)

objectification of females (p. 186)

objective scales (p. 190)

prejudice (p. 179)

realistic conflict theory (p. 199)

recategorization (p. 208)

risk averse (p. 180)

shifting standards (p. 190)

singlism (p. 191)

social identity theory (p. 201)

social learning view (of prejudice) (p. 207)

stereotypes (p. 183)

subjective scales (p. 190)

subtype (p. 194)

superordinate goals (p. 200)

threat (p. 197)

tokenism (p. 189)

zero-sum outcomes (p. 199)

CHAPTER 7

Interpersonal Attraction, Close Relationships, and Love

D ORIS AND WENDELL ROBERTS RECENTLY CELEBRATED THEIR 75th anniversary. During these long decades, they raised three daughters, ran a successful bee-keeping business, and lived in several different homes. They went through very hard times during the 1930s, when they lived on $52 a week and bought only one item on credit (a refrigerator) for which the payments were $4.00 per month. And they generally got along very well. They seldom argued and as Doris puts it, "Never enough that we got up and left." And yes, according to both, they had a good and active sex life. During their years together, their respect for each other grew, and they came to count on one another as true life partners and helpers. They are both in their 90s, and are now living in an assisted-living facility; their fondest wish, as Doris puts it, is "I just hope we can go at the same time. I don't know how we can manage it, but I hope we can do it." How do they feel about celebrating 75 years of marriage—an accomplishment few couples ever reach? "A lot of it's been hard work," Doris says. "A lot of it's been luck" is Wendell's comment . . .

In 2008, Tricia Walsh-Smith was informed by her husband that he was divorcing her—and also faced with his demand that she immediately vacate their luxurious New York apartment on Park Avenue. Ms. Walsh-Smith was so angered by her husband's treatment that she made a video and put it on YouTube. It was entitled "One more crazy day in the life of a Phoenix rising from the ashes," after the myth of the Phoenix, a bird that rises from its own ashes over and over again. In it, she truly displays the couple's "dirty laundry"—everything from their nonexistent sex life to the prenuptial agreement her husband "pressured" her into signing. The video is so extreme that it has become legendary, and has been viewed by more than 1 million people . . .

"Will you marry me?" That's a statement that occurs between almost all couples as they contemplate making their relationship permanent. But until recently, no one had ever made such a proposal publicly on the Internet through a social network. All that changed when Greg Rewis sent those words to Stephanie Sullivan in a Twitter message he made available to the entire Twitter universe. Stephanie replied, again making her message available to everyone on Twitter, "Ummmm . . . I guess in front of the whole twitter-verse I'll say—I'd be happy to spend the rest of my geek life with you." The couple met at Web conferences, and have conducted a long-term relationship through Twitter and cell phones for several years. Now, as their friends note, they'll be turning their virtual relationship and partnership into a real one . . .

Together, these three incidents offer lots of food for thought. On the one side are a marriage that has survived (and prospered) for an entire lifetime and one that is beginning via a public declaration of love on Twitter; on the other side is a relationship that, like others, began in love, but is now ending in bitterness, anger, and in this case, very public disclosure. Together, these incidents—all very real—raise intriguing and truly important questions about the social side of life. How do relationships get started—why are people attracted to one another in the first place? How does such attraction deepen into love—one of the most powerful feelings of which we are capable? And why do some of these relationships strengthen and prosper over time, while others dissolve—often in very painful ways? Finally, why, given the obvious risks involved in forming deep relationships with others, do we do it? Why, as one old song put it, are most of us so willing to "take a chance on love"?

The answer lies in how most of us would respond to the question, What would make you *truly* happy? Clearly, there are as many different answers as there are human beings, but many would include words to this effect: "A close, long-term relationship with someone I truly love and who loves me." As Angelina Jolie put it (July 2010): "I've always wanted a great love . . . something that feels big and full, really honest. . . . It is hard to find all that in a relationship, but it is what we all are looking for, isn't it?" Jolie, for one, believes that there are many kinds of love. In describing her mother and her recent death, she remarked: "When she [her mother] passed away, I brought my son to church to light a candle for her . . . " and sobbing she adds, *"Forgive me . . . I loved her so much . . . "* As these words suggest, forming and maintaining long-term relationships with others is truly a central part of our social lives. And although Angelina Jolie didn't mention it, we should add that most people also have a strong desire to have good friends—ones they can really trust and to whom they can reveal their deepest thoughts and desires.

Social psychologists have recognized these desires for long-term relationships for decades, and have, in their research, carefully considered all of the questions listed above—which are worth repeating: Why do people like or dislike each other? Why do they fall in love? Are there several kinds of love or just one? Why do some relationships gradually move toward deeper and deeper levels of commitment, while others fizzle or end in acrimony? We don't yet have full answers to these questions, but decades of careful research has provided many insights about them (e.g., Hatfield & Rapson, 2009). That's the knowledge we present in this chapter.

First, we examine the nature of interpersonal attraction, considering the many factors that influence whether, and to what extent, people like or dislike each other. As we soon see, many factors play a role, and these range from the basic need to affiliate with others, through similarity to them, frequent contact with them, and their physical appearance. After considering interpersonal attraction, we turn to the close relationships that often develop when attraction is high or when other powerful factors operate (kinship relationships). These are lasting social bonds we form with family, friends, lovers, and spouses, and we examine how such relationships form, the nature of love—the powerful force that holds them together—and factors that sometimes cause relationships to end (see Figure 7.1) . While the risk of painful endings to even the closest relationships is always present, it is a risk almost everyone is willing to bear because life without such ties and without love, is—for most of us—truly unthinkable. We reserve discussion of several related topics—how to build successful relationships and how to cope with loneliness—for a later chapter (Chapter 12).

Internal Sources of Attraction: The Role of Needs and Emotions

When most people think about attraction—liking others—they tend to focus on factors relating to these individuals: Are they similar or dissimilar to us in important ways? Do we find their appearance appealing or unappealing? In fact, as we'll soon see, these factors

FIGURE 7.1 Close Relationships: Some Succeed, Others Fail
The desire for close and lasting personal relationships is a very powerful one, and plays a crucial role in most people's lives. It can lead to great happiness (left photo), but—sadly—to disappointment and misery, too. Why do relationships begin, and why do some succeed while others fail? These have been central topics of research by social psychologists.

do play a powerful role in attraction. In addition, though, our initial feelings of liking or disliking for others also stem from internal sources—our basic needs, motives, and emotions. We begin by focusing on those sources of attraction.

The Importance of Affiliation in Human Existence— and Interpersonal Attraction

Much of our life is spent interacting with other people, and this tendency to affiliate (i.e., associate with them) seems to have a neurobiological basis (Rowe, 1996). In fact, the need to affiliate with others and to be accepted by them may be just as basic to our psychological well-being as hunger and thirst are to our physical well-being (Baumeister & Leary, 1995; Koole, Greenberg, & Pyszczynski, 2006). From an evolutionary perspective, this makes perfect sense: cooperating with other people almost certainly increased our ancestors' success in obtaining food and surviving danger. As a result, a strong desire to affiliate with others seems to be a basic characteristic of our species. Human infants, for instance, are apparently born with the motivation and ability to seek contact with their interpersonal world (Baldwin, 2000), and even newborns tend to look toward faces in preference to other stimuli (Mondloch et al., 1999).

INDIVIDUAL DIFFERENCES IN THE NEED TO AFFILIATE   Although the need to affiliate with others appears to be very basic among human beings, people differ greatly in the strength of this tendency—known as **need for affiliation.** These differences, whether based on genetics or experience, constitute a relatively stable *trait* (or *disposition*). Basically, we tend to seek the amount of social contact that is optimal for us, preferring to be alone some of the time and in social situations some of the time (O'Connor & Rosenblood, 1996).

When their affiliation needs are not met, how do people react? When, for example, other people ignore you, what is the experience like? Most people find it highly unpleasant, and being "left out" by others hurts, leaves you with the sense that you have lost control, makes you feel both sad and angry because you simply don't belong (Buckley, Winkel, & Leary, 2004). Social exclusion leads to increased sensitivity to interpersonal information (Gardner, Pickett, & Brewer, 2000) and actually results in less effective cognitive functioning (Baumeister, Twenge, & Nuss, 2002).

need for affiliation
The basic motive to seek and maintain interpersonal relationships.

FIGURE 7.2   The Need for Affiliation: Evidence That We All Have it
Some individuals claim that they have little or no need for affiliation—for connections to other people. But research findings indicate that even such persons really do have affiliation needs. How do we know that's true? When such people learn that they have been accepted by others, both their moods and self-esteem increase. That would only be expected to happen if such acceptance satisfied a basic need for affiliation.

ARE THERE PEOPLE WHO DON'T NEED OTHER PEOPLE?   Decades of research by social psychologists indicate that although the need to affiliate with others is both strong and general (e.g., Baumeister & Twenge, 2003; Koole et al., 2006) there are some people who show what is known as the *dismissing avoidant attachment style*—a pattern in which they claim to have little or no need for emotional attachments to others, and who, in fact, tend to avoid close relationships (e.g., Collins & Feeney, 2000). Are such people really an exception to the general rule that as human beings, we have a strong need to affiliate with others (see Figure 7.2)? This is a difficult question to answer because such people strongly proclaim that they do not have these needs. Social psychologists are ingenious, though, and research findings (e.g., Carvallo & Gabriel, 2006) indicate that in fact, even people who claim to have little or no need for affiliation do, at least to some extent. True—they may be lower on this dimension than most other people, but even they show increased self-esteem and improved moods when they find out that they are accepted by others—the people they claim not to need. (We provide more complete coverage of attachment styles and their effects on social relationships in a later section.)

In short, all human beings—even people who claim otherwise—have strong needs for affiliation—to feel connected to others. They may conceal these needs under a mask of seeming indifference, but the needs are still there no matter how much such people try to deny them. In fact, we should add that these needs, and differences in *attachment style*—the ways in which we form emotional bonds and regulate our emotions in close relationships—are a very basic aspect of the social side of life. Research by Gillath and his colleagues (e.g., Gillath, Selcuk, & Shaver, 2008; Gillath & Shaver, 2007) indicates that attachment styles exert strong effects on both our thinking about others and our relationships with them, and that such effects, in turn, influence important aspects of our behavior, such as the tendency to seek their support or engage in *self-disclosure*—revealing our innermost thoughts and feelings. Individual differences in attachment style can even be measured at the level of brain functioning. For instance, the higher individuals are in fear of rejection and abandonment by others (*attachment anxiety*), the greater the activation they show in parts of the brain linked to emotion when they think about negative outcomes in relationships, such as conflict, breakups, or the death of partners (Gillath, Bunge,Wendelken, & Mikulincer, 2005). In sum, attachment style clearly plays an important role in our relationships with others and in the cognitive and neural processes that underlie these relationships.

SITUATIONAL INFLUENCES ON THE NEED TO AFFILIATE   While people differ with respect to their need to affiliate with others, external events can temporarily boost or reduce this need. When people are reminded of their own mortality, for example, a common response is the desire to affiliate with others (Wisman & Koole, 2003). Similarly, after highly disturbing events such as natural disasters, many people experience an increased desire to affiliate with others—primarily to obtain help and comfort and reduce negative feelings (Benjamin, 1998; Byrne, 1991). One basic reason for responding to stress with friendliness and affiliation was first identified by Schachter (1959). His early work revealed that participants in an experiment who were expecting to receive an electric shock preferred to spend time with others facing the same unpleasant prospect rather than being alone. Those in the control group, not expecting an unpleasant electric shock, preferred to be alone or didn't care whether they were with others or not. One conclusion from this line of research was that "misery doesn't just love any kind of company, it loves only miserable company" (Schachter, 1959, p. 24).

Why should real-life threats and anxiety-inducing laboratory manipulations arouse the need to affiliate? Why should frightened, anxious people want to interact with other frightened, anxious people? One answer is that such affiliation provides the opportunity for *social comparison*. People want to be with others—even strangers—in order to communicate about what is going on, to compare their perceptions, and to make decisions about what to do. Arousing situations lead us to seek "cognitive clarity" in order to know what is happening and "emotional clarity" (Gump & Kulik, 1997; Kulik et al., 1996). Contact with other humans that is likely to include both conversations and hugs can be a real source of comfort.

Liking or disliking for others (high or low levels of attraction) often seem subjectively to involve strong emotional compotnents. Is this true? And more generally, what role do feelings (our moods and emotions) play in attraction? This intriguing issue is discussed in the section "EMOTIONS AND ATTRACTION: Feelings as a Basis for Liking," below.)

EMOTIONS *and* ATTRACTION

Feelings as a Basis for Liking

As we have seen in other chapters, positive and negative affect are complex: they vary in intensity (valence) and arousal (low to high), and perhaps other dimensions as well. But despite this complexity, one basic principle has emerged over and over again in careful research: the presence of positive affect, regardless of its source, often leads to positive evaluations of other people (i.e., liking for them), whereas negative affect often leads to negative evaluations (i.e., disliking for them) (Byrne, 1997; Dovidio, Gaertner, Isen, & Lowrance, 1995). These effects occur in two different ways.

First, emotions have a direct effect on attraction. When another person says or does something that makes you feel good or bad, these feelings influence liking for that person. It probably does not come as a surprise to be informed that you like someone who makes you feel good and dislike someone who makes you feel bad (Ben-Porath, 2002; Reich, Zautra, & Potter, 2001). More surprising, though, are *indirect effects of emotions or feelings on attraction*—effects sometimes known as the *associated effect* of emotions on attraction. This occurs when another person is simply present at the same time that one's emotional state is aroused

(continued)

EMOTIONS *and* ATTRACTION *(continued)*

by something or someone else. Even though the individual toward whom you express liking or disliking is not in any way responsible for what you are feeling, you nevertheless tend to evaluate him or her more positively when you are feeling good and more negatively when you are feeling bad. For example, if you come in contact with a stranger shortly after you receive a low grade on an exam, you tend to like that person less than someone you meet shortly after you receive a high grade, or some other positive event.

These associated (or indirect) influences of affective states on attraction have been demonstrated in many experiments involving emotional states based on a variety of diverse external causes. Examples include the subliminal presentation of pleasant versus unpleasant pictures—for example, kittens versus snakes (Krosnick et al., 1992), the presence of background music that college students perceived as pleasant versus unpleasant—for example, rock and roll versus classical jazz (May & Hamilton, 1980), and even the positive versus negative mood states that the research participants reported before the experiment began (Berry & Hansen, 1996).

How can we explain such indirect effects of affect on attraction? As is true for all attitudes (and liking or disliking can be viewed as a special kind of attitude toward another person), *classical conditioning,* a basic form of learning, plays

a role (see our discussion of this topic in Chapter 5). When a neutral stimulus (e.g., another person we are meeting for the first time) is paired with a positive stimulus (something that makes us feel good), it is evaluated more positively than a neutral stimulus that has been paired with a negative stimulus (something that makes us feel bad), even when we are not aware that such pairings occurred (Olson & Fazio, 2001) and might even deny that they have any effect on our feelings of attraction toward a stranger.

Advertisers and others who seek to influence us seem to be well aware of this basic process, so they often seek to generate positive feelings and emotions among the people they want to sway, and then associate these with the products—or political candidates!—they want to promote. The goal is to make us like whatever or whoever is being "sold" by linking it with positive feelings. This can be accomplished by using highly attractive models in ads and commercials for products and by associating the products with happy times and pleasant experiences (see Figure 7.3). Political candidates use the same basic principal by associating their image or their presence with happy celebrations, and often arrange to have truly committed supporters present at political rallies so that they will be shown surrounded by cheering crowds (Figure 7.3). Again, the goal is

FIGURE 7.3   Affect Influences Liking and Liking in Turn, Plays a Role in Our Product Purchases and Even Our Voting Behavior
Advertisers and politicians often use the indirect effects of emotion to induce liking for their products or candidates. The basic idea is to the extent these products of candidates are associated with positive feelings, they will be liked. Liking, in turn, can lead to purchasing the products or voting for the candidates.

to increase liking through the candidates' association with positive feelings.

Are such attempts to influence our liking for various items or people by influencing our moods (affect) really effective? Research findings indicate that they are (e.g., Pentony, 1995). Overall, it seems clear that irrelevant affective states—ones induced by factors unrelated to the candidates, products, or items being sold—can indeed influence our liking for them, and hence our overt actions (our votes, our purchase decisions). Keep this point in mind the next time you are exposed to any kind of message that is clearly designed to cause you to experience positive or negative feelings: The ultimate goal may be persuasion or influence, not merely making you feel good!

KEYPOINTS

- *Interpersonal attraction* refers to the evaluations we make of other people—the positive and negative attitudes we form about them.

- Human beings have a strong **need for affiliation,** the motivation to interact with other people in a cooperative way. The strength of this need differs among individuals and across situations, but even people who claim they do not have it show evidence that they do.

- Positive and negative affect influence attraction both directly and indirectly. Direct effects occur when another person is responsible for arousing the emotion. Indirect effects occur when the source of the emotion is elsewhere, and another person is simply associated with its presence.

- The indirect (associated) effects of emotion are applied by advertisers and politicians who understand that associating the products and candidates they wish to promote with positive feelings can influence decisions to purchase the products or vote for the candidate.

External Sources of Attraction: The Effects of Proximity and Physical Beauty

Whether or not two specific people ever come in contact with each other is often determined by accidental, unplanned aspects of where they live, work, or play. For example, two students assigned to adjoining classroom seats are more likely to interact than those two given seats several rows apart. Once physical **proximity** brings about contact, additional factors play an important role. One of these is outward appearance—others' **physical attractiveness.** Another is the extent to which the two people find that they are similar in various ways. We examine the effects of proximity and physical appearance here, and examine the effects of similarity—which are often powerful—in the next section.

The Power of Proximity: Unplanned Contacts

More than 6.7 billion people now live on our planet, but you will probably interact with only a relatively small number of them during your lifetime. In the absence of some kind of contact, you obviously can't become acquainted with other people or have any basis on which to decide whether you like or dislike them, so in a sense, proximity (physical nearness to others) is a basic requirement that must be met before feelings of attraction can develop. Actually, that was true in the past, but now, social networks and other electronic media make it possible for people to interact and form initial feelings of liking or disliking without direct face-to-face contact. Ultimately, of course, such contact must occur for close relationships to develop beyond the "virtual world." But overall, although physical

proximity
In attraction research, the physical closeness between two individuals with respect to where they live, where they sit in a classroom, where they work, and so on. The smaller the physical distance, the greater the probability that the two people will come into repeated contact experiencing repeated exposure to one another, positive affect, and the development of mutual attraction.

physical attractiveness
The combination of characteristics that are evaluated as beautiful or handsome at the positive extreme and as unattractive at the negative extreme.

proximity was a requirement for interpersonal attraction in the past, that may no longer be true. Now, though, let's take a look at classic research on the role of proximity in liking (or disliking) for others—research conducted long before the advent of the Internet.

WHY DOES PROXIMITY MATTER?: REPEATED EXPOSURE IS THE KEY   Picture yourself in a large lecture class on the first day of school. Let's say that you don't see anyone you know and that the instructor has a chart that assigns students to seats alphabetically. At first, this roomful of strangers is a confusing blur of unfamiliar faces. Once you find your assigned seat, you probably notice the person sitting on your right and the one on your left, but you may or may not speak to one another. By the second or third day of class, however, you recognize your "neighbors" when you see them and may even say hello. In the weeks that follow, you may have bits of conversation about the class or about something that is happening on campus. If you see either of these two individuals at some other location, there is mutual recognition and you are increasingly likely to interact. After all, it feels good to see a familiar face. Numerous early studies in the United States and in Europe revealed that students are most likely to become acquainted if they are seated in adjoining chairs (Byrne, 1961a; Maisonneuve, Palmade, & Fourment, 1952; Segal, 1974). In addition to proximity in the classroom, investigations conducted throughout the 20th century indicated that people who live or work in close proximity are likely to become acquainted, form friendships, and even marry one another (Bossard, 1932; Festinger, Schachter, & Back, 1950). But why does proximity to others and the contacts it generates influence attraction to them?

The answer appears to lie in the **repeated exposure effect** (Zajonc, 1968). Apparently, the more often we are exposed to a new stimulus—a new person, a new idea—a new product—the more favorable our evaluation of it tends to become. This effect is subtle—we may not be aware of it—but it is both powerful and general. Research findings indicate that it occurs for people, words, objects—almost everything. Moreover, it is present very early in life: Infants tend to smile more at a photograph of someone they have seen before but not at a photograph of someone they are seeing for the first time (Brooks-Gunn & Lewis, 1981).

A very clear demonstration of such effects is provided by a study conducted in a classroom setting (Moreland & Beach, 1992). In a college course, one female assistant attended class 15 times during the semester, a second assistant attended class 10 times, a third attended five times, and a fourth did not attend the class at all. None of the assistants interacted with the other class members. At the end of the semester, the students were shown slides of the four assistants and were asked to indicate how much they liked each one. As shown in Figure 7.4, the more times a particular assistant attended class, the more she was liked. In this and many other experiments, repeated exposure was found to have a positive effect on attraction.

Zajonc (2001) explains the effect of repeated exposure by suggesting that we ordinarily respond with at least mild discomfort when we encounter anyone or anything new and unfamiliar. It is reasonable to suppose that it was adaptive for our ancestors to be wary of approaching anything or anyone for the first time. Whatever is unknown and unfamiliar is at least, potentially, dangerous. With repeated exposure, however, negative emotions decrease and positive emotions increase (Lee, 2001). A familiar face, for example, elicits positive affect, is evaluated positively, and activates facial muscles and brain activity in ways associated with positive emotions (Harmon-Jones & Allen, 2001). Not only does familiarity elicit positive affect, but positive affect elicits the perception of familiarity (Monin, 2003). For example, even when it is seen for the first time, a beautiful face is perceived as being more familiar than an unattractive one.

repeated exposure effect
Zajonc's finding that frequent contact with any mildly negative, neutral, or positive stimulus results in an increasingly positive evaluation of that stimulus.

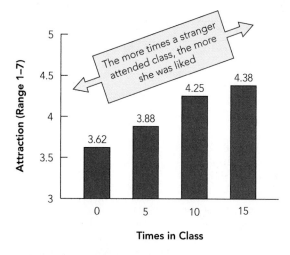

FIGURE 7.4   Frequency of Exposure and Liking in the Classroom

To test the repeated exposure effect in a college classroom, Moreland and Beach (1992) employed four female research assistants who pretended to be members of a class. One of them did not attend class all semester, another attended class five times, a third attended ten times, and a fourth came to class fifteen times. None of them interacted with the actual students. At the end of the semester, the students were shown photos of the assistants and were asked to indicate how much they liked each one. The more times the students had been exposed to an assistant, the more they liked her. (Source: Based on data from Moreland & Beach, 1992).

As powerful as the repeated exposure effect has been found to be, it fails to operate when a person's initial reaction to the stimulus is very negative. Repeated exposure in this instance not only fails to bring about a more positive evaluation, it can even lead to greater dislike (Swap, 1977). You may have experienced this yourself when a song or a commercial you disliked at first seems even worse when you hear it over and over again. So sometimes, increasing familiarity can result in contempt rather than attraction.

Observable Characteristics of Others: The Effects of Physical Attractiveness

"Love at first sight," "Struck with a lightning bolt"—different cultures have different phrases, but they all refer to the fact that sometimes just seeing someone for the first time can be the basis for powerful feelings of attraction toward that person. And although we are warned repeatedly against being too susceptible to others' physical charms ("Don't judge a book by its cover"), it is all too clear that others' physical appearance does have a strong effect on us, and often plays a powerful role in interpersonal attraction and influences many aspects of social behavior (e.g., Vogel, Kutzner, Fiedler, & Freytag, 2010). How strong are these effects? Why do they occur? What is physical attractiveness? And do we believe that "what is beautiful is good"—that attractive people possess many desirable characteristics aside from the physical beauty? These are the questions we now examine.

BEAUTY MAY BE ONLY SKIN DEEP, BUT WE PAY A LOT OF ATTENTION TO SKIN

Certainly, at some point in your life, you have heard the saying "Beauty is only skin deep." It warns us to avoid assigning too much weight to outward appearance—especially how people look. But existing evidence indicates that even if we want to, we can't really follow this advice because physical appearance is a powerful factor in our liking for others , and even in our selection of prospective and actual mates (Collins & Zebrowitz, 1995; Perlini & Hansen, 2001; Van Straaten, Engels, Finkenauer, & Holland, 2009).

Both in experiments and in the real world, physical appearance determines many types of interpersonal evaluations. For instance, attractive defendants are found guilty by judges and juries less often than unattractive ones (e.g., Downs & Lyons, 1991). Furthermore, attractive people are judged to be healthier, more intelligent, more trustworthy, and as possessing desirable social characteristics such as kindness, generosity, and warmth to a greater extent than less attractive ones (Lemay, Clark, & Greenberg, 2010). People even respond more positively to attractive infants than to unattractive ones (Karraker & Stern, 1990). As we'll see in our later discussions of romantic relationships, physical appearance also plays an important role in mate selection. Now, though, let's consider the fact that attractive people are generally viewed more favorably than unattractive ones along many dimensions—not just physical beauty.

THE "WHAT IS BEAUTIFUL IS GOOD" EFFECT

We have already noted that attractive people are viewed as possessing desirable characteristics such as intelligence, good health, kindness, and generosity, to a greater extent than less attractive people. Why is this so? One possibility, first suggested by Dion, Berscheid, and Walster (1972), is that we possess a very positive stereotype for highly attractive people—a physical attractiveness stereotype. Evidence for this interpretation has been obtained in many studies (Langlois et al., 2000; Snyder, Tanke, & Berscheid, 1977), and it has been the most widely accepted view for many years. Certainly, it makes good sense: If we do possess a favorable stereotype for physically attractive people, then, as is true with all stereotypes (see Chapter 6), this cognitive framework strongly shapes our perceptions of others and our thinking about them.

Recently, though, an alternative interpretation for the "good is beautiful" effect has been suggested. Lemay et al. (2010) propose that three steps are involved. First, we desire

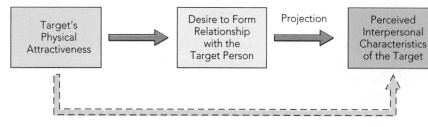

FIGURE 7.5 **The "What Is Beautiful Is Good" Effect: Why It Occurs**

Recent findings (Lemay et al., 2010) indicate that one reason why we tend to perceive "beautiful people as also good" (i.e., as having desirable characteristics), is that our own desire to form relationships with them leads us to project similar feelings to them. We want to get close to them, so we project these feelings onto them, and rate them more favorably. (Source: Based on suggestions by Lemay et al., 2010).

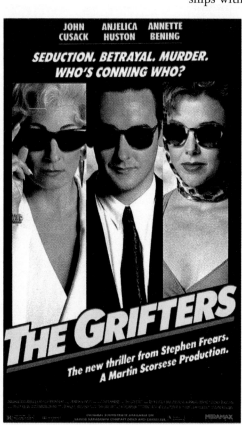

FIGURE 7.6 **Beautiful People Are Not Necessarily Also Good!**

Shown here are the stars of "The Grifters," a movie about swindlers who used their attractiveness to deceive and cheat other people as their full-time career. The characters in the film are fictitious, but many confidence artists are indeed high in attractiveness, and this helps them take advantage of their victims—who falsely assume that "What is beautiful is also good."

to form relationships with attractive people. Second, this strong desire leads us to perceive them as interpersonally responsive in return—as kinder, more outgoing, and socially warmer than less attractive people. In other words, we project our own desire to form relationships with these people to them, and it is this projection that generates very positive perceptions of them. To test this theory, Lemay and colleagues performed several studies. In one, participants first viewed photos of strangers rated very high or below average in physical attractiveness (8.5 or higher or 5 and below on a 10-point scale). Then they rated their own desire to form relationships with these people, and the extent to which the attractive and unattractive people desired to form relationships with others (their affiliation motive). In addition, they rated the target people's interpersonal traits—the extent to which they were kind, generous, extraverted, warm, and so on.

It was predicted that attractive people would be viewed as higher in affiliation motive than those lower in attractiveness, and would also be rated more favorably in terms of various interpersonal traits. Most important, it was predicted that these effects would be mediated by participants' desire to form relationships with the attractive and unattractive strangers. In fact, when the effects of this factor were removed statistically, effects of the target people's attractiveness disappeared. In other words, it was the projection of their own desire to get to know the attractive strangers that led participants to perceive these strangers in favorable terms (see Figure 7.5).

Before leaving the "what is beautiful is good" effect, we should comment on one other question: Is it accurate? Are "beautiful people" also more socially poised, kinder, more outgoing, and so on, than less attractive ones? Despite widespread acceptance of these beliefs, most of them appear to be incorrect (Feingold, 1992; Kenealy, Gleeson, Frude, & Shaw, 1991). For instance, extremely evil people, such as confidence artists, can be good looking (and often are), and many people who do not look like movie stars—for instance, Bill Gates or Warren Buffet—are often intelligent, interesting, kind, and generous. A few ideas contained in the "what is beautiful" effect are accurate; for instance, attractiveness is associated with popularity, good interpersonal skills, and high self-esteem (Diener, Wolsic, & Fujita, 1995; Johnstone, Frame, & Bouman, 1992). Perhaps this is so because very attractive people spend their lives being liked and treated well by other people who are responding to their appearance (Zebrowitz, Collins, & Dutta, 1998). And, not surprisingly, people who are very attractive to others are often aware that they are pretty or handsome (Marcus & Miller, 2003) and often try to use this characteristic for their own advantage—for instance, in persuading or influencing others (Vogel et al., 2010). In other words, attractiveness in and of itself does not create excellent social skills and high self-esteem, but may contribute to their development because attractive people are treated very well by most of the people they meet. Whether they use these skills for good or evil, however, appears to be independent of physical attractiveness itself (see Figure 7.6).

WHAT, EXACTLY, Is "ATTRACTIVENESS"?   Now for another interesting question: What exactly makes another person attractive? Researchers assume that there must be some underlying basis because there is surprisingly good agreement about attractiveness both within and between cultures (Cunningham, Roberts, Wu, Barbee, & Druen, 1995; Fink & Penton-Voak, 2002; Marcus & Miller, 2003). Despite general agreement about who is and is not attractive, it is not easy to identify the precise cues that determine these judgments—what factors make people high or low in attractiveness.

In attempting to discover just what these factors are, social psychologists have used two quite different procedures. One approach is to identify a group of individuals who are rated as attractive and then to determine what they have in common. Cunningham (1986) asked male undergraduates to rate photographs of young women. The women who were judged to be most attractive fell into one of two groups, as shown in Figure 7.7. Some had "childlike features" consisting of large, widely spaced eyes and a small nose and chin. Women like Meg Ryan and Amy Adams fit this category and are considered "cute" (Johnston & Oliver-Rodriguez, 1997; McKelvie, 1993a). The other category of attractive women had mature features with prominent cheekbones, high eyebrows, large pupils, and a big smile—Angelina Jolie is an example. These same two general facial types are found among fashion models, and they are commonly seen among white, African American, Hispanic, and Asian women (Ashmore, Solomon, & Longo, 1996). Although there is less evidence on this point, the same general categories seem to exist for men—being highly attractive can mean looking "cute" or "boyish," or mature and masculine.

A second approach to the determination of what is meant by attractiveness was taken by Langlois and Roggman (1990). They began with several facial photographs, and then used computer digitizing to combine multiple faces into one face. The image in each photo is divided into microscopic squares, and each square is translated into a number that represents a specific shade. Then the numbers are averaged across two or more pictures, and the result is translated back into a composite image.

You might reasonably guess that a face created by averaging would be rated as average in attractiveness. Instead, composite faces are rated as more attractive than most

FIGURE 7.7   Two Types of Attractive Women: Cute or Mature
The study of physical attractiveness has identified two types of women who are rated most attractive. One category is considered cute—childlike features, large widely spaced eyes, with a small nose and chin—for example, Amy Adams. The other category of attractiveness is the mature look—prominent cheekbones, high eyebrows, large pupils, and a big smile—for example, Angelina Jolie.

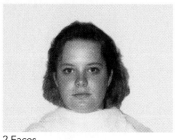

2 Faces

4 Faces

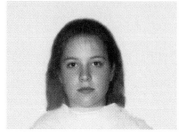

8 Faces

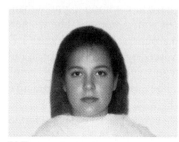

16 Faces

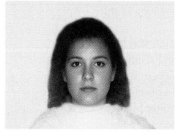

32 Faces

FIGURE 7.8 Averaging Multiple Faces Results in an Attractive Face

When computer images of several different faces are combined to form a composite, the resulting average face is seen as more attractive than the individual faces that were averaged. As the number of faces contributing to the average increases, the attractiveness of the composite increases.

of the individual faces used to make the composite (Langlois, Roggman, & Musselman, 1994; Rhodes & Tremewan, 1996). In addition, the more faces that are averaged, the more beautiful the resulting face. As shown in Figure 7.8, when you combine as many as 32 faces, " . . . you end up with a face that is pretty darned attractive" (Judith Langlois, as quoted in Lemley, 2000, p. 47). (You might find it interesting to visit the following website, showing how personal beauty can be enhanced by technology: http://campaignforrealbeauty.com/flat4.asp?id=6909.) As shown at this, the faces presented in ads and on billboards are not nearly as attractive in reality as they appear when advertisers—and beauty specialists—get through "enhancing" them!

Why should composite faces be especially attractive? It is possible that each person's schema of women and of men is created in our cognitions in much the same way that the averaged face is created. That is, we form such schemas on the basis of our experiences with many different images, so a composite face is closer to that schema than is any specific face. If this is an accurate analysis, a composite of other kinds of images should also constitute the most attractive alternative, but this does not work with composite dogs or composite birds (Halberstadt & Rhodes, 2000). It may be that our perception of human composites is different because it was historically more important to our species to recognize potential friends, enemies, and mates than to recognize dogs and birds.

In addition to the details of facial features, perceptions of attractiveness are also influenced by the situation. As suggested by Mickey Gilley's song about searching for romance in bars, "The girls all get prettier at closing time." In fact, both "girls" and "boys" are perceived as more attractive by members of the opposite sex as the evening progresses (Nida & Koon, 1983; Pennebaker et al., 1979). Ratings of same-sex strangers do not improve as closing time approaches, so alcohol consumption (which might impair judgment!) does not explain the effects (Gladue & Delaney, 1990). Rather, as people pair off and the number of available partners decreases, the resulting scarcity leads to more positive evaluations of those who remain unattached.

RED REALLY IS INDEED SEXY—AND ATTRACTIVE When archeologists open Egyptian tombs that have been sealed for thousands of years, they often find cosmetics, and among these are lipstick and rouge that is red (see Figure 7.9). In fact, in many ancient cultures, as well as many modern ones, the color red has been associated with increased attractiveness, at least for women. This belief is also shown in literature, as in Nathaniel Hawthorn's classic story, *The Scarlet Letter*, and is associated with famous "red-light districts" throughout the world. Interestingly, outside our own species, many primate females display red on their genitals, chest, or face during ovulation—when they are, at least from a reproductive point of view, at their sexiest. These observations have led social psychologists to suggest that perhaps the color red does have special significance, and can increase women's attractiveness to men. In a sense, then, beauty is generated not only by the face or body, but may involve other, seemingly peripheral environmental cues.

Evidence for this suggestion has been reported by Elliot and Niesta (2008). These social psychologists performed several studies in which both male and female participants saw photos of strangers who were shown either against a red background or one of a different color (white, gray, green), and who either wore a red shirt or a shirt of another color (blue). Then they rated the attractiveness and sexual appeal of these people. Results were clear in every study performed: the color red did indeed significantly boost ratings of the female strangers. Moreover, this effect occurred for male participants, but not for females (see Figure 7.10). For men, for instance, when photos of the female strangers were shown against a red background, they assigned higher ratings of attractiveness to the stranger than when the same people were shown against a white background. For women, however, the background color did not make a significant difference. So, as Elliot and Niesta suggest, red is indeed romantic and carries a special meaning in the language of love—or at least, attraction—among men.

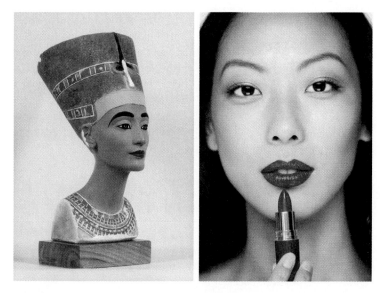

FIGURE 7.9   Does the Color Red Enhance Women's Physical Attractiveness?

Many cultures—both ancient and modern—accept the view that red on the lips and the face, and perhaps in clothing too, can enhance women's physical appeal. Recent research by social psychologists suggests that there may be a sizable grain of truth in this belief.

OTHER ASPECTS OF APPEARANCE AND BEHAVIOR THAT INFLUENCE ATTRACTION   When we meet someone for the first time, we usually know, very quickly, whether our reactions to them are positive or negative—in other words, as discussed in Chapter 3, we form first impressions of others from "thin slices" of information about them, and feelings of liking or disliking are often part of these initial impressions. What specific factors, aside from facial features, influence our initial level of interpersonal attraction? One is physique or body build. Although the stereotypes associated with different body builds are often misleading or just plain wrong, many people tend to associate a round body build with an easygoing disposition, relaxed personality, and a lack of personal discipline. A hard and muscular body, in contrast, is perceived as indicating not merely good health, but also high energy and vigor, while a thin and angular body is perceived as a sign of intelligence and perhaps an introspective personality (Gardner & Tuckerman, 1994). Recently, of course, the growing proportion of the population who is overweight or actually obese has brought these stereotypes into sharper focus. There is a strong "anti-fat" attitude in many cultures (although certainly not all), and this can work against overweight people in many areas of life, from dating to their careers (e.g., Crandall & Martinez, 1996).

Observable differences in actual behavior also elicit stereotypes that influence attraction. A person with a youthful walking style elicits a more positive response than one who walks with an elderly style, regardless of gender or actual age (Montepare & Zebrowitz-McArthur, 1988). A person with a firm handshake is perceived as being extroverted and emotionally expressive—positive characteristics (Chaplin et al., 2000). People respond positively to someone whose behavior is animated (Bernieri, Gillis, Davis, & Grahe, 1996) and who acts modestly rather than arrogantly (Hareli & Weiner, 2000).

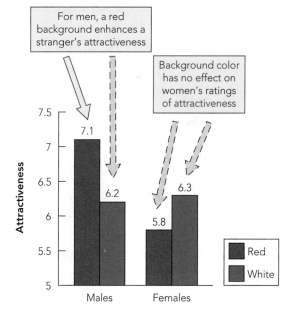

FIGURE 7.10   Evidence That the Color Red Is Indeed Romantic

When men saw photos of a female stranger against a red background, they rated her as more attractive than when the same stranger was shown against a white background. This effect did not occur for women, whose ratings of the stranger were unaffected by color of the background. (Source: Based on data from Elliot & Niesta, 2008).

One of the most surprising influences on interpersonal perceptions of others, and initial liking or disliking for them, is a person's first name. Names go in and out of favor, and a person with a name that is now viewed as "old-fashioned" may be at a disadvantage. How, for instance, would you react to someone named Gertrude, Mildred, Otto, or Delbert? These were once popular names, but now you might well assume that the people having them are very old, or have other undesirable characteristics (Macrae, Mitchell, & Pendy, 2002). So, names do indeed matter, as many expectant parents realize as they carefully consider hundreds of possible choices.

KEY POINTS

- The initial contact between two people is very often based on the **proximity**—they are near each other in physical space.

- Proximity, in turn, leads to repeated exposure, and that often produces positive affect and increased attraction (the mere exposure effect).

- Attraction toward others is often strongly influenced by their observable characteristics, especially their **physical attractiveness.**

- We often assume that "what is beautiful is good," apparently because we want to form relationships with

attractive people, and so project positive interpersonal traits to them.

- Red does indeed appear to be "sexy" and enhances women's attractiveness, as many cultures have believed throughout recorded history.

- In addition to attractiveness, many other observable characteristics influence initial interpersonal evaluations, including physique, weight, behavioral style, and even first names, and other superficial characteristics.

Factors Based on Social Interaction: Similarity and Mutual Liking

Although our own need for affiliation, proximity, repeated exposure, and others' physical appearance can exert strong effects on interpersonal attraction, these factors are far from the entire story. Additional variables that strongly affect attraction only emerge as we interact with others, communicate with them, and acquire more information about them. Among these, two have been found to be the most influential: our degree of similarity to others and the extent to which they like us.

Similarity: Birds of a Feather Actually Do Flock Together

Writing about friendship more than 2,000 years ago, Aristotle (330 BC, 1932) suggested that similarity is often the basis for this important kind of relationship. Empirical evidence for this view—known as the *similarity hypothesis*—was not available until many centuries later, when Sir Francis Galton (1870/1952) obtained correlational data on married couples, indicating that spouses did in fact resemble one another in many respects. In the first half of the 20th century, additional correlational studies continued to find that friends and spouses expressed a greater than chance degree of similarity (e.g., Hunt, 1935). Because the research was correlational in nature, though, these findings could have meant either that similarity leads to liking or that liking leads to similarity—people who like each other become more similar over time. In a study that is a true "classic" of social psychology, however, Newcomb (1956) found that similar attitudes predicted subsequent liking between students. In his research, he reasoned that if attitudes were measured before people had even met, and it was found that later, the more similar their attitudes the more they liked each other, it could be concluded that similarity produced such attraction. To test this hypothesis, he studied transfer students—ones who had not met each other before coming to the university. He measured their attitudes about issues such as family, religion, public affairs, and race relations by mail, before the students reached campus. Then, their liking for one another was assessed weekly after they came to campus. Results indicated that in fact, the more similar the students were initially, the more they liked each other by the end of the semester. This was strong evidence that similarity produced attraction rather than vice versa. Newcomb's initial findings were confirmed in many later studies (Byrne, 1961b; Schachter, 1951), so just as Aristotle and others had suggested, research findings tend to confirm the similarity hypothesis: the more similar two people are, the more they tend to like each other.

This conclusion probably seems reasonable, but what about the idea that "opposites attract"? Don't we sometimes find people who are very different from ourselves to be attractive? Informal evidence suggests that this might be so. You have probably observed couples who seemed to be radically different from each other, yet had happy relationships (see Figure 7.11). And many films have a theme of attraction between people from very different social backgrounds or lives. What has careful research on this issue revealed? Overall, the major conclusion is clear: similarity is a much stronger basis for attraction than differences.

In early research on this topic, the proposed attraction of opposites was often phrased in terms of *complementarities*—differences that complemented each other. For instance, it was suggested that dominant individuals would be attracted to submissive ones, talkative people to quiet ones, sadists to masochists, and so on. The idea was that such complementary characteristics would be mutually reinforcing (i.e., beneficial to both people in the relationships) and hence a good basis for attraction. Surprisingly, though, direct tests of these propositions failed to support complementarity as a determinant of attraction, even

FIGURE 7.11   Do Opposites Attract? Sometimes, But Even Then, There Are Underlying Similarities

Though the belief that opposites attract is a familiar one in fiction, similarity is a much better predictor of attraction. Even when people who seem very different do attract one another (as in the couples shown here), they usually have a great deal in common—though this similarity may not be visible to casual, outside observers.

with respect to dominance and submissiveness (Palmer & Byrne, 1970). With respect to attitudes, values, personality characteristics, bad habits, intellectual ability, income level, and even minor preferences such as choosing the right-hand versus left-hand aisle in a movie theater, similarity was found to result in attraction (Byrne, 1971). So overall, there is little if any evidence for the suggestion that opposites attract. Of course, there can be exceptions to this general rule (see Figure 7.11), but overall, attraction seems to derive much more strongly from similarity than complementarity.

One such exception occurs in situations in which a male and a female are interacting. Specifically, when one person engages in dominant behavior, the other then responds in a submissive fashion (Markey, Funder, & Ozer, 2003; Sadler & Woody, 2003). This specific kind of complementarity leads to greater attraction than when the second person copies the first person (i.e., is also dominant; Tiedens & Fragale, 2003). So opposites may in fact attract, at least in one context: dominance versus submission in male–female interactions. With respect to other kinds of interaction (e.g., a person who is verbally withdrawn and unresponsive interacting with someone who is verbally expressive and critical), however, opposite styles not only fail to attract, they are quite incompatible and more likely to lead to rejection and avoidance than liking and attraction (Swann, Rentfrow, & Gosling, 2003). Overall, then, the evidence is both strong and consistent: Similarity—not complementarity (opposites)—seems to be the basis for attraction across many kinds of situations and many kinds of relationships.

SIMILARITY–DISSIMILARITY: A CONSISTENT PREDICTOR OF ATTRACTION Much of the early work on the **similarity–dissimilarity effect** focused on **attitude similarity,** but this phrase was generally used as a shorthand term that included not only similarity of attitudes, but also of beliefs, values, and interests. The initial laboratory experiments on this topic consisted of two steps. First, the attitudes of the participants were assessed and second, these individuals were exposed to the attitudes of a stranger and asked to evaluate this person (Byrne, 1961b). The results were straightforward in that people consistently indicated that they liked similar strangers much better than they liked dissimilar ones. Not only do we like people who are similar to ourselves, we also judge them to be more intelligent, better informed, more moral, and better adjusted than people who are dissimilar. As you might suspect on the basis of our discussion of affect earlier in this chapter, similarity arouses positive feelings and dissimilarity arouses negative feelings.

Many such investigations, with a variety of populations, procedures, and topics, revealed that people respond to similarity–dissimilarity in a surprisingly precise way. Attraction is determined by the **proportion of similarity.** That is, when the number of topics on which two people express similar views is divided by the total number of topics on which they have communicated, the resulting proportion can be inserted in a simple formula that allows us to predict attraction (Byrne & Nelson, 1965). The higher the proportion of similarity, the greater the liking. No one knows exactly how attitudinal information is processed to produce that outcome, but it is as if people automatically engage in some kind of cognitive addition and division, manipulating the units of positive and negative affect they experience.

The effect of attitude similarity on attraction is a strong one, and it holds true regardless of the number of topics on which people express their views and regardless of how important or trivial the topics may be. It holds equally true for males and females, regardless of age, educational, or cultural differences (Byrne, 1971). The general level of attraction may vary and the total impact of proportion may vary, based on dispositional factors, but the basic proportion effect remains true (Kwan, 1998; Michinov & Michinov, 2001).

One serious challenge to the validity of such findings was offered by Rosenbaum (1986) when he proposed that using proportion as the independent variable made it impossible to separate the effect of similarity from the effect of dissimilarity. Based on

similarity–dissimilarity effect
The consistent finding that people respond positively to indications that another person is similar to themselves and negatively to indications that another person is dissimilar from themselves.

attitude similarity
The extent to which two individuals share the same attitudes.

proportion of similarity
The number of specific indicators that two people are similar divided by the number of specific indicators that two people are similar plus the number of specific indicators that they are dissimilar.

data he gathered, Rosenbaum proposed the **repulsion hypothesis** as an alternative to the similarity–dissimilarity effect. The basic idea is that information about similarity has no effect on attraction—people are simply repulsed by information about dissimilarity. Later research was able to show that the idea is wrong (Smeaton, Byrne, & Murnen, 1989), but there was a grain of truth in the repulsion hypothesis. Specifically, under most circumstances information about dissimilarity has a slightly stronger effect on attraction than the same amount of information about similarity (Chen & Kenrick, 2002; Singh & Ho, 2000; Tan & Singh, 1995). That goes along with the general finding that negative information has a more powerful effect on several aspects of our cognition than positive information—a finding summarized by Baumeister, Bratslavsky, Finkenaurer, and Vohs (2001) as "bad is stronger than good," at least where social cognition is concerned (see Chapter 2).

Beyond attitudes and values, many kinds of similarity–dissimilarity have been investigated, and in each instance people prefer those similar to themselves rather than dissimilar. Examples include similarity–dissimilarity with respect to smokng marijuana (Eisenman, 1985), religious practices (Kandel, 1978), self-concept (Klohnen & Luo, 2003), being a "morning person" versus an "evening person" (Watts, 1982), and finding the same jokes amusing (Cann, Calhoun, & Banks, 1995). One of the most interesting areas of research on the effects of similarity, though, involves physical attractiveness, so let's take a closer look at that work.

DO PEOPLE SEEK SIMILARITY IN PHYSICAL ATTRACTIVENESS?: THE MATCHING HYPOTHESIS REVISITED Suppose someone gave you a magic potion you could use to make anyone you wish fall in love with you. What kind of romantic partner would you choose? Many people would select those people they found most attractive—those extremely high in physical attractiveness. Such a potion or spell is, of course, only fiction, and most of us realize we can't, in general, have any partner we wish. We also know that the more attractive potential partners are, the more they will be sought after by others, and the more likely they are to reject our advances, especially if, like most people, we are only average in attractiveness. These considerations suggest what is known as the **matching hypothesis**—the idea that although we would prefer to obtain extremely attractive romantic partners, we generally focus on obtaining ones whose physical beauty is about the same as our own. This view was first proposed by Berscheid, Dion, and Walster and Walster (1971), who found that couples who were similar in attractiveness were more likely to continue dating than those who were very different. Over the years, though, very little additional evidence for this very reasonable idea of matching in terms of physical attractiveness was obtained. In fact, several studies indicated that overall, people don't match—they "go for the best"—they try to obtain the most attractive partners available (e.g., Kalick & Hamilton, 1996).

More recently, though, van Straaten, Engles, Fainkenauer, and Holland (2009) have reported findings that offer strong support for the matching hypothesis. These researchers had male and female strangers interact briefly in a study supposedly concerned with student preferences in daily life. These interactions were videotaped, and the attractiveness of the two participants was rated by observers. In addition, the extent to which each partner engaged in efforts to make a favorable impression on the other person was also rated. Finally, participants also rated their interest in dating the stranger.

If the matching hypothesis is accurate, then it would be expected that participants would invest more effort in trying to impress their partner when they were similar to this person in attractiveness than when they were different. However, the more attractive the partner, the stronger their interest in dating this person would be (remember, according to this hypothesis, we prefer very attractive partners, but focus on obtaining ones who match our own level of attractiveness). Results confirmed these predictions for men: They invested more effort in building a relationship with the stranger when they were

repulsion hypothesis
Rosenbaum's provocative proposal that attraction is not increased by similar attitudes but is simply decreased by dissimilar attitudes. This hypothesis is incorrect as stated, but it is true that dissimilar attitudes tend to have negative effects that are stronger than the positive effects of similar attitudes.

matching hypothesis
The idea that although we would prefer to obtain extremely attractive romantic partners, we generally focus on obtaining ones whose physical beauty is about the same as our own.

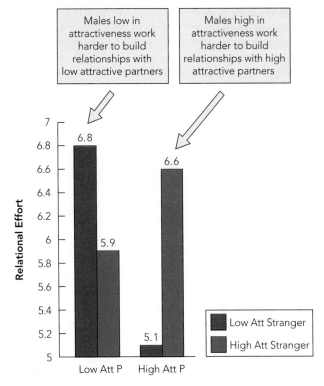

FIGURE 7.12 Evidence for the Matching Hypothesis

Participants in the study illustrated here interacted with an opposite sex stranger. Their behavior was videotaped, and the extent to which they invested effort in trying to form a relationship with the partner was rated. Men invested more effort in this respect when they were similar to their partner in physical attractiveness than when they were very different. The same pattern did not emerge for women, who were more reluctant to engage in overt relationship-building actions. (Only date for men are shone). *(Source: Based on data from van Straaten et al., 2009).*

balance theory
The formulations of Heider and of Newcomb that specify the relationships among (1) an individual's liking for another person, (2) his or her attitude about a given topic, and (3) the other person's attitude about the same topic. Balance (liking plus agreement) results in a positive emotional state. Imbalance (liking plus disagreement) results in a negative state and a desire to restore balance. Nonbalance (disliking plus either agreement or disagreement) leads to indifference.

similar to this person in attractiveness than when they were different. For women, however, this pattern did not emerge (see Figure 7.12). This was not surprising because it has been found that women are generally much less willing to express overt interest in a potential romantic partner than men, so they "played it safe" and did not engage in strong efforts to impress their partner regardless of whether they were similar to this person or not.

Overall, these findings suggest that although we may daydream about incredibly attractive romantic partners, we focus most of our effort and energy on obtaining ones who closely match our own level of attractiveness. This may not lead to the fulfillment of our dreams or fantasies, but does provide the basis for relationships that are mutually desired, and have a better chance to survive and prosper.

Together, a large body of research findings indicate that similarity is indeed an important determinant of attraction. But why is this so? Why do we like others who are similar to ourselves but tend to dislike others who are different? That's a key question, and one to which we turn next.

EXPLAINING THE EFFECT OF SIMILARITY–DISSIMILARITY ON ATTRACTION To ask the same question in a slightly different way, why does similarity elicit positive affect (i.e., feelings) while dissimilarity elicits negative affect? The oldest explanation—**balance theory**—was proposed independently by Newcomb (1961) and by Heider (1958). This framework suggests that people naturally organize their likes and dislikes in a symmetrical way (Hummert, Crockett, & Kemper, 1990). When two people like each other and discover that they are similar in some specific respect, this constitutes a state of *balance*, and balance is emotionally pleasant. When two people like each other and find out that they are dissimilar in some specific respect, the result is *imbalance*. Imbalance is emotionaly unpleasant, causing the individuals to strive to restore balance by inducing one of them to change and thus create similarity, by misperceiving the dissimilarity, or simply by deciding to dislike one another. Whenever two people dislike one another, their relationship involves *nonbalance*. This is not especially pleasant or unpleasant because each individual is indifferent about the other person's similarities or dissimilarities.

These aspects of balance theory are helpful, but they do not deal with the question of why similarity should matter in the first place. So, a second level of explanation is needed. Why should you care if someone differs from you with respect to musical preferences, belief in God, or anything else? One answer is provided by Festinger's (1954) **social comparison theory.** Briefly stated, you compare your attitudes and beliefs with those of others because the only way you can evaluate the accuracy of your views and their "normality" is by finding that other people agree with you. This is not a perfect way to determine the truth, but it is often the best we can do. For example, if you are the only one who believes that global warming is happening so quickly that the seas will flood many coastlines next year, the odds are that you are incorrect. No one wants to be in that position, so we turn to others to obtain *consensual validation*—evidence that they share our views. When you learn that someone else holds the same attitudes and beliefs that you do, it feels good because such information suggests that you have sound judgment, are in contact with reality, and so on. Dissimilarity suggests the opposite, and that creates negative feelings, unless such dissimilarity comes from outgroup members, whom we expect to be different from ourselves (Haslam, 2004).

Reciprocal Liking or Disliking: Liking Those Who Like Us

Everyone (or at least, nearly everyone!) wants to be liked. Not only do we enjoy being evaluated positively, we welcome such input even when we know it is inaccurate and is simply undeserved flattery. To an outside observer, false flattery may be perceived accurately for what it is, but to the person being flattered, it is likely to appear accurate, even if not completely honest (Gordon, 1996; Vonk, 1998, 2002). Only if it is totally obvious does flattery sometimes fail (see Chapter 3).

Research findings offer strong support for the powerful effects of others' liking for *us* on our liking for *them* (e.g., Condon & Crano, 1988; Hayw, 1984), so, overall, it appears that the rule of reciprocity—which applies to many aspects of social life—operates with respect to attraction, too. In general, we tend to like those who express liking toward us, and dislike others who indicate that as far as they are concerned, we don't really measure up.

What Do We Desire in Others?: Designing Ideal Interaction Partners

In this discussion so far, we have focused on the factors that lead individuals to like—or dislike—each other. But now, consider a different but closely related question: What do people desire in others? In other words, suppose you could design the perfect person for a particular kind of relationship—a romantic interest, a work-group member, someone to play sports with. What characteristics would you want these people to have? In other words, what would make you like these imaginary individuals very much—more, perhaps, than anyone else you have actually met? That question has been addressed by social psychologists (e.g., Kurzbam & Neuberg, 2005), and in a sense, it serves as a good link to the discussion of relationships that forms the next major topic of this chapter.

While many studies have investigated this issue, one of the most revealing was conducted by Cottrell, Neuberg, and Li (2007). These researchers began by asking undergraduate students to "create an ideal person" by rating 31 positive characteristics in terms of how important each was for their ideal person to have. Included among the characteristics were trustworthiness, cooperativeness, agreeableness, extraversion (outgoing, sociable), emotionally stable, physical health, and physical attractiveness. Results indicated that trustworthiness and cooperativeness were seen as the most important traits, followed by agreeableness (being kind, interpersonally warm) and extraversion (being outgoing and sociable). These initial findings indicate that overall, there are indeed characteristics that most people desire in others. They do not, however, address another question: Do these characteristics vary with the kind of relationship in question? In other words, do we desire different traits in friends, work partners, lovers, friends, or employees?

To find out, the researchers asked male and female students to imagine creating ideal members of several different groups and relationships—work project team members, final exam study group members, golf team members, sorority members, fraternity members, close friends, and employees. For each task or relationship, they rated the extent to which 75 different traits were important for this ideal person to possess. As shown in Table 7.1, results were revealing. First, across all seven relationships, trustworthiness and cooperativeness were rated as most important. Agreeableness followed closely, as did extraversion. As you might expect, though, other traits were viewed as more or less important, depending on the kind of relationship participants had with this imaginary "ideal" person. For instance, intelligence was rated as very important for

social comparison theory
Festinger (1954) suggested that people compare themselves to others because, for many domains and attributes, there is no objective yardstick with which to evaluate the self, so we compare ourselves to others to gain this information.

TABLE 7.1   What Do We Desire in Others? It Depends on The Context

As shown here, several traits (trustworthiness, cooperativeness, agreeableness) are viewed as important in "ideal partners" across many different kinds of relationships (project teams, employees, friends, etc.). The importance of other traits, however, varies with the kind of relationship in question. For instance, attractiveness is important in a sorority member, but not in a project team or study group member. (High ratings for various traits are shown in italic and indicate that the traits in question were rated as very important by research participants.)

TRAIT	PROJECT TEAM	STUDY GROUP	GOLD TEAM	SORORITY	FRATERNITY	CLOSE FRIEND	EMPLOYEE
Trustworthiness	*7.35*	*6.87*	*7.74*	*7.45*	*7.33*	*7.68*	*7.78*
Cooperativeness	*6.39*	*5.93*	*5.70*	*6.51*	*6.29*	*6.79*	*6.28*
Agreeableness	*6.36*	*5.65*	*5.38*	*6.99*	*6.50*	*7.14*	*6.76*
Attractiveness	2.84	2.68	3.17	*6.36*	*5.24*	4.73	3.74
Intelligence	*7.67*	*7.74*	5.52	6.04	5.97	6.51	*7.39*
Humor	5.17	4.48	5.02	*6.61*	*6.92*	*7.53*	5.49
Wealth	3.43	2.17	3.70	4.82	4.92	3.94	4.45

Source: Based on data from Cottrell et al., 2006.

project teams and study groups, but much less important for fraternity or sorority members. Similarly, humor was rated as very important for close friends, but less important for employees or project team and study group members. In other words, overall, the results pointed to two major conclusions. First, there are several traits (trustworthiness, cooperativeness, agreeableness, extraversion) that we value in *everyone*—no matter what kind of relationship we have with them. Second, we value other traits differentially—that is, to a greater or lesser degree—depending on the kind of relationship we have with the other person.

In sum, although we can't always explain why we like or dislike other people, it seems clear that our reactions in these respects are somewhat predictable. They are influenced by a number of factors, including our similarity to other people, their liking for us, their appearance, how frequently we interact with them, and their possession of certain key traits. From the perspective of social psychology, therefore, interpersonal attraction loses some of its mystery—but at the same time, becomes much more understandable and predictable, which is precisely the kind of knowledge social psychologists seek.

KEY POINTS

- One of the many factors determining attraction toward another person is similarity to that individual in terms of attitudes, beliefs, values, and interests.

- Despite the continuing popularity of the idea that opposites attract (complementarity), that rarely seems to be true in the real world.

- Though dissimilarity tends to have a greater impact on attraction than similarity, we respond to both, and the larger the proportion of similar attitudes, the greater the attraction.

- The beneficial effects of similarity is even found with respect to physical attractiveness, where recent

- evidence supports the matching hypothesis—the view that we tend to actually choose romantic partners who are similar to ourselves in terms of attractiveness.

- Several theoretical perspectives (balance theory, social comparison theory, an evolutionary perspective) offer explanations for the powerful effects of similarity on attraction.

- We especially like other people who indicate that they like us. We very much dislike those who dislike and negatively evaluate us.

- The traits we desire in other people depend on the context.

Close Relationships: Foundations of Social Life

In a sense, interpersonal attraction is the beginning of many relationships. If we have a choice, we tend to spend time with people we like, and to develop friendships, romances, or other long-term relationships with them. In other cases, of course, relationships are not voluntary in this way. We have long-term relationships with family members (our parents, siblings, grandparents, etc.) that exist from birth, and continue throughout life—sometimes whether we like it or not! And still other relationships are related to our jobs, careers, or education. Most people have coworkers and bosses, some of whom they like and others they would prefer to avoid. Regardless of whether relationships are formed voluntarily or are the result of birth or external constraints (where we work), they certainly play a crucial role in the social side of life.

Social psychologists are fully aware of the central role of relationships in our lives, and have turned growing attention to understanding basic questions about them: How and why are they formed? How do they develop? What functions do they serve? And how, and why, do they sometimes end in unhappy or even personally devastating ways, such as divorce, conflict, or even physical violence? In this discussion, we provide an overview of findings of social psychological research on these and related questions (e.g., Adams, 2006; Arriaga, Reed, Goodfriend, & Agnew, 2006). We start with family relationships and friendships, and then turn to romantic relationships, where we consider the nature of love. As we'll soon see, love is a multifaceted process, and romantic love—although one of the most dramatic forms—is just one of several different types. Before turning to the nature of these relationships and the factors that affect them, however, we want to begin by emphasizing the fact that relationships are strongly influenced by the cultures in which they develop. To see what we mean, consider two very basic kinds of relationships, found all over the world: marriage and parent–child relationships.

Different cultures have very different expectations concerning marriage. For instance, cultures that accept only monogamous marriages have very different expectations concerning the roles, obligations, and responsibilities of marriage partners from a culture in which individuals can be married to several partners at the same time. Similarly, consider the responsibilities of parent–child relationships. In the United States and many other Western cultures, the responsibilities of parents are emphasized, and in fact, they often find themselves in the position of caring for or providing help to children long after they have become adults (see Figure 7.13). The children, in contrast, are not expected to care for their parents directly as they age

"Well, this is one way to keep the kids from moving back home."

FIGURE 7.13   Parent–Child Relationships: Responsibilities Differ Greatly Across Cultures

In some cultures (such as in the United States), parents are expected to help and support their children even after they are adults—although, as this cartoon suggests, some don't like it! In other cultures, in contrast, children are expected to care for their parents as they grow older. (Source: The New Yorker, July 12, 2010).

and perhaps become ill. Nursing homes are an acceptable way to handle such obligations. In many other cultures, in contrast, children who fail to care directly for their aging parents would be strongly condemned as ungrateful, irresponsible, or worse! So, clearly, cultural factors often play a powerful role in determining the nature of important social relationships. Having made that basic point, let's turn to important forms of relationships and the insights research provides about them.

Relationships with Family Members: Our First—and Most Lasting—Close Relationships

In the 1950s and 1960s, situation comedies on television often showed family relationships in a very favorable light: mothers were caring, fathers were wise, brothers and sisters—if sometimes annoying—were shown as generally getting along well. And grandparents, aunts, uncles, and cousins shared experience, support, and advice freely and openly with their relatives. While few families can match the ideal shown in those TV shows, one fact is clear: Relations with family members are important throughout our lives. They certainly change as we mature and move through different phases of life, but they remain as a constant foundation of our social existence. The same can be said for friends. Many people form friendships during childhood or adolescence that they carry with them throughout life. And even if separated by thousands of miles, they remain in contact and are present in each other's thoughts often. Let's take a closer look at these very basic relationships, examining the many benefits—and costs—they often involve.

RELATIONSHIPS WITH PARENTS   Parent–child interactions are of basic importance because this is usually one's first contact with another person. We come into the world ready to interact with other humans (Dissanayake, 2000), but the specific characteristics of those interactions differ from person to person and family to family. It is those details that seem to have important implications for our later interpersonal behavior.

During the first year of life, when the range of possible behaviors is obviously limited, human infants are extremely sensitive to facial expressions, body movements, and the sounds people make. The person taking care of the baby is often the mother, and she, in turn, is equally sensitive to what the infant does (Kochanska, Lange, & Martel, 2004). As they interact, the two individuals communicate and reinforce the actions of one another (Murray & Trevarthen, 1986; Trevarthen, 1993). The adult shows interest in the infant's communication in various ways such as engaging in baby talk and displaying exaggerated facial expressions. The infant, in turn, shows interest in the adult by attempting to make appropriate sounds and expressions. Overall, such reciprocal interactions tend to be a positive educational experience for both.

THE LASTING IMPORTANCE OF PARENT–CHILD INTERACTIONS: THEIR ROLE IN ATTACHMENT STYLE   Early relationships between parents and children have primarily been studied by developmental psychologists, but the fact that these relationships affect the nature of later interpersonal behavior has led social psychologists to look more closely at how what happens to us in childhood shapes our social relationships throughout life. One framework for understanding such effects was offered by Bowlby (1969, 1973). On the basis of careful studies of mothers and infants, Bowlby developed the concept of **attachment style,** the degree of security an individual feels in interpersonal relationships. Infants, Bowlby suggests, acquire two basic attitudes during their earliest interactions with an adult. The first is an attitude about self, *self-esteem.* The behavior and the emotional reactions of the caregiver provide information to the infant that he or she is a valued, important, loved individual or, at the other extreme, someone who is without value, unimportant, and unloved. The second basic attitude concerns other people, and involves general expectancies and beliefs about them. This attitude is **interpersonal trust,**

attachment style
The degree of security experienced in interpersonal relationships. Differential styles initially develop in the interactions between infant and caregiver when the infant acquires basic attitudes about self-worth and interpersonal trust.

interpersonal trust
An attitudinal dimension underlying attachment styles that involves the belief that other people are generally trustworthy, dependable, and reliable as opposed to the belief that others are generally untrustworthy, undependable, and unreliable. This is the most successful and most desirable attachment style.

and is based largely on whether the caregiver is perceived by the infant as trustworthy, dependable, and reliable or as relatively untrustworthy, undependable, and unreliable. Research findings suggest that we develop these basic attitudes about self and about others long before we acquire language skills.

Based on the two basic attitudes, infants, children, adolescents, and adults can be roughly classified as having a particular style involving relationships with others. If you think of self-esteem as one dimension and interpersonal trust as another, then four possible patterns exist: one in which an individual is high on both dimensions, another in which the individual is low on both, and two others in which the person involved is high on one and low on the other. These four contrasting attachment styles can be described as follows.

- A person with a **secure attachment style** is high in both self-esteem and trust. Secure individuals are best able to form lasting, committed, satisfying relationships throughout life (Shaver & Brennan, 1992).

- Someone low in both self-esteem and interpersonal trust has a **fearful-avoidant attachment style.** Fearful-avoidant individuals tend not to form close relationships or to have unhappy ones (Mikulincer, 1998; Tidwell, Reis, & Shaver, 1996).

- Low self-esteem combined with high interpersonal trust produces a **preoccupied attachment style.** Individuals showing this pattern of attachment want closeness (sometimes excessively so), and they readily form relationships. They cling to others, but expect eventually to be rejected because they believe themselves to be unworthy (Lopez et al., 1997; Whiffen, Aube, Thompson, & Campbell, 2000).

- Finally, those with a **dismissing attachment style** (a style we examined briefly previously) are high in self-esteem and low in interpersonal trust. This combination leads to the belief that one is very much deserving of good relationships, but because these individuals don't trust others, they fear genuine closeness. They are the kind of people who state that they don't want or need close relationships with others (Carvello & Gabriel, 2006).

These contrasting styles of attachment can strongly shape the relationships individuals have with others. For instance, those with a secure attachment style are more likely to have positive long-term relationships, whereas those with a fearful-avoidant style often avoid such relationships or have ones that fail—often very badly. Attachment styles, although formed early in life, are not set in stone; they can be changed by life experiences. For instance, a painful divorce or relationship breakup may reduce an individual's self-esteem and undercut feelings of security. But they tend to be stable over long periods of time (Klohnen & Bera, 1998), and for that reason, can have strong implications for a wide range of life outcomes. For example, adolescents with an insecure attachment style often do worse in school than ones with secure attachment styles, form fewer friendships, and often turn into "outsiders." Such people also experience higher levels of stress when they have conflict with relationship partners (Powers, Pietromonaco, Gunlicks, & Sayer, 2008). Perhaps worst of all, those with insecure attachment (and especially a fearful-avoidant style), are more likely to commit suicide (Orbach, 2007). We return to the effects of attachment styles in a discussion of romantic relationships because they appear to play a key role in that context.

THE ROLE OF OTHER FAMILY MEMBERS   Besides the mother (or caregiver), other family members also interact with infants and young children. Research is beginning to reveal the importance of fathers as well as mothers, and of grandparents and others (Lin & Harwood, 2003; Maio, Fincham, & Lycett, 2000). Because these people differ in personality characteristics, children can be influenced in a variety of ways (Clark, Kochanska, & Ready, 2000). For example, the negative effects of having a withdrawn, unreliable mother can be partly offset by the presence of an outgoing, dependable grandfather. Every interaction is potentially important as the young person is developing

secure attachment style
A style characterized by high self-esteem and high interpersonal trust. This is the most successful and most desirable attachment style.

fearful-avoidant attachment style
A style characterized by low self-esteem and low interpersonal trust. This is the most insecure and least adaptive attachment style.

preoccupied attachment style
A style characterized by low self-esteem and high interpersonal trust. This is a conflicted and somewhat insecure style in which the individual strongly desires a close relationship but feels that he or she is unworthy of the partner and is thus vulnerable to being rejected.

dismissing attachment style
A style characterized by high self-esteem and low interpersonal trust. This is a conflicted and somewhat insecure style in which the individual feels that he or she deserves a close relationship but is frustrated because of mistrust of potential partners. The result is the tendency to reject the other person at some point in the relationship to avoid being the one who is rejected.

attitudes about the meaning and value of such factors as trust, affection, self-worth, competition, and humor (O'Leary, 1995). When an older person plays games with a youngster, learning involves not only the game itself, but also how people interact in a social situation, follow a set of rules, behave honestly or cheat, and how they deal with disagreements. All of this affects the way the child interacts with other adults and with peers (Lindsey, Mize, & Pettit, 1997).

RELATIONSHIPS BETWEEN AND AMONG SIBLINGS   Approximately 80 percent of us grow up in a household with at least one sibling, and sibling interactions contribute to what we learn about interpersonal behavior (Dunn, 1992). Among elementary school-children, those who have no siblings are found to be less liked by their classmates and to be more aggressive or to be more victimized by aggressors than those with siblings, presumably because having brothers or sisters provides useful interpersonal learning experiences (Kitzmann, Cohen, & Lockwood, 2002). Sibling relationships, unlike those between parent and child, often combine feelings of affection, hostility, and rivalry (Boer, Westenberg, McHale, Updegraff, & Stocker, 1997). A familiar theme is some version of "Mom always liked you best" or "They always did more for you than me." Parents, though, seldom admit that they feel any such favoritism.

Most of us have experienced (or observed in others) multiple examples of sibling rivalry and we have heard a great many adults complain about events involving competition between siblings that occurred in the distant past. In fact, though, most siblings get along fairly well. There are certainly major exceptions to this rule, but in general, sibling rivalry is ultimately far surpassed by the shared memories and affection that siblings feel for one another (see Figure 7.14).

close friendship
A relationship in which two people spend a great deal of time together, interact in a variety of situations, and provide mutual emotional support.

FIGURE 7.14   Relationships with Siblings: Usually (Although Not Always) Positive

Although sibling rivalry certainly exists, it is generally less important in relationships between siblings than their many shared experiences and genuine affection for one another. (Shown here is one family, consisting of five brothers and a sister; they are standing in order of age—oldest on the left to youngest on the right; and they enjoy excellent and mutually supportive social relationships.)

Friendships: Relationships Beyond the Family

Beginning in early childhood, most of us establish casual friendships with peers who share common interests. These relationships generally begin on the basis of proximity (we are in the same class in school or live in the same neighborhood), or as a result of parental friendships, that bring the children into contact. Such relationships are maintained in part by mutual interests and by positive rather than negative experiences together, and sometimes develop into much stronger social ties.

CLOSE FRIENDSHIPS   Many childhood friendships simply fade away. At times, however, a relationship begun in early childhood can mature into a **close friendship** that involves increasingly mature types of interaction. Such friendships can survive for decades—and, sometimes, for an entire life (see Figure 7.15).

FIGURE 7.15   Long-Term Friendships: Friends for Life
Many friendships formed during childhood fade away, but a few survive for decades—or even an entire lifetime.

These long-term friendships have several important characteristics. For example, many people tend to engage in self-enhancing behavior (such as bragging) when interacting with a wide range of others, but they exhibit modesty when interacting with their long-term friends (Tice, Butler, Muraven, & Stillwell, 1995). Friends are less likely to lie to one another, unless the lie is designed to make the friend feel better (DePaulo & Kashy, 1998). And friends begin to speak of "we" and "us" rather than "she and I" or "he and I" (Fitzsimmons & Kay, 2004).

Once established, a close friendship results in the two individuals spending increasing amounts of time together, interacting in varied situations, self-disclosing, and providing mutual emotional support (Laurenceau, Barrett, & Pietromonaco, 1998; Matsushima & Shiomi, 2002). A close friend is valued for his or her generosity, sensitivity, and honesty—someone with whom you can relax and be yourself (Urbanski, 1992). But cultural differences exist with respect to friendship, too. For instance, Japanese college students describe a "best friend" as someone in a give-and-take relationship, a person with whom it is easy to get along, who does not brag, and is considerate and not short-tempered (Maeda & Ritchie, 2003). American students describe close friends in a similar way except they also value as friends individuals who are spontaneous and active.

GENDER AND FRIENDSHIPS   Women report having more close friends than men do (Fredrickson, 1995). Women also place more importance on intimacy (e.g., self-disclosure and emotional support) than is true for men (Fehr, 2004).

There are many benefits to having close friends, but there can also be pain when you lose a friend or have to separate. For example, when a friendship is interrupted by college graduation, the two individuals must adapt to the emotional threat of separation. As a result, graduating seniors, especially women, report more intense emotional involvement when interacting with close friends than is true for students not facing graduation (Fredrickson, 1995). The importance of friendships extends far beyond the undergraduate years, and even plays a role in the social position of professionals in the world of business (Gibbons & Olk, 2003).

IS SIMILARITY THE BASIS FOR FRIENDSHIP?   Earlier, we noted that similarity is an important basis for interpersonal attraction: The more similar people are in any of many different ways (attitudes, personality, interests, values), they more they tend to like one another. Is this also a basis for friendship? To find out, Selfhout, Denissen, Branje, and Meeus (2009) conducted research with individuals who were becoming acquainted and forming friendships. These research participants were freshmen at a European university, and during orientation sessions, they completed measures of several key aspects of personality (the "Big Five" dimensions—extraversion, agreeableness, openness to experience, etc.). On this questionnaire, they rated both themselves and other students they were just meeting in terms of these dimensions. Then they completed similar questionnaires once a month for several months. This provided information both on *actual similarity* between participants in the study and on their *perceived similarity*—how similar they perceived themselves to be. In addition, ratings by peers were also included. Finally, students also provided information on their developing friendships—the extent to which they were friends with other participants in the study.

The key question was, Would actual similarity or perceived similarity be a better predictor of friendship formation? Although many previous studies suggest that actual similarity should play a key role, other research indicates that determining actual similarity takes a long time and is often an uncertain process. Perceived similarity, however, can develop almost immediately and exert its effects from the very start of a relationship. Results offered support for this alternative prediction. In fact, actual similarity did not predict who became friends, while perceived similarity predicted this outcome very well. For people who are just beginning to get acquainted, then, perception appears to be more important than underlying reality in terms of friendship formation.

KEY POINTS

- Our first relationships are within the family, and we acquire an **attachment style** (which is based on level of self-esteem and degree of interpersonal trust) in the context of these relationships.
- These attachment styles influence the nature of other relationships, and also play an important role in many life outcomes.
- Other family relationships include those between siblings and between children and other relatives.
- Friendships outside of the family begin in childhood and are initially based simply on such factors

as proximity and the relationship between parents. With increasing maturity, it becomes possible to form close friendships that involve spending time together, interacting in many different situations, providing mutual social support, and engaging in self-disclosure.

- Although actual similarity between individuals is an important factor in interpersonal attraction, research findings indicate that perceived similarity plays a more important role in the early stages of friendship, when individuals are first becoming acquainted.

Romantic Relationships and the (Partially Solved) Mystery of Love

While not everyone would agree that love is the only ingredient necessary for personal happiness, most would accept the idea that it is one of the most important components. And countless singers, novelists, and poets would concur. But what, precisely, *is* love? What role does it play in romantic relationships? How does it develop? Does it develop naturally from other relationships, or is it something special that occurs when the "right" two people meet—the "bolt of lightning" that strikes unexpectedly and without warning? Given love's obvious importance in the social side of life, social psychologists have attempted to unravel these and other mysteries. While they have not yet obtained complete answers to these questions, their research definitely offers important new insights into the nature and impact of love. Please be ready for some surprises, because efforts to study love scientifically have sometimes provided answers that are very different from those provided by poets, philosophers, or popular singers. We begin with a discussion of love, and then turn to its role in romantic relationships.

LOVE: ITS BASIC NATURE   **Love** is certainly one of the most popular topics in songs, movies, and novels. And most people would agree that it plays a key role in our lives—and our personal happiness. It is a familiar experience in many (but not all) cultures, and recent polls indicate that almost three out of four Americans say they are currently "in love." In part, love is an emotional reaction that seems as basic as sadness, happiness, and fear (Shaver, Morgan, & Wu, 1996). And in fact, love may actually be good for you in terms of psychological adjustment. Research by social psychologists indicates that falling in love leads to an increase in self-efficacy and self-esteem (see Chapter 4)—two important ingredients in psychological health and happiness. So, what exactly is love?

Some clues to the meaning of love can be found in the spontaneous definitions people offer when asked what it means. When asked "What is love?", answers like these are common (Harrison, 2003): "Love is offering your partner the last bite of your favorite food," "Love is when you look at your partner when they first wake up and still think they are beautiful"; "Love is like an elevator; you can ride it to the top or end up in the basement, but eventually you'll choose which floor to get off." You probably have your own answer—and it may well be very different from these.

Surprisingly, social psychologists did not attempt to study love systematically until the 1970s, when one (Rubin, 1970) developed a measure of romantic love, and others (Berscheid & Hatfield, 1974), proposed a psychological theory of love. Since then, though, love has been a major topic of interest for social psychologists. As a result of such research, we now know, fairly clearly, what love is *not*. It is not merely a close friendship extended to physical intimacy, and it involves more than merely being romantically or sexually interested in another person. The specific details appear to vary from culture to culture (Beall & Sternberg, 1995), but there is reason to believe that the basic experience we call love is a relatively universal one (Hatfield & Rapson, 1993). Here is an overview of what research tells us about its major cognitive and emotional aspects.

PASSIONATE LOVE   Aron, Dutton, Aron, and Iverson (1989) pointed out that many people fall in love, but no one ever seems to have "fallen in friendship." Unlike attraction, or even romance, **passionate love** involves an intense and often unrealistic emotional reaction to another person. Passionate love usually begins as a sudden, overwhelming, surging, all-consuming positive reaction to another person—a reaction that feels as if it's beyond control. The title of a film that won many awards several decades ago captures this basic aspect of love: *Swept Away* (see Figure 7.16). And indeed, love often occurs suddenly, seems overwhelming, and drives away thoughts of almost anything else when it occurs.

Is sexual attraction an essential component of passionate love? Meyers and Berscheid (1997) propose that it is, but that it is not sufficient in and of itself for concluding that we are in love with another person. You can be sexually attracted to someone without being in love, but you aren't likely to be in love in the absence of sexual attraction. Surveys indicate that college students agree (Regan, 1998). For many people, love makes sex more acceptable; and sexual activity tends to be romanticized (Goldenberg, Pyszczynski, Greenberg, McCoy, & Solomon, 1999). That's why it is more acceptable for two people to "make love" than simply to copulate like animals in heat.

In addition to sex, passionate love includes strong emotional arousal, the desire to be physically close, and an intense need to be loved as much as you love the other person. Loving and being loved are positive experiences, but they are accompanied by a recurring

love
A combination of emotions, cognitions, and behaviors that often play a crucial role in intimate relationships.

passionate love
An intense and often unrealistic emotional response to another person. When this emotion is experienced, it is usually perceived as an indication of true love, but to outside observers it appears to be infatuation.

FIGURE 7.16   Passionate Love: Swept Away by Powerful Emotions
A film originally made in the 1970s (and then made again in 2002), was titled "Swept Away." It describes two people who start, on a boat cruise, with intense dislike of each other. After being marooned on an island, though, they are soon swept away by a passion that overcomes all their restraints and inhibitions—as well as major barriers between them in terms of wealth and education.

fear that something may happen to end the relationship. Hatfield and Sprecher (1986b) developed a scale to measure the various elements of passionate love (the Passionate Love Scale) and it contains items such as "For me, _____ is the perfect romantic partner" and "I would feel deep despair if _____ left me."

Though it sounds like something that only happens in movies, most people, when asked, say they have had had the experience of suddenly falling in love with a stranger—*love at first sight* (Averill & Boothroyd, 1977). Often, sadly, just one person falls in love, and his or her feelings are not returned by the partner; that's known as **unrequited love.** Such one-way love is most common among people with a conflicted attachment style (Aron, Aron, & Allen, 1998). In one large survey investigation, about 60 percent of the respondents said that they had experienced this kind of love within the past 2 years (Bringle & Winnick, 1992).

Two social psychologists who have studied love for many years, Hatfield and Walster (1981), suggest that passionate love requires the presence of three basic factors. First, you have to have an idea or concept of passionate love—you must have a basic idea of what it is and believe that it exists (Sternberg, 1996). Second, an appropriate love object must be present. "Appropriate" tends to mean a physically attractive person of the opposite sex who is not currently married—although again, this differs in cultures and in various groups within a culture. Third, the individual must be in a state of physiological arousal (sexual excitement, fear, anxiety, or whatever) that can then be interpreted as the emotion of love (Dutton & Aron, 1974; Istvan, Griffitt, & Weidner, 1983). Together, these three components are the basic ingredients of love.

WHAT IS THE ORIGIN OF LOVE?   The answer is that no one knows for sure. One possibility is that love is simply a pleasant fantasy that people belonging to a given culture share at certain times of life—much like belief in Santa Claus or the Tooth Fairy when we are children. Another explanation involves the fact that when our early ancestors first began to walk in an upright position, they hunted for meat and gathered edible vegetables that could be carried back to a place of shelter (Lemonick & Dorfman, 2001). Their survival, and that of the entire species, depended on their reproductive success (Buss, 1994), and such success was more likely if heterosexual pairs were erotically attracted to one another and if they were willing to invest time and effort in feeding and protecting any offspring they produced. These two important characteristics (desire and interpersonal commitment) are presumably based on biology. We experience sexual desire and the desire to bond with mates and our children because such motivations were adaptive (Rensberger, 1993)—they helped our species to reproduce and survive. Our ancestors were more than simply sex partners, however. It was also beneficial if they liked and trusted one another and if they could divide tasks such as hunting and childcare. Altogether, bonding with a mate and with one's offspring was important to the success of the species. As a consequence, today's humans may be genetically primed to seek sex, fall in love, and become loving parents. Monogamy may depend in part on brain chemistry (Insel & Carter, 1995), and most young adults say they expect to have a monogamous relationship with the person they love (Wiederman & Allgeier, 1996). Keep in mind that cultural influences can affect both desire and commitment through religious teachings, civil laws, and the way love and marriage is represented in our songs and stories (Allgeier & Wiederman, 1994).

SEVERAL KINDS OF LOVE   Though passionate love is a common occurrence, it is too intense and too overwhelming to be maintained as a long-term emotional state. There are other kinds of love, however, that can be much more lasting. One, **companionate love** (Hatfield, 1998), is the " . . . affection we feel for those with whom our lives are deeply entwined." Unlike passionate love, companionate love is based on a very close friendship in which two people are sexually attracted, have a great deal in common, care about each other's well-being, and express mutual liking and respect (Caspi & Herbener, 1990). Perhaps it's not as exciting as passionate love nor as interesting a theme for music and fiction, but it does serve as a foundation for lasting, committed relationships.

unrequited love
Love felt by one person for another who does not feel love in return.

companionate love
Love that is based on friendship, mutual attraction, shared interests, respect, and concern for one another's welfare.

A different conception of the meaning of love is provided by Sternberg's (1986) **triangular model of love,** shown in Figure 7.17. This theory suggests that each love relationship is made up of three basic components that are present in varying degrees in different couples (Aron & Westbay, 1996). One component is **intimacy**—the closeness two people feel and the strength of the bond that holds them together. Intimacy is essentially companionate love. Partners high in intimacy are concerned with each other's welfare and happiness, and they value, like, count on, and understand one another. The second component, **passion,** is based on romance, physical attraction, and sexuality—in other words, passionate love. Men are more likely to stress this component than women (Fehr & Broughton, 2001). The third component, **decision/commitment,** represents cognitive factors such as the decision that you love and want to be with the other person plus a commitment to maintain the relationship on a permanent basis. When all three angles of the triangle are equally strong and balanced, the result is **consummate love**—defined as the ideal form, but something difficult to attain.

Though research on attraction has long stressed the effects of physical attractiveness on liking, its effect on love have been somewhat overlooked until recently. In research conducted in Spain, almost 2,000 individuals ranging in age from 18 to 64 were asked questions about physical attractiveness, falling in love, and each of the components of Sternberg's model (Sangrador & Yela, 2000). Findings suggest that appearance is not simply important with respect to passion, but with respect to intimacy and decision/commitment as well. Also, attractiveness is as important in the later stages of a relationship as it is at the beginning. In the words of these Spanish psychologists, "What is beautiful is loved." This focus on external appearance may not be wise, but these investigators suggest that we should at least acknowledge the reality of the influence of physical attractiveness on relationships.

triangular model of love
Sternberg's conceptualization of love relationships.

intimacy
In Sternberg's triangular model of love, t.he closeness felt by two people—the extent to which they are bonded.

passion
In Sternberg's triangular model of love, the sexual motives and sexual excitement associated with a couple's relationship.

decision/commitment
In Sternberg's triangular model of love, these are the cognitive processes involved in deciding that you love another person and are committed to maintain the relationship.

consummate love
In Sternberg's triangular model of love, a complete and ideal love that combines intimacy, passion, and decision (commitment).

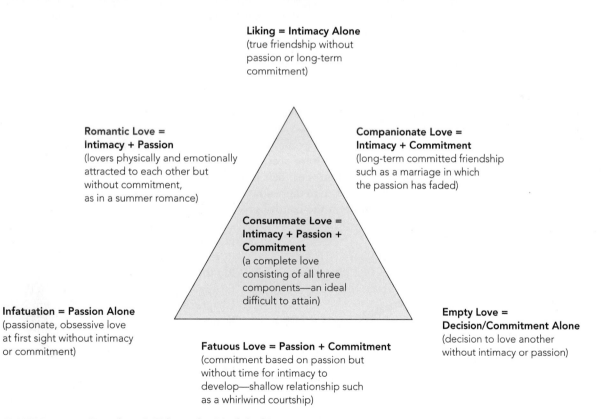

Liking = Intimacy Alone
(true friendship without passion or long-term commitment)

Romantic Love = Intimacy + Passion
(lovers physically and emotionally attracted to each other but without commitment, as in a summer romance)

Companionate Love = Intimacy + Commitment
(long-term committed friendship such as a marriage in which the passion has faded)

Consummate Love = Intimacy + Passion + Commitment
(a complete love consisting of all three components—an ideal difficult to attain)

Infatuation = Passion Alone
(passionate, obsessive love at first sight without intimacy or commitment)

Empty Love = Decision/Commitment Alone
(decision to love another without intimacy or passion)

Fatuous Love = Passion + Commitment
(commitment based on passion but without time for intimacy to develop—shallow relationship such as a whirlwind courtship)

FIGURE 7.17   Sternberg's Triangular Model of Love
Sternberg suggests that love has three basic components: intimacy, passion, and decision/commitment. For a given couple, love can be based on any one of these three components, on a combination of any two of them, or on all three. These various possibilities yield seven types of relationships, including the ideal (consummate love) that consists of all three basic components equally represented. (Source: © 1986 by the American Psychological Association. Reproduced with permission).

Jealousy: An Internal Threat to Relationships— Romantic and Otherwise

Jealousy has often been described as the "green-eyed monster," and with good reason. Feelings of *jealousy*—concerns that a romantic partner or other person about whom we care deeply might transfer their affection or loyalty to another—are deeply distressing. While most people think about jealousy primarily in connection with romantic relationships, it can occur in other contexts too; all that is essential is that a valued relationship with another person is threatened by a rival (e.g., DeSteno, 2004). But despite this fact, it seems clear that jealousy may exert its strongest and most dangerous effects in the context of romantic triads: one person becomes jealous over the possibility that his or her partner is interested in a rival (Harris, 2003). In fact, government statistics indicate that jealousy is a major factor in a large proportion of homicides against women; women are most likely to be murdered by current or former jealous partners (U.S. Department of Justice, 2003). But why, precisely, does jealousy occur? Is it "built into" our emotional reactions by genetic factors (Buss, Larsen, Westen, & Semmelruth, 1992)? Or are other factors involved? In fact, growing evidence now points to the conclusion that jealousy is largely the result of threats to one's self-esteem. In other words, we experience jealousy because anticipated or actual social rejection threatens our self-esteem.

Clear evidence for this view is provided by research conducted by DeSteno, Valdesolo, and Bartlett (2006). These researchers arranged for participants in their study to perform a problem-solving task with a partner, who was actually an assistant of the researchers. This person praised the real subject's work, smiled at her (participants were all females), and provided lots of encouragement. The result was that the assistant and the real subject formed a very pleasant working relationship. Then, this relationship was threatened by a rival—a third person who entered the room, apologizing for being late. The three people (two assistants and the one real subject) then worked on another task and during this activity, the experimenter informed them that they could work either as pairs or alone. That meant that one person would be "out"—she would have to work alone. In the jealousy-inducing condition, the partner—with whom the real subject had previously worked so well—chose to work with the newly arrived rival. In a control condition, not designed to induce jealousy, the partner suddenly remembered that she had another appointment and had to leave. In this condition, too, she ended the enjoyable working relationship with the real subject, but in a way that would not be expected to produce jealousy.

After these procedures were over, participants in both conditions (jealousy and no jealousy) completed measures of their jealousy and their self-esteem. The researchers predicted that those exposed to the jealousy-inducing conditions would experience stronger jealousy than those in the control group, and this is precisely what was found. In addition, and more importantly, these feelings of jealousy stemmed from reductions in self-esteem (which was measured explicitly through a questionnaire, and implicitly through procedures based on the IAT; see Chapter 4). In fact, as shown in Figure 7.18, it appeared that jealousy operated largely through reductions in self-esteem.

So jealousy, it appears, stems largely from threats to self-esteem—threats that occur whenever someone we care about (a lover, work partner, good friend) seem ready to desert us for a rival. As we'll see in Chapter 10, such feelings are not merely unpleasant and distressing, but they can sometimes lead to overt violence against

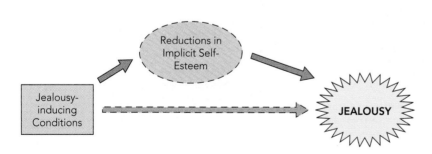

FIGURE 7.18 Jealousy and Threats to Self-Esteem
Research findings indicate that jealousy stems primarily from threats to self-esteem (thick, upper arrows). These threats involve the possibility that someone we care about (a romantic partner, a work partner, etc.) may desert us for a rival. (Source: Based on suggestions by DeSteno, Valdesolo, & Bartlett, 2006).

others, especially in cultures that emphasize the importance of protecting one's "honor." In this respect, the "green-eyed monster" really *is* a monster, and can pose a serious threat not just to personal happiness, but to safety and even life as well.

We should note, of course, that jealousy is just one reason why romantic relationships end. There are many others, too—everything from partners' discovery that they really don't have a lot in common, through sheer boredom and intense, prolonged conflicts (Salvatore, Kuo, Steele, Simpson, & Collins, 2011). Whatever the cause of a breakup, though, it is often painful, and often very hard for the person who wants "out" to do. Is there help for this difficult task? Surprisingly, there is, and we describe it in the section "SOCIAL LIFE IN A CONNECTED WORLD: Breaking Up Is Hard to Do, But Help Is Available."

SOCIAL LIFE *in a* CONNECTED WORLD

Breaking Up Is Hard to Do, But Help is Available

A hit record many years ago was titled "Breaking Up is Hard to Do" (it was sung by Neil Sedaka in 1962). Although many years have passed and the world has changed tremendously, the words of the song are still very true: Ending a romantic relationship is indeed a difficult task (Vangelisti, 2006). Moreover, it is one many people dread. They are reluctant to shatter another person's ego by telling them that they no longer want to be in a relationship with them and perhaps no longer love them. In the past, most people handled this painful task face to face. They would gather their courage and tell their former partner that it was all over between them. That's still the way many people deal with this situation, but now, they also do it via e-mail messages (e.g., a text message saying, essentially, "We're through," or over social networks, where, unfortunately, their rejection of their partner can be very public).

In addition, there is another way that more and more people are using: Internet companies now exist to handle this task for you. For instance, one is known as "Au Revoir Breakup Service" (French for goodbye). This company offers the service of dealing with rejection on your behalf. They advertise that they will act as a mediator to convey your feelings and bring closure to a relationship so you can avoid the emotional repercussion that the situation will bring. Other companies offer the same basic services—for instance, iBreakUp.net, which is specifically designed for people who meet online—and want to break up the same way.

Is this a reasonable way to proceed if you want to end a relationship, but don't want to do it directly? Perhaps, but views about this differ greatly. Alison Arnold, a psychologist who specializes in helping people solve interpersonal problems, puts it simply: "The news of a breakup should never be broken over text or e-mail. Texting a breakup is the coward's way out." Others, however, feel that breaking up indirectly, via text messages, social networks, or Internet break-up services, *is* acceptable.

Research on this topic is just beginning, but already some revealing findings have been reported. For instance, Sprecher, Zimmerman, and Abrahams (2010) asked male and female students to rate the extent to which various strategies for ending a relationship are compassionate, that is, show consideration and concern for the former partner. Results indicated that face-to-face approaches emphasized the good things gained from the relationship, avoided blaming the partner for the breakup, and tried to prevent the partner leaving with "hard feelings," were rated as most compassionate. On the other hand, the following tactics were rated as very low in compassion: using instant messenger to list the reasons for the breakup, informing the partner of negative feelings in an e-mail, text messaging the partner to tell him or her about the pending breakup, or asking a third party—including Internet services—to break the news to the partner.

On the basis of such evidence, it appears that using technology to end a romantic relationship is viewed by many people as not the kindest or most considerate approach. Given the anguish many people feel over confronting their partner directly, however, it seems clear that they will continue to be used even if, as psychologist Alison Arnold suggests, they are not the way many people would prefer to receive such news.

KEYPOINTS

- As is true for attraction and friendship, romantic attraction is influenced by factors such as physical proximity, appearance and similarity. In addition, romance includes sexual attraction and the desire for total acceptance by the other person.
- The reproductive success of our ancient ancestors was enhanced by not only by sexual attraction between males and females, but also by bonding between mates and between parents and their offspring.
- **Passionate love**—a sudden, overwhelming emotional response to another person—is just one kind of love.

- Another, **companionate love,** resembles a close friendship that includes caring, mutual liking, and respect. Sternberg's **triangular model of love** includes these two components, plus a third—**decision/commitment**—that is a cognitive decision to love and to be committed to a relationship.
- Jealousy is a powerful emotion, and research findings suggest that it is often triggered by threats to our self-esteem—threats arising when we fear that someone we love or care about will desert us for a rival.

Selecting Romantic Partners: Do Women and Men Differ in What They Seek?

What do we seek in romantic partners? Research on attraction suggests that similarity probably plays a role, and research on passionate love indicates that physical attractiveness is important too. Are other factors also important? And do women and men seek different qualities in potential romantic partners—including long-term ones? Research on these issues suggests that several factors are important, and that women and men may differ in terms of the weight or importance they attach to some of these (e.g., Geary, Vigil, & Byrd-Craven, 2004; Li, Bailey, Kenrick, & Linsenmeier, 2002).

THE ROLE OF PHYSICAL ATTRACTIVENESS   From the perspective of evolutionary determinants, it would be expected that youth and beauty would weigh heavily in the balance because these characteristics are associated with reproductive potential: young people and ones we find attractive are generally healthier and more fit than older people or ones who are not attractive, so both women and men might well be expected to prefer romantic partners who show these characteristics. In general, that's true, but existing evidence indicates that even today, these qualities count more heavily for men than for women. In other words, women's physical appeal and youth play a stronger role in men's preferences for them than men's physical appeal and youth play in women's choice of romantic partners (Scutt, Manning, Whitehouse, Leinster, & Massey, 1997). But the overall situation is more complex than this, as we now explain.

POSSIBLE FUTURE SELVES AND MATE PREFERENCES   What would your ideal mate be like? Would you want the same things in such a person regardless of anything else—such as, for instance, whether you work outside the home or choose to be a homemaker? Perhaps not. In fact, that's what Eagly, Eastwick, and Johannesen-Schmidt (2009) suggested recently, in research designed to investigate this issue. They reasoned that if individuals anticipate pursuing a career outside the home, they might seek a mate who would be high in the skills necessary to be a homemaker, while if they anticipated being a homemaker themselves, they might prefer a mate who is likely to be a good provider. In other words, they would expect to divide tasks between themselves and their partner, at least to some extent. So the social roles people expect to play in life would be an important factor in determining what they sought in a possible future mate. In fact, Eagly and colleagues reasoned that this would be more important than gender, although some differences between women and men might still exist.

To study these possibilities, they asked male and female participants to imagine that in the future, they are married with children, and that they would be either the primary provider for their family or the primary homemaker. Participants then indicated the extent to which various mate characteristics would be important to them, from irrelevant to indispensable. Several of these characteristics related to being a good provider (ambition, industriousness), while others related to being a good homemaker (desire to have a home and children, good cook and housekeeper).

Results indicated that the role individuals expected to play did influence the skills or traits they would find important in a mate. For both men and women, when participants expected to be a provider, they rated homemaker skills in their potential mate as more important than provider-related skills. When they expected to be a homemaker themselves, however, they rated provider skills in potential mates as more important than homemaker skills (see Figure 7.19). In other words, they sought someone with whom they could readily divide key tasks or responsibilities. In addition, some gender differences were also observed.

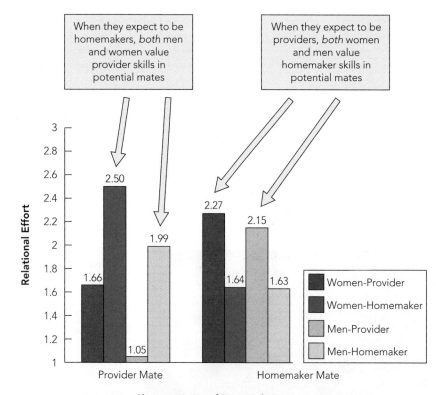

FIGURE 7.19 Future Roles and Mate Preference
For both women and men, the characteristics they sought in a potential mate varied in terms of the social role they expected to play—primary provider or primary homemaker. When participants expected to be a homemaker, they valued provider skills and traits more highly than homemaker skills and traits, while when they expected to be a provider, they valued homemaker skills more highly. So anticipated future roles strongly affect what we seek in a potential mate. (Source: Based on data from Eagly et al., 2009).

Regardless of the role they expected to play themselves, women valued good provider skills or traits more highly than did men. In addition, women also expressed a preference for mates older than themselves, while men expressed a preference for ones younger.

What is the source of these relatively small differences, which have persisted despite major changes in current gender roles? According to an evolutionary perspective, the reason that females are less concerned about male youth and attractiveness is explained by the fact that while women have a limited age span during which reproduction is possible, men are usually able to reproduce from puberty well into old age. For prehistoric females, reproductive success was enhanced by choosing a mate who had the ability to protect and care for her and for their offspring (Kenrick, Neuberg, Zierk, & Krones, 1994; Kenrick, Sundie, Nicastle, & Stone, 2001).

Many studies of contemporary men and women suggest that even today, mate preferences are consistent with this evolutionary description. For example, a study in the Netherlands of men and women from 20 to 60 years of age reported that men preferred women who were more attractive than themselves whereas women preferred men who were higher in income, education, self-confidence, intelligence, dominance, and social position than themselves (Buunk, Dukstra, Fetchenhauer, & Kenrick, 2002). These differential preferences often result in couples consisting of a younger, attractive woman and an older, wealthier man, both in movies and in real life (Gallo & Byrne, 2004). In addition the findings of a meta-analysis of sex differences in romantic attachment can be interpreted as consistent with the evolutionary perspective. In this research, men were found to show greater avoidance of long-term relationships than women, who, in contrast, showed higher levels of anxiety over romantic relationships (aDel Guidice, 2011).

As compelling as this evidence and the evolution-based explanation of gender differences may be, it is not universally accepted (see Miller, Putcha-Bhgavatula, & Pedersen, 2002). Cultural factors are important, and research findings indicate that both men and women prefer a wealthy and healthy mate (Miller et al., 2002). The fact that they do makes more sense in terms of cultural values than genetic influences (Hanko et al., 2004). With this point in mind, it is interesting to note that both George Washington and Thomas Jefferson chose to marry wealthy widows (Wood, 2004), even though, it would seem, they had a large choice of potential mates.

FIGURE 7.20   Secret Romances: Alluring, but Often Dangerous

Are these people shown here trying to conceal their identity because they are involved in a secret romance? We can't tell, but one fact is clear: Research on the effects of secret romances suggests that such relationships, although sometimes appealing, are costly both to the relationship and to the health of the people involved in them.

IS THE "MATING GAME" A COMPETITIVE ONE—OR CAN IT INVOLVE COOPERATION, TOO?   As we noted earlier in our discussion of physical attractiveness, almost everyone expresses a preference for romantic partners they find physically appealing. Furthermore, depending on the role they expect to play in the future, people generally seek mates with skills and characteristics that will complement their own; if they expect to be a primary provider, they want a mate who is high in homemaking skills, while if they expect to be a homemaker, they want a mate who will support them and their children very well. This suggests that obtaining a desirable mate is a highly competitive activity: To succeed, we have to somehow eliminate and defeat potential rivals for the romantic partners we desire.

Certainly, that's true to an important degree. On the other hand, though, there appears to be room for cooperation with respect to obtaining desirable mates. How can this be? Ackerman and Kenrick (2009) suggest that it could stem from the fact that women generally are more selective in obtaining mates than men—they seek to erect barriers to keep undesirable mates away. In contrast, men are less selective, and are more intent on gaining access to females—especially ones they find desirable. In following these general strategies, both women and men might find help and cooperation from friends to be useful. For instance, female friends might help each other to avoid people they are not interested in. In contrast, male friends might help each other to gain access to desirable females, perhaps by praising their friends and building up their "image." In a series of studies, Ackerman and Kenrick found support for these predictions. Women reported that they often helped their friends to avoid contact with men in whom they were not interested, and men reported that they often helped their male friends to gain access to romantic partners they desired. Overall, women engaged in more cooperative behavior in the "mating game" than men—a finding consistent with previous research—but both genders clearly engaged in cooperative as well as competitive actions. In sum, in their efforts to obtain attractive romantic partners—ones they want—both women and men employ a wide range of strategies, and competition is only one of these.

SECRET ROMANCES: ENTICING, BUT DANGEROUS   Have you ever been involved in a romantic relationship that you wanted or had to keep secret? (See Figure 7.20.) There are many possible reasons for being in this situation: parents and others don't approve of your romantic partner, one or both partners are participating in another relationship, or there are actual rules against such relationships. For instance, many universities prohibit romantic relationships between faculty and students in their classes, and many businesses prohibit romantic relationships between coworkers or between supervisors and their subordinates. Whatever the reason, though, secret romantic relationships are not rare.

It is clear that such relationships are somewhat enticing: Many people like a little mystery and danger in their lives, and being involved in a secret romance is one way to obtain these experiences. But are such relationships beneficial for the people in them? Research findings suggest that often, the costs of secret relationships may be substantial. To investigate the effects of secret romances, Lehmiller (2009) recruited hundreds of couples who were romantically involved (mainly over the Internet). These individuals completed a questionnaire designed to measure the extent to which they were involved in a secret romance. In addition, they provided information on their feelings of commitment to the relationship, the extent to which there were limitations and barriers in interacting with their partners, and their personal physical and psychological well-being. Results indicated that keeping a romance secret was related to reduced commitment to it, and to reduced cognitive interdependence between the partners; they could not get close in important ways. In addition, people involved in secret romances also reported negative effects on their physical and psychological health; the stress involved in keeping the romances secret took a heavy toll on them in these respects.

In additional research, Lehmiller (2009) found support for a basic model suggesting that romantic secrecy leads to reduced commitment to the relationships, to negative feelings about the relationships, and so to lowered self-esteem and reduced personal health. After considering these findings, Lehmiller (p. 1465) reached a clear conclusion: " . . . the costs associated with maintaining a secret romance tend to outweigh any benefits derived from the sense of mystery or excitement thought to accompany such relationships." In this case, then, "forbidden fruits" definitely leave a bitter aftertaste.

KEY POINTS

- Ending romantic relationships is often very difficult, and as a result, a growing number of people are using technology (e-mail, text messages, Internet breakup services) to carry out this painful task.

- What do we seek in romantic partners? Research findings indicate that this depends, to an important extent, on what role we expect to play in the future—provider or homemaker.

- Mate selection often involves competition for the most desirable mates, but new evidence indicates that both women and men often cooperate with their friends in this context. Women' friends help them avoid contact with undesirable partners, while men's friends help them gain access to desirable ones.

- Secret romances are exciting, but generally appear to have adverse effects on the relationships themselves and on the people involved in them.

SUMMARY *and* REVIEW

- *Interpersonal attraction* refers to the evaluations we make of other people—the positive and negative attitudes we form about them. Human beings have a strong **need for affiliation,** the motivation to interact with other people in a cooperative way. The strength of this need differs among individuals and across situations, but even people who claim they do not have it show evidence that they do. Positive and negative affect influence attraction both directly and indirectly. Direct effects occur when another person is responsible for arousing the emotion. Indirect effects occur when the source of the emotion is elsewhere, and another person is simply associated with its presence.

- The indirect (associated) effects of emotion are applied by advertisers and political tacticians who understand that associating the products and candidates they wish to promote with positive feelings can influence decisions to purchase the products or vote for the candidate. The initial contact between two people is very often based on the **proximity**—they are near each other in physical space. Proximity, in turn, leads to **repeated exposure**, and that often produces positive affect and increased attraction (the mere exposure effect).

- Attraction toward others is often strongly influenced by their observable characteristics, especially their **physical attractiveness.** We often assume that "what is beautiful is good," apparently because we want to form relationships with attractive people, and so project positive interpersonal traits to them. Red does indeed appear to be "sexy" and enhance women's attractiveness, as many cultures have believed throughout recorded history.

- In addition to attractiveness, many other observable characteristics influence initial interpersonal evaluations, including physique, weight, behavioral style, and even first names, and other superficial characteristics. One of the many factors determining attraction toward another person is similarity to that individual in terms of attitudes, beliefs, values, and interests. Despite the continuing popularity of the idea that opposites attract (complementarity), that rarely seems to be true in the real world. Though dissimilarity tends to have a greater impact on attraction than similarity, we respond to both, and the larger the proportion of similar attitudes, the greater the attraction. The beneficial effects of similarity were even found with respect to physical attractiveness, where recent evidence supports the **matching hypothesis**—the view that we tend to actually choose romantic partners who are similar to ourselves in terms of attractiveness.

- Several theoretical perspectives **(balance theory, social comparison theory,** and evolutionary perspective) offer explanations for the powerful effects of similarity on attraction. We especially like other people who indicate that they like us. We very much dislike those who dislike and negatively evaluate us.

- Our first relationships are within the family, and we acquire an **attachment style** (which is based on level of self-esteem and degree of **interpersonal trust**) in the context of these relationships. These attachment styles influence the nature of other relationships, and also play an important role in many life outcomes. Other family relationships include those between siblings and between children and other relatives. Friendships outside of the family begin in childhood and are initially based simply on such factors as proximity and relationship between parents. With increasing maturity, it becomes possible to form **close friendships** that involve spending time together, interacting in many different situations, providing mutual social support, and engaging in self-disclosure. Although actual similarity between individuals is an important factor in interpersonal attraction, research findings indicate that perceived similarity plays a more important role in the early stages of friendship, when individuals are first becoming acquainted.

● As is true for attraction and friendship, romantic attraction is influenced by factors such as physical proximity, appearance, and similarity. In addition, romance includes sexual attraction and the desire for total acceptance by the other person. The reproductive success of our ancient ancestors was enhanced by not only sexual attraction between males and females, but also by bonding between mates and between parents and their offspring. **Passionate love,** a sudden, overwhelming emotional response to another person is just one type of **love.** Others include **companionate love,** which involves caring, mutual liking, and respect. Sternberg's **triangular model of love** includes these two components, plus a third—**decision/commitment**—that is a cognitive decision to love and to be committed to a relationship.

● Jealousy is a powerful emotion, and research findings suggest that it is often triggered by threats to our self-esteem—threats arising when we fear that someone we love or care about will desert us for a rival.

● Ending romantic relationships is often very difficult, and as a result, an increasing number of people are using technology (e-mail, text messages, Internet breakup services) to carry out this painful task.

● What do we seek in romantic partners? Research findings indicate that this depends, to an important extent, on what role we expect to play in the future—provider or homemaker. Mate selection often involves competition for the most desirable mates, but new evidence indicates that both women and men often cooperate with their friends in this context. Women's friends help them avoid contact with undesirable partners, while men's friends help them gain access to desirable ones. Secret romances are exciting, but generally appear to have adverse effects on the relationships themselves and on the people involved in them.

KEY TERMS

attachment style (p. 236)

attitude similarity (p. 230)

balance theory (p. 232)

close friendship (p. 238)

companionate love (p. 242)

consummate love (p. 243)

decision/commitment (p. 243)

dismissing attachment style (p. 237)

fearful-avoidant attachment style
　(p. 237)

interpersonal trust (p. 236)

intimacy (p. 243)

love (p. 241)

matching hypothesis (p. 231)

need for affiliation (p. 217)

passion (p. 243)

passionate love (p. 241)

physical attractiveness (p. 221)

preoccupied attachment style
　(p. 237)

proportion of similarity (p. 230)

proximity (p. 221)

repeated exposure effect (p. 222)

repulsion hypothesis (p. 231)

secure attachment style (p. 237)

similarity–dissimilarity effect
　(p. 230)

social comparison theory (p. 232)

triangular model of love (p. 243)

unrequited love (p. 242)

Social Influence

Changing Others' Behavior

*I*N THOSE LONG-AGO DAYS BEFORE THE INTERNET, CONFIDENCE artists worked their scams in the flesh: they usually had to meet their potential victims to somehow induce them to give them (the swindlers) their wealth and possessions. But now, they never see their potential victims; rather, they visit them electronically and lure them into the traps they have set via enticing e-mail messages. Have you ever opened your In-box to discover a message from what *looks* like your own bank—a message asking you to 'confirm' your security code and other personal information? If so, watch out! You may well be the target of *phishing*—a fraudulent effort to obtain information that will permit the people who sent it to gain access to your accounts—and perhaps your life savings! But even if you do not receive a message like that, you can still be the intended victim of *pharming*—an even more sinister technique for invading your privacy, and stealing your money. Pharming doesn't require you to click on phoney e-mail links; rather, it simply redirects your own Web browser to what looks like your bank, utility company, or other secure locations, so that you to log in, just as you would on the genuine sites. And of course, that gives the "pharmers" what they want—access to your funds.

But those are not the only ways in which scammers turn the Internet into their personal—and profitable—playground. Have you ever received an unsolicited e-mail stating that you have won a prize in a lottery? Or a message stating that your computer has been invaded by a virus that will destroy it—unless you purchase software from a "concerned" company that can protect you? If so, you have experienced other ways in which evil, but creative, criminals seek to tap the Internet for their profit—and *your* loss. In fact, the last scam we just described was recently practiced on a grand scale by Shaileshkumar P. Jain, Bjorn Daniel Sundin, and James Reno, who sent messages to millions of unsuspecting recipients, warning them that their computers had been infected by "malware" and offering them a solution in terms of products such as "Error-Safe" or "DriveCleaner"—programs that did little or nothing, but cost $30–70. So many people fell for this scheme that the swindlers collected more than $100 million from victims in 60 different countries. They were recently found guilty of these crimes and would be serving time in prison—if they could be found!

So, yes, the Internet is a joy and, like you, we use it every day; but it does pose risks that didn't exist before by providing dishonest people with new "cyber" ways to invade your life—and turn you into an unknowing victim.

Why do we begin with this unsettling array of sad but realistic facts? Because we want to echo the theme, first stated in Chapter 1, that the social side of life is indeed being tremendously affected by technology. Even the topic that is the focus of this chapter—**social influence,** one very close to the central core of social psychology—is not immune to such effects. What is social influence? A general definition is that it involves efforts by one or more people to change the behavior, attitudes, or feelings of one or more others (Cialdini, 2000, 2006). Confidence artists, including the electronic scammers described above, are intent on changing the behavior of their intended victims so that these people give them what they want—money, valuables, or confidential personal information. But people exert social influence for many reasons, not just to swindle others. Sometimes they exert influence in order to help the people involved (e.g., by getting them to stop smoking or stick to their diets). Or—and less altruistically— they may try to get them to do personal favors, buy certain products, or vote for specific candidates—the goals are almost infinite. The means used for inducing such change—for exerting social influence—vary greatly too, ranging from direct personal requests to clever commercials and political campaigns (see Figure 8.1). Whatever the goals, though, social influence always involves efforts by one or more people to induce some kind of change in others. Efforts to change others' attitudes involve persuasion, a topic we discussed in Chapter 5. Direct efforts to change others' overt behavior through requests are often labeled compliance (or seeking compliance); these involve specific requests to which the people who receive them can say "Yes," "No," or "Maybe." Often, efforts to change others' behavior involve the impact of rules or guidelines indicating what behavior is appropriate or required in a given situation. These can be formal, as in speed limits, rules for playing games or sports, and dress codes (if any still exist!); or they can be informal, such as the general rule "Don't stare at strangers in public places." This kind of influence is known as conformity, and is an important part of social life. Finally, change can be produced by direct orders or commands from others—*obedience*. In this chapter, we examine all of these forms of social influence (persuasion was discussed in Chapter 5).

To provide you with a broad overview of the nature—and power—of social influence, we proceed as follows. First, because it was one of the first aspects of social influence studied by social psychology, we examine **conformity**—pressures to behave in ways that are viewed as acceptable or appropriate by a group or society

FIGURE 8.1   Social Influence: Many Techniques, Many Goals

Each day, we try to influence others—and are on the receiving end of many influence attempts from them. Such efforts take many different forms, ranging from the sales pitches of used car salespersons (top photo), through political speeches (middle), and clever ads (bottom).

social influence
Efforts by one or more persons to change the behavior, attitudes, or feelings of one or more others.

conformity
A type of social influence in which individuals change their attitudes or behavior to adhere to existing social norms.

in general. Next, we turn to **compliance**—direct efforts to get others to change their behavior in specific ways (Cialdini, 2006; Sparrowe, Soetjipto, & Kraimer, 2006).

After that, we examine what is, in some ways, the most intriguing form of social influence—influence that occurs when other people are not present and are not making any direct attempts to affect our behavior (e.g., Fitzsimons & Bargh, 2003). We refer to such effects as **symbolic social influence** to reflect the fact that it results from our mental representations of other people rather than their actual presence or overt actions. Finally, after considering this indirect form of social influence, we examine another kind that is, in some respects, its direct opposite: **obedience**—social influence in which one person simply orders one or more others to do what they want.

Conformity: Group Influence in Action

During an exam, another student's cell phone begins to ring loudly. What does this person do?

You are driving on a street when you see and hear an ambulance approaching you from behind. What do you do?

In a supermarket, a new checkout line suddenly opens, right next to a checkout with a long line of shoppers. Who gets to go first in that new line?

In each of these situations, the people involved could, potentially, behave in many different ways. But probably you can predict with great certainty what they will do. The student with the loud cell phone will silence it immediately—and perhaps apologize to other members of the class sitting nearby. When you hear an ambulance, you will pull over to the right and perhaps stop completely until it passes. The checkout line is a little trickier. People near the front of the long checkout line *should* get to be first in the new line—but this might not happen. Someone from the back of the long line might beat them to it. In contexts where norms are more obvious, greater conformity by most people can be expected compared to contexts like this where norms are less clear about what action is the "correct" one.

The fact that we can predict others' behavior (and our own) with considerable confidence in these and many other situations illustrates the powerful and general effects of pressures toward *conformity*—toward doing what we are expected to do in a given situation. Conformity, in other words, refers to pressures to behave in ways consistent with rules indicating how we *should* or *ought to* behave. These rules are known as **social norms,** and they often exert powerful effects on our behavior. The uncertainty you might experience in the checkout line situation stems from the fact that the norms in that situation are not as clear as in the others; it's uncertain whether people in the front or the back of the existing line should go first.

In some instances, social norms are stated explicitly and are quite detailed. For instance, governments generally function through written constitutions and laws; chess and other games have very specific rules; and signs in many public places (e.g., along highways, in parks, at airports) describe expected behavior in considerable detail (e.g., *Stop!*; *No Swimming; No Parking; Keep Off the Grass*). As another example, consider the growing practice, in many restaurants, of showing tips of various sizes on the bill (e.g., 15 percent, 17 percent, 20 percent, etc.). In a sense, these numbers establish social norms concerning tipping, and in fact, research findings (Setter, Brownlee, & Sanders, 2011) indicate that they are effective: when they are present, tips are higher than when they are absent.

In other situations, norms may be unspoken or implicit, and, in fact, may have developed in a totally informal manner. For instance, we all recognize such unstated rules as "Don't make noise during a concert" and "Try to look your best when going on a job interview." Regardless of whether social norms are explicit or implicit, formal or informal,

compliance
A form of social influence involving direct requests from one person to another.

symbolic social influence
Social influence resulting from the mental representation of others or our relationships with them.

obedience
A form of social influence in which one person simply orders one or more others to perform some action(s).

social norms
Rules indicating how individuals are expected to behave in specific situations.

though, one fact is clear: *Most people follow them most of the time.* For instance, virtually everyone regardless of personal political beliefs stands when the national anthem of their country is played at sports events or other public gatherings. Similarly, few people visit restaurants without leaving a tip for the server. In fact, so powerful is this social norm that most people leave a tip of around 15 percent *regardless of the quality of the service they have received* (Azar, 2007).

At first glance, this strong tendency toward conformity—toward going along with society's or a group's expectations about how we should behave in various situations—may seem objectionable. After all, it does place restrictions on personal freedom. Actually, though, there is a strong basis for so much conformity: without it, we would quickly find ourselves facing social chaos. Imagine what would happen outside movie theaters, stadiums, or at supermarket checkout counters if people did not obey the norm "Form a line and wait your turn." And consider the danger to both drivers and pedestrians if there were not clear and widely followed traffic regulations. In many situations, then, conformity serves a very useful function. If you have ever driven in a country where traffic rules are widely ignored or viewed as mere suggestions (!), you know what we mean: When people don't follow social norms, their actions are unpredictable—and sometimes, that can be dangerous! (See Figure 8.2.)

Another reason people conform is, simply, to "look good" to others—to make a positive impression on them. For instance, at work, many employees adopt what are known as *facades of conformity*—the appearance of going along with the values and goals of their organizations, even if they really do not (Hewlin, 2009). For instance, they often say things they don't really believe, suppress personal values different form those of the organization, and keep certain things about themselves confidential. They may find doing so to be unpleasant but necessary to further their careers, and are more likely to engage in them when they feel that they have little input into how things are run (including their own jobs), and intend to leave—thus assuring that they will get a positive recommendation! In short, people often use conformity as a tactic of self-presentation, a process we described in Chapter 4.

FIGURE 8.2   Conformity: It Makes Life More Predictable
When norms telling people how to behave don't exist—or are largely ignored—chaos can develop. Countries in which traffic regulations are taken lightly provide a clear illustration of this fact—and of why conformity can sometimes be very useful.

How Much Do We Conform? More Than We Think

Conformity is a fact of social life: We tend to wear the same styles of clothing as our friends, listen to the same music, see the same movies, and read the same books and magazines. Overall, we feel much more comfortable when we are similar to our friends and family than when we are different from them. But do we recognize just how much we are influenced in this way? Research findings indicate that we do not. Rather, we think of ourselves as standing out in what amounts to a crowd of sheep! Others may conform, but us? No way! In the United States, we believe that we tend to be independent, and "do our own thing" regardless of others' actions or choices. Evidence for such effects is provided by the fact that in many classic experiments (several of which we review later), participants who conformed to the actions of others often denied that they had been influenced, even though it was clear that they were influenced.

More direct evidence for the fact that we believe we are less susceptible to conformity pressure than other people is provided by research conducted by Pronin, Berger, and Molouki (2007). They reasoned that people underestimate the impact of social influence on their own actions because in trying to understand these actions, they tend to focus on internal information rather than on the overt actions. As in the famous *actor–observer* difference (discussed in Chapter 3), we each know much more about our own thoughts and feelings than we do about the thoughts and feelings of others, so when we estimate how much they and we are influenced by conformity pressure, we tend to conclude that social influence is less important in shaping our actions than those of other people. For instance, we "know" that we choose to dress in popular styles because we like them—not because others are wearing them. But when making the same judgment about other people, we assume that they are "sheep" following the herd. Pronin and colleagues call this the **introspection illusion**, to refer to the fact that often, conformity occurs nonconsciously, and so escapes our introspection (or notice).

To test this reasoning, they conducted several studies. In one, participants read a series of recommendations about student life and learned that these recommendations had been endorsed or not endorsed by a group of fellow students. They then voted on each proposal themselves, indicating whether they supported it or did not support it. This provided a measure of their conformity to the panel's recommendations. Students then rated the extent to which they believed these recommendations had influenced their own behavior, and also the behavior (i.e., voting) of another student, whose answers they were shown. The stranger agreed with the panel on precisely the same number of recommendations as did the students, so they actually showed equal conformity. But when they rated how much they and the other person had conformed, results were clear: Participants in the study rated the other person as being significantly more influenced than they were (see Figure 8.3). In contrast, they viewed themselves as being *more* influenced than the other person by the contents of each proposal rather than the panel's recommendations.

In short, it appears that although we show conformity in many contexts—and for good reason!—we underestimate the extent to which others' actions influence us in this way. We should add that this may be true to a greater extent in individualistic cultures such as the United States; in such cultures, people prefer to think of themselves as "lone wolves" in a world of sheep. But in more collectivist societies, such as Japan, conforming has no negative implications attached to it, and as a result, people may be more willing to admit that they conform because doing so is seen as a good thing!

Given the importance and prevalence of conformity, it is surprising that it received relatively little attention in social psychology until the 1950s. At that time, Solomon Asch (1951), whose research on impression formation we considered in Chapter 3, carried out a series of experiments on conformity that yielded dramatic results. Asch's research was clearly a "classic" of social psychology. But, in fact, it was modern in some respects too so we describe it here in order to illustrate the lengths we go to avoid being different from other people, so that we stick out like the proverbial "sore thumb."

introspection illusion
Our belief that social influence plays a smaller role in shaping our own actions than it does in shaping the actions of others.

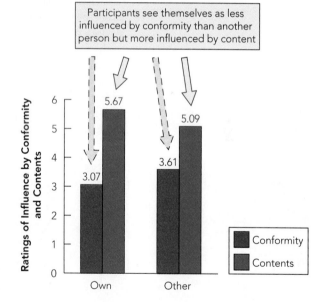

FIGURE 8.3   The Illusion That We Are Less Influenced by Conformity Than Others
Participants reported that they were less influenced by conformity to a group's judgments than was another person (a stranger). In fact, they actually conformed as much as this person did—whose ratings on various issues were designed to conform precisely the same as each participant. Still, despite this objective fact, they perceived the other person as showing more conformity. (Source: Based on data from Pronin, Berger, & Molouki, 2007).

Asch's Research on Conformity: Social Pressure—the Irresistible Force?

Suppose that just before an important math exam, you discover that your answer to a homework problem—a problem of the type that will be on the test—is different from that obtained by one of your friends. How would you react? Probably with some concern. Now imagine that you learn that a second person's answer, too, is different from yours. To make matters worse, it agrees with the answer reported by the first person. How would you feel now? The chances are good that your anxiety will increase. Next, you discover that a third person agrees with the other two. At this point, you know that you are in big trouble. Which answer should you accept? Yours or the one obtained by these three other people? The exam is about to start, so you have to decide quickly.

Life is filled with such dilemmas—instances in which we discover that our own judgments, actions, or conclusions are different from those reached by other people. What do we do in such situations? Important insights into our behavior were provided by studies conducted by Solomon Asch (1951, 1955).

Asch created a compelling social dilemma for his participants whose task was ostensibly to simply respond to a series of perceptual problems such as the one in Figure 8.4. On each of the problems, participants were to indicate which of three comparison lines matched a standard line in length. Several other people (usually six to eight) were also present during the session, but unknown to the real participant, all were assistants of the experimenter. On certain occasions known as *critical trials* (12 out of the 18 problems) the accomplices offered answers that were clearly wrong; they unanimously chose the wrong line as a match for the standard line. Moreover, they stated their answers *before* the real participants responded. Thus, on these critical trials, the people in Asch's study faced precisely the type of dilemma described above. Should they go along with the other individuals present or stick to their own judgments? The judgments seemed to be very simple ones, so the fact that other people agreed on an answer different from the one the participants preferred was truly puzzling. Results were clear: A large majority of the people in Asch's research chose conformity. Across several different studies, fully 76 percent of those tested went along with the group's false answers at least once; and overall, they voiced agreement with these errors 37 percent of the time. In contrast, only 5 percent of the participants in a control group, who responded to the same problems alone, made such errors.

Of course, there were large individual differences in this respect. Almost 25 percent of the participants never yielded to the group pressure. (We have more to say about such people soon.) At the other extreme, some individuals went along with the majority nearly all the time. When Asch questioned them, some of these people stated: "I am wrong, they are right"; they had little confidence in their own judgments. Most, however, said they felt that the other people present were suffering from an optical illusion or were merely sheep following the responses of the first person. Yet, when it was their turn, these people, too, went along with the group. They knew that the others were wrong (or at least, *probably* wrong), but they couldn't bring themselves to disagree with them.

In further studies, Asch (1959, 1956) investigated the effects of shattering the group's unanimity by having one of the accomplices break with the others. In one study, this person gave the correct answer, becoming an "ally" of the real participant; in another study, he chose an answer in between the one given by the

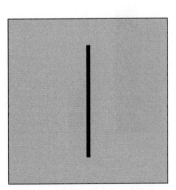
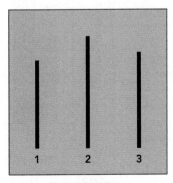

Standard Line   Comparison Lines

FIGURE 8.4   Asch's Line Judgment Task
Participants in Asch's research were asked to report their judgments on problems such as this one. Their task was to indicate which of the comparison lines (1, 2, or 3) best matched the standard line in length. To study conformity, he had participants make these judgments out loud, only after hearing the answers of several other people—all of whom were Asch's assistants. On certain critical trials the assistants all gave wrong answers. This exposed participants to strong pressures toward conformity.

group and the correct one; and in a third, he chose the answer that was even more incorrect than that chosen by the majority. In the latter two conditions, in other words, he broke from the group but still disagreed with the real participants. Results indicated that conformity was reduced under all three conditions. However, somewhat surprisingly, this reduction was greatest when the dissenting assistant expressed views even more extreme (and wrong) than the majority. Together, these findings suggest that it is the unanimity of the group that is crucial; once it is broken, no matter how, resisting group pressure becomes much easier.

There's one more aspect of Asch's research that is important to mention. In later studies, he repeated his basic procedure, but with one important change: Instead of stating their answers out loud, participants wrote them down on a piece of paper. As you might guess, conformity dropped sharply because the participants didn't have to display the fact that they disagreed with the other people present. This finding points to the importance of distinguishing between *public conformity*—doing or saying what others around us say or do—and *private acceptance*—actually coming to feel or think as others do. Often, it appears, we follow social norms overtly, but don't actually change our private views (Maas & Clark, 1984). This distinction between public conformity and private acceptance is an important one, and we refer to it at several points in this book.

Sherif's Research on the Autokinetic Phenomenon: How Norms Emerge

A clear illustration of private acceptance of social influence was provided many years ago by another founder of social psychology—Muzafer Sherif (1937). Sherif was interested in several questions, but among these, two were most important: (1) How do norms develop in social groups? and (2) How strong is their influence on behavior once they (the norms) emerge? To examine these issues, he used a very interesting situation, one involving the **autokinetic phenomenon.** This refers to the fact that when placed in a completely dark room and exposed to a single, stationary point of light, most people perceive the light as moving about. This is because in the dark room, there are no clear cues to distance or location. The perceived movement is known as the autokinetic phenomenon.

Sherif (1937) realized that he could use this situation to study the emergence of social norms. This is so because there is considerable ambiguity about how much the light is moving and different people perceive it as moving different distances. Thus, when placed in this setting with several others and asked to report how much they perceive the light to be moving, they influence one another and soon converge on a particular amount of movement; that agreement, in a sense, constitutes a group norm. If the same individuals are then placed in the situation alone, they continue to give estimates of the light's movement consistent with the group norm, so clearly, the effect of such norms persist. This suggests that these effects reflect changes in what participants in these studies actually believe—private acceptance or commitment; after all, they continue to obey the group norm even if they are no longer in the group!

Sherif's findings also help explain why social norms develop in many situations— especially ambiguous ones. We have a strong desire to be "correct"—to behave in an appropriate manner—and social norms help us attain that goal. As we note below, this is one key foundation of social influence; another is the desire to be accepted by others and liked by them—which sometimes involves the "facades of conformity" studied by Hewlin (2009), and discussed above. Together, these two factors virtually ensure that social influence is a powerful force—one that can often strongly affect our behavior.

Asch's research was the catalyst for much activity in social psychology, as many other researchers sought to investigate the nature of conformity to identify factors that influence it, and to establish its limits (e.g., Crutchfield, 1955; Deutsch & Gerard, 1955). Indeed, such research is continuing today, and is still adding to our understanding of the factors that affect this crucial form of social influence (e.g., Baron, Vandello,

autokinetic phenomenon
The apparent movement of a single, stationary source of light in a dark room. Often used to study the emergence of social norms and social influence.

& Brunsman, 1996; Bond & Smith, 1996; Lonnqvist, Leikas, Paunonen, Nissinen, & Verkasalo, 2006).

Factors Affecting Conformity: Variables That Determine the Extent to Which We "Go Along"

Asch's research demonstrated the existence of powerful pressures toward conformity, but even a moment's reflection suggests that conformity does not occur to the same degree in all settings. Why? In other words, what factors determine the extent to which individuals yield to conformity pressure or resist it? Research findings suggest that many factors play a role; here, we examine the ones that appear to be most important.

COHESIVENESS AND CONFORMITY: BEING INFLUENCED BY THOSE WE LIKE   One factor that strongly influences our tendency to conform—to go along with whatever norms are operating in a given situation—is **cohesiveness**—the extent to which we are attracted to a particular social group and want to belong to it (e.g., Turner, 1991). The greater cohesiveness is, the more we tend to follow the norms (i.e., rules) of the group. This is hardly surprising: the more we value being a member of a group and want to be accepted by the other members, the more we want to avoid doing anything that will separate us from them. So prestigious fraternities and sororities can often extract very high levels of conformity from would-be members (see Figure 8.5) who are very eager to join these highly selective groups. Similarly, acting and looking like others is often a good way to win their approval. So, in very basic terms, the more we like other people and want to belong to the same group as they do, and the more we are uncertain of winning their acceptance, the more we tend to conform (Crandall, 1988; Latané & L'Herrou, 1996; Noel, Wann, & Branscombe, 1995). In other words, cohesiveness and the desire to be accepted can be viewed as factors that intensify the tendency to conform.

cohesiveness
The extent to which we are attracted to a social group and want to belong to it.

FIGURE 8.5   Cohesiveness: A Magnifier of Conformity Pressure
The more strongly we are attracted to a group to which we belong or would like to belong, the more likely we are to conform to the norms of this group, especially if we feel less uncertain about our acceptance by the group. For instance, "pledges" hoping to join popular sororities or fraternities tend to show high levels of conformity to the norms of these groups.

CONFORMITY AND GROUP SIZE: WHY MORE IS BETTER WITH RESPECT TO SOCIAL PRESSURE   Another factor that produces similar effects is the size of the group that is exerting influence. Asch (1956) and other early researchers (e.g., Gerard, Wilhelmy, & Conolley, 1968) found that conformity increases with group size, but only up to about three or four members; beyond that point, it appears to level off or even decrease. However, more recent research has failed to confirm these early findings concerning group size (e.g., Bond & Smith, 1996). Instead, these later studies found that conformity tends to increase with group size up to eight group members and beyond. In short, the larger the group—the greater the number of people who behave in some specific way—the greater our tendency to conform and "do as they do."

DESCRIPTIVE AND INJUNCTIVE SOCIAL NORMS: HOW NORMS AFFECT BEHAVIOR
Social norms, as we have already seen, can be formal or informal in nature—as different as rules printed on large signs and informal guidelines such as "Don't leave your shopping cart in the middle of a parking spot outside a supermarket." This is not the only way in which norms differ, however. Another important distinction is that between **descriptive norms** and **injunctive norms** (e.g., Cialdini, Kallgren, & Reno, 1991; Reno, Cialdini, & Kallgren, 1993). Descriptive norms are ones that simply describe what most people do in a given situation. They influence behavior by informing us about what is generally seen as effective or adaptive in that situation. In contrast, injunctive norms specify what *ought* to be done—what is approved or disapproved behavior in a given situation. For instance, there is a strong injunctive norm against cheating on exams—such behavior is considered to be ethically wrong. The fact that some students disobey this norm does not change the moral expectation that they should obey it. Both kinds of norms can exert strong effects upon our behavior (e.g., Brown, 1998).

Since people obviously do disobey injunctive norms in many situations (they speed on highways, cut into line in front of others), a key question is this: When, precisely, do injunctive norms influence behavior? When are they likely to be obeyed? One answer is provided by **normative focus theory** (e.g., Cialdini, Reno, & Kallgren, 1990). This theory suggests that norms will influence behavior only to the extent that they are *salient* (i.e., relevant, significant) to the people involved at the time the behavior occurs.

In other words, people will obey injunctive norms only when they think about them and see them as relevant to their own actions. This prediction has been verified in many different studies (e.g., Reno, Cialdini & Kallgren, 1993; Kallgren, Reno, & Cialdini, 2000), so it seems to be a general principle that norms influence our actions primarily when we think about them and view them as relevant to our behavior. When, in contrast, we do not think about them or view them as irrelevant, their effects are much weaker, or even nonexistent (see Figure 8.6). In fact, this is one reason why people sometimes disobey even strong injunctive norms: they don't see these norms as applying to them.

Social Foundations of Conformity: Why We Often Choose to "Go Along"

As we have just seen, several factors determine whether and to what extent conformity occurs. Yet, this does not alter the essential point: Conformity is a basic fact of social life. Most people conform to the norms of their groups or societies much, if not most, of the time. Why is this so? Why do people often choose to go along with these social rules instead of resisting them? The answer seems to involve two powerful motives possessed by all human beings: the desire to be liked or accepted by others and the desire to be right—to have accurate understanding of the social world (Deutsch & Gerard, 1955; Insko, 1985)—plus cognitive processes that lead us to view conformity as fully justified after it has occurred (e.g., Buehler & Griffin, 1994).

descriptive norms
Norms simply indicating what most people do in a given situation.

injunctive norms
Norms specifying what ought to be done; what is approved or disapproved behavior in a given situation.

normative focus theory
A theory suggesting that norms will influence behavior only to the extent that they are focal for the people involved at the time the behavior occurs.

FIGURE 8.6   Why People Sometimes Disobey Even Strong Injunctive Norms: Please Don't Drive Like This!

One reason people disobey even strong and clear injunctive norms (norms indicating what they are expected to do or should do) is because they don't see these norms as applying to them. This may be one reason why many people text message, watch the displays on their GPS, or put on make-up while driving. They know that "in general" such actions are not approved by many other people and can be risky, but they are convinced that they can handle the challenges of multi-tasking, so they see these norms as not applying to them!

NORMATIVE SOCIAL INFLUENCE: THE DESIRE TO BE LIKED   How can we get others to like us? This is one of the eternal puzzles of social life. As we saw in Chapters 4 and 7, many tactics can prove effective in this regard. One of the most successful of these is to appear to be as similar to others as possible. From our earliest days, we learn that agreeing with the people around us, and behaving as they do, causes them to like us. Parents, teachers, friends, and others often heap praise and approval on us for showing such similarity (see our discussion of attitude formation in Chapter 5). One important reason we conform, therefore, is this: we have learned that doing so can help us win the approval and acceptance we crave. This source of conformity is known as **normative social influence,** since it involves altering our behavior to meet others' expectations.

THE DESIRE TO BE RIGHT: INFORMATIONAL SOCIAL INFLUENCE   If you want to know your weight, you can step onto a scale. If you want to know the dimensions of a room, you can measure them directly. But how can you establish the accuracy of your own political or social views, or decide which hairstyle suits you best? There are no simple physical tests or measuring devices for answering these questions. Yet we want to be correct about such matters, too. The solution to this dilemma is obvious: to answer such questions, we refer to other people. We use their opinions and actions as guides for our own (see Chapter 5 on the important role that others play in the attitudes we form). Such reliance on others, in turn, is often a powerful source of the tendency to conform. Other people's actions and opinions define social reality for us, and we use these as a guide for our own actions and opinions. This basis for conformity is known as **informational social influence,** since it is based on our tendency to depend on others as a source of information about many aspects of the social world.

Research evidence suggests that because our motivation to be correct or accurate is very strong, informational social influence is a powerful source of conformity. However, as you might expect, this is more likely to be true in situations where we are highly uncertain about what is "correct" or "accurate" than in situations where we have more confidence in our own ability to make such decisions (e.g., Baron et al., 1996).

How powerful are the effects of social influence when we are uncertain about what is correct and what is not? Research findings suggest a chilling answer: extremely powerful. Because such effects often operate to encourage negative behaviors—ones with harmful social effects—we now describe them in more detail. But please note: Before we

normative social influence
Social influence based on the desire to be liked or accepted by other people.

informational social influence
Social influence based on the desire to be correct (i.e., to possess accurate perceptions of the social world).

proceed, we should be clear that sometimes conformity can be helpful in such situations; for instance, when confronted with an emergency (e.g., a fire), we can sometimes escape from danger by doing what others do—for instance, following them to the nearest safe exit.

The Downside of Conformity: Why Good People Sometimes Do Evil Things

Earlier, we noted that the tendency to conform—to obey social norms—can produce positive effects. The fact that most people comply with most social norms most of the time introduces a large measure of predictability into social relations: we know how we and others are expected to behave, and can proceed on the assumption that these expectations will be met. Other motorists will drive on the correct side of the street (whatever that is in one's own society) and stop for red lights; people waiting for service in a store will form a line and wait their turn. But as we have already noted, there is definitely a downside to conformity, too. In fact, recent research by social psychologists suggests that pressures to conform, and our tendency to surrender to such pressures, can sometimes result in very harmful effects. In fact, we now discuss what is perhaps the most dramatic research illustrating such effects—a famous study by Philip Zimbardo, which showed, among other things, the powerful impact of norms concerning various social roles.

Do good people ever do bad things? The answer, of course, is yes. History is filled with atrocities performed by people who, most of the time, were good neighbors, parents, friends, and spouses, and who often showed kindness and concern for others in their daily lives. Yet, under some conditions, they seem to surrender all these positive qualities and engage in actions that most of us—and they, too—would find inexcusable. The key question for social psychologists is, Why? What makes good people turn bad—at least sometimes? There is no single answer, and later in this chapter, we discuss *obedience*—a form of social influence that sometimes induces good people to do bad things. But now we focus on the answer provided by one very famous study in social psychology, one known simply as Zimbardo's prison study. Here's how this unique and famous study took place:

> *Imagine that one peaceful Sunday you hear a loud knock on your door. When you go to answer, you find yourself face to face with several police officers. Without any explanation, they arrest you and take you downtown to be photographed, fingerprinted, and "booked." (Participants knew that they volunteered to participate in social psychological research, but still, these events were surprising for many of them.) Next, you are blindfolded and driven to a prison whose location you can only guess. Once there, you are stripped of all your clothes and are forced to dress in an uncomfortable, loose-fitting gown and a tight nylon cap. All of your personal possessions are removed and you are given an I.D. number instead of a name. Then you are locked in an empty cell containing only the bare necessities. All guards in the prison wear identical uniforms and reflecting sunglasses and they carry clubs, whistles, and other signs of their authority.*
>
> *As a prisoner, you are expected to obey a long set of rules under threat of severe punishment. You must remain silent during rest periods and after lights are turned out each night. You must eat only at mealtimes; you must address other prisoners only by their I.D. numbers and your guards as "Mr. Correctional Officer." And you must ask their permission to do anything—from reading and writing to going to the bathroom.*

How would you react to such conditions? Would you obey? Rebel? Become angry? Depressed? Resentful? And what if you were a guard instead of a prisoner? Would you treat prisoners with respect or would you seek to humiliate them? These are the questions Zimbardo and his colleagues investigated in the famous Stanford Prison Study. It was conducted in the basement of the Stanford University psychology building, and all guards and prisoners were paid volunteers. In fact, whether a volunteer became a guard or a prisoner was determined completely at random.

The main purpose of the study was to determine whether participants would come to behave like real guards and real prisoners—whether they would, in a sense, conform to the norms established for these respective roles. The answer was clear: they did. The prisoners were rebellious at first, but then became increasingly passive and depressed. And the guards grew increasingly brutal and sadistic. They harassed the prisoners constantly, forced them to make fun of one another, and assigned them to difficult, senseless tasks. They also tended to dehumanize the prisoners, coming to perceive them as inferior to themselves and "less than human." In fact, these changes in behavior were so large that it was necessary to stop the study after only 6 days; initial plans called for it to last 2 weeks.

So what do we learn from this striking and thought-provoking research? Zimbardo, who planned the research and served as "prison warden," contends that it drives home a key point about human behavior: it is the *situations* in which people find themselves—not their personal traits—that largely determine their behavior. Yes, people do differ in many ways, but place them in a powerful situation like this one, and such differences tend to disappear. Zimbardo (2007) suggests that it is this tendency to yield to situational pressures—including conformity pressures—that is responsible for much evil behavior. As he puts it: " . . . we all like to think that the line between good and evil is impermeable—that people who do terrible things . . . are on the other side of the line—and we could never get over there . . . . My work began by saying no, that line is permeable. The reason some people are on the good side of the line is that they've never been fully tested . . . ." In other words, according to Zimbardo, placed in the wrong kind of situation, virtually all of us—even those who have always been good, upstanding citizens—might commit atrocities.

Zimbardo leaves some room for personal heroism: He recognizes that some people seem able to resist even powerful situational or conformity pressures (and we'll soon present research that explains why). But most of us, he contends, cannot—situations are often stronger than our ability to resist and remain true to our values. (As we'll soon see, though, several factors can reduce the "press" of the situation on us, so that we can resist its influence and the pressure to conform (e.g,. Galinsky, Magee, Gruenfeld, Whitson, & Liljenquist, 2008). In the past few years, Zimbardo has related his famous study to the disturbing events that occurred in the Abu Ghraib prison in Iraq in 2005—events in which American soldiers humiliated and physically abused Iraqi prisoners. Zimbardo's explanation for these events is much the same as for the findings of the Stanford Prison Study: The soldiers found themselves in a situation where prevailing norms pushed them toward viewing the prisoners as less than human, where they (the soldiers) were anonymous, and where they could alleviate their boredom by turning the prisoners into playthings.

If Zimbardo is correct, then our tendency to "go along" with prevailing norms and with requirements of the roles we play in life can truly sometimes lead good people to perform evil acts. But please take heart: More recent research, including another dramatic prison study (this time conducted jointly by social psychologists and the BBC) offers a much more optimistic set of conclusions (Reicher & Haslam, 2006). In this research, volunteers were, again, placed in a kind of "prison" and were randomly assigned to be either guards or prisoners. And once more, the guards were given means to enforce their authority over the prisoners (e.g., they could place disobedient prisoners in an isolation cell as punishment). Overall, then, the BBC prison study was similar in many respects to Zimbardo's famous research. Important differences did exist, however.

For instance, it was explained to the guards and prisoners that they had been chosen for these roles on the basis of extensive psychological tests (all volunteers were actually assessed by trained psychologists prior to their selection as participants in the study). Furthermore, it was explained that the guards could "promote" prisoners they selected to become guards, and in fact, one prisoner *was* promoted to become a guard. After this event, however, it was made clear that guards would remain guards and prisoners would remain prisoners, so no chance of further changes existed. Then, 3 days later, both guards and prisoners were told that careful observations indicated that in fact, no differences existed between the two groups. However, since it would be impractical to change the roles now, they would remain unchanged for the rest of the study. In a sense, this removed any legitimacy of assignments to these roles.

These differences turned out to have dramatic effects on the results. In contrast to the findings of the Stanford Prison Study, guards and prisoners in the BBC research did *not* passively accept their roles. Rather, the guards actually rejected their power over the prisoners while the prisoners, in contrast, identified closely with one another and actually took action to gain equal power. They succeeded, and for a time, the "prison" adopted a democratic structure in which guards and prisoners had relatively equal rights (see Figure 8.7). When this new structure seemed to fail, however, both groups moved toward acceptance of a rigidly authoritarian approach in which the prisoners surrendered almost totally and no longer offered any resistance to their inequality.

These findings point to an important conclusion: Social norms and the social structure from which they arise do *not* necessarily produce acceptance of inequalities. On the contrary, whether individuals go along with roles (and norms) that impose inequality depends on the extent to which the people involved identify with these roles; if their identification is low, they may resist and seek social change rather than simply resign themselves to their disadvantaged fate. As noted by one social psychologist (Turner, 2006), this is why social change occurs: People decide to challenge an existing social structure rather than accept it, as happened in the 1950s and 1960s in the civil rights movement in the United States, and the women's movement of the 1970s and 1980s. Large numbers of people challenged the "status quo," and the result was major social change. In sum, the power of social norms and social roles to induce conformity is strong. But as we'll note once again in a later discussion of obedience, it is not invincible and sometimes, under the right conditions, individuals challenge existing social orders and the rules they impose, and actively seek social change. As Turner (2006, p. 45) puts it, social psychologists realize that social structures are not set in stone; on the contrary, " . . . the future is created in the social present" and change as well as stability is a common aspect of the social side of life.

Why We Sometimes Choose *Not* to Go Along: The Effects of Power, Basic Motives, and the Desire for Uniqueness

Our discussion so far may have left you with the impression that pressures toward conformity are so strong that they are all but impossible to resist. But as the Reicher and Haslam (2006) BBC prison study illustrated, this is simply not the case. Individuals—or

FIGURE 8.7 Conformity: Sometimes, It Leads Good People to Do Evil Things—But Not Always!
In a recent study that replicated Zimbardo's famous Stanford prison experiment, volunteers were also placed in a simulated "prison" and played the roles of prisoners and guards. Initially, they showed behavior consistent with these roles, but soon the guards rejected the norms of their assigned roles, and the prisoners formed a cohesive collective identity and rebelled against the existing power structure.

FIGURE 8.8 **The Pressure for Conformity Is Strong—But Some People Manage to Resist**

Most people conform most of the time to most social norms. But few people show total conformity, and some stand out as people who refuse to "go along"—for instance, college students with conservative political views, which are generally not popular on their campuses. Research findings help explain why they are able to resist even powerful pressures to conform.

groups of individuals—*do* resist conformity pressure. This was certainly true in Asch's research where, as you may recall, most of the participants yielded to social pressure, but *only part of the time.* On many occasions, they stuck to their guns even in the face of a unanimous majority that disagreed with them. If you want other illustrations of resistance to conformity pressures, just look around you: You will find that while most people adhere to social norms most of the time, some do not. And most people do not go along with all social norms; rather, they pick and choose, conforming to most but rejecting at least a few. For instance, some people choose not to dress or wear their hair in the current style, whatever it happens to be. Similarly, some people choose to hold and express unpopular political or social views, and continue to do so even in the face of strong pressure to conform (see Figure 8.8). So, conformity pressures are *not* irresistible. What accounts for our ability to resist them? Many factors appear to play a role, but here we focus on factors identified in recent research as ones that seem to tip the balance away from conformity and toward independent thought and action.

POWER AS A SHIELD AGAINST CONFORMITY

Power . . . the very word conjures up images of people who are truly in charge—political leaders, generals, heads of huge corporations. Such people often seem to enjoy more freedoms than the rest of us: They make the rules (or at least they can change them), and they can shape situations rather than be molded by them. Does this also make them immune—or at least resistant—to social influence? Several social psychologists have suggested that it does. For instance, Keltner, Gruenfeld, and Andeson (2003) have noted that the restrictions that often influence the thought, expression, and behavior of most people don't seem to apply to the powerful. And in fact, there are several reasons why this might be so.

First, powerful people are less dependent on others for obtaining social resources. As a result, they may not pay much attention to threats from others or efforts to constrain their actions in some way. Third, they may be less likely to take the perspective of other people and so be less influenced by them. Instead, their thoughts and actions are more directly shaped by their own internal states; in other words, there is a closer correspondence between their traits and preferences and what they think or do than is true for most people. Overall, then, situational information might have less influence on their attitudes, intentions, actions, and creative expressions.

Is this really true? Research conducted by Galinsky et al. (2008) indicates that it is. In a series of related studies, they found that people who possessed power, or were merely primed to think about it, were in fact less likely to show conformity to the actions or judgments of others than people lower in power. In one study, for instance, participants were asked to think either about a situation in which they had power over someone (high power) or a situation in which someone else had power over them (low power). In a third condition they did not think about power one way or the other. Following these conditions, they performed a tedious word construction task—one that most people do not find interesting or enjoyable. Then, they were asked to rate this task. Before doing so, however, they learned that 10 other students rated it very high on both dimensions.

(In a control, baseline condition, they did not receive this information.)

It was predicted that the people primed to think about times when they had power over others would rate the task less favorably than those who thought about times when others had power over them—in other words, their feelings of power would affect the extent to which they were influenced by the judgments of other people. In contrast, those not asked to think about power would be influenced by others' opinions and therefore rate the task more favorably. As you can see from Figure 8.9, this is precisely what happened. People in the high-power group did rate the task as less enjoyable and interesting than those in the low-power group. In fact, they rated it as low as those who received no bogus ratings supposedly provided by other students. In sum, while power may indeed corrupt, it also seems to free those who possess it from situational control, and to make them relatively resistant to the conformity pressures that strongly influence most of us much of the time. And in fact, we sometimes admire powerful people who ignore the rules and view their independent actions as further proof that they are somehow deserving of the power they possess.

SEXUAL MOTIVES AND NONCONFORMITY: WHY THE DESIRE TO ATTRACT DESIRABLE MATES MAY SOMETIMES COUNTER CONFORMITY PRESSURES— AT LEAST AMONG MEN

As we pointed out earlier, people have strong reasons for conforming: to win social approval, interpret unfamiliar situations correctly, make a favorable impression on others. These are powerful motives, so it is not at all surprising that most people do conform most of the time. But what about nonconformity? What are the reasons for thinking or acting in ways that are different from, or even contrary to, what most others are thinking or doing? One possibility, of course, is that people do this because they want to do what they believe is right—not what is acceptable or expedient. In addition, however, there may be other motives for refusing to "go along"—for remaining independent. Griskevicius, Goldstein, Mortensen, Cialdini, and Kenrick (2006) suggest that one of these motives may be that of attracting a desirable mate. They reason that for men, but perhaps not necessarily for women, standing up to group pressure may add to their attractiveness and help them win desirable romantic partners. This is so because gender stereotypes often include assertiveness and independence for men, but do not necessarily include these characteristics for women. Furthermore, research on what women find attractive in men suggests characteristics such as assertiveness, decisiveness, independence, and willingness to take risks—all of which can be shown by nonconformity—are rated as desirable. In contrast, men don't report finding such traits attractive in women, so women would have less reason to use nonconformity to increase their own attractiveness.

In a series of ingenious studies, Griskevicius and colleagues (2006) found clear support for this reasoning. In particular, they found that when the motive to attract desirable mates was activated in participants (by asking them to imagine having met someone to whom they were passionately attracted), men *were* less conforming in a situation where they could demonstrate conformity or independence. In contrast, women

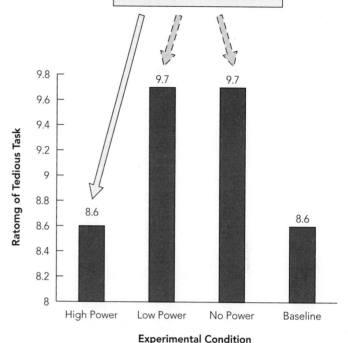

FIGURE 8.9   Power Reduces Conformity

Participants asked to remember times when they had power over others (high power) were less influenced by ratings of a tedious task supposedly provided by other students than participants who thought about times when others had power over them (low power) or who did not think about power. (In the baseline conditions, participants didn't think about power.) (Source: Based on data from Galinsky et al., 2008).

were, if anything *more* conforming when their mate-attraction motive had been activated. Presumably, women know that seeming to be agreeable is more attractive to many men (because it is consistent with gender stereotypes) than seeming independent and assertive. In a sense, then, both groups were showing conformity to gender stereotypes, which were made salient by the dating situation. For men this implied less conformity, while for women it did not. So these findings don't suggest that men and women differ in overall tendency to conform; rather, they merely show that both tend to go along with gender stereotypes, so they may conform or not conform in different situations. In short, this research, and that of related studies, suggests that just as people have strong reasons for conforming, they often have strong motives for nonconformity—for refusing to go along with the group, especially if this puts them in a favorable light or is consistent with gender stereotypes. Once again, therefore, we see that social pressures to conform, although strong, are not irresistible.

THE DESIRE TO BE UNIQUE AND NONCONFORMITY   Do you remember the research by Pronin and colleagues (2007), indicating that most people believe that they conform less than others? In a sense, this is far from surprising because we all want to believe that we are unique individuals (see Snyder & Fromkin, 1980). Yes, we may dress, speak, and act like others most of the time, but in some respects, we are still unique. Could this desire be a factor in resisting conformity pressure? Two social psychologists—Imhoff and Erb (2009)—have obtained evidence indicating that, as other researchers (Snyder & Fromkin) suggested, it is. They reasoned that people have a motive to be unique—the need for uniqueness—and that when it is threatened (when they feel their uniqueness is at risk)—they will actively resist conformity pressures to restore their sense of uniqueness (see Figure 8.10).

To test this prediction, they had participants complete a questionnaire that, supposedly, assessed several key personality traits. They then either provided feedback indicating either that the participant was "exactly average" on these traits, or offered no feedback. The first group, of course, experienced a threat to their uniqueness, so they were expected to be motivated to resist pressures to conform. Conformity was measured in terms of the extent to which they went along with what were supposedly majority opinions about the desirability of a nearby lake as a good spot for a vacation. For half of the participants, a majority of other people endorsed the lake, while for the remainder, they rated it lower. What would participants now do? If raising their uniqueness

FIGURE 8.10   The Desire to Be Unique: A Source of Nonconformity
Although most of us conform most of the time and in most situations (see left photo), we still want to hold onto our uniqueness—to believe that we are unique people in some ways (right photo).

motivation resulted in less conformity, those who had learned they were "just average" on key personality traits would be less likely to go along with the majority than those who had not received this bogus information. Results supported this prediction, so it appeared that when the motive to be somewhat unique was threatened, individuals did respond by showing nonconformity—they refused to endorse the views supported by a majority of other people.

In sum, many factors contribute to nonconformity, so its occurrence is definitely not an accident; nor does it always stem from Shakespeare's advice "To thine own self be true." Just as conformity stems from a variety of causes and motives, so, too, does independence (see Chapter 5 for more information on when we maintain attitude independence). But this in itself is encouraging, for it suggests that while conformity is often a safe, convenient, and even useful approach to social life, there is lots of room for independence and individuality, too! Do emotions play a role in social influence? For evidence that they do, please see the section "EMOTIONS AND SOCIAL INFLUENCE: Emotional Contagion," below.)

EMOTIONS *and* SOCIAL INFLUENCE

Emotional Contagion

Suppose one of your good friends suddenly enters the room. She is overflowing with joy—happy, smiling, and bubbling over with enthusiasm. You ask her to explain why she's feeling so great, but even before she does so, do you think you would "catch her mood"—would you begin to feel a little boost in your own emotions, so that you, too, start to feel happy? Probably you have had experiences like this one because it is clear that often we *are* influenced by others' moods or emotions. And if you have ever cried while watching someone in a movie show sadness, or experienced joy when a character in a film or play shows happiness, you know about these kinds of reactions from firsthand experience (see Figure 8.11).

Social psychologists refer to such effects (through which moods spread from one person to another) as *social contagion,* and view it as another, and very basic, form of social influence. The fact that moods or emotions are indeed "catching" is clear; but *why* does this occur? What mechanisms permit one person's moods to influence those of another, even if this person is not intending to produce such effects?

Initial research on this topic (e.g., Hatfield, Cacioppo, & Rapson, 1994), emphasized a very basic process: When we observe emotions in others, we tend to physically match their feelings. If they are happy, we begin to smile; if they are sad, we may frown. These effects occur automatically, and the result is that we come to feel what the other person is feeling. Certainly, this is correct to some extent. But it doesn't explain another interesting and important fact: Sometimes when we observe emotions in others we don't experience what they are feeling, but something very different. For

instance, if you witness joy on the part of a team that has just defeated your own school's team, you will probably not feel happy. On the contrary, you may feel disappointment or even anger at their happy reactions. The German language has a specific word for this kind of reaction—*Schadenfreude*—which means malicious pleasure in others' sorrow or disappointment. Have you ever experienced such feelings? Unless you are a complete saint (!), you probably have; when others triumph over us, we are supposed to be "good losers," but it is sometimes easier to recommend such graciousness than to achieve it.

The fact that we sometimes experience the same emotions as others and sometimes ones quite different from theirs suggest that the situation is not simply one of "automatic mimicry." Rather, cognition too must be involved. We not only notice others' emotions, but interpret them, too. For instance, Parkinson and Simons (2009) suggest that sometimes we interpret others' reactions as a source of information about how *we* should feel. For instance, if they are showing lots of anxiety and excitement while making a decision, we conclude that the decision is very important, and may begin to feel similar reactions. This is very different from a direct effect in which we observe their reactions and feel the same emotion automatically. The researchers obtained evidence supporting this proposal from a diary study in which participants reported on their own feelings, and those of another person who was important in their lives (e.g., a spouse or lover), while making various decisions. Findings indicated that the reactions of the other person generated automatic

(continued)

EMOTIONS *and* SOCIAL INFLUENCE *(continued)*

FIGURE 8.11 **Emotional Contagion: A Very Basic Form of Social Influence**
When we are exposed to the emotions of others, we often experience similar feelings or moods; this is known as emotional contagion. Sometimes, however, we experience emotions or feelings opposite to theirs—an effect known as counter-contagion. Our similarity to these persons is often a strong determinant of which kind of reaction we experience.

emotional reactions *and* influenced appraisals of the situation (and these feelings) too.

In addition, other research (Epstude & Mussweiler, 2009) indicates that similarity to other people showing emotion is important in determining our own reactions. If we perceive ourselves as similar to them, then through social comparison processes, we tend to experience the emotions they are showing. If we perceive ourselves as dissimilar to them, then we may experience *counter-contagion*—emotions different from or even opposite to theirs. To test these predictions, the researchers conducted a study in which participants were first induced to think about similarity or dissimilarity. (This was accomplished by having them examine some pictures, and describe either similarities or differences between them.) Then they listened to an audiotape in which an actor

of their own gender read a passage; the actor was either in a slightly happy or slightly sad mood. Finally, participants rated their own mood. It was predicted that when primed to think about similarity, participants would perceive the actor as similar to themselves, and report being happier after hearing the happy actor than the sad one. When primed to think about dissimilarity, however, the opposite would be true. Results confirmed both predictions.

Overall, then, it is clear that our own feelings and emotions are often influenced by those of other people and that, moreover, this occurs even if they do not intend to affect us in this way. Emotional contagion, then, is a very basic and pervasive form of social influence, and one that may well play an important role in many ways in the social side of life.

Do Women and Men Differ in the Tendency to Conform?

Consider the following statement by Queen Victoria of England, one of the most powerful rulers in the history of the world: "We women are not made for governing—and if we are good women, we must dislike these masculine occupations . . . " (Letter dated February 3, 1852). This and many similar quotations suggest that women do not like to be in charge—they would prefer to follow rather than lead. And that idea, in turn, suggests that they may be more conforming than men. As informal evidence for this view, many people who accept it point to the fact that in general, women seem to be more likely than men to adopt new fashions in clothing and hairstyles. But does this mean that they are really more likely to conform in general? Early studies on conformity (e.g., Crutchfield, 1955) seemed to suggest that they are, but more recent—and more sophisticated research—points to a different conclusion.

For instance, Eagly and Carli (1981) conducted a meta-analysis of 145 different studies in which more than 20,000 people participated. Results indicated the existence of a very small difference between men and women, with women being slightly more accepting of social influence than men. So if such gender differences existed, they were much smaller than was once widely believed.

But that's not the end of the story. Additional research has further clarified when and why these small differences may exist—if they exist at all. With respect to "when," it appears that both genders are more easily influenced when they are uncertain about how to behave or about the correctness of their judgments. And careful examination of many studies on conformity indicates that the situations and materials used were ones more familiar to men than women. The result? Men were more certain about how to behave and so showed less conformity. Direct evidence for this reasoning was obtained by Sistrunk and McDavid (1971) who found that when males and females were equally familiar with the situations or materials employed, differences between them in terms of conformity disappeared.

Turning to "why" any gender differences in conformity might exist, the answer seems to involve differences in status between men and women. In the past—and even to some extent today—men tend to hold higher status jobs and positions in many societies than do women. And there is a relationship between status and susceptibility to social influence: Lower status leads to greater tendencies to conform (Eagly, 1987). So, when and if gender differences in conformity exist, they seem to be linked to social factors such as differences in status and gender roles—*not* to any basic, "built-in" differences between the two genders. These factors (e.g., women's status in society and gender roles and stereotypes) are certainly changing, and recent polls indicate that in the United States, a large majority of voters state that they would readily cast their ballots for a woman candidate for President (Eagly, 2007).

Overall, and contrary to what many once expected, women are generally *not* more susceptible to conformity pressures (or social influence) than men. In fact, any differences between the two genders that do exist are very small. And when such factors as confidence in one's own judgments (as determined by familiarity with the situation) and social status are considered, these differences totally disappear. Once again, therefore, we see how the careful, scientific approach adopted by social psychology helps us to clarify and refine "commonsense" views about important social issues, as we emphasized in Chapter 1.

Minority Influence: Does the Majority Always Rule?

As we noted earlier, individuals can, and often do, resist group pressure. Lone dissenters or small minorities can dig in their heels and refuse to go along. Yet there is more going on in such situations than just resistance; in addition, there are instances in which such people—minorities within their groups—actually turn the tables on the majority and *exert* rather than merely *receive* social influence. History provides many examples of such events. Giants of science, such as Galileo, Pasteur, and Freud, faced virtually unanimous majorities who initially rejected their views. Yet, over time, these famous people overcame such resistance and won widespread acceptance for their theories.

More recent examples of minorities influencing majorities are provided by the successes of environmentalists. Initially, such people were viewed as wild-eyed radicals with strange ideas. Gradually, however, they succeeded in changing the attitudes of the majority so that today, many of their views are widely accepted. For instance, many people are deeply concerned about global warming, which results in part from the burning of fossil fuels, such as the gasoline we use to run our cars (see Figure 8.12).

FIGURE 8.12 **Minorities Can Sometimes Carry the Day**
In the 1960s, environmentalists were viewed as weird radicals. Now, however, the views they stated are accepted by very large numbers of persons throughout the world. Shown here is Al Gore receiving the Nobel Prize peace prize, awarded for his efforts to combat global warming.

But when, precisely, do minorities succeed in influencing majorities? Research findings suggest that they are most likely to do so under certain conditions (Moscovici, 1985). First, the members of such groups must be consistent in their opposition to majority opinions. If they waiver, or seem to be divided, their impact is reduced. Second, members of the minority must avoid appearing to be rigid and dogmatic (Mugny, 1975). A minority that merely repeats the same position over and over again is less persuasive than one that demonstrates a degree of flexibility. Third, the general social context in which a minority operates is important. If a minority argues for a position that is consistent with current social trends (e.g., conservative views at a time of growing conservatism), its chances of influencing the majority are greater than if it argues for a position out of step with such trends. Of course, even when these conditions are met, minorities face a tough uphill fight. But both history and research findings (e.g., Kenworthy & Miller, 2001) indicate that they can sometimes prevail.

For instance, only a minority of the people living in the United States were in favor of gaining independence from Britain when the Revolutionary War began; but that minority did prevail and they founded a new nation that has served as a model for many others over the intervening centuries.

KEY POINTS

- **Social influence**—the many ways in which people produce changes in others—in their behavior, attitudes, or beliefs—is a common part of life.

- Most people behave in accordance with social norms most of the time; in other words, they show strong tendencies toward **conformity.**

- Conformity was first systematically studied by Solomon Asch, whose classic research indicated that many people will yield to social pressure from a unanimous group. Many factors determine whether, and to what extent, conformity occurs. These include **cohesiveness**—degree of attraction felt by an individual toward some group, group size, and type of social norm operating in that situation—*descriptive* or *injunctive.*

- Norms tend to influence our behavior primarily when they are relevant to us.

- Two important motives underlie our tendency to conform: the desire to be liked by others and the desire to

be right or accurate. These two motives are reflected in two distinct types of social influence, **normative** and **informational.**

- Emotional contagion occurs when one or more people are influenced by the emotions of one or more others. Such contagion can lead to similarity or opposite emotional reactions on the part of the people involved, depending on, for instance, the extent to which we feel similar to them.

- Several factors encourage *nonconformity*—refusing to "go along" with the group. These include the desire to attract a desirable mate, which may encourage men to demonstrate nonconformity, power, and the desire to be unique (which are consistent with the male gender stereotype).

- The effects of social influence are powerful and pervasive, but tend to be magnified in situations where we are uncertain about our own judgments of what is correct.

- Pressures to conform often produce harmful effects and cause even good people to perform bad actions. This was dramatically illustrated by Zimbardo's famous prison study.

- When we see others showing various emotions, we often experience the same feelings ourselves—an effect known as *emotional contagion*. However, if they are dissimilar to ourselves in important ways,

we may experience *counter-contagion*—emotions opposite to theirs, for instance, sorrow in response to their joy.

- Gender differences in conformity are much smaller than was once assumed, and appear to exist only in very special circumstances.

- Under some conditions, minorities can induce even large majorities to change their attitudes or behavior.

Compliance: To Ask—Sometimes—Is to Receive

Suppose that you wanted someone to do something for you; how would you go about getting this person to agree? If you think about this question for a moment, you'll quickly realize that you have many tactics for gaining *compliance*—for getting others to say yes to your requests (e.g., Gueguen, in press) (One unusual approach is shown in Figure 8.13.) What are these techniques and which ones work best? These are among the questions we now consider. Before doing so, however, we introduce a basic framework for understanding the nature of these techniques and why they often work.

Compliance: The Underlying Principles

Some years ago, Robert Cialdini, a well-known social psychologist, decided that the best way to find out about compliance was to study what he termed *compliance professionals*—people whose success (financial or otherwise) depends on their ability to get others to say yes. Who are such people? They include salespeople, advertisers, political lobbyists, fund-raisers, politicians, con artists, professional negotiators, and many others. Cialdini's technique for learning from these people was simple: He temporarily concealed his true identity and took jobs in various settings where gaining compliance is a way of life. In other words, he worked in advertising, direct (door-to-door) sales, fund-raising, and other compliance-focused fields. On the basis of these firsthand experiences, he concluded that although techniques for gaining compliance take many different forms, they all rest to some degree on six basic principles (Cialdini, 1994, 2008):

"I really need this completed before we suddenly let you go on friday."

FIGURE 8.13   Compliance: Getting Others to Say "Yes"
We all use—and are exposed to—many different techniques for gaining compliance—for getting others to do what we would like them to do. The one shown here is unusual, but suggests just how varied approaches for gaining compliance can be! (Source: The New Yorker).

- *Friendship/liking:* In general, we are more willing to comply with requests from friends or from people we like than with requests from strangers or people we don't like.
- *Commitment/consistency:* Once we have committed ourselves to a position or action, we are more willing to comply with requests for behaviors that are consistent with this position or action than with requests that are inconsistent with it.
- *Scarcity:* In general, we value, and try to secure, outcomes or objects that are scarce or decreasing in availability. As a result, we are more likely to comply with requests that focus on scarcity than ones that make no reference to this issue.
- *Reciprocity:* We are generally more willing to comply with a request from someone who has previously provided a favor or concession to us than to someone who has not. In other words, we feel obligated to pay people back in some way for what they have done for us.
- *Social validation:* We are generally more willing to comply with a request for some action if this action is consistent with what we believe people similar to ourselves are doing (or thinking). We want to be correct, and one way to do so is to act and think like others.
- *Authority:* In general, we are more willing to comply with requests from someone who holds legitimate authority—or simply appears to do so.

According to Cialdini (2008), these basic principles underlie many techniques used by professionals—and ourselves—for gaining compliance from others. We now examine techniques based on these principles, plus a few others as well.

Tactics Based on Friendship or Liking: Ingratiation

We've already considered several techniques for increasing compliance through liking in our discussion of *impression management* (Chapter 3)—various procedures for making a good impression on others. While this can be an end in itself, impression management techniques are often used for purposes of *ingratiation*—getting others to like us so that they will be more willing to agree to our requests (Jones, 1964; Liden & Mitchell, 1988).

What ingratiation techniques work best? A review of existing studies on this topic (Gordon, 1996) suggests that *flattery*—praising others in some manner—is one of the best. Another is known as *self-promotion*—informing others about our past accomplishments or positive characteristics ("I'm really very organized" or "I'm really easy to get along with"; Bolino & Turnley, 1999). Other techniques that seem to work are improving one's own appearance, emitting many positive nonverbal cues, and doing small favors for the target people (Gordon, 1996; Wayne & Liden, 1995). Since we described many of these tactics in detail in Chapter 3, we won't repeat that information here. Suffice it to say that many of the tactics used for purposes of impression management are also successful from the point of view of increasing compliance.

Still another means of increasing others' liking for us—and thus increasing the chances that they will agree to requests we make—involves what has been termed *incidental similarity*—calling attention to small and slightly surprising similarities between them and ourselves. In several recent studies, Burger, Messian, Patel, del Pardo, and Anderson (2004) found that research participants were more likely to agree to a small request (make a donation to charity) from a stranger when this person appeared to have the same first name or birthday as they did than when the requester was not similar to them in these ways. Apparently, these trivial forms of similarity enhance liking or a feeling of affiliation with the requester and so increase the tendency to comply with this person's requests.

Tactics Based on Commitment or Consistency: The Foot-in-the-Door and the Lowball

When you visit the food court of your local shopping mall, are you ever approached by people offering you free samples of food? If so, why do they do this? The answer is simple: They know that once you have accepted this small, free gift, you will be more willing to buy something from their booth. This is the basic idea behind an approach for gaining compliance known as the **foot-in-the-door technique.** Basically, this involves inducing target people to agree to a small initial request ("Accept this free sample") and then making a larger request—the one desired all along. The results of many studies indicate that this tactic works—it succeeds in inducing increased compliance (e.g., Freedman & Fraser, 1966). Why is this the case? Because the foot-in-the-door technique rests on the principle of *consistency:* Once we have said yes to the small request, we are more likely to say yes to subsequent and larger ones, too, because refusing these would be inconsistent with our previous behavior. For example, imagine that you wanted to borrow one of your friend's class notes since the start of the semester. You might begin by asking for the notes from one lecture. After copying these, you might come back with a larger request: the notes for all the other classes. If your friend complied, it might well be because refusing would be inconsistent with his or her initial yes (e.g., DeJong & Musilli, 1982).

The foot-in-the-door technique is not the only tactic based on the consistency/commitment principle, however. Another is the **lowball procedure.** In this technique, which is often used by automobile salespersons, a very good deal is offered to a customer. After the customer accepts, however, something happens that makes it necessary for the salesperson to change the deal and make it less advantageous for the customer—for example, the sales manager rejects the deal. The totally rational response for customers, of course, is to walk away. Yet, often they agree to the changes and accept the less desirable arrangement (Cialdini, Cacioppo, Bassett, & Miller, 1978). In instances such as this, an initial commitment seems to make it more difficult for individuals to say no, even though the conditions that led them to say yes in the first place have now been changed.

Clear evidence for the importance of an initial commitment in the success of the lowball technique is provided by research conducted by Burger and Cornelius (2003). These researchers phoned students living in dorms and asked them if they would contribute $5.00 to a scholarship fund for underprivileged students. In the lowball condition, she indicated that people who contributed would receive a coupon for a free smoothie at a local juice bar. Then, if the participant agreed to make a donation, she told them that she had just run out of coupons and couldn't offer them this incentive. She then asked if they would still contribute. In another condition (the interrupt condition), she made the initial request but before the participants could answer yes or no, interrupted them and indicated that there were no more coupons for people who donated. In other words, this was just like the lowball condition, except that participants had no opportunity to make an initial commitment to donating to the fund. Finally, in a third (control) condition, participants were asked to donate $5.00 with no mention of any coupons for a free drink. Results indicated that more people in the lowball condition agreed to make a donation than in either of the other two conditions.

These results indicate that the lowball procedure does indeed rest on the principles of commitment: Only when individuals are permitted to make an initial public commitment—when they say yes to the initial offer—does it work. Having made this initial commitment, they feel compelled to stick with it, even though the conditions that lead them to say yes in the first place no longer exist. Truly, this is a subtle yet powerful technique for gaining compliance.

foot-in-the-door technique
A procedure for gaining compliance in which requesters begin with a small request and then, when this is granted, escalate to a larger one (the one they actually desired all along).

low-ball procedure
A technique for gaining compliance in which an offer or deal is changed to make it less attractive to the target person after this person has accepted it.

Tactics Based on Reciprocity: The Door-in-the Face and the "That's-Not-All" Approach

Reciprocity is a basic rule of social life: we usually "do unto others as they have done unto us." If they have done a favor for us, therefore, we feel that we should be willing to do one for them in return. While this is viewed by most people as being fair and just, the principle of reciprocity also serves as the basis for several techniques for gaining compliance. One of these is, on the face of it, the opposite of the foot-in-the-door technique. Instead of beginning with a small request and then escalating to a larger one, people seeking compliance sometimes start with a very large request and then, after this is rejected, shift to a smaller request—the one they wanted all along. This tactic is known as the **door-in-the-face technique** (because the first refusal seems to slam the door in the face of the requester), and several studies indicate that it can be quite effective. For example, in one well-known experiment, Cialdini and his colleagues (1975) stopped college students on the street and presented a huge request: Would the students serve as unpaid counselors for juvenile delinquents 2 hours a week for the next *2 years!* As you can guess, no one agreed. When the experimenters then scaled down their request to a much smaller one—would the same students take a group of delinquents on a 2-hour trip to the zoo—fully 50 percent agreed. In contrast, less than 17 percent of those in a control group agreed to this smaller request when it was presented cold rather than after the larger request.

Recently, it has been found that this tactic works on the Internet, as well as in face-to-face situations. Gueguen (2003) set up a website supposedly to help children who are the victims of mines in war zones. More than 3,600 people were contacted and invited to visit the site, and 1,607 actually did. Once there, they received either a very large request (the door-in-the-face condition): Would they volunteer 2–3 hours per week for the next 6 months to increase awareness of this problem? In contrast, those in a control group were simply invited to visit a page where they could make a donation to help the children. It was expected that very few people would agree with the large request—only two did. But the key question was, Would more people who had received and refused the first request visit the donation site and actually begin the process of making a donation? As you can see in Figure 8.14, this is precisely what happened. Higher percentages of the door-in-the-face group than in the control group went to the donation page and activated the link to make a donation. So clearly, this tactic can work in cyberspace as well as in person.

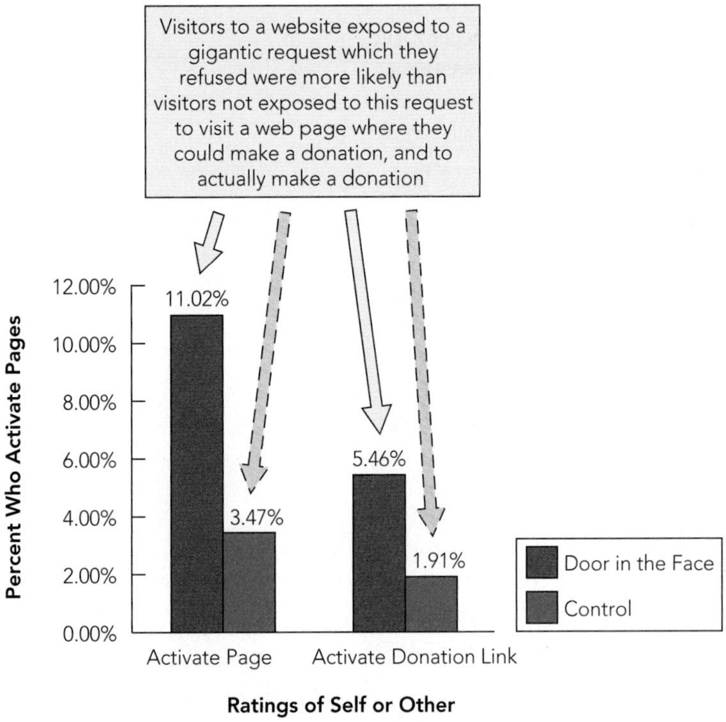

A related procedure for gaining compliance is known as the **that's-not-all technique.** Here, an initial request is followed, *before the target person can say yes or no,* by something that sweetens the deal—a small extra incentive from the people using this tactic (e.g., a reduction in price, "throwing in" something additional for the same price). For example, television commercials for various products frequently offer something extra to induce viewers to pick up the phone and place an order—for instance a "free" knife or a "free" cookbook (see Figure 8.13). Several studies confirm informal observations suggesting that the that's-not-all technique really works (e.g., Burger, 1986). Why is this so? One possibility is that this tactic succeeds because it is

door-in-the-face technique
A procedure for gaining compliance in which requesters begin with a large request and then, when this is refused, retreat to a smaller one (the one they actually desired all along).

that's-not-all technique
A technique for gaining compliance in which requesters offer additional benefits to target people before they have decided whether to comply with or reject specific requests.

FIGURE 8.14   The Door-in-the-Face on the Internet

People who visited a website concerned with helping children injured by mines in war zones who received a very large request they refused (door-in-the-door condition), later were more likely to visit a page on which they could make a donation to the children or actually begin the process of donating than those who never received the large request (control).   (Source: Based on Data from Gueguen, 2003).

based on the principle of reciprocity: People on the receiving end of this approach view the "extra" thrown in by the other side as an added concession, and so feel obligated to make a concession themselves. The result: They are more likely to say "yes."

Tactics Based on Scarcity: Playing Hard to Get and the Fast-Approaching-Deadline Technique

It's a general rule of life that things that are scarce, rare, or difficult to obtain are viewed as being more valuable than those that are plentiful or easy to obtain. Thus, we are often willing to expend more effort or go to greater expense to obtain items or outcomes that are scarce than to obtain ones that are in large supply. This principle serves as the foundation for several techniques for gaining compliance. One of the most common of these is **playing hard to get**—a tactic often used in the area of romance. What it involves is actions by a person using this technique suggesting that they have very little interest in the target person—the one toward whom playing hard to get is directed. For instance, a person playing hard to get might drop hints to the effect that a potential partner (the target person) has a lot of competition—many rivals. When it works, this tactic can fan the flames of passion in the people who are on the receiving end (e.g., Walster, Walster, Piliavin, & Schmidt, 1973).

The playing-hard-to-get tactic is also not limited to dating and romance, however; research findings indicate that it is also sometimes used by job candidates to increase their attractiveness to potential employers, and hence to increase the likelihood that these employers will offer them a job. People using this tactic let the potential employer know that they have other offers and so are a very desirable employee. And in fact, research findings indicate that this technique often works (Williams, Radefeld, Binning, & Suadk, 1993).

A related procedure also based on the "what's-scarce-is-valuable" principle is one frequently used by department stores. Ads using this **deadline technique** state that a special sale will end on a certain date, implying that after that, the prices will go up. In many cases, the time limit is false: the prices won't go up after the indicated date and may, in fact, continue to drop if the merchandise remains unsold. Yet many people reading such ads believe them and hurry down to the store to avoid missing out on a great opportunity. So when you encounter an offer suggesting that "the clock is ticking" and may soon run out, be cautious: this may simply be a technique for boosting sales.

In sum, there are many different tactics for gaining compliance—for changing others' behavior in ways we desire. And remember that such efforts work both ways: we try to influence others, and they, in turn, often attempt to influence us. Thus, it's wise to always remember these words, written by Eric Hoffer (1953): "It would be difficult to exaggerate the degree to which we are influenced by those we influence." (People seek compliance in many situations, but one that has recently received lots of attention is Internet dating. Please see the section "SOCIAL LIFE IN A CONNECTED WORLD: The Use of Social Influence Tactics by Scammers on the Web—Internet Daters, Beware!" for a discussion of compliance in this very personal context.)

playing hard to get
A technique that can be used for increasing compliance by suggesting that a person or object is scarce and hard to obtain.

deadline technique
A technique for increasing compliance in which target people are told that they have only limited time to take advantage of some offer or to obtain some item.

KEYPOINTS

- Individuals use many different tactics for gaining *compliance*—getting others to say yes to various requests. Many of these rest on basic principles well known to social psychologists.

- Two widely used tactics, the **foot-in-the-door** and the **lowball procedure,** rest on the principle of commitment/consistency. In contrast, the **door-in-the-face** and **that's-not-all** techniques rest on the principle of reciprocity.

- Research findings indicate that the door-in-the-face technique works on the Internet as well as in face-to-face situations.

- **Playing hard to get** and the **deadline technique** are based on the principle of scarcity—what is scarce or hard to obtain is valuable.

SOCIAL LIFE *in a* CONNECTED WORLD

The Use of Social Influence Tactics by Scammers on the Web—Internet Daters, Beware!

Ads for Internet dating services often show happy couples who started wonderful long-term relationships through their service (see Figure 8.15). Such couples certainly do exist and in fact, many people believe that Internet dating services fill important needs. But *watch out*—they are also a place where ruthless people who seek to prey upon unsuspecting victims through the use of various tactics of social influence sometimes operate (Johnson, McKenna, Postmes, & Reips, 2007). Consider, for instance, the true case of Annette, one young woman who sought her perfect mate through eHarmony.com, a well-known and widely used dating service (this story was reported on elAMB.org, a Web page that specializes in unmasking scams on the Internet).

Annette soon found someone who seemed just right: a 41-year-old Christian engineer named John from California who was working in Nigeria, accompanied by his daughter Hailey (elAMB.org, June 27, 2010). Over several months, Annette communicated frequently with John and gradually built up what was, for her, a very appealing online relationship. The only problem was that just as he was about to return to the United States for a happy meeting with Annette, John—who was supposedly quite wealthy—experienced a series of major setbacks. First, his luggage containing all his traveler's checks was impounded at the airport. This meant that he didn't have enough funds to pay for tickets for himself and his daughter. Could Annette wire him $1,300? Thinking "He must really need the money—it's not a large amount," she did. But that was just the start. John then learned that he'd have to bribe the customs officials to release his luggage; that would cost several thousands more. And then the worst thing of all happened: his daughter Hailey was kidnapped and held for ransom. Could Annette help again?

The upshot was that ultimately Annette sent "John" more than $40,000. She only stopped when she had nothing

FIGURE 8.15   Internet Dating Services: Potential Benefits, Real Risks
Internet dating services often run ads like this one, showing happy couples who met and formed long-term relationships on their network. Such happy outcomes certainly occur, but watch out! There are unprincipled criminals out there just waiting to lure into a situation where you trust them enough to send them money. You'll never meet them—and in fact, they don't exist as described in their profiles—but you'll also never see your money again, either.

left to send. Her family was shocked because Annette had always been a level-headed and stable person; how did she fall victim to this confidence artist who, of course, never existed—his identity and everything about him was manufactured by the person seeking to work this swindle.

The answer is complex, involving many principles of compliance. John started with a small request and only after it was granted, moved to larger ones later—the foot-in-the-door tactic. He also used guilt against Annette, writing, "If you don't give me the money, it means you don't love me." And he put pressure on his victim by indicating that if she didn't help immediately, he'd be unable to get out of Nigeria and come to see her. There's more, too, but as you can see, swindlers like this use effective compliance tactics when seeking victims through Internet dating services.

Annette's case is a real one, but it is only one of many because scams involving Internet dating appear to use basic techniques for gaining compliance from the victims that are well known to social psychologists. This means that you should always *be cautious* when using such services.

The losses you can experience go far beyond financial ones; many people report experiences in which they have sent money to "the love of their dreams" to help them come to the United States, only to wait at the airport for someone who never arrives. The result is a painful broken heart. How can you avoid such experiences? Here are some guidelines to follow—ones endorsed by many consumer protection organizations:

Be skeptical of claims of love that occur before you have even met the person sending them. As we saw in Chapter 7, love develops over time—it doesn't usually result from one photo and a few e-mail messages.

Run—don't walk—away from people who ask you for money, who ask inappropriate questions, or ask for confidential information such as your password.

Be suspicious of people who want to speed up the pace of the relationship, so that it is outside your comfort zone.

Be wary of people who give vague answers to specific questions, or tell stories with inconsistencies and that sound too good to be true.

Ditto for people who suddenly experience a series of heart-rending events and blame others, or forces beyond their control.

Don't be lulled into a sense of security if your online relationship has continued for weeks or even months; these swindlers play a long-term game, and realize that it may take quite a while before their victims will be ready to send cash.

Does this mean that you should avoid Internet dating services entirely? Not at all. They can help people find suitable and desirable romantic partners. But the guidelines for all such dealings—as it should be in *everything* you do on the Internet—should emphasize caution, prudence, and vigilance. And above all, be on the watch for tactics of influence and persuasion such as the ones described in this chapter.

Symbolic Social Influence: How We Are Influenced by Others Even When They Are Not There

That other people can influence us when they are present and trying to do so is not surprising; they have many techniques at their disposal for getting us to say, think, or do what they want. But growing evidence suggests that others can influence us even when they are *not* present and *not* trying to change our behavior or thoughts. Although the evidence is new, the basic idea is not; in fact, writing in what was perhaps the first textbook on social psychology, Floyd Allport (1924, p. 32) defined influence as: "the ways in which the thoughts, feelings, and behaviors of individuals are influenced by the actual, *imagined,* or *implied presence of others.*" Ultimately, of course, other people do not produce such effects: *we* do. Our mental representations of others—what they want or prefer, our relationships with them, how we think they would evaluate us or our current actions—can exert powerful effects on us, even, it appears, when we are not consciously aware that they are occurring (e.g., Bargh, Gollwitzer, Lee-Chai, Barndollar, & Trotschel, 2001). For example, in one well-known study—which initially triggered interest in this topic—Baldwin, Carrell, and Lopez (1990) found that graduate students evaluated their own research ideas more negatively after being exposed, subliminally, to the face of their scowling department chair. In other words, the chair's face was shown for so short a period of time that the graduate students were not aware of having seen him. Yet his negative facial expression exerted significant effects on their evaluations of their own work anyway.

How can the psychological presence of others in our mental representations of them influence our behavior and thought? Two mechanisms seem to be involved, and both may involve goals—objectives we wish to attain. First, to the extent other people are present in our thoughts (and even if we are not aware that they are), this may trigger *relational schemas*—mental representations of people with whom we have relationships, and of these relationships themselves. When these relational schemas are triggered, in turn, goals relevant to them may be activated, too. For instance, if we think of a friend, the goal of being helpful may be activated; if we think of our mother or father, the goal of making them proud of us may be triggered. These goals, in turn, can affect our behavior, our thoughts about ourselves, and our evaluations of others. For instance, if the goal of helping others is triggered, then we may become more helpful. If the goal of being physically attractive is activated, we may refuse that delicious dessert when it is offered.

Second, the psychological presence of others may trigger goals with which that person is associated—goals they want us to achieve. This, in turn, can affect our performance on various tasks and our commitment to reaching these goals, among other things (e.g., Shah, 2003). For instance, if we have thoughts about our father, we know that he wants us to do well in school, and our commitment to this goal may be increased and we may work harder to attain it—especially if we feel very close to him.

In other words, to the extent that others are psychologically present in our thoughts, the nature of our relationships with them, goals we seek in these relationships, or goals these people themselves want us to attain can all be stimulated, and these ideas and knowledge structures, in turn, can strongly affect our behavior.

While many different studies have recently reported such effects, research conducted on this topic by Fitzsimons and Bargh (2003) is especially revealing. In one such study, people at an airport were approached and asked to think either of a good friend or a coworker. Then, they were asked to write down the initials of the person of whom they were thinking and to answer a series of questions about that person (describe his or her appearance, how long they had known this person, his or her age, etc.). Finally, participants were asked if they would be willing to help the researcher by answering a longer set of questions. It was predicted that those who thought about a friend would be more willing to help because thinking about a friend would trigger the goal of helping—something we often do for friends. This is precisely what happened: more people who thought about a friend than a coworker were willing to help. Note that they were not asked to help their friend; rather, they were asked to assist a stranger—the researcher. But still, thoughts of the friend affected their current behavior.

Findings such as these, and those reported in a growing number of other studies (e.g., Shah, 2003), suggest that we can be strongly influenced by other people when they are not physically present on the scene and trying to affect us, as long as they are psychologically present (in our thoughts).

KEYPOINTS

- Internet dating works well for some people, but there are confidence artists "out there" waiting to entrap unwary people seeking romance through the use of *social influence* tactics. For that reason, it's important to be very cautious with respect to such relationships.

- Other people can influence us even when they are not present through our mental representations of them and our relationship with them. This is known as *symbolic social influence*.

- Such influence often involves goals relevant to our relationships with them, or goals with which these people themselves are associated.

- To the extent that others are psychologically present in our thoughts, goals we seek in our relationships with them or goals these people themselves seek or want us to attain can be stimulated, and these, in turn, can strongly affect our behavior.

Obedience to Authority: Would You Harm an Innocent Stranger If Ordered to Do So?

Have you ever been ordered to do something you didn't want to do by someone with authority over you—a teacher, your boss, your parents? If so, you are already familiar with another major type of social influence—*obedience*—in which one person directly orders one or more others to behave in specific ways. Obedience is less frequent than conformity or compliance because even people who possess authority and could use it often prefer to exert influence in less obvious ways—through requests rather than direct orders (e.g., Yukl & Falbe, 1991). Still, obedience is far from rare, and occurs in many settings, ranging from schools to military bases. Obedience to the commands of people who possess authority is far from surprising; they usually have effective means for enforcing their orders. More unexpected is the fact that often, people lacking in such power can also induce high levels of submission from others. The clearest and most dramatic evidence for such effects was reported by Stanley Milgram in a series of famous but still controversial studies (1963, 1965a, 1974).

Obedience in the Laboratory

In his research, Milgram wished to find out whether individuals would obey commands from a relatively powerless stranger requiring them to inflict what seemed to be considerable pain on another person—a totally innocent stranger. Milgram's interest in this topic derived from tragic events in which seemingly normal, law-abiding people actually obeyed such directives. For example, during World War II, troops in the German army frequently obeyed commands to torture and murder unarmed civilians. In fact, the Nazis established horrible but highly efficient death camps designed to eradicate Jews, Gypsies, and other groups they felt were inferior or a threat to their own "racial purity."

In an effort to gain insights into the nature of such events, Milgram designed an ingenious, if unsettling, laboratory simulation. The experimenter informed participants in the study (all males) that they were taking part in an investigation of the effects of punishment on learning. One person in each pair of participants would serve as a "learner" and would try to perform a simple task involving memory (supplying the second word in pairs of words they had previously memorized after hearing only the first word). The other participant, the "teacher," would read these words to the learner, and would punish errors by the learner (failures to provide the second word in each pair) through electric shock. These shocks would be delivered by means of the equipment shown in Figure 8.16, and as you can see from the photo, this device contained 30 numbered switches ranging from "15 volts" (the first) through 450 volts (the 30th). The two people present—a real participant and a research assistant—then drew slips of paper from a hat to determine who would play each role; as you can guess, the drawing was rigged so that the real participant always became the teacher. The teacher was then told to deliver a shock to the learner each time he made an error on the task. Moreover—and this is crucial—teachers were told *to increase the strength of the shock each time the learner made an error*. This meant that if the learner made many errors, he would soon be receiving strong jolts of electricity. It's important to note that this information was false: In reality, the assistant (the learner) *never received any shocks during the experiment*. The only real shock ever used was a mild pulse from button number three to convince participants that the equipment was real.

During the session, the learner (following prearranged instructions) made many errors. Thus, participants soon found themselves facing a dilemma: Should they continue punishing this person with what seemed to be increasingly painful shocks? Or

FIGURE 8.16 **Studying Obedience in the Laboratory**

The left photo shows the apparatus Stanley Milgram used in his famous experiments on destructive obedience. The right photo shows the experimenter (right front) and a participant (rear) attaching electrodes to the learner's (accomplice's) wrist. (Source: From the film Obedience, *copyright 1968 by Stanley Milgram, copyright renewed 1993 by Alexandra Milgram and distributed by Penn State Media Sales).*

should they refuse? If they hesitated, the experimenter pressured them to continue with a graded series "prods": "Please continue"; "The experiment requires that you continue"; "It is absolutely essential that you continue"; and "You have no other choice; you *must* go on."

Since participants were all volunteers and were paid in advance, you might predict that most would quickly refuse the experimenter's orders. In reality, though, *fully 65 percent showed total obedience*—they proceeded through the entire series to the final 450-volt level. Many participants, of course, protested and asked that the session be ended. When ordered to proceed, however, a majority yielded to the experimenter's influence and continued to obey. Indeed, they continued doing so even when the victim pounded on the wall as if in protest over the painful shocks (at the 300-volt level), and then no longer responded, as if he had passed out. The experimenter told participants to treat failures to answer as errors; so from this point on, many participants believed that they were delivering dangerous shocks to someone who might already be unconscious!

In further experiments, Milgram (1965b, 1974) found that similar results could be obtained even under conditions that might be expected to reduce obedience. When the study was moved from its original location on the campus of Yale University to a run-down office building in a nearby city, participants' level of obedience remained virtually unchanged. Similarly, a large proportion continued to obey even when the accomplice complained about the painfulness of the shocks and begged to be released. Most surprising of all, about 30 percent obeyed even when they were required to grasp the victim's hand and force it down upon a metal shock plate! That these chilling results are not restricted to a single culture is indicated by the fact that similar findings were soon reported in several different countries (e.g., Jordan, Germany, Australia) and with children as well as adults (e.g., Kilham & Mann, 1974; Shanab & Yanya, 1977). Thus, Milgram's findings seemed to be alarmingly general in scope.

Psychologists and the public both found Milgram's results highly disturbing. His studies seemed to suggest that ordinary people are willing, although with some reluctance, to harm an innocent stranger if ordered to do so by someone in authority—in a sense, echoing the theme stated by Zimbardo in his famous "Stanford Prison Study" and more recent writings (Zimbardo, 2007).

At this point, you might be tempted to conclude: "OK, in 1960 people obeyed a man in a white laboratory coat. But today, people are much more sophisticated, so they would never hold still for this kind of thing. They'd just refuse to play the game." That's a comforting thought, but in fact, one social psychologist (Burger, 2009), replicated Milgram's research just recently. He made a few changes to protect participants from the extreme stress Milgram's procedures generated. For instance, he screened them to make sure that they had no medical problems that would make them especially susceptible to the harmful effects of stress. In addition, if they agreed to continue after the learner protested (150 volts), he stopped the study, thus avoiding further stress for the participants. Burger reasoned that he could do this because almost all of the participants in Milgram's original research who continued past 150 volts went all the way to the end of the series. In addition, both females and males participated in the research; in Milgram's studies, only males took part.

What were the results? Almost identical to those found by Milgram 45 years earlier. As you can see in Figure 8.17, a very high proportion (66.7 percent for men, 72.7 percent for women) continued past the 150-volt level—the point at which the victim protested and said he wanted to stop the experiment. This is very similar to the figure reported by Milgram. Furthermore, when procedures were used in which an assistant of the experimenter refused to continue, this did *not* increase participant's willingness to stop—fully 54.5 percent of men and 68.4 percent of women continued despite seeing another person refuse to obey.

So what do these results tell us? That the pressures to obey in a situation like the one Milgram created are difficult to resist—so difficult that many people yield to them, even if this means harming an innocent stranger who has done nothing to harm them. What are these pressures? What factors lie behind this tendency to obey in such situations? That's the question we consider next.

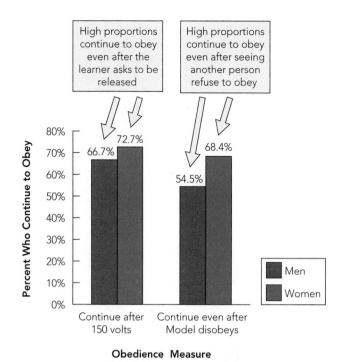

FIGURE 8.17   Obedience: Still a Powerful Form of Social Influence

In a recent replication of Milgram's famous research, high proportions of both men and women and obeyed the experimenters commands to deliver shocks to an innocent victim. They continued even after the victim asked to stop the study (150 volts), and even if they saw another person (a model) refuse to obey. (Source: Based on data from Burger, 2009).

Destructive Obedience: Why It Occurs

As we noted earlier, one reason why Milgram's results are so disturbing is that they seem to parallel many real-life events involving atrocities against innocent victims such as the murder of millions of Jews and other people by the Nazis, the genocide advocated by the Hutu government in Rwanda in which 800,000 Tutsis were killed in less than 3 months in 1994, and the massacre of more than 1 million Armenians by Turkish troops in the early years of the 20th century. To repeat the question we raised above: Why does such destructive obedience occur? Why were participants in these experiments—and so many people in these tragic situations outside the laboratory—so willing to yield to this form of social influence? Social psychologists have identified several factors that seem to play a role, and together, these combine to make an array of situational pressures most people find very hard to resist.

First, in many situations, the people in authority relieve those who obey of the responsibility for their own actions. "I was only carrying out orders" is the defense many offer after obeying harsh or cruel commands. In life situations, this transfer of responsibility may be implicit; the person in charge (e.g., the military or police officer) is assumed to have the responsibility for what happens. This seems to be what happened in the tragic events at Abu Ghraib prison camp in Iraq, when U.S. soldiers—both men and women—were filmed abusing and torturing prisoners. The soldiers' defense? "I was only following orders . . . I was told to do this and a good soldier always obeys!" In Milgram's experiments, this transfer of responsibility was explicit. Participants were told at the start that the experimenter (the authority figure), not they, would be responsible for the learner's well-being. In view of this fact, it is not surprising that many obeyed; after all, they were completely off the hook.

Second, people in authority often possess visible badges or signs of their status. They wear special uniforms or insignia, have special titles, and so on. These serve to remind many individuals of the social norm "Obey the people in charge." This is a powerful norm, and when confronted with it, most people find it difficult to disobey. After all, we do not want to do the wrong thing, and obeying the commands of those who are in charge usually helps us avoid such errors. In Milgram's study, the experimenter wore a white lab coat, which suggested that he was a doctor or someone with authority. So it's not surprising that so many participants obeyed the commands this person issued (e.g., Bushman, 1988; Darley, 1995).

A third reason for obedience in many situations where the targets of such influence might otherwise resist involves the gradual escalation of the authority figure's orders. Initial commands may call for relatively mild actions, such as merely arresting people. Only later do orders come to require behavior that is dangerous or objectionable (see Staub, 1989). For example, police or military personnel may at first be ordered only to question or threaten potential victims. Gradually, demands are increased to the point where these personnel are commanded to beat, torture, or even murder unarmed civilians. In a sense, people in authority use the foot-in-the-door technique, asking for small actions first but ever-larger ones later. In a similar manner, participants in Milgram's research were first required to deliver only mild and harmless shocks to the victim. Only as the sessions continued did the intensity of these "punishments" rise to potentially harmful levels.

Finally, events in many situations involving destructive obedience move very quickly: demonstrations turn into riots, arrests into mass beatings or murder, and so on, quite suddenly. The fast pace of such events gives participants little time for reflection or systematic thought: People are ordered to obey and—almost automatically—they do so. Such conditions prevailed in Milgram's research; within a few minutes of entering the laboratory, participants found themselves faced with commands to deliver strong electric shocks to the learner. This fast pace, too, may tend to increase obedience.

In sum, the high levels of obedience generated in Milgram's studies are not as mysterious as they may seem. A social-psychological analysis of the conditions existing both there and in many real-life situations identifies several factors that, together, may make it very difficult for individuals to resist the commands they receive (these are summarized in Figure 8.18). The consequences, of course, can be truly tragic for innocent and often defenseless victims.

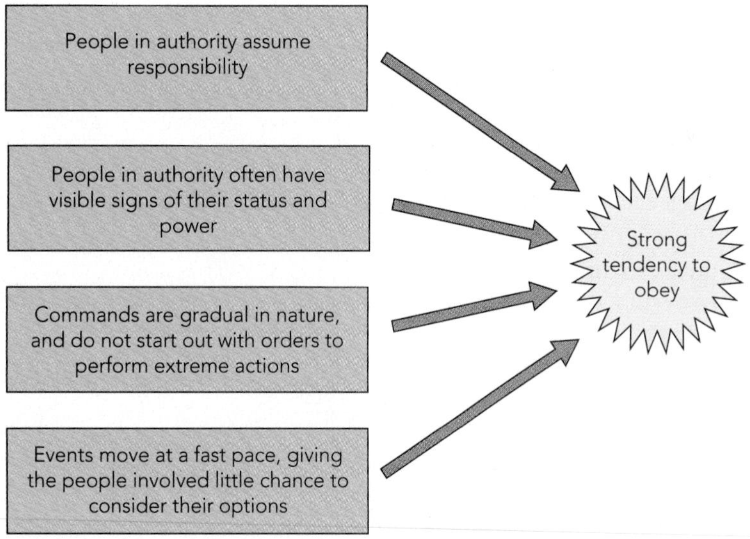

| People in authority assume responsibility |
| People in authority often have visible signs of their status and power |
| Commands are gradual in nature, and do not start out with orders to perform extreme actions |
| Events move at a fast pace, giving the people involved little chance to consider their options |

→ Strong tendency to obey

FIGURE 8.18   Obedience to Authority: Why It Often Occurs
As shown here, several factors combine to make it all too easy to obey orders from persons in authority—even if these commands involve harming others and violating our own ethical or moral standards.

Destructive Obedience: Resisting Its Effects

Now that we have considered some of the factors responsible for the strong tendency to obey sources of authority, we turn to a related question: How can this type of social influence be resisted? Several strategies may be helpful in this respect.

First, individuals exposed to commands from authority figures can be reminded that *they*—not the authorities—are responsible for any harm produced. Under these conditions, sharp reductions in the tendency to obey have been observed (e.g., Hamilton, 1978; Kilham & Mann, 1974).

Second, individuals can be provided with a clear indication that beyond some point, total submission to destructive commands is inappropriate. One procedure that can be effective in this regard involves exposing individuals to the actions of *disobedient models*—people who refuse to obey an authority figure's commands. Research findings indicate that such models can reduce unquestioning obedience (e.g., Rochat & Modigliani, 1995)—although as Burger (2009) reported, not always.

Third, individuals may find it easier to resist influence from authority figures if they question the expertise and motives of these figures. Are those in authority really in a better position to judge what is appropriate and what is not? What motives lie behind their commands—socially beneficial goals or selfish gains? Dictators always claim that their brutal orders reflect their undying concern for their fellow citizens and are in their best interest, but to the extent large numbers of people question these motives, the power of such dictators can be eroded and perhaps, ultimately, be swept away.

Finally, simply knowing about the power of authority figures to command blind obedience may be helpful in itself. Some research findings (e.g., Sherman, 1980) suggest that when individuals learn about the results of this social psychological research, they often recognize these as important (Richard, Bond, & Stokes-Zoota, 2001), and sometimes change their behavior to take into account this new knowledge. With respect to destructive obedience, there is some hope that knowing about this process can enhance individuals' resolve to resist. To the extent this is so, then even exposure to findings as disturbing as those reported by Milgram can have positive social value.

The power of authority figures to command obedience is certainly great, but it is not irresistible. Under appropriate conditions, it can be countered or reduced. As in many other areas of life, there is a choice. Deciding to resist the commands of people in authority can, of course, be highly dangerous: they usually control most of the weapons, the army, and the police. Yet, history is filled with instances in which the authority of powerful and entrenched regimes has been resisted by courageous people who ultimately triumphed, despite the long odds against them (see Turner, 2006). Indeed, the American Revolution began in just this way: Small bands of poorly armed citizens decided to make a stand against Britain, the most powerful country on Earth at the time. Their success in winning their independence became a model for many other people all over the world—and changed history. The lesson from this and related events is clear: Power is never permanent and, ultimately, victory often goes to those who stand for freedom and decency rather than to those who wish to control the lives of their fellow human beings.

KEYPOINTS

- *Obedience* is a form of social influence in which one person orders one or more others to do something, and they do so. It is, in a sense, the most direct form of social influence.

- Research by Stanley Milgram indicates that many people readily obey orders from a relatively powerless source of authority, even if these orders require them to harm another innocent person.

- A recent replication of this study reported results very similar to those obtained by Milgram.

- Such destructive obedience, which plays a role in many real-life atrocities, stems from several factors. These include the shifting of responsibility to the authority figure; outward signs of authority that remind many people of the norm "obey those in authority"; a gradual escalation of the scope of the commands given (related to the *foot-in-the-door technique*); and the rapid pace with which such situations proceed.

- Several factors can help to reduce the occurrence of destructive obedience. These include reminding individuals that they share in the responsibility for any harm produced; reminding them that beyond some point, obedience is inappropriate; calling the motives of authority figures into question; and informing the general public of the findings of social psychological research on this topic.

SUMMARY *and* REVIEW

- **Social influence**—the many ways in which people produce changes in others—in their behavior, attitudes, or beliefs—is a common part of life. Most people behave in accordance with **social norms** most of the time; in other words, they show strong tendencies toward **conformity.** Conformity was first systematically studied by Solomon Asch, whose classic research indicated that many people will yield to social pressure from a unanimous group. Many factors determine whether, and to what extent, conformity occurs. These include **cohesiveness**—the degree of attraction felt by an individual toward some group, group size, and type of social norm operating in that situation—**descriptive** or **injunctive.** Norms tend to influence our behavior primarily when they are relevant to us.

- Two important motives underlie our tendency to conform: the desire to be liked by others and the desire to be right or accurate. These two motives are reflected in two distinct types of social influence, *normative* and *informational.*

- Emotional contagion occurs when one or more people are influenced by the emotions of one or more others. Such contagion can lead to similarity or opposite emotional reactions on the part of the people involved, depending on, for instance, the extent to which we feel similar to them.

- Several factors encourage *nonconformity*—refusing to "go along" with the group, These include the desire to attract a desirable mate, which may encourage men to demonstrate nonconformity, power, and the desire to be unique (which are consistent with the male gender stereotype). The effects of social influence are powerful and pervasive, but tend to be magnified in situations where we are uncertain about our own judgments of what is correct. Pressures to conform often produce harmful effects and cause even good people to perform bad actions. This was dramatically illustrated by Zimbardo's famous prison study.

- When we see others showing various emotions, we often experience the same feelings ourselves—an effect known as **emotional contagion.** However, if they are dissimilar to ourselves in important ways, we may experience counter-contagion—emotions opposite to theirs, for instance, sorrow in response to their joy.

- Gender differences in conformity are much smaller than was once assumed, and appear to exist only in very special circumstances. Under some conditions, minorities can induce even large majorities to change their attitudes or behavior.

- Individuals use many different tactics for gaining **compliance**—getting others to say yes to various requests. Many of these rest on basic principles well known to social psychologists. Two widely used tactics, the **foot-in-the-door** and the **lowball procedure,** rest on the principle of commitment/consistency. In contrast, the **door-in-the-face** and **that's-not-all** techniques rest on the principle of reciprocity. Research findings indicate that the door-in-the-face technique works on the Internet as well as in face-to-face situations. **Playing hard to get** and the **deadline technique** are based on the principle of scarcity—what is scarce or hard to obtain is valuable. Internet dating works well for some people, but there are confidence artists out there waiting to entrap unwary people seeking romance through the use of social influence tactics. For that reason, it's important to be very cautious with respect to such relationships.

- Other people can influence us even when they are not present through our mental representations of them and our relationship with them. This is known as **symbolic social influence**. Such influence often involves goals relevant to our relationships with them, or goals with which these people themselves are associated.

- To the extent that others are psychologically present in our thoughts, goals we seek in our relationships with them or goals these people themselves seek or want us to attain can be stimulated, and these, in turn, can strongly affect our behavior.

- **Obedience** is a form of social influence in which one person orders one or more others to do something, and they do so. It is, in a sense, the most direct form of social influence. Research by Stanley Milgram indicates that many people readily obey orders from a relatively powerless source of authority, even if these orders require them to harm others. A recent replication of this study reported results very similar to those obtained by Milgram. Such *destructive obedience,* which plays a role in many real-life atrocities, stems from several factors. These include the shifting of responsibility to the authority figure; outward signs of authority that remind many people of the norm "obey those in authority"; a gradual escalation of the scope of the commands given (related to the foot-in-the-door technique); and the rapid pace with which such situations proceed.

- Several factors can help to reduce the occurrence of destructive obedience. These include reminding individuals that they share in the responsibility for any harm produced, reminding them that beyond some point obedience is inappropriate, calling the motives of authority figures into question, and informing the general public of the findings of social psychological research on this topic.

KEY TERMS

autokinetic phenomenon (p. 259)

cohesiveness (p. 260)

compliance (p. 255)

conformity (p. 254)

deadline technique (p. 277)

descriptive norms (p. 261)

door-in-the-face technique (p. 276)

foot-in-the-door technique (p. 275)

informational social influence (p. 262)

injunctive norms (p. 261)

introspection illusion (p. 257)

low-ball procedure (p. 275)

normative focus theory (p. 261)

normative social influence (p. 262)

obedience (p. 255)

playing hard to get (p. 277)

social influence (p. 254)

social norms (p. 255)

symbolic social influence (p. 255)

that's-not-all technique (p. 276)

Prosocial Behavior

Helping Others

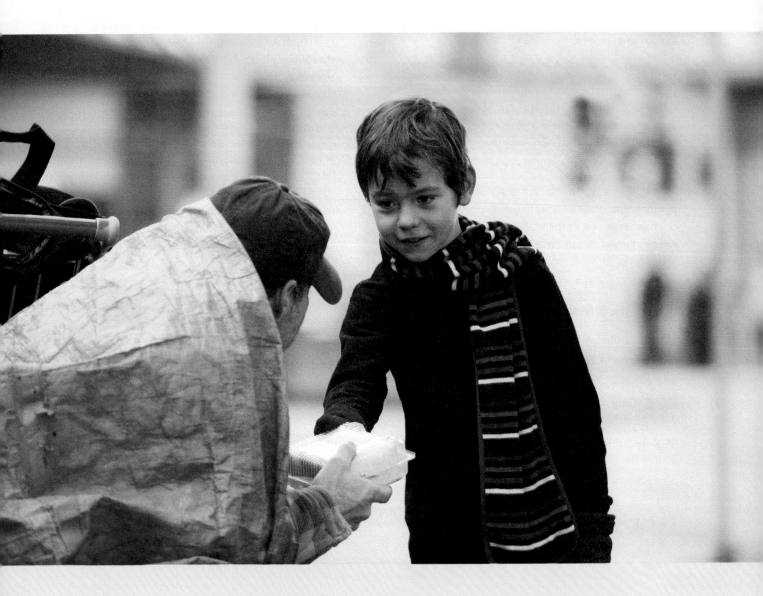

WATCHING THE EVENING NEWS ON TELEVISION OR MERELY reading newspaper headlines can, we believe, lead to serious doubts about human nature and human behavior. The vast majority of the stories presented focus on negative events and trends: war atrocities, crime, cruelty, hatred, natural disasters such as the damage caused by the oil spill in the Gulf of Mexico . . . The topics of the featured stories are very disturbing and seem to lead to the conclusion that the social side of life is both dangerous and mainly negative. In fact, though, this is only a small part of the total picture. For most of us, most of the time, social life is filled with small acts of kindness—ones we perform or ones we receive from others. And in emergency situations, some people, at least, perform actions that help others that are truly heroic. So helping, kindness, generosity, and self-sacrifice are far from rare; in fact, they are as much a part of the social side of life as the darker themes so often emphasized by the media.

Want some examples? Then consider these, which start with small acts of kindness and move, ultimately, to truly courageous efforts to help others:

Donna Delfino Dugay of Harper Woods, Michigan, remembers a day when she was 11 years old and her parents took the family to the beach. Donna's mother brought a picnic lunch and served the food (fried chicken and potato salad). But while serving, her mother noticed a man who was picking his way through a nearby trashcan. Without hesitation, she fixed another plate and carried it to the stranger. Not a word was spoken, but he gladly accepted the food and smiled in thanks. Years later, Donna asked her mother if she remembered the incident, which had a major impact on her. "Not at all," her mother said, because for her, small acts of kindness like this were nothing special.

David Hutmacher of Marietta, Georgia, had been ill and as a result, missed many days of work. When his December 1 paycheck arrived, it was for only a small fraction of the usual amount. He was worried because Christmas was approaching, and he and his wife were barely paying their bills—they had little or nothing left to celebrate the holiday with their two daughters. Two weeks later, however, David received another paycheck. It was for his usual salary *plus* the part of his previous check that had been deducted. When he tried to find out what had happened, he learned that all the other employees had donated their remaining vacation time so that he could get the extra pay. "I cried," says David, "It was truly a good deed."

It was really raining hard in London one day when Fred Parkhurst passed an elderly woman sitting on a bench in the pouring rain. He asked if she was OK, and she replied that she was a little tired and needed to rest for a few minutes. At that point, he asked her if she would hold his umbrella for a little while. He handed it to her and walked away and never returned—happy to help a stranger in this way.

One afternoon, Joe Autrey was standing on a subway platform in New York City when he saw another passenger fall down; he was clearly having an epileptic seizure. The man, 20-year-old Cameron Hollopter, sprawled on the platform, and Autrey rushed over, inserting a pen into his mouth to prevent him from swallowing his tongue. But the incident wasn't over. The young man struggled to his feet but then fell onto the tracks, just as a train was approaching. Autrey didn't hesitate; he jumped onto the tracks and tried to get the man back onto the platform. Confused, Hollopter struggled, and was still resisting as the train rushed toward them. Autrey then did the only thing he could: he wrestled Hollopter into a face-down position and told him: "Don't move or we'll both die!" The train stopped, but not until two cars had passed over them—without harming either one. When the train backed away, all the other passengers cheered Autrey for his heroic actions . . .

Perhaps you've never handed a plate of food to a hungry person on the beach, given your umbrella to an elderly woman sitting unprotected in the rain, or rescued someone from subway tracks. We're certain, though, that you *have* helped others in various ways, and been helped by them, in turn, when you needed assistance (see Figure 9.1). In fact, **prosocial behavior**—actions by individuals that help others (often, with no immediate benefit to the helper)—are a very common part of social life. We want to emphasize that fact right at the start because such kind, helpful actions are definitely an important part of social life. The fact that they are, however, raises an intriguing question: Why,

prosocial behavior
Actions by individuals that help others with no immediate benefit to the helper.

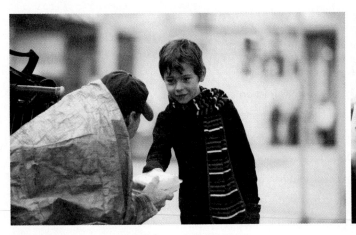 

FIGURE 9.1   Prosocial Behavior: An Important Part of Social Life
Although the media tend to emphasize stories about the negative side of social life (crime, violence, prejudice, etc.), the positive side—prosocial behavior—*should not be overlooked. On the contrary, it is an important aspect of our daily lives.*

precisely, do people help others frequently when they are not required to do so, and often at considerable cost to themselves? What are the motives behind such behavior? And when do people help or fail to help? In other words, what factors influence this very positive side of social life?

We examine all of these questions, plus several others, in the present chapter. Specifically, our discussion of prosocial behavior will proceed as follows. First, we examine the basic motives behind helpful actions—why, in short, people perform them, often at considerable cost to themselves. Second, we consider helping in emergencies—why people sometimes engage in heroic acts like the ones described above or, more disturbingly, why they *don't*. Third, we describe situational factors that influence helping, focusing both on factors that increase the tendency to help others and ones that block or reduce our helpful tendencies. Finally, we examine the effects of helping others both on the recipients and on the helpers.

Why People Help: Motives for Prosocial Behavior

Why do people help others? That's a very basic question in efforts to understand the nature of prosocial behavior. As we'll soon see, many factors play a role in determining whether, and to what extent, specific people engage in such actions. Several aspects of the situation are important, and a number of personal (i.e., dispositional) factors are also influential. We focus on these factors in later discussions. Here, though, we focus on the basic question, What motives underlie the tendency to help others? Several seem to play an important role.

Empathy-Altruism: It Feels Good to Help Others

One explanation of prosocial behavior involves **empathy**—the capacity to be able to experience others' emotional states, feel sympathetic toward them, and take their perspective (e.g., Eisenberg, 2000; Hodges, Kiel, Kramer, Veach, & Villaneuva, 2010). In other words, we help others because we experience any unpleasant feelings they are experiencing vicariously, and want to help bring their negative feelings to an end. This is unselfish because it leads us to offer help for no extrinsic reason, but it is also selfish, in one sense, since the behavior of assisting others helps us, too: it can make us feel better. Reflecting these basic observations, Batson, Duncan, Ackerman, Buckley, and Birch (1981) offered the **empathy-altruism hypothesis,** which suggests that at least some prosocial acts are motivated solely by the desire to help someone in need (Batson & Oleson, 1991). Such motivation can be sufficiently strong that the helper is willing to engage in unpleasant, dangerous, and even life-threatening activities (Batson & Batson et al., 1995). Compassion for other people outweighs all other considerations (Batson, Klein, Highberger, & Shaw, 1995; Goetz, Keltner, & Simon-Thomas, 2010).

In fact, research findings indicate that empathy consists of three distinct components: an emotional aspect (*emotional empathy*, which involves sharing the feelings and emotions of others), a cognitive component, which involves perceiving others' thoughts and feelings accurately (*empathic accuracy*), and a third aspect, known as *empathic concern*, which involves feelings of concern for another's well-being (e.g., Gleason, Jensen-Campbell, & Ickes, 2009). This distinction is important because it appears that the three components are related to different aspects of prosocial behavior, and have different long-term effects. For instance, consider the effects of empathic accuracy. This appears to play a key role in social adjustment—the extent to which we get along well with others.

empathy
Emotional reactions that are focused on or oriented toward other people and include feelings of compassion, sympathy, and concern.

empathy-altruism hypothesis
The suggestion that some prosocial acts are motivated solely by the desire to help someone in need.

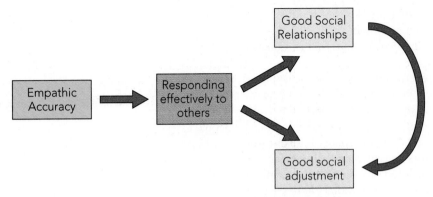

FIGURE 9.2   Empathic Accuracy: An Important Aspect in Social Adjustment

Recent research indicates that empathic accuracy—the ability to accurately understand others' feelings and thoughts (sometimes termed "everyday mind-reading") plays an important role in social adjustment. Adolescents who are high in this skill have more friends, greater acceptance from their peers, and are victimized less by others than adolescents who are low in this skill. In contrast, those low in empathic accuracy tend to develop problems of social adjustment.   (Source: Based on suggestions by Gleason et al., 2009).

In an informative study on this topic, Gleason and colleagues (2009) hypothesized that the higher adolescents are in empathic accuracy—that is, the better their skill in what has been termed "everyday mind-reading" (accurately understanding what others are thinking and feeling), the better their social adjustment: the more friends they will have, the more they will be liked by their peers, the better the quality of their friendships, and the less they will be victims of bullying or social exclusion. Basically, the researchers reasoned that empathic accuracy would help the students respond appropriately to others; this in turn would lead to better relationships and better adjustment (see Figure 9.2). Empathic accuracy was assessed by showing the participants in the study a videotape in which a student interacted with a teacher. The tape was stopped at specific points, and participants wrote down what they thought the other people were thinking or feeling; accuracy was assessed by comparing their responses to what the people in the tape reported actually thinking and feeling.

Results indicated that the higher students were in empathic accuracy, the better their social adjustment in terms of all the dimensions listed above (number of friends, peer acceptance, etc.). In short, a high level of empathic accuracy—clear understanding of others' feelings and thoughts—contributed strongly to their ability to get along well with others. Of course, we should quickly add that it is possible that people who get along well with others become more empathetic, perhaps as a result of pleasant interactions with lots of other people. We mention this possibility not because we think it is more likely to be accurate, but mainly to remind you that establishing causality is always a difficult and tricky task, even in excellent research like this.

IS EMPATHY DECLINING? AND IF SO, WHY?   Before concluding this discussion, we should mention recent evidence indicating that empathy is declining among U.S. college students (Konrath, O'Brien, & Hsing, 2011). Students at the present time report lower levels of empathy than students in previous decades. The declines are small, but significant for two aspects of empathy: empathic concern (concern for the feelings and well-being of others) and empathic perspective taking (being able to take the perspective of others). Why is empathy declining? As Konrath et al. (2011) note, many factors probably play a role. For instance, increasing exposure to violence in the media and even in schools may tend to reduce important aspects of empathy. Similarly, increased emphasis in schools and other settings on building individual self-esteem may reduce the tendency to focus on others and their needs. Reality television shows, which are viewed by tens of millions of people, tend to emphasize such messages as "winners take all," or "put yourself first and to heck with others . . ." Perhaps most intriguing possibility is that the social media are contributing to this trend toward reduced empathy. Facebook, Twitter, and other social media reduce face-to-face contacts between people, who form "friends" and relationships online rather than in person. This, in turn, can reduce empathic feelings toward others because it is easier to ignore the needs and feelings of others when we "meet" them only as online representations rather than as flesh-and-blood people.

Of course, at present, all of these explanations are simply interesting, but unproven possibilities. Regardless of the precise causes, though, it seems clear that empathy is indeed declining, and that this trend can have important implications for the incidence and scope of all forms of prosocial behavior.

Negative-State Relief: Helping Sometimes Reduces Unpleasant Feelings

Another possible motive for helping others is, in a sense, the mirror image of empathy: Instead of helping because we care about the welfare of another person (empathic concern), understand their feelings (empathic accuracy), and share them (emotional empathy), we help because such actions allow us to reduce our own negative emotions. In other words, we do a good thing in order to stop feeling bad. The knowledge that others are suffering, or more generally, witnessing those in need can be distressing. To decrease this distress in ourselves, we help others.

This explanation of prosocial behavior is known as the **negative-state relief model** (Cialdini, Baumann, & Kenrick, 1981). Research indicates that it doesn't matter whether the bystander's negative emotions were aroused by something unrelated to the emergency or by the emergency itself. That is, you could be upset about receiving a bad grade or about seeing that a stranger has been injured. In either instance, you engage in a prosocial act primarily as a way to improve your own negative mood (Dietrich & Berkowitz, 1997; Fultz, Shaller, & Cialdini, 1988). In this kind of situation, unhappiness leads to prosocial behavior, and empathy is not a necessary component (Cialdini et al., 1987).

Empathic Joy: Helping as an Accomplishment

It is generally true that it feels good to have a positive effect on other people. This fact is reflected in the **empathic joy hypothesis** (Smith, Keating, & Stotland, 1989), which suggests that helpers enjoy the positive reactions shown by others whom they help. For instance, do you recall how good it felt seeing someone you care about smile and show pleasure when you gave them a gift? That is an example of empathic joy.

An important implication of this idea is that it is crucial for the person who helps to know that his or her actions had a positive impact on the victim. If helping were based entirely on emotional empathy or empathic concern, feedback about its effects would be irrelevant since we know that we "did good" and that should be enough. But it would not guarantee the occurrence of empathic joy. To test that prediction, Smith et al. (1989) asked participants to watch a videotape in which a female student said she might drop out of college because she felt isolated and distressed. She was described as either similar to the participant (high empathy) or dissimilar (low empathy). After participants watched the tape, they were given the opportunity to offer helpful advice. Some were told they would receive feedback about the effectiveness of their advice while others were told that they would not be able to learn what the student eventually decided to do. It was found that empathy alone was not enough to produce a prosocial response. Rather, participants were helpful only if there was high empathy and they also received feedback about their action's impact on the victim.

Why Nice People Sometimes Finish First: Competitive Altruism

The three theoretical models described so far (summarized in Figure 9.3) suggest that the affective state (feelings) of the person engaging in a prosocial act is a crucial element. All three formulations rest on the assumption that people engage in helpful behavior either because they want to reduce others' negative feelings or because doing so helps *them* feel better—it counters negative moods or feelings. This general idea is carried one step further by another perspective on prosocial behavior—the *competitive*

negative-state relief model
The proposal that prosocial behavior is motivated by the bystander's desire to reduce his or her own uncomfortable negative emotions or feelings.

empathic joy hypothesis
The view that helpers respond to the needs of a victim because they want to accomplish something, and doing so is rewarding in and of itself.

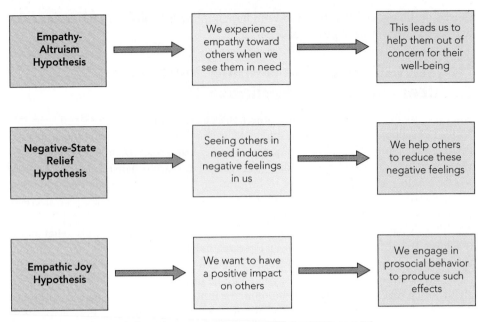

FIGURE 9.3   The Origins of Prosocial Behavior: Three Different Views

What are the origins of prosocial behavior—actions that help others? The views summarized here are among the varied explanations offered by social psychologists.

altruism approach. This view suggests that one important reason why people help others is that doing so boosts their own status and reputation and, in this way, ultimately brings them large benefits, ones that more than offset the costs of engaging in prosocial actions.

FIGURE 9.4   Why Alums Sometimes Make Huge Gifts to Their Colleges: Competitive Altruism in Action

According to the competitive altruism theory, people sometimes engage in prosocial behavior because doing so provides them with large gains in status. This kind of outcome is visible on many university campuses, where buildings or entire schools are named after persons who make large donations. T. Boone Pickens (shown here in the center), is a graduate of Oklahoma State University, and recently donated $100,000,000 to the university. But please note: We don't mean to imply that this was his only or primary reason for making such a large donation. In fact, we're sure it derived largely from his deep commitment to Oklahoma State University and his personal kindness.

Why might helping others confer status? Because often, helping others is costly, and this suggests to other people that the individuals engaging in such behavior have desirable personal qualities; they are definitely the kind of people a group—or society—wants to have around. For the people who engage in prosocial actions, the gains too may be substantial. High status confers many advantages, and people who engage in prosocial behavior may be well compensated for their kind and considerate actions. For instance, as you probably know, many people who donate large amounts of money to universities are treated like stars when they visit their alma mater, and they may have entire buildings named after them—as is true at the university where one of us works (see Figure 9.4). Research findings confirm that the motive to experience a boost in social status does lie behind many acts of prosocial behavior—especially ones that bring public recognition (e.g., Flynn, Reagans, Amanatullah, & Ames, 2006). So, overall, this appears to be an important motive for helping others.

Kin Selection Theory: Helping Ourselves by Helping People Who Share Our Genes

A very different approach to understanding prosocial behavior is offered by the **kin selection theory** (Cialdini, Brown, Lewis, Luce, & Neuberg, 1997; Pinker, 1998). From an evolutionary perspective, a key goal for all organisms—including us—is getting our genes into the next generation. Support for this general prediction has been obtained in many studies, suggesting that, in general, we are more likely to help others to whom we are closely related than people to whom we are not related (e.g., Neyer & Lang, 2003). For example, Burnstein, Crandall, and Kitayama (1994) conducted a series of studies in which participants were asked whom they would choose to help in an emergency. As predicted on the basis of genetic similarity, participants were more likely to say they would help a close relative than either a distant relative or a nonrelative. Furthermore, and also consistent with kin selection theory, they were more likely to help young relatives, who have many years of reproductive life ahead of them, than older ones. For example, given a choice between a female relative young enough to reproduce and a female relative past menopause, help would go to the younger individual.

Overall, then, there is considerable support for kin selection theory. There is one basic problem, though, that you may already have noticed: we don't just help biological relatives; instead, often we *do* help people who are unrelated to us. Why do we do so? According to kin selection theory, this would not be useful or adaptive behavior since it would not help us transmit our genes to future generations. One answer is provided by *reciprocal altruism theory*—a view suggesting that we may be willing to help people unrelated to us because helping is usually reciprocated: If we help them, they help us, so we do ultimately benefit, and our chances of survival could then be indirectly increased (e.g., Korsgaard, Meglino, Lester, & Jeong, 2010).

Defensive Helping: Helping Outgroups to Reduce Their Threat to One's Ingroup

As we saw in our discussion of prejudice (Chapter 6), people often divide the social world into two categories: their own *ingroup* and *outgroups*. Furthermore, they often perceive their own group as distinctive from other groups, and as superior in several ways. Sometimes, however, outgroups achieve successes that threaten the supposed superiority of one's own group. Can that provide a motive for helping? Recent research suggests that it can because one way of removing the threat posed by outgroups is to help them—especially in ways that make them seem dependent on such help, and therefore as incompetent or inadequate (e.g., Sturmer & Snyder, 2010). In other words, sometimes people help others—especially people who do not belong to their own ingroup—as a means of defusing status threats from these people. Such actions are known as **defensive helping** because they are performed not primarily to help the recipients, but rather to "put them down" in subtle ways and so reduce their threat to the ingroup's status. In such cases, helping does not stem from empathy, positive reactions to the joy or happiness it induces among recipients, but, rather, from a more selfish motive: protecting the distinctiveness and status of one's own group.

Evidence for precisely such effects has been reported by Nadler, Harpaz-Gorodeisky, and Ben-David (2009). They told students at one school that students at another school scored either substantially higher than students at their own school on a test of cognitive abilities (this posed a high threat to the superiority of their own group), while students at a third school scored about the same as students at their school (this was low threat to their own group's superiority). When given a chance to help students at these two schools, participants offered more help to the high-threat school, presumably as a way of reducing the status threat from this rival institution.

kin selection theory
A theory suggesting that a key goal for all organisms—including human beings—is getting our genes into the next generation; one way in which individuals can reach this goal is by helping others who share their genes.

defensive helping
Help given to members of outgroups to reduce the threat they pose to the status or distinctiveness of one's own ingroup.

Findings such as these emphasize the fact that helping others can stem from many different motives. Like many forms of social behavior, then, prosocial actions are complex not only in the forms they take and the factors that affect them, but with respect to the underlying motives from which they spring. Whatever the precise causes of such behavior, though, it is clear that helping is an important and fairly common part of the social side of life—one with many beneficial effects both for helpers and those who receive assistance.

KEYPOINTS

- Several different motives may underlie prosocial behavior. The **empathy-altruism hypothesis** proposes that, because of empathy, we help those in need because we experience empathic concern for them.

- Empathy actually consists of three distinct components—emotional empathy, empathic accuracy, and empathic concern. All three components can serve as a basis for helping others.

- The **negative-state relief model** proposes that people help other people in order to relieve and make less negative their own emotional discomfort.

- The **empathic joy hypothesis** suggests that helping stems from the positive reactions recipients show when

they receive help (e.g., gifts), and the positive feelings this, in turn, induces in helpers.

- The *competitive altruism theory* suggests that we help others as a means of increasing our own status and reputation—and so benefit from helping in important ways.

- **Kinship selection theory** suggests that we help others who are related to us because this increases the likelihood that our genes will be transmitted to future generations.

- Another motive for helping behavior is that of reducing the threat posed by outgroups to one's own ingroup, known as **defensive helping.**

Responding to an Emergency: Will Bystanders Help?

When an emergency arises, people often rush forward to provide help—as was true in the subway incident described at the start of this chapter. But we also often learn of situations in which witnesses to an emergency stand around and do nothing; they take no action while victims suffer or perhaps even die. What can explain such dramatic differences in people's behavior? Let's see what social psychologists have discovered about this important question.

Helping in Emergencies: Apathy—or Action?

Consider the following situation. You are walking across an icy street, lose your footing as you step up on the curb, and fall, injuring your knee. Because of your pain and the slickness of the ice, you find that you can't get back on your feet. Suppose (1) the block is relatively deserted, and only one person is close enough to witness your accident or (2) the block is crowded, and a dozen people can see what happened. Common sense suggests that the more bystanders that are present, the more likely you are to be helped. In the first situation, you are forced to depend on the assistance of just one individual and that person's decision to help or not help you. In the second situation, with 12 witnesses, there would seem to be a much greater chance that at least one of them (and quite possibly more) will be motivated to behave in a prosocial way. So, is there really safety in numbers? The more witnesses present at an emergency, the more likely the victims are to receive help? Reasonable as this may sound, research by social psychologists suggests that it may be wrong—dead wrong!

The reasons why it may be incorrect were first suggested by John Darley and Bibb Latané, two social psychologists who thought long and hard about this issue after learning of a famous murder in New York City. In this tragic crime, a young woman (Kitty Genovese) was assaulted by a man in a location where many people could see and hear what was going on; all they had to do was look out of their apartment windows. Yet, despite the fact that the attacker continued to assault the victim for many minutes, and even left and then returned to continue the assault later, *not a single person reported the crime to the police.* When news of this tragic crime hit the media, there was much speculation about the widespread selfishness and indifference of people in general or, at least, of people living in big cities. Darley and Latané, however, raised a more basic question: Common sense suggests that the greater the number of witnesses to an emergency (or in this case, a crime), the more likely it is that someone will help. So why wasn't this the case in the tragic murder of Kitty Genovese? In their efforts to answer this question, Darley and Latané developed several possible explanations and then tested them in research that is certainly a true "classic" of social psychology. Their ideas—and the research it generated—have had a lasting impact on the field. Let's take a closer look at this work.

Is There Safety in Numbers? Sometimes, But Not Always

In their attempts to understand why no one came to Kitty Genovese's aid—or even phoned the police—Darley and Latané considered many possible explanations. The one that seemed to them to be most promising, however, was very straightforward: Perhaps no one helped because *all the witnesses assumed that someone else would do it!* In other words, all the people who saw or heard what was happening believed that it was OK for them to do nothing because others would take care of the situation. Darley and Latané referred to this as **diffusion of responsibility,** and suggested that according to this principle, the greater the number of strangers who witness an emergency, the less likely are the victims to receive help. After all, the greater the number of potential helpers, the less responsible any one individual will feel, and the more each will assume that "someone else will do it." We should add, however, that if the person needing help appears to be a member of one's own ingroup, they are more likely to get help (Levine, Prosser, Evans, & Reicher, 2005).

To test this reasoning, they performed an ingenious but disturbing experiment in which male college students were exposed to an apparent—but fictitious—emergency. During an experiment, a fellow student apparently had a seizure, began to choke, and was clearly in need of help. The participants interacted by means of an intercom, and it was arranged that some believed they were the only person aware of the emergency, one of two bystanders, or one of five bystanders. Helpfulness was measured in terms of (1) the percentage of participants in each experimental group who attempted to help and (2) the time that passed before the help began.

Darley and Latané's predictions about diffusion of responsibility were correct. The more bystanders participants believed were present, the lower the percentage who made a prosocial response (offered help to the apparent victim; see Figure 9.5) and the longer they waited before responding. Applying this to the example of a fall on the ice described earlier, you would be more likely to be helped if you fell with only one witness present than if 12 witnesses were present.

Over the years, additional research on prosocial behavior has identified a great many other factors that determine how people respond to an

diffusion of responsibility
A principle suggesting that the greater the number of witnesses to an emergency the less likely victims are to receive help. This is because each bystander assumes that someone else will do it.

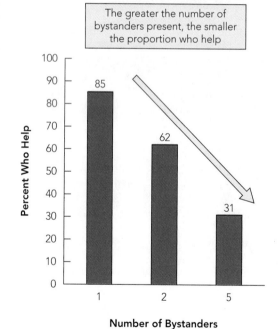

FIGURE 9.5 **Diffusion of Responsibility and Helping in Emergncies**
The greater the number of witnesses to a staged emergency, the less likely they were to help the apparent victim. This illustrates the powerful inhibiting effect of diffusion of responsibility in such situations. (Source: Based on data from Darley & Latané, 1968).

FIGURE 9.6 When Bystanders Do React to an Emergency: United Flight 93

Passengers on United Airlines Flight 93 took action in an emergency: they overpowered the four hijackers who tried to seize the plane and crash it into a public building in Washington. Instead, it crashed in a rural area of Pennsylvania, killing all on board. The passengers who took action in this emergency are viewed as heroes and heroines by people all over the world.

emergency. For instance, Kuntsman and Plant (2009) suggests that race of the victim and the helper may play a role, with black victims less likely to receive help from white bystanders, especially if they are high in *aversive racism* (negative emotional reactions to black people). We discuss evidence concerning the reasons why people don't help in a later section, but it is important to note at this point that group membership of the potential helpers and the person in need can play a critical role in whether helping is received. Overall, however, the bystander effect is clearly an important basic discovery concerning the social side of life with respect to helping between strangers, and one that common sense would not have predicted.

Understanding the Bystander Effect: Five Crucial Steps in Deciding to Help—or Not

As the study of prosocial behavior expanded beyond the initial concern with the number of bystanders, Latané and Darley (1970) proposed that the likelihood of a person engaging in prosocial actions is determined by a series of decisions that must be made quickly in the context of emergency situations. Indeed, such decisions must be made quickly, or, in many cases, it will be too late! (Recall how quickly Joe Autrey decided to try to pull a stranger who had fallen onto subway tracks to safety, and how quickly he decided to make him lie flat when it was clear that they could not get out before a train arrived.)

Any one of us can sit in a comfortable chair and figure out instantly what bystanders should do. The witnesses to the assault on Kitty Genovese should either have called the police immediately or perhaps even intervened directly by shouting at the attacker or attempting to stop the attack. Indeed, on September 11, 2001, the passengers on one of the hijacked planes apparently responded jointly, thus preventing the terrorists from accomplishing their goal of crashing into the U.S. Capitol (see Figure 9.6). Why did they do so? Perhaps, as Levine and colleagues (2005) note, because they could see each other and interact directly. In contrast, when bystanders fail to help in emergency situations, as in the ones used by Darley and Latané, they can't interact directly, and this seems to be an important basis for their failure to act.

In a similar manner, the students in the laboratory experiment conducted by Darley and Latané (1968) should have rushed out of the cubicle to help their fellow student who was, apparently, having a medical emergency. Why didn't they do so? One answer is that when we are suddenly and unexpectedly faced with an emergency, the situation is often complex and hard to interpret. Before acting, we must first figure out what, if anything, is going on, and what we should do about it. This requires a series of decisions, and at each step—and for each decision—many factors determine the likelihood that we will fail to help. Here's a summary of the decisions involved, and the factors that play a role in each one.

1. *Noticing, or failing to notice, that something unusual is happening.* An emergency is obviously something that occurs unexpectedly, and there is no sure way to anticipate that it will take place or to plan how best to respond. We are ordinarily doing something else and thinking about other things when we hear a scream outside our window, observe that a fellow student is coughing and unable to speak, or observe that some of the other passengers on our airplane are holding weapons in their hands. If we are asleep, deep in thought, concentrating on something else, we may simply fail to notice that something unusual is happening. The passengers on Flight 93 saw the weapons of the hijackers and learned from the captain that the plane was being taken over by these people. In addition, they used their cell phones to learn of the other attacks (e.g., on the World Trade Center), so they knew that something very terrible was occurring, and this made it easier for them to take action.

2. *Correctly interpreting an event as an emergency.* Even after we pay attention to an event, we often have only limited and incomplete information as to what exactly is happening. Most of the time, whatever catches our attention does not turn out to be an emergency and so does not require immediate action. Whenever potential helpers are not completely sure about what is going on, they tend to hold back and wait for further information. After all, responding as if an emergency is occurring when one is not can lead to considerable embarrassment. It's quite possible that in the early morning when Kitty Genovese was murdered, her neighbors could not clearly see what was happening, even though they heard the screams and knew that a man and a woman were having a dispute. It could have just been a loud argument between a woman and her boyfriend. Or perhaps the couple were just joking with each other. Either of these two possibilities is actually more likely to be true than the fact that a stranger was stabbing a woman to death. With ambiguous information as to whether one is witnessing a serious problem or something trivial, most people are inclined to accept the latter, and take no action (Wilson & Petruska, 1984).

This suggests that the presence of multiple witnesses may inhibit helping not only because of the diffusion of responsibility, but also because it is embarrassing to misinterpret a situation and to act inappropriately. Making such a serious mistake in front of several strangers might lead them to think you are overreacting in a stupid way. And when people are uncertain about what's happening they tend to hold back and do nothing.

This tendency for an individual surrounded by a group of strangers to hesitate and do nothing is based on what is known as **pluralistic ignorance.** Because none of the bystanders knows for sure what is happening, each depends on the others to provide cues. Each individual is less likely to respond if the others fail to respond. Latané and Darley (1968) provided a dramatic demonstration of just how far people will go to avoid making a possibly ridiculous response to what may or may not be an emergency. They placed students in a room alone or with two other students and asked them to fill out questionnaires. After several minutes had passed, the experimenters secretly and quietly pumped smoke into the research room through a vent. When a participant was working there alone, most (75 percent) stopped what they were doing when the smoke appeared and left the room to report the problem. When three people were in the room, however, only 38 percent reacted to the smoke. Even after it became so thick that it was difficult to see, 62 percent continued to work on the questionnaire and failed to make any response to the smoke-filled room. The presence of other people clearly inhibits responsiveness. It is as if risking death is preferable to making a fool of oneself.

This inhibiting effect is much less if the group consists of friends rather than strangers, because friends are likely to communicate with one another about what is going on (Rutkowski, Gruder, & Romer, 1983). The same is true of people in small towns who are likely to know one another as opposed to big cities where most people are strangers (Levine, Martinez, Brase, & Sorenson, 1994). Also, and not surprisingly, any anxiety about the reactions of others and thus the fear of doing the wrong thing is reduced by alcohol. As a result, people who have been drinking show an increased tendency to be helpful (Steele, Critchlow, & Liu, 1988)—another finding that is, perhaps, counterintuitive. But of course, they sometimes show other changes in behavior that are not so beneficial!

3. *Deciding that it is your responsibility to provide help.* In many instances, the responsibility for helping is clear. Firefighters are the ones to do something about a blazing building, police officers take charge when cars collide, and medical personnel deal with injuries and illnesses (see Figure 9.7). If responsibility is not clear, people assume that anyone in a leadership role must take responsibility—for instance, adults with children, professors with students. As we have pointed out earlier, when there is only one bystander, he or she usually takes charge because there is no alternative.

pluralistic ignorance
Refers to the fact that because none of the bystanders respond to an emergency, no one knows for sure what is happening and each depends on the others to interpret the situation.

FIGURE 9.7 **Whose Responsibility Is It to Help?**

When people feel responsible for helping in an emergency, they often spring into action—like the lifeguards shown here. If responsibility for helping is less clear, however, bystanders are uncertain what to do—and often do nothing.

4. *Deciding that you have the knowledge and/or skills to act.* Even if a bystander progresses as far as Step 3 and assumes responsibility, a prosocial response cannot occur unless the person knows *how* to be helpful. Some emergencies are sufficiently simple that almost everyone has the necessary skills to help. If someone slips on the ice, most bystanders are able to help that person get up. On the other hand, if you see someone parked on the side of the road, peering under the hood of the car, you can't be of direct help unless you know something about cars and how they function. The best you can do is offer to call for assistance.

When emergencies require special skills, usually only a portion of the bystanders are able to help. For example, only good swimmers can assist a person who is drowning. With a medical emergency, a registered nurse is more likely to be helpful than a history professor (Cramer, McMaster, Bartell, & Pragma, 1988).

5. *Making the final decision to provide help.* Even if a bystander passes the first four steps in the decision process, help does not occur unless he or she makes the ultimate decision to engage in a helpful act. Helping at this final point can be inhibited by fears (often realistic ones) about potential negative consequences. In effect, potential helpers engage in "cognitive algebra" as they weigh the positive versus the negative aspects of helping (Fritzsche, Finkelstein, & Penner, 2000). As we note in a later discussion, the rewards for being helpful are primarily provided by the emotions and beliefs of the helper, but there are a great many varieties of potential costs. For example, if you intervened in the Kitty Genovese attack, you might be stabbed yourself. You might slip while helping a person who has fallen on the ice. A person might be asking for assistance simply as a trick leading to robbery or worse (Byrne, 2001).

In sum, deciding to help in an emergency situation is not a simple, one-time decision. Rather, it involves a number of steps or decisions and only if all of these decisions are positive does actual helping occur. (Figure 9.8 summarizes these steps.)

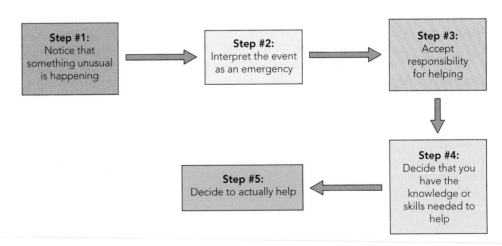

FIGURE 9.8 **Five Steps on the Path to Helping in Emergencies**

As shown here, deciding to actually offer help to the victims of emergencies depends on five steps. Only if these steps or decisions are positive does actual helping occur. *(Based on suggestions by Latané and Darley, 1970).*

KEYPOINTS

- When an emergency arises and someone is in need of help, a bystander may or may not respond in a prosocial way—responses can range from apathy (and doing nothing) to heroism.

- In part because of **diffusion of responsibility,** the more bystanders present as witnesses to an emergency, the less likely each of them is to provide help and the greater the delay before help occurs (the *bystander effect*).

- This is true for helping between strangers, but is less likely to occur for helping among people who belong to the same groups.

- When faced with an emergency, a bystander's tendency to help or not help depends in part on decisions made at five crucial steps. First, it is necessary for the bystander to pay attention and be aware that an unusual event is occurring.

- Second, the bystander must correctly interpret the situation as an emergency.

- Third, the bystander must assume responsibility to provide help.

- Fourth, the bystander must have the required knowledge and skills to be able to act.

- In a final step, the bystander must decide to take action.

Factors That Increase or Decrease the Tendency to Help

As we noted earlier, interest in prosocial behavior by social psychologists was first inspired by the question, Why do bystanders at an emergency sometimes help and sometimes fail to do anything? We have already considered one important factor to emerge from research on this question: the number of bystanders present. Here, we examine additional aspects of the situation that influence the tendency to help others. Then, we turn to a number of internal factors (e.g., emotions, personal characteristics) that also influence such behavior.

Situational (External) Factors Influence Helping: Similarity and Responsibility

Are all victims equally likely to receive help? Or are some more likely to get assistance than others? And is the tendency to help others affected by social influence—for instance, by the actions of others who might also help? Research by social psychologists offers intriguing insights into these and related questions.

HELPING PEOPLE WE LIKE   Most of the research we now discuss has focused on providing help to *strangers* because it is obvious that most people are very likely to help family members and friends when they need assistance. But the situation is less clear-cut when strangers are involved. Suppose, for instance, that you observe what seems to be an emergency, and the victim is a stranger. If this person is similar to you with respect to age, nationality, or some other factor, are you more likely to help than you would be if the victim were very different from yourself—for instance, much older, a member of a group different from your own? The answer provided by careful research is yes—we are indeed more likely to help people who are similar to ourselves than people who are dissimilar (Hayden, Jackson, & Guydish, 1984; Shaw, Borough, & Pink, 1994). Why?

Research by Hodges and colleagues (2010) suggests that part of the answer may involve the fact that similarity to others increases our empathic concern for them, and our understanding of what they are experiencing. This research compared three groups: new mothers, women who were pregnant, and women who had never been pregnant. All three groups watched videotapes showing new mothers, in which they described their experiences in this role. The participants then completed measures of empathic concern (e.g., how moved they felt in response to seeing the video), a measure of empathic accuracy, and their self-reported ability to understand the person shown in the video. It was reasoned that new mothers would be most similar to the woman shown in the tape, pregnant women would be less similar, and those who had never been pregnant would be least similar to the new mothers. If similarity increases empathy generally, then the three groups (new mothers, pregnant women, women who had never been pregnant) should differ on all three measures. However, if similarity influences some aspects of empathy more than others, they might differ only on some components. That's precisely what was found. Similarity to the person in the tape influenced empathic concern, but did *not* significantly influence empathic accuracy (see Figure 9.9). So although similarity is an important factor influencing empathy, it seems to primarily influence the emotional component of empathy, not the cognitive component (i.e., empathic accuracy).

HELPING THOSE WHO ARE NOT RESPONSIBLE FOR THEIR PROBLEM

If you were walking down the sidewalk early one morning and passed a man lying unconscious by the curb, would you help him? You know that helpfulness would be influenced by all of the factors we have discussed—from the presence of other bystanders to interpersonal attraction. But there is an additional consideration, too. Why is the man lying there? If his clothing is stained and torn and an empty wine bottle in a paper sack is by his side, what would you assume about his problem? You might well decide that he is a hopeless drunk who passed out on the sidewalk. In contrast, what if he is wearing an expensive suit and has a nasty cut on his forehead? These cues might lead you to decide that this man had been brutally mugged on his way to work.

Based on your attributions about the reasons for a man lying unconscious on the sidewalk, you would be less likely to help the victim with the wine bottle than the one with the cut on his head. In general, we are less likely to act if we believe that the victim is to blame (Higgins & Shaw, 1999; Weiner, 1980). The man in the business suit did not choose to be attacked, so we are more inclined to help him.

Exposure to Live Prosocial Models

In an emergency, we know that the presence of bystanders who fail to respond inhibits helpfulness. It is equally true, however, that the presence of a helpful bystander provides a strong *social model*, and the result is an increase in helping behavior among the remaining bystanders. An example of such modeling is provided by a field experiment in which a young woman (a research assistant) with a flat tire parked her car just off the road. Motorists were much more inclined to stop and help this woman if they had previously driven past a staged scene in which another woman with car trouble was observed receiving assistance (Bryan & Test, 1967). Even the symbolic presence of one or more helping models can increase prosocial behavior. Have you ever visited a museum and then, on the way out, passed by a large glass case asking for donations? Often, the museums will place money in the case (including a few bills of large denominations—$10s or $20s)—in an effort to increase donations. And the tactic works: many people passing the case think "Others

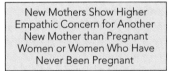

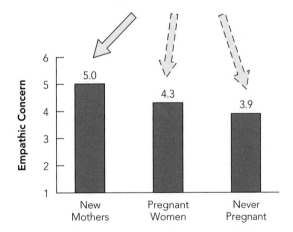

FIGURE 9.9   Similarity, Empathy, and Helping
Research findings indicate that similarity to others increases the tendency to help by increasing empathic concern. It does not increase empathic accuracy, however. (Source: Based on data from Hodges et al., 2010).

have donated, so perhaps I should too" and then they actually reach into their pockets or purses for a donation.

Playing Prosocial Video Games

That exposure to other people, either "in the flesh" or symbolically, who behave in a helpful manner increases helping is not surprising. As we saw in Chapter 8, we are often strongly influenced by the actions of others, especially when we are uncertain about what is the best or most appropriate way to act ourselves. But what about another, and very different, source of exposure to prosocial behavior—video games? Many of these games, as we'll see in Chapter 10, are aggressive in nature—they involve a wide range of assaults against various targets within the games. But some video games, in contrast, involve prosocial actions: characters in the game help and support one another (see Figure 9.10). Does playing such games increase the tendency to engage in similar actions? Several recently proposed theoretical frameworks (e.g., Bushman & Anderson, 2002; Gentile & Gentile, 2008) suggest that there are important reasons why this might be the case. For instance, playing prosocial video games might prime prosocial thoughts and schemas—cognitive frameworks related to helping others. Repeated exposure to such games might, over time, generate attitudes favorable to prosocial actions, emotions consistent with them (e.g., positive feelings associated with helping others), and other lasting changes in the ways in which individuals think that, together, could facilitate prosocial actions.

That such effects actually occur and are both strong and lasting in nature is indicated by a growing body of recent research (e.g., Gentile et al., 2009). For instance, in a

FIGURE 9.10 **Effects of Playing Prosocial Video Games**
Recent research indicates that playing prosocial video games in which characters help and support each other (e.g., Lemmings) can increase the tendency to engage in prosocial actions. Such effects appear to be lasting rather than merely short-term in nature. In contrast, playing aggressive video games (e.g., Crash Twinsanity) tends to reduce prosocial actions and increase aggressive ones (see Chapter 10).

series of studies by Greitmeyer and Osswald (2010), participants played either prosocial (e.g., Lemmings), aggressive (e.g., Lamers), or neutral (Tetris) video games. Then they were exposed to a situation in which they could engage in spontaneous helping: the experimenter spilled a cup of pencils on the floor. As expected, a higher proportion of those who had played the prosocial video games (57 percent) helped pick up the pencils, whereas lower proportions of those who had played the neutral game (33 percent) or the aggressive game (28 percent) helped. In a follow-up study, participants played either prosocial or neutral video games and were again presented with an opportunity to help another person; in this case, though, helping involved intervening when a male assistant harassed a female experimenter. Again, a higher proportion who had played the prosocial video game intervened (56 percent), versus only 22 percent who had played the neutral game. Finally, to obtain evidence on the underlying mechanisms through which prosocial video games increased helping, the researchers conducted another study in which participants indicated what they had been thinking about while playing the video games. As predicted, those who played the prosocial game reported more thoughts about helping others than those who played the neutral game. So, consistent with the theoretical models mentioned above, playing prosocial video games influenced actual helping by influencing participants' thoughts.

Similar, confirming evidence has been reported in other studies (e.g,. Gentile et al, 2009), including a longitudinal study in which the amount of time participants played prosocial video games was related to their helping of others several months later. As expected, the more they played prosocial games, the more likely they were to report engaging in such actions as "helping a person who was in trouble" months later. These findings indicate that playing prosocial video games produces not merely short-term effects, but ones of a more lasting nature.

In sum, video games—which have often been criticized as a waste of time and as having negative effects on the people who play them—appear to be neutral in and of themselves. Depending on their content, they can facilitate either harmful, aggressive actions (see Chapter 10) or beneficial, prosocial ones. Apparently, it is the nature of the games—not the games themselves—that is crucial with respect to the social side of life.

Gratitude: How It Increases Further Helping

Everyone wants to be appreciated, and where helping others is concerned, that often implies that the recipient of the help says "Thank you!" in no uncertain terms. While some people who engage in prosocial behavior prefer to remain anonymous, most want to be thanked for their help publicly and graciously. In fact, as we noted before, some request that schools, hospitals, or buildings be named after them in recognition of their help (in the form of financial gifts). It is far from surprising, therefore, that gratitude—thanks expressed by the recipients of help—has been found to increase subsequent helping. "Thank me," helpers and donors seem to say, "and I'll do it again." Research findings provide strong support for such effects, indicating that when helpers are thanked by the beneficiaries of their assistance, they are more willing to help them again—or even to help other people (McCullough, Kilpatrick, Emmons, & Larson, 2001).

But why, specifically, do expressions of gratitude facilitate further prosocial actions? According to Grant and Gino (2010), two clear possibilities exist. First, being thanked may add to the sense of self-efficacy—helpers feel that they are capable and competent, and have acted effectively (and in good ways). Second, it may add to helpers' feelings of self-worth, their belief that they are valued by others. Which, if either, is more important? Research by Grant and Gino points strongly to the latter: Expressions of gratitude increase helping by increasing helpers' feelings of self-worth. In their research, Grant and Gino asked participants to help another student by suggesting ways in which this person could improve a cover letter being sent with a job application. In one condition, the person helped offered thanks, saying "I just wanted to let you know that I received your feedback on my cover letter. Thanks you so much! I am really grateful." In another condition, he did not express such gratitude, saying merely "I just wanted to let you know that I received your feedback on my cover letter." In both conditions, this person then asked for help with a second cover letter. As expected, a higher proportion of participants who were thanked for their help agreed to help again (55 percent vs. 25 percent). In addition, gratitude increased both self-efficacy and feelings of self-worth, but—and this is crucial—only boosts in self-worth were related to subsequent helping. These findings were repeated in several other studies, including one conducted with volunteer fundraisers for a university. These people were either thanked or not thanked for their help by the manager of the fundraising project, and once again, those thanked showed more helping—they made 50 percent more calls than the people not thanked. Furthermore, this effect of gratitude was, as in the earlier study, mediated by increases in self-worth, but not by increases in self-efficacy.

Overall, then, it appears that gratitude increases helping in a very straightforward way—by making the people who are thanked for their help feel that they are indeed valued by others, especially by the people who benefit from their prosocial actions. Clearly, then, saying thank you is not only the polite and correct thing to do if you receive help from another person—it is also an effective strategy for increasing the likelihood that they will help you again if the need arises (see Figure 9.11).

KEYPOINTS

- We are more likely to help others who are similar to ourselves than others who are dissimilar. This leads to lower tendencies to help people outside our own social groups.

- We are also more likely to help people we like than those we don't like, and those who are not responsible for their current need for help.

- Helping is increased by exposure to prosocial models; it can also be increased by playing prosocial video games.

- Prosocial video games increase subsequent helping by priming prosocial thoughts, building cognitive frameworks related to helping, and related effects.

- Gratitude increases prosocial behavior, primarily by enhancing helpers' feelings of self-worth.

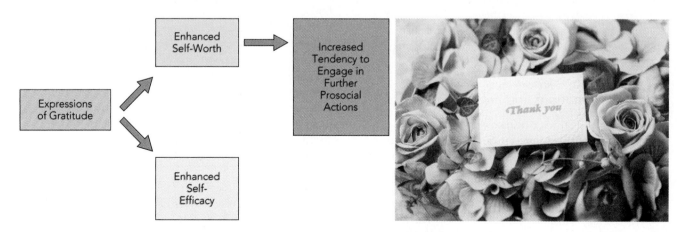

FIGURE 9.11 **Expressions of Gratitude: Why They Increase Prosocial Behavior**
Expressions of gratitude from the recipients of helping have been found to increase helpers' tendencies to assist the same people (or even others) again. Gratitude increases helpers' self-efficacy and feelings of self-worth, but only the latter contribute to increased helping on future occasions. This is one more reason to always say "Thank You!" when you are helped by another person.

EMOTIONS *and* PROSOCIAL BEHAVIOR

Mood, Feelings of Elevation, and Helping

Suppose you want to ask another person for a favor; when would you do this? When he or she is in a very good mood or when she or he is in a very sad or angry mood? The answer is obvious: Most people know that other people—and they themselves—are more likely to engage in prosocial behavior when in a good mood than a bad mood. But research findings indicate that the situation is a bit more complicated than that.

Positive Emotions and Prosocial Behavior

Many ingenious studies have been performed to investigate the potential link between good moods and helping. In general, this research indicates that people are more willing to help a stranger when their mood has been elevated by some recent experience—for instance, listening to a comedian (Wilson, 1981), finding money in the coin return slot of a public telephone (Isen & Levin, 1972), spending time outdoors on a pleasant day (Cunningham, 1979), or receiving a small unexpected gift (Isen, 1970). Even a pleasant fragrance in the air can increase prosocial behavior (e.g., Baron, 1990; Baron & Thomley, 1994)—something department stores know very well. That's why they often pump pleasant smells into the air in various departments in the hope that this will increase purchases by customers.

Under certain specific circumstances, however, a positive mood can *decrease* the probability of responding in a prosocial way (Isen, 1984). Why? Because being in a good mood can lead us to interpret various situations—especially emergencies—as not really serious. And even if it is clear that an emergency exists, people in a good mood sometimes help less than those in a neutral mood if helping involves actions that are difficult (Rosenhan, Salovey, & Hargis, 1981) or will detract from their current good mood.

Negative Emotions and Prosocial Behavior

If positive moods increase helping, do negative moods reduce such behavior? Some research findings offer support for this view (Amato, 1986). As is true of positive emotions, though, specific circumstances can strongly influence or even reverse this general trend. For example, if the act of helping others generates positive feelings, people in a bad mood may actually be more likely to help than those in a neutral or even positive mood because they want to make themselves feel better, and helping others can help them accomplish this goal (Cialdini, Kenrick, & Baumann,

1982). This is consistent with the negative-state relief model described earlier. A negative mood or emotion is most likely to increase prosocial behavior if the negative feelings are not too intense, if the emergency is clear-cut rather than ambiguous, and if the act of helping is interesting and satisfying rather than dull and unrewarding (Cunningham, Shaffer, Barbee, Wolff, & Kelley, 1990).

Feelings of Elevation and Helping Others

When we see another person engaging in a kind or helpful act, this can have a strong effect on our emotions. In particular, it can trigger feelings of *elevation*—it can make us feel inspired, uplifted, and optimistic about human nature (despite what the media often feature in this respect). Does it also increase our tendency to engage in prosocial behavior too? Recent evidence indicates that it does. Schnall, Roper, and Fessler (2010) conducted a series of studies in which participants were exposed either to an elevating video film, showing prosocial actions by others; a neutral video clip (a clip about the ocean); or a videotape showing a funny comedian (mirth condition). The mirth condition was included as a control for the possibility that the effects of seeing other people behave in a prosocial manner merely increase positive affect, and as we noted above, positive moods do often increase helping in and of themselves.

After watching the tapes, participants in the research had an opportunity to act in a prosocial manner. In one study, for instance, they were asked if they would help the experimenter by completing a questionnaire described as boring. The measure of helping was how many minutes participants volunteered. It was predicted that those exposed to a videotape designed to induce feelings of elevation (feelings of being uplifted, inspired, etc.) would volunteer more time, and as you can see in Figure 9.12, this is precisely what happened. In fact, participants who viewed the elevating videotape volunteered about twice as much time as those in the other two conditions. The fact that the mirth condition (exposure to a funny comedian) did not increase helping indicates that feelings of elevation do indeed involve more than merely positive affect. The moral of such research is clear, and fits well with research on the effects of playing prosocial video games. Apparently, the tendency to perform prosocial actions can be increased by exposure to others engaging in such actions. Kindness, in short, is "contagious" and can be encouraged by witnessing it in the actions of others.

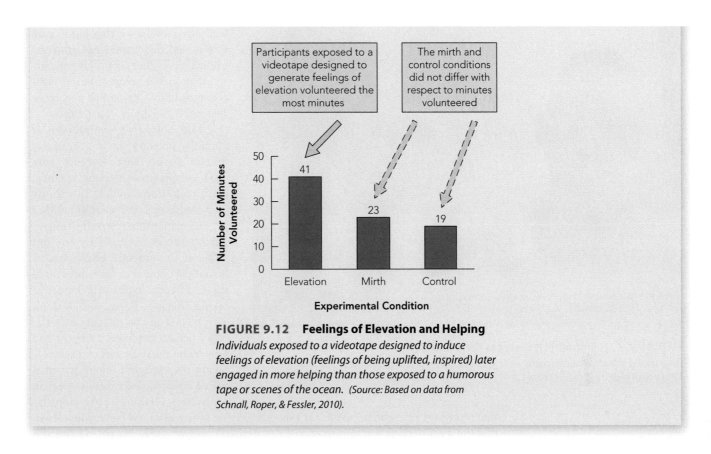

FIGURE 9.12   Feelings of Elevation and Helping

Individuals exposed to a videotape designed to induce feelings of elevation (feelings of being uplifted, inspired) later engaged in more helping than those exposed to a humorous tape or scenes of the ocean. (Source: Based on data from Schnall, Roper, & Fessler, 2010).

Empathy: An Important Foundation for Helping

Many factors have been identified as affecting prosocial behavior, and people facing the same situation often do not respond in an identical way. Some are more helpful than others, and these individual differences are visible in a wide range of contexts. Among the various personal factors that influence helping, the one that appears to be most important is the tendency to experience *empathy* toward others—emotional reactions that are focused on or oriented toward other people, and include feelings of compassion, sympathy, and concern (e.g., Batson & Oleson, 1991). As we noted earlier, empathy involves several components: affective and cognitive responses to another person's emotional state and the capacity to take the perspective of the other person (Batson et al., 2003). An empathetic person feels what another person is feeling and understands why that person feels as he or she does (Azar, 1997; Darley, 1993; Duan, 2000). For instance, if another person is experiencing embarrassment, someone experiencing empathy toward this individual will experience (vicariously) this embarrassment, too (Stocks, Lishner, Waits, & Downum, 2011). Individual differences in the tendency experience empathy appear to be relatively consistent over time. For example, children who are prosocial in early childhood behave in a similar way in adolescence (Caprara, Barbaranelli, Pastorelli, Bandura, & Zimbardo, 2000; Eisenberg et al., 2002). Thus, personal characteristics or predispositions are often an important factor in the decision to help or not help others.

The affective component (emotional empathy) is an important component of empathy, and children as young as 12 months seem to clearly feel distress in response to the distress of others (Brothers, 1990; see Figure 9.13). This same characteristic is also observed in other primates (Ungerer et al., 1990) and probably among many animal species (Azar, 1997). For instance, cats and dogs often hate going to the vet. Why? One possibility is because they

FIGURE 9.13 Empathy: It Emerges Early in Life
Even young infants show empathy—for instance, they will cry when exposed to another infant who is distressed and crying.

hear other animals crying out in pain or fear and they experience empathy toward these other pets. This is mainly speculation, but seems to be a reasonable possibility—given that pets experience the social side of life too!

The cognitive component of empathy appears to be a uniquely human quality that develops only after we progress beyond infancy. Such cognitions include the ability to consider the viewpoint of another person, sometimes referred to as *perspective taking*—the ability to "put yourself in someone else's shoes." Social psychologists have identified three different types of perspective taking (Batson, Early, & Salvarani, 1997): (1) You can imagine how the other person perceives an event and how he or she must feel as a result—taking the "imagine other" perspective. Those who take this perspective experience relatively pure empathy that motivates altruistic behavior. (2) You can imagine how you would feel if you were in that situation—taking the "imagine self" perspective. Those who take this perspective also experience empathy, but they tend to be motivated by self-interest, which can interfere with prosocial behavior. (3) The third type of perspective taking involves fantasy—feeling empathy for a fictional character. In this instance, there is an emotional reaction to the joys, sorrows, and fears of a person (or an animal) in a book, movie, or TV program. Many children (and adults, too) may cry when Bambi discovers that his mother has been shot, or cringe in fear when the Wicked Witch of the West threatens Dorothy and "your little dog, too."

EMPATHY AND HELPING ACROSS GROUP BOUNDARIES   Does empathy occur across group boundaries? Is it more difficult to experience empathy toward people outside our own social group than people within it? And if so, could this help explain why people belonging to one social group often fail to help those in other groups when they face emergencies or are in need of assistance for other reasons? Research findings suggest that this may indeed be the case (e.g,. Pryor, Reeder, Yeadon, & Hesson-McInnis, 2004; Stuermer et al., 2006).

A clear example of such findings is provided by research conducted by Stuermer, Snyder, Kropp, and Siem (2006). In this study, two groups of male students in Germany—ones of German cultural background and others of Muslim cultural background—performed a task in which they learned about a serious problem being experienced by another person: he was out of money and could not find a place to live in the city to which he had just moved. This person was presented as being either a member of their own group or of the other group. After learning of the stranger's problem, participants completed a measure of empathy toward this person, and also indicated the likelihood that they would help him. The researchers predicted that empathy would encourage helping, but that this effect would be much stronger within groups than across groups. In other words, empathy would increase helping for members of one's own group but would have weaker or no effect for members of another group. This is exactly what was found.

Overall, these results indicate that empathy does indeed increase pro-social behavior, but that such effects are stronger for people whom we categorize as members of our own group than for people we categorize as members of some other group.

HOW DOES EMPATHY DEVELOP?   How does empathy develop? People differ a great deal in how they respond to the emotional distress of others. At one extreme are those willing to risk their lives to help another person. At the other extreme are those who enjoy inflicting pain and humiliation on a helpless victim. As with most individual characteristics, the answer seems to lie in a combination of biological differences and contrasting experiences.

What kinds of specific experiences might enhance or inhibit the development of empathy? Having a secure attachment style facilitates an empathic response to the needs of others (Mikulincer et al., 2001). In addition, parents can be models of empathy and exert powerful effects on their children in this way, demonstrating concern for the well-being of others and showing negative reactions to their difficulties or negative feelings (e.g., sadness, pain). Children do learn much by observing what their parents do and say in their everyday lives (Bandura, 1986). In addition, they learn from other children and from teachers in school (Ma, Shek, Cheung, & Tam, 2002).

Either because of genetic differences or because of different socialization experiences, women express higher levels of empathy than do men (Trobst, Collins, & Embree, 1994). Does this lead to greater helping on the part of women? Research findings indicate that it does, but not in all situations. For instance, the results of a careful meta-analysis of acts of heroism—actions in which individuals physically intervene to rescue victims in very dangerous emergency situations—indicate that men outnumber women by a large margin. This is true of Carnegie Medal winners in the United States—people who are awarded medals for voluntarily risking their own life to an extraordinary degree while saving or trying to save the life of another person. On the other hand, in many other situations involving risk to the people involved, and which also involve heroism, women outnumber men. This holds for kidney donors, volunteering for the Peace Corps, or for Doctors of the World. And, notably, it is also true among non-Jews who rescued Jews during the Holocaust, thus placing their own lives in jeopardy: Women outnumber men by more than two to one (Anderson, 1993; Becker & Eagly, 2004) (see Figure 9.14). So the fact that women are higher in empathy than men does seem to lead to greater helping in many contexts.

FIGURE 9.14   Prosocial Behavior: No Gender Boundaries
Irena Sendler, almost 100 years old at her death in May 2008, rescued more than 2,500 Jewish children from the Nazis by smuggling them out of the Warsaw ghetto where they were destined for certain death. She was recently honored by the Polish government for her heroism and was a candidate for the 2007 Nobal Peace Prize. Ms. Sendler is just one of many women who engaged in similar actions; in fact, many more women than men risked their own lives to rescue Jews from the Nazi death-machine.

KEY POINTS

- Emotions exert strong effects on the tendency to help others. Positive feelings increase this tendency, whereas negative ones tend to reduce it.

- In addition, feelings of *elevation*—being inspired by others' kind or helpful acts—increases our own tendency to help.

- Positive and negative emotional states can either enhance or inhibit prosocial behavior, depending on specific factors in the situation and on the nature of the required assistance.

- Empathy is an important determinant of helping behavior. It is weaker across group boundaries than within social groups.

Factors That Reduce Helping: Social Exclusion, Darkness, and Putting an Economic Value on Our Time and Effort

To some extent, engaging in prosocial behavior involves the belief, among potential helpers, that they are part of a *community*—a group or society in which people will engage in mutual help, support, and kindness. Such beliefs can encourage empathy toward others, and as we have already seen, empathy is a powerful force for helping. But what happens when people feel that they have been excluded (**social exclusion**)? One possibility, suggested recently by Twenge, Baumeister, DeWall, Ciarocco, and Bartels (2007), is that the emotional reactions that make us feel close to others and encourage helping might be reduced or eliminated. Being socially excluded is a painful experience, and one that may leave people who experience it with few emotional resources: They are too busy trying to deal with their own feelings of rejection and abandonment to have much emotion left for experiencing empathy concerning the problems of others!

Evidence for this reasoning has recently been reported by Twenge et al. (2007) in a series of related studies. In several of these experiments, some participants were made to feel excluded by being told that their responses to a personality test indicated that they would probably be alone later in life. Others, in contrast, were told that their responses predicted that they would probably enjoy a future rich in personal relationships. Participants in two control groups were either given no information about their future social lives, or were told that they were likely to experience accidents in the future (a negative outcome unrelated to social exclusion).

The tendency to help others was measured by asking participants how much of their payment for being in the study they wanted to contribute to a fund to help needy students. Results were clear: those told they would have a rich future social life gave much more than those told they would probably be excluded. Participants in the two control conditions (misfortune, no feedback) who were not expected to experience feelings that would block empathy also gave more than those in the social exclusion condition.

In further studies, Twenge et al. (2007) obtained evidence indicating that when people experience social exclusion, they adopt a cautious attitude toward social relations. They want to have good relations with others, but because they have recently been rejected, they are reluctant to expose themselves to the risk of even further exclusion. As a result, they are less likely to experience empathy toward others, and less likely to use prosocial actions as a way of winning new friends and social support. This suggests that exclusion can sometimes have lasting effects, since it effectively prevents people who experience it from building the new social relationships they so badly want. Truly, then, social exclusion—which is far from rare—may be very damaging to the people who experience it, in addition to reducing their tendency to help others.

DARKNESS: FEELINGS OF ANONYMITY REDUCE THE TENDENCY TO HELP OTHERS
Darkness has often been linked to disinhibited behavior—under "cover" of darkness, people often engage in actions they would be reluctant to perform in broad daylight (see Figure 9.15). Why? One reason is that they feel anonymous; others can't see them or evaluate their actions. If prosocial behavior sometimes occurs because it can be observed by others and win their approval, then darkness should reduce or eliminate this motive. In other words, people would be less likely to help others, or engage in other forms of prosocial behavior, in the presence of darkness—or merely when they believe that conditions provide them with anonymity.

Classic studies in social psychology on *deindividuation*—a reduced state of self-awareness that encourages wild, impulsive behavior (see Chapter 12 for discussion of this research)—indicate that this reasoning is correct: When people feel anonymous, they do perform actions they would not perform under other conditions. However, it

social exclusion
Conditions in which individuals feel that they have been excluded from some social group.

FIGURE 9.15   A Lot Happens Under "Cover of Darkness"—But Prosocial Behavior Does Not
Research findings indicate that darkness (or anything else that encourages feelings of anonymity) can reduce the occurrence of prosocial behavior.

may not be merely feelings of anonymity that are operating: When people are part of a large crowd, they are more likely to obey the norms of that group, and do what others are doing (Postmes & Spears, 1998), so this may be an important factor in such situations. But does darkness itself encourage such feelings? And does this, in turn, reduce prosocial behavior? Evidence reported by Zhong, Bohns, and Gino (2010) suggest that it does. In an ingenious study, the researchers placed participants in a slightly darkened room, or in a room with bright lighting, and had them perform a task involving finding two numbers in matrixes of numbers that added up to 10. They were told that if they performed very well, they could receive an extra $10. Participants recorded their own scores, and these could then be compared with their actual scores. Zhong and colleagues predicted that participants would be more likely to exaggerate their scores (i.e., to be dishonest) in a dark room than a bright one, and in fact this is what happened. Fully 50 percent of the participants who performed the task in the dark room overstated their performance, while only 24.4 percent of those in the bright room did. Their performance itself was not different from that of people who performed in a bright room, so it appeared that darkness did in fact reduce their tendency to help another person. Similar findings were obtained when room lighting was not varied, but participants either wore or did not wear dark sunglasses, which, presumably, would give them feelings of anonymity. In this study, those wearing the glasses were more likely to act in a selfish manner, taking more of an available prize for themselves and giving less to their partners.

PUTTING AN ECONOMIC VALUE ON OUR TIME REDUCES PROSOCIAL BEHAVIOR
As we have seen in this chapter, many factors influence the tendency to help others in various ways. Emotional factors certainly play a role (empathy, current moods, feelings of elevation) and cognitive factors (our accuracy in perceiving others' feelings and so in understanding their need for help), too, are important. An additional cognitive factor might be the extent to which we think about helping others in terms of the economic costs to us: Time used in helping others can't be used for other activities, including ones that generate income. To the extent that we think about helping in this way (e.g., the

*"Listen. It's at the quiet moments like this that you can
actually hear the meter running."*

**FIGURE 9.16   Putting Economic Value on Our
Time Reduces Our Willingness to Help Others:
The Effects of Billable Hours**

*As shown here, attorneys, who often bill their clients in
terms of tenths of an hour (six-minute segments) keep a very
careful record of the time they use on a client's case. Research
findings indicate that thinking about time in economic terms
may reduce the willingness to help others. In short, a focus on
"billable hours" may cause the "milk of human kindness" to
dry up quickly!*

economic costs of volunteering our time), we may be less likely to
engage in prosocial behavior. Two researchers, DeVoe and Pfeffer
(2010), have recently suggested that this is the case. When people
think about the economic value of their time, they may be less
likely to volunteer it to help others.

Certain professions, of course, train their members to think
in just these ways. While physicians bill patients according to the
procedures they perform, attorneys (and other professionals such
as accountants) bill in terms of their time. In fact, many attorneys
bill in tenths of an hour—for each 6-minute period they use in
working on clients' cases. So like the attorneys in Figure 9.16,
they are oriented to take carful note of their time. Does this
make them less likely to engage in prosocial behavior? Findings
reported by DeVoe and Pfeffer (2010) indicate that it does. In one
study, third-year law students, who had not yet practiced billing
for their time, were asked to complete a questionnaire concerning their willingness to volunteer their time to organizations they
cared about. Then, 5 months later, after graduating and taking
jobs, they completed the same survey. Results indicated that as
the researchers predicted, the now-practicing attorneys expressed
less willingness to volunteer their time than they had as law students; moreover, this was true even when their initial willingness
to volunteer was taken into account through statistical procedures.

To further test the same predictions, the researchers conducted additional studies in which participants (students who
were not in law school) performed tasks in which they kept care-
ful track of how much time they have spent in various activities (billing treatment) or
were not asked to do this (nonbilling). Later, they were asked how much time they
were willing to volunteer to worthy causes. Results again indicated that those in the
billing condition, who focused on time and its use, expected to spend fewer hours on
volunteer work than those in the control condition. Several other studies confirmed the
same findings, and research by others indicates that to the extent we attach economic
value to our time, we may be less likely to donate it to helping others (e.g., Leboeuf &
Shafir, in press). The milk of human kindness, it appears, dries up when it is measured
precisely in 10ths of an hour! (Does helping in the age of the Internet take different
forms than it did before? For information on this issue, please see the section "SOCIAL
LIFE IN A CONNECTED WORLD: Helping Others via the Internet—the Case of
Kiva.")

SOCIAL LIFE *in a* CONNECTED WORLD

Helping Others via the Internet—the Case of Kiva

Prosocial behavior often occurs between people
who meet face to face. For instance, a young
mother walked down the aisle of an Amtrak train
explaining to other passengers that she and her daughters
were trying to get home, but had run out of money. She
asked, "Might someone please help us?" Many passengers
dug into their pockets or purses and gave her some money.
Was she being honest? The passengers on the train couldn't
be sure—but they wanted to help, and probably experienced positive feelings from doing so.

But how can you help people you never met, and perhaps help them to help themselves? Many individuals do not want charity; they simply want the opportunity to gain a better life for themselves and their families through hard work, and one way of doing so is to start their own businesses. But they need funds to get started. In short, they want to be entrepreneurs—but they need help to do so.

Here is where the Internet comes to the rescue. In recent years, an organization known as *Kiva* has been formed to accomplish precisely this goal—to help people in developed countries loan (not give!) small amounts of money to people in developing countries so that they can become entrepreneurs. This is the way it works: A potential lender signs on to *www.kiva.org* and looks through the people seeking small loans. He or she then chooses one or more, and using a credit card, provides a small amount ($25.00 is the minimum). Local organizations known as Field Partners then disburse the loan to the entrepreneur; they also protect lenders against changes in the values of currencies, which might reduce the amount they receive as repayment. The entrepreneurs then open their businesses (usually with just a few hundred dollars) and repay the lenders out of their profits. They give these funds to the Field Partners who then forward them to the lenders. The money can then be reloaned or withdrawn as the lender wishes.

Here's an example of one entrepreneur and how she used the funds she received (just a few hundred dollars). Her name is Pando Luisi. She is 27 years old and she lives in the African nation of Tanzania (see Figure 9.17). She wanted a loan to convert her small snack shop (started with a previous loan) into a café, and to expand her door-to-door cosmetics business. Her previous business was successful, and the new ones—expanded or started with the most recent loan—have grown rapidly. The result is that now, she is earning over $200 per month—a very good income in Tanzania. As Pando notes, she could never have done this without money loaned to her through Kiva, the Internet loan website (which is aimed at transferring help from the wealthy with resources to those in need).

Does Kiva work—does it really increase helping between people who don't know each other and will probably never meet? Research on the outcomes it produces suggests that it is highly effective. This work has been conducted in the context of what is known as *social entrepreneurship*—instances in which individuals start their own businesses, or help others start them, not mainly to earn economic benefits, but primarily because they want to do some good in the world—to help many other people live better (e.g., Brooks, 2008). And overall, it suggests that Kiva is effective in helping many people living in impoverished countries toward a much richer and happier life.

So, although helping others is as old as human society and has always been part of social life, today it can occur in ways no one dreamed possible in the past—and enrich the lives of a large number of people who will never meet the people who help them, but who are very grateful for the assistance they receive from far away!

FIGURE 9.17   Kiva: Helping People to Help Themselves
Kiva helps people in developing countries to live better by starting their own businesses. It provides these entrepreneurs with small loans from funds provided by lenders around the world. One such entrepreneur—Pando Luisi of Tanzania—is shown with the snack bar she started with one loan. She paid the original loan back promptly, and has since received another loan to start a café and expand her door-to-door cosmetic sales business.

KEY POINTS

- Positive and negative emotional states can either enhance or inhibit prosocial behavior, depending on specific factors in the situation and on the nature of the required assistance.

- Empathy is an important determinant of helping behavior. It is weaker across group boundaries than within

social groups. **Social exclusion** often reduces prosocial behavior because people who experience it have reduced capacity to feel empathy toward others.

- Several factors reduce the tendency to help others. These include social exclusion, darkness, and putting an economic value on our time.

The Effects of Being Helped: Why Perceived Motives Really Matter

Being helped when we need assistance is wonderful in many ways, and often generates strong feelings of gratitude on the part of the people who are helped. But is this always the case? Do people always react positively to receiving help? If you have ever received a gift you didn't want, or had someone insist on doing a favor for you that you really didn't need, you already know that our reactions to help from others are not always positive. In fact, they can sometimes they can generate negative feelings, such as resentment at being "indebted" to the those who offer assistance (see Figure 9.18).

FIGURE 9.18 Does Helping Always Produce Positive Reactions?
As this pet owner has just discovered, engaging in prosocial behavior does not always generate gratitude and thanks from the recipients. Rather, like the fish shown here, they may react negatively and actually "bite the hand that feeds (helps) them." (Source: The New Yorker).

This fact is confirmed by research indicating that people who receive help from others sometimes experience negative rather than positive reactions to such assistance. Why does this occur? In part because when people receive help, their self-esteem can suffer. This is especially likely to occur when the person on the receiving end is lower in status than the helper. In such cases, receiving help drives home the status difference between them (e.g., Penner, Dovidio, Piliavin, & Schroeder, 2005). For instance, in several studies, Nadler and Halabi (2006) exposed participants—Jewish Israelis and Arab Israelis—to situations in which they received or did not receive help from members of their own group or the other group. The researchers predicted that in general, people belonging to low-status groups are reluctant to receive help from high-status groups, especially when they try to gain equality—to boost their own status. Specifically, they expected that Arab-Israelis, who have lower status in Israel than Jewish Israelis, would react negatively to help from Jewish Israelis, especially when they perceived such help as threatening their quest for equality by suggesting that they are dependent on the high-status group. This is precisely what was found: members of the low-status group (Arab-Israelis) reacted negatively in several respects (more negative feelings, lower evaluations of the other group—and the helper—to unsolicited help). Findings such as this drive home the key point: being helped by others is not always a positive experience and in fact, under some conditions, can be viewed negatively by the people on the receiving end (DePaulo, Brown, Ishii, & Fisher, 1981; Nadler, Fisher, & Itzhak, 1983).

On the other hand, more positive reactions to help often occur when the person receiving assistance believes that the help was offered because of positive feelings on the part of the helper (Ames, Flynn, & Weber, 2004) or stemmed from personal motivation to help—*autonomous* motivation. In contrast, when helping seems to stem from conditions that more or less forced the helper to extend assistance—*controlled* motivation (e.g., they would "look bad" to others if they did not, or their job or role requires them to help)—reactions on the part of the person being helped tend to be far less positive (Weinstein & Ryan, 2010). In fact, both the recipient and the helper have less favorable reactions under these conditions.

Research by Weinstein and Ryan (2010) illustrates these effects very clearly. In one of their studies, participants (university students) were given an opportunity to help an experimenter who needed assistance with her research. In the autonomous help condition, they were told that it was entirely their choice as to whether they wanted to help. In the controlled help condition, it was suggested that they more or less had an obligation to help. Finally, in a control condition, they were not given an opportunity to help. After these experiences, participants completed measures of positive affect, self-esteem, and vitality—important aspects of subjective well-being. It was predicted that both helpers and recipients would have more positive feelings and reactions in the autonomous than controlled help condition, and less positive reactions in the control (no-help) condition. As you can see from Figure 9.19, results confirmed these predictions. In short, it appears that the

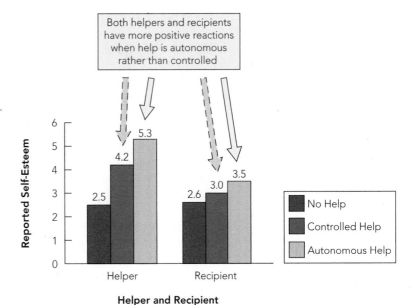

FIGURE 9.19   Motives for Helping: They Strongly Influence Reactions of Both the Helper and Receipient

As shown here, when helping stems from autonomous (i.e., internal) motives, it generates more positive reactions in both the helper and the recipient than when it stems from controlled (i.e., external) motives.   (Source: Copyright © 2010 by the American Psychological Association. Reproduced with permissions. 'When Helping Helps: Autonomous Motivation for Prosocial Behavior and Its influence on Well-Being for the Helper and Recipient' Netta Weinstein and Richard M. Ryan, JOURNAL OF PERSONALITY AND SOCIAL PSYCHOLOGY, 98, PP. 222–224. Feb. 2010.).

motivation behind helping behavior is crucial in determining reactions of both the helper and the recipient to such actions. When helping seems to be autonomous—to stem from internal motives on the part of the helper—both helpers and recipients experience more positive feelings and reactions than when it seems to be dictated or controlled by the situation or external factors. So, when you help others, try to be sure that you are doing it because you *want* to; if, instead, you help because you feel it is required or because you are obligated to assist them, the likelihood that neither you nor they will feel very good about the experience is high.

KEY POINTS

- Receiving help does not always generate positive reactions in the recipients. In fact, under some conditions, they are more likely to experience feelings of resentment and unwanted obligations to the helper.

- An important factor determining how recipients react to help is the motivation underlying such behavior. If it seems to stem from internal motives (e.g., a genuine

- desire to help), positive feelings and reactions may result. If, instead, it stems from external motives (i.e., the helper felt obligated to extend assistance), reactions tend to be far less favorable.

- Similar effects occur among helpers, too: they react more positively to helping others when such behavior stems from internal, voluntary motives than when it is somehow required by external conditions.

Final Thoughts: Are Prosocial Behavior and Aggression Opposites?

Helping and hurting—at first glance, they certainly seem to be opposites. Rushing to the aid of victims in emergencies, donating to charity, volunteering to help the wildlife harmed by the oil spill in the Gulf of Mexico, giving directions to people who are lost—these and countless other helpful actions seem opposite in many ways to *aggression*, which social psychologists generally define as intentional efforts to harm others in some way (see Chapter 10). But are helping and aggression really opposites? If you stopped 100 people at random, showed them a line, and asked them to place helping and aggression along it, almost all of them would in fact place these forms of social behavior at opposite sides.

But get ready for a surprise: Social psychologists have thought long and hard about this issue and reached the conclusion that in many ways, prosocial behavior and aggression are *not* opposites. In fact, they overlap much more than you might expect. First, consider the motives underlying such actions. The motivation for helping, you might assume, is simply to do something beneficial for the recipient; the motivation for aggression, in contrast, is to do something to harm the recipient in some way. But look a bit more closely: As we have seen in this chapter, people sometimes engage in prosocial actions not primarily to help the recipients but, rather, to boost their own status, to incur obligations, and to gain a positive reputation. Their motivation, in short, is not necessarily to do something beneficial for the recipients. Certainly, that motive does exist in the form of empathy-based helping; but it is often not the primary one responsible for helpful actions toward others.

Now consider aggression. Is the motivation behind such behavior always to harm the victim in some way? Perhaps, but consider the following situation. A sports coach, dissatisfied with the effort an athlete is investing in practice and angry at this person, orders the athlete to take "10 laps around the field" and then also confines the athlete to his or her room that evening: no parties or getting together with friends. Do these actions—which might seem to be aggressive (at least potentially from the recipient's point of view)—stem from a motive to harm the athlete? Far from it. The coach takes these actions to help the athlete improve—or at least become more motivated. We could offer many other examples, but the main point is clear: The motives behind prosocial behavior and aggression sometimes overlap and can't be easily separated. In this respect, certainly, they are not polar opposites.

Now think about the specific actions involved in prosocial behavior and aggression. These, you might guess, *are* direct opposites. Prosocial actions help the recipients in some way, while aggressive actions harm them, so they involve very different kinds of actions. Perhaps. But now imagine the following scene. A young woman takes a sharp needle and uses it to puncture the skin of another person, who cries out in pain. Is she behaving aggressively? Maybe yes, maybe no. What if she is placing a tattoo on the supposed "victim's" body—one she has requested and paid for in advance? So while these actions might appear to be aggressive, they may actually have little or nothing to do with harming the "victim." Not all aggressive and prosocial actions overlap in this sense, but some do and this suggests that these two aspects of social behavior are *not* direct opposites.

Finally, contemplate the effects of aggression and prosocial behavior. By definition, aggression produces harm and prosocial actions produce benefits, but again, not always. For instance, consider someone who uses a very sharp knife to cut into the body of another person. Is this aggression? On the surface it may appear to be. But what if the person performing this action is a skilled surgeon, trying to save the other person's life? The short-term effects might seem harmful (the "victim" bleeds profusely), but the long-term effects are actually beneficial: the patient's health is restored. Similarly, prosocial actions can seem beneficial in the short term but harm the recipient in the long term. Help we don't request or want can undermine our self-esteem and confidence, so short-term benefits can soon turn into long-term harm.

Finally, we should mention the fact that research findings (e.g., Hawley, Card, & Little, 2007) indicate that aggression and prosocial behavior are sometimes used by the same people to gain popularity and status. Specifically, such research indicates that individuals who behave aggressively can be highly attractive to others—rather than merely alarming—if they combine such actions with prosocial ones. Such people are "tough" and assertive, but also possess social skills that allow them to be charming and helpful; and they know when to "turn" their tough sides on and off. Hawley and her colleagues (2007) describe this as "the allure of mean friends" (the appeal of people who are indeed aggressive but also have other skills that help them to attain important goals), and have found that this combination of toughness and prosocial action is seductive, and far from rare.

As you can see, then, the question of whether helping and aggression are opposites is far more complex than at first meets the eye. The motives from which these forms of behavior spring, the behaviors themselves, and the effects they produce are complex and overlap much more than you might initially guess. And that's not really surprising because *all* social behavior is complex; generally, it stems from many different motives, takes a wide range of forms, and produces many different effects. So yes, indeed, helping and hurting *are* very different in several respects, but not, perhaps, as different as common sense suggests.

SUMMARY *and* REVIEW

● Several different motives may underlie **prosocial behavior.** The **empathy-altruism hypothesis** proposes that, because of empathy, we help those in need because we experience empathic concern for them. **Empathy** actually consists of three distinct components: emotional empathy, empathic accuracy, and empathic concern. All three components can serve as a basis for helping others. The **negative-state relief model** proposes that people help other people in order to relieve and make less negative their own emotional discomfort. The **empathic joy hypothesis** suggests that helping stems from the positive reactions recipients show when they receive help (e.g., gifts), and the positive feelings this, in turn, induces in helpers. The *competitive altruism theory* suggests that we help others as a means of increasing our own status and reputation—and so benefit from helping in important ways. **Kin ship selection theory** suggests that we help others who are related to us because this increases the likelihood that our genes will be transmitted to future generations.

● Another motive for helping behavior is that of reducing the threat posed by outgroups to one's own ingroup, known as **defensive helping.** When an emergency arises and someone is in need of help, a bystander may or may not respond in a

prosocial way—responses can range from apathy (and doing nothing) to heroism. In part because of **diffusion of responsibility,** the more bystanders present as witnesses to an emergency, the less likely each of them is to provide help and the greater the delay before help occurs (the *bystander effect*). This is true for helping between strangers, but is less likely to occur for helping among people who belong to the same groups.

● When faced with an emergency, a bystander's tendency to help or not help depends in part on decisions made at five crucial steps. First, it is necessary for the bystander to pay attention and be aware that an unusual event is occurring. Second, the bystander must correctly interpret the situation as an emergency. Third, the bystander must assume responsibility to provide help. Fourth, the bystander must have the required knowledge and skills to be able to act. In a final step, the bystander must decide to take action. We are more likely to help others who are similar to ourselves than others who are dissimilar. This leads to lower tendencies to help people outside our own social groups.

● We are also more likely to help people we like than those we don't like, and those who are not responsible for their current need for help. Helping is increased by exposure to prosocial models; it can also be increased by playing prosocial video games. Prosocial video games increase subsequent helping by priming prosocial thoughts, building cognitive frameworks related to helping, and related effects. Gratitude increases prosocial behavior, primarily by enhancing helpers' feelings of self-worth. Emotions exert strong effects on the tendency to help others. Positive feelings increase this tendency, whereas negative ones tend to reduce it. In addition, feelings of *elevation*—being inspired by others' kind or helpful acts—increases our own tendency to help.

- Positive and negative emotional states can either enhance or inhibit prosocial behavior, depending on specific factors in the situation and on the nature of the required assistance. Empathy is an important determinant of helping behavior. It is weaker across group boundaries than within social groups. **Social exclusion** often reduces prosocial behavior because people who experience it have reduced capacity to feel empathy toward others. Several factors reduce the tendency to help others. These include social exclusion, darkness, and putting an economic value on our time.

- Receiving help does not always generate positive reactions in the recipients. In fact, under some conditions, they are more likely to experience feelings of resentment and unwanted obligations to the helper. An important factor determining how recipients react to help is the motivation underlying such behavior. If it seems to stem from internal motives (e.g., a genuine desire to help), positive feelings and reactions may result. If instead it stems from external motives (i.e., the helper felt obligated to extend assistance), reactions tend to be far less favorable. Similar effects occur among helpers, too: they react more positively to helping others when such behavior stems from internal, voluntary motives than when it is somehow required by external conditions. Although it is tempting to assume that helping and aggression are direct opposites, careful examination of these important forms of social behavior indicates that this idea is not correct.

KEY TERMS

defensive helping (p. 295)

diffusion of responsibility (p. 297)

empathic joy hypothesis (p. 293)

empathy (p. 291)

empathy-altruism hypothesis (p. 291)

kin selection theory (p. 295)

negative-state relief model (p. 293)

pluralistic ignorance (p. 299)

prosocial behavior (p. 290)

social exclusion (p. 310)

Aggression

Its Nature, Causes, and Control

HEN PHILLIP ALPERT, AN 18-YEAR-OLD IN ORLANDO,
Florida, had an argument with his girlfriend, he decided to "get even"
in a very special way: he'd post a naked photo of her on the Internet
and send it to dozens of her friends and family, too. That's just what he did, and the
results were *not* what he expected: he was arrested and charged with sending child
pornography. That's a serious crime in most places, and he had little or no defense, so
he was rapidly convicted and sentenced to 5 years of probation. Most important, he
was required to register as a sex offender. Alpert's life, he now knows, will never be
the same. He must remain on the sex offender list until he is 43, has been kicked out
of college, and cannot travel out of the county where he lives without making prior
arrangements with his probation officer.

Bad as these results of seeking to harm others through electronic media, they
were even worse for Jessica Logan. When Jessica and her boyfriend split, he sent nude
photos of her (ones she previously provided) to other girls in her high school. They
then began a campaign of taunting her, both in person and on the Web, calling her a
"slut and a whore." Jessica's mother noted that her daughter was so distressed by this
treatment that she started skipping school. And when the verbal and electronic abuse
continued, she came home one day and . . . took her own life. Her mother is now trying to sue school authorities, claiming that they should have protected her daughter.
As Parry Aftab, an expert on Internet security, explains, however, both she and her
boyfriend violated the law by sending nude photos of her via e-mail and posting them
on the Web. And, sadly, Aftab adds, "It is normal kids just like Jessica who fall victim
to the perils of the Internet and the easy exchange of information on cell phones . . ."

Do you find these events disturbing? We certainly do. And they are not isolated
incidents; in fact, recent surveys suggest that more than 40 percent of teenagers
are involved in sexting (sending explicit sexual photos over the Web), almost half
have received messages containing such photos, and fully 15 percent of teenage
boys send photos of their former girlfriends to others after they break up. Why
do we mention these facts and the tragic incidents above? Because we want to
illustrate a very basic and important point: Although people have always engaged

in **aggression**—actions designed to harm others in some way—the modern, connected world in which we currently live offers new ways of accomplishing this goal. In the past, aggression involved face-to-face assaults against others, either verbal or physical) or indirect efforts to harm them through such tactics as spreading malicious rumors about them. But now, there are many new—and deadly—ways to harm others. Sexting can be one of them, but so, too, can using the Web to spread embarrassing photos with other kinds of content and "smear campaigns," designed to harm the targets' reputations. In one college course offered at Indiana University, the professor Googles students prior to the first day of class—and then reports to them embarrassing postings this process has uncovered. Not surprisingly, there are always a few posts the students wish would disappear—for example, photos of them posing half naked, or engaging in actions they now find embarrassing and wish had never occurred.

Overall, many people believe that we are now living in an age when humiliating others is viewed as more acceptable than it was in the past. Do you ever watch *American Idol?* Then you know what happens to performers who are dismissed early on: often, they are ridiculed harshly before millions of viewers (see Figure 10.1). And special websites designed to demean strangers now exist (e.g., PeopleofWalmart.com, which shows photos of shoppers at Walmart in very unattractive poses and clothing). So yes, we do live in a new age, but the age-old desire to harm others can find many new forms of expression. And, of course, more "traditional" forms of aggression—from terrorism through serial killings and genocide—are still very much with us and remain an unsettling part of the human story.

Given the pervasiveness of aggression and violence (and its human costs), it is not surprising that social psychologists have sought to obtain a greater understanding of the roots of aggression—to gain insights into its nature and causes. The ultimate goal of such research is to use this increased knowledge to develop improved techniques for reducing aggression in many different contexts (e.g., Anderson et al., 2010; Baumeister, 2005). In the present chapter, we summarize the knowledge gained by social psychologists through several decades of careful research. To do this, we proceed as follows.

First, we describe several *theoretical perspectives* on aggression, contrasting views about its nature and origins. Next, we examine research illustrating important determinants of human aggression. These include *basic social factors*, the words or actions of other people, either "in the flesh" or as shown in the mass media (e.g., Fischer & Greitemeyer, 2006); *cultural factors*, such as norms requiring that individuals respond aggressively to insults to their honor; aspects of *personality*, traits that predispose some people toward aggressive outbursts; and *situational factors*, aspects of the external world such as high temperatures and alcohol. After examining the effects of all these factors, we turn our attention to a very common but disturbing form of aggression to which children and teenagers are often exposed: *bullying* (repeated victimization of specific people by

aggression

Behavior directed toward the goal of harming another living being who is motivated to avoid such treatment.

FIGURE 10.1   Do We Live in a World Where Humiliating Others Is Acceptable?

On popular shows such as "American Idol," contestants who are eliminated are often ridiculed by the host, panel, and audience. In short, they are humiliated in front of millions of viewers. Many believe that such actions—which are a form of aggression—are now more common than in the past.

one or more other people). Finally, we examine various techniques for the prevention and control of aggression.

Perspectives on Aggression: In Search of the Roots of Violence

Have you flown lately? If so, you know that, although the system is operating better than in the past, getting through airport security can still sometimes take a long time, and be somewhat stressful. In fact, on a recent trip, one of us had his very small overnight bag pulled off the line and carefully searched. What was the problem? A water bottle he had forgotten to empty before getting on line. The inspector took it away, and that was the end of the process . . . but it was not pleasant. In the past, this kind of intense inspection—including full body scans—was not part of flying, so why do we have it now? You almost certainly know the answer: because of acts of aggression against innocent victims known as *terrorism*. The tragic events of 9/11 were a "wake-up" call for Americans—and the citizens of every other country—reminding them that there were people out there who were perfectly willing to kill and injure other people they didn't know and who had done them no harm. This, of course, raises a very basic question: Why do human beings aggress against others in such savage and frightening ways? Social psychologists—along with many other thoughtful people—have pondered these questions for centuries and offered many explanations. Here, we examine several that have been especially influential, ending with those that have recently emerged from social psychological research.

The Role of Biological Factors: Are We Programmed to Aggress?

The oldest and probably most famous explanation for human aggression attributed it to biological factors, our basic nature as a species. The most famous supporter of this theory was Sigmund Freud, who held that aggression stems mainly from a powerful *death wish* (*thanatos*) we all possess. According to Freud, this instinct is initially aimed at self-destruction, but is soon redirected outward, toward others. A related view was proposed by Konrad Lorenz, a Nobel Prize–winning ethologist, who suggested that aggression springs mainly from an inherited *fighting instinct*, which ensures that only the strongest males will obtain mates and pass their genes on to the next generation (Lorenz, 1966, 1974).

Until recently, most social psychologists rejected such ideas. Among the many reasons they did were these: (1) human beings aggress against others in many different ways—everything from excluding them from social groups to performing overt acts of violence against them. How can such a huge range of behaviors all be determined by genetic factors? (2) The frequency of aggressive actions varies tremendously across human societies, so that is much more likely to occur in some than in others (e.g., Fry, 1998). If that's so, social psychologists wonder, "How can aggressive behavior be determined by genetic factors?"

With the growth of the *evolutionary perspective* in psychology, however, the situation has changed. While most social psychologists continue to reject the view that human aggression stems largely from innate (i.e., genetic) factors, some now accept the possibility that genetic factors may indeed play *some* role in human aggression. For instance, consider the following reasoning, based on an evolutionary perspective (recall our discussion of this theory in Chapter 1). In the evolutionary past (and even at present to some extent), males seeking desirable mates found it necessary to compete with other males. One way of eliminating such competition is through successful aggression, which drives such rivals away. Since males who were adept at such behavior may have been more successful in securing mates and in transmitting their genes to offspring, this may have led to the development of a genetically influenced tendency for males to aggress against other males. In contrast, males would not be expected to possess a similar tendency to aggress against females; in fact, development of such tendencies might be discouraged because females would tend to reject as mates males who are aggressive toward them or even ones who are aggressive in public, thus exposing themselves and their mates to unnecessary danger. As a result, males may have weaker tendencies to aggress against females than against other males. In contrast, females might aggress equally against males and females, or even more frequently against males than other females.

Some research findings are consistent with this reasoning. For instance, males tend to be more aggressive toward other males than toward females (although, of course, domestic violence is often perpetrated by males against females). In contrast, similar differences do not exist (or are weaker) among females (e.g., Hilton, Harris, & Rice, 2000) (As we'll note later in this chapter, though, gender differences in aggression are not nearly as large as many people seem to believe; Hawley et al., 2007). In addition, recent research by Griskevicius and colleagues (2009) indicates that when men's mating motivation is activated (by reading a story about meeting a very attractive woman)—they do indeed become more aggressive toward other men, which is consistent with their goal of driving off potential rivals. Moreover, this is especially likely to occur when only other males can observe their behavior; if females are present, they do not become more aggressive, thus avoiding the possibility of turning off these potential mates (many women find men who are aggressive in public to be frightening rather than attractive). Findings such as these have led some social psychologists to conclude that biological or genetic factors do indeed play a role in human aggression because such behavior is closely linked to certain forms of status, which in turn is related to success in obtaining attractive mates (Grisakevicius et al., 2007) (see Figure 10.2). As we noted in Chapter 1, however, the fact that a given form of behavior is influenced by genetic factors does not mean that such behavior must occur or is an essential part of "human nature." It simply means that a potential for engaging in such behavior exists, and is generated, at least in part, by biological factors.

drive theories (of aggression)
Theories suggesting that aggression stems from external conditions that arouse the motive to harm or injure others. The most famous of these is the frustration-aggression hypothesis.

FIGURE 10.2   Do Genetic Factors Play a Role in Aggression? Aggression Confers Status, and Status Often Attracts Desirable Mates
Some research findings are consistent with the view that genetic factors underlie human tendencies to aggress. Successful aggression sometimes confers status on those who perform it, and this, in turn, increases their attractiveness to at least some potential mates. (Shown here are female fans showing admiration for aggressive male athletes).

Drive Theories: The Motive to Harm Others

When social psychologists rejected the instinct views of aggression proposed by Freud and Lorenz, they countered with an alternative of their own: the view that aggression stems mainly from an externally elicited drive to harm others. This approach is reflected in several different **drive theories** of aggression (e.g., Berkowitz, 1989; Feshbach, 1984).

These theories propose that external conditions—especially frustration—arouse a strong motive to harm others. This aggressive drive, in turn, leads to overt acts of aggression (see Figure 10.3). It can be initiated by several factors discussed below (e.g., provocations from others), or even by the presence of a weapon in the room (Anderson, 1998).

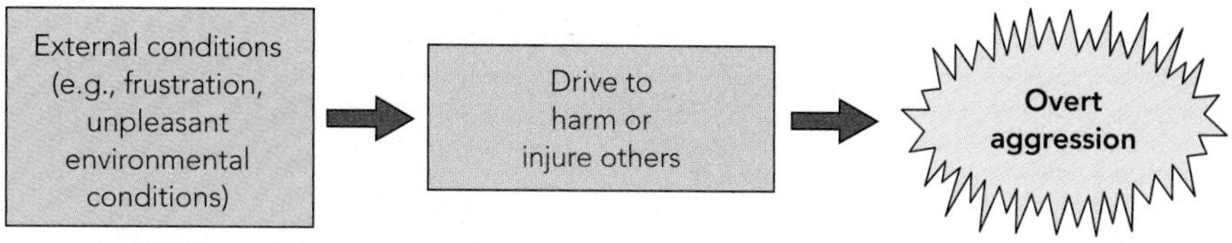

By far the most famous of these theories is the well-known *frustration-aggression hypothesis* (Dollard, Doob, Miller, Mowerer, & Sears, 1939), and we discuss it in some detail in a later section. Here, we just want to note that this theory suggests that frustration—anything that prevents us from reaching goals we are seeking—leads to the arousal of a drive whose primary goal is that of harming some person or object—primarily the perceived cause of frustration (Berkowitz, 1989). Furthermore, the theory suggests that frustration is the strongest, or perhaps the *only*, cause of aggression. Social psychologists now realize that this theory is somewhat misleading, but it still enjoys widespread acceptance outside our field, and you may sometimes hear your friends refer to it in such statement as, "He was so frustrated that he finally blew up" or "She was feeling frustrated, so she took it out on her roommate." We explain later why such statements are often truly misleading.

FIGURE 10.3   Drive Theories of Aggression: Motivation to Harm Others

Drive theories of aggression suggest that aggressive behavior is pushed from within by drives to harm or injure others. These drives, in turn, stem from external events such as frustration. Such theories are no longer accepted as valid by most social psychologists, but one such view—the famous frustration-aggression hypothesis–continues to influence modern research, and many people's beliefs about the causes of aggression.

Modern Theories of Aggression: The Social Learning Perspective and the General Aggression Model

Unlike earlier views, modern theories of aggression (e.g., Anderson & Bushman, 2002; Berkowitz, 1993; Zillmann, 1994) do not focus on a single factor (instincts, drives, frustration) as the primary cause of aggression. Rather, they draw on advances in many areas of psychology in order to gain added insight into the factors that play a role in the occurrence of such behavior. One such theory, known as the *social learning perspective* (e.g., Bandura, 1997), begins with a very reasonable idea: Human beings are not born with a large array of aggressive responses at their disposal. Rather, they must acquire these in the much the same way that they acquire other complex forms of social behavior: through direct experience or by observing the behavior of others (i.e., social models—live people or characters on television, in movies, or even in video games who behave aggressively; Anderson et al., 2010; Anderson & Bushman, 2001; Bushman & Anderson, 2002). Thus, depending on their past experience and the cultures in which they live, individuals learn (1) various ways of seeking to harm others, (2) which people or groups are appropriate targets for aggression, (3) what actions by others justify retaliation or vengeance on their part, and (4) what situations or contexts are ones in which aggression is permitted or even approved. In short, the social learning perspective suggests that whether a specific person will aggress in a given situation depends on many factors, including the person's past experience, the current rewards associated with past or present aggression, and attitudes and values that shape this person's thoughts concerning the appropriateness and potential effects of such behavior.

Building on the social learning perspective, a newer framework known as the **general aggression model (GAM)** (Anderson & Bushman, 2002), provides an even more complete account of the foundations of human aggression. According to this theory, a chain of events that may ultimately lead to overt aggression can be initiated by two major types of *input variables:* (1) factors relating to the current situation (situational

general aggression model (GAM)

A modern theory of aggression suggesting that aggression is triggered by a wide range of input variables that influence arousal, affective stages, and cognitions.

factors) and (2) factors relating to the people involved (person factors). Variables falling into the first category include frustration, some kind of provocation from another person (e.g., an insult), exposure to other people behaving aggressively (*aggressive models*, real or in the media), and virtually anything that causes individuals to experience discomfort—everything from uncomfortably high temperatures to a dentist's drill or even an extremely dull lecture. Variables in the second category (*individual differences across people*) include traits that predispose some individuals toward aggression (e.g., high irritability), certain attitudes and beliefs about violence (e.g., believing that it is acceptable and appropriate), a tendency to perceive hostile intentions in others' behavior, and specific skills related to aggression (e.g., knowing how to fight or how to use various weapons).

According to the general aggression model (GAM), these situational and individual (personal) variables lead to overt aggression through their impact on three basic processes: *arousal*—they may increase physiological arousal or excitement; *affective states*—they can arouse hostile feelings and outward signs of these (e.g., angry facial expressions); and *cognitions*—they can induce individuals to think hostile thoughts or can bring beliefs and attitudes about aggression to mind. Depending on individuals' interpretations (*appraisals*) of the current situation and restraining factors (e.g., the presence of police or the threatening nature of the intended target person), they then engage either in thoughtful action, which might involve restraining their anger, or impulsive action, which can lead to overt aggressive actions (see Figure 10.4 for an overview of this theory).

Bushman and Anderson (2002) have expanded this theory to explain why individuals who are exposed to high levels of aggression—either directly, in the actions of others, or in films and video games—may tend to become increasingly aggressive themselves. Repeated exposure to such stimuli serves to strengthen *knowledge structures* related to aggression—beliefs, attitudes, schemas, and scripts (see Chapter 2) relevant to aggression. As these knowledge structures related to aggression grow stronger, it is easier for these to be activated by situational or person variables. The result? The people in question are truly "primed" for aggression.

The GAM is certainly more complex than earlier theories of aggression (e.g., the famous frustration-aggression hypothesis; Dollard et al., 1939). In addition, because it fully reflects recent progress in the field—growing understanding of the fact that what people *think* is crucial in determining in what they actually do—it seems much more likely to provide an accurate view of the nature of human aggression than these earlier theories—and that, of course, is what scientific progress is all about!

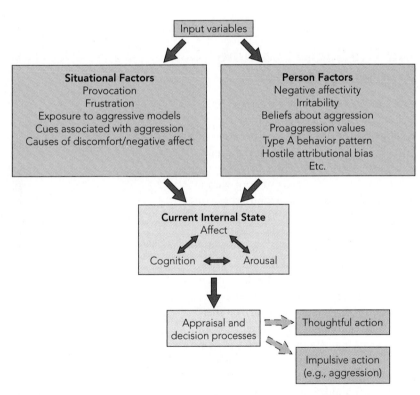

FIGURE 10.4   The GAM: A Modern Theory of Human Aggression

As shown here, the general aggression model (GAM) suggests that human aggression stems from many different factors. Input variables relating to the situation or person influence cognitions, affect, and arousal, and these internal states plus other factors such as appraisal and decision mechanism determine whether, and in what form, aggression occurs.   (Source: Based on suggestions by Bushman & Anderson, 2002).

KEY POINTS

- **Aggression** is the intentional infliction of harm on others. While most social psychologists reject the view that human aggression is strongly determined by genetic factors, evolution-oriented theorists claim that genetic factors play some role in such behavior.

- **Drive theories** suggest that aggression stems from externally elicited drives to harm or injure others. The

frustration-aggression hypothesis is the most famous example of such theories.

- Modern theories of aggression, such as the **general aggression model,** recognize the importance of learning various eliciting input variables, individual differences, affective states, and, especially, cognitive processes.

Causes of Human Aggression: Social, Cultural, Personal, and Situational

Here's an actual incident that occurred not very long ago in a bar. Charles Barkley, a professional basketball player (see Figure 10.5), entered a local bar at the same time as another man. (Barkley stands 6' 6" and weighs 252 pounds.) Both stepped up to the bar and Barkley ordered a drink. Seemingly, without provocation, the other fellow picked up a glass of water and hurled the contents at Barkley. What should Barkley do? Water is harmless and will dry very quickly; the two men are strangers who will probably never see each other again. In addition, Barkley is a stranger in town and it is possible that the water-throwing offender has many friends standing by, ready to help him; in other words, it could be a setup for Barkley—something professional athletes sometimes encounter from fans of rival teams. Rationally, therefore, Barkley should just look the other way and avoid trouble, right? What do you think he actually did? Without hesitation, he simply picked up the offender and threw him through the front window of the bar.

What would you do in a similar situation? Would you, too, lose your temper and react strongly? Or would you follow a less dangerous course of action, such as leaving the scene? This would probably depend on many factors: Are you as tall and powerful as Barkley, so that you easily handle people like this stranger who annoyed you? Have you already had several drinks or none? Who else is present—friends, strangers, perhaps undercover police officers? Are you in a good mood or a bad one? Is it pleasant in the bar, or hot, steamy, and uncomfortable? What explanations for this stranger's provocation pass through your mind? Research by social psychologists has shown that *all* of these factors—and many others, too—can play a role. In other words, aggression doesn't stem from one primary factor or just a few; rather, as modern theories of aggression suggest (e.g., Anderson & Bushman, 2002; DeWall, Twenge, Gitter, & Baumeister, 2009), it is influenced by a wide range of social, cultural, personal, and situational conditions. We now review some of the most important of these factors—conditions that increase the likelihood that people will engage in some form of aggression.

FIGURE 10.5   Charles Barkley: One Famous Athlete Who Responded Strongly to Provocation
Would you provoke this famous and powerful athlete? Only if you like to live dangerously! When one stranger annoyed Barkley in a bar, he picked up this person up and threw him through the bar's front window!

Basic Sources of Aggression: Frustration and Provocation

Aggression, like other forms of social behavior, is often a response to something in the social world around us. In other words, it often occurs in response to something other people have said or done. Here are several ways in which this can—and often does—occur.

FRUSTRATION: WHY *NOT* GETTING WHAT YOU WANT (OR WHAT YOU EXPECT) CAN SOMETIMES LEAD TO AGGRESSION Suppose that you asked 20 people you know to name the single most important cause of aggression. What would they say? The chances are good that most would reply *frustration*. And if you asked them to define frustration, many would state: "The way I feel when something—or someone—prevents me from getting what I want or expect to get in some situation." This widespread belief in the importance of frustration as a cause of aggression stems, at least in part, from the famous **frustration-aggression hypothesis** mentioned in our discussion of drive theories of aggression (Dollard et al., 1939). In its original form, this hypothesis made two sweeping assertions: (1) Frustration *always* leads to some form of aggression and (2) aggression *always* stems from frustration. In short, the theory held that frustrated people always engage in some type of aggression and that all acts of aggression, in turn, result from frustration. Bold statements like these are appealing, but it does not mean that they are necessarily accurate. In fact, existing evidence suggests that both portions of the frustration-aggression hypothesis assign far too much importance to frustration as a determinant of human aggression. When frustrated, individuals do not always respond with aggression. On the contrary, they show many different reactions, ranging from sadness, despair, and depression on the one hand, to direct attempts to overcome the source of their frustration on the other. In short, aggression is definitely not an automatic response to frustration.

Second, it is equally clear that not all aggression stems from frustration. As we have already noted, people aggress for many different reasons and in response to many different factors. Why, for instance, did Jessica Logan's classmates heap abuse on her after her boyfriend posted nude photos of her on the Internet? Were they frustrated in any way? Was Jessica the cause of such feelings? Probably not. Many factors other than frustration no doubt played a role.

In view of these basic facts, few social psychologists now accept the idea that frustration is the only, or even the most important, cause of aggression. Instead, most believe that it is simply one of many factors that can potentially lead to aggression. We should add that frustration can serve as a powerful determinant of aggression under certain conditions—especially when it is viewed as illegitimate or unjustified (e.g., Folger & Baron, 1996). For instance, if a student believes that she deserves a good grade on a term paper but then receives a poor one, with no explanation, she may conclude that she has been treated very unfairly—that her legitimate needs have been thwarted. The result: She may have hostile thoughts, experience intense anger, and seek revenge against the perceived source of such frustration—in this case, her professor.

DIRECT PROVOCATION: WHEN AGGRESSION (OR EVEN TEASING) BREEDS AGGRESSION Major world religions often suggest that when provoked by another person, we should "turn the other cheek"—in other words, the most appropriate way to respond to being annoyed or irritated by another person is to do our best to ignore this treatment. In fact, however, research findings indicate that this is easier to say than to do, and that physical or verbal **provocation** from others is one of the strongest causes of human aggression. When we are on the receiving end of some form of provocation from others—criticism we consider unfair, sarcastic remarks, or physical assaults—we tend to reciprocate, returning as much aggression as we have received—or perhaps even more, especially if we are certain that the other person *meant* to harm us.

frustration-aggression hypothesis
The suggestion that frustration is a very powerful determinant of aggression.

provocation
Actions by others that tend to trigger aggression in the recipient, often because they are perceived as stemming from malicious intent.

What kinds of provocation produce the strongest push toward aggression? Existing evidence suggests that *condescension*—expressions of arrogance or disdain on the part of others—is very powerful (Harris, 1993). Harsh and unjustified criticism, especially criticism that attacks *us* rather than our behavior, is another powerful form of provocation, and when exposed to it, most people find it very difficult to avoid getting angry and retaliating in some manner, either immediately or later on (Baron, 1993b). Still another form of provocation to which many people respond with annoyance is **teasing**—provoking statements that call attention to an individual's flaws and imperfections, but can be, at the same time, somewhat playful in nature (e.g., Kowalski, 2001). Teasing can range from mild, humorous remarks (e.g., "Hey—you look like your hair just went through an electric mixer!") through nicknames or comments that truly seem designed to hurt. Research findings indicate that the more individuals attribute teasing to hostile motives—a desire to embarrass or annoy them—the more likely they are to respond aggressively (Campos, Keltner, Beck, Gonzaga, & John, 2007).

In addition, research findings indicate that actions by others that somehow threaten our status or public image are important triggers of aggression. For instance, in one revealing study (Griskevicius et al., 2009), participants (male and female college students) were asked to describe the primary reason why they had performed the most recent act of direct aggression against another person. A substantial proportion—48.3 percent of men and 45.3 percent of women—described concerns about their status or reputation as the main cause of their aggression—threats to their self-identity (see Chapter 4). In sum, others' actions—especially when they are interpreted as stemming from hostile motives—from a desire to harm *us* are often a very powerful cause of aggression.

What about emotion? Does it, too, play an important role in triggering aggression? Your first reaction is probably "Of course! People aggress when they are feeling frustrated or angry—not when they are happy or relaxed." But in fact, the situation is more complex than this, as we explain in the special section "EMOTIONS AND AGGRESSION: Does Arousal Play a Role?" below.

teasing
Provoking statements that call attention to the target's flaws and imperfections.

EMOTIONS *and* AGGRESSION

Does Arousal Play a Role?

The view that strong emotions underlie many aggressive acts makes good sense, and seems intuitively obvious. But think again: Do all instances of aggression involve strong emotions or feelings? Actually, they do not. For instance, people who have a grudge against someone sometimes wait for long periods of time before attempting to harm their enemies—they wait until conditions are "right" for doing the most damage with the least risk to themselves. An old Italian saying captures this idea: "Revenge is the only dish best served cold." It suggests that when seeking revenge, it is sometimes best to do so *after* intense emotions have cooled—the result may be a more effective strategy! Here's another example: Paid assassins—professional killers who murder specific people—do so simply because they are paid for completing this task. Usually, as many movies have illustrated, they don't know these individuals, and feel no anger toward them; but this is their job, and the most effective ones do it coolly, with no emotional "baggage" to get in their way.

And here's another complication in the simple idea that "aggression stems from or always involves strong emotion." Experts on emotion generally agree that often, our moods involve two basic dimensions: a positive–negative dimension (happy to sad) and an activation dimension (low to high). This raises an intriguing question about the role of the "feeling side" of life in aggression: Can heightened arousal facilitate aggression even if it is unrelated to this behavior in any direct way? Suppose, for instance, that you are driving to the airport to meet a friend. On the way there, another driver cuts you off and you almost have an accident. Your heart pounds wildly and your blood pressure shoots through the roof; but fortunately, no accident occurs. Now you arrive at the airport. You

(continued)

EMOTIONS *and* AGGRESSION *(continued)*

park and rush inside because you are already late for your flight. When you get to the security line, a person in front of you is very slow to open his briefcase and also slow to remove his shoes. In addition, he hasn't placed his liquids in a separate small bag, so the agent must sort through them now, while you wait. Quickly, you become highly irritated by this person, and say, mainly to yourself, "What a jerk; why don't people like that stay home? I may miss my flight because of his stupidity . . . " And if you could, you would push him out of the way and move forward to catch your plane.

Now for the key question: Do you think that your recent near miss in traffic may have played any role in your sudden surge of anger at this other passenger's slowness? Could the emotional arousal from that incident, which has persisted, be affecting your feelings and actions inside the airport? Research evidence suggests that it could (Zillmann, 1988, 1994). Under some conditions, heightened arousal—whatever its source—can enhance aggression in response to provocation, frustration, or other factors. In fact, in various experiments, arousal stemming from such varied sources as participation in competitive games (Christy, Gelfand, & Hartmann, 1971), exercise (Zillmann, 1979), and even some types of music (Rogers & Ketcher, 1979) has been found to increase subsequent aggression. Why is this the case? A compelling explanation is offered by **excitation transfer theory** (Zillmann, 1983, 1988).

This theory suggests that because physiological arousal tends to dissipate slowly over time, a portion of such arousal may persist as a person moves from one situation to another. In the example above, some portion of the arousal you experienced because of the near-miss in traffic may still be present as you approach the security gate in the airport. Now, when you encounter a minor annoyance, that arousal, which is no longer salient to you, remains and intensifies your emotional reactions to the annoyance. The result: You become enraged rather than just mildly irritated. Excitation theory further suggests that such effects are most likely to occur when the people involved are relatively unaware of the presence of residual arousal—a common occurrence, since small elevations in arousal are difficult to notice (Zillmann, 1994). In fact, the theory may even help us to understand why tragic events such as the abuse of prisoners in the Abu Ghraib prison by U.S. soldiers occurred and why it aroused such strong reactions in many people who learned about it (Breen & Matusitz, 2009).

Excitation transfer theory also suggests that such effects are likely to occur when the people involved recognize their residual arousal but attribute it to events occurring in the present situation (Taylor, Helgeson, Reed, & Skokan, 1991). In the airport incident, for instance, your anger would be intensified if you recognized your feelings of arousal but attributed them to the elderly man's actions rather than the driver who nearly cut you off (see Figure 10.6). Overall, it's clear that the relationship between emotion and aggression is more complex than common sense suggests.

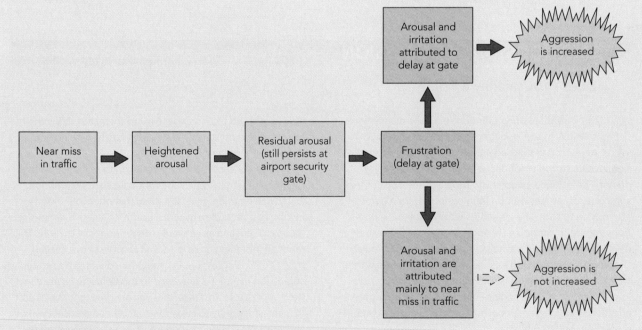

FIGURE 10.6 Excitation Transfer Theory
This theory suggests that arousal occurring in one situation can persist and intensify emotional reactions in later, unrelated situations. For instance, the arousal produced by a near miss in traffic can intensify feelings of annoyance stemming from delays at an airport security gate. (Source: Based on suggestions by Zillmann, 1994).

Social Causes of Aggression: Social Exclusion and Exposure to Media Violence

What does it feel like to be excluded—rejected by others? Clearly, this is an unpleasant experience, and one most of us would prefer to avoid. Exclusion not only means that we can't enjoy the benefits of social relations with others; it also reflects negatively on our self-image. After all, if other people don't want us around, that seems to indicate that we have undesirable rather than desirable characteristics. Does rejection by others increase our likelihood of aggressing against them? Doing so would allow us to "even the score," but on the other hand, aggressive people are often excluded from groups or rejected by others *because* they are aggressive. Research findings, however, indicate that despite such issues, social rejection *is* often a powerful trigger for aggression (e.g., Leary, Twenge, & Quinlivan, 2006). Being rejected or excluded by others often leads to increases in aggression against them by the excluded individuals, which, in turn, could lead to even more exclusion—a kind of self-perpetuating, negative cycle. But why, precisely, does this occur? Does the emotional distress generated by being excluded lead to "lashing out" against the sources of rejection? That seems like a reasonable explanation, but studies designed to find out if emotional distress following rejection leads to aggression have not confirmed this idea. Negative emotions do not appear to mediate the effects of rejection on aggression. Another possibility is that rejection by others initiates a *hostile cognitive mind-set*—it activates cognitive structures in our minds that lead us to perceive ambiguous or neutral actions by others as hostile in nature, and to perceive aggression as common in social interactions and as an appropriate kind of reaction (e.g., as suggested by the general aggression model; Anderson & Bushman, 2002; Tremblay & Belchevski, 2004). Evolutionary theory, too, suggests that a hostile cognitive mind-set or bias might follow from exclusion. In the past, human beings needed others—and cooperation with them—to survive. So, being excluded from the group was a very serious and threatening matter. This, in turn, suggests that exclusion by others would be interpreted as a very hostile action.

To test this reasoning, and find out if hostile cognitive bias does indeed underlie the effects of social exclusion on aggression, DeWall et al. (2009) conducted a series of studies. In one, some participants learned that their partner in an experiment had actively rejected them—refused to work with them—while others learned that their partner couldn't work with them because of factors beyond the partner's control—another appointment. To find out if rejection triggered hostile cognitive bias, both groups were then asked to complete word fragments that could be completed to form aggressive or nonaggressive words (e.g., "r _ pe" can be either *rape* or *ripe*). It was predicted that those who had been rejected would be more likely to complete the words in an aggressive way, and that was just what was found. In a follow-up study, participants completed a personality test and then were told that their scores indicated that they would either spend the future alone (i.e., they would be rejected by others) or that they would spend the future closely connected with other people in meaningful relationships. Next, they read a story in which another person acted in ambiguous ways. Afterward, they rated the extent to which the actions of the person in the story were accurately described by several adjectives related to hostility (e.g., *angry, hostile, dislikable, unfriendly*). It was predicted that learning that they would be socially excluded in the future would generate a hostile cognitive bias and lead participants in this group to rate a stranger's ambiguous actions as hostile. Again, this prediction was confirmed by the results. Finally, to determine if this hostile bias increased aggression, participants in both groups were given an opportunity to aggress against the stranger in the story; they were told that this person was seeking a position as a research assistant, which they needed badly, and were asked evaluate the stranger's suitability for the position. Negative evaluations, of course, would prevent this person from obtaining the needed position. It was predicted that participants told they would experience social exclusion

excitation transfer theory
A theory suggesting that arousal produced in one situation can persist and intensify emotional reactions occurring in later situations.

FIGURE 10.7 Social Exclusion: It Hurts, and Can Lead to Aggression

Being rejected or excluded by others is a painful experience. Research findings indicate that it results in a hostile mind-set, which leads us to perceive actions by others as stemming from hostility, even when they do not. This, in turn, can increase aggression.

in the future would rate this person lower than those told they would experience a rich, full social life. Once more, the findings confirmed these predictions.

Overall, the results of this study, and several others, indicate that social exclusion does indeed operate through the generation of a hostile cognitive mind-set or bias (see Figure 10.7). In short, rejection by others is indeed a strong antecedent of aggression, and it has such effects because it leads us to perceive others' actions as stemming from hostile motives and a desire on their part to harm us. Yes, rejection hurts and causes a lot of emotional distress, but it appears to be the cognitive effects it produces rather than the emotional ones that are most strongly responsible for the fact that excluded people do often become highly aggressive—not simply toward the people who have excluded them, but toward others as well.

MEDIA VIOLENCE: THE POTENTIALLY HARMFUL EFFECTS OF FILMS, TELEVISION, AND VIDEO GAMES What's the last film you saw at the movies? Did it contain aggression or violence? How often did characters attack others and attempt to harm others? For instance, consider one giant hit of a few years back: *Avatar*. Certainly it was exciting in many ways, but didn't it contain a tremendous amount of violence? In fact, a large proportion of the action on the screen fit into this category (see Figure 10.8). And indeed, systematic surveys of the content of recent films, television shows, and other media indicate that violence is very frequent in the popular offerings of the mass media (Bushman & Anderson, 2001; Reiss & Roth, 1993; Waters, Block, Friday, & Gordon, 1993).

This fact raises an important question that social psychologists have studied for decades: Does exposure to such materials increase aggression among children or adults? Literally hundreds of studies have been performed to test this possibility, and the results seem clear: *Exposure to media violence may indeed be one factor contributing to high levels of violence in countries where such materials are viewed by large numbers of people* (e.g., Anderson et al., 2003; Bushman & Anderson, 2009; Paik & Comstock, 1994). In fact, in a summary of research findings in this area (Anderson, Berkowitz, et al., 2004), leading experts on this topic who have provided testimony in U.S. Senate hearings on media and violence offered the following basic conclusions:

1. Research on exposure to violent television, movies, video games, and music indicates that such materials significantly increase the likelihood of aggressive behavior by people exposed to them.
2. Such effects are both short term and long term in nature.
3. The magnitude of these effects is large—at least as large as the various medical effects considered to be important by physicians (e.g., the effect of aspirin on heart attacks).

In other words, social psychology's leading experts on the effects of media violence agree that these effects are real, lasting, and substantial—effects with important implications for society and for the safety and well-being of millions of people who are the victims of aggressive actions each year. Many different types of research support these conclusions. For example, in short-term laboratory experiments, children or adults exposed to violent films and television programs have been found to show more aggression than others exposed to nonviolent films or programs (e.g., Bushman & Huesmann, 2001). The earliest research of this type was conducted by Albert Bandura and his colleagues in the early 1960s—a time when social psychology was still, in many respects, a new and rapidly growing science. To address this question, Bandura's team of researchers (e.g., Bandura, Ross, & Ross, 1963a, 1963b) devised an ingenious approach. Instead of using actual television programs, they constructed their own TV shows in which an adult model was shown aggressing against a large inflated toy clown (a Bobo doll) in unusual ways. For instance, the model sat on the doll, punched it repeatedly in the nose, struck it on the head with a toy mallet, and kicked it about the room. This "program" or one in which the model showed no aggressive actions toward the Bobo doll were then shown to nursery school–age children.

FIGURE 10.8   Violence in the Media: More Than Ever?
Despite decades of research indicating that exposure to media violence can increase aggression among viewers, recent hit films such as "Avatar" are literally loaded with scenes like this one.

Following exposure to one of the two programs, the children were placed in a room containing many toys, several of which had been used by the adult model in his or her attacks against the doll. They were allowed to play freely for 20 minutes and during this period their behavior was carefully observed to see if, perhaps, they would show actions similar to those of the model in the aggressive program. Results were clear: Young children exposed to the actions of an aggressive adult model showed strong tendencies to imitate these behaviors (see Figure 10.9). In contrast, those exposed to a nonaggressive adult model (the one who sat quietly in the room and didn't attack the inflated doll) did not show similar actions. Bandura and his associates reasoned that the children had learned new ways of aggressing from the "program" they watched and that in a similar manner, children could also learn new ways of aggressing against others— and also learn that aggression is an acceptable form of behavior—from watching actual television shows and films.

Other research on the effects of media violence, in contrast, has employed longitudinal procedures, in which the same participants are studied for many years (e.g., Anderson & Bushman, 2002; Huesmann & Eron,

FIGURE 10.9   Bandura's "Bobo Doll" Studies: Early Evidence for the Effects of Televised Violence
In these famous studies, children saw a "television program" in which an adult model either attacked an inflated plastic doll (top row of photos) or sat quietly. When given a chance to play with the same toys, children imitated the actions of the aggressive model (bottom two rows of photos). These findings suggested that exposure to violence in the media may lead to similar actions by viewers.

1984, 1986). Results of such research, too, are clear: The more violent films or television programs participants watched as children, the higher their levels of aggression as teenagers or adults—for instance, the higher the likelihood that they have been arrested for violent crimes. Such findings have been replicated in many different countries—Australia, Finland, Israel, Poland, and South Africa (Botha, 1990). Thus, they appear to hold across different cultures. Furthermore, such effects are not restricted only to actual programs or films; they appear to be produced by violence in news programs, by violent lyrics in popular music (e.g., Anderson, Carnagey, & Eubanks, 2003), and by violent video games (Anderson, 2004; Anderson & Bushman, 2001).

This last media source—*violent video games*—has recently become the subject of intense study because these games are very popular and are played (often, for hours each day) by many millions of people all over the world. A large number of studies have sought to determine if playing such games produces effects similar to those produced by watching violent films or television shows, and the results are both consistent and, in one sense, alarming. For instance, a recent meta-analysis that examined the findings of all available well-conducted studies on the effects of aggressive video games (Anderson et al., 2010) concluded that playing such games increases aggressive cognitions (thoughts related to harming others), aggressive affect (feelings of hostility, anger, and revenge), and subsequent aggressive behavior. In addition, playing aggressive video games reduces empathy for others and the tendency to engage in prosocial behavior. Such effects occur in Eastern (i.e., Asian) countries as well as Western ones (Europe, North America), and appear to generate long-term effects—relatively long-lasting increases in aggressive cognitions, affect, and overt behavior. Indeed, such effects are found in short-term laboratory studies as well as long-term longitudinal studies that follow the same participants for months or years. After reviewing this extensive evidence, Anderson et al. (2010, p. 171) offer the following somewhat unsettling conclusion: "Video games are neither inherently good nor inherently bad. But people learn. And content matters." When the content being learned is aggression, it is likely to have substantial and large-scale undesirable social implications.

FIGURE 10.10 Why Do People Play Violent Video Games?
Research findings indicate that contrary to popular belief, people who play violent video games do not do so because of their violent content. Rather, they play these games because they enjoy the feeling of mastery and competence they provide. These effects are especially strong for people high in trait aggressiveness.

One more question arises concerning the impact of violent video games: Why do so many people like to play them? An initial guess was that it is the violent content that makes them so popular; people find violence (especially in the safe context of a video game) exciting and enjoyable, so they purchase these games and play them. This suggestion is so compelling that it has generally been accepted as *the* explanation for the immense popularity of violent video games (see Figure 10.10). But is this really so? Research by Przybylski, Ryan, and Rigby (2009) indicates that in fact it is not. Drawing on cognitive evaluation theory (Ryan & Deci, 2000, 2007)—they suggest that, in fact, it is not the violence in games such as "Grand Theft Auto" that make them so appealing, but rather the sense of autonomy and competence that the games provide. In other words, people enjoy playing violent video games because they provide players with a sense of being in control—acting independently—and because they provide opportunities for experiencing competence by exercising their skills or abilities. To test this reasoning, members of an Internet forum for discussion of video games completed measures of their feelings of competence and mastery while playing various games (e.g.,"I experienced a lot of freedom in the game," "The game provides me with interesting options and choices"). In addition, they rated their enjoyment of the games, their absorption in them, and their interest in a sequel (e.g., "I would buy a sequel to this game"). Finally, violent content in various games was coded by three raters; a rating of 1 was assigned to games with no violent content (e.g., "Tetris"), 2 was assigned to games with abstract violence (e.g., "Super Mario"), 3 to games with impersonal violence (e.g., "Civilization"), 4 to games with fantasy violence ("Starfox"), and 5 to games with realistic violence (e.g., "God of War 2").

Results indicated that the extent to which the games satisfied needs for autonomy and competence were related to enjoyment of the games, absorption in them, and interest in purchasing a sequel, but were *not* related to violent content. So it appeared that the popularity of these games was not due primarily to their violent content, but rather to other factors. In several follow-up studies, the same authors examined the possibility that people who are high in aggressiveness would be more likely to prefer, enjoy, and become immersed in violent games relative to nonviolent ones. In these studies, participants played either a violent or nonviolent game, and then rated their preference for future play. Those high in trait aggressiveness did in fact prefer the violent games to the nonviolent ones, whereas people low in trait aggressiveness preferred the nonviolent games. However—and this is key—when the extent to which the games satisfied their needs for mastery and competence were held constant, this difference (between people high and low in aggressiveness) disappeared. This, too, suggests that it is not the violent content of these games that makes them appealing, even for highly aggressive people.

Overall, results of the research by Przybyilski and colleagues (2009) indicate that although highly aggressive people are indeed attracted to violent video games, in general, it is *not* the violent content of these games but rather the opportunity for autonomy and competence they provide that makes them so popular. This suggests that games that provide such experiences, but without violent content, might well be as popular as those with such content. So it may be possible for players of video games to enjoy important benefits *without* simultaneously experiencing the negative effects that often stem from violent games. Now, if only the manufacturers of video games will give this possibility a try . . . !

THE EFFECTS OF MEDIA VIOLENCE: WHY DO THEY OCCUR?   By now, you may be wondering about a very basic question: Why does exposure to media violence (of many different kinds) increase aggression among people exposed to it? A compelling answer has been provided by Bushman and Anderson (2002), who suggest that the effects of media violence can be readily understood within the context of the general aggression model (GAM) presented earlier in this chapter. As you may recall, this model suggests that both personal and situational factors influence individuals' internal states—their feelings, thoughts, and arousal—and that these internal states, in turn, shape individuals' appraisal of a given situation and their decision as to how to behave in it—aggressively or nonaggressively. Bushman and Anderson suggest that repeated exposure to media violence can strongly affect cognitions relating to aggression, gradually creating a *hostile expectation bias*—a strong expectation that others will behave aggressively. This, in turn, causes individuals to be more aggressive themselves; after all, they perceive provocations from others everywhere, even when they really don't exist! Studies designed to test this reasoning (e.g., Bushman & Anderson, 2002;) have generated results consistent with it, so it appears that the GAM and the processes it describes do indeed play an important role in the effects of media violence.

THE EFFECTS OF MEDIA VIOLENCE: NEUROSCIENCE EVIDENCE FOR THE IMPACT OF DESENSITIZATION One other factor that may also play an important role is *desensitization* to violence. In other words, as a result of exposure to large amounts of violent content in television programs, films, and video games, individuals become less sensitive to violence and its consequences (Anderson et al., 2003). Research findings suggest that such effects do occur, and can contribute to increased aggression by people exposed to media violence (e.g., Funk, Bechtoldt-Baldacci, Pasold, & Baumgartner, 2004). For example, Krahe et al. (2011) measured the skin conductance (a measure of physiological arousal) among individuals who reported watching media violence (films, violent games) often or relatively rarely as they viewed either a violent or sad film. As expected, those with a history of frequent exposure to violent materials showed less arousal to the violent film than those who were rarely exposed to such materials. Apparently, their frequent exposure to violence had reduced their emotional reactions to such scenes of even extreme violence. Perhaps even more dramatic evidence for such desensitization, however, is provided by research using a social neuroscience perspective.

Actually, the research by Bartholow, Bushman, and Sestir (2006) provides a clear example of this approach. Individuals in that study reported on the extent to which they had played violent and nonviolent video games in the past and then participated in a competitive reaction time task in which they could determine the loudness of unpleasant sounds delivered to another person (who did not actually exist) when that person lost the competition. Before playing the competitive game, participants first viewed a series of neutral images (e.g., a man on a bicycle) and violent images (e.g., a person holding a gun to another person's head). Activity in their brains was recorded while they watched these images. In particular, activity that had been found in previous research to indicate the extent to which incoming emotion-provoking stimuli are being processed and categorized was carefully analyzed. (This is known as P300 activity—one kind of *event-related brain potential*—changes in brain activity that occur as certain kinds of information are processed.) Presumably, if individuals have been desensitized to violent images by their past experience in playing video games, P300 activity would be smaller when they view violent images. In fact, that's exactly what happened: Individuals who had previously played violent video games frequently showed smaller P300 reactions when viewing violent images than individuals who reported previously having played mainly nonviolent games. These findings suggest that exposure to media violence does indeed desensitize the people who view it. Other findings (e.g., Bartholow et al., 2006) indicate that the degree of such desensitization, in turn, predicts the likelihood that such people will aggress against others.

Overall, it appears that exposure to violence in films, television, or video games increases the tendency to aggress against others in several ways. First, as we just saw, it reduces individuals' emotional reactions to such events so that, in a sense, they perceive them as "nothing out of the ordinary." Second, it strengthens beliefs, expectations, and other cognitive processes related to aggression. In other words, as a result of repeated exposure to violent movies, TV programs, or video games, individuals develop strong *knowledge structures* relating to aggression—structures reflecting, and combining, these beliefs, expectations, schemas, and scripts. When these knowledge structures are then activated by various events, people feel, think, and act aggressively because this is what, in a sense, they have learned to do.

Whatever the precise underlying mechanisms, 40 years of research on this issue suggests strongly that exposure to media violence can have very harmful effects on society. So why, then, is there so much of it on television, in movies, and in video games? The answer, sad to relate, is that violence *sells*—people seem to find it exciting and enjoyable. Moreover, because advertisers assume this is true, they "put their money where the action is" (Bushman, 1998). In short, this is one more case in which economic motives take precedence over everything else. We know what to do, as a society, with respect to media violence: We should reduce it, if decreasing violence is our goal. But as long as people are willing to pay to see aggressive shows and films or buy violent video games, there seems little chance this will happen. But we are optimists by nature, so we can always hope!

KEY POINTS

- Contrary to the famous **frustration-aggression hypothesis**, all aggression does not stem from frustration, and frustration does not always lead to aggression. Frustration is a strong elicitor of aggression only under certain limited conditions.

- In contrast, **provocation** from others is a powerful elicitor of aggression. Even mild **teasing** can stimulate aggression, although such effects are stronger in certain cultures than others.

- Heightened arousal can increase aggression if it persists beyond the situation in which it was induced and is unknowingly interpreted as anger generated in the new context.

- Exposure to media violence has been found to increase aggression among viewers. This is due to several factors, such as the priming of aggressive thoughts and a weakening of restraints against aggression, and also to desensitization to such materials.

- Playing violent video games increases aggressive cognition, aggressive affect, and overt aggressive behavior. It also reduces empathy toward others and prosocial behavior.

- Individuals like to play these games not because of the aggressive content but because the games satisfy motives for competence and mastery.

Cultural Factors in Aggression: "Cultures of Honor," Sexual Jealousy, and the Male Gender Role

While aggression is often triggered by the words or deeds of other people, it can also stem from *cultural factors*—beliefs, norms, and expectations in a given culture—suggesting that aggression is appropriate or perhaps even required under certain circumstances. Social psychologists have taken careful note of this fact in recent research on what is known as **cultures of honor**—cultures in which there are strong norms indicating that aggression is an appropriate response to insults to one's honor. This is a theme in many films about the Old West, in which characters felt compelled to have a shoot-out with another person because their honor had somehow been sullied and is also seen in Asian films that present epic battles between warriors who possess seemingly magical powers.

Why did such norms develop? Cohen and Nisbett (1994, 1997) suggest that they may be traced to the fact that in some geographic areas, wealth was once concentrated mainly in assets that could readily be stolen (e.g., cattle and, sad to relate, slaves). For this reason, it became important for individuals to demonstrate that they would not tolerate such thefts, or any other affront to their honor. The result? Norms condoning violence in response to insults to one's honor emerged and were widely accepted.

Research findings indicate that such norms are definitely *not* a thing of the past; on the contrary, they are alive and well in many parts of the world (e.g., Vandello & Cohen, 2003). For instance, in one study, white baseball pitchers were more likely to hit batters in situations where their honor had been, in a sense, insulted: after another batter had hit a home run or after one of their own teammates had been hit by a pitched ball (Timmerman, 2007). While cultural beliefs condoning or even requiring aggression in response to affronts to one's honor operate in many different contexts, their impact is especially apparent with respect to *sexual jealousy*.

cultures of honor
Cultures in which there are strong norms indicating that aggression is an appropriate response to insults to one's honor.

SEXUAL JEALOUSY Infidelity—real or imagined—occurs in every society, even in ones that greatly restrict informal contact between women and men. But even if actual infidelity does not occur, *sexual jealousy*—the suspicion or fear that it might—can be a powerful motivator of aggressive behavior (e.g., Kaighobadi, Schackelford, & Goetz, 2009; Kaighobadi, Starratt, Schackelford, & Popp, 2008). In cultures of honor, such behavior by women is viewed as especially threatening to male honor (e.g., Baker, Gregware, & Cassidy, 1999), and can result in drastic responses—severe punishment for both the women and men involved in such contacts.

Not surprisingly, sexual jealousy is related to aggression against one's unfaithful partner. In fact, in the United States, 20 percent of all reported incidents of nonfatal violence against women are performed by intimate partners (Bureau of Justice Statistics, 2003)—some 600,000 assaults each year! Moreover, 30 percent of all female homicide victims are killed by an intimate partner (Bureau of Justice Statistics, 2007). Although sexual jealousy did not play a key role in all of these events, it has been found to be present in a large proportion of them. In one sense, the link between sexual jealousy and aggression is not surprising: Jealousy is a powerful emotion and is often closely associated with intense feelings of betrayal and anger. On the other hand, assaulting intimate partners—the ones we love most—is also puzzling. How do people overcome strong restraints against seeking to harm people with whom they enjoy such close and intimate bonds?

An evolutionary perspective suggests that sexual jealousy, although present in both men and women, may have somewhat different foundations. For men, it may stem primarily from concern that children in the relationship are not, in fact, theirs—they are the offspring of sexual rivals. For women, in contrast, it may stem from the need for the resources and support that a mate provides. In fact, for men, sexual jealousy is focused on sexual infidelity, whereas for women, it is often focused on emotional infidelity—the withdrawal of emotional support by a mate who is involved with other females (Buss, 2000; Thomson, Patel, Platek, & Shackelford, 2007). However, recent evidence suggests that this difference is not as clear-cut as was previously believed, and that in fact, the two genders overlap with respect to the factors that lead them to experience sexual jealousy (Eagly & Wood, in press).

Evolutionary theory further suggests that to lessen sexual jealousy—and avoid the rage it often generates—men engage in *mate-retention behaviors*—actions designed to prevent a partner from engaging in infidelity. These include keeping a partner under close surveillance, threats of punishment for infidelity, showing affect and care, public signals of possession, and actions designed to drive off or threaten potential rivals. The more attractive a mate, or the younger she is, the more men tend to engage in such actions (Starratt, Shakelford, Goetz, & McKiddin, 2007).

How can evolutionary theory account for dangerous assaults against intimate partners, and more violent fatal ones? One hypothesis is that this stems from paternal uncertainty—men's inability to know, with absolute certainty, that their children are theirs (i.e., genetically). This may have led to a tragic tendency to eliminate unfaithful mates—and their offspring. While such a hypothesis is very controversial and drastic in nature, it is consistent with the fact that men are most likely to kill their intimate partners when they threaten to leave the relationship, thus confirming suspicions of sexual infidelity.

Whatever the actual causes of the strong link between sexual jealousy and aggression, it is clear that jealousy is indeed a powerful cause of aggression and that, moreover, violence stemming from it—or from other factors that threaten a man's honor—are excused or condoned in many cultures, including, especially, in cultures of honor (e.g., Puente & Cohen, 2003; Vanandello & Cohen, 2003). Clearly, then, cultural factors play a key role in both the occurrence of aggression and in how it is perceived and evaluated.

PRECARIOUS MANHOOD: THE MALE GENDER ROLE AND OVERT AGGRESSION Different cultures define "manhood" in contrasting ways, but around the world, it seems to involve more than mere maturation—attaining full growth and sexual maturity. Rather, the transition to manhood is often marked by special ceremonies, and involves a boost in status. Unfortunately, this status can be readily challenged or even lost. For instance, when asked how a person might lose his "manhood," many people list a large number of factors, such as "being unable to support his family," "letting others down," or "losing face in front of his wife or friends." In contrast, people find it more difficult to come up with ways in which a woman could lose her womanhood, and these were much more drastic in scope (e.g., having a sex-change operation). If "manhood" does confer increased status and other benefits (and in many cultures it does), then threats to it might lead to actions designed to protect or restore and these might—as you can readily guess—involve aggression. Moreover, physical aggression is part of men's culturally defined gender role in many cultures. So what happens when manhood is challenged? Bosson, Vandello, Burnaford, Weaver, and Wasti (2009), predicted that the result would be increased physical aggression. To obtain evidence on this prediction, they asked men either to braid a rope or braid the hair on a female mannequin's head. The first task was relatively neutral, but the second was one designed to expose the men to a mild threat to their manhood; after all, braiding hair is *not* a typical activity for most men. After this experience, they were asked to perform a task in which they punched a punching bag. The force of their blows was recorded, and as predicted, the men who had braided the mannequin's hair hit the punching bag significantly harder than those who had braided the rope.

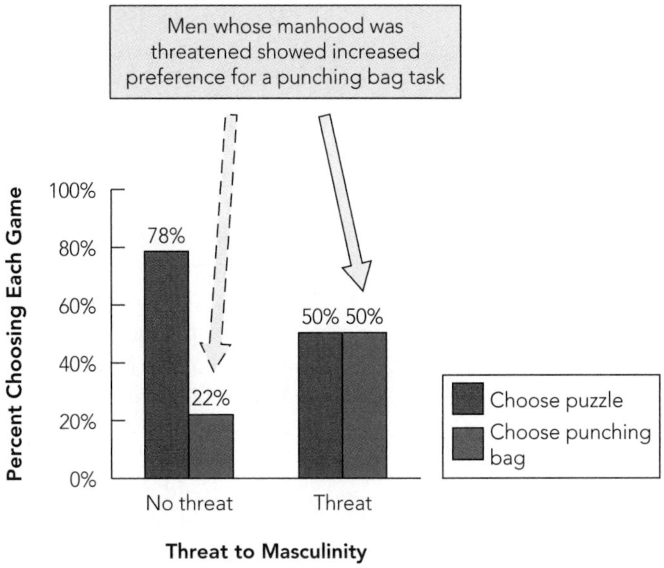

In a follow-up study, men once again braided either a rope or a dummy's hair, then were given a choice between performing two tasks: punching the punching bag or working on a puzzle. It was predicted that the men whose manhood was threatened would choose the punching bag task, and as you can see from Figure 10.11, that's what happened: fully 50 percent of them chose the punching bag task, while only 22 percent of those who braided the rope did so. In other words, when their manhood had been challenged, even mildly, men were more likely to choose an aggressive task, presumably as a means of reducing or eliminating the threat they experienced. So once again, we see that cultural factors—in this case, cultural definitions of the male gender role—often play an important role in aggression.

FIGURE 10.11 **Threats to Masculinity: A Cause of Aggression**

Men who braided a mannequin's hair, and so experienced a mild threat to their "manhood," later showed a strong preference for punching a punching bag rather than playing a puzzle game. In contrast, men who braided a rope (and whose "manhood" was not threatened), were more likely to choose the puzzle task. (Source: Based on data from Bosson et al., 2009).

KEY POINTS

- **Cultures of honor** are ones in which strong norms indicate that slights to one's honor require an aggressive response. Such norms are still in existence today, and help explain differences in rates of aggression in different geographic locations.

- Sexual jealousy is a major cause of aggression between partners in intimate relationships.

- An evolutionary perspective suggests that men experience jealousy over sexual infidelity because of their parental uncertainty, while women experience jealousy over emotional infidelity because of their need for assistance from mates in child rearing.

- Manhood is, it appears, more precarious than womanhood: manhood can be lost through many events (e.g., an inability to support one's family). This suggests that threats to manhood may encourage aggression as a means of restoring or protecting manhood. Research findings offer support for this view, and highlight the importance of culturally defined gender roles in aggression.

Personality, Gender, and Aggression

Are some people more likely to aggress than others? Informal observation suggests that this is so. While some individuals rarely lose their tempers or engage in aggressive actions, others seem to be forever "losing it," with potentially serious consequences. And in fact, recent evidence (Carre, McCormick, & Moundloch, 2009) indicates that we can even accurately estimate others' aggressiveness from the appearance of their faces! In this surprising research, participants looked at the photos of male strangers and then estimated how aggressive they were likely to be. When aggression by these individuals was actually measured in a special laboratory game involving the choice between taking points away from or giving them to an opponent, their predictions of the stranger's aggressiveness were found to be accurate. What aspect of the face did they use for making such predictions? The width-to-height ratio of strangers' faces (i.e., the wider they are relative to how high they are). The larger this ratio, the more aggressive were the strangers predicted to be. And indeed, width-to-height ratios *were* significantly related to actual aggression. Why would this be so? Perhaps, as an evolutionary perspective suggests, people with a large width-to-height ratio appear more fierce and so are better able to drive away potential rivals for mates (see Figure 10.12). Whatever the reason, it is clear that even facial appearance can be a predictor of actual aggression, so clearly characteristics possessed by individuals are related to the occurrence of this dangerous form of behavior.

In the remainder of this section, we consider several characteristics—aspects of personality—that also seem to play an important role in aggression. First, though, we begin with a brief discussion of how personality characteristics can influence aggression—and many other forms of behavior.

TASS model

The traits as situational sensitivities model. A view suggesting that many personality traits function in a threshold-like manner, influencing behavior only when situations evoke them.

THE TASS MODEL: TRAITS AS SENSITIVITIES TO VARIOUS SITUATIONS In everyday speech, we often talk about people as possessing discrete traits. For instance, we say, "She is very friendly," "He is lazy," or "She is really smart." And as we saw in Chapter 3 in our discussion of the *fundamental attribution error*, we often go further, assuming that others' traits and characteristics largely determine their behavior. Social psychologists, in contrast, hold a somewhat different view. They note that *situations* are important too, and that social behavior often derives from a complex interaction between situational factors and personal traits or other characteristics (e.g., Kammrath, Mendoza-Denton, & Mischel, 2005). One theory that takes careful account of this fact is known as the **TASS model**—the traits as situational sensitivities model. This model suggests that many aspects of personality function in a threshold-like manner: Only when situational factors are strong enough to trigger them do they influence behavior. (In contrast, a more traditional model of how personality factors influence behavior suggests that such factors are most likely to exert strong or clear effects in ambiguous or "weak" situations—ones that don't require people to behave in certain ways.)

When applied to aggression, the TASS model makes the following prediction: The tendency to behave aggressively (sometimes known as *trait aggressiveness*) will only influence overt behavior when situational factors are strong enough to activate it. For people high in this trait, even weak provocations will stimulate an aggressive reaction; for people low in this trait,

FIGURE 10.12   Is the Tendency to Aggress Revealed in Peoples' Faces?

Surprising as it may seem, research findings indicate that we can accurately predict others' level of overt aggression from certain aspects of their faces. In particular, the higher the width-to-height ratio of others' faces, the more aggressive we perceive them as being—and in fact, the more aggressive they actually are! The person on the right has the higher width-to-height ratio.

in contrast, much stronger levels of provocation are required to trigger aggression. Evidence for this view has recently been reported by Marshall and Brown (2006). They first measured the trait aggressiveness of a large number of students, and then placed them in a situation where they were exposed to either no provocation from another person, moderate provocation, or strong provocation. Then, participants in all three groups were given an opportunity to aggress against this other person (by setting the intensity of bursts of noise this person would receive if she lost on a competitive reactions time task). The researchers predicted that for people high in trait aggressiveness, even a moderate level of provocation would trigger intense aggressive reactions; for people low in trait aggressiveness, however, a moderate provocation would trigger little or no aggression. Only a strong provocation would result in overt aggression. This is precisely what happened. People high in the tendency to aggress (high in trait aggressiveness) literally "exploded" when they received even a mild provocation from another person (a mildly negative evaluation of an essay they wrote). In contrast, people low in trait aggressiveness showed little or no reaction to a mild provocation, but they *did* respond with strong aggression when they received a very powerful provocation (an unfairly negative evaluation of their work, describing it as "the worst I've ever read").

These findings, and those of many other studies, indicate that personal dispositions and traits do indeed influence and are indeed associated with aggression—just as they are linked to many other forms of social behavior. But we don't know for certain that they are *causes* of aggressive actions (much of the research on their effects is correlational in nature). And it seems clear that if they do affect aggression, they don't do so directly; rather, they interact in complex ways with many situational factors, and it is the combination that often proves deadly!

THE TYPE A BEHAVIOR PATTERN: WHY THE *A* IN TYPE A COULD STAND FOR AGGRESSION   Do you know anyone you could describe as (1) extremely competitive, (2) always in a hurry, and (3) especially irritable and aggressive? If so, this person shows the characteristics of what psychologists term the **Type A behavior pattern** (Glass, 1977; Strube, 1989). At the opposite end of the continuum are people who do not show these characteristics—individuals who are not highly competitive, who are more relaxed and not always fighting the clock, and who do remain calm even in the face of strong provocation; such people are described as showing the **Type B behavior pattern.**

Given the characteristics mentioned above, it seems only reasonable to expect that type As would tend to be more aggressive than type Bs in many situations. In fact, the results of several experiments indicate that this is actually the case (Baron, Russell, & Arms, 1985; Carver & Glass, 1978; Beaman, Gladue & Taylor, 1993).

Additional findings indicate that Type As are truly hostile people; they don't merely aggress against others because this is a useful means for reaching other goals, such as winning athletic contests or furthering their own careers. Rather, they are more likely than Type Bs to engage in what is known as **hostile aggression**—aggression in which the prime objective is inflicting some kind of harm on the victim (Strube et al., 1984). In view of this fact, it is not surprising to learn that Type As are more likely than Type Bs to engage in such actions as child abuse or spousal abuse (Strube, Turner, Cerro, Stevens, & Hinchey, 1984). In contrast, Type As are *not* more likely than Type Bs to engage in **instrumental aggression**—aggression performed primarily to attain other goals aside from harming the victim, goals such as control of valued resources or praise from others for behaving in a "tough" manner.

NARCISSISM, EGO-THREAT, AND AGGRESSION: ON THE DANGERS OF WANTING TO BE SUPERIOR   Do you know the story of Narcissus? He was a character in Greek mythology who fell in love with his own reflection in the water and drowned trying to

type A behavior pattern
A pattern consisting primarily of high levels of competitiveness, time urgency, and hostility.

type B behavior pattern
A pattern consisting of the absence of characteristics associated with the type A behavior pattern.

hostile aggression
Aggression in which the prime objective is inflicting some kind of harm on the victim.

instrumental aggression
Aggression in which the primary goal is not to harm the victim but rather attainment of some other goal—for example, access to valued resources.

reach it. His name has now become a synonym for excessive self-love—for holding an overinflated view of one's own virtues or accomplishments—and research findings indicate that this trait may be linked to aggression in important ways. Specifically, research findings indicate that people high in *narcissism* (ones who agree with items such as "If I ruled the world it would be a much better place" and "I am more capable than other people") react with exceptionally high levels of aggression when their egos are threatened—when other people say or do something that puts their inflated self-image in danger (e.g., Bushman & Baumeister, 1998; Thomaes, Bushman, Stegge, & Olthof, 2008). These findings raise important questions concerning the strategy, now used in many schools, of attempting to boost students' egos in various ways. In fact, it seems possible that raising students' self-esteem to unrealistic levels might increase their sensitivity to events that threaten their excessive egos! For instance, narcissistic people may react strongly to even mild provocations because they believe that they are so much better than other people, and as a result, perceive even very mild critical comments from others as strong slurs on their inflated self-image. This latter possibility was investigated by McCullough, Fincham, and Tsang (2003).

These researchers reasoned that narcissistic people, because of their inflated self-image, perceive themselves as the victims of transgressions more often than non-narcissistic people. To test this prediction, they asked college students to complete a measure of narcissism, and then to keep a diary for 14 days in which they recorded the number of times in which other people offended them in some way. As expected, the higher participants' scored in narcissism, the greater the number of transgressions by others they reported. This was especially true for one aspect of narcissism relating to exploiting others or being entitled to wonderful treatment by them (e.g., strong agreement with statements such as "I insist on getting the respect that is due me"). More recent study (e.g., Thomaes, de Castro, Cohen, & Denissen, 2009) have carried this work one step further, demonstrating that activities that help restore threatened egos reduce aggression by narcissistic people. We return to such research in more detail in a later discussion of the prevention and control of aggression. Here, we simply want to emphasize the point made above: While boosting students' egos in various ways can indeed produce important benefits, it's possible to go too far in this direction. If such esteem-building tactics are overdone and cause children to hold opinions of themselves that are unrealistically high (i.e., narcissistic), their tendency to aggress when these views are threatened may be increased (see Figure 10.13). Clearly, this is a possibility worthy of further careful study.

GENDER DIFFERENCES IN AGGRESSION: DO THEY EXIST?   Are males more aggressive than females? Folklore suggests that they are, and research findings suggest that in this case, informal observation is correct: when asked whether they have ever engaged in any of a wide range of aggressive actions, males report a higher incidence of many aggressive behaviors than do females (Harris, 1994). On close examination, however, the picture regarding gender differences in the tendency to aggress becomes more complex. On the one hand, males are generally more likely than females both to perform aggressive actions and to serve as the target for such behavior (Bogard, 1990; Harris, 1992, 1994). Furthermore, this difference seems to persist throughout the lifespan, occurring even among people in their 70s and 80s (Walker, Richardson, & Green, 2000). On the other hand, the size of these differences appears to vary greatly across situations.

First, gender differences in aggression are much larger in the absence of provocation than in its presence. In other words, males are significantly more likely than females to aggress against others when they have *not* been provoked in any manner (Bettencourt & Miller, 1996). In situations where provocation *is* present, and especially when it is intense, such differences tend to disappear.

Second, the size—and even direction—of gender differences in aggression seems to vary greatly with the *type* of aggression in question. Research findings indicate that men are more likely than women to engage in various forms of *direct* aggression—actions aimed directly at the target that clearly stem from the aggressor (e.g., physical assaults, pushing, shoving, throwing something at another person, shouting, making insulting remarks; Bjorkqvist, Österman, & Lagerspetz, 1994). Interestingly, though, the size of such differences appears to be decreasing (Odgers et al., 2007) and rates of direct aggression—including violent behavior—are increasing among women (Graves, 2007).

Similarly, although it was once widely believed that large gender differences exist with respect to various forms of *indirect* aggression—actions that allow the aggressor to conceal his or her identity from the victim, and that, in some cases, make it difficult for the victim to know that they have been the target of intentional harm-doing—such differences, too, appear to be decreasing and may in fact have vanished (e.g., Richardson & Hammock, 2007). Indirect forms of aggression include spreading vicious rumors about the target person, gossiping behind this person's back, telling others not to associate with the intended victim, making up stories to get them in trouble, and so on. Research findings indicate that while gender differences with respect to indirect aggression are present among children (Bjorkqvist, Lagerspetz, & Kaukiainen, 1992; Osterman et al., 1998), they may not persist into adulthood (Richardson & Hammock, 2007).

FIGURE 10.13   Narcissism: Falling in Love With Our Own Virtues as a Source of Aggression
Research findings indicate that when exposed to threats to their inflated egos, people high in narcissism often lash out at others—they become highly aggressive.

Third, recent findings indicate that for women as well as men, being aggressive can be a social "plus," conferring high status and appeal on the people who demonstrate it (Hawley et al., 2007). This is especially true for individuals who combine aggression with high levels of relationship-enhancing actions (e.g., high social skills, high levels of extraversion). Such people combine high levels of aggression with prosocial, relationship-boosting actions, which seems to reflect their overall high levels of extraversion. As a result, they are often very successful in gaining access to valued rewards (e.g., high status, approval from others), and become very popular with their peers. This pattern—which Hawley and her colleagues describe as "the bright side of bad behavior" (Hawley, Little, & Rodin, 2007)—is equally frequent among females and males, and this fact suggests, too, that gender differences in aggression have been overstated in the past. We discussed this fascinating research in more detail in Chapter 9, when we noted that the popular but *inaccurate* view that aggression and helping (prosocial behavior) are opposites may in fact be wrong.

In sum, although some gender differences with respect to aggression do exist, they are far smaller in magnitude than formerly believed, and appear to be decreasing. We wish we could note that this is due to the fact that aggression by both genders is decreasing, but existing evidence—alas!—suggests that it is due to the fact that women are becoming more aggressive while men are maintaining their high levels of this dangerous form of behavior. But stay tuned for future developments; as societies all over the world change, gender differences in aggression may be affected in ways impossible to predict.

KEYPOINTS

- Personality traits interact with situational factors to influence aggression; only if the situational factors (e.g., provocation) are above threshold do these personal traits enhance aggression. But when the situation is strong and clear (e.g., high provocation), individual differences are also eliminated.

- People showing the **Type A behavior pattern** are more irritable and aggressive than people with the **Type B behavior pattern**.

- People high in narcissism hold an overinflated view of their own worth. They react with exceptionally high levels of aggression to feedback that threatens their inflated egos. They also view themselves, more than

- other people, as victims of the transgressions of others, and this may contribute to their heightened aggression.

- Males are more aggressive overall than females, but this difference is highly dependent on the situation and is eliminated in the context of strong provocation. Males are more likely to use direct forms of aggression, but females are more likely to use indirect forms of aggression.

- Both women and men who combine aggression with relationship-enhancing skills are very popular, and this, too, suggests that gender differences in aggression are smaller and more complex than was suggested in the past.

Situational Determinants of Aggression: The Effects of Heat and Alcohol

While aggression is often strongly influenced by social factors and is sometimes predicted by personal traits, it is also affected by factors relating to the situation or context in which it occurs. Here, we examine two of the many situational factors that can influence aggression: uncomfortably high temperatures and alcohol.

IN THE HEAT OF ANGER: TEMPERATURE AND AGGRESSION *Boiling mad, hot-tempered, in a white-hot rage . . .* Phrases like these suggest that there may well be a link between temperature (and perhaps anything else that makes people feel uncomfortable!) and human aggression. And in fact, many people report that they often feel especially irritable and short-tempered on hot and steamy days (see Figure 10.14). Is there really a link between climate and human aggression? Social psychologists have studied this question for more than three decades, and during this period the methods they have used and the results they have obtained have become increasingly sophisticated.

The earliest studies on this topic (e.g., Baron, 1972) were experiments, conducted under controlled laboratory conditions, in which temperature was systematically varied as the independent variable. For instance, participants were exposed either to comfortably pleasant conditions (temperatures of 70–72° Fahrenheit), or to uncomfortably hot conditions (temperatures of 94–98° Fahrenheit), and were then given opportunities to

FIGURE 10.14   The Long, Hot Summer: Is There a Real Effect?
Research on the effects of uncomfortable heat on aggression suggests that there is indeed a link:
People are more likely to behave aggressively when uncomfortably hot than when comfortably cool.
Does this contribute to the fact that many violent riots occur during the summer months? Some
evidence indicates that this is so.

aggress against another person. (In fact, they only *believed* they could harm this person; ethical considerations made it necessary to ensure that no harm could actually take place.) Results were surprising: High temperature *reduced* aggression for both provoked and unprovoked people. The initial explanation of these findings was that the high temperatures were so uncomfortable that participants focused on getting away from them—and this caused them to reduce their aggression. After all, aggression might lead to unfriendly encounters with the victim and this would prolong their own misery.

This seemed reasonable—when they are very hot, people do seem to become lethargic and concentrate on reducing their discomfort rather than on "evening the score" with others. However, these early studies suffered from important drawbacks that made it difficult to determine the validity of this interpretation. For instance, the exposure to the high temperatures lasted only a few minutes, while in the real world, this occurs over much longer periods. Subsequent studies, therefore, used very different methods (e.g., Anderson, 1989; Anderson & Anderson, 1996; Bell, 1992). Specifically, they examined long-term records of temperatures and police records of various aggressive crimes to determine whether the frequency of such crimes increased with rising temperatures. For instance, consider a careful study conducted by Anderson, Bushman, and Groom (1997).

These researchers collected average annual temperatures for 50 cities in the United States over a 45-year period (1950–1995). In addition, they obtained information on the rate of both violent crimes (aggravated assault, homicide) and property crimes (burglary, car theft), as well as another crime that has often been viewed as primarily aggressive in nature: rape. They then performed analyses to determine if temperature was related to these crimes. In general, hotter years did indeed produce higher rates of violent crimes, but did *not* produce increases in property crimes or rape. This was true even though the effect of many other variables that might also influence aggressive crimes (e.g., poverty, age distribution of the population) were eliminated. These findings, and those of related studies (e.g., Anderson, Anderson, & Deuser, 1996), suggest that heat is indeed linked to aggression.

Excellent as this research was, however, it did not fully resolve one key question: Does this heat–aggression relationship have any limits? In other words, does aggression increase with heat indefinitely, or only up to some point, beyond which aggression actually declines as temperatures continue to rise? As you may recall, that is the pattern obtained in initial laboratory studies on this topic.

Additional research by Rotton and Cohn (Cohn & Rotton, 1997; Rotton & Cohn, 2000) have carefully addressed this issue. These researchers reasoned that if people do indeed try to reduce their discomfort when they are feeling very uncomfortable (e.g., when temperatures are very high), the relationship between heat and aggression should be stronger in the evening hours than at midday. Why? Because temperatures fall below their peak in the evening. In other words, a finer-grained analysis would reveal a curvilinear relationship between heat and aggression during the day, but a linear one at night. This is just what they found.

In sum, research on the effects of heat on aggression suggests that there is indeed a link between heat and aggression: When people get hot, they become irritable and may be more likely to lash out at others—especially when they have been provoked in some way. For instance, in an analysis of 57,293 (!) major league baseball games, Larrickk Timmerman, Carton, & Abrevaya (2011) found that the probability that batters would be hit by pitched balls increased with temperature, especially when the pitchers' teammates had previously been hit by the opposing pitcher. So it was the combination of high temperature and provocation that increased aggression. There may be limits to the relationship between heat and aggression, however—limits deriving from the fact that after prolonged exposure to high temperatures, people become so uncomfortable that they are lethargic and focus on reducing their discomfort—not on attacking others. Short of these extreme conditions, however, there is a big grain of truth in the phrase "the heat of anger," and when temperatures rise, tempers may, too—with serious social consequences. That is certainly something to consider in the context of global warming and the very real possibility that all of us will soon be exposed to uncomfortably hot outdoor temperatures more frequently than was true in the past.

ALCOHOL AND AGGRESSION: TRULY A DANGEROUS MIX It is widely assumed that people become more aggressive when they consume alcohol. This idea is supported by the fact that bars and nightclubs are often the scene of violence. However, while alcohol is certainly consumed in these settings, other factors might be responsible for the fights—or worse—that often erupt: competition for desirable partners, crowding, and even cigarette smoke (where it is legal), which irritates many people (Zillmann, Baron, & Tamborini, 1981). What does systematic research reveal about a possible link between alcohol and aggression? Interestingly, it tends to confirm the existence of such a link.

In several experiments, participants who consumed substantial amounts of alcohol—enough to make them legally drunk—have been found to behave more aggressively, and to respond to provocations more strongly than those who did not consume alcohol (e.g., Bushman & Cooper, 1990; Gustafson, 1992). For example, Giancola and colleagues (2009) had men and women participants consume either drinks containing alcohol (one gram per kilogram of body weight for men, 0.90 grams per kilogram for women) or no alcohol (although a few drops were floated on the top to equate the smell of the two kinds of drinks). (An ounce contains 28 grams and a kilogram is about 2.2 pounds.) Then, the participants played a game in which they and an opponent competed in terms of reaction time—who could respond quicker. Both participants set electric shocks for each other, and were supposed to receive these shocks if they lost on each trial. However, there was no opponent. At first, the opponent set very weak shocks (which participants actually received after giving their permission to do so). But then, the opponent set extreme shocks at the highest level. How would the participants respond? As you can see from Figure 10.15, men were more aggressive than women in terms of the shocks they set for their opponents, but for both genders, extreme aggression (trials in which participants selected the strongest available shock for their opponents) was increased by alcohol. The effect was stronger for men than for women, but was present for both.

But why does alcohol produce such effects? Does it simply eliminate inhibitions against acting in an impulsive, and possibly dangerous, way? Or does it make people especially sensitive to provocations, so that they are more likely to behave aggressively (e.g., Gantner & Taylor, 1992)? In other words, does it lower their threshold for responding aggressively to provocations? All of these possibilities are reasonable and

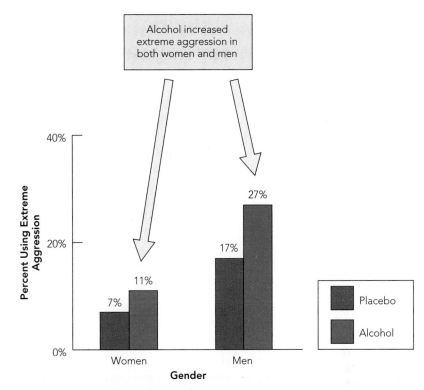

FIGURE 10.15   Alcohol: Evidence That It Increases Aggression for Both Genders

Although women were less aggressive than men while playing a competitive reaction time task, aggression by both genders was increased by alcohol consumption. (Source: Based on data from Giancola et al., 2009).

are supported by some evidence, but recent findings suggest that the effects of alcohol on aggression may stem, at least in part, from reduced cognitive functioning and what this does, in turn, to social perception. Specifically, the findings of several studies (e.g., Bartholow, Pearson, Gratton, & Fabian, 2003), indicate that alcohol impairs higher-order cognitive functions such as evaluation of stimuli and memory. This may make it harder for individuals to evaluate others' intentions (hostile or nonhostile) and to evaluate the effects that various forms of behavior on their part, including aggression, may produce (e.g., Hoaken, Giancola, & Pihl, 1998). For instance, people who have consumed alcohol show reductions in their capacity to process positive information about someone they initially dislike. This means that if such a person provoked them, but then apologized, those who have consumed alcohol might be less able to process this information carefully, and so would remain likely to aggress, despite the apology. This is speculation at present, but does seem to fit other findings concerning the impact of alcohol (e.g., Bartholow et al., 2003).

 KEY POINTS

- High temperatures tend to increase aggression, but only up to a point. Beyond some level, aggression declines as temperatures rise.

- Consuming alcohol can increase aggression in both men and women, perhaps because this drug reduces the individual's capacity to process some kinds of information.

Bullying: Singling Out Others for Repeated Abuse

When you were in school, did you know any bullies—other students who frequently picked on various victims and made their lives truly miserable? Unfortunately, bullying is far from rare. Almost everyone has either experienced or observed the effects of **bullying**—a form of behavior in which one person repeatedly assaults one or more others who have little or no power to retaliate (Olweus, 1996). In other words, in bullying relationships, one person does the aggressing, and the other is on the receiving end. While bullying has been studied primarily as something that occurs between children and teenagers, it is also common in other contexts too, such as workplaces and prisons (e.g., Ireland & Archer, 2002; Neuman & Baron, in press) (see Figure 10.16). Indeed, research findings indicate that fully 50 percent of people in prison are exposed to one or more episodes of bullying each week (Ireland & Ireland, 2000). In this discussion, therefore, we consider research on bullying in many different contexts.

Why Do People Engage in Bullying?

A very basic question about bullying, of course, is why does it occur? Why do some individuals choose targets they then terrorize over and over again? While there is no simple answer to this question, two motives appear to play a key role: the motive to hold power over others and the motive to be part of a group that is "tough" and therefore high in status (e.g., Olweus, 1999; Roland, 2002). These motives are clearly visible in research conducted by Roland (2002). In this study, more than 2,000 children in Norway answered questions designed to measure their desire to exercise power over others, their desire to be part of powerful groups, and their tendency to be unhappy or depressed. (Previous research had suggested that feeling depressed is another cause of bullying—it makes the bullies feel better!) A measure of bullying was obtained by asking the children to indicate

bullying
A pattern of behavior in which one individual is chosen as the target of repeated aggression by one or more others; the target person (the victim) generally has less power than those who engage in aggression (the bullies).

FIGURE 10.16   Bullying: When Aggressors Choose Defenseless Victims
Bullying is a common occurrence among children in schools, but also occurs frequently in workplaces, too, where abusive bosses sometimes pick on particular employees.

how often they had bullied other children (i.e., never, now and then, weekly, daily). Such self-reports of bullying have generally been found to be accurate when compared with teachers' ratings.

Results revealed some interesting gender differences. Among boys, both the desire to gain power and to be part of powerful groups were significantly related to bullying, while feeling depressed was not. For girls, all three motives were related to bullying. This suggests that for girls, at least, aggressing against someone who can't retaliate is one technique for countering the negative feelings of depression. While many other factors also play a role in bullying, the motives mentioned here have been found to be among the most important causes of such behavior.

The Characteristics of Bullies and Victims

Are bullies always bullies and victims always victims? While common sense suggests that these roles would tend to be relatively fixed, research findings indicate that, in fact, they are not. Many people who are bullies in one context become victims in other situations, and vice versa (Neuman & Baron, in press). So there are various combinations to consider—those who appear to be pure bullies (people who are always and only bullies), pure victims (people who are always and only victims), and bully-victims (people who switch back and forth between these roles, depending on the context).

But what, aside from the motives for power and belonging we described earlier, makes some people become bullies in the first place? Findings of careful research on bullying point to the following factors. First, bullies tend to believe that others act the way they do intentionally or because of lasting characteristics (Smorti & Ciucci, 2000). In contrast, victims tend to perceive others as acting as they do at least in part because they are responding to external events of conditions, including how others have treated them.

Another difference is that bullies (and also bully-victims) tend to be lower in self-esteem than other people. As a result, they aggress against others to build up their self-image. In addition, bullies tend to adopt a ruthless, manipulative approach to life and to dealing with other people (e.g., Andreou, 2000; Mynard & Joseph, 1997). They believe that others are not to be trusted, so they feel it is totally justified to break their word and take unfair advantage of others (e.g., to attack them when their guard is down).

Finally, bullies and bully-victims believe that the best way to respond to bullying is with aggression. They believe, more than other people, that being highly aggressive will bring them high levels of respect (Ireland & Archer, 2002).

Reducing the Occurrence of Bullying: Some Positive Steps

Bullying can have truly devastating effects on its victims. In fact, there have been several cases in which children who have been repeatedly bullied by their classmates have actually committed suicide (O'Moore, 2000), and similar results often occur in prisons, where people who are brutalized by their fellow inmates see death as the only way out. These distressing facts lead to the question, What can be done to reduce or even eliminate bullying? Many research projects—some involving entire school or prison systems in several countries—have been conducted to find out, and the results have been at least moderately encouraging. Here is an overview of the main findings:

- First, bullying must be seen to be a serious problem by all parties involved—teachers, parents, students, prisoners, guards, fellow employees, and supervisors (if bullying occurs in work settings).

- If bullying occurs, people in authority (teachers, prison guards, supervisors) must draw attention to it and take an unequivocal stand against it.

- Potential victims must be provided with direct means for dealing with bullying—they must be told precisely what to do and who to see when bullying occurs.

- Outside help is often useful in identifying the cause of bullying and in devising programs to reduce it.

Programs that have emphasized these points have produced encouraging results. Overall, then, there appears to be grounds for optimism; bullying *can* be reduced, provided it is recognized as being a serious problem and steps to deal with it are implemented. (Does bullying occur only in face-to-face contexts? Or can it also occur in cyberspace? For a discussion of this topic, please see the section "SOCIAL LIFE IN A CONNECTED WORLD: Cyberbullying," below).

cyberbullying
Bullying (repeated assaults against specific target persons) occurring in chatrooms and other Internet locations.

SOCIAL LIFE *in a* CONNECTED WORLD

Cyberbullying

As noted above, bullying is repeated aggression by one person against one or more others (e.g., Scheithauer & Hayer, 2007). In general, it has been studied as something that occurs between students in school, or between coworkers in the workplace. But in fact, growing evidence suggests that it can occur in chatrooms, by e-mail, and perhaps in other Internet contexts as well. **Cyberbullying** can take many different forms, including insults, exclusion, or even blackmail (Newman & Murray, 2005), and, like face-to-face bullying, it is far from rare, and may, sadly, be increasing. A recent study by Katzer, Fetchenhauer, and Belschak (2009) illustrates these points.

This research focused on students in German schools (average age 14) and involved completion of a Bully/Victim Questionnaire and other measures by the students (e.g., their parents' childrearing practices). Results were both informative—and unsettling. First, sizeable proportions of the students reported that they experienced cyberbullying fairly often—more than once a month. For instance, 24.7 percent indicated that they were insulted during chat sessions, and 36.2 percent indicated that other chatters broke into their conversations. Almost 10 percent reported that they were excluded from chat sessions, and over 16 percent indicated that they were slandered by other chatters. Almost 4 percent said that they had been blackmailed during chat sessions, and 12 percent reported that other chatters made fun of them during chat sessions. Furthermore, these events were much more common for some children than others, as in face-to-face settings (e.g., in school)

some were being singled out by others for abuse, in this case, electronic rather than face-to-face abuse.

Several characteristics predicted who would become victims. For instance, less popular students were more likely to be victimized, as were students who often lied in chatrooms. Students who visited chatrooms known to be "risky" were more likely to be victimized than those who stayed away from such locations. And, not surprisingly, students who were victims in school were also likely to be victims in chatrooms.

After considering these findings, the authors offered several recommendations designed to protect students from this kind of electronic victimization. First, schools should initiate programs designed to alert students to these dangers, and to provide them with a mechanism for reporting cyberbullying. Second, students should be warned carefully about "dangerous places" on the Web so that they can avoid Internet environments where they are likely to be victimized. Third, "cyberpolice," perhaps students themselves, should supervise popular Internet chatrooms and provide help to victimized students. Finally, online help for victims of cyberbullying could be provided, perhaps in the form of "virtual helpers" who could be contacted by victims without revealing their real identity.

Overall, the message of this research seems clear: bullying, like other forms of aggression, now occurs in contexts that did not even exist 10 or 20 years ago. And factors that affect face-to-face aggression may also play a role in the occurrence of this less direct, but often very painful, kind of aggression.

KEYPOINTS

- **Bullying** involves repeated aggression against individuals who, for various reasons, are unable to defend themselves against such treatment. Bullying occurs in many contexts, including schools, workplaces, and prisons. Few children are solely bullies or victims; more play both roles. Bullies and bully-victims appear to have lower self-esteem than children who are not involved in bullying.

The Prevention and Control of Aggression: Some Useful Techniques

If there is one idea we hope you'll remember and take away with you from this chapter, this is it: Aggression is *not* an inevitable or unalterable form of behavior. On the contrary, since it stems from a complex interplay between cognitions, situational factors, and personal characteristics, it *can* be prevented or reduced. With that optimistic thought in mind, we now examine several techniques that, when used appropriately, can be highly effective in reducing the frequency or intensity of human aggression.

Punishment: Just Desserts or Deterrence?

In most societies throughout the world, **punishment**—delivery of aversive consequences—is a major technique for reducing aggression. People who engage in such behavior receive large fines, are put in prison, and in some countries are placed in solitary confinement or receive physical punishment for their aggressive actions (see Figure 10.17). In many cases, this involves spending time in prison, but in some locations, extreme cases of violence such as mass murder may result in *capital punishment*—legal execution of the convicted criminals. Why do so many societies punish aggressive acts? Basically, for two major reasons (e.g., Darley, Carlsmith, & Robinson, 2000).

punishment
Procedures in which aversive consequences are delivered to individuals when they engage in specific actions.

First, there is a widespread belief that individuals who engage in acts of aggression viewed as inappropriate in their societies *deserve* to be punished. They have inflicted harm on others—and on society in general—and should suffer to make amends for this harm. This perspective suggests that the amount of punishment people should receive should be matched to the magnitude of harm they have caused (e.g., breaking someone's arm should deserve less punishment than permanently harming them or killing them). In addition, the magnitude of punishment should take account of extenuating circumstances—for instance, was there some "good" motive for the aggressive action, such as self-defense or defense of one's family?

FIGURE 10.17   Punishment: An Effective Detererrent to Aggression?
Most societies use punishment for aggressive actions (e.g., fines, prison terms, or worse) to deter such behavior. Are these procedures effective? Existing evidence on this complex issue is mixed.

The second reason for punishing people who commit aggressive actions is to deter them (or others) from engaging in such behavior in the future. This basis for punishment implies that ease of detection of the crime should be given careful attention; if aggressive actions are hard to detect (e.g., they involve hidden or covert forms of harming others), they should be strongly punished because only strong punishment will deter people from engaging in actions they believe they can "get away with." Similarly, public punishment would be expected to be more effective in deterring future crimes than private punishment, especially in cultures where public shame is viewed as a truly negative outcome.

Which of these two perspectives are most important in determining the magnitude of punishment people feel is justified for specific aggressive acts or other offenses? Research by Carlsmith, Darley, and Robinson (2002) suggests that in general, the first perspective tends to dominate. So across many different contexts, most people seem to believe that "the punishment should fit the crime."

There is still another rationale for using punishment to reduce aggressive behavior that we have not yet mentioned: some kinds of punishment, at least, remove dangerous people from society (e.g., by placing them in prison), and in this way, prevent them from repeating their aggressive actions with new victims in the future. Is there any support for this view? In fact, statistics indicate that once people engage in violent crimes, they are likely to do so again. If that's true, then removing them from society can indeed help prevent additional acts of aggression against others (although not against other prisoners!). This is one rationale for giving people convicted of aggressive crimes long prison sentences, although it is rarely stated by judges or prosecuting attorneys.

Another important question relating to punishment is simple: Does it work? Can it reduce the tendency of specific people to engage in harmful acts of aggression? Here, existing evidence is relatively clear. Punishment *can* reduce aggression, but only if it meets four basic requirements: (1) it must be *prompt*—it must follow aggressive actions as quickly as possible; (2) it must be *certain to occur*—the probability that it will follow aggression must be very high; (3) it must be *strong*—strong enough to be highly unpleasant to potential recipients; and (4) it must be perceived by recipients as *justified* or deserved.

Unfortunately, these conditions are typically not met in the criminal justice systems of many nations. In most societies, the delivery of punishment for aggressive actions is delayed for months or even years. Similarly, many criminals avoid arrest and conviction, so the certainty of punishment is low. The magnitude of punishment itself varies from one city, state, or even courtroom to another and is often harsher for minority group members than other people. And often, punishment does not seem to fit the crime—it does not seem to be justified or deserved. In such cases, the people who are punished may view such treatment as aggression against them—as a kind of provocation. And as we saw earlier, provocation is a very powerful trigger for aggression. In view of these facts, it is hardly surprising that the threat of punishment—even severe punishment—does not seem to be effective in deterring violent crime. The conditions necessary for it to be effective simply do not exist, and probably, given the nature of most legal systems, cannot exist. For this reason, we must conclude that the belief that severe punishment for aggressive crimes will successfully deter such behavior are wildly optimistic (and inaccurate). But read on: Other techniques for reducing aggression, including several based on principles of social cognition, can be much more effective.

Self-Regulation: Internal Mechanisms for Controlling Aggression

From an evolutionary perspective, aggression can be viewed as adaptive behavior, at least in some situations. For instance, competition for desirable mates is often intense, and one way to "win" in such contests is through aggression against potential rivals.

So, especially for males, strong tendencies to aggress against others can yield beneficial outcomes. On the other hand, living together in human society often requires restraining aggressive behavior. Lashing out at others in response to every provocation is definitely not adaptive, and can greatly disrupt social life. For this reason, it is clear that we possess effective internal mechanisms for restraining anger and overt aggression (e.g., Baumeister, 1997, 2005). Such mechanisms are described by the term *self-regulation* (or self-control), and refer to our capacity to regulate many aspects of own behavior, including aggression.

Unfortunately, such self-regulation often requires a lot of cognitive effort, so one reason why this internal system of restraint sometimes fails is that we simply don't have the resources required. In other words, aggression often erupts because we have invested so much cognitive effort in other tasks that we don't have enough left to perform this important but demanding function. In fact, the results of many studies indicate that self-control can, like other resources, be depleted by tasks that require its exercise (e.g., Baumeister, Vohs, & Tice, 2007; De Wall et al., 2007). And in fact, in such research, when participants had used up their self-control (e.g., by resisting the temptation to eat a delicious-looking donut), they were in fact more aggressive than those who had not depleted their self-control.

Encouragingly, though, other research findings (e.g., Mauss, Evers, Wilhelm, & Gross, 2006) indicate that self-control of aggressive impulses does not necessarily involve the use of cognitive resources. In fact, when individuals have positive implicit attitudes toward regulating their own emotions, they may be able to restrain aggression almost effortlessly—simply because they have positive attitudes toward exerting such emotional control. Furthermore, it appears that one way in which individuals self-regulate their behavior so as to avoid aggressing involves thinking *prosocial thoughts*—thinking about helping others, caring for them (see Chapter 9). The more readily people can bring such thoughts to mind when provoked or exposed to conditions that normally tend to trigger aggression, the less likely they are to behave in an aggressive manner (Meier, Robinson, & Wilkowski, 2006).

So where does this intriguing research leave us? With the suggestion that one effective means of reducing human aggression—perhaps a very effective one—is strengthening the *internal mechanisms* that usually operate to control such behavior. We all possess these mechanisms, so the major task is making them stronger and ensuring that they are not overwhelmed by other demands on our cognitive resources. How can internal restraints against aggression be strengthened? In several different ways. For instance, exposure to other people who show restraint even in the face of strong provocation (nonaggressive models; e.g., Baron & Richardson, 1994) might help, as would providing training designed to strengthen internal restraints. In addition, individuals can be taught to recognize when their cognitive resources are being "stretched," since those are the occasions on which inappropriate aggression is most likely to occur.

Catharsis: Does "Blowing Off Steam" Really Help?

When one of us (Robert) was a child, his grandmother used to greet temper tantrums by saying, "That's OK darling, let it out . . . don't keep it bottled up inside—that's bad for you." In other words, she was a true believer in the **catharsis hypothesis**—the view that if individuals give vent to their anger and hostility in nonharmful ways, their tendencies to engage in more dangerous types of aggression will be reduced (Dollard et al., 1939).

Is this actually true? Most people seem to believe that it is; for instance, newspaper columnists (including "Dear Abby") often urge people to express their aggressive emotions and thoughts as a means of reducing them. This belief has given rise to a minor industry providing toys and games that, supposedly, allow people to "get rid" of their aggressive

catharsis hypothesis
The view that providing angry people with an opportunity to express their aggressive impulses in relatively safe ways will reduce their tendencies to engage in more harmful forms of aggression.

FIGURE 10.18　Catharsis: Does It Really Work?
Many people believe that "releasing aggressive impulses" through relatively safe activities, such as hitting a punching bag, reduces overt aggression. In fact, however, research findings indicate that such activities are more likely to facilitate aggression than reduce it.

impulses (see Figure 10.18). But systematic research on catharsis by social psychologists calls such advice into doubt; widespread faith in the effectiveness of catharsis does not seem justified. On the contrary, it appears that so-called *venting* activities such as watching, reading about, or imagining aggressive actions, or even engaging in "play" aggression such as punching a punching bag, are more likely to *increase* subsequent aggression than to reduce it (e.g., Bushman, 2001; Bushman, Baumeister, & Stack, 1999). A clear demonstration of this fact is provided by research conducted by Anderson et al. (2003).

These researchers reasoned that if catharsis really works, then exposure to songs with violent lyrics would allow people to "vent" aggressive thoughts or feelings; as a result, they would show lower levels of hostility and lower levels of aggressive thoughts. However, if catharsis does not work—and on the basis of previous findings, the researchers did not expect that it would—exposure to songs with violent lyrics might actually increase hostility and aggressive cognitions. To test these competing predictions, they conducted a series of studies in which participants listened to violent or nonviolent songs and then completed measures of their current feelings (hostile or friendly) and their aggressive cognitions (e.g., how much similarity they perceived between aggressive and ambiguous words—ones that could have both an aggressive and nonaggressive meaning such as *alley* or *police*; how quickly they pronounced aggressive and nonaggressive words that appeared on a computer screen). Results of all the studies were consistent: After hearing songs with violent lyrics, participants showed an increase both in hostile feelings and in aggressive thoughts. So catharsis definitely did *not* occur.

Why does "letting it out" fail to reduce aggression? For several reasons. First, anger may actually be increased when individuals think about wrongs they have suffered at the hands of others and imagine ways of harming these people. Second, watching aggressive scenes, listening to songs with aggressive lyrics, or merely thinking about revenge and other aggressive activities may activate even more aggressive thoughts and feelings. These, in turn, may color interpretations of actual social interactions so that ambiguous actions by others are more likely to be perceived as hostile ones. (As we saw earlier, research on the effects of playing violent video games confirms this suggestion.) As a result of such effects, aggression is increased—*not* reduced by activities that, according to the catharsis hypothesis, should decrease it. Third, even if catharsis did occur, the effects would probably be temporary; whatever made the people involved angry might well occur again, so any benefits would be short term at best.

Is there even a small grain of truth in the catharsis hypothesis? Perhaps only this: Giving vent to angry feelings may make individuals feel better emotionally. Anyone who has punched their own pillow or shouted angrily at other drivers who can't hear them has experienced such effects. But research findings indicate that such effects do not really reduce the long-term tendency to engage in aggressive actions. In fact, since reduced tension is pleasant, the long-term effects, again, may be a strengthening rather than a weakening of aggressive impulses.

In short, systematic research by social psychologists suggests that in this case, "commonsense" beliefs about the effectiveness of catharsis (as well as suggestions to this effect by Freud and others) are not really justified. So resist the urging of those newspaper columnists and do not put your faith in catharsis as a useful means for keeping your own anger—and aggression—in check.

Reducing Aggression by Bolstering Self-Esteem

Do you recall our earlier discussion of narcissism—inflated and unjustified views of their own value held by certain individuals? If so, you may recall that such people are especially likely to lash out at others when their egos are threatened—when something threatens to deflate their overinflated self-image (Thomaes, Stegge, Bushman, Olthof, & Denissen, 2008). Given that boosting students' self-image appears to be a key goal sought by many schools, narcissism may well be on the rise. And if that's so, then an interesting question arises: Can anything be done to minimize aggression by people high in narcissism? Presumably, procedures designed to protect or bolster such people' self-esteem might prevent them from engaging in aggression because the threat to their inflated self-image would be reduced. A study by Thomaes and his colleagues (2009) tested this prediction. Students 12–15 years old first completed a measure of narcissism and—in two different groups—later performed a task designed either to bolster or not bolster their self-esteem. To bolster self-esteem, students were asked to write about their most important personal values and why they held them. This would bolster self-esteem by giving students a chance to engage in **self-affirmation.** In contrast, the other condition (writing about their least important values) would not produce such effects. Information on the participants' actual aggression was then obtained from ratings by classmates, and results indicated that high-narcissism students were in fact more aggressive toward their classmates than low-narcissism students in the no-ego-boost condition. In the condition designed to bolster self-esteem, in contrast, high-narcissism students were *not* more aggressive than those low in narcissism. In other words, the self-affirmation intervention did prevent slights to their egos—which students' reported occurred regularly in school—from triggering aggression.

These findings suggest, once again, the key point we wish to make: Aggression is *not* inevitable, even among people who, because of certain characteristics, are likely to engage in such behavior. Rather, under appropriate conditions, and with effective interventions, it *can* be prevented—with benefits both for aggressors and their potential victims.

self-affirmation
Refers to the tendency to respond to a threat to one's self-concept by affirming one's competence in another area (different from the threat).

 # KEY POINTS

- **Punishment** can be effective in reducing aggression, but only when it is delivered under certain conditions that are rarely met.

- The **catharsis hypothesis** appears to be mainly false. Engaging in vigorous activities may produce reductions in arousal, but these are only temporary. Similarly, the likelihood of subsequent aggression is *not* reduced by engaging in apparently "safe" forms of aggression.

- Aggression is often restrained by internal self-regulatory processes. If the cognitive resources needed by these processes are depleted, however, aggression is more likely to occur.

- Techniques that bolster self-esteem can be effective in reducing aggression by people high in narcissism by preventing threats to their egos from triggering aggression.

SUMMARY *and* REVIEW

- **Aggression** is the intentional infliction of harm on others. While most social psychologists reject the view that human aggression is strongly determined by genetic factors, evolutionary-oriented theorists claim that genetic factors play some role in such behavior. **Drive theories** suggest that aggression stems from externally elicited drives to harm or injure others. The **frustration-aggression hypothesis** is the most famous example of such theories. Modern theories of aggression, such as the **general aggression model,** recognize the importance in aggression of learning various eliciting input variables, individual differences, affective states, and, especially, cognitive processes.

- Contrary to the famous frustration-aggression hypothesis, all aggression does not stem from frustration, and frustration does not always lead to aggression. Frustration is a strong elicitor of aggression only under certain limited conditions. In contrast, **provocation** from others is a powerful elicitor of aggression. Even mild **teasing** can stimulate aggression, although such effects are stronger in certain cultures than in others. Heightened arousal can increase aggression if it persists beyond the situation in which it was induced and is unknowingly interpreted as anger generated in the new context.

- Exposure to media violence has been found to increase aggression among viewers. This is due to several factors, such as the priming of aggressive thoughts and a weakening of restraints against aggression, and also to desensitization to such materials. Playing violent video games increases aggressive cognition, aggressive affect, and overt aggressive behavior. It also reduces empathy toward others and prosocial behavior. Individuals like to play these games not because of the aggressive content but because the games satisfy motives for competence and mastery.

- **Cultures of honor** are ones in which strong norms indicate that slights to one's honor require an aggressive response. Such norms are still in existence today, and help explain differences in rates of aggression in different geographic locations. Sexual jealousy is a major cause of aggression between partners in intimate relationships. An evolutionary perspective suggests that men experience jealousy over sexual infidelity because of their parental uncertainty, whereas women experience jealousy over emotional infidelity, because of their need for assistance from mates in childrearing. Manhood is, it appears, more precarious than womanhood: manhood can be lost through many events (e.g., an inability to support one's family). This suggests that threats to manhood may encourage aggression as a means of restoring or protecting manhood. Research findings offer support for this view, and highlight the importance of culturally defined gender roles in aggression.

- Personality traits interact with situational factors to influence aggression; only if the situational factors (e.g., provocation) are above threshold do these personal traits enhance aggression. But when the situation is strong and clear (e.g., high provocation), individual differences are also eliminated. People showing the **type A behavior pattern** are more irritable and aggressive than people with the **type B behavior**

pattern. People high in narcissism hold an overinflated view of their own worth. They react with exceptionally high levels of aggression to feedback that threatens their inflated egos. They also view themselves, more than other people, as victims of the transgressions of others, and this may contribute to their heightened aggression.

● Males are more aggressive overall than females, but this difference is highly dependent on the situation and is eliminated in the context of strong provocation. Males are more likely to use direct forms of aggression, but females are more likely to use indirect forms of aggression. Both women and men who combine aggression with relationship-enhancing skills are very popular, and this, too, suggests that gender differences in aggression are smaller and more complex than was suggested in the past.

● High temperatures tend to increase aggression, but only up to a point. Beyond some level, aggression declines as temperatures rise. Consuming alcohol can increase aggression in both men and women, perhaps because this drug reduces the individual's capacity to process some kinds of information.

● **Bullying** involves repeated aggression against individuals who, for various reasons, are unable to defend themselves against such treatment. Bullying occurs in many contexts, including schools, workplaces, and prisons. Few children are solely bullies or victims; more play both roles. Bullies and bully-victims appear to have lower self-esteem than children who are not involved in bullying.

● **Punishment** can be effective in reducing aggression, but only when it is delivered under certain conditions that are rarely met. The **catharsis hypothesis** appears to be mainly false. Engaging in vigorous activities may produce reductions in arousal, but these are only temporary. Similarly, the likelihood of subsequent aggression is not reduced by engaging in apparently "safe" forms of *aggression*. Aggression is often restrained by internal self-regulatory processes. If the cognitive resources needed by these processes are depleted, however, aggression is more likely to occur. Techniques that bolster self-esteem can be effective in reducing aggression by people high in narcissism by preventing threats to their egos from triggering aggression.

KEY TERMS

aggression (p. 322)

bullying (p. 348)

catharsis hypothesis (p. 353)

cultures of honor (p. 337)

cyberbullying (p. 350)

drive theories (of aggression) (p. 324)

excitation transfer theory (p. 330)

frustration-aggression hypothesis (p. 328)

general aggression model (GAM) (p. 325)

hostile aggression (p. 341)

instrumental aggression (p. 341)

provocation (p. 328)

punishment (p. 351)

self-affirmation (p. 355)

TASS model (p. 340)

teasing (p. 329)

type A behavior pattern (p. 341)

type B behavior pattern (p. 341)

CHAPTER 11

Groups and Individuals

The Consequences of Belonging

*T*HE FINANCIAL CRISIS OF 2008 CAME INTO CONSCIOUS AWARENESS when George W. Bush's Treasury Secretary, Henry Paulson, and Federal Reserve Chairman Ben Bernanke became involved in efforts to convince members of the U.S. Senate that a $700 billion emergency bailout plan was needed to deal with the mortgage and banking crisis. But prior to Bernanke's warning that the economy would collapse without a massive bailout and stimulus spending bill, various decisions going back to the mid-1990s appear to have contributed to this crisis in the mortgage and banking systems. During this time, there were many players, both groups and individuals—all of whom had a hand in the events leading to the crisis. One group, the Securities and Exchange Commission, which is the major government entity that regulates banks when they are involved in investment activities, and Freddie Mac and Fannie Mae, both quasi-governmental agencies, were instrumental in facilitating large amounts of subprime mortgage lending.

The BP oil spill, another major crisis, with substantial economic consequences for Americans, started with an explosion at its Deepwater Horizon well in the Gulf of Mexico on April 20, 2010. Approximately 3 months later, on July 15, the well was capped, although there remains some doubt as to whether that will stop all oil leaking from the drill pipe under the seabed. Apart from the obvious responsibility of BP itself, there is ample evidence of long-term ignorance and irresponsibility on the part of a government agency, the Minerals Management Service, a division of the Interior Department.

In each of these cases, an individual representative has commanded the public's attention. For the financial crisis, Goldman Sachs CEO Lloyd Blankfein tried to defend his company's actions, while following the oil spill CEO Tony Hayward as BP's spokesman attempted to do so as well. Soon after both these respective disasters, with some of their consequences shown in Figure 11.1, both these CEOs appeared to generate more anger from the public than they were able to squash.

As onlookers (and victims), people are prone to blaming individual CEOs when disasters occur—partly because the CEOs are salient spokespeople—and they almost certainly played a role. In addition, given the oversized compensation that CEOs receive currently, this might even seem fair. But many people also have the idea that groups, compared to individuals, are more likely to make

FIGURE 11.1   Individual or Group Decision Making: Which Leads to Disasters?
Was the problem the people at the top of these organization (CEOs), or was it groups and the decisions they made that lead to the financial and oil spill crises?

disaster-prone decisions. In this chapter, we consider research addressing this question—do individuals or groups make more risky (or worse) decisions? Probably both individuals and groups bear responsibility for creating the environments in which both of these crises were likely (some would say inevitably) to occur. In this chapter we also address the question of whether individuals act differently when in a group compared to when they act alone. Such a possibility is important because, if it is true that individuals are affected by processes that occur in groups, then understanding group life is critical to gaining insight into how these kinds of disasters may be prevented. When things go wrong—catastrophically wrong—as they did in both the financial crisis and oil spill, understanding both the pitfalls and strengths of group decision making is needed.

Because groups cannot be eliminated from our lives—even if being a member of a group can sometimes involve negative aspects—we seek to understand both the costs and benefits of belonging to groups. Let's first consider a few of the potential hitches that come with joining a group. If it is a *cohesive group*—one where there are strong bonds among the members—it could be difficult to even get admitted, or it might result in some initiations we would wish to avoid. And what if, after getting in a group, we discover that there are group norms that we don't like? When a person is new to a group, one's status is likely to be low, which would make it difficult to change the group's norms. Moreover, as a newcomer, one's performance in the group may be judged by more established members, resulting in some evaluation anxiety. Some conflict is likely within almost any group, and managing such difficult interactions might be quite effortful. For this reason, people sometimes ask themselves whether they might have to put more effort into a group than the rewards they'd get from being a member. Realistically, some groups do require major commitments of time. But it is also the case that some benefits can only be obtained by belonging to groups. For that reason, we first turn to the question of why people join and stay in groups. Can we realistically just dispense with them, or might groups critically shape who we are?

Is being in groups a fundamental part of our evolutionary history? No one individual can know all the information necessary—particularly in our technologically complex world—to always make the best decisions alone on all issues. Perhaps we have to rely on other people for collective knowledge and information sharing, and perhaps being connected to groups is essential to our survival as a species. Brewer and Caporael (2006) argue that interdependence among group members is the *primary* strategy for survival among humans, with the group providing a critical buffer between the individual and the physical habitat. Such social coordination could be therefore central to our survival.

What implications does an evolutionary perspective have for our attitudes toward groups in the here-and-now? Schachter (1959) concluded that the arousal of *any* strong emotion in humans tends to create the need to compare this reaction with others. This suggests that the complex emotional lives of humans may, in fact, be one of the causes of the human need for group affiliation. Indeed, it is under the most threatening or uncertain conditions that we seem to need our groups most. In these instances, for psychological security, we may increasingly identify with our social groups (Hogg, 2007). In fact, among the best predictors of psychological well-being across people is degree of connectedness to others (Diener & Oishi, 2005; Lyubomirsky, King, & Diener, 2005).

Are all groups equally important to us? While we are born into some of our groups, such as our family or ethnic group, others are self-selected—we choose to join groups such as fraternities and sororities, work organizations, and sports teams. Some groups are temporary, coming into existence to accomplish a specific purpose such as completing a team project, while others are longer lasting and less linked to specific goals (e.g., being a member of your university student community). Some groups such as a workplace organization are joined explicitly because of the benefits (i.e, a paycheck) that they provide. Despite this material benefit, people do form occupational identities that are of considerable importance to them, and many people also come to strongly identify with the organizations in which they are employed (Ashforth, Harrison, & Corley, 2008; Haslam, 2004). In fact, if you ask people "Who are you?", many reply in terms of their occupations: "I'm a student" or "I'm a psychologist, engineer, accountant, etc." Might you someday show equal pride in your occupational or organizational group and its accomplishments, as the people shown in Figure 11.2?

For other groups, clear material benefits of membership might be hard to see, although those groups too can have considerable relevance for our identities (e.g., a peer or friendship group). In fact, leaving behind our old friendship groups as we make life transitions such as moving from high school to college can be a stressful process (Iyer, Jetten, & Tsivrikos, 2008). Thus, we have emotional connectedness to groups—we like them, like being in them, and often develop strong bonds with the people in them. Perhaps that is the point: joining groups, and staying in them, feels

FIGURE 11.2 Will You Identify Strongly with the Occupation You Join?
These photos illustrate people who appear to be highly attached to their work group and its accomplishments. Research reveals that people who identify with the organization that employs them exhibit greater commitment to it and show positive organizational citizenship behavior that goes beyond the "call of duty."

perfectly natural—we really *want* to belong, and *freely choose* to join! And, when we are deprived of a connection to the group, when given an opportunity we often work hard to re-connect to group members, even if only via Facebook (Sheldon, Abad, & Hinsch, 2011).

Now, let's turn to the issues of whether there are different types of groups, when we join them and why, and what determines when we choose to quit them. Then, we will examine the impact of what is, in some ways, the most basic group effect: the mere presence of others. As we'll see, the presence of others, even if we are not in a formal group with them, can affect our performance on many tasks, as well as other important aspects of our behavior. Third, we briefly examine the nature of cooperation and conflict in groups—why these contrasting patterns emerge and the effects they produce. After that, we address the closely related question of perceived *fairness* in groups. Finally, we turn to *decision making* in groups, and the unexpected dangers this process can pose.

Groups: When We Join . . . and When We Leave

group
A collection of people who are perceived to be bonded together in a coherent unit to some degree.

common-bond groups
Groups that tend to involve face-to-face interaction and in which the individual members are bonded to each other.

common-identity groups
Face-to-face interaction is often absent, and the members are linked together via the category as a whole rather than each other.

What is a group? Do we know one when we see it? Look at the photos in Figure 11.3. Which one would you say shows a group? You would probably identify the photo on the right as a group, but the one on the left as a mere collection of people waiting in line. Perhaps that is because you have a definition of the term group that is close to the one adopted by many social psychologists—a **group** involves people who *perceive themselves to be part of a coherent unit that they perceive as different from another group* (Dasgupta, Banaji, & Abelson, 1999; Haslam, 2004).

The basis of this perceived coherence differs in different types of groups (Prentice, Miller, & Lightdale, 1994). In **common-bond groups,** which tend to involve face-to-face interaction among members, the individuals in the group are bonded *to each other.* Examples of these kinds of groups include the players on a sports team, friendship groups, and work teams. In contrast, in **common-identity groups** the members are *linked via the category as a whole* rather than to each other, with face-to-face interaction often being

FIGURE 11.3 **What Makes a Group a Group?**
The photo on the left shows a collection of people who just happen to be in the same place; they are not part of a group. The photo on the right shows a real group, where the members interact with one another in a coordinated way and have shared goals and outcomes. Moreover, they feel that they are, in fact, part of a group.

entirely absent. Our national, linguistic, university, and gender groups, where we might not even know personally all or even most of the other group members, are good examples of groups that we might identify with strongly, but not because of the bonds we have with specific other individual members. As you'll see in this chapter, both of these types of group memberships can be important to people.

Groups can also differ dramatically in terms of their **entitativity**— the extent to which they are perceived as coherent wholes (Campbell, 1958). Entitativity can range from, at the low end, a mere collection of individuals who happen to be in the same place at the same time and who have little or no connection with one another, to at the high end, where members of intimate groups such as families share a name, a history, and an identity. As shown in Table 11.1, when people are asked to freely name different types of groups, there is considerable agreement about which types of groups are perceived to be high and low in entitativity (Lickel et al., 2000). Those groups that are rated as high in entitativity also tend to be groups that people rate as relatively important to them. Groups high in entitativity are also perceived as persisting across time, although the specific members may change, whereas those low in entitativity are often not seen as possessing such continuity (Hamilton, Levine, & Thurston, 2008).

What determines whether, and to what extent, we perceive a group as an entity? Groups high in entitativity tend to have the following characteristics: (1) members interact with one another often, although not necessarily in a face-to-face setting (it could be over the Internet, for example); (2) the group is important in some way to its members; (3) members share common goals; and (4) they are similar to one another in important ways. The higher groups are on these dimensions, the more they will be seen by their members and nonmembers alike as forming coherent entities—real groups that can, and often do, exert powerful effects upon their members.

Highly entitative groups are more likely to be stereotyped than are groups low in entitativity (Yzerbyt et al., 2001). People even use different language to describe entitative groups compared to those low in entitativity (Spencer-Rodgers, Hamilton, & Sherman, 2007). Specifically, abstract language is used to imply that high entitativity groups are enduring and that they possess distinct characteristics that differentiate them from other groups, whereas groups low in entitativity are seen as less distinctive and members are less likely to be characterized as sharing attributes. Perhaps, surprisingly, it is not the size of a group per se that matters for entitativity—some small and some large groups are perceived to be high in entitativity. It is behavioral features such as sharing of resources, reciprocating favors among group members, recognition of group authorities, and adherence to group norms that tend to result in greater entitativity rather than structural features of groups (Lickel, Rutchick, Hamilton, & Sherman, 2006).

Groups: Their Key Components

Before turning to the specific ways in which groups affect various aspects of our behavior and thought, it is useful to consider several basic features of groups—ones that are present in virtually every group. These features are *status*, *roles*, *norms*, and *cohesiveness*.

STATUS: HIERARCHIES IN GROUPS When the President of the United States, or the leader of any other nation for that matter, enters the room, everyone stands; and no one sits down until the President has taken a seat. Why? Although the President is an

TABLE 11.1 Is the Importance of a Group Dependent on Its Entitativity?

As you can see here, groups clearly vary in their perceived entitativity—the extent to which they are perceived to be a distinct group. While some groups are seen as being high in entitativity (1 = not a group; 9 = very much a group), others are not. The perceived importance of a group to its members was strongly correlated ($r = .75$) with how much of an entity it was perceived to be.

TYPE OF GROUP	ENTITATIVITY	IMPORTANCE TO SELF
Families	8.57	8.78
Friends/romantic partners	8.27	8.06
Religious groups	8.20	7.34
Music groups	7.33	5.48
Sports groups	7.12	6.33
Work groups	6.78	5.73
Ethnic groups	6.67	7.67
Common interest groups	6.53	5.65
National groups	5.83	5.33
Students in a class	5.76	4.69
Gender groups	4.25	3.00
Region of country	4.00	3.25
Physical attributes	3.50	2.50

Source: Based on data from Lickel et al., 2000.

entitativity
The extent to which a group is perceived as being a coherent entity.

American, like the rest of us, he (or she) occupies a special position within the group. Many groups have hierarchies like this, with members differing in **status**—their rank within the group. Sometimes it is an "official position" as in the case of the President, and sometimes it is not so explicit and instead is simply the "old-timers" in a group who are accorded higher status compared to "newcomers." People are often extremely sensitive to their status within a group because it is linked to a wide range of desirable outcomes—everything from respect and deference from other group members to material benefits such as salary received.

Evolutionary psychologists attach considerable importance to status attainment within a group, noting that in many different species, including our own, high status confers important advantages on those who possess it (Buss, 1999). But how, precisely, do people acquire high status? Physical attributes such as height may play some role—taller men and women have a consistent edge, especially in the workplace (Judge & Cable, 2004). Those who are taller are held in higher esteem compared to shorter people—they are literally "looked up to." Meta-analyses have revealed that taller people earn more in salary, are perceived as having more skills, and are more likely to be nominated as leader of groups relative to shorter people (Judge & Cable, 2004). Height even predicts who wins the American Presidency, within each election year's set of candidates. In fact, people judge those who have just won an election to be taller than they were before winning, while the losers of the election are seen as shorter (Higham & Carment, 1992)! And in fact, the average height of all Presidents is much higher than for the general population. This may change, of course, when women Presidents are elected, but even they, perhaps, will be taller than the average woman!

Factors relating to individuals' behavior also play a critical role in status acquisition. People who are seen as prototypical—by embodying the group's central attributes—are particularly likely to be accorded status and be selected as leader of a group (Haslam & Platow, 2001). Longevity or seniority in a group too can result in higher status—to the extent that it is seen as reflective of wisdom or knowledge of ingroup ways (Haslam, 2004).

Once status within a group is obtained, people with high status actually behave differently than those with lower status. Guinote, Judd, and Brauer (2002) observed that high-status group members are more "idiosyncratic and variable" in their behavior than are lower-status group members. Indeed, there appears to be an awareness of the need to conform to group norms more strongly among those who are junior in a group and therefore have lower status (Jetten, Hornsey, & Adarves-Yorno, 2006). Across a number of different samples from professional to student groups where status varied, people with high status report conforming less than people with lower status. As shown in Figure 11.4, when surveyed about "how susceptible to group influence" they were, social psychologists who were very senior in terms of number of years in a professional organization reported being less conforming than those who had few years in the organization or those who had just recently joined. By portraying themselves as open to group influence, low-status group members may be helping to ensure they become accepted in the organization. In fact, newcomers who lack status in a group are more likely to be subjected to punishments if they fail to yield to those with higher status (Levine, Moreland, & Hausmann, 2005). Thus, there can be little doubt that differences in status are an important fact of life in most groups.

ROLES: DIFFERENTIATION OF FUNCTIONS WITHIN GROUPS   Think of a group to which you belong or have belonged—anything from a sports team to a sorority or fraternity. Now consider this question: Did everyone in the group perform the same functions? Your answer is probably *no*. Different people performed different tasks and were expected to accomplish different things for the group. In short, they played different **roles.** Sometimes roles are assigned; for instance, a group may select different individuals to serve as its leader, treasurer, or secretary. In other cases, individuals gradually acquire certain roles

status
The individual's position or rank within the group.

roles
The set of behaviors that individuals occupying specific positions within a group are expected to perform.

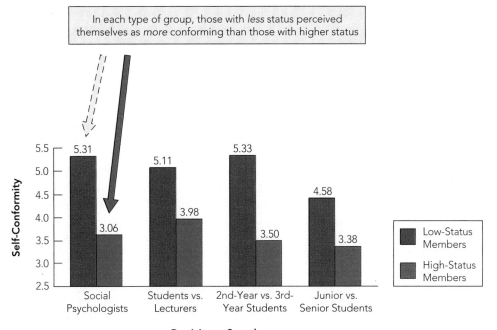

FIGURE 11.4   Status Matters for Conformity
As you can see, in every participant sample, those who were relatively high in status or more senior rated themselves personally as less conforming to the in-group's norms than did persons who were lower in status or more junior members of their group. Status would appear to grant freedom on group members! (Source: Based on data from Jetten, Hornsey, & Adarves-Yorno, 2006).

without being formally assigned to them. Regardless of how roles are acquired, in many groups, someone often serves as the "good listener," taking care of members' emotional needs, while another person tends to specialize in "getting things done."

To the extent that people *internalize* their social roles—those roles are linked to key aspects of the self-concept—they can have important implications for psychological well-being. Indeed, enacting a role well can lead people to feel that their behavior reflects their *authentic* self. Consider students in one study whose key self-perceptions were first measured and then they were randomly assigned to fulfill a particular role in a class task (Bettencourt, Molix, Talley, & Sheldon, 2006). The behaviors called for when assigned to the "idea generating" role are rather different than the behaviors required when assigned to the "devil's advocate" role. The results showed that for those people whose traits were consistent with whichever role they were assigned, they perceived their behavior during the task as authentically reflecting themselves, exhibited more positive mood, and enjoyed the class task more than people for whom there was a discrepancy between their self-perceptions and the role they had enacted.

As we noted in Chapter 8, a simulated prison study obtained new answers concerning the question of when and why role assignments affect our behavior (Reicher & Haslam, 2006). The adult participants in this study were first randomly assigned to the role of either prisoner or guard. Over the course of the study, those assigned to be guards failed to identify with their role, in part because of their concerns with being liked by the prisoners and how others might perceive them when the study was over (and was televised). In contrast, the prisoners showed significant increases over the course of the study in the degree to which they identified with their role. Did this difference in identification with their assigned role make a difference for the behavior that was observed? The answer was a definite yes. Because the guards did not identify with their role, they failed to impose their authority collectively, and they were eventually overcome by the other group whose members were highly identified with their group. The guards also showed increased stress responses that the prisoners did not show—both self-reported burnout and greater cortisol reactivity, which is a physiological indicator of stress (Haslam & Reicher, 2006). Those assigned to the prisoner role, however, showed increasing identification with the other prisoners, developed a norm of rebellion, and showed reductions in depression over the course of the study.

So, while roles are not *automatic* determinants of behavior, when they are internalized they can affect how we see ourselves, who we identify with, and our actions. Once people identify with a role, the norms—or appropriate ways for "people like us" to act—guide our behavior and, as we'll see below, even our emotions.

NORMS: THE RULES OF THE GAME   Groups powerfully affect the behavior of their members via **norms**—implicit rules that inform people about what is expected of them. Although we discussed the influence of norms on behavior in Chapter 9, here we want to consider how different norms can operate in different groups, and what happens when we deviate from what is normatively expected of us.

Have you ever considered the possibility that there might be "norms" that guide our emotions? Sometimes those are explicit **feeling rules**—expectations about the emotions that are appropriate to express (Hochschild, 1983). For example, as shown in Figure 11.5, many employers demand that service providers (cashiers, restaurant servers, and flight attendants) "always smile" at customers, no matter how annoying or rude they may be! In this case, norms for displaying positive feelings are specific to these kinds of employment settings. If one were employed as a funeral director, there would be explicit instructions to interact with the bereaved family in a "sincere" way, and to display only a "serious face" while trying to communicate empathy. But perhaps socialization into groups involves more than being told how to "act" emotionally. Potentially, learning "how to be a good group member" may be guided by subtle emotional experience norms.

An interesting study of Evangelical Christians that was conducted by Wilkins (2008) reveals how emotion norms reflect group membership acquisition. She found that initially, new converts did not perceive their participation in church lessons and meetings as

norms
Rules or expectations within a group concerning how its members should (or should not) behave.

feeling rules
Expectations about the appropriate emotions to display or express.

FIGURE 11.5   Some Roles or Groups Have Emotion Norms: Happiness on Demand!
Members of some social groups are told, or otherwise learn, how they are supposed to feel. These norms can be in the form of explicit rules: MacDonald's employees and flight attendants are told they must always smile at customers. Or, they can be more subtle, where learning to be a "good" group member means claiming to be "happier than you were before" you joined the group.

pleasant. But over time, and through interactions with other community members, new members learned to model their emotions on others. A new emotional vocabulary was acquired; new members were encouraged to publicly talk about their old, pre-Christian self as unhappy and anxiety-ridden and to present their new Christian self as happy. Most participants in this study reported initially having to be pushed to devote the time to learning the new faith practices but, after doing so, they came to perceive themselves as having acquired an "authentic Christian self," in which negative emotions are disallowed. According to this research, to maintain this new identity and be fully accepted within this community, feeling happy appears to be necessary. For these participants, because happiness is equated with moral goodness, feeling happy with one's life is necessary to be perceived as a good group member.

An important norm that varies considerably across cultures, but can also apply differentially to groups within a culture, is **collectivism** versus **individualism.** In collectivist groups, the norm is to maintain harmony among group members, even if doing so might entail some personal costs; in such groups, disagreement and conflict among members are to be avoided. In contrast, in individualistic groups, the norm is to value standing out from the group and be different from others; individual variability is to be expected and disagreeing with the group is often seen as courageous. Therefore, greater tolerance might be expected for those who deviate from group norms in individualist groups than in collectivist groups. Of course, people do differ in how much they value being a member of any particular group. Considerable research has illustrated that when being a member of a particular group is important to our self-concept (we highly identify with it), we are more likely to be guided by its norms, but ignore or even act contrary to its norms when we are not identified with that group (Jetten et al., 1997; Moreland & Levine, 2001). How then do people who are high or low in identification with an individualist or a collectivist group respond to someone who deviates from their group?

This question was addressed in a series of studies by Hornsey, Jetten, McAuliffe, and Hogg (2006). First, participants were selected who were either high or low in identification with their university. Then, the norm of their "student culture" was described as being "collectivist," with an emphasis on members achieving goals that will benefit the group as a whole rather than the students' personal goals, or as "individualist," where meeting personal goals is emphasized by members over achieving the goals of the student group as a whole. Responses to a student who was described as dissenting from the position of most students on an issue were then measured. As can be seen in Figure 11.6, among those who highly identify with their student group, a dissenter was liked when the norm was individualist, but that same dissenter was disliked when the norm was collectivist. Among those low in identification with their student group, the norm did not affect evaluations of the dissenting student. This research illustrates the potential costs of violating a group's norms—at least in the eyes of those who highly value that group.

COHESIVENESS: THE FORCE THAT BINDS Consider two groups. In the first, members like one another very much, strongly concur with the goals their group is seeking, and feel that they could not possibly find another group that would better satisfy their

collectivism
Groups in which the norm is to maintain harmony among group members, even if doing so might entail some personal costs.

individualism
Groups where the norm is to stand out and be different from others; individual variability is expected and disagreement among members is tolerated.

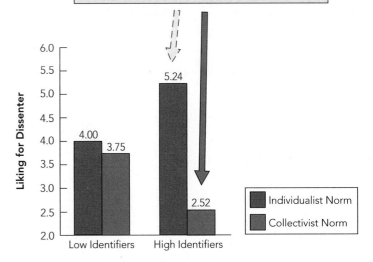

FIGURE 11.6   Responses to a Dissenting Group Member: It Depends on the Group Norm
Dissent, or disagreeing with other group members, can result in negative evaluations by those who highly identify with the group when the group's norm is collectivist and conflict is to be avoided. In contrast, when the group's norm is individualist, those who highly identify with the group are tolerant of dissenting group members. The norm of the group does not affect how low identifiers evaluate a dissenting fellow group member. (Source: Based on data from Hornsey et al., 2006).

needs. They have formed a group identity, and as a result are likely to perform their tasks well together. In the second, the opposite is true: members don't like one another very much, don't share common goals, and are actively seeking other groups that might offer them a better deal. They lack a shared identity and are less likely to successfully perform tasks together. The reason for this difference in the experience and performance of these two groups is what social psychologists refer to as **cohesiveness**—all the forces that cause members to remain in the group (Ellemers, de Gilder, & Haslam, 2004).

Cohesive groups have a sense of *solidarity;* they see themselves as homogenous, supportive of ingroup members, cooperative with ingroup members, aim to achieve group goals rather than individual goals, have high morale, and perform better than noncohesive groups (Hogg, 2007; Mullen & Cooper, 1994). As shown in Figure 11.7, outgroup members may find it difficult to gain acceptance in cohesive groups—they may not "fit" the norms all that well!

The presence of an outgroup or other form of competitive threat tends to increase cohesion and commitment to local community groups (Putnam, 2000). It fact, within nations during times of war, support for ingroup leaders dramatically increases (Landau et al., 2004). What might be less obvious is the effect that perceiving one's group to be potentially indistinguishable from another group has on emotions and actions aimed at protecting the ingroup's distinctiveness. Recent studies have revealed that French Canadians who worry about not being able to maintain their culture as distinct from English Canadians favor the separation of Quebec from Canada (Wohl, Giguère, Branscombe, & McVicar, 2011). Likewise, English Canadians who are threatened with the possibility of a ficticious "North American Union" in which their distinctive Canadian identity might be lost by such a merger with their "superpower neighbor"—the United States—favor putting limits on the amount of American media shown in Canada and indicate they intend to vote for candidates who see Canada as too closely involved with the United States (Wohl et al., 2011). As shown in Figure 11.8, the more general threat that your group's future might be in jeopardy can encourage all sorts of groups to advocate actions aimed at creating greater ingroup cohesion (Wohl, Branscombe, & Reysen, 2010).

cohesiveness
All forces (factors) that cause group members to remain in the group.

"Let's face it: you and this organization have never been a good fit."

FIGURE 11.7 Cohesive Groups Can Be Hard to Enter!
As this dog is learning, fitting into a cohesive "cat-run" organization may be difficult, if not impossible—at least for a dog! (Source: The New Yorker, December 18, 2000).

FIGURE 11.8   If Your Group's Future Might Be in Jeopardy, Actions That Will Make the InGroup More Cohesive Increase

Imagining how the future of your group might be in jeopardy—either by a union with another nation, your university is destroyed by a tornado, or merely thinking about a historical attempt to eliminate your group—can result in actions aimed at strengthening the ingroup. Such perceived jeopardy induces feelings of collective anxiety, which in turn can affect preferences that will create greater cohesion (e.g., marrying other ingroup members, educating children in schools for ingroup members only, voting for politicians who will protect the ingroup). (Source: Based on Wohl et al., 2010; Wohl et al., in press).

 # K E Y P O I N T S

- Groups are an indispensible part of our lives; evolutionary theorists suggest that groups are necessary for human survival.

- There are different kinds of groups: **common-bond groups** where the individual members have bonds with each other and **common-identity groups** where the members are linked via the category as a whole.

- **Groups** are composed of people who perceive themselves and are perceived by others as forming a coherent unit to some degree. The extent to which the group is perceived to form a coherent entity is known as **entitativity.**

- Basic features of groups include **status, roles, norms,** and **cohesiveness.**

- People gain status in a group for many reasons, ranging from physical characteristics (e.g., height) to various aspects of their behavior (e.g., conforming to group norms). Status tends to be higher for those who are prototypical of the group, or those who have seniority within the group.

- The effects of roles on our behavior are often very powerful, primarily when we have internalized the role as part of our identity.

- In some groups there are norms or explicit **feeling rules** about the emotions we should express.

- Deviating from group norms can affect how other group members, especially those who highly identify with their group, evaluate us. Norms can be **collectivist** or **individualist.**

- Another important feature of groups is their level of cohesiveness—the sum of all the factors that cause people to want to remain members. Perceiving a threat to one's group can encourage actions that increase group cohesiveness.

The Benefits—and Costs—of Joining

If you consider how many different groups you belong to, you may be surprised at the length of the list—especially if you consider both common-bond (face-to-face) and common-identity (social categories) groups. While some people belong to more groups than others, most of us put forth effort to gain admittance to and maintain membership in at least some groups. Why, then, if we work hard to get in and the benefits of group membership can be great, do we sometimes choose to leave groups? Withdrawing from a group to which we have belonged for months, years, or even decades can be a stressful experience. Here's what social psychologists have found out about why we join groups and the processes involved in leaving them.

THE BENEFITS OF JOINING: WHAT GROUPS DO FOR US   That people sometimes go through a lot to join a specific group is clear: membership in many groups is by "invitation only," and winning that invitation can be difficult! Perhaps more surprising is that once they gain admission, many people will stick with a group even when it experiences hard times. For instance, consider some sports fans and how they remain loyal to their team when it has a miserable season, even when it is the target of ridicule and gains a reputation as "the worst of the worst." What accounts for this strong desire to join—and remain a part of—social groups?

First, we often gain *self-knowledge* from belonging to various groups (Tajfel & Turner, 1986). Our membership in them tells us what kind of person we are—or perhaps, would like to be—so group membership becomes central to our self-concept. The result? Once we belong, we can find it hard to imagine not belonging because it makes our life meaningful by defining to some extent who we are. Indeed, to be rejected by a group—even one we have recently joined—can be among the most painful of experiences (Williams, 2001). Being ostracized from just an online computer group can lower feelings of control and self-esteem both immediately after it occurs and even after a 45-minute delay. Such harmful effects are particularly acute among people who are high in social anxiety and who fear rejection (Zadro, Boland, & Richardson, 2006).

Another obvious benefit of belonging to some groups is that they help us reach our goals. One important goal is attaining prestige. When an individual is accepted into a certain type of group—a highly selective school, an exclusive social club, a varsity sports team—self-esteem can increase. Just how important is this boost from joining and identifying with particular groups? As you can probably guess, the more an individual is seeking *self-enhancement*—boosting one's own public image—the more important will a group's status be to that person and the more strongly he or she will identify with it (Roccas, 2003).

People are also attracted to groups when they fit our goals—even if those goals are relatively transient. Suppose you feel willing to take risks and try something new or, conversely, want to feel secure and are a little cautious. How might these orientations affect the kind of group you would join and value being in? Would you prefer a relatively high-power group (that is able to exert influence and get things done) or a relatively low-power group with less of those capabilities? Research findings indicate that people like being in a group best when that group matches their current goal orientation (Sassenberg, Jonas, Shah, & Brazy, 2007).

Another important benefit of joining groups is that doing so often helps us to accomplish goals we could not achieve alone (i.e., social change). How can members of groups that have been the target of oppression attain equal rights? One way such groups cope with the discrimination they experience is to increasingly turn to and identify with their group (Branscombe, Schmitt, & Harvey, 1999). As a result of recognizing shared grievances, people can develop a **politicized collective identity,** which prepares them to engage in a power struggle on behalf of their group. As shown in Figure 11.9, by joining together, people who have been the victims of prejudice gain "social clout" and can succeed in winning better treatment for their group (Simon & Klandermans, 2001). Clearly, then, we derive many benefits—some personal and some collective—from belonging to and identifying with various groups.

THE COSTS OF GETTING ACCEPTED INTO A GROUP   Many groups erect barriers to entry: they want only *some* people to join, and they insist that those who do be highly motivated to enter. Steep initiation fees, substantial efforts to prove one's credentials as suitable, and long trial or probationary periods are common methods of restricting group membership.

Social psychologists have addressed the question, What are the consequences of undergoing severe admission processes in terms of their impact on commitment to the group? Does paying a very high price to secure membership in such selective groups require us to cognitively justify our time and effort in doing so, and might that make it difficult to later admit that joining might have been a mistake?

To increase our commitment to a group because we have paid a heavy material or psychological price to join it might at first appear to be a rather strange idea. In

politicized collective identity
Recognizing shared grievances and engaging in a power struggle on behalf of one's devalued group.

a classic experiment, Aronson and Mills (1959) illustrated why this sometimes happens. In order to imitate an initiation rite, students in their study were asked to read either very embarrassing material in front of a group, mildly embarrassing material, or they did not read any material aloud. As we saw in Chapter 5, according to cognitive dissonance theory, people feel discomfort when their attitudes and behavior are discrepant. When we have put forth considerable effort to achieve membership in a group, we may change our attitudes toward that group in a positive direction in order to justify our effort. As a result, after going through an initiation in order to be admitted to a group and then learning that the group is unattractive after all, our commitment toward that group should actually *increase*. As these researchers predicted, liking for the group was greater as the severity of the initiation increased; the more embarrassing the material the students had to read, the more attractive they subsequently found this boring group.

FIGURE 11.9   Producing Social Change: One Reason Why People Join Groups
One potential benefit individuals obtain from joining groups is social change. For instance, by joining together, members of gay rights groups can collectively attempt to change the law to allow same-sex marriage.

THE COSTS OF MEMBERSHIP: WHY GROUPS SOMETIMES SPLINTER   While groups can help us to reach our goals, help to boost our status along the way, and form an important part of who we are, they also impose certain costs. First, group membership often restricts personal freedom. Members of various groups are expected to behave in certain ways—and if they don't, the group may impose sanctions or even expel such violators from membership. For instance, in the United States, it is considered inappropriate for military officers to make public statements about politics. Even high-ranking generals who do so may be strongly reprimanded. In 2010, President Barack Obama removed General Stanley McChrystal as commander in Afghanistan for his remarks about administration officials.

Groups often make demands on members' time, energy, and resources, and they must meet these demands or surrender their membership. Some churches, for instance, require that their members donate 10 percent of their income to the church. People wishing to remain in these groups must comply—or face expulsion. Finally, groups can adopt positions or policies of which some members disapprove. Again, the dissenting members either must remain silent, speak out and run the risk of strong sanctions, or withdraw.

Withdrawing from some groups can be a major step with lasting repercussions. Why might individuals take this ultimate action—exiting a group they perhaps once highly valued? One intriguing answer is provided by a series of studies involving political parties and church groups (Sani, 2005, 2009). When individuals identify with these sorts of groups, other members of the group are categorized together with the self to in effect become "we." To the extent that people identify themselves and others as part of the same category, then they may choose to withdraw from groups that they no longer see as meeting the definition of the "we-ness" they initially adopted. Thus, individuals may decide to leave a group, and a group may splinter, when members conclude that some subset of the group has changed sufficiently that they can no longer be viewed as part of "us." This is particularly likely when differences in **ideology**—the philosophical and political values

ideology
The philosophical and political values that govern a group.

FIGURE 11.10   Groups Change: Women Become Priests in the Church of England

In 1994, the first women were ordained as priests in the Church of England. Some existing clergy found this change ideologically intolerable and left the church, while others saw the admission of women to the priesthood as enhancing their group identity.

schism
Splintering of a group into distinct factions following an ideological rift among members.

of a group—among different factions become so disparate that some members cannot see themselves as sharing a social identity with other members of the group.

Evidence for this ideological splintering process among members of the Church of England was obtained by Sani (2005). In 1994, the first women were ordained as priests, and as a result, hundreds of clergy, who objected to this ideological change from the 500-year tradition of permitting only males to enter the priesthood, decided to leave the church (see Figure 11.10). Why did they feel this drastic action was necessary? After all, they had been officials of this church for much of their lives and their identities were strongly bound up with it.

To investigate what led to this upheaval among members, over 1,000 priests and deacons in the Church of England were asked to express their views about the new policy of ordaining women as priests, the extent to which they felt this had changed the church greatly, how much they identified with the Church of England, the degree to which they felt emotionally distressed by the change, and whether they believed their views (if they were opposed to the policy change) would be heard. Results indicated that clergy who left the church did so because they felt this policy change altered fundamental doctrines so much that it was no longer the same organization as the one they originally joined and that it no longer represented their views. Furthermore, they felt strongly that no one would pay attention to their dissenting opinions and that this left them no choice but to withdraw. As shown in Figure 11.11, perceiving their group identity as being subverted by this change resulted in emotional distress, reduced the perception that the church was an entitative group, and lowered identification with the church. These processes lead to a **schism**—splintering of the group into distinct factions that could not stay united by a single identity. For those members who felt compelled to leave, the emotional distress experienced reflected the loss of this important identity and was akin to bereavement.

This potential for splintering as groups undergo change is not restricted to religious groups. On the contrary, Sani (2009) notes that similar splits have occurred in

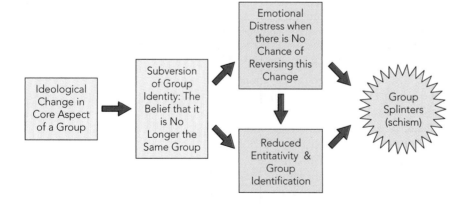

FIGURE 11.11   Why Groups Sometimes Splinter

Research indicates that groups splinter when members perceive that the group has changed so much (subversion) that it is no longer the same entity (group) they originally joined, and when they conclude that no one will listen to their protests over this change (there is no chance of reversing it), the group splinters apart.   (Source: Based on suggestions by Sani, 2009).

other groups—political parties, social movements, and, in fact, can occur in any group that is based on shared beliefs and values. Groups change, and when they do so to the extent that members feel that they can no longer identify with the group, the final outcome is inevitable: some members will withdraw because, they believe, the group is no longer the same as the one they originally joined.

KEYPOINTS

- Joining groups confers important benefits on members, including increased self-knowledge, progress toward important goals, enhanced status, and, when a **politicized collective identity** is formed, a means of attaining social change.

- However, group membership also exacts important costs, such as loss of personal freedom and heavy demands on time, energy, and resources.

- The desire to join exclusive and prestigious groups may be so strong that individuals are willing to undergo painful and dangerous initiations in order to become

members. After doing so, people must justify to themselves their efforts to join the group, and therefore show increased positive attitude change toward that group.

- Individuals withdraw from groups when they feel that the group's **ideology** has changed so much that it no longer reflects their basic values or beliefs. When a **schism** or splintering of a group into distinct factions occurs, some members experience emotional distress, feel they can no longer identify with the group, and no longer see the group as the cohesive one they originally joined.

Effects of the Presence of Others: From Task Performance to Behavior in Crowds

The fact that our behavior is often strongly affected by the groups to which we belong is far from surprising; after all, in these groups there are usually well-established norms that tell us how we are expected to behave. Perhaps much more surprising is the fact that often we are strongly affected by the *mere presence of others*, even if we, and they, are not part of a formal group. You are probably already familiar with such effects from your own experience. For instance, suppose you are sitting alone in a room studying. You may sit any old way you find comfortable, including putting your feet up on the furniture. But if a stranger enters the room, all this may change. You will probably refrain from doing some things you might have done when alone, and you may change many other aspects of your behavior—even though you don't know this person and are not directly interacting with him or her (see Figure 11.12). So clearly, we are often affected by the mere physical presence of others. While such effects take many different forms, we focus here on two that are especially important: the effects of the presence of others on our performance of various tasks, and the effects of being in a large crowd.

Social Facilitation: Performing in the Presence of Others

Sometimes, when we perform a task, we work totally alone; for instance, you might study alone in your room. In many other cases, even if we are working on a task by ourselves, other people are present—for instance, you might study at a café, or in your room while your roommate also studies. How does the presence of others affect our performance, and why does having an audience matter?

Imagine that you have to give a speech in a class—and that you are preparing for this important performance (most of your grade depends on how you do). You repeatedly

FIGURE 11.12   Effects of the Mere Presence of Others

Often, the mere presence of other persons, even if they are total strangers, can strongly affect our behavior. We change from casual slouching and having our feet on the furniture to a more "socially acceptable" posture.

practice your speech alone. Finally, the big day arrives and you walk out onto the stage to find a large audience seated there waiting to hear you. How will you do? Most of us can recall times when we have been nervous about performing in front of others (I can still remember the first time I ever lectured in a big undergraduate class). Some of us have even "choked" when the time came, whereas others have felt that their abilities really shone with an audience. Evidence from several different studies confirms that the presence of others can affect our performance—sometimes positively and sometimes negatively.

More than 40 years ago, Zajonc, Heingartner, and Herman (1969) conducted a seemingly zany experiment. They arranged to have cockroaches run a maze. That would have been strange enough for social psychologists, but these researchers added a curious twist to the roach maze—they constructed clear plastic boxes close enough to the maze so that a roach "audience" could observe the maze-running "participants." With this setup the roaches in the maze would also "know" they were being watched—they would be aware of the presence of the onlooking audience.

As it turned out, those cockroaches who were watched by other roaches ran the maze faster than cockroaches without an audience. Zajonc and his colleagues (1969) were intent on making a point about a group phenomenon called *social facilitation* (i.e., the effects of the presence of others on performance). Although, as social psychologists, we typically study human, as opposed to cockroach, behavior, why did Zajonc et al. choose to conduct an animal experiment of this type?

Zajonc (1965) argued that the mere presence of others would *only* facilitate a well-learned response, but that it could inhibit a less-practiced or "new" response. Why? He noted that the presence of others increases physiological arousal (our bodies become more energized) and, as a result, any *dominant response* will be facilitated. This means that we can focus better on something we *know* or have *practiced* when we're aroused, but that same physiological arousal will create problems when we're dealing with something *new* or *complex*. This reasoning—depicted in Figure 11.13—became known as the *drive theory of social facilitation* because it focuses on arousal or drive-based effects on performance. The presence of others will improve individuals' performance when they are highly skilled at the task in question (in this case their dominant responses would tend to be correct), but will interfere with performance when they are not highly skilled—for instance, when they are learning to perform it (for their dominant responses would not be correct in that case).

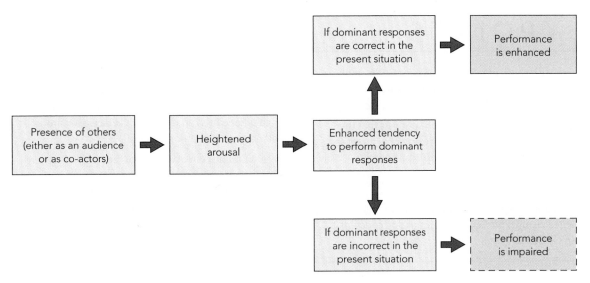

FIGURE 11.13   The Drive Theory of Social Facilitation
According to the drive theory of social facilitation (Zajonc, 1965), the presence of others, either as an audience or co-actors, increases arousal and this, in turn, strengthens the tendency to perform dominant responses. If these responses are correct, performance is improved; if they are incorrect, performance is harmed.

However, other researchers thought that performance might sometimes be disrupted by the presence of an audience because of apprehension about having their performance evaluated (remember the professor who will be grading your speech!). This **evaluation apprehension** idea was studied by Cottrell, Wack, Sekerak, and Rittle (1968). In fact, several of their experiments found that social facilitation did *not* occur when an audience was blindfolded, or displayed no interest in watching the person performing the task, which lent support to the interpretation that concerns about evaluation might play a role. But Zajonc did not believe the fear of potential evaluation was *necessary* for social facilitation to occur, so that was why he performed the cockroach experiment. Given that we can assume that cockroaches do not worry about their maze-running abilities being evaluated, it is safe to say that social facilitation does not *require* evaluation apprehension to work, at least for some species.

CAN HAVING AN AUDIENCE DISTRACT US?   Some have suggested that the presence of others, either as an audience or as co-actors, can be distracting and, for this reason, it can produce cognitive overload (e.g., Baron, 1986). Because performers must divide their attention between the task and the audience, such increased cognitive load can result in a tendency to restrict one's attention so as to focus only on essential cues or stimuli while "screening out" nonessential ones. Several findings offer support for this view, known as **distraction conflict theory.** So, which is more important—increased arousal with an audience (Zajonc, 1965) or this tendency toward a narrowed attentional focus?

Hetherington, Anderson, Norton, and Newson (2006) applied these ideas to understand the effects of others on eating as a function of distraction. Caloric intake was measured in male participants under differing distraction conditions. Both eating with friends and while watching TV increased eating. Because both friends and TV can be distracting, it can result in a greater focus on the food and thus lead to "improved" eating performance (i.e., greater caloric intake). In contrast, eating in the presence of strangers was less distracting, and, therefore, caused no increased focus on food and no increased caloric intake. One advantage of this cognitive perspective is that it helps explain when and why animals, as well as people, are affected by the presence of an audience that differs in how distracting it is to the performer. After all, animals, too (even cockroaches), can experience conflicting tendencies to work on a task *and* pay attention to an audience.

evaluation apprehension
Concern over being evaluated by others. Such concern can increase arousal and so contribute to social facilitation effects.

distraction conflict theory
A theory suggesting that social facilitation stems from the conflict produced when individuals attempt, simultaneously, to pay attention to the other people present and to the task being performed.

KEYPOINTS

- The mere presence of other people either as an audience or as co-actors can influence our performance on many tasks. Such effects are known as *social facilitation*.

- The *drive theory of social facilitation* suggests that the presence of others is arousing and can either increase or reduce performance, depending on whether dominant responses in a given situation are correct or incorrect.

- The **evaluation apprehension** view suggests that an audience disrupts performance because of concerns about being evaluated.

- The **distraction conflict** perspective suggests that the presence of others induces conflicting tendencies to focus on the task being performed and on the audience or co-actors. This can result both in increased arousal and narrowed attentional focus.

- Recent findings offer support for the view that several kinds of audiences produce narrowed attentional focus among people performing a task. Both the arousal and cognitive views of social facilitation can help explain why social facilitation occurs among animals as well as people.

Social Loafing: Letting Others Do the Work

additive tasks

Tasks for which the group product is the sum or combination of the efforts of individual members.

FIGURE 11.14   Does Everyone Do Their Share of the Work?

When several people work together to accomplish a task like this, it is probable that they will not all exert the same amount of effort. Some will work very hard, others will do less, and perhaps a few will do nothing at all, while pretending to work hard! Social loafing in groups tends to reduce their output overall.

You have probably had the experience of seeing a construction crew in which some appear to be working hard while others seem to be standing around not doing much at all. When it comes to a task like the rowing shown in Figure 11.14, do you think everyone will fully "pitch in" and exert equal effort? Probably not. Some will contribute by taking on as much of the load as they can, while some will pretend to be rowing as hard as they can when, in fact, they are not.

This pattern is quite common in situations where groups perform what are known as **additive tasks**—ones in which the contributions of each member are combined into a single group output. On such tasks, some people will work hard, while others goof off and do less than they would if working alone. Social psychologists refer to such effects as **social loafing**—reductions in effort when individuals work collectively compared to when they work individually (Karau & Williams, 1993).

Social loafing has been demonstrated in many different task contexts. For example in one of the first studies on this topic, Latane, Williams, and Harkins (1979) asked groups of male students to clap or cheer as loudly as possible at specific times, supposedly so that the experimenter could determine how much noise people make in social settings. To make sure participants were not affected by the actual noise of other participants, they wore headphones, through which noise-making was played at a constant volume. Furthermore, they could not see the other participants, but were only told how many others they were shouting with. They performed these tasks in groups of two, four, or six people. Results indicated that although the total amount of noise rose as group size increased, the amount produced *by each participant* dropped. In other words, each person put out less and less effort as the size of the group increased.

Such effects appear to be quite general in scope, and occur with respect to many different tasks—cognitive ones as well as those involving physical effort (Weldon & Mustari, 1988; Williams & Karau, 1991). As anyone who has worked as a server in a restaurant knows, tips are proportionally less as the size of the group increases, which may be one reason why a standard tip is often added by the restaurant when there are six or more in a party.

To ask whether social loafing occurs in school settings might elicit a "duh" response from students. Englehart (2006) suggests that social loafing can explain patterns of student participation as a function of the size of the class; students participate less in larger classes. Likewise, social loafing occurs among students working on team projects. Price, Harrison, and Gavin (2006) identified several psychological factors that affect students' social loafing on team projects. First, those who felt "dispensable" to the group were more likely to loaf. Second, the more fairness that was perceived in the group generally, the less likely students were to loaf. What determined these two perceptions—dispensability and fairness? When participants had substantial knowledge and skills relating to the task, they felt less dispensable. So, in effect, being able to offer task-relevant help to the group served to counteract loafing. In addition, dissimilarity from the other group members led participants to feel more dispensable, and thus more likely to loaf. So what can be done to reduce social loafing?

REDUCING SOCIAL LOAFING: SOME USEFUL TECHNIQUES The most obvious way of reducing social loafing involves making the output or effort of each participant readily identifiable (Williams, Harkins, & Latané, 1981). Under these conditions, people can't sit back and let others do their work, so social loafing is reduced. When people believe their contribution matters, and a strong performance on the part of the group will lead to a desired outcome, individuals also tend to try harder (Shepperd & Taylor, 1999). So, pooling contributions to a task—such as co-writing a paper—will be effective only to the extent that each writer's contribution is clear; even better is when each person feels uniquely skilled to write their own part.

Second, groups can reduce social loafing by increasing group members' commitment to successful task performance (Brickner, Harkins, & Ostrom, 1986). Pressures toward working hard will then serve to offset temptations to engage in social loafing. Third, social loafing can be reduced by increasing the apparent importance or value of a task (Karau & Williams, 1993). Fourth, people are less likely to loaf if they are given some kind of standard of performance—either in terms of how much others are doing or their own past performance (Williams et al., 1981). An interesting study with students in a marketing class showed that group members themselves can provide such feedback to each other over the course of a joint project and that doing so reduces social loafing (Aggarwal & O'Brien, 2008). Together, use of these tactics can sharply reduce social loafing—and the temptation to "goof off" at the expense of others.

Effects of Being in a Crowd

Have you ever attended a football or basketball game at which members of the crowd screamed insults, threw things at the referees, or engaged in other violent behavior they would probably never show in other settings? Most of us haven't, since such extreme events are relatively rare, although, interestingly enough, this is part of the "stereotype" of how people behave in crowds, particularly those at sporting events. English soccer fans have become especially famous for **hooliganism**—incidents throughout Europe of serious disorder at matches involving England's team (Stott, Hutchison, & Drury, 2001). Such effects in crowds—where there is a drift toward wild, unrestrained behavior, were initially termed **deindividuation** because they seemed to stem, at least in part, from the fact that when people are in a large crowd they tend "to lose their individuality" and instead act as others do. More formally, the term deindividuation was used to indicate a psychological state characterized by reduced self-awareness and personal identity salience, brought on by external conditions such as being an anonymous member of a large crowd.

Initial research on deindividuation (Zimbardo, 1970) seemed to suggest that being in a crowd makes people anonymous and therefore less responsible or accountable for their own actions, which encourages unrestrained, antisocial actions. More recent evidence, though, indicates that deindividuation leads to greater normative behavior, not less. When we are part of a large crowd we are more likely to obey the norms of this group—whatever those may be (Postmes & Spears, 1998). For instance, at a sporting event, when norms in that situation suggest that it is appropriate to boo the opposing

social loafing
Reductions in motivation and effort when individuals work in a group compared to when they work individually.

hooliganism
Negative stereotype about how people behave in crowds at sporting events, especially applied to incidents involving England's soccer fans.

deindividuation
A psychological state characterized by reduced self-awareness brought on by external conditions, such as being an anonymous member of a large crowd.

team, that is what many people—especially highly identified fans—will do. Certainly that seems to have been the norm that was active for "English hooligans" at soccer games in the past. However, recent evidence indicates that, as a result of social psychological intervention with police agencies, those norms can be changed (Stott, Adang, Livingstone, & Schreiber, 2007). As a result, at more recent soccer matches, England's fans no longer defined hooliganism as characteristic of their fan group; they self-policed by marginalizing those few English fans who attempted to create conflict, and no violent incidents have taken place.

Overall, then, being part of a large crowd and experiencing deindividuation does not necessarily lead to negative or harmful behaviors; it simply increases the likelihood that crowd members will follow the norms of the group. Those norms might be of "showing respect" by silently crying—behaviors demonstrated at the immense gatherings following Diana, Princess of Wales' death, or at the vigils that took place on the campus of Virginia Tech in Blacksburg following the shooting deaths that took place there in 2007. Or, the critical norms might involve working together for a purpose—coordinating efforts to save people from crumbled buildings after the earthquake in Haiti in 2010, or praying and singing joyously together at huge Christian revival meetings. When people are in large crowds, as shown in Figure 11.15, what behavior they will exhibit—for good or ill—will depend on what norms are operating.

KEYPOINTS

- When individuals work together on an **additive task,** where their contributions are combined, **social loafing**—reduced output by each group member—frequently occurs. Such loafing has been found on physical, cognitive, and verbal tasks among both adults and children.

- Social loafing can be reduced in several ways: by making outputs individually identifiable or unique, ensuring individuals do not feel dispensable, providing feedback on

each person's performance, and increasing commitment to the success of the task.

- When we are part of a large crowd, **deindividuation**—where we are less aware of our personal self and morals—can occur. People act on the basis of the norms operative in crowds, which differ depending on what group identity is salient. Those norms can sanction either antisocial or prosocial actions.

FIGURE 11.15   The Crowd: Conforming to Norms for Good or Ill
Crowds sometimes engage in actions that individual members would never dream of performing if they were alone. Those actions can be dramatically destructive as shown in the picture on the left, or peaceful as shown in the picture on the right. Depending on what norms are salient, identifying with others in a crowd can strongly affect our behavior and encourage conformity to the norms governing that particular crowd.

Coordination in Groups: Cooperation or Conflict?

Cooperation—helping that is mutual, where both sides benefit—is common in groups working together to attain shared goals. As we discussed in the beginning of this chapter, by cooperating, people can attain goals they could never hope to reach by themselves. Surprisingly, though, cooperation does not always develop in groups. Sometimes, group members may perceive their personal interests as incompatible, and instead of coordinating their efforts, may work against each other, often producing negative results for all. This is known as **conflict,** and can be defined as a process in which individuals or groups perceive that others have taken, or will soon take, actions incompatible with their own interests (DeDreu, 2010). Conflict is indeed a process, for, as you probably know from your own experience, it has a nasty way of escalating—from simple mistrust, through a spiral of anger, to actions designed to harm the other side. Let's see what social psychologists have learned about both patterns of behavior. (For information on cooperating on work tasks over the Internet, and avoiding the pitfalls that can lead to conflict, please see the section "SOCIAL LIFE IN A CONNECTED WORLD: Working with Others via Computer-Mediated Communication," below.)

cooperation
Behavior in which group members work together to attain shared goals.

conflict
A process in which individuals or groups perceive that others have taken or will soon take actions incompatible with their own interests.

social embeddedness
Having a sense of that you know other persons because you know their reputations, often by knowing other people they know too.

SOCIAL LIFE *in a* CONNECTED WORLD

Working with Others via Computer-Mediated Communication

In the world of work, communicating over the Internet with people you don't know well, or at all, is becoming increasingly common (Brandon & Hollingshead, 2007). Attempting to work on group projects with people you don't know always raises questions about how they will turn out. This is especially true when you consider that such projects often require considerable trust and cooperation. To get students prepared for working in this sort of environment, some universities require students to work on a cooperative project with other students in the same course at another school. All the work has to be done on the Internet.

So, now, imagine that you've been given this assignment. You are one of two students at your school who was assigned to work on a paper with two students at another school who you had never met. When you did briefly meet face-to-face with the other student at your school, she said she thought you all could work well together over the Internet and the professor required that you do the task this way.

Part of what makes for good cooperation is **social embeddedness,** which is a sense of knowing the reputation of the other parties involved, often by knowing someone else who knows them (Riegelsberger, Sasse, & McCarthy, 2007). Although the student you would be working with at your home university happened to know from high school one of the students at the other university, no one knew anything about the other student. Aside from your partner believing that the student she knew had a reputation for

being a team player, you were sort of in the dark about what these other people would be like to work with.

Because social embeddedness was low, none of the students would be likely to trust their virtual workmates all that well. And the communications were going to be strictly written—text only—at least initially! You wonder how do you judge a workmate's response to an idea if you cannot see his or her face? Research has shown that people communicating via video are more likely to develop trustworthy relationships than people communicating via voice alone (i.e., over the phone). However, both these methods guarantee greater trust developing than communicating only by text-based chat (Green, 2007).

Naturally, you are wary of communicating by text only. Something you might say could be misunderstood, and it might be difficult to gauge the effect of what you say about the other students' work. Kruger, Epley, Parker, and Ng (2005) found that the *apparent advantage* of **asynchronous forms of communication**—communication in which people have a period of time during which to think about their response, as in e-mail and other forms of text messaging—can cause problems in people being accurately understood by others. In their study, pairs of friends were separated and told their task was to identify which of their friend's 20 statements about general topics were sarcastic or serious. Then, using other friend-pairs, these same statements were communicated either via instant message

(continued)

SOCIAL LIFE *in a* **CONNECTED WORLD** *(continued)*

or over the phone. Because tone of voice, a nonverbal expression that helps detect sarcasm, is absent in the text condition (but text writers fail to appreciate this important point), they will think others understand them when they do not. Thus, the senders of the message thought they were equally likely to be understood, regardless of the method of communication, but the text message's sarcasm was lost on the message receiver (i.e., it was less likely to be accurately detected in the text condition compared to the voice condition).

Interpersonal cues, while they are absent in a computer-mediated situation, play a role in establishing trust between participants. Consider an experiment by Rickenberg and Reeves (2000) that used animated characters that showed only simplistic interpersonal cues. Even without a genuinely human element, the presence of such cues increased trust, even without a rational basis for such trust!

In addition to concerns about the lack of interpersonal cues because you were confined to using text only, you and the other student on your campus feared there might be a disagreement with the students on the other campus about what to include in the paper because, after all, you had different instructors who might have emphasized different things in class. Because this could lead to conflict—the very opposite of

cooperation—if disagreements like that arose, it could result in your virtual group failing.

Fortunately, after 2 weeks, the group moved to text plus once-a-week audio-visual conversations using Skype. This change seemed like real progress because any disagreements that occurred could be more effectively talked through on Skype, allowing you and the other students to move toward settling differences about what should go in the paper. Over time, you and the other students became more trusting of your virtual associates, mostly because you ended up getting a lot of good work done. The virtual writing team turned out to be a success, and you all received A's! If you have to do an assignment with someone using the Internet in the future, maybe the setup employed by the people shown in Figure 11.16 could be you.

FIGURE 11.16   To Skype or Not to Skype: That Is the Question
Increasingly people are working and socializing on the internet. At present, many social activities that used to take place face-to-face can now be done using Skype, or other video conferencing programs, which allows for all the normal interpersonal cues to be present during long distance communication.

Cooperation: Working with Others to Achieve Shared Goals

asynchronous forms of communication
Unlike face-to-face communication where there is no delay, asynchronous forms such as e-mail and other forms of text messaging give people a period of time during which they can think about their response before responding.

negative interdependence
A situation where if one person obtains a desired outcome, others cannot obtain it.

Cooperation is often highly beneficial to the people involved. So why don't group members always cooperate? One answer is straightforward: because some goals that people seek simply can't be shared. Several people seeking the same job or romantic partner can't combine forces to attain these goals: the rewards can go to only one. Social psychologists refer to this situation as one of **negative interdependence**—where if one person obtains a desired outcome, others cannot (DeDreu, 2010). Likewise, if I want to look "good," I might not want to cooperate with others because that would mean I would have to share the glory (the exact opposite of the two authors of this textbook!).

In many other situations, however, cooperation could develop but does not. Social psychologists study these kinds of situations with the aim of identifying the factors that tip the balance either toward or away from cooperation. Often the people involved in such conflicts don't realize that a compromise *is* possible. Consider the following example. Suppose we wanted to go on vacation together. You say you want to go to Switzerland, and I say I want to go to Hawaii. Does this conflict seem solvable, without one person losing? Yes, it could be. One thing conflict mediators do know is that to solve this kind of conflict—without one person simply capitulating to the other—we have to get to the essence of what lies behind each person's demands. Now suppose your "real" goal is to see some mountains (which Switzerland certainly has, but so do many other places), and my "real" goal is to be by the sea and swim in warm water. Once this underlying goal of each party is known, it can often be settled, with the help of a little imagination. In this case, we could go to Greece—visit some mountains *and* the beach on some lovely Greek island! Of course, all social conflicts are not solvable by this method, but many are. Let's examine now classic research on dilemmas where a lack of cooperation frequently results in poor outcomes for all parties involved.

SOCIAL DILEMMAS: WHERE COOPERATION COULD OCCUR, BUT OFTEN DOESN'T   **Social dilemmas** are situations in which each person can increase his or her individual gains by acting in a purely selfish manner, but if all (or most) people do the same thing, the outcomes experienced by all are reduced (Komorita & Parks, 1994; Van Lange & Joireman, 2010). A classic illustration of this kind of situation is known as the *prisoner's dilemma*—a situation faced by two suspects who have been caught by the police. Here, either or both people can choose to cooperate (e.g., stay silent and not confess) or compete (e.g., "rat the other person out"). If both cooperate with each other, then they both experience large gains. If both compete, each person loses substantially. What happens if one chooses to compete while the other chooses to cooperate? In this case the one who competes experiences a moderate gain, while the trusting one loses. Social psychologists have used this type of situation to examine the factors that tip the balance toward trust and cooperation or mistrust and competition (Insko et al., 2001; Rusbult & Van Lange, 2003).

It might be reasonable to suppose that decreasing the attractiveness of competition should increase cooperation. One way to do this would be to increase the sanctions given in a social dilemma for noncooperative choices. But doing so might change how people perceive such situations—from one involving trust in others to one based on economic self-interest. When seen as based in trust, cooperation should be higher than when the dilemma is seen as a situation in which people act on their own self-interests. To what degree, then, does the presence of sanctions for noncooperation undermine people's subsequent cooperative behavior—the exact opposite of its intended effect?

Mulder, van Dijk, De Cremer, and Wilke (2006) addressed this question by first telling their participants about a "game" that "other participants in a prior study" were said to have engaged in. All participants were told about a situation in which four group members had to decide whether to keep chips for themselves or donate them to the group. The total number of chips that were donated by the members to the group would be doubled in value by the experimenter and then equally divided among the members. This information phase of the study was included so that the presence of sanctioning for noncooperative group members could be varied. The crucial manipulation was whether a sanctioning system—applied to the two lowest chip-donating people—was said to have been operating or not. Later, when the participants took part in a different social dilemma where no sanctioning was mentioned, the influence of exposure to the prior sanctioning system for noncooperation could be assessed.

As you can see in Figure 11.17, prior exposure to the sanctioning for noncooperation subsequently lowered cooperation when the participants made their behavioral choices in a social dilemma. The reduction in cooperation among those exposed to a sanctioning system stemmed from changes in participants' perceptions of the extent to which they could trust that others will behave cooperatively. So, having sanctions be present, over time, has the opposite effect on cooperation than might be intended! In fact, recent research has revealed that merely thinking about the law as a sanctioning system fosters people's

social dilemmas
Situations in which each person can increase his or her individual gains by acting in one way, but if all (or most) people do the same thing, the outcomes experienced by all are reduced.

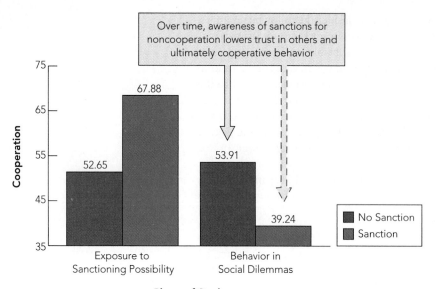

FIGURE 11.17 **Awareness of Sanctions for Noncooperation Can Undermine Trust and Cooperation**

At first, as shown on the left side of the graph, awareness that there are sanctions for noncooperation might serve to ensure people cooperate with others. However, as shown on the right side of the graph, later responses to a new social dilemma may be less cooperative following exposure to sanctions for noncooperation because it serves to undermine trust in others. *(Source: Based on data from Mulder, van Dijk, De Cremer, & Wilke, 2006).*

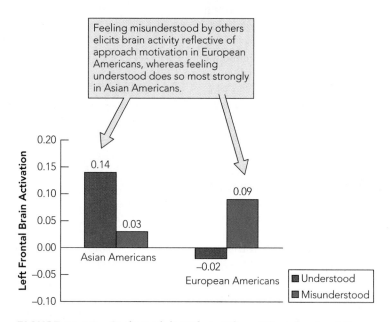

FIGURE 11.18 **Brain Activity When Others Misunderstand You**

Shown here is EEG left frontal brain activity in Asian American and European Americans when they felt either misunderstood by others or understood by them. Brain activation in this area is thought to reflect approach motivation. Thus, when European Americans felt misunderstood they prepared to confront, while Asian Americans were less likely to do so. In fact, they showed evidence of withdrawal motivation when they felt misunderstood. *(Source: Based on research by Lun et al., 2010).*

beliefs that others are competitive, that they cannot be trusted, and leads people to make more competitive choices during a prisoner's dilemma game (Callan, Kay, Olson, Brar, & Whitefield, 2010).

Responding to and Resolving Conflicts: Some Useful Techniques

Most definitions of conflict emphasize the existence of incompatible interests. But conflict can sometimes occur when the two sides don't really have opposing interests—they simply believe that these exist (DeDreu & Van Lang, 1995). Indeed, errors concerning the causes of others' behavior—*faulty attribution*—can play a critical role in conflict (Baron, 1990).

How do you feel when someone misunderstands your actions? Do you attempt to make him or her "see the light" or do you "simply withdraw," assuming there is nothing you can do to change his or her mind no matter how hard you try? "Feeling misunderstood" by others leads to different responses in members of various ethnic groups. In a series of studies by Lun, Oishi, Coan, Akimoto, and Miao (2010), electroencephalogram (left prefrontal) brain activity was measured when group members were subjected to a "misunderstood or understood by others" manipulation. Because European Americans were expected to feel challenged and be prepared to confront others when they felt misunderstood, whereas Asian Americans were expected to be motivated to withdraw from the same situation, brain activity in the area reflecting approach motivation should be differentially observable in these circumstances. As shown in Figure 11.18, that is exactly what occurred. European Americans showed elevated activity reflective of approach motivation when they were misunderstood, while Asian Americans showed reductions in such activity in this case. Conversely, Asian Americans' brain activation was especially high when they felt understood, whereas European Americans appeared not to be motivated to approach when they felt understood.

Conflicts within groups are often likely to develop under conditions of scarce resources where group members must compete with each other to obtain them. What begins as a task conflict can rapidly generate into relationship conflict (DeDreu,

2010). Imagine that you and your sibling are told you have to clean out the garage and you are told that whoever completes their half of the task first gets to use your parent's car for the weekend. Both of you can't have the car—a desirable resource—so conflict is likely to happen! And, you can easily imagine how conflict over who gets to use the vacuum cleaner first and so on could rapidly deteriorate into name calling and other actions that would ultimately harm your relationship. So, a variety of social factors can play a strong role in initiating and intensifying conflicts. Because conflicts are often very costly, people are often motivated to resolve them as quickly as possible. What steps are most useful for reaching this goal? Two seem especially useful: *bargaining* and *superordinate goals*.

BARGAINING: THE UNIVERSAL PROCESS By far the most common strategy for resolving conflicts is **bargaining** or *negotiation* (Pruitt & Carnevale, 1993). In this process, opposing sides exchange offers, counteroffers, and concessions, either directly or through representatives. If the process is successful, a solution acceptable to both sides is attained, and the conflict is resolved. If, instead, bargaining is unsuccessful, costly deadlock may result and the conflict is likely to intensify. What factors determine which of these outcomes occurs?

First, and perhaps most obviously, the outcome of bargaining is determined, in part, by the specific tactics adopted by the bargainers. Many of these are designed to accomplish a key goal: reduce the opponent's *aspirations* (i.e., hopes or goals), so that this person or group becomes convinced that it cannot get what it wants and should, instead, settle for something less favorable to their side. Tactics for accomplishing this goal include (1) beginning with an extreme initial offer—one that is very favorable to the side proposing it; (2) the "big-lie" technique—convincing the other side that one's break-even point is much higher than it is so that they offer more than would otherwise be the case; for example, used-car salespeople may claim that they will lose money on the deal if the price is lowered when in fact this is false; and (3) convincing the other side that you can go elsewhere and get even better terms (Thompson, 1998).

A second, and very important, determinant of the outcome of bargaining involves the overall orientation of the bargainers to the process (Pruitt & Carnevale, 1993). People taking part in negotiations can approach such discussions from either of two distinct perspectives. In one, they can view the negotiations as "win–lose" situations in which gains by one side are necessarily linked with losses for the other. In the other, they can approach negotiations as potential "win–win" situations, in which the interests of the two sides are not necessarily incompatible and in which the potential gains of both sides can be maximized.

This approach produces more favorable results in the long run—and is typically what is used when negotiating national conflicts such as the one between the Israelis and Palestinians or the conflict between Protestants and Catholics in Northern Ireland. Such peace agreements, when achieved, are known as *integrative agreements*—ones that offer greater joint benefits than would be attained by simply splitting all differences down the middle, or one side simply giving in to the demands of the other side. This is very much like the situation we described earlier in which there was a conflict between two individuals about picking a vacation destination. When the two parties communicate clearly about their underlying needs, a new option that satisfies both parties' needs can often be found. This technique—called *bridging*—is one of many techniques for attaining such integrative solutions to conflicts (Table 11.2).

Often negotiators believe that displaying anger at the other party will further their interests (i.e., lead the other party to make larger concessions). However, there are cultural differences in the norms concerning the appropriateness of expressing anger in negotiations, so this strategy

bargaining (negotiation)
A process in which opposing sides exchange offers, counteroffers, and concessions, either directly or through representatives.

TABLE 11.2 Tactics for Reaching Integrative Agreements

Many strategies can be useful in attaining integrative agreements—ones that offer better outcomes than simple compromise. Several of these are summarized here.

TACTIC	DESCRIPTION
Broadening the pie	Available resources are increased so that both sides can obtain their major goals.
Nonspecific compensation	One side gets what it wants; the other is compensated on an unrelated issue.
Logrolling	Each party makes concessions on low-priority issues in exchange for concessions on issues it values more highly.
Bridging	Neither party gets its initial demands, but a new option that satisfies the major interests of both sides is developed.
Cost cutting	One party gets what it desires, and the costs to the other party are reduced in some manner.

must be used with care. In a series of studies on this issue, Adam, Shirako, and Maddux (2010) found that expressing anger in a negotiation resulted in greater concessions from European Americans, but smaller concessions from Asian Americans. These researchers showed that this difference stemmed from the adherence to different cultural norms. When the relevant norms were directly manipulated so that members of both cultural groups perceived anger expression as appropriate to the negotiation context, both cultural groups made concessions to the apparently angry opponent. So the effectiveness of different bargaining strategies involving displays of emotion appear to depend on cultural norms.

SUPERORDINATE GOALS: WE'RE ALL IN THIS TOGETHER   As we saw in Chapter 6, members of groups in conflict often divide the world into two opposing camps—"us" and "them." They perceive members of their own group (us) as quite different from, and usually better than, people belonging to other groups (them). These tendencies to magnify differences between one's own group and others and to disparage outsiders are very powerful and often play a role in the occurrence and persistence of conflicts. Fortunately, they can be countered through the induction of **superordinate goals**— goals that both sides seek, and that tie their interests together rather than driving them apart (Sherif et al., 1961). When opposing sides can be made to see that they share overarching goals, conflict is often sharply reduced and may, in fact, be replaced by overt cooperation.

superordinate goals
Goals that both sides to a conflict seek and that tie their interests together rather than driving them apart.

KEYPOINTS

- **Cooperation**—working together with others to obtain shared goals—is a common aspect of social life. However, cooperation does not develop in many situations where it is possible, partly because such situations involve **social dilemmas** in which individuals can increase their own gains by defection.

- Cooperation in teams such as might occur during computer-mediated communication can be difficult to develop because of the absence of interpersonal cues that are present during face-to-face interactions.

- **Negative interdependence**—where if one person obtains a desired outcome, others cannot—lowers the likelihood of cooperation. Social dilemmas such as the *prisoner's dilemma* is an instance where cooperation could occur and both parties would benefit, but where it rarely occurs.

- Having sanctions for noncooperation can change the extent to which people trust others, and thereby lower the extent to which they engage in cooperation.

- Conflict often begins when individuals or groups perceive that others' interests are incompatible with their own interests. Social factors such as *faulty attributions* can play a role in conflict.

- Members of different ethnic groups often respond differently when they feel misunderstood by others. European Americans appear to prepare for confrontation and Asian Americans seem to withdraw under these conditions.

- Conflict can be reduced in many ways, but **bargaining** and the induction of **superordinate goals** can be particularly effective.

Perceived Fairness in Groups: Its Nature and Effects

Have you ever been in a situation where you felt that you were getting less than you deserved from some group to which you belong? If so, you probably experienced anger and resentment in response to such *perceived unfairness or injustice* (Cropanzano, 1993). Were you ready to act to rectify it and attempt to get whatever it was you felt you deserved, or were you afraid of potential retaliation (Miller, Cronin, Garcia, & Branscombe, 2009). Social psychologists have conducted many studies to understand (1) the factors that lead individuals to decide they have been treated fairly or unfairly and (2) what they do about it—their efforts to deal with perceived unfairness (Adams, 1965; Walker & Smith, 2002). We now consider both of these questions.

Basic Rules for Judging Fairness: Distributive, Procedural, and Transactional Justice

Deciding whether we have been treated fairly in our relations with others can be quite tricky. First, we rarely have all the information needed to make such a judgment accurately (van den Bos & Lind, 2002). Second, even if we did, perceived fairness is very much "in the eye of the beholder," so is subject to many forms of bias. Despite such complexities, research on perceived fairness in group settings indicates that, in general, we make these judgments by focusing on three distinct aspects or rules.

The first, known as **distributive justice** involves the *outcomes* we and others receive. According to the equity rule, available rewards should be divided among group members in accordance with their contributions: the more they provide in terms of effort, experience, skills, and other contributions to the group, the more they should receive. For example, we expect people who have made major contributions toward reaching the group's goals to receive greater rewards than people who have contributed very little. In short, we often judge fairness in terms of the ratio between the contributions group members have provided and the rewards they receive (Adams, 1965).

While people are concerned with the outcomes they receive, this is far from the entire story where judgments of fairness are concerned. In addition, people are also interested in the fairness of the procedures through which rewards have been distributed, what is known as **procedural justice** (Folger & Baron, 1996; Tyler & Blader, 2003). We base our judgments about it on factors such as (1) the extent to which the procedures are applied in the same manner to all people; (2) there are opportunities for correcting any errors in distributions; and (3) decision makers avoid being influenced by their own self-interest.

Evidence that such factors really do influence our judgments concerning procedural justice has been obtained in many studies (Tyler & Blader, 2003). For instance, in one investigation, when people perceived authorities as holding attitudes that are biased against them, and when they believed they lack "voice" (e.g., cannot complain or won't be listened to), the more they report procedural injustice (van Prooijen, van den Bos, Lind, & Wilke, 2006). In a large study of people who had been laid off from their jobs, those who felt the procedures used to decide who would be let go were unfair expressed greater hostility and intentions to retaliate against organizational authorities (Barclay, Skarlicki, & Pugh, 2005).

We also judge fairness in terms of the way information about outcomes and procedures is given to us. This is known as **transactional justice,** and two factors seem to play a key role in our judgments about it: the extent to which we are given clear and rational reasons for why rewards were divided as they were (Bies, Shapiro, & Cummings, 1988), and the courtesy or respect with which we are informed about these divisions (Greenberg, 1993; Tyler, Boeckmann, Smith, & Huo, 1997).

In sum, we judge fairness in several different ways—in terms of the rewards we have received (distributive justice), the procedures used to reach these divisions (procedural justice), and the style in which we are informed about these divisions (transactional justice). All three forms of justice can have strong effects on our behavior.

In many situations in which we ask the question "Am I being treated fairly?" we do not have sufficient information about the outcomes or procedures used to clearly apply rules of distributive and procedural justice. We don't know exactly what rewards others have received (e.g., their salaries), and we may not know all the procedures or whether

distributive justice (fairness)
Refers to individuals' judgments about whether they are receiving a fair share of available rewards—a share proportionate to their contributions to the group or any social relationship.

procedural justice
Judgments concerning the fairness of the procedures used to distribute available rewards among group members.

transactional justice
Refers to the extent to which people who distribute rewards explain or justify their decisions and show respect and courtesy to those who receive the rewards.

they were consistently followed when distributing rewards to group members. What do we do in such situations? Meta-analyses (Barsky & Kaplan, 2007) have revealed that we treat our feelings as a source of information and base our judgments on them, reasoning "If I feel good, this must be fair" or "If I feel bad, this must be unfair." (For more on the role of emotion in groups and responses to perceived injustice, please see the section "EMOTIONS AND GROUPS: When Members of One Group Perceive Members of Another Group as Rejecting Them," below).

meta-stereotypes
Beliefs about how one's group is viewed by another group; these are often negative.

EMOTIONS *and* GROUPS

When Members of One Group Perceive Members of Another Group as Rejecting Them

Often members of one group have to interact with and get along with members of another group. Corporations may merge—some successfully (Disney and Pixar) and others not so successfully (Daimler-Benz and Chrysler)—requiring employees of each organization (often former competitors) to get along.

Such group mergers can trigger threat in members of each group. Among those who were members of the lower-status group, particularly those who were highly identified with the original organization, negative social comparisons with the higher-status merger group can be stressful (Amiot, Terry, & Callan, 2007). For members of the former high-status group, if the merger is seen as diminishing their distinctiveness or creating a sense that their group may be dragged down by the lower-status group that they are merging with, such experienced threat can have undesirable interaction consequences (Boen, Vanbeselaere, & Wostyn, 2010). In both cases, members of each of the merged groups may fail to identify with the new corporate entity, and instead show hostility toward members of the other group and favoritism toward members of their old group (Gleibs, Noack, & Mummendey, 2010).

Such potential for negative emotion is not only the case for corporate groups experiencing a merger. Because people are profoundly sensitive to the evaluations of others, whenever group members perceive another group as potentially rejecting their group, negative emotions can be elicited, creating awkward social interactions and even intensifying conflict between groups (Vorauer, 2006).

Let's consider first how members of high-status or majority groups respond when they are concerned about how interactions with members of a lower-status or minority group will go. In some cases, existing **meta-stereotypes**—beliefs about how one's group is viewed by another group— are negative. This can create anxiety about such interactions and overt awkwardness in behavior toward members of the minority group, and thereby undermine the likelihood of friendships developing (Shelton, Richeson, & Vorauer, 2006).

For example, in studies by Vorauer, Hunter, Main, and Roy (2000), white Canadians who expected to have a discussion with a Native Canadian about social issues believed they would be regarded as prejudiced and closed minded. This meta-stereotype activation affected actual interaction with a Native Canadian differently depending on whether the white Canadians in the research were high or low in levels of prejudice toward Native Peoples. Higher-prejudiced whites are more likely to believe that the meta-stereotype of their group will be applied to themselves, so they experience greater threat when expecting to interact with members of this minority group compared to lower-prejudiced whites who expect that Native Canadians will see them personally as different from other whites. What happens, though, when the social context makes this assumption of lower prejudiced white participants—that they personally will be seen as different from other whites who are prejudiced—questionable?

To answer this question, Vorauer (2003) had low- and high-prejudiced white Canadians first discuss prejudice-relevant issues accompanied by other ingroup members, and then they were told that an "observer" who was either white or native would view and evaluate the videotape of their discussion. As you can see in Figure 11.19, when participants were asked to predict how the observer would perceive them, low-prejudiced participants felt vulnerable and expected to be judged as more prejudiced by a Native observer when they were viewed in the company of other ingroup members who exhibited prejudiced behaviors than when they were viewed by a white observer. In this case, being seen as "just like other members of your own group" was threatening to the low-prejudiced white Canadians.

Studies involving other dominant and minority groups have revealed that interethnic behavior is affected by meta-stereotype activation. For example, white Americans for whom the meta-stereotype about their group had been activated (e.g., bigoted) sat further away from an African American with whom they expected to discuss racial profiling compared to when they expected to discuss interpersonal relationships (Goff, Steele, & Davies, 2008). So emotions in group settings can affect how interactions proceed.

But is it only dominant or high-status groups that fear rejection by minority group members and exhibit distancing as a consequence of this? Interesting recent research by Barlow, Louis, and Terry (2010) has revealed that minority group members can sometimes show similar fears with respect to members of another minority group. In their research, Asian Australians, particularly those who were highly identified with their ethnic group, who perceived Aboriginal Australians as rejecting them expressed greater intergroup anxiety, advocated avoiding Aboriginal Australians, and reported being against the Australian government apologizing for its historical treatment of Aboriginal people.

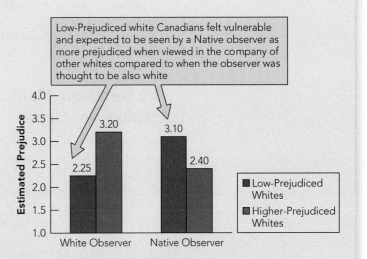

FIGURE 11.19   Do You Think You Will Be Seen as Prejudiced, Like Others in Your Group?
As shown here, white Canadians who had discussed prejudice-related topics with other whites in a group who then expected to be evaluated by a fellow ingroup member believed they would be seen as lower in prejudice than when they believed they would be evaluated by a Native Canadian observer.   (Source: Based on research by Vorauer, 2003).

KEYPOINTS

- Individuals wish to be treated fairly by the groups to which they belong. Fairness can be judged in terms of outcomes (**distributive justice**), in terms of procedures (**procedural justice**), or in terms of how the treatment is delivered (**transactional justice**).

- People may not have the necessary information to determine whether their outcomes or the procedures used are fair or not. When such information is unknown, people may use their feelings as a basis for judging perceived fairness.

- When formerly distinct groups merge, members of both groups can feel threatened and consequently show favoritism toward members of their old group.

- Group members can feel anxiety about how members of another group see them; that is, **meta-stereotypes**—beliefs another group are thought to hold about one's own group—can be negative. When such meta-stereotypes are activated, it can negatively affect interactions between members of both high- and low-status groups.

Decision Making by Groups: How It Occurs and the Pitfalls It Faces

One of the most important activities that groups perform is **decision making**—deciding on one out of several possible courses of action. Governments, corporations, and many other organizations entrust key decisions to groups. Why? As we noted in our opening about the financial and oil spill crises, people often believe that groups reach better decisions than individuals. After all, they can pool the expertise of their members and avoid the biases and extreme decisions that might be made by individuals acting alone. But are such beliefs about group decision making accurate? Do groups really make better decisions than individuals?

decision making
Processes involved in combining and integrating available information to choose one out of several possible courses of action.

In their efforts to address this issue, social psychologists have focused on three major questions: (1) How do groups *actually* make their decisions and reach a consensus? (2) Do decisions reached by groups differ from those made by individuals? (3) What accounts for the fact that groups sometimes make disastrous decisions?

The Decision-Making Process: How Groups Attain Consensus

When groups first begin to discuss any issue, their members rarely start out in complete agreement. Rather, they come to the decision-making task with a range of views (Brodbeck, Kerschreiter, Mojzisch, Frey, & Schulz-Hardt, 2002; Larson, Foster-Fishman, & Franz, 1998). After some period of discussion, however, groups usually do reach a decision. How is this accomplished, and can the final outcome be predicted from the views initially held by the members of the group?

THE DECISION QUALITY OF GROUPS: LESS OR MORE EXTREME?   Many suppose that groups are far less likely than individuals to make extreme decisions. Is that view correct? A large body of evidence indicates that groups are actually *more* likely to adopt extreme positions than if its members made those same decisions alone. Across many different kinds of decisions and many different contexts, groups show a pronounced tendency to shift toward views that are more extreme than the ones with which they initially began (Burnstein, 1983; Rodrigo & Ato, 2002). This is known as **group polarization**, and its major effects can be summarized as follows: whatever the initial leaning or preference of a group prior to its discussions, this preference is strengthened during the group's deliberations. As a result, groups make more extreme decisions than individuals. Initial research on this topic (Kogan & Wallach, 1964) suggested that groups move toward riskier alternatives as they discuss important issues—a change described as the *risky shift*. But additional research showed that the shift was not always toward risk—the shift toward risk *only* happened in situations where the initial preference of the group leaned in that direction. The shift could be in the opposite direction—toward increased caution—if caution was the group's initial preference.

Why do groups tend to move, as shown in Figure 11.20, over the course of their discussions, toward increasingly extreme views and decisions? Two major factors are involved. First, *social comparison* plays a role. If we all want to be "above average" where opinions are concerned, this implies holding views that are "better" than other group members. Being "better" would mean holding views that are more prototypical of the group's overall preference, but even more so (Turner, 1991). So, for example, in a group of liberals, "better" would mean "more liberal." Among a group of conservatives, better would mean "more conservative."

group polarization
The tendency of group members to shift toward a more extreme position than initially held by those individuals as a result of group discussion.

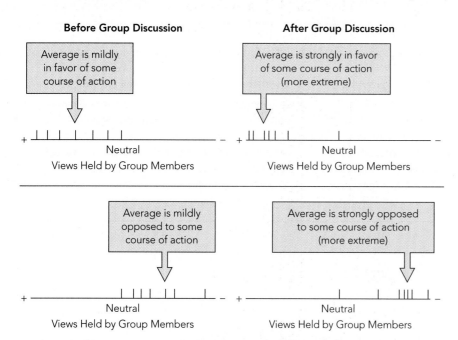

FIGURE 11.20   Group Polarization: How It Works
As shown here, group polarization involves the tendency for decision-making groups to shift toward views that are more extreme than the ones with which the groups initially began, but in the same general direction. Thus, if groups start out slightly in favor of one view or position, they often end up holding this view more strongly or extremely after discussion. This shift toward extremity can be quite dangerous in many settings.

A second factor involves the fact that during group discussion, most arguments favor the group's initial preference. As a result of hearing such arguments, members shift, increasingly, toward the majority's view. Consequently, the proportion of discussion favoring the group's initial preference increases so that ultimately, members convince themselves that this must be the "right" view (Vinokur & Burnstein, 1974). In support of this idea, recent research has revealed that if other group members' opinions are not known before discussion, group decisions improve because more diverse arguments are considered (Mojzisch & Schulz-Hardt, 2010).

The Downside of Group Decision Making

The drift of many decision-making groups toward polarization is a serious problem—one that can interfere with their ability to make sound decisions, but this is not the only process that can exert such negative effects (Hinsz, 1995). Among the most important of these other processes are (1) groupthink and (2) groups' seeming inability to share and use information held by only some of their members.

GROUPTHINK: WHEN COHESIVENESS IS DANGEROUS Earlier we described how high levels of cohesiveness in groups has benefits: it can increase members' commitment to the group and make those groups more satisfying. But, like anything else, there can be too much of a good thing. When cohesiveness reaches very high levels, **groupthink** may develop. This is a strong tendency for decision-making groups to "close ranks" around a decision, to assume that the group *can't* be wrong, with pressure for all members to support the decision strongly, and to reject any information contrary to the decision. Research indicates that once groupthink develops, groups become unwilling to change their decisions, even when initial outcomes suggest that those decisions were very poor ones (Haslam et al., 2006).

Consider the decisions of three United States Presidents (Kennedy, Johnson, and Nixon) to escalate the war in Vietnam. Each escalation brought increased American casualties and no progress toward the goal of ensuring the survival of South Vietnam as an independent country. Likewise, President George W. Bush and his cabinet chose to invade Iraq, without critically considering the assumption that is now known to be incorrect—that Saddam Hussein possessed weapons of mass destruction. According to Janis (1982), the social psychologist who originated the concept of groupthink, this process—and the fact that it encourages an unwillingness among members of cohesive groups to consider alternative courses of action—may well have contributed to these events.

Why does groupthink occur? Research findings (Kameda & Sugimori, 1993; Tetlock, Peterson, McGuire, Change, & Feld, 1992) suggest that two factors are crucial. One of these is a very high level of *cohesiveness* among group members and the fact that supportive group members in the leader's "inner circle" exert a disproportional impact on the ultimate decision making (Burris, Rodgers, Mannix, Hendron, & Oldroyd, 2009). The second is *emergent group norms*—norms suggesting that the group is infallible, morally superior, and because of these factors, there should be no further discussion of the issues at hand; the decision has been made, and the only valid response is to support it as strongly as possible. Closely related to these effects is a tendency to reject any criticism by outside sources. Criticism from outsiders is viewed with suspicion and attributed negative motives. The result? It is largely ignored, and may even tend to strengthen the group's cohesiveness, as members rally to defend the group against perceived assaults by outsiders!

Such rejection of criticism on the part of outsiders has been reported by Hornsey and Imani (2004). They asked Australian college students to read comments supposedly made during an interview that were either positive ("When I think of Australians I think of them as being fairly friendly and warm people . . . ") or negative ("When I think of

groupthink
The tendency of the members of highly cohesive groups to assume that their decisions can't be wrong, that all members must support the group's decisions strongly, and that information contrary to it should be ignored.

Australians I think of them as being fairly racist . . . "). The comments were attributed either to another Australian (an ingroup member), a person from another country who had never lived in Australia (inexperienced outgroup), or to a person from another country who had once lived in Australia and therefore had experience with Australians (experienced outgroup). Participants then evaluated the source of the comments and rated the extent to which this person's comments were designed to be constructive.

Hornsey and Imani (2004) reasoned that when the comments were negative, both the speaker and the comments would receive lower ratings when this person was an outgroup member than an ingroup member. Furthermore, an outgroup member's experience with the ingroup (having lived in Australia) would not make any difference because this person was still not a member of the ingroup. When the comments were positive, such effects were not expected to occur; after all, praise is acceptable no matter what its source!

This is precisely what happened. When the stranger's comments were positive, whether this person was an Australian or not, made no difference. But when this person made negative comments, both the speaker and the comments were viewed more negatively when this person was from an outgroup—regardless of degree of experience with Australia—than when this person was a member of the ingroup. Furthermore, when criticism of the ingroup is voiced, if it is aired in front of an outgroup audience, evaluations of the critic are even worse than if the criticism were voiced to the ingroup only (Hornsey et al., 2005).

THE FAILURE TO SHARE INFORMATION UNIQUE TO EACH MEMBER   A second potential source of bias in decision-making groups involves the fact that such groups do not always pool their resources—share information and ideas unique to each member. In fact, research (Gigone & Hastie, 1997; Stasser, 1992) indicates such pooling of resources or information may be the exception rather than the rule. The result: The decisions made by groups tend to reflect the shared information. This is not a problem if such information points to the best decision. But consider what happens when information pointing to the best decision is *not* shared by most members. In such cases, the tendency of group members to discuss mainly the information they all already possess may prevent them from reaching the best decision. Consequently, the presence of dissent in groups can be critical; it can lead members to consider nonshared information and this improves decision quality (Schulz-Hardt, Brodbeck, Mojzisch, Kerschreiter, & Frey, 2006).

BRAINSTORMING: IDEA GENERATION IN GROUPS   When groups work on creative tasks together they tend to produce different kinds of solutions than when working alone (Adarves-Yorno, Postmes, & Haslam, 2007). But are they better solutions? In **brainstorming**—a process whereby people meet as a group to generate new ideas—it has generally been assumed that more creative output will emerge than when the same people work as individuals (Stroebe, Diehl, & Abakoumkin, 1992). But in contrast to this expectation, brainstorming does not on the whole result in more creative ideas being generated than if the same people worked alone. So why doesn't such a great idea in theory work in practice?

Dugosh and Paulus (2005) investigated both cognitive and social aspects of brainstorming, particularly the effects of idea exposure. This is especially important because the benefits of brainstorming were assumed to result from group members' exposure to others' creativity. These researchers considered whether exposure to common or unique ideas by other group members would result in similar quality ideas being generated by the other participants, as well as whether people engage in social comparison during brainstorming. Some research has suggested that "performance matching" could lead to lowered motivations for idea output (i.e., everyone sort of "dumbing down" to conform to a low-output norm). Munkes and Diehl (2003) have suggested, however, that such social comparison ought to result in *competition* and raise the quality of the ideas generated.

brainstorming
A process in which people meet as a group to generate new ideas freely.

Dugosh and Paulus's (2005) study tested this idea by having some participants believe that the ideas they were exposed to were selected by a computer from an "idea database," whereas other participants were told that the ideas came from people similar to themselves. First, exposure to a larger quantity of ideas did in fact result in more ideas being generated by participants. Moreover, participants who were led to believe they were being exposed to people-generated ideas, as opposed to computer-selected ideas, produced more high-quality ideas—presumably because participants felt the need to be as creative as those "other people."

Nemeth, Personnaz, Personnaz, and Goncalo (2004) point out that dissent or debating competing views are widely valued as stimuli for creative ideas. These researchers gave two different instructions to brainstorming groups, either traditional instructions to just listen without evaluating or instructions encouraging people to debate the merits of ideas. In general, debate instructions produced results superior to traditional instructions. Thus a central tenet of brainstorming, the lack of criticism of new ideas, seems, on balance, to add less in the way of stimulation of idea production than does the cognitive stimulation provided by dissent and debate.

 # KEY POINTS

- It is often supposed that groups make better decisions than individuals. However, research findings indicate that groups are often subject to **group polarization,** which leads them to make more extreme decisions than individuals. This occurs for two reasons: members want to hold views that are more prototypical than others, which means more extreme than average, and because during group discussions members are persuaded by the arguments that other members make and, therefore, they subsequently move their own views in that direction.

- In addition, groups often suffer from **groupthink**—a tendency for highly cohesive groups to assume that they can do no wrong and that information contrary to the group's view should be rejected.

- Groups do tend to reject criticism from outgroup members relative to the identical criticism from ingroup members. It is also more distressing to hear one's ingroup criticized in front of an outgroup compared to when the audience consists of other ingroup members only.

- Group members often fail to share information during discussion that only some members possess. Instead, discussions tend to focus on the information that all members already know, so the decisions they make tend to reflect this shared information. One way to prevent this is to ensure group members do not know other members' views and what information they have before discussion.

- **Brainstorming**—generating ideas in a group without critically evaluating them—does not result in more creativity than were those individuals producing the ideas on their own. Debate about ideas, though, does tend to stimulate more creative idea production.

The Role of Leadership in Group Settings

Leadership—the very word conjures up images of heroic figures leading their followers toward something better: victory, prosperity, or social justice. But what, precisely, is *leadership?* Researchers in several different fields have considered this question for decades, and the result is that at present, there is general agreement that leadership involves *influence*—influencing others in a group by establishing a direction for collective effort and then encouraging the activities needed to move in that direction (Turner, 2005; Yukl, 2006; Zaccaro, 2007). Consistent with that definition, being a *leader* involves exerting *influence*—changing the behavior and thoughts of other members of the group so that they work together to attain the group's common goals.

Research on leadership has been part of social psychology for many years (Haslam, Reicher, & Platow, 2010). Here, we consider three key aspects of the findings of research on this topic in terms of (1) why some individuals, but not others, become leaders; (2) when nontraditional leaders are most likely to emerge; and (3) how leaders influence group members' satisfaction with their performance.

Why do some people become leaders, but not others? Are some people simply born to lead? Indeed, some famous leaders were born to the job (e.g., Queen Elizabeth I). Others clearly were not: Abraham Lincoln, Nelson Mandela, Adolf Hitler, Bill Gates, Barack Obama, to name a few—all of whom, frankly, came from rather ordinary circumstances. Although leaders tend to reflect dominant majorities in their societies (Chin, 2010), and in the case of the United States that means they have been, historically, white, heterosexual, Protestant males, to explain *which* individual from within those categories becomes a leader, early researchers formulated the *great person* theory of leadership—the view that great leaders possess certain traits that set them apart from other human beings—traits that differentiate them from those who are merely followers.

Early research designed to test this notion was not encouraging. Try as they might, researchers could not come up with a short list of key traits shared by all great leaders (Yukl, 1998). Although the relationships obtained have been consistently weak—generally accounting for less than 5 percent of the variability across people—some attributes do appear to differentiate between leaders and nonleaders: leaders tend to be slightly more intelligent, socially skilled, open to new experiences, and extroverted than nonleaders (Haslam, 2004; Hogg, 2001). Of course, we cannot know from such studies whether these attributes resulted in those individuals becoming leaders as is assumed, or if experience as a leader resulted in the development of those attributes.

So if leaders and followers can't be differentiated from one another so easily in terms of the traits they possess, perhaps effective and ineffective leaders can be. Not really. Research seeking to predict U.S. Presidential leader effectiveness has found that Presidents rated effective by historians are more intelligent and they were not involved in scandals compared to those rated ineffective leaders (Simonton, 2009), but otherwise aspects of the context appear to be more important in predicting effectiveness (they were President during war—ensuring there was high national cohesiveness and certainty of the priorities to achieve).

In a sense, there can be no leadership without followers. The importance of followers is given consideration in modern theories of leadership. For instance, experts on leadership (Hackman & Wageman, 2007; Turner, 2005) suggest that leaders and followers are both essential parts of the leadership relationship, and that all theories of leadership should note that *both* play a crucial role and that both exert influence as well as receive it. For this reason, recent research has considered whether some people are more likely to become leader in some contexts (or times), while others emerge as leaders in other contexts.

In 2008, Barack Obama was elected U.S. President, after competing for the leadership for his party with then Senator Hillary Clinton (see Figure 11.21). What is notable here is that not only were both these leaders from "underrepresented leadership groups," but they came to the fore during a period of national crisis. This is precisely the kind of context in which Ryan and Haslam (2005) predict the selection of nontraditional leaders will occur. In a study of appointments of women to CEO positions, Haslam, Ryan, Kulich, Trojanowski, and Atkins (2010) found that women were appointed to these positions when the organization was in crisis and there was a high risk of failure, whereas men were more likely to be appointed when the organization was doing well and the likelihood of failure was low. In an archival study of appointments to the board of directors in major corporations listed on the London Stock Exchange, Ryan and Haslam (2005) found that when men were appointed, the share price of the company had been relatively stable before the appointment. However, women were appointed to boards of directors only after consistently poor share performance in the months preceding their appointments.

These findings were characterized in terms of nontraditional group members being appointed to leadership positions only when a **glass cliff** exists—that is, when the leadership position can be considered precarious or relatively risky because the organization is in crisis. What this research suggests is that being seen as "leader material" may depend more on the "times" than on the "person."

What role do leaders play in enhancing group members' satisfaction with the group and its performance? Research has documented that, for a variety of kinds of groups, having a leader that is seen as prototypical of the group (rather than different from group members) predicts both member satisfaction (Cicero, Pierro, & van Knippenberg, 2007) and perceived leader effectiveness (Fielding & Hogg, 1997). Why does the leader being seen as prototypical of the group have such important conse-

FIGURE 11.21 **Leaders from Underrepresented Groups: More Likely to Be Selected in Risky or Difficult Situations**
Both Barack Obama and Hillary Clinton are members of "nontraditional" political candidate groups. Were they selected because the context was precarious or especially risky in terms of being able to produce successful outcomes?

quences? Giessner and van Knippenberg (2008) propose that it is due to its impact on group members' trust in the leader. Sometimes leaders have to make choices that all group members do not experience as positive, or as consistent with their own interests. Furthermore, sometimes leader decisions can lead to failure to achieve group goals. But leaders who are seen as prototypical of the group are seen as more likely to take actions that serve the group's interests, and trust in the leader's intentions enables group members to weather such poor outcomes. Giessner and van Knippenberg found that even when participants knew their leader's decision had resulted in failure to reach an important goal, because the leader who was prototypical of the group was seen as trustworthy, the leader was more likely to be forgiven than when the leader was non-prototypical of the group.

glass cliff
When women and minorities are seen as better leaders because of their ability to manage crises. They are more likely to be selected as leader when the situation contains more risk.

KEY POINTS

- Leadership researchers long sought personality characteristics that differentiate leaders from followers. There is evidence that leaders may be somewhat more intelligent and sociable than nonleaders. However, despite its intuitive appeal, traits explain little of the variability and do a poor job differentiating leaders from nonleaders, or even effective leaders from ineffective leaders.

- Nontraditional leaders tend to emerge in periods of crisis—which means they can find themselves on **glass**

cliffs where failure is more likely because the situation they are attempting to lead in contains greater risk.

- Leaders that are seen as prototypical of the group (rather than different from other group members) instill greater member satisfaction and perceived leader effectiveness. The greater trust felt in leaders who are prototypical of the group allows group members to weather poor outcomes and forgive the leader for failures relative to leaders who are seen as not prototypical of the group.

SUMMARY *and* REVIEW

- **Groups** are collections of people who perceive themselves as forming a coherent unit to some degree. Groups have played a critical role in human evolutionary history. In **common-bond groups**, the members tend to be bonded with each other, whereas in **common-identity groups**, members tend to be linked via the category as a whole. The extent to which the group is perceived to form a coherent entity is known as **entitativity**.

- Basic aspects of groups involve **status, roles, norms,** and **cohesiveness**. People achieve high status—position or rank within a group—for many reasons, ranging from physical characteristics (e.g., height), how long they have been members of the group, how prototypical of the group they are, and various aspects of their behavior. To the extent that people internalize their social roles, where those roles are linked to aspects of their self-concept, they can have important implications for behavior and well-being. Being assigned to act as "prisoner" or "guard" in a prison simulation (e.g., the BBC Prison Experiment) resulted in behavioral changes to the extent that people identified with those roles and were guided by the norms associated with them. Group norms—implicit rules about what is appropriate—can affect our emotional expressions and experience. Norms of **individualism** and **collectivism** can affect our willingness to tolerate dissent within groups. Cohesiveness—the factors that cause people to want to remain members—produces a sense of solidarity among group members. Anxiety about our group's future distinctiveness from another group can encourage actions aimed at strengthening ingroup cohesion.

- Joining groups confers important benefits on members, including increased self-knowledge, progress toward important goals, enhanced status, and the possibility of attaining social change. However, group membership also exacts important costs, such as loss of personal freedom and heavy demands on time, energy, and resources. The desire to join exclusive and prestigious groups may be so strong that individuals are willing to undergo painful and dangerous initiations in order to become members. Undergoing severe

- initiation processes to obtain admission in a group frequently increases commitment to that group.

- Individuals often withdraw from groups when they feel that the group has changed so much that it no longer reflects their basic values or beliefs. When a group undergoes a **schism**—splintering into distinct factions—it can produce emotional distress in those who feel compelled to leave.

- The mere presence of other people either as an audience or as co-actors can influence our performance on many tasks. Such effects are known as *social facilitation*. The *drive theory of social facilitation* suggests that the presence of others is arousing and can either increase or reduce performance, depending on whether dominant responses in a given situation are correct or incorrect. The **distraction conflict theory** suggests that the presence of others induces conflicting tendencies to focus on the task being performed and on an audience or co-actors. This can result both in increased arousal and narrowed attentional focus, explaining why social facilitation occurs in many species. The **evaluation apprehension** view suggests that an audience disrupts our performance because we are concerned about their evaluation of us.

- When individuals work together on a task, **social loafing**—reduced output by each group member—sometimes occurs. Social loafing can be reduced in several ways: by making outputs individually identifiable, by increasing commitment to the task and task importance, and by ensuring that each member's contributions to the task are unique.

- Being part of a large crowd has been stereotyped as inducing **hooliganism**—violent and antisocial incidents—due to the reduction in self-awareness that occurs with **deindividuation**. Contrary to this idea, anonymity in a crowd actually induces more normative or conforming behavior. The norms operating in some crowds may be changed, and the likelihood of violence reduced. Deindividuation can intensify either aggressive or prosocial behavior, depending on what norms are operating in a particular crowd context.

- **Cooperation**—working together with others to obtain shared goals—is a common aspect of social life. However, cooperation does not develop in many situations where it is possible, partly because such situations involve **social dilemmas** in which individuals can increase their own gains at the expense of the other. Sanctioning for noncooperation, though, can decrease people's trust in others and thereby undermine subsequent willingness to cooperate.

- **Conflict** is a process that begins when individuals or groups perceive that others have interests that are incompatible with their own. Members of different cultural groups respond differently to feeling misunderstood by others. Conflict can be reduced in many ways, but **bargaining** and the induction of **superordinate goals** seem to be most effective.

- Individuals wish to be treated fairly by the groups to which they belong. Fairness can be judged in terms of outcomes (**distributive justice**), in terms of procedures (**procedural justice**), or in terms of courteous treatment (**transactional justice**). When individuals feel that they have been treated unfairly, they often take steps to restore fairness. **Meta-stereotypes**—negative beliefs about how one's group is viewed by members of another group—can inhibit or disrupt social interactions by group members.

- Research findings indicate that groups are often subject to **group polarization**, which leads them to make more extreme decisions than individuals. This occurs for two reasons: group members want to be "good" group members, which means holding views that are prototypical of the group, and members are influenced by the group's discussion, which tends to focus on arguments that favor the group's initial preference. In addition, groups often suffer from **groupthink**—a tendency to assume that they can't be wrong and that information contrary to the group's view should be rejected. Groups do tend to reject criticism from outgroup members relative to identical criticism from ingroup members. Groups often fail to share information that only some members possess and this can lead to biased decisions.

- People tend to believe that **brainstorming**—where people attempt to generate new ideas in a group—will be more effective than individuals working alone. Research illustrates that this is generally not true. In fact, dissent and debate in group discussions tends to produce more creative ideas.

- The *great person theory of leadership* suggested that leaders and nonleaders have different traits. This largely turns out not to be the case. Nontraditional leaders often emerge during times of crisis—the **glass cliff**—conditions that carry a greater risk of failure. Leaders who are seen as prototypical of their group are perceived as more effective, and even when they fail they are more likely to be forgiven because they are seen as more trustworthy than leaders who are nonprototypical of the group.

KEY TERMS

additive tasks (p. 376)

asynchronous forms of communication (p. 379)

bargaining (negotiation) (p. 383)

brainstorming (p. 390)

cohesiveness (p. 368)

collectivism (p. 367)

common-bond groups (p. 362)

common-identity groups (p. 362)

conflict (p. 379)

cooperation (p. 379)

decision making (p. 387)

deindividuation (p. 377)

distraction conflict theory (p. 375)

distributive justice (fairness) (p. 385)

entitativity (p. 363)

evaluation apprehension (p. 375)

feeling rules (p. 366)

glass cliff (p. 393)

group (p. 362)

groupthink (p. 389)

group polarization (p. 388)

hooliganism (p. 377)

ideology (p. 371)

individualism (p. 367)

meta-stereotypes (p. 386)

negative interdependence (p. 380)

norms (p. 366)

politicized collective identity (p. 370)

procedural justice (p. 385)

roles (p. 364)

schism (p. 372)

social dilemmas (p. 381)

social embeddedness (p. 379)

social loafing (p. 376)

status (p. 364)

superordinate goals (p. 384)

transactional justice (p. 385)

Social Psychology

A Guide to Dealing with Adversity and Achieving a Happy Life

Difficulty ... is the nurse of greatness ...

William Cullen Bryant (1842)

A S THIS QUOTATION SUGGESTS, LIFE IS NOT ALWAYS EASY—FAR from it! Instead, it is filled with adversity—setbacks, disappointments, obstacles, and defeats: a low grade on an important exam, the painful breakup of a romance, bad news about the health of a relative, failure to receive an important promotion . . . the list is endless.

On the other hand, life also offers a wealth of positive events and experiences—times when we enjoy great happiness and the sense of excitement that follows from achieving key goals: we win an award, receive unexpected good news, meet someone who sets us tingling—and even better, they seem to like *us* too! So in fact, life is a very "mixed bag" of highs and lows, and lots of feelings in between. Having said that, though, it is obvious that most people seek and expect to be happy; they want to overcome the adversities they experience and go on to enjoy a life that is not only happy, but meaningful, too. The journey to that goal is never easy, and along the way, most of us do encounter problems and obstacles. Can social psychology help us to handle these setbacks and to become what are often described as flourishing, happy people? We believe that it can. In fact, we believe that the knowledge acquired by social psychologists is invaluable in this respect: if carefully applied, it can help us turn adversity into strength, achievement, and contentment.

Certainly, there are no easy or simple strategies for achieving these goals—for assuring that life's setbacks (or at least their negative effects) are minimized, while its triumphs are enhanced. But research by social psychologists offers important insights into the causes and effects of personal adversity, and suggests important means for overcoming them on the way to a rich, fulfilling life. In this chapter, we summarize some of these contributions. In other words, we provide an overview of some of the important ways in which social psychology—with its basically scientific approach to the social side of life—can help us attain key personal goals. To accomplish this complex and challenging task, we proceed as follows. First, we examine some of the key sources of adversity in the social side of life. These include loneliness and the social isolation and failure of personal relationships that often leads to it. Research by social psychologists provides important insights into the causes and effects of these painful experiences (e.g., Jetten, Haslam, Haslam, & Branscombe, 2009), and also offers hope in the form of steps individuals can take to cope with loneliness and build enduring and mutually satisfying personal relationships (friendships, romantic ties).

Next, we turn to the social side of personal health, focusing primarily on the social causes of obesity and the adverse effects of stress, with special attention to social techniques for reducing these effects. Good personal health is essential for living a happy and fulfilling life, and as you'll see, social psychology has much to contribute to helping people attain this important goal (e.g., Cohen & Jenicki-Deverts, 2009). After that, we consider the contributions of social psychology to an important practical goal: making our legal system more open, fair, and effective. As it exists now, the legal system in the United States and many other countries makes certain assumptions about human beings that may, in fact, be wrong—dead wrong! For instance, it assumes that juries can, when instructed to do so, ignore the race, attractiveness, or other characteristics of defendants. Can they? Research findings indicate "probably not." And what about police lineups? Are they really helpful in identifying the people who have performed various crimes? Perhaps, but research by social psychologists suggests that lineups are effective only when used in certain ways. The goal of research by social psychologists working on such issues is straightforward: help make the legal system one that better protects and promotes human rights to "life, liberty, and the pursuit of happiness."

Finally, we turn to what research by social psychologists tells us about the causes and effects of personal happiness. What are the major ingredients that play a role in increasing—or reducing—happiness? Does wealth bring happiness—or reduce it? Does being happy merely feel good, or does it actually confer real advantages on the people who attain it? What can individuals do to become truly happy? Please be ready for some surprises here, because the answers to these questions are probably not what you guess. Another question we consider is this: Can people be *too* happy? Can there be "too much of a good thing" when it comes to happiness or life satisfaction? If you guessed *no,* you'll be surprised to find that in fact the answer is *yes,* at least in some situations and in some respects.

Overall, we believe that the information presented in this concluding chapter accomplishes two major goals. First, it serves to pull together and integrate the vast array of knowledge gathered by social psychologists and presented in earlier chapters, primarily by showing how this knowledge can advance human happiness. And second, it will serve to underscore the fact that not only is social psychology interesting (it certainly is!): it is also of tremendous potential value both to individuals and society. It is, in short, a field that can help you in your own quest to build the happy and fulfilling life we all seek.

Some Basic Causes of Social Adversity—and Coping with Them

Have you ever felt truly lonely—completely alone, without anyone around who cares about you, or to whom you can turn for help, guidance, or just a little talk? If so, welcome to the club, because most people have felt lonely at some time in their lives. I know I felt this way when I was a visiting professor in a foreign city where I was not fluent in the local language. As a result, when the university was closed and I couldn't access my e-mail (because it was only available at the office), I counted the hours until it opened again, and I could get back, once again, into contact with my friends and family back home—my network of social support.

Fortunately, for most of us, loneliness is a temporary state. We belong to many different groups and as we'll soon see, this not only prevents us from feeling isolated, it also has beneficial effects on our physical and psychological well-being (Jetten et al., 2009). For some people, of course, social isolation is a choice; they prefer to live their lives without any close ties to others (Burger, 1995), and, as a result, they don't feel deprived of social contact. But many others lead lives of desperate isolation and loneliness not by choice, but because they have not been successful in forming bonds with others—or they *have*, and these ties have been severed for some reason (divorce, death of loved ones). In other words, they experience involuntary *loneliness*, a state social psychologists describe as involving emotional and cognitive reactions to having fewer and less satisfying relationships than an individual desires (Archibald, Bartholomew, & Marx, 1995). Loneliness is an all-too-common human experience, occurring in many cultures all around the world (Goodwin, Cook, Young, 2001; Rokach & Neto, 2000; Shams, 2001), and as we'll now see, it is indeed an important source of social adversity (see Figure 12.1). It truly feels bad or "hurts" to feel alone, as anyone who has experienced loneliness knows, and it does more than this: It can adversely affect our psychological and personal health. Clearly, then, it is a topic worthy of our careful attention.

FIGURE 12.1   Loneliness: Alone, But Not By Choice
Some people choose isolation because they prefer it, but a much greater number are alone not by choice, but because they lack close relationships with others. Such persons often experience intense, and unpleasant, feelings of loneliness.

Loneliness: Life Without Relationships

What are the negative consequences of **loneliness**—of being socially isolated? Research by social psychologists offers many insights into the nature of these effects.

THE CONSEQUENCES OF BEING LONELY   Not surprisingly, people who feel lonely tend to spend their leisure time in solitary activities, to have very few connections that are important to them, and have only casual friends or acquaintances (Berg & McQuinn, 1989). Lonely individuals feel left out and believe they have very little in common with those they meet (Bell, 1993). Even if a child has only *one* friend, that is enough to reduce such reactions (Asher & Paquette, 2003). Loneliness is unpleasant, and the negative feelings it involves include depression, anxiety, unhappiness, dissatisfaction, pessimism about the future, self-blame, and shyness (Anderson, Miller, Riger, Dill, & Sedikides, 1994; Jackson, Soderlind, & Weiss, 2000; Jones, Carpenter, & Quintana, 1985). From the perspective of others, lonely individuals are often perceived as maladjusted—people we prefer to avoid, if we can (Lau & Gruen, 1992; Rotenberg & Kmill, 1992). Even worse, loneliness is associated with poor health and with lower life expectancy (Cacioppo, Hawkley, & Berntson, 2003; Hawkley, Burleson, Berntson, & Cacioppo, 2003). For instance, in one recent study, Jetten, Haslam, Pugliesse, Tonks, and Haslam (2010) studied first-year students at a university for several months, both before they came to the university and afterward. Students completed several measures of their personal health (e.g., a measure of depression) and also reported on the number of groups to which they belonged before coming to campus. Results indicated that the greater this number, the less likely they were to become depressed. In short, membership in many groups buffered them against the high levels of stress freshmen generally encounter.

loneliness
The unpleasant emotional and cognitive state based on desiring close relationships but being unable to attain them.

Additional studies with older people (Jetten, Haslam, & Haslam, 2011) indicate that among these people, the more groups to which they belong—or even, the more groups to which they *believe* they belong, the healthier they feel. Overall, then, it seems clear that *not* belonging to groups—*not* being socially connected, which is a key component of loneliness—does indeed have strong negative effects on personal health.

WHY ARE SOME PEOPLE LONELY?　The origins of loneliness, like all complex forms of social behavior, are complex. They appear to include a combination of genetic factors, attachment style (e.g., an avoidant or dismissive style; see Chapter 7), and a lack of opportunity for early social experiences with peers. In an intriguing study designed to examine the possible role of genetic factors in loneliness, McGuire and Clifford (2000) conducted a behavioral genetic investigation of loneliness among children aged 9–14. The participants included pairs of biological siblings, pairs of unrelated siblings raised in adoptive homes, and pairs of identical and fraternal twins. The data consistently indicated that loneliness is based in part on inherited factors. For example, identical twins are more similar in loneliness than are fraternal twins, indicating that greater genetic similarity is associated with greater similarity with respect to loneliness.

But loneliness was also found to be influenced by environmental conditions, as indicated by the fact that unrelated siblings raised in adoptive homes are more similar in loneliness than random pairs of children. As the investigators point out, the fact that there is a genetic component to loneliness does not explain just how it operates. For example, the relevant genes could affect feelings of depression or hostility; if so, differences in loneliness could be the result of rejection based on differences in interpersonal behavior. In other words, there is no "gene" for loneliness; rather, a combination of genetic and social behavioral factors may, quite literally, drive other people away!

Another possible source of loneliness—one we just mentioned above—involves attachment style (Duggan & Brennan, 1994). Both fearful-avoidant or dismissive styles (see Chapter 7) involve patterns in which individuals fear intimacy and so tend to avoid establishing relationships (Sherman & Thelen, 1996). Such people do not have sufficient trust in other people to risk being close to them. In general, insecure attachment is associated with social anxiety and loneliness (Vertue, 2003). A third factor that is correlated with loneliness is failure to develop social skills, and this can occur for a variety of reasons (Braza, Braza, Carreras, & Munoz, 1993). In part, children learn interpersonal skills by interacting with peers. As a result, children who have attended preschool or otherwise had the opportunity to engage in play-related interactions with multiple peers are liked better in elementary school than those lacking such experiences (Erwin & Letchford, 2003). Without appropriate social skills, a child may engage in self-defeating behaviors such as avoidance of others, verbal aggression such as teasing, or physical aggression. As a result of such actions, he or she may be rejected as a playmate, and the seeds for loneliness can be planted (Johnson, Poteat, & Ironsmith, 1991; Ray, Cohen, Secrist, & Duncan, 1997). Factors that influence loneliness are summarized in Figure 12.2.

Without some form of intervention to improve social skills, interpersonal difficulties typically continue throughout childhood and adolescence and into

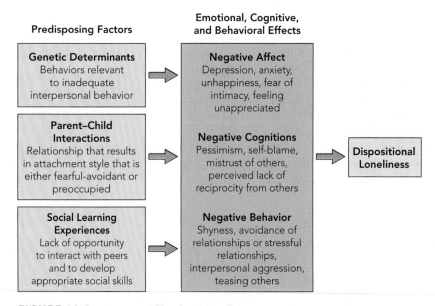

FIGURE 12.2　Factors Affecting Loneliness

As shown here, the tendency to be chronically lonely appears to stem from several different factors: genetic factors, certain aspects of a person's attachment style, and early social learning experience.

adulthood—they do not simply "go away" with the passage of time (Asendorpf, 1992; Hall-Elston & Mullins, 1999). To reduce loneliness, active steps are often needed, and several of these have been identified by social psychologists.

Whatever its causes, loneliness and the social isolation it involves is truly an important source of social adversity. As social psychologists Jetten et al. (2009) put it, ". . . we are *social animals* who live . . . in groups. For humans membership in groups is an indispensable part of who we are and what we need to be and lead rich and fulfilling lives."

REDUCING LONELINESS   Those who function badly in social interactions are usually well aware that they have a problem (Duck, Pond, & Leatham, 1994). They know that they are unhappy, dissatisfied, and unpopular (Furr & Funder, 1998; Meleshko & Alden, 1993), but often, they don't know why. Are there any effective ways to reduce this problem and the pain it produces?

Once loneliness develops, it is obviously not possible to change the individual's history by providing different genes or by altering what occurred during early parent–child interactions. It is, however, possible to acquire new and more appropriate *social skills*—more effective ways of getting along with others. Social skills include the ability to "read" others accurately—to know what they are thinking or feeling (social perception), the ability to make a good first impression on others (impression management), the ability to regulate our own emotions, and the ability to adapt to new social situations (e.g., Ferris, Davidson, & Perrewe, 2006). Most people learn social skills gradually as they interact with others at home, in school, and in many other locations. But for various reasons, some individuals don't seem to acquire these basic skills, and one result of this may be that they are good candidates for loneliness.

Fortunately, social skills can be acquired, and psychologists have developed several procedures for helping people acquire such skills. One involves having individuals interact with strangers, and then showing them tapes of their own behavior. Many people low in social skills are sincerely surprised: They don't realize that they are behaving in ways that "turn others off" and make them want to avoid further contact with them. For instance, they don't know that when they make a request, it sounds more like an order than an appeal. Similarly, they may not realize that they cut other people off as they try to speak. By viewing videotapes of their own behavior, and with guidance from experts in social skills, they can learn to do much better in these and other respects (e.g., Hope, Holt, & Heimberg, 1995). Another approach involves cognitive therapy, which is designed to get the people receiving treatment to think differently about others, and to develop more realistic expectations about social interactions. For instance, they learn that most people are very sensitive to criticism, and that, as a result, it should be used very carefully.

In sum, just as people can be taught engineering, table manners, and how to drive a car, they can also be taught social skills and how to interact with other people in more effective ways. Acquiring improved social skills can be an important step toward reducing loneliness, since these skills make interactions with others more pleasant for both parties, and that can be the start of the lasting relationships that lonely people lack. Of course, it is not easy to change long-established patterns of thought and behavior, but the important point is that they *can* be altered, and to the extent they are, the factors that cause people to lead lives of lonely desperation can be changed.

The Shattering—and Building—of Relationships

If, as existing evidence strongly suggests, loneliness is harmful to our physical and psychological well-being (Hawkley, Thisted, Masi, & Cacioppo, 2010), then it is even more important than most people realize to form and maintain social relationships with others—to feel connected with friends, romantic partners, family, neighbors, to mention just a few. We discussed the factors that influence acquaintance and the formation of relationships in Chapter 7. Here we focus on the factors that play a role in whether relationships, once formed, strengthen and deepen over time, or end, either fading gradually away or crashing down with pain and emotional turmoil. Because they are important in most people's lives, we focus to some extent on romantic relationships and marriage, which, aside from family relationships, are the longest-lasting and perhaps most important relationships we form during our lives. But please note that we don't wish to imply that these are the only kinds of relationships that fulfill our needs for being connected with others or establishing a clear social identity. Consider, for example, individuals who join religious organizations that require them to live in isolation away from society, and that may specifically forbid them to marry (e.g., priests and nuns in the Catholic church). These people fill their needs for feeling connected through their relationship with their church and the roles they fill within it, even though they don't join many other groups and don't form romantic relationships or marry. Other people identify closely with organizations for which they work or to which they belong, and fulfill their need to feel socially connected in this way. What's basic is the need to have social connections, which often involve group memberships; such connections do *not* have to take the form of romantic relationships or marriage—far from it. Having clarified that crucial point, we now discuss romantic relationships and marriage because for most people around the world, these kinds of relationships do indeed play an important role in their lives and their quest for happiness. But as we do, please keep in mind that these are *not* the only important social connections in people's lives, and that human beings find fulfillment in many kinds of social connections and networks.

FIGURE 12.3   Marriage: From Happy Beginnings to . . . ?

Most people marry at some point during their lives, but in many countries, including the United States, more than half of these relationships end in divorce or separation. Why? And how can these odds be changed? Research by social psychologists is providing useful answers.

WHAT MAKES RELATIONSHIPS—INCLUDING LONG-TERM RELATIONSHIPS SUCH AS MARRIAGE—HAPPY?

Even today, when many people live in long-term relationships without formal marriage, being happily married is still an important goal for many, even if they never achieve it. And even today, most people do get married at some point in their lives (see Figure 12.3). Sadly, though, half or more of these relationships fail, and the same is true for other kinds of long-term romantic relationships. People who live together for years or even decades without going through a formal marriage ceremony also separate and for them, too, the breakup of the relationships can be painful and traumatic. Clearly, then, knowing what factors contribute to the survival and happiness of romantic relationships, and the factors that undermine their survival, would be helpful from the point of view of increasing human happiness. Much research has focused on this issue because, especially when children are involved (and having children is one key reason why many people enter long-term relationships or choose to get married), stressful, and often angry, breakups are devastating.

One important factor that contributes to the survival of romantic relationships (and other kinds too), is *commitment*—a strong desire to maintain a relationship, regardless of forces acting to break it apart. Such commitment can involve fear of loneliness: "What will I do if he/she leaves me . . . ?" That plays a role, but is not as effective as commitment based on the *positive* rewards of a continuing relationship (Frank & Branstatter, 2002). In a long-term relationship, many problems can arise over time—financial problems, family-related problems, issues relating to children, and of course, as we saw in Chapter 7, jealousy. But aside from such problems, research findings indicate that there are several factors present even before the wedding that predict whether, and to what extent, marriages will succeed or fail. We now examine some of these.

SIMILARITY AND ASSUMED SIMILARITY   In Chapter 7 we noted that similarity plays an important role in attraction. Does it also play a role in long-term relationships such as marriage? Decades of research, starting with classic studies conducted in the 1930s (Terman & Buttenwieser, 1935a, 1935b) indicate that it does. Overall, these studies emphasized the importance of similarity in the long-term survival and happiness of relationships, and extended our understanding of its effects. For instance, longitudinal research that followed couples from the time they became engaged through 20 years of marriage indicated that couples whose relationships survive are generally quite similar in many respects (attitudes, values, goals; Caspi, Herbener, & Ozer, 1992). Furthermore, such similarity does not change much over time. In short, people tend to marry others similar to themselves, and they remain similar—or even become *more* similar—with the passage of years. Not only do similar people marry, but in happy marriages, the partners believe they are even more similar than they actually are; they show high levels of *assumed similarity* (Byrne & Blaylock, 1963; Schul & Vinokur, 2000). Moreover, both actual and *assumed* similarity appear to contribute to relationship satisfaction. Interestingly, dating couples are higher than married couples with respect to assumed similarity, perhaps reflecting the operation of romantic illusions. We return to this issue later, when we discuss the role of positive illusions in romantic relationships.

DISPOSITIONAL FACTORS   Having a happy and lasting marriage is also correlated with specific personality dispositions. In other words, some individuals appear to be better able to maintain a positive relationship than others, and they are better bets as marriage partners. For example, *narcissism* refers to an individual who feels superior to most other people, someone who seeks admiration and lacks empathy (American Psychiatric Association, 1994). Narcissists report feeling less commitment to a relationship (Campbell & Foster, 2002). As an exception to the similarity rule, two narcissists are not likely to have a happy relationship (Campbell, 1999). Other important personality dispositions that predict the success of a relationship are those associated with interpersonal behavior and attachment styles. Thus, individuals with preoccupied or fearful–avoidant styles have less satisfying relationships than those with secure or dismissing styles (Murray, Holmes, Griffin, Bellavia, & Rose, 2001).

CAN WE PREDICT WHETHER LOVE—AND RELATIONSHIPS—WILL LAST?: THE ROLE OF IMPLICIT PROCESSES   Similarity, personality characteristics, commitment—all these factors certainly play a role in the stability and mutual happiness of long-term relationships. A major theme of modern social psychology, though, is that often, implicit or subconscious processes strongly influence our cognition and behavior (see, e.g., Chapters 2 and 4). Do they also play a role in long-term relationships? In other words, can feelings we cannot accurately report influence the course of romance, friendship, and marriage? Growing evidence indicates that they can. For example, in a recent study, Lee, Rogge, and Reis (2010) asked partners in romantic relationships to supply their partner's first name and two other words that related to that person—for instance, a pet name or

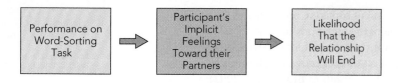

FIGURE 12.4   Predicting Whether Love—and Relationshps—Will Last

Recent findings indicate that implicit feelings about one's partner—feelings people can't easily put into words, and of which they may not be aware—are a better predictor of the future of their relationships than their conscious or explicit reports about the strength of the relationship.   (Source: Based on data from Rogge, Lee, & Reis, 2010).

a word related to one of their key characteristics (e.g., *intelligent, strong*). Participants then watched a monitor as three kinds of words were presented: words with a positive valence (e.g., *vacation, peace*), words with negative meanings (e.g., *tragedy, criticize*), and the partner-related words (the ones they had supplied). They were then asked to press the space bar on a keyboard whenever a target word appeared, but to refrain from pressing the space bar when other (distractor) words appeared. For one condition, target words (e.g., words like *peace* or *gift*) and partner-related words were good stimuli. Bad words (e.g., *death, accident*) were not targets—they were distractors. For another condition, target words (e.g., *death, accident*) were bad stimuli and partner-related words, while good words, were distracters. Presumably, the more positive participants' attitudes toward their partners, the better they will do on this task when partner-related words and *good* stimuli are targets, but the worse they will do when *bad* words and target-related words are targets. Furthermore, the implicit feelings revealed by this task should predict the future outcome of the relationship: The more positive they are, the lower the likelihood that the relationship will break up. Results offered support for these predictions. The more positive participants' implicit attitudes or feelings toward their partners, the less likely was the relationships to break up. In fact, these implicit feelings were better predictors of such outcomes than their explicit reports concerning the strength of their relationships, provided at the start of the study (see Figure 12.4). In short, subtle and implicit feelings of which we may not even be aware may predict the course of our relationships, so uncovering them, and becoming aware of them, can be very helpful from the point of view of giving us clear warning about the storms that may lie ahead!

WHY RELATIONSHIPS FAIL—AND HOW TO MAKE THEM STRONGER   Most people enter a relationship with high hopes and very positive views of their partners; yet, more than 50 percent of marriages in the United States and many other countries end in divorce (McNulty & Karney, 2004). Despite these statistics, unmarried respondents estimate for themselves only a 10 percent chance of a divorce when they marry (Fowers, Lyons, Montel, & Shaked, 2001). In other words, people expect their own marriages to succeed, despite the fact that most marriages fail. Why is it, then, that so many romantic relationships and marriages fail? As you can probably guess, the answer is complex and involves many different factors.

PROBLEMS BETWEEN PARTNERS   One factor is the failure to understand the reality of a relationship. That is, no spouse (including oneself) is perfect. No matter how ideal the other person may have seemed through the mist of romantic images, it eventually becomes obvious that he or she has negative qualities as well as positive ones. For example, there is the disappointing discovery that the *actual* similarity between partners or spouses is less than the assumed similarity (Sillars et al., 1994). Also, over time, negative personality characteristics in one's partner (e.g., selfishness, a bad temper, chronic sloppiness) may become less and less tolerable. Minor personality and behavioral flaws that once seemed acceptable can come to be perceived as annoying and unlikable (Felmlee, 1995; Pines, 1997). If you are initially drawn to someone because that person is very different from yourself, or perhaps even unique, chances are good that disenchantment will eventually set in (Felmlee, 1998).

Some problems experienced by couples are universal, and probably unavoidable, because being in any kind of close relationship involves some degree of compromise. When you live alone, you can do as you wish, which is one important reason why many people choose to remain single, or why people who have been in a relationship that ends sometimes choose not to enter another one. When two people are together, however, they must somehow decide what to eat for dinner, who prepares it, and when and how to serve the meal. Similar decisions must be made about whether to watch TV and which programs to watch, whether to wash the dishes after dinner or let them wait for the next day, where to set the thermostat, whether to have sex right now or some other time—the list of decisions—and compromises—is endless. Because both partners have needs and preferences, there is an inevitable conflict between the desire for independence and the need for closeness (Baxter, 1990). As a consequence, 98.8 percent of married couples report that they have disagreements, and most indicate that serious conflicts arise once a month or more often (McGonagle, Kessler, & Schilling, 1992). Because disagreements and conflicts are essentially inevitable, what becomes crucial is how those conflicts are handled.

PERCEIVING LOVE—OR AT LEAST APPROVAL—AS CONTINGENT ON SUCCESS

Another problem that troubles many long-term relationships is a growing tendency on the part of one or both partners to perceive that their partner's love and approval is linked to external success—achievements in their careers, jobs, or at school. In other words, partners come to expect that their partners will be kind and loving, and express approval of them, only when they are successful (Murray, Holmes, & Griffin, 2004). Such beliefs can badly erode even very loving relationships. Even worse, such perceptions may be especially likely to develop among people low in self-esteem. This idea is demonstrated very clearly in research by Murray, Griffin, Rose, and Bellavia (2006). They asked 173 couples (either married or cohabiting) to complete questionnaires that measured their self-esteem and their satisfaction with their relationship. In addition, the couples completed daily event diaries for 21 days, reporting (each day) on their personal successes, personal failures, felt rejection, and felt acceptance by their spouses. The key question was whether members of these couples would report feeling less acceptance from their spouses (and more rejection) on days when they experienced failures than on days when they experienced successes. A related question was whether people low in self-esteem would be more likely to perceive such negative outcomes than ones high in self-esteem. This is precisely what was found. People low in self-esteem felt less accepted and less loved on days when they had failures in their professional lives (i.e., their jobs, careers, or school). People high in self-esteem, however, did not report such effects.

In sum, for people low in self-esteem, personal failures on the job or at school spilled over into their relationships, causing them to feel less accepted and more rejected by their partners. Clearly, to the extent such effects occur, they can be devastating for relationship happiness.

BUILDING STRONGER RELATIONSHIPS: MAKING THEM LAST—AND HAPPY

Now that we've discussed why relationships fail, we want to return to a question we considered earlier: What makes them succeed? As we have already seen, factors such as high levels of similarity between the partners in a relationship are a "plus" and so too are certain personal characteristics (e.g., a secure attachment style) and positive feelings (implicit or explicit) toward one's partner. In a sense, though, these are the factors people bring with them into a relationship. Here, we want to address a related question: Once in a relationship, what can the partners do to strengthen their ties and help their relationship to grow and strengthen, rather than wither and die? While there are no simple "no-fail" tactics for achieving these goals, research by social psychologists offers some important suggestions, and we now review some of the most important of these findings.

KNOWING WHAT BEHAVIORS ENHANCE RELATIONSHIPS

One important factor in building strong and satisfying relationships is very basic: knowledge of what behaviors build relationships and what behaviors do not. This sounds so basic that your first reaction might be, "Doesn't everyone know what is good for relationships and what is bad for them?" In fact, research evidence indicates that people differ greatly in this respect (e.g., Turan & Horowitz, 2007). For instance, while some people recognize that noticing a partner's moods and asking about these feelings helps to build relationships, others do not. And while some recognize that "ignoring other people in the street" is *not* crucial to relationships, others think it is just as important as being sensitive to the partner's emotions and needs. Research by Turan and Vicary (2010) indicates that, in fact, the better individuals are at recognizing what actions are relationship-building and which ones are not, the more satisfied they are in their personal relationships, and the better they are at choosing partners who will be supportive when needed.

Closely related to knowledge of relationship-building behaviors is the motivation to attain a supportive partner. Again, people differ greatly on this dimension, and those who value partner supportiveness highly tend to be the ones who choose such people and have successful relationships. Attachment style seems to play an important role in the extent to which individuals learn to recognize relationship-enhancing behaviors. Those high in attachment anxiety (they worry about losing their partners or being rejected) are slower to learn which actions help to build relationships and which tend to undermine them. In short, existing evidence indicates that as informal knowledge suggests, building successful and lasting personal relationships involves a considerable amount of work. First, individuals must increase their understanding of what actions on their part and by their partner help to strengthen such relationships, and then they must actually perform them. Fortunately, such knowledge can be learned and the overall conclusion is that happy relationships are within most people's grasp—*if* they are willing to expend the effort needed to attain them.

BEING POSITIVE—OR BEING CONSTRUCTIVE? Which is better in terms of building strong relationships: focusing on building *positive feelings* between the partners by such actions as praising them often, expressing confidence in them, and attributing any negative actions on their part to factors beyond their control or focusing on dealing with important problems even if this means being less positive toward one's partner? In the past, most evidence suggested that building positive feelings is crucial. Partners who praised one another and held very positive expectations about each other definitely seemed to have more successful relationships than ones who were less positive (e.g., criticized each other often; Murray, Holmes, & Griffin, 1996). The results of recent studies, however, suggest that, in fact, there can definitely be "too much of a good thing" where such actions are concerned. In other words, up to a point, expressing positive feelings about one's partner and viewing them favorably does strengthen relationships, but these actions—useful as they are—can be overdone. In fact, research by McNulty (2010) indicates that couples who continue to express positive expectancies, make positive attributions about each other, and always forgive each other for negative actions tend to show larger declines in relationship satisfaction over time relative to ones who show a more balanced approach—*sometimes* expressing lower expectancies about their partners, *sometimes* withholding forgiveness, and *sometimes* attributing their negative actions to internal causes such as lack of sensitivity rather than to external factors beyond their control (see Figure 12.5).

These differences are relative; most couples show some decline in satisfaction over time, as the "honeymoon effect" wears off, but the differences across couples are both real and significant. More importantly, the declines in satisfaction are greater among couples who focus on always being positive than those who do not—especially when the couples face serious problems, life events require that they come to grips with problems rather than just make each other feel good or happy. Why is this so? Perhaps because in couples who focus on being positive, the contrast between their high expectations and reality is especially great; when their high expectations are disconfirmed, the larger and more distressing it would be if they did not uniformly express positive expectancies and attributions. So should couples always focus on building positive feelings into their relationships? Existing evidence suggests that in general this is useful, but as McNulty (2010, p. 170) puts it: "Couples experiencing . . . severe problems may benefit from . . . thoughts and behaviors that motivate them to directly address and resolve those problems . . ." and that includes actions once frowned upon as relationship-destroying, such as blaming their partners for negative actions and withholding forgiveness. In attaining happy relationships, in short, it appears that a balance between the ideal and the real is a crucial ingredient.

GIVING ONLY WHAT YOU RECEIVE—OR GIVING WHAT YOUR PARTNER NEEDS Love, most people agree, should imply caring as much for one's partner as for oneself. Is this always the case? In fact, it is not. Although many relationships begin this way, with both partners promising that they will always love and cherish one another ("I'll always love you; I'll always make you happy"), for many couples, this is gradually replaced with an approach that is based on *social exchange or reciprocity:* "I'll do things for you, but only if you give me equal benefit in return." The return benefit doesn't have to involve the same activities (e.g., it doesn't have to be "you do the dishes tonight, and I'll do them tomorrow"). Rather, what's crucial is that each partner expects to receive *something* back from the other that is equivalent to their own contributions. That kind of approach contrasts sharply with a **communal approach,** which suggests that each partner should try to meet the other's needs and not seek to balance the benefits that each receives from the relationship.

Which approach do you think builds stronger relationships? If you guessed the communal approach or norm, you are correct. In fact, recent findings (Clark, Lemay, Graham, Pataki, & Finkel, 2010) indicate that while most people perceive the communal perspective or norm as ideal, it often fades with time. Moreover, the greater the extent to which a communal approach is replaced by an exchange one in which the benefits provided by the two partners should be equal or balanced, the lower the satisfaction with the relationship. In addition, this shift toward an exchange rather than a communal approach appears to be more likely to occur among people who are securely attached than ones who have avoidant or anxiety attachment styles.

The message in these findings for building stronger and more satisfying relationships is clear: strive to stay as close as possible to the ideal of taking care of the partner's needs, and do not drift into a situation where the focus is on achieving balance in the benefits provided by each person. That, it appears, can be an important early warning that love—and the relationship—are beginning to die.

Maintain love's illusions, if you can. Most couples start their relationships with very positive feelings about their chosen partners; after all, they are in love! In addition, they often hold very positive beliefs concerning each other—beliefs that are often inflated. In other words, they view each other as possessing more positive characteristics, and being much closer to perfect, than is actually the case. Do such positive illusions lead to disaster—to becoming disillusioned with and disappointed in one's spouse? While some early research suggested this might be so, more recent evidence points strongly

FIGURE 12.5 Should Couples Always Be Positive toward One Another?

In the past it was widely believed (on the basis of research findings) that to build strong relationships, couples should always express positive feelings and thoughts (e.g., positive expectations about each other). Recent evidence, however, indicates that a more balanced approach that permits the couples to address important problems may actually be better.

communal approach

In the context of long-term relationships, a principle suggesting that each partner should try to meet the other's needs, and *not* seek to balance the benefits that each receives from the relationship.

to the opposite conclusion: Couples who begin their relationships with idealized views of each other usually develop more satisfying and happier relationships than those who do not (e.g., Miller, Caughlin, & Huston, 2003). Moreover—and perhaps even more important—maintaining such illusions over time seems to encourage strengthening of the relationship (e.g., Miller et al., 2003). In one longitudinal study, newly married couples were studied for 13 years. The research occurred in four phases: after the couples had been married for 2 months, after 1 year, 2 years, and after approximately 13 years. During each phase, the researchers conducted face-to-face interviews with the 168 couples in the study, obtaining measures of the agreeableness or disagreeableness of their spouse's behavior, ratings of their spouse's overall agreeableness, and their love for their spouses. Agreeable behaviors included such actions as expressing approval or complimenting the spouse, saying "I love you," kissing, hugging, and cuddling the spouse. Disagreeable behaviors included yelling, snapping, raising his or her voice, criticizing or complaining about something the spouse did, or seeming bored and uninterested in the partner.

During the first phase of the study, participants kept diaries in which they reported such actions by their partners on a daily basis. During this and later phases, they also rated the extent to which their partners showed traits related to agreeableness (cheerful, pleasant, friendly, happy, easygoing, patient). Positive illusions were measured in terms of the extent to which partners perceived each other to be more agreeable (in terms of the trait ratings) than would be expected on the basis of actual agreeable or disagreeable behavior (as reported in the daily diaries). Results indicated that the stronger the tendency of the couples to hold positive illusions about each other (to perceive their partners are more agreeable than their actual behavior indicated), the greater love they reported and the smaller the declines in love they experienced during the period studied (13 years). In short, positive illusions about one's spouse predicted marital happiness well beyond the "newlywed" period (see Figure 12.6).

FIGURE 12.6   Illusions: The Cement of Lasting Relationships?

Growing evidence indicates that to the extent couples maintain positive illusions about their partners, perceiving them as better than they actually are, their relationships may be strengthened. In a sense, then, positive illusions about one's partner are one of the foundations of lasting and mutually satisfying relationships. The moral: try to maintain them, because doing so may strengthen your relationship.

So in one sense, viewing our relationship partners more favorably than they actually deserve can provide an important boost to continued love and happiness. Again, the lesson for making relationships last—and prosper—is clear: Hold onto those illusions; they will get you through the difficult times. Besides, communicating positive expectations and beliefs to one's partner may encourage them to live up to these "halos" and to actually become a better partner than they already are! Please note that this doesn't imply *not* providing negative feedback occasionally; as the research by McNulty (2010) suggests, it is possible to go too far in the direction of positive feelings and thoughts about one's partner. What seems to matter most, then, is obtaining a good balance: The early "glow" of a relationship is maintained, but adjusted in the face of the adversities couples confront and the unavoidable frictions of living closely together. Such a balance helps to strengthen relationships, and to make them mutually satisfying over the long haul.

KEYPOINTS

- **Loneliness** occurs when a person has fewer and less satisfying relationships than he or she desires.

- One negative consequence of loneliness is depression and the feelings of anxiety that may accompany it.

- Loneliness seems to stem from many different factors, including genetic predispositions, an insecure attachment style, and lack of early social experiences with peers.

- Lonely people can often benefit from treatments designed to enhance their social skills such as seeing themselves in interaction with others, so they see what they are doing that "turns people off."

- Relationships strengthen—or fail—for many reasons. They strengthen when partners are similar to one another, have certain personal characteristics, and both have positive implicit feelings about each other.

- They fail when problems develop between spouses, or when partners are too positive toward one another and thus fail to face important issues.

- Relationships also fail when partners adopt an exchange rather than communal perspective on the relationship, and fail to maintain at least some positive illusions about each other.

- When partners avoid these pitfalls and develop good balance in their relationships, the relationships often grow stronger and deeper over time.

The Social Side of Personal Health

Overcoming social adversity is certainly one important step toward attaining a happy life. Another, though, involves achieving and maintaining good health. As anyone who has ever been seriously ill knows, health-related problems make it difficult, if not impossible, to focus on personal growth and progress toward important life goals. Clearly, many variables that influence personal health are outside our direct control—genetic factors, exposure to disease-producing organisms, environmental conditions where we live, and so on. Other important factors, though, involve the social side of life. Our interactions with other people, their influence on us, and the problems we experience in our dealings with them should be included in any list of the factors that influence personal health.

Social psychologists have long been aware of the important role of the social side of life in personal health, and their research not only clarifies the influence of these factors, it also offers suggestions as to how to improve personal health through attention to these factors. Research on the interface between the social side of life and personal health is varied in scope (e.g., Jetten et al., 2009), but here we focus on two issues that clearly illustrate importance of social variables in health, and also illustrate how the knowledge uncovered by social psychologists can help us achieve and retain high levels of personal health. These issues are (1) the role of social factors in the epidemic of obesity that is now sweeping the globe and (2) the role of social factors in stress, and coping effectively with it.

Obesity: Why Its Roots Are Social as Well as Biological

Around the globe, the percent of people who are *obese*—who substantially exceed their ideal, healthy weight—is increasing (see Figure 12.7). In fact, it is estimated that in the United States 66 percent exceed their ideal weight. (To be classified as truly obese, individuals must exceed this figure by at least 20 percent or have a body mass index of 30 or higher.) But you don't need statistics to demonstrate this fact: just go to any nearby shopping mall or theater and observe the crowd. You will soon have

Percentage of total population who have a BMI (body mass index) greater than 30 Kg/sq.meters.

RANK	COUNTRIES	AMOUNT ▼
1	United States	30.6%
2	Mexico	24.2%
3	United Kingdom	23.0%
4	Slovakia	22.4%
5	Greece	21.9%
6	Australia	21.7%
7	New Zealand	20.9%
8	Hungary	18.8%
9	Luxembourg	18.4%
10	Czech Republic	14.8%
11	Canada	14.3%
12	Spain	13.1%
13	Ireland	13.0%
14	Germany	12.9%
15	Portugal	12.8%
15	Finland	12.8%
17	Iceland	12.4%
18	Turkey	12.0%
19	Belgium	11.7%
20	Netherlands	10.0%
21	Sweden	9.7%
22	Denmark	9.5%
23	France	9.4%
24	Austria	9.1%
25	Italy	8.5%
26	Norway	8.3%
27	Switzerland	7.7%
28	Japan	3.2%
28	South Korea	3.2%
	Weighted average	**14.1%**

FIGURE 12.7 **The Worldwide Obesity Epidemic: Does It Have Social Roots?**

Although increasing rates of obesity are related to biological and genetic causes, growing evidence indicates that social factors, too, play an important role.

your own evidence that Americans (and people in many other countries, too) are truly becoming "supersized." Since obesity is clearly harmful to personal health—it increases the risk of heart disease, bone disease, and a host of other illnesses—two key questions arise: What factors—especially social factors—are responsible for this growing problem? What, if anything, can be done to reverse the trend?

You are probably already familiar with genetic and environmental variables that play a role in the growing problem of obesity. With respect to genetic factors, it is clear that because of the conditions of feast-or-famine faced by our ancestors, we all have a tendency to store excess calories very effectively. This means that if we overeat (something many people tend to do), we gain weight; our bodies simply "turn on" our efficient calorie-storing systems. Environmental factors, too, play an important role. In recent years, the size of portions of many foods has increased dramatically (Ritzer, 2011). Do you ever take food home from a restaurant? In the past that was rare, but now it is very common, mainly because portions are so much larger. In addition, many fast-food chains have increased the size of the items they sell. Thirty years ago, a Coke or Pepsi was eight ounces; now, one-liter bottles (about 32 ounces) are being offered as a single serving. Similarly, McDonald's hamburgers were small and thin and contained 250 calories; now, most people purchase double cheeseburgers or Big Macs containing 440 or 540 calories. Since people tend to eat their entire portion of food, no matter how big it is, this, too, may be a factor in the rising rate of obesity (see Figure 12.8).

In addition—and most central to this discussion—social factors play an important role. First, people don't walk as much as they did in the past. In cities, fear of crime has stopped many people from walking to stores and other locations. In addition, people simply take their cars everywhere instead of walking, which reduces calories expended and, of course, also contributes to growing air pollution. Similarly, shopping malls have brought a large number of stores to one location, with parking just outside the door. In the past, people had to walk many blocks to visit as many different shops—and often rode public transportation to reach them because parking was so difficult. Now, most people do their shopping at malls or in shopping centers where the stores are close together. And school buses tend to stop in front of every house, thus assuring that even children have less opportunity to exercise than was true in the past. This means that people burn fewer calories, while they are consuming ever-larger portions. It is not surprising that the result is increasing waistlines! In addition, low-calorie, healthy foods such as fresh fruit and vegetables tend to be expensive relative to the high-calorie foods served by fast-food outlets. This is one reason why obesity is more common among poorer and disadvantaged groups in society than among wealthier and better-educated ones.

Another social factor involves ever more enticing media campaigns for high-calorie meals and snacks. Who can resist the foods shown in television commercials, on billboards, and in magazines? Fewer and fewer people, it seems, so caloric intake—and weight gain—is increased by this factor too.

Yet another factor involves the fact that the sit-down dinner is fast disappearing. Instead of eating their meals together, a growing number of families eat at different times, often away from home. This can lead to a situation in which people snack all day; after all, there is no reason to save their appetites for a family meal! Research findings indicate that it is much harder for our built-in bodily mechanisms to regulate eating when it occurs in this manner, so this is yet another social factor that contributes to expanding waistlines.

FIGURE 12.8   Hamburgers: Then and Now
One reason for increasing rates of obesity is that the size of items sold in many restaurants has increased greatly. Compare the hamburger of the 1960s (left photo) with ones sold today (right photo). The difference is truly astounding!

Finally, consider social norms concerning weight: "thin" is definitely "in," and most people report that they want to weigh less than they do. Yet, despite such attitudes, the number of extremely large people continues to increase. As it does, overweight individuals can, perhaps, take consolation from the fact that they are not alone. In fact, one organization (the National Association to Advance Fat Acceptance) has arisen, in part to counteract the stigma against the overweight. This organization, and other similar ones, provide a shelter against the strong "anti-fat" stigma that pervades many societies and, in addition, send the following message: Since so many people are now obese, let's just accept it and move on to other, and perhaps more important, problems.

In sum, many social factors appear to play a role in the trend toward obesity occurring in many countries in recent years. If social factors contribute to obesity, social psychologists reason, they can be changed and this perhaps can help stem the "rising" tide of weight. Some steps in that direction have already been taken. For instance Michelle Obama, First Lady of the United States, has recently launched a campaign to combat childhood obesity. While it involves changing the foods available to children in school (see Figure 12.9), it also emphasizes increased exercise and suggests restrictions on advertising of high-calorie foods aimed principally at children. In addition, legislation now requires restaurants in many cities to post calories next to the foods on their menus. The idea is that if people know how many calories are in even supposedly low-calories foods such as salads, they may make healthier choices. This is a use of social influence techniques to counter growing obesity. While such efforts are just beginning, recognition of the fact that obesity has important social as well as biological and dietary causes is a step in the right direction, and allows for the application of social psychological knowledge and findings to this important problem. (Can the Internet help people lose weight? For some surprising information on this issue, please see the section "SOCIAL LIFE IN A CONNECTED WORLD: Can Internet Sites Help People Lose Weight?")

FIGURE 12.9   Michelle Obama's Campaign Against Childhood Obesity
Michelle Obama, First Lady of the United States, has launched a campaign to counter growing childhood obesity. Although many of the steps in this program focus on healthy eating, others indicate growing recognition of the social factors that contribute to obesity.

SOCIAL LIFE *in a* CONNECTED WORLD

Can Internet Sites Help People Lose Weight?

In the past, when being overweight was relatively rare, people who wanted to shrink their waistlines kept this goal—and their problem with being overweight—very private. They purchased diet books in bookstores—or through the mail, in brown paper wrappers! Or they joined special groups such as *Weight Watchers,* often keeping their membership a secret from friends and family. Now, though, when being overweight seems to be the norm rather than the exception, many people are much more willing to acknowledge this problem publicly, and to seek help wherever they can find it. One place they are going with increasing frequency is the Internet, where many sites offer free advice on how to lose weight.

While these sites vary greatly in content and quality (see Figure 12.10), most offer advice on eating a healthy (and less-fattening) diet, on increasing exercise—often through small changes in behavior, such as climbing stairs instead of automatically taking the elevator or parking far from stores at the mall rather than as close as possible. In addition, they often provide access to personal logs that people can use to record their weight, exercise, and progress toward their goals. In general, there is nothing unusual or "magical" about the advice provided by these sites, or the steps they suggest for losing weight and keeping it off. But growing evidence suggests that they may be quite effective, perhaps because they provide individuals with ready access to information such as comparative information ("How well am I doing compared to other people using this site?") and feedback on their progress. In fact, some research findings seem to confirm the value of these Internet-based weight-loss programs.

For instance, one study published recently online in the *Journal of Medical Internet Research* used a very straightforward research design. People who came to a site established for the study first went through a kind of "qualifying" phase in which they were given information on losing weight by changes in their diet and increased exercise. Those who lost 9 pounds or more during this phase were then permitted to continue in the study. These individuals were assigned to one of three weight maintenance programs: one that was self-directed (no outside help), one that involved monthly meetings with a health counselor, and one that was entirely Internet-based. The Internet condition focused on helping people monitor their weight as well as obtain information on their diets, exercise, and specific goals. Participants in this group interacted through a bulletin board, and continued using the same basic strategies (diet, exercise) they used in the first phase of the study.

Results indicated that people who visited the Internet site regularly gained back the smallest amount of weight; those in the other two conditions (self-directed weight loss, monthly meetings with a counselor) gained more. Of course, we don't know enough about this research to evaluate it carefully, but it does seem consistent with basic

FIGURE 12.10   Internet Sites for Weight Loss
In recent years, many sites that offer free advice on weight loss have appeared on the Internet. Are they helpful? We certainly don't know for certain, but some research findings indicate that they may be helpful if they follow basic principles effective in changing many forms of behavior.

psychological principles found to be effective in changing almost any behavior: choice of specific goals, information on how to attain these goals, and frequent feedback concerning progress toward them.

To the extent Internet weight-loss sites provide this kind of help, they may indeed assist individuals to regulate their own weight—and in this way, to improve both their personal health and the overall quality of their lives, certainly goals worth achieving!

We should note that research by social psychologists on the issue of weight control is also very enlightening—and somewhat encouraging. For instance, Baumeister, Heatherton, and Tice (1994) report studies indicating that obesity is related to *self-control,* the ability to do the things we know are good for us (like sticking to a diet) while avoiding the actions we know are bad for us (e.g., continuing to overeat). Certainly, there are important lessons in this research for anyone wishing to control their weight.

KEYPOINTS

- Achieving and maintaining good personal health is an important step on the way toward attaining a happy and fulfilling life, so social psychologists have long been interested in the role of social factors in health.

- One growing threat to personal health is obesity, which is increasing worldwide. Although obesity certainly involves biological and genetic factors (e.g., our inherited tendency to store extra calories as fat in "good times"), it also involves many social factors.

- Because of changes in social conditions, people walk less, do not eat sit-down family meals as often as in the past, and eat higher-calorie meals, mainly because the portion sizes in restaurants has increased greatly over the years.

- Many sites on the Internet offer free advice for people who want to reduce their weight, and some of these sites do provide useful information. However, they should be approached with great caution, since they are largely free of any government controls and safeguards.

Stress: Social Tactics for Reducing Its Harmful Effects

Have you ever felt that you were right at the edge of being overwhelmed by negative events in your life or by pressures you could no longer handle? If so, you are already quite familiar with **stress:** our response to events that disrupt, or threaten to disrupt, our physical or psychological functioning (Lazarus & Folkman, 1984; Taylor, 2002). Unfortunately, stress is a common part of modern life—something few of us can avoid altogether. Partly for this reason, and partly because it seems to exert negative effects on both physical health and psychological well-being, stress has become an important topic of research in psychology—and social psychologists have made major contributions to this work. We now review the key findings of this research, with special attention to its links to major principles of social psychology.

MAJOR SOURCES OF STRESS AND THEIR EFFECTS ON PERSONAL HEALTH   What factors contribute to stress? Unfortunately, the list is a very long one; many conditions and events can add to our total "stress quotient." Among the most important of these, though, are major stressful life events related to our relationships with other people (e.g., the death of a loved one or a painful divorce). What are the effects of such events—and high levels of stress they generate—on health? The answer is clear: devastating. In fact, existing evidence indicates that people who experience high levels of stress are much more likely to become seriously ill than people who do not, and that overall, stress is a key contributing factor to a very wide range of medical problems (Cohen, 1998; Cohen & Janicki-Deverts, 2009; Holmes & Rahe, 1967).

stress
Our response to events that disrupt, or threaten to disrupt, our physical or psychological functioning.

We should add that while certain major life events such as the death of a loved one are dramatic and deeply disturbing, they are not the only social cause of stress in our lives. In fact, the minor annoyances of daily life—often termed *hassles*—are also important, making up for their relatively low intensity by their much higher frequency. That such daily hassles are an important cause of stress is suggested by the findings of several studies by Lazarus and his colleagues (e.g., DeLongis, Folkman, & Lazarus, 1988; Lazarus, Opton, Nomikes, & Rankin, 1985). These researchers developed a Hassles Scale on which individuals indicate the extent to which they have been "hassled" by common events during the past month. The items included in this scale deal with a wide range of everyday events, such as having too many things to do at once, misplacing or losing things, troublesome neighbors, and concerns over money. While such events may seem relatively minor when compared with the life events discussed earlier, they appear to be quite important. When scores on the Hassles Scale are related to reports of psychological symptoms, strong positive correlations are obtained (Lazarus et al., 1985). In short, the more stress people report as a result of daily hassles, the poorer their psychological well-being.

HOW DOES STRESS AFFECT HEALTH? We hope that by now you are convinced that stress plays an important role in personal health. But how, exactly, do these effects occur? While the precise mechanisms involved remain to be determined, growing evidence suggests that the process goes something like this: By draining our resources, inducing negative affect, and keeping us off balance physiologically, stress upsets our complex internal chemistry. In particular, it may interfere with efficient operation of our *immune system*—the mechanism through which our bodies recognize and destroy potentially harmful substances and intruders, such as bacteria, viruses, and cancerous cells. When functioning normally, the immune system is nothing short of amazing: Each day it removes or destroys many potential threats to our health. Unfortunately, prolonged exposure to stress seems to disrupt this system. Chronic exposure to stress can reduce circulating levels of *lymphocytes* (white blood cells that fight infection and disease) and increase levels of the hormone *cortisol*, a substance that suppresses aspects of our immune system (Kemeny, 2003).

One model of how stress can affect our health suggests that stress exerts both direct and indirect effects upon us. The direct effects are the ones just described (e.g., on our immune system and other bodily functions). The indirect effects involve influences on the lifestyles we adopt—our health-related behaviors (e.g., whether we seek medical care promptly when we need it) and fitness-related behaviors (e.g., the diet we choose, exercise). While this model may not include all the ways in which stress can affect our health, it offers a useful overview of several ways in which such effects may arise.

SOCIAL TACTICS FOR COPING WITH STRESS: THE BENEFITS OF SOCIAL SUPPORT
Since stress is an inescapable part of life, the key task we face is not trying to eliminate or avoid it, but, rather, to *cope* with it effectively—in ways that reduce its adverse effects while helping us deal with its causes. You are already familiar with several effective means for coping with stress such as improving your physical fitness (e.g., Brown, 1991) and eating a healthy diet—which can provide the added benefit of regulating your weight. Maintaining a stable weight is a very important outcome. Since we've already considered that topic, though, here we focus on one strategy for reaching that goal that is closely related to social psychology and the social side of life: seeking **social support**—drawing on the emotional and other resources provided by others. More specifically, social support refers to the perception or experience that one is loved and cared for by others, is valued and esteemed, and is part of a social network of mutual assistance (Taylor et al., 2010).

social support
Drawing on the emotional and task resources provided by others as a means of coping with stress.

What do you do when you feel stressed? Many people turn to friends or family, seeking their advice, help, and sympathy. And research findings indicate that this can be a highly effective means of protecting our health from the ravages of stress (House, Landis, & Umberson, 1998). In fact, the availability of social support has been found to reduce psychological distress, including depression and anxiety, and to promote better adjustment to high levels of stress that are chronic—ones that continue over time (e.g., Taylor, 2007). Just being with those you like can be helpful; even monkeys seek contact with others in stressful situations (Cohen, Kaplan, Cunnick, Manuck, & Rabin, 1992). As you might also guess on the basis of research on the effects of similarity, people who desire social support tend to turn to others who are similar to themselves in various ways (Morgan, Carder, & Neal, 1997). But you don't have to have contact with another person to experience such benefits: Findings indicate that having a pet can help reduce stress (e.g., Allen, 2003) (see Figure 12.11).

FIGURE 12.11   Pets Can Reduce Stress
As shown in this photo, for many people, interacting with a pet is an important aid to reducing stress.

In one intriguing study (Allen, Shykoff, & Izzo, 2001), stockbrokers who lived alone and described their work as very stressful, and who all had high blood pressure, were either randomly selected to receive a pet cat or dog from an animal shelter or to not receive a pet. Results indicated that the pets were an excellent source of social support, reducing stress among those who received them. In fact, when exposed to high levels of stress, those who had acquired pets cut their blood pressure increases by half compared to those who did not receive pets. Why are pets so effective in this regard? One possibility is that they provide nonjudgmental social support: they love their owners under all conditions. Whatever the precise reasons, it seems clear that pets can be an important aid in coping with stress—at least for people who enjoy having them.

In contrast, a lack of a reliable social support network can actually increase a person's risk of dying from disease, accidents, or suicide. People who are divorced or separated from their spouses often experience reduced functioning in certain aspects of their immune system, compared to individuals who are happily married (Kiecolt-Glaser et al., 1987, 1988). Recent findings indicate that social support is not always effective in reducing stress—for instance, when concerns over being evaluated by others are strong, social support from those doing the evaluating may not counter the high levels of stress generated (e.g., Taylor et al., 2010). But overall, it seems clear that receiving social support is important to health. Indeed, recent findings indicate that providing social support to others may be just as important for our health. In one revealing study, Brown, Nesse, Vinokur, and Smith (2003) isolated and compared the unique effects of giving and receiving social support on mortality in a sample of 846 elderly married people. The researchers initially measured the extent to which participants received and gave support to their spouse and to others (friends, relatives, neighbors) and then monitored mortality rates over a 5-year period. Participants who reported providing high levels of support to others were significantly less likely to die over the 5-year period than participants who had provided little or no support to others. By contrast, receiving social support, from one's spouse or from others, did not appear to affect mortality among people in this group. In short, these findings suggest it may be even better to give than to receive, especially when it comes to personal health! In any case, evidence provided by social psychologists indicates that social conditions (e.g., high levels of support and acceptance from others) can go a long way toward reducing the harmful effects of even high levels of stress on personal health.

KEYPOINTS

- **Stress** involves feelings of being overwhelmed—of being no longer able to cope.

- Stress exerts negative effects on personal health, in part because it undermines the immune system, and also because it leads us to adopt less healthy lifestyles.

- Many tactics for reducing stress exist and are well known (e.g., getting in shape, eating a healthy diet).

- Other ways of dealing with stress involve the social side of life, such as obtaining **social support** from one's friends and family. Although this is not always effective, it can often go a long way toward reducing stress and protecting personal health. So get—and stay—connected! Doing so may be beneficial to your health as well as your happiness.

Making the Legal System More Open, Fair, and Effective: The Social Side of the Law

Is justice really blind? It is shown this way (blindfolded) on many court buildings throughout the world (see Figure 12.12), and this is the ideal: All people should be equal before the law and treated in the same impartial manner. After reading the chapters in this book, however, you probably realize that while this is an admirable ideal, it may be very hard to achieve in real life. As we saw in earlier chapters (e.g., Chapters 2 and 6), it is very difficult, if not impossible, for us to ignore the words, behaviors, or personal characteristics of other people, or to dismiss the preconceived ideas, beliefs, and stereotypes that we have developed over the years from our thinking and decision making. So while we might wish that justice could be totally impartial and fair, we must recognize that making it—and our legal system—live up to these goals is a very tall order! To move toward it, many social psychologists believe we must first understand the potential sources of error and bias that either creep into the legal system or, in some cases, are actively introduced by its key players—attorneys, judges, and police (e.g., Frenda, Nichols, & Loftus, 2011). Once we understand the possible risks, we may be able to take steps to correct these problems and reduce, if not totally eliminate, them from the system. By doing so, justice could indeed be more fair and impartial. What are some of these potential pitfalls and how can we seek to reduce them? Let's see what research has revealed.

FIGURE 12.12   Is Justice Really Blind?
Although we hope that justice is blind—completely impartial and fair—research by social psychologists suggests that this ideal is more difficult to attain than most people believe.

Social Influence and the Legal System

In a sense, most legal proceedings—trials, interrogation of suspects in a crime—involve an element of social influence. During trials, for instance, attorneys attempt to persuade jurors and perhaps the presiding judge of the guilt or innocence of the people on trial. And during interrogation of suspects, police often attempt to influence the individuals they question to confess—or at least tell the full truth. Clearly, social influence is, potentially, a major factor in these activities and this is widely recognized by attorneys, police, and other participants in the legal system. It is one reason why defense attorneys often urge their clients to dress conservatively and groom neatly: doing so can help them make a better impression on jurors and so perhaps exert subtle influence on them in the direction of a favorable judgment.

Social influence can also play an important role in events that happen before a case goes to trial. While this can occur in many different ways, we focus here on one that is especially interesting, and related to our basic theme of how social psychology can help make the legal system more fair and impartial: the role of social influence in police lineups.

LINEUPS: HOW SUBTLE SOCIAL PRESSURE SOMETIMES LEADS TO DISASTROUS ERRORS One technique commonly used by police to help identify suspects is the **lineup**—a procedure in which witnesses to a crime are shown several people, one or more who may be suspects in a case, and asked to identify any that they recognize as the person who committed the crime. Witnesses may look either at the real people involved or at photos of them. Although these procedures are designed to get at the truth—to allow witnesses to identify the real criminals—they are clearly subject to several forms of bias related to social influence.

For instance, consider the way in which suspects are presented. In *sequential lineups* the suspects are presented one at a time and witnesses indicate whether they recognize each one. In *simultaneous lineups*, in contrast, all the suspects are shown at once and witnesses are asked to indicate which one (if any) they recognize. Results of many studies indicate that sequential lineups are better in the sense that they reduce the likelihood that witnesses will make a serious mistake—identify someone who did not commit the crime (Steblay, Dysart, Fulero, & Lindsay, 2001).

Perhaps the most disturbing findings concerning lineups relate to the impact of instructions to witnesses—which can be viewed as involving subtle forms of social influence. Totally neutral instructions simply ask them to identify the person who committed the crime, and don't make any statements about whether this person is or is not present in the lineup. In contrast, *biased* instructions suggest that the criminal is present and that their task as witnesses is to pick this person out from the others (e.g., Pozzulo & Lindsay, 1999). Such instructions expose witnesses to a subtle form of social influence: they may feel pressured to identify someone, even if no one they recognize is present.

Research by Pozzulo and Dempsey (2006) illustrates this danger very clearly. They had both children and adults watch a videotape of a staged crime—one in which a woman's purse was stolen. Both groups were then shown a lineup consisting of photos of people who resembled the people who committed the crime. Simultaneous presentation of the photos was used. A key aspect of the study involved instructions to the participants. In one condition (neutral instructions), they were told that the criminal might or might not be present in the lineup. In the biased instructions condition, they were led to believe that this person was indeed present in the lineup. In fact, though, this person was *not* included in the lineup, so the key question was: Would the biased instructions lead participants to falsely identify someone— an innocent person—as the culprit? That's exactly what happened. As shown in Figure 12.13, both adults and children were more likely to falsely identify an innocent person after hearing the biased instructions (ones leading them to conclude that the criminal was present) than after hearing the neutral instructions.

These findings indicate that social influence is at work in police lineups, and that stringent procedures should be adopted to avoid such effects. Instructions to witnesses should be neutral and not imply the guilty party is actually present, and sequential rather than simultaneous lineups should be used whenever possible. Social influence is a powerful and often very subtle process, so guarding against it is a difficult task. Doing so, however, may help increase the likelihood that lineups, which are used very commonly around the world, will be helpful in identifying actual criminals, and be less likely to point to people who are actually innocent of the crimes in question.

lineup
A procedure in which witnesses to a crime are shown several people, one or more of whom may be suspects in a case, and asked to identify those that they recognize as the person who committed the crime.

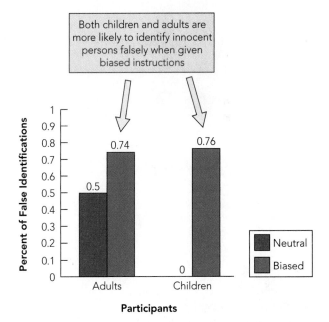

FIGURE 12.13 Instructions to Witnessses: Subtle Social Influence at Work in the Legal System
As shown here, when given instructions suggesting that the person who committed a crime was present in a lineup (actually, he was not), both children and adults showed an increased tendency to identify someone falsely (an innocent person) as the criminal. When such instructions were not provided, they were less likely to make such serious errors. (Source: Based on data from Pozzulo & Dempsey, 2006).

FIGURE 12.14 Defendants' Appearance: It Shouldn't Matter—But It Does

Justice should, ideally be blind, but research findings indicate that attractive defendants (top photo) have an important edge with juries and even judges, during legal proceedings. They are less likely to be found guilty, and receive milder sentences if they are convicted.

The Influence of Prejudice and Stereotypes on the Legal System

If justice were truly blind—the ideal we described above—then it would be completely unaffected by race, gender, ethnic background, and other factors. In other words, decisions by judges and juries would be based entirely on evidence, and the characteristics of defendants would have no effect. Having read the chapters in this book on social cognition, attitudes, and prejudice, however, you probably realize that this is a difficult, if not impossible, goal to attain. As human beings, each of us enters any social situation, including legal proceedings, with complex sets of attitudes, beliefs, values, and—unfortunately—stereotypes concerning various groups. These can then interact in many ways with information concerning the particular case in question, and so influence the decisions we reach as jurors. How common are such effects? And what can be done to eliminate them? These are the issues to which we turn next (e.g., Levine & Wallach, 2001).

CHARACTERISTICS OF DEFENDANTS AND JURORS, AND HOW THEY INFLUENCE LEGAL PROCEEDINGS Let's begin with the characteristics of defendants—the people on trial. These include race, gender, and ethnic background, and all these factors have been found to influence jury decisions and other outcomes. In the United States, African American defendants have generally been found to be at a disadvantage. For example, they are more likely than whites to be convicted of murder and to receive the death penalty and are therefore proportionally overrepresented on death row (Sniffen, 1991).

Race, however, is not the only characteristic of defendants that can play a role in legal proceedings. In addition, physical appearance (attractiveness), gender, and socioeconomic status are also important. For example, people accused of most major crimes are less likely to be found guilty if they are physically attractive, female, and of high rather than low socioeconomic status (Mazzella & Feingold, 1994). Attractiveness has been studied the most, and in real as well as mock trials, attractive defendants have a major advantage over unattractive ones with respect to being acquitted, receiving a light sentence, and gaining the sympathy of the jurors (Downs & Lyons, 1991; Quigley, Johnson, & Byrne, 1995; Wuensch, Castellow, & Moore, 1991) (see Figure 12.14). In addition to race and attractiveness, another visible characteristic—gender—also plays an important role in legal proceedings. In general, female defendants tend to be treated more leniently by juries and courts than male defendants, but this depends on the specific crime. For instance, in cases involving assault, female defendants are actually more likely to be found guilty than male defendants, perhaps because assault is considered an even more unacceptable and unusual behavior for women than men (Cruse & Leigh, 1987). The gender of jurors, too, can be important. One of the consistent differences between male and female jurors is in reaction to cases involving sexual assault. In judging what occurred in cases of rape, men are more likely than women to conclude that the sexual interaction was consensual (Harris & Weiss, 1995). Schutte and Hosch (1997) analyzed the results of 36 studies of simulated cases of rape and child abuse. In responding to defendants accused of either crime, women were more likely than men to vote for conviction.

CAN THESE BIASING EFFECTS ON LEGAL PROCEEDINGS BE REDUCED?   Our comments so far in this section seem to paint a picture in which the decisions reached by jurors and perhaps even judges are influenced by factors we all wish *did not* exert such effects. But don't despair: growing evidence suggests that although the factors we have discussed do indeed influence outcomes, these effects may not be as large as was previously suspected, and may be overcome—at least to a considerable extent—by some aspects of legal processes or by improved techniques for interviewing witnesses that have been developed by psychologists (e.g., Fisher, Milne, & Bull, 2011).

Perhaps the most encouraging evidence in this respect is provided by research conducted by Bothwell, Piggott, Foley, and McFatter (2006). Taking account of past research on prejudice and stereotypes, these researchers reasoned that often these cognitive factors operate at an automatic or unconscious level; they influence behavior, but do so in subtle rather than overt ways, and the people who hold such views often state—vigorously!—that they are *not* prejudiced. This suggests that such prejudiced views would be more likely to influence their private judgments than their public decisions as jurors. In other words, while specific jurors might well have subtle negative views about various racial or ethnic groups, these views would be more likely to find expression in their private judgments and thoughts than in their actual decisions as jurors. Jury deliberations, which are often lengthy and detailed, might serve to reduce the impact of subtle and nonconscious forms of prejudice, and so help make the process more fair.

To test this reasoning, Bothwell et al. (2006) conducted research in which both students and prospective jurors in actual legal cases read about a sexual harassment suit in which a supervisor demanded sexual favors from a subordinate. Race of the supervisor and the subordinate (who had made the complaint) was varied so that each could be either black or white; gender, too, was a factor in the study, so that the supervisor and the subordinate could each be either a man or a woman. Participants read a case that presented one of these various combinations (e.g., a black male supervisor and a white female subordinate; a white female supervisor and a black male subordinate). Participants then rated the responsibility of the person making the complaint and how much monetary compensation the victim should receive from the company. Results for these measures indicated that racial and gender prejudice exerted significant effects. For instance, the person making the complaint was held more responsible for what happened to him or her when the supervisor was black than when this person was white. Similarly, they awarded less compensation when the supervisor was black than when he or she was white. Participants reasoned—at the private level—that when the supervisor was black, the subordinates "should have known better" than to go to this person's hotel room for a drink.

After making the private decisions and judgments, a mock trial was held in which jurors met and then recommended compensation for the victim. Here's the interesting—and encouraging finding: At the end of the mock trials, the effects of race and gender *largely disappeared*. In other words, although the impact of these variables was present prior to actual jury deliberations, it was essentially eliminated by jury deliberations. For instance, as shown in Figure 12.15, as individuals, participants in the study privately awarded

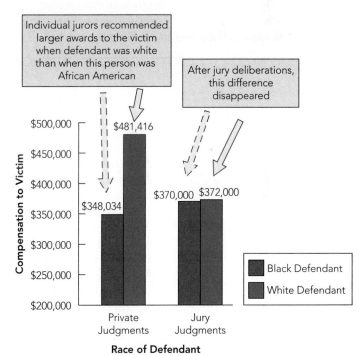

FIGURE 12.15   Do Juries Overcome Bias in Legal Proceedings?

When participants in the study shown here made individual (private) recommendations for compensation to a victim of sexual harassment, they recommended larger awards when the defendant was white than when he or she was black. After jury deliberation, however, this difference—and others reflecting racial and gender bias—tended to disappear. These findings suggest that jury deliberations may help to reduce the impact of prejudices held by individual jurors, prejudices related to the race, gender, and attractiveness of defendants. (Source: Based on data from Bothwell et al., 2006).

much less compensation to the victim of sexual harassment when the defendant (the supervisor) was black than when he or she was white. After jury discussion, however, this difference totally disappeared.

These findings, and those in related studies (e.g., Greene & Bornstein, 2003), suggest that while justice is certainly not entirely blind, the procedures used for reaching legal decisions can, at least sometimes, help to counter the impact of various characteristics of defendants, and perhaps of jurors, too. So while our existing system is far from perfect, it may operate more effectively than some experts have feared. In any case, the knowledge provided by social psychologists can certainly help make the system even better—more fair, impartial, and accurate—and that is truly an important goal.

KEY POINTS

- To make the legal system more fair, impartial, and protective of basic human rights, it is necessary to take account of the fact that it involves many aspects of social thought and behavior.

- For instance, the legal system often involves social influence: attorneys seek to influence jurors, and police influence defendants through many actions, often unintentionally. Such effects are readily visible in **lineups** and how they are conducted.

- Prejudice also plays an important role in legal proceedings because defendants' race, age, and physical attractiveness often strongly influence jurors' perceptions of them, and judgments of innocence or guilt.

- Fortunately, careful deliberations by juries as they discuss available evidence tend to reduce such effects, although not, of course, in all instances.

Personal Happiness: What It Is, and How to Attain It

Personal happiness is a key life goal for most of us. We all want to be happy and satisfied with our lives, but what does that mean, specifically? After decades of research on the nature, causes, and effects of personal happiness, most social psychologists agree that such evaluations involve four basic components: *global life satisfaction*—feeling generally happy with our lives; *satisfaction with important life domains*—being satisfied with our work, relationship, and family; *positive feelings*—experiencing positive emotions and moods often; and *negative feelings*—experiencing negative feelings or emotions less often or, preferably, rarely (Diener, 2000). In short, happiness seems to rest on several foundations, and to the extent these are present in our lives, they strongly influence how happy we are and the extent to which we see our lives as meaningful and fulfilling (Krause, 2007). Efforts to investigate personal happiness often focus on these components, but because they are highly correlated, researchers frequently use short and simple measures of happiness—ones in which individuals respond to such straightforward questions as "How satisfied or dissatisfied are you with your life overall?" (Weiss, Bates, & Luciano, 2008). What does research on personal happiness indicate? We now present an overview of some of the key findings, and once again, get ready for surprises, because it appears that the ingredients in **personal happiness** are different, in important ways, from what many people might guess.

personal happiness
Refers to subjective well-being, which involves global life satisfaction, satisfaction with specific life domains, frequent positive feelings, and relatively few negative feelings.

How Happy Are People Generally?

Let's begin with a very basic question: How happy are people in general with their lives? In other words, what level of *subjective well-being* do most people report? Surprisingly, despite hugely varied living conditions around the world, most people—no matter where they live, their standard of living, gender, age, and health—report that they are quite happy. In fact, about 80 percent of all respondents in large surveys indicate that they are very happy and satisfied (Diener, Lucas, & Scollon, 2006; European Values Study Group & World Values Survey Association, 2005). How can this be so? How can people leading very different lives in very different settings all be happy? As we'll now see, the answer seems to involve the fact that there are indeed many sources of happiness, and human beings are very adept at securing many of these—and thus their own personal happiness can be high for different reasons (Diener, Ng, Harter, & Arora, 2010). In addition, as we've noted at several points in this book, people generally have a strong tendency to look on the bright side—to be optimistic and upbeat in a wide range of situations (e.g., Diener & Subh, 1998). Given that most people report being happy, let's consider some of the factors that appear to contribute to happiness.

Factors That Influence Happiness

What makes people happy with their lives, even if these might appear to someone from an advantaged country to be lives filled with grinding poverty and deprivation? Here's what research reported by social psychologists has indicated. First, happy people report experiencing higher levels of positive emotion and lower levels of negative emotion than less happy people (Lyubomirsky et al., 2005). According to psychologist Barbara Fredrickson, high levels of positive emotion lead people to think, feel, and act in ways that help to broaden and build their emotional, physical, and social resources (e.g., Fredrickson, 2001; Fredrickson & Joiner, 2002). Second, good social relations with other people—close friends, family, romantic partners—appear to be an important ingredient for being happy. Such close relationships are certainly available to people everywhere, in all cultures, regardless of personal wealth (see Figure 12.16). In fact, close family relationships may be more the rule in less wealthy societies than in wealthy ones, where people move around frequently and may live hundreds or even thousands of miles from their relatives, or from close friends whom they must leave behind when they take a new job or move for other reasons.

Additional findings (Diener, Suh, Lucas, & Smith, 1999) suggest that personal happiness may be influenced by other factors, too. One of these involves having goals and the resources—personal, economic, and otherwise—necessary to reach them. Many

FIGURE 12.16   Close Family Relationships: An Important Factor in Happiness
Research findings indicate that close relationships with family, friends, and others are an important source of personal happiness. Such relationships are available to people everywhere, regardless of their own wealth or that of their societies.

studies indicate that people who have concrete goals, especially goals that they have a realistic chance of reaching, and who feel (realistically or otherwise) that they are making progress toward these, are happier than people lacking in such goals (Sanderson & Cantor, 1999).

"OK," we can almost hear you saying, "so happiness derives from many different things. But what about wealth? Doesn't *that* make people happy? After all, wealthy people can have anything they want and can lead the lives they prefer." This is such a widespread assumption, and raises such complex issues, that we now examine it in detail. In fact, economists have long assumed that the wealth of a nation (gross domestic product) should be the primary measure of its well-being. But is this correct? Let's see what social psychologists have discovered about this intriguing issue.

Wealth: An Important Ingredient in Personal Happiness?

Does money equal happiness? Many people—not just economists—seem to believe that it does. They assume that wealth will buy the things and conditions that produce happiness. After all, if you can have anything you want and live any lifestyle you wish, shouldn't that make you happy? While these ideas seem like reasonable ones, research on the link between wealth and happiness indicates that it is far, far more complex than this. Overall, recent findings (Diener et al., 2010; Kahneman, Diener, & Schwarz, 2003), indicate that there is some connection between wealth and happiness, at least at certain points in the income distribution, but that it is far from as powerful as many people assume. For instance, around the globe, household income is related to global feelings of well-being, and so is gross national product per capita, but primarily at the low income levels. Think about it—if you are worried about how you will get food for your kids, lack of money is likely to make you unhappy; without it, you can't meet your basic needs or those of the people you care about. At higher income levels, however, income is not strongly correlated with happiness: People already have all the basics and some of the luxuries, so increasing wealth still further does not strongly increase their happiness or life satisfaction. In sum, although wealth—both at the individual and societal level—does play *some* role in personal happiness, it has a much smaller one than many people guess.

Furthermore—and this is an important point—wealth is *not* associated with positive feelings, another important component of happiness. In fact, Diener and colleagues (2010) report that wealth is not clearly linked to the social side of life and happiness. In fact, one reason this is the case is that such factors as being treated with respect and having friends and family one can count on in an emergency (what has been discussed in Chapter 4 as "social capital ") are independent of income. In fact, many countries high in societal wealth (gross domestic product) are relatively *low* in terms of social measures or positive feelings (see Table 12.1), which are typically derived from having strong community ties (see Putnam, 2000). As Diener et al. (2010, p. 60) put it: "Some nations that do well in economic terms do only modestly well in social psychological prosperity, and some nations that rank in the middle in economic development are stars . . . in social psychological prosperity."

So why doesn't wealth necessarily result in personal happiness? Additional findings reported by social psychologists have shed light on this puzzling question. First, consider research by Boyce, Brown, and Moore (2010). They found that it is not wealth itself that is important, but, rather, *relative* judgments about one's wealth that matter most. People seem to care more about how their income (wealth) compares with that of others than they do about its absolute level. When individuals were asked to report on the number of people in their society who have income worse than or better than theirs, these relative judgments were in fact strongly

TABLE 12.1 Does Wealth = Happiness?

As shown here, countries ranked high in income (e.g., the United States) do not necessarily rank high in social prosperity (respect from others, good relationships with friends, family, etc.), or in positive feelings. So wealth does not automatically generate all components of happiness.

COUNTRY	INCOME	SOCIAL PROSPERITY	POSITIVE FEELINGS
U.S.	1	19	26
Italy	18	33	67
South Korea	24	83	58
India	61	85	63
Tanzania	89	58	52

Source: Based on data from Diener, Ng, Harter, & Arora, 2010.

related to life satisfaction. On the other hand, absolute income was not. So what we seem to care about is doing better than others, not just being wealthy ourselves—here again we see the important role that social comparison plays even in our own subjective well-being. This is one reason why even when countries experience rising standards of living, people living in them don't necessarily report that they are happier—because others with whom they compare also are experiencing a rise in income. In the United States, for instance, per capita income (adjusted for inflation) rose more than 50 percent in recent decades, but people do not report being happier. In fact, they report being *less* happy than in the "good old days" when they were actually poorer! So a rising tide may indeed float all boats, as one expression goes, but it doesn't make the people in the boats happier.

In addition, while wealth may give us the material possessions we want, and lots of comforts, it may take away something just as important: the capacity to savor and enjoy the little pleasures of life. When people get used to enjoying the "best," and to having everything they want when they want it, they may become so accustomed to these benefits that it leads them to enjoy them less. Direct evidence for such effects has been reported by Quoidbach, Dunn, Petrides, and Mikolajcazk (2010) in an intriguing study. They gave participants in the study (students at a Canadian university) a piece of chocolate and then observed their reactions as they ate it. Before receiving the chocolate, some participants saw photos of Canadian money—they were primed to think about wealth and their desire for it, while others saw a neutral photo unrelated to money. Observers rated the amount of enjoyment shown by the participants as they ate the chocolate from 1 (not at all) to 7 (a great deal), and also how long they spent enjoying the treat. Results were clear: Those who had looked at photos of money and were primed to think about wealth enjoyed the chocolate less and spent less time eating it than those who saw a neutral photo. These findings suggest that while money may provide many of the things we want, it may actually reduce our ability to savor life's pleasures. If that's so, then it is hardly surprising that money does not automatically guarantee personal happiness!

Is Happiness Having What You Want, or Wanting What You Have?

Here's another basic question about personal happiness that raises some fascinating issues: Does happiness consist primarily in having what you want—getting the things you desire in life—or wanting (enjoying) what you have? The research by Quoidbach and colleagues (2010) suggests that, in fact, having what we want may not really add to our happiness, since it may reduce our capacity to enjoy these items once we have them. But other findings seem to indicate that both sides of the equation are important. Happiness, in other words, comes from *both* having what we want and wanting (enjoying) what we have. This issue has been investigated by Larsen and McKibben (2008) in research in which participants reported on what they had (in terms of material possessions) and how much they wanted (enjoyed) these items. Information on these issues was used to predict their life satisfaction (an important component of personal happiness), and results were clear: Both having what you want *and* wanting what you have play a role in this aspect of happiness. The basic meaning of these findings is that neither things, nor having them, are closely related to happiness. Rather, happiness comes from valuing the things we have—being grateful for them and enjoying them.

Sadly, many people seem to lose the latter capacity when they attain wealth. They continue to believe that if they obtain just *one more thing*—that new car, new and larger home, more items to complete their wardrobe, one more tool for their workshop, one more piece of jewelry, one more piece of art—they will finally attain the happiness they seek (see Figure 12.17). But in fact, if they obtain these possessions, the happiness they experience is fleeting, and they are soon focusing on the *next* item needed to complete their happiness. Truly, that's a very sad and frustrating cycle to enter, and one—we hope!—reading this chapter will help you avoid!

FIGURE 12.17 Having What We Want or Wanting What We Have? Which Brings Happiness?

Research by social psychologists indicates that having what we want does not in and of itself bring happiness. Rather, it is both having what we want and appreciating what we have that together generates high levels of happiness. This is one reason why many people who have lots of possessions and high levels of wealth are not happy: they constantly expand their list of "wants" and take little pleasure in these items when they actually obtain them.

The Benefits of Happiness

Being happy certainly feels good—it is the state most of us would prefer to be in most, if not all, of the time. But does it do more than this? Does being happy and satisfied with our life confer other benefits, too? A rapidly growing body of evidence indicates that the answer is definitely *yes*. Happy people generally experience many tangible benefits related to their high levels of life satisfaction (Lyubomirsky et al., 2005). With regard to work, individuals high in subjective well-being are more likely to experience better work outcomes, including increased productivity, higher quality of work, higher income, more rapid promotions, and greater **job satisfaction** (Borman, Penner, Allen, & Motowidlo et al., 2001; Weiss et al., 1999; Wright & Cropanzano, 2000). They also tend to have more and higher quality social relationships—more friends, more satisfying romantic relationships, and stronger social support networks—than do less happy people (e.g., Lyubomirsky, King, & Diener, 2005; Pinquart & Sorensen, 2000). In addition, happy people tend to report better health and fewer unpleasant physical symptoms, and deal with illness more effectively when it does occur (Lyubomirsky et al., 2005).

Additional health-related benefits associated with higher levels of well-being include increased resistance to cold and flu viruses (Cohen et al., 2003), better ability to deal with pain (Keefe et al., 2001), a lower incidence of depression (Maruta, Colligan, Malinchoc, & Offord et al., 2000), and improved recovery from surgery (Kopp et al., 2003). Perhaps most intriguing of all, they actually seem to live longer (Maruta, 2000). For instance, in one recent study, Xu and Roberts (2010) related subjective well-being to longevity in a very large sample of people living in a large county in California. They examined death from all causes and specifically from natural causes over a 28-year period. Measures of global life satisfaction, positive feelings, negative feelings, and satisfaction with important life domains were all available because the people in their research were participating in a countywide longitudinal public health study.

Results were compelling: All the components of personal happiness (life satisfaction, satisfaction with important life domains, high positive affect, low negative affect) were related to longevity. In other words, the higher people were on these factors, the less likely they were to die during the study or, conversely, the longer they tended to live. Interestingly, these findings were found among both younger and older adults, and were especially strong among healthy adults. Being happy, it appears, not only makes our lives more enjoyable, it prolongs them, too. Clearly, then, it is something to seek—which leads us to the next question: How can it be increased?

Can We Increase Personal Happiness?

Initial research on happiness seemed to suggest that it is relatively fixed: because of a large genetic component, people are born with strong tendencies to be happy or unhappy and these are difficult to change. In other words, some people tend to be happy even under very difficult life circumstances, whereas others tend to be unhappy, even if they are blessed with wealth and material possessions. Support for this view was provided by studies indicating that subjective well-being remains fairly stable over time (Eid & Diener, 2004). In addition, research involving twins provided evidence that happiness is, as we noted earlier, influenced by genetic factors. For instance, identical twins tend to be more similar in their levels of happiness than fraternal twins or other less-closely related family members (Tellegen et al., 1988). A third source of evidence came from the idea that emotions, including happiness, vary, but do so around a *set point* that is fairly stable throughout life. Thus, after experiencing emotion-generating events (e.g., winning the lottery, receiving harsh criticism from one's boss), people tend to return to their basic set point (e.g., Fredrick & Loewenstein, 1999), and this seems to apply to happiness as well as current moods or affect.

Although genetic factors do play an important role in happiness, however, growing evidence points to the more optimistic conclusion that it *can* be changed. Happiness varies considerably across individuals (Diener & Lucas, 1999; Diener, Lucas, & Scollon, 2006) and there are three primary types of factors that determine happiness: the set point we mentioned earlier, life circumstances, and intentional activity (Lyubomirsky, Sheldon, & Schkade, 2005). Genetic factors, it appears, account for about 50 percent of happiness (Lykken & Tellegen, 1996; Tellegen et al., 1988) and external life circumstances account for approximately 10 percent (Diener et al., 1999). This suggests that a significant amount of happiness—up to 40 percent—is determined by a person's thoughts and actions, and is, therefore, subject to change. Interventions targeting intentional activity have been shown to produce relatively lasting effects on happiness. For example, careful research has confirmed that relatively simple behavioral interventions, such as asking participants to exercise regularly or be kind to others, and cognitive interventions, such as having people pause to count and consider their blessings, can exert lasting effects on measures of happiness (Lyubomirsky et al., 2005; Seligman, Steen, Park, & Peterson, 2005). In sum, a growing body of evidence suggests we can increase our level of happiness through interventions that target intentional activity—a term used to describe things that people think and do in their daily lives. Here are some other steps you can take to increase your personal happiness:

- **Start an upward spiral.** Experiencing positive emotions appears to be one way of "getting the ball rolling," so to speak. Positive emotions help us adopt effective ways of coping with life's unavoidable problems, and this, in turn, can generate even more positive emotions. So the hardest step, as in many tasks, may be the first: Once you begin experiencing positive feelings, it may quickly become easier to experience more of them.

- **Build close personal relationships.** Although no single factor can grant you personal happiness, it is clear that one of the most important ingredients in being happy is having good, mutually supportive relations with friends, family members, and romantic partners—knowing that we have others who care about us and will be there for us if we need them. Developing and maintaining good relationships requires a lot of hard work and may involve joining several groups, but the rewards appear to make this effort well worthwhile. In fact, this may be the single most important thing you can do to increase your own happiness. So start thinking more about the people who are important to you and how you can make them happy. The result may be a major boost to your own life satisfaction.

- **Build personal skills that contribute to being happy.** Happy people possess a number of personal characteristics that contribute to their happiness. These include being friendly and outgoing (extroverted), agreeable (i.e., approaching others with the belief that you will like and trust them), and emotionally stable. So figure out where you stand on these dimensions, and then begin working on them—preferably with the help of close friends.

- **Stop doing counterproductive things.** Because everyone wants to be happy, we all take many steps to enhance our positive emotions. Some of these—like the ones listed in this feature—are helpful. Others (e.g., abusing drugs, worrying about anything and everything, trying to be perfect, setting impossible goals for yourself) are

job satisfaction
Attitudes individuals hold concerning their jobs.

optimum level of well-being theory
A theory suggesting that for any specific task, there is an optimum level of subjective well-being. Up to this point, performance increases, but beyond it, performance on the task declines.

not. They may work temporarily (see Chapter 10 for more discussion), but in the long run, they will not contribute to your personal happiness. So start now to eliminate them from your life! And may you soon become one of those fortunate, very happy people! (Happiness is clearly a desirable state, but can people be *too* happy? Can too much happiness have a serious "downside?" For information on this possibility, please see the section "EMOTIONS AND PERSONAL HAPPINESS: Is It Possible to Be *Too* Happy?", below.)

EMOTIONS *and* PERSONAL HAPPINESS

Is It Possible to Be *Too* Happy?

Happiness is certainly one of the goals most people seek. And as noted earlier, it confers important benefits in terms of success and achievement, personal relationships, and health. But is it possible for people to be *too* happy? Initially, you might be tempted to answer "No! The more the better!" But a basic principle of life is that there can, sometimes, be too much of a good thing. For instance, have you ever heard the expression "Too smart for his/her own good?" That captures an important idea: Even characteristics or conditions that are generally beneficial can be overdone, with the result that they produce negative rather than positive outcomes. Another example: People can be *too* confident, so that they try to perform tasks or activities beyond their capabilities, and get into serious trouble.

Does this apply to personal happiness? Surprisingly, there are strong grounds for suggesting that it does. First, a theory proposed by Oishi, Diener, and Lucas (2007) concerned with the effects of well-being on task performance (**optimum level of well-being theory**) suggests the existence of a curvilinear relationship between positive affect and performance of many tasks. This theory proposes that for any specific task, there is an *optimum* (i.e., best) level of subjective well-being. This theory suggests that for any task or life domain, there is an optimum level of well-being (or in the present context, positive affect)—a level that is associated with maximum performance. Up to that point, performance on many different tasks improves, but beyond it, performance declines.

Research findings provide strong support for this prediction. Across studies involving hundreds of thousands of participants, performance on many different tasks relating to career success, income, and educational attainment, performance has been found to increase with subjective well-being, but only up to a specific point, beyond which further increments in well-being are linked to declines. As you might guess, the precise pattern of findings varies with the tasks or life domain being considered. For instance, although income, educational attainment, and career success show a curvilinear relationship with positive affect, measures of

satisfaction with social relationships do not: rather, they continue to increase with further increments in positive affect (or well-being). Oishi et al. (2007) explain these contrasting patterns as follows. For tasks related to achievement (e.g., career success, education), very high levels of positive affect may foster complacency or satisfaction, with the result that motivation and effort are reduced (Baron, Hmieleski, & Henry, in press). Thus, performance declines at very high levels of positive affect. For personal relationships, in contrast, high levels of satisfaction may contribute to happier relationships and reduced desire to seek other partners. Whatever the precise reason, existing evidence does offer support for the view that for many tasks involving achievement or accomplishment—which play a key role in entrepreneurial activity—the relationship between positive affect (as a proxy for well-being) and performance is curvilinear rather than linear in nature.

Why, specifically, would very high levels of subjective well-being lead to reductions in performance on many tasks? Several possibilities exist. For example, very high levels of subjective well-being may be related to cognitive errors, such as the ones we examined in Chapter 2: overoptimism, overconfidence, and the planning fallacy (the false belief that more can be accomplished in a given period of time than is actually true). Furthermore, it may encourage heuristic thinking (Chapter 2), which sometimes can prevent individuals from recognizing important information in a new situation. High levels of subjective well-being can also lead to complacency: When people are feeling very satisfied with their lives, they have little reason to exert effort and work hard on various tasks. Rather, they may "take it easy," since they are already quite satisfied. Research evidence indicates that all these effects actually do occur, and in a wide range of settings. For instance, entrepreneurs' success in running their new businesses increases as their dispositional tendency to feel positive or happy increases, but only up to a point; beyond that, their success (and that of their businesses) declines. And these declines appear to stem from the fact that very high levels of dispositional positive affect (i.e., a tendency to be very happy much of the time) can interfere with basic processes involved in task performance—motivation, perception, certain aspect of cognition. Finally, with respect to personal health, very high levels of subjective well-being may lead people to believe that they can "get away" with doing things that are dangerous or harmful to their health. They can eat or drink too much, engage in risky actions, and so on, and "get away with it." This kind of illusion can, of course, be very harmful and undermine the benefits

to personal health conferred by subjective well-being. For these and other reasons, very high levels of subjective well-being can have harmful as well as beneficial effects. So, in sum, growing evidence suggests that there can indeed be too much of a good thing where subjective well-being is concerned. While being a happy person is generally beneficial and helps people lead productive, satisfying lives, even this tendency can be overdone. And when it is, the results may be that being happy has a real, and important, "downside."

KEY POINTS

- Everyone seeks **personal happiness,** and systematic research on this topic suggests that it involves four basic components: global life satisfaction, satisfaction with specific life domains, a high level of positive feelings, and a minimum of negative feelings.

- Around the world, regardless of wealth, standard of living, gender, or age, a large proportion of people report that they are very happy, perhaps because human beings are adept at finding sources of happiness in their lives. One important source of happiness is close ties with friends and family—being part of an extended social network. Other factors involve having concrete goals and attaining them.

- Wealth (both personal and societal) is surprisingly not strongly related to happiness, and its relationship to positive feelings is even weaker.

- It is not wealth itself that makes people happy, but *relative* wealth—knowing that they are wealthier than others. In addition, thinking about money or wealth seems to reduce the capacity to savor (enjoy) pleasant experiences.

- Overall, what makes people happy seems to be having some of the things they want *and* wanting the things they have—valuing them.

- Personal happiness stems, in part, from genetic factors, but environmental conditions too strongly affect it, so there are many steps people can take to increase their own happiness.

- Surprisingly, it appears that people can be *too* happy—extreme levels of happiness can generate excessive levels of optimism and confidence, and so interfere with the performance of many important life tasks. In short, there appears to be an *optimum* level of happiness.

SUMMARY *and* REVIEW

- Loneliness occurs when a person has fewer and less satisfying relationships than he or she desires. One negative consequence of loneliness is depression and feelings of anxiety that may accompany it. Loneliness seems to stem from many different factors including genetic factors, an insecure attachment style, and lack of early social experiences with peers. Lonely people can often benefit from treatments designed to enhance their social skills such as seeing themselves in interaction with others, so they see what they are doing that "turns people off."

- Relationships strengthen—or fail—for many reasons. They strengthen when partners are similar to one another, have

certain personal characteristics, and both have positive implicit feelings about each other. They fail when problems develop between spouses, or when partners are too positive toward one another and thus fail to face important issues. Relationships also fail when partners adopt an exchange rather than communal perspective on the relationship, and fail to maintain at least some positive illusions about each other. When partners avoid these pitfalls and develop good balance in their relationships, the relationships often grow stronger and deeper over time.

- Achieving and maintaining good personal health is an important step on the way toward attaining a happy and fulfilling life, so social psychologists have long been interested in the role of social factors in health. One growing threat to personal health is obesity, which is increasing worldwide. Although obesity certainly involves biological and genetic factors (e.g., our inherited tendency to store extra calories as fat in "good times"), it also involves many social factors. Because of changes in social conditions, people walk less, do not eat sit-down family meals as often as in the past, and eat higher calorie meals, mainly because the portion sizes in restaurants have increased greatly over the years. Many sites on the Internet offer free advice for people who want to reduce their weight, and some of these sites do provide useful information. However, they should be approached with great caution, since they are largely free of any government controls and safeguards.

- **Stress** involves feelings of being overwhelmed—of being no longer able to cope. Stress exerts negative effects on personal health, in part because it undermines the immune system, and also because it leads us to adopt less healthy lifestyles.

- Many tactics for reducing stress exist and are well known (e.g., getting in shape, eating a healthy diet). Other ways of dealing with stress involve the social side of life, such as obtaining **social support** from one's friends and family. Although this is not always effective, it can often go a long way toward reducing stress and protecting personal health. So get—and stay—connected! Doing so may be beneficial to your health as well as your happiness.

- To make the legal system more fair, impartial, and protective of basic human rights, it is necessary to take account of the fact that it involves many aspects of social thought and behavior. For instance, the legal system often involves social influence: attorneys seek to influence jurors, and police influence defendants through many actions, often unintentionally. Such effects are readily visible in **lineups** and how they are conducted.

- Prejudice also plays an important role in legal proceedings because defendants' race, age, and physical attractiveness often strongly influence jurors' perceptions of them and judgments of innocence or guilt. Fortunately, careful deliberations by juries as they discuss available evidence tend to reduce such effects, although not, of course, in all instances.

- Everyone seeks **personal happiness,** and systematic research on this topic suggests that it involves four basic components: global life satisfaction, satisfaction with specific life domains, a high level of positive feelings, and a minimum of negative feelings.

- Around the world, regardless of wealth, standard of living, gender, or age, a large proportion of people report that they are very happy, perhaps because human beings are adept at finding sources of happiness in their lives. One important source of happiness is close ties with friends and family—being part of an extended social network. Other factors involve having concrete goals and attaining them. Wealth (both personal and societal) is surprisingly not strongly related to happiness, and its relationship to positive feelings is even weaker. It is not wealth itself that makes people happy, but *relative* wealth—knowing that they are wealthier than others. In addition, thinking about money or wealth seems to reduce the capacity to savor (enjoy) pleasant experiences. Overall, what makes people happy seems to be having some of the things they want *and* wanting the things they have—valuing them. Personal happiness stems, in part, from genetic factors, but environmental conditions too strongly affect it, so there are many steps people can take to increase their own happiness. Surprisingly, it appears that people can be *too* happy—extreme levels of happiness can generate excessive levels of optimism and confidence, and so interfere with the performance of many important life tasks. In short, there appears to be an *optimum* level of happiness.

KEY TERMS

communal approach
     (p. 407)

job satisfaction (p. 424)

lineup (p. 417)

loneliness (p. 399)

optimum level of well-being theory
     (p. 426)

personal happiness (p. 420)

social support (p. 414)

stress (p. 413)

Glossary

above average effect   The tendency for people to rate themselves as above the average on most positive social attributes.

action identification   The level of interpretation we place on an action; low-level interpretations focus on the action itself, whereas higher-level interpretations focus on its ultimate goals.

actor-observer effect   The tendency to attribute our own behavior mainly to situational causes but the behavior of others mainly to internal (dispositional) causes.

additive tasks   Tasks for which the group product is the sum or combination of the efforts of individual members.

affect   Our current feelings and moods.

affective forecasts   Predictions about how we would feel about events we have not actually experienced.

aggression   Behavior directed toward the goal of harming another living being who is motivated to avoid such treatment.

anchoring and adjustment heuristic   A heuristic that involves the tendency to use a number of value as a starting point to which we then make adjustments.

asynchronous forms of communication   Unlike face-to-face communication where there is no delay, asynchronous forms such as e-mail and other forms of text messaging give people a period of time during which they can think about their response before responding.

attachment style   The degree of security experienced in interpersonal relationships. Differential styles initially develop in the interactions between infant and caregiver when the infant acquires basic attitudes about self-worth and interpersonal trust.

attitude   Evaluation of various aspects of the social world.

attitude similarity   The extent to which two individuals share the same attitudes.

attitude-to-behavior process model   A model of how attitudes guide behavior that emphasizes the influence of attitudes and stored knowledge of what is appropriate in a given situation on an individual's definition of the present situation. This definition, in turn, influences overt behavior.

attribution   The process through which we seek to identify the causes of others' behavior and so gain knowledge of their stable traits and dispositions.

autobiographical memory   Concerned with memory of the ourselves in the past, sometimes over the life course as a whole.

autokinetic phenomenon   The apparent movement of a single, stationary source of light in a dark room. Often used to study the emergence of social norms and social influence.

automatic processing   This occurs when, after extensive experience with a task or type of information, we reach the stage where we can perform the task or process the information in a seemingly effortless, automatic, and non-conscious manner.

availability heuristic   A strategy for making judgments on the basis of how easily specific kinds of information can be brought to mind.

balance theory   The formulations of Heider and of Newcomb that specify the relationships among (1) an individual's liking for another person, (2) his or her attitude about a given topic, and (3) the other person's attitude about the same topic. Balance (liking plus agreement) results in a positive emotional state. Imbalance (liking plus disagreement) results in a negative state and a desire to restore balance. Nonbalance (disliking plus either agreement or disagreement) leads to indifference.

bargaining (negotiation)   A process in which opposing sides exchange offers, counteroffers, and concessions, either directly or through representatives.

body language   Cues provided by the position, posture, and movement of others' bodies or body parts.

bona fide pipeline   A technique that uses priming to measure implicit racial attitudes.

brainstorming   A process in which people meet as a group to generate new ideas freely.

bullying   A pattern of behavior in which one individual is chosen as the target of repeated aggression by one or more others; the target person (the victim) generally has less power than those who engage in aggression (the bullies).

catharsis hypothesis   The view that providing angry people with an opportunity to express their aggressive impulses in relatively safe ways will reduce their tendencies to engage in more harmful forms of aggression.

central route to persuasion   Attitude change resulting from systematic processing of information presented in persuasive messages.

classical conditioning   A basic form of learning in which one stimulus, initially neutral, acquires the capacity to evoke reactions through repeated pairing with another stimulus. In a sense, one stimulus becomes a signal for the presentation or occurrence of the other.

close friendship   A relationship in which two people spend a great deal of time together, interact in a variety of situations, and provide mutual emotional support.

cognitive dissonance   An internal state that results when individuals notice inconsistency between two or more attitudes or between their attitudes and their behavior.

cohesiveness (Chapter 8)   The extent to which we are attracted to a social group and want to belong to it.

cohesiveness (Chapter 11)   All forces (factors) that cause group members to remain in the group.

collective guilt   The emotion that can be experienced when we are confronted with the harmful actions done by our ingroup against an outgroup. It is most likely to be experienced when the harmful actions are seen as illegitimate.

collectivism   Groups in which the norm is to maintain harmony among group members, even if doing so might entail some personal costs.

common ingroup identity model   A theory suggesting that to the extent individuals in different groups view themselves as members of a single social entity, intergroup bias will be reduced.

common-bond groups   Groups that tend to involve face-to-face interaction and in which the individual members are bonded to each other.

common-identity groups   Face-to-face interaction is often absent, and the members are linked together via the category as a whole rather than each other.

communal approach   In the context of long-term relationships, a principle suggesting that each partner should try to meet the other's needs, and *not* seek to balance the benefits that each receives from the relationship.

companionate love   Love that is based on friendship, mutual attraction, shared interests, respect, and concern for one another's welfare.

compliance   A form of social influence involving direct requests from one person to another.

conditioned stimulus   The stimulus that comes to stand for or signal a prior unconditioned stimulus.

conditions of uncertainty   Where the "correct" answer is difficult to know or would take a great deal of effort to determine.

conflict   A process in which individuals or groups perceive that others have taken or will soon take actions incompatible with their own interests.

conformity   A type of social influence in which individuals change their attitudes or behavior to adhere to existing social norms.

consensus   The extent to which other people react to some stimulus or even in the same manner as the person we are considering.

consistency   The extent to which an individual responds to a given stimulus or situation in the same way on different occasions (i.e., across time).

consummate love   In Sternberg's triangular model of love, a complete and ideal love that combines intimacy, passion, and decision (commitment).

contact hypothesis   The view that increased contact between members of various social groups can be effective in reducing prejudice between them.

cooperation   Behavior in which group members work together to attain shared goals.

correlational method   A method of research in which a scientist systematically observes two or more variables to determine whether changes in one are accompanied by changes in the other.

correspondence bias (fundamental attribution error)   The tendency to explain others' actions as stemming from dispositions even in the presence of clear situational causes.

correspondent inference   A theory describing how we use others' behavior as a basis for inferring their stable dispositions.

counterfactual thinking   The tendency to imagine other outcomes in a situation than the ones that actually occurred ("What might have been").

cultures of honor   Cultures in which there are strong norms indicating that aggression is an appropriate response to insults to one's honor.

cyberbullying   Bullying (repeated assaults against specific target persons) occurring in chatrooms and other Internet locations.

deadline technique   A technique for increasing compliance in which target people are told that they have only limited time to take advantage of some offer or to obtain some item.

debriefing   Procedures at the conclusion of a research session in which participants are given full information about the nature of the research and the hypothesis or hypotheses under investigation.

deception   A technique whereby researchers withhold information about the purposes or procedures of a study from people participating in it.

decision making   Processes involved in combining and integrating available information to choose one out of several possible courses of action.

decision/commitment   In Sternberg's triangular model of love, these are the cognitive processes involved in deciding that you love another person and are committed to maintain the relationship.

defensive helping   Help given to members of outgroups to reduce the threat they pose to the status or distinctiveness of one's own ingroup.

deindividuation   A psychological state characterized by reduced self-awareness brought on by external conditions, such as being an anonymous member of a large crowd.

dependent variable   The variable that is measured in an experiment.

descriptive norms   Norms simply indicating what most people do in a given situation.

diffusion of responsibility   A principle suggesting that the greater the number of witnesses to an emergency the less likely victims are to receive help. This is because each bystander assumes that someone else will do it.

discrimination   Differential (usually negative) behaviors directed toward members of different social groups.

dismissing attachment style   A style characterized by high self-esteem and low interpersonal trust. This is a conflicted and somewhat insecure style in which the individual feels that he or she deserves a close relationship but is frustrated because of mistrust of potential partners. The result is the tendency to reject the other person at some point in the relationship to avoid being the one who is rejected.

distinctiveness The extent to which an individual responds in the same manner to different stimuli or events.

distraction conflict theory A theory suggesting that social facilitation stems from the conflict produced when individuals attempt, simultaneously, to pay attention to the other people present and to the task being performed.

distributive justice (fairness) Refers to individuals' judgments about whether they are receiving a fair share of available rewards—a share proportionate to their contributions to the group or any social relationship.

door-in-the-face technique A procedure for gaining compliance in which requesters begin with a large request and then, when this is refused, retreat to a smaller one (the one they actually desired all along).

downward social comparison A comparison of the self to another who does less well than or is inferior to us.

drive theories (of aggression) Theories suggesting that aggression stems from external conditions that arouse the motive to harm or injure others. The most famous of these is the frustration-aggression hypothesis.

ego-depletion (Chapter 4) The lowered capacity to exert subsequent self-control following earlier efforts to exert self-control. Performance decrements are typically observed when people's ego strength has been depleted by prior efforts at self-control.

ego-depletion (Chapter 5) When our capacity to self-regulate has been reduced because of prior expenditures of limited resources.

elaboration-likelihood model (ELM) A theory suggesting that persuasion can occur in either of two distinct ways, differing in the amount of cognitive effort or elaboration the message receives.

empathic joy hypothesis The view that helpers respond to the needs of a victim because they want to accomplish something, and doing so is rewarding in and of itself.

empathy Emotional reactions that are focused on or oriented toward other people and include feelings of compassion, sympathy, and concern.

empathy-altruism hypothesis The suggestion that some prosocial acts are motivated solely by the desire to help someone in need.

entitativity The extent to which a group is perceived as being a coherent entity.

essence Typically some biologically based feature that is used to distinguish one group and another; frequently can serve as justification for the differential treatment of those groups.

evaluation apprehension Concern over being evaluated by others. Such concern can increase arousal and so contribute to social facilitation effects.

evolutionary psychology A new branch of psychology that seeks to investigate the potential role of genetic factors in various aspects of human behavior.

excitation transfer theory A theory suggesting that arousal produced in one situation can persist and intensify emotional reactions occurring in later situations.

experimentation (experimental method) A method of research in which one or more factors (the independent variables) are systematically changed to determine whether such variations affect one or more other factors (dependent variables).

explicit attitudes Consciously accessible attitudes that are controllable and easy to report.

fear appeals Attempting to change people's behaviors by use of a message that induces fear.

fearful-avoidant attachment style A style characterized by low self-esteem and low interpersonal trust. This is the most insecure and least adaptive attachment style.

feeling rules Expectations about the appropriate emotions to display or express.

foot-in-the-door technique A procedure for gaining compliance in which requesters begin with a small request and then, when this is granted, escalate to a larger one (the one they actually desired all along).

forewarning Advance knowledge that one is about to become the target of an attempt at persuasion. Forewarning often increases resistance to the persuasion that follows.

frustration-aggression hypothesis The suggestion that frustration is a very powerful determinant of aggression.

fundamental attribution error (correspondence bias) The tendency to overestimate the impact of dispositional cues on others' behavior.

gender stereotypes Stereotypes concerning the traits possessed by females and males and that distinguish the two genders from each other.

general aggression model (GAM) A modern theory of aggression suggesting that aggression is triggered by a wide range of input variables that influence arousal, affective stages, and cognitions.

glass ceiling Barriers based on attitudinal or organizational bias that prevent qualified females from advancing to top-level positions.

glass cliff When women and minorities are seen as better leaders because of their ability to manage crises. They are more likely to be selected as leader when the situation contains more risk.

glass cliff effect Choosing women for leadership positions that are risky, precarious, or when the outcome is more likely to result in failure.

group A collection of people who are perceived to be bonded together in a coherent unit to some degree.

group polarization The tendency of group members to shift toward a more extreme position than initially held by those individuals as a result of group discussion.

groupthink   The tendency of the members of highly cohesive groups to assume that their decisions can't be wrong, that all members must support the group's decisions strongly, and that information contrary to it should be ignored.

habit   Repeatedly performing a specific behavior so responses become relatively automatic whenever that situation is encountered.

heuristic processing   Processing of information in a peruasive message that involves the use of simple rules of thumb or mental shortcuts.

heuristics   Simple rules for making complex decisions or drawing inferences in a rapid manner and seemingly effortless manner.

hooliganism   Negative stereotype about how people behave in crowds at sporting events, especially applied to incidents involving England's soccer fans.

hostile aggression   Aggression in which the prime objective is inflicting some kind of harm on the victim.

hypocrisy   Publicly advocating some attitudes or behavior and then acting in a way that is inconsistent with these attitudes or behavior.

hypothesis   An as yet unverified prediction concerning some aspect of social behavior or social thought.

ideology   The philosophical and political values that govern a group.

illusion of truth effect   The mere repetition of information creates a sense of familiarity and more positive attitudes.

implementation plan   A plan for how to implement our intentions to carry out some action.

implicit associations   Links between group membership and trait associations or evaluations that the perceiver may be unaware of. They can be activated automatically based on the group membership of a target.

implicit attitudes   Unconscious associations between objects and evaluative responses.

implicit personality theories   Beliefs about what traits or characteristics tend to go together.

implicit self-esteem   Feelings about the self of which we are not consciously aware.

impression formation   The process through which we form impressions of others.

impression management (self-presentation)   Efforts by individuals to produce favorable first impressions on others.

incidental feelings   Those feelings induced separately or before a target is encountered; as a result, those feelings are irrelevant to the group being judged but can still affect judgments of the target.

independent variable   The variable that is systematically changed (i.e., varied) in an experiment.

individualism   Groups where the norm is to stand out and be different from others; individual variability is expected and disagreement among members is tolerated.

information overload   Instances in which our ability to process information is exceeded.

informational social influence   Social influence based on the desire to be correct (i.e., to possess accurate perceptions of the social world).

informed consent   A procedure in which research participants are provided with as much information as possible about a research project before deciding whether to participate in it.

ingratiation   When we try to make others like us by conveying that we like them; praising others to flatter them.

injunctive norms   Norms specifying what ought to be done; what is approved or disapproved behavior in a given situation.

instrumental aggression   Aggression in which the primary goal is not to harm the victim but rather attainment of some other goal—for example, access to valued resources.

instrumental conditioning   A basic form of learning in which responses that lead to positive ourcomes or which permit avoidance of negative outcomes are strengthened.

intergroup comparisons   Judgments that result from comparisons between our group and another group.

interpersonal trust   An attitudinal dimension underlying attachment styles that involves the belief that other people are generally trustworthy, dependable, and reliable as opposed to the belief that others are generally untrustworthy, undependable, and unreliable. This is the most successful and most desirable attachment style.

intimacy   In Sternberg's triangular model of love, the closeness felt by two people—the extent to which they are bonded.

intragroup comparisons   Judgments that result from comparisons between individuals who are members of the same group.

introspection   To privately contemplate "who we are." It is a method for attempting to gain self knowledge.

introspection illusion   Our belief that social influence plays a smaller role in shaping our own actions than it does in shaping the actions of others.

job satisfaction   Attitudes individuals hold concerning their jobs.

kin selection theory   A theory suggesting that a key goal for all organisms—including human beings—is getting our genes into the next generation; one way in which individuals can reach this goal is by helping others who share their genes.

less-leads-to-more effect   The fact that offering individuals small rewards for engaging in counterattitudinal behavior often produces more dissonance, and so more attitude change, than offering them larger rewards.

lineup   A procedure in which witnesses to a crime are shown several people, one or more of whom may be suspects in a case, and asked to identify those that they recognize as the person who committed the crime.

linguistic style   Aspects of speech apart from the meaning of the words employed.

loneliness   The unpleasant emotional and cognitive state based on desiring close relationships but being unable to attain them.

love   A combination of emotions, cognitions, and behaviors that often play a crucial role in intimate relationships.

low-ball procedure   A technique for gaining compliance in which an offer or deal is changed to make it less attractive to the target person after this person has accepted it.

magical thinking   Thinking involving assumptions that don't hold up to rational scrutiny—for example, the belief that things that resemble one another share fundamental properties.

matching hypotheses   The idea that although we would prefer to obtain extremely attractive romantic partners, we generally focus on obtaining ones whose physical beauty is about the same as our own.

mediating varible   A variable that is affected by an independent variable and then influences a dependent variable. Mediating variables help explain why or how specific variables influence social behavior or thought in certain ways.

mere exposure   By having seen before, but not necessarily remembering having done so, attitudes toward an object can be formed.

metaphor   A linguistic device that relates or draws a comparison between one abstract concept and another dissimilar concept.

meta-stereotypes   Beliefs about how one's group is viewed by another group; these are often negative.

microexpressions   Fleeting facial expressions lasting only a few tenths of a second.

minimal groups   When we are categorized into different groups based on some "minimal" criteria we tend to favor others who are categorized in the same group as ourselves compared to those categorized as members of a different group.

modern racism   More subtle beliefs than blatant feelings of superiority. It consists primarily of thinking minorities are seeking and receiving more benefits than they deserve and a denial that discrimination affects their outcomes.

mood congruence effects   The fact that we are more likely to store or remember positive information when in a positive mood and negative information when in a negative mood.

mood dependent memory   The fact that what we remember while in a given mood may be determined, in part, by what we learned when previously in that mood.

moral disengagement   No longer seeing sanctioning as necessary for perpetrating harm that has been legitimized.

multicultural perspective   A focus on understanding the cultural and ethnic factors that influence social behavior.

need for affiliation   The basic motive to seek and maintain interpersonal relationships.

negative interdependence   A situation where if one person obtains a desired outcome, others cannot obtain it.

negative-state relief model   The proposal that prosocial behavior is motivated by the bystander's desire to reduce his or her own uncomfortable negative emotions or feelings.

noncommon effects   Effects produced by a particular cause that could not be produced by any other apparent cause.

nonverbal communication   Communication between individuals that does not involve the content of spoken language. It relies instead on an unspoken language of facial expressions, eye contact, and body language.

normative focus theory   A theory suggesting that norms will influence behavior only to the extent that they are focal for the people involved at the time the behavior occurs.

normative social influence   Social influence based on the desire to be liked or accepted by other people.

norms   Rules or expectations within a group concerning how its members should (or should not) behave.

obedience   A form of social influence in which one person simply orders one or more others to perform some action(s).

objectification of females   Regarding them as mere bodies that exist for the pleasure of others.

objective scales   Those with measurement units that are tied to external reality so that they mean the same thing regardless of category membership (e.g., dollars earned, feet and inches, chosen or rejected).

observational learning   A basic form of learning in which individuals acquire new forms of behavior as a result of observing others.

optimistic bias   Our predisposition to expect things to turn out well overall.

optimum level of well-being theory   A theory suggesting that for any specfic task, there is an optimum level of subjective well-being. Up to this point, performance increases, but beyond it, performance on the task declines

overconfidence accuracy   The tendency to have more confidence in the accuracy of our own judgments than is reasonable.

passion   In Sternberg's triangular model of love, the sexual motives and sexual excitement associated with a couple's relationship.

passionate love   An intense and often unrealistic emotional response to another person. When this emotion is experienced, it is usually perceived as an indication of true love, but to outside observers it appears to be infatuation.

peripheral route to persuasion   Attitude change that occurs in response to peripheral persuasion cues, which is often based on information concerning the expertise or status of would-be persuaders.

perseverance effect   The tendency for beliefs and schemas to remain unchanged even in the face of contradictory information.

personal happiness   Refers to subjective well-being, which involves global life satisfaction, satisfaction with specific life domains, frequent positive feelings, and relatively few negative feelings.

personal-versus-social identity continuum   At the personal level, the self is thought of as a unique individual, whereas at the social identity level, the self is seen as a member of a group.

persuasion   Efforts to change others' attitudes through the use of various kinds of messages.

physical attractiveness The combination of characteristics that are evaluated as beautiful or handsome at the positive extreme and as unattractive at the negative extreme.

planning fallacy The tendency to make optimistic predictions concerning how long a given task will take for completion.

playing hard to get A technique that can be used for increasing compliance by suggesting that a person or object is scarce and hard to obtain.

pluralistic ignorance (Chapter 5) When we collectively misunderstand what attitudes others hold and believe erroneously that others have different attitudes than us.

pluralistic ignorance (Chapter 9) Refers to the fact that because none of the bystanders respond to an emergency, no one knows for sure what is happening and each depends on the others to interpret the situation.

politicized collective identity Recognizing shared grievances and engaging in a power struggle on behalf of one's devalued group.

possible selves Image of how we might be in the future—either a "dreaded" potential to be avoided or "desired" potential that can be strived for.

prejudice Negative emotional responses based on group membership.

preoccupied attachment style A style characterized by low self-esteem and high interpersonal trust. This is a conflicted and somewhat insecure style in which the individual strongly desires a close relationship but feels that he or she is unworthy of the partner and is thus vulnerable to being rejected.

priming A situation that occurs when stimuli or events increase the availability in memory or consciousness of specific types of information held in memory.

procedural justice Judgments concerning the fairness of the procedures used to distribute available rewards among group members.

proportion of similarity The number of specific indicators that two people are similar divided by the number of specific indicators that two people are similar plus the number of specific indicators that they are dissimilar.

prosocial behavior Actions by individuals that help others with no immediate benefit to the helper.

prototype Summary of the common attributes possessed by members of a category.

provocation Actions by others that tend to trigger aggression in the recipient, often because they are perceived as stemming from malicious intent.

proximity In attraction research, the physical closeness between two individuals with respect to where they live, where they sit in a classroom, where they work, and so on. The smaller the physical distance, the greater the probability that the two people will come into repeated contact experiencing repeated exposure to one another, positive affect, and the development of mutual attraction.

punishment Procedures in which aversive consequences are delivered to individuals when they engage in specific actions.

random assignment of participants to experimental conditions A basic requirement for conducting valid experiments. According to this principle, research participants must have an equal chance of being exposed to each level of the independent variable

reactance Negative reactions to threats to one's personal freedom. Reactance often increases resistance to persuasion and can even produce negative attitude change or opposite to what was intended.

realistic conflict theory The view that prejudice stems from direct competition between various social groups over scarce and valued resources.

recategorization Shifts in the boundaries between our ingroup ("us") and some outgroup ("them"). As a result of such recategorization, people formerly viewed as outgroup members may now be viewed a belonging to the ingroup and consequently are viewed more positively.

reference groups Groups of people with whom we identify and whose opinions we value.

relationships Our social ties with other persons, ranging from casual acquaintance or passing friendships, to intense, long-term relationships such as marriage or lifetime friendships.

repeated exposure effect Zajonc's finding that frequent contact with any mildly negative, neutral, or positive stimulus results in an increasingly positive evaluation of that stimulus.

representativeness heuristic A strategy for making judgments based on the extent to which current stimuli or events resemble other stimuli or categories.

repulsion hypothesis Rosenbaum's provocative proposal that attraction is not increased by similar attitudes but is simply decreased by dissimilar attitudes. This hypothesis is incorrect as stated, but it is true that dissimilar attitudes tend to have negative effects that are stronger than the positive effects of similar attitudes.

risk averse We weigh possible losses more heavily than equivalent potential gains. As a result, we respond more negatively to changes that are framed as potential losses than positively to changes that are framed as potential gains.

roles The set of behaviors that individuals occupying specific positions within a group are expected to perform.

salience When someone or some object stands out from its background or is the focus of attention.

schemas Mental frameworks centering on a specific theme that help us to organize social information.

schism Splintering of a group into distinct factions following an ideological rift among members.

secure attachment style A style characterized by high self-esteem and high interpersonal trust. This is the most successful and most desirable attachment style.

selective avoidance   A tendency to direct attention away from information that challenges existing attitudes. Such avoidance increases resistance to persuasion.

self-affirmation   Refers to the tendency to respond to a threat to one's self-concept by affirming one's competence in another area (different from the threat).

self-construal   How we characterize ourselves, which can vary depending on what identity is salient at any given moment.

self-control   Achieved by refraining from actions we like and instead performing actions we prefer not to do as a means of achieving a long-term goal.

self-deprecating   Putting ourselves down or implying that we are not as good as someone else.

self-esteem   The degree to which we perceive ourselves positively or negatively; our overall attitude toward ourselves. It can be measured explicitly or implicitly.

self-evaluation maintenance model   This perspective suggests that to maintain a positive view of ourselves, we distance ourselves from others who perform better than we do on valued dimensions and move closer to others who perform worse than us. This view suggests that doing so will protect our self-esteem.

self-promotion   Attempting to present ourselves to others as having positive attributes.

self-regulation   Limited capacity to engage our willpower and control our own thinking and emotions.

self-serving bias   The tendency to attribute positive outcomes to internal causes (e.g., one's own traits or characteristics) but negative outcomes or events to external causes (e.g., chance, task difficulty).

self-verification perspective   Theory that addresses the processes by which we lead others to agree with our views of ourselves; wanting others to agree with how we see ourselves.

shifting standards   When we use one group as the standard but shift to use another group as the comparison standard when judging members of a different group.

similarity-dissimilarity effect   The consistent finding that people respond positively to indications that another person is similar to themselves and negatively to indications that another person is dissimilar from themselves.

singlism   Negative stereotyping and discrimination directed toward people who are single.

social capital   The number of social ties each person has to others; typically these are connections people can draw on for knowledge, assistance, or other social goods.

social cognition   The manner in which we interpret, analyze, remember, and use information about the social world.

social comparison   The process through which we compare ourselves to others to determine whether our view of social reality is, or is not, correct.

social comparison theory   Festinger (1954) suggested that people compare themselves to others because for many domains and attributes there is no objective yardstick to evaluate ourselves against, and other people are therefore highly informative.

social dilemmas   Situations in which each person can increase their individual gains by acting in one way, but if all (or most) people do the same thing, the outcomes experienced by all are reduced.

social embeddedness   Having a sense of that you know other persons because you know their reputations, often by knowing other people they know too.

social exclusion   Conditions in which individuals feel that they have been excluded from some social group.

social identity theory (Chapter 4)   Addresses how we respond when our group identity is salient. Suggests that we will move closer to positive others with whom we share an identity but distance from other ingroup members who perform poorly or otherwise make our social identity negative.

social identity theory (Chapter 6)   A theory concerned with the consequences of perceiving ourselves as a member of a social group and identifying with it.

social influence   Efforts by one or more persons to change the behavior, attitudes, or feelings of one or more others.

social learning   The process through which we acquire new information, forms of behavior, or attitudes from other people.

social learning view (of prejudice)   The view prejudice is acquired through direct and vicarious experiences in much the same manner as other attitudes.

social loafing   Reductions in motivation and effort when individuals work in a group compared to when they work individually.

social networks   Composed of individuals with whom we have interpersonal relationships and interact with on a regular basis.

social norms   Rules indicating how individuals are expected to behave in specific situations.

social perception   The process through which we seek to know and understand other people.

social support   Drawing on the emotional and task resources provided by others as a means of coping with stress.

staring   A form of eye contact in which one person continues to gaze steadily at another regardless of what the recipient does.

status   The individual's position or rank within the group.

stereotype threat   Can occur when people believe that they might be judged in light of a negative stereotype about their group or that, because of their performance, they may in some way confirm a negative stereotype of their group.

stereotypes   Beliefs about social groups in terms of the traits or characteristics that they are believed to share. Stereotypes are cognitive frameworks that influence the processing of social information.

stress   Our response to events that disrupt, or threaten to disrupt, our physical or psychological functioning.

subjective scales   Response scales that are open to interpretation and lack an externally grounded referent, including scales labeled from good to bad or weak to strong. They are said to be subjective because they can take on different meanings depending on the group membership of the person being evaluated.

subliminal conditioning Classical conditioning of attitudes by exposure to stimuli that are below individuals' threshold of conscious awareness.

subtype A subset of a group that is not consistent with the stereotype of the group as a whole.

superordinate goals (Chapter 6) Those that can only be achieved by cooperation between groups.

superordinate goals (Chapter 11) Goals that both sides to a conflict seek and that tie their interests together rather than driving them apart.

survey method A method of research in which a large number of people answer questions about their attitudes or behavior.

symbolic social influence Social influence resulting from the mental representation of others or our relationships with them.

systematic observation A method of research in which behavior is systematically observed and recorded.

systematic processing Processing of information in a persuasive message that involves careful consideration of message content and ideas.

TASS model The traits as situational sensitivities model. A view suggesting that many personality traits function in a threshold-like manner, influencing behavior only when situations evoke them.

teasing Provoking statements that call attention to the target's flaws and imperfections.

terror management Our efforts to come to terms with certainty of our own death and its unsettling implications.

that's-not-all technique A technique for gaining compliance in which requesters offer additional benefits to target people before they have decided whether to comply with or reject specific requests.

theory of planned behavior An extension of the theory of reasoned action, suggesting that in addition to attitudes toward a given behavior and subjective norms about it, individuals also consider their ability to perform the behavior.

theory of reasoned action A theory suggesting that the decision to engage in a particular behavior is the result of a rational process in which behavioral options are considered, consequences or outcomes of each are evaluated, and a decision is reached to act or not to act. That decision is then reflected in behavioral intentions, which strongly influence overt behavior.

thin slices Refers to small amounts of information about others we use to form first impressions of them.

threat It primarily concerns fear that our group interests will be undermined or our self-esteem is in jeopardy.

tokenism Tokenism can refer to hiring based on group membership. It can concern a numerically infrequent presence of members of a particular category or it can refer to instances where individuals perform trivial positive actions for members of out-groups that are later used as an excuse for refusing more meaningful beneficial actions for members of these groups.

transactional justice Refers to the extent to which people who distribute rewards explain or justify their decisions and show respect and courtesy to those who receive the rewards.

triangular model of love Sternberg's conceptualization of love relationships.

type A behavior pattern A pattern consisting primarily of high levels of competitiveness, time urgency, and hostility.

type B behavior pattern A pattern consisting of the absence of characteristics associated with the type A behavior pattern.

unconditioned stimulus A stimulus that evokes a positive or negative response without substantial learning.

unpriming Refers to the fact that the effects of the schemas tend to persist until they are somehow expressed in thought or behavior and only then do their effects decrease.

unrequited love Love felt by one person for another who does not feel love in return.

upward social comparison A comparison of the self to another who does better than or is superior to us.

zero-sum outcomes Those that only one person or group can have. So, if one group gets them, the other group can't.

Ackerman, J. M., & Kenrick, D. T. (2009). Cooperative courtship: Helping friends raise and raze relationships barriers. *Personality and Social Psychology Bulletin, 35,* 1285–1300.

Adam, H., Shirako, A., & Maddux, W. W. (2010). Cultural variance in the interpersonal effects of anger in negotiations. *Psychological Science, 21,* 882–889.

Adams, G., Biernat, M., Branscombe, N. R., Crandall, C. S., & Wrightsman, L. S. (2008). Beyond prejudice: Toward a sociocultural psychology of racism and oppression. In *Commemorating Brown: The social psychology of racism and discrimination* (pp. 215–246). Washington, DC: American Psychological Association.

Adams, J. S. (1965). Inequity in social exchange. In L. Berkowitz (Ed.), *Advances in experimental social psychology* (Vol. 2, pp. 267–299). New York: Academic Press.

Adarves-Yorno, I., Postmes, T., & Haslam, S. A. (2007). Creative innovation or crazy irrelevance? The contribution of group norms and social identity to creative behavior. *Journal of Experimental Social Psychology, 43,* 410–416.

Aggarwal, P., & O'Brien, C. L. (2008). Social loafing on group projects: Structural antecedents and effect on student satisfaction. *Journal of Marketing Education, 30,* 255–264.

Ajzen, I. (1987). Attitudes, traits, and actions: Dispositional prediction of behavior in personality and social psychology. In L. Berkowitz (Ed.), *Advances in experimental social psychology* (Vol. 20). San Diego, CA: Academic Press.

Ajzen, I. (1991). The theory of planned behavior: Special issue: Theories of cognitive self-regulation. *Organizational Behavior and Human Decision Processes, 50,* 179–211.

Ajzen, I. (2001). Nature and operation of attitudes. *Annual Review of Psychology, 52,* 27–58.

Ajzen, I., & Fishbein, M. (2005). The influence of attitudes on behavior. In D. Albarracin, B. T. Johnson, & M. P. Zanna (Eds.), *The handbook of attitudes* (pp. 173–221). Mahwah, NJ: Lawrence Erlbaum.

Ajzen, I., & Fishbein, M. (1980). *Understanding attitudes and predicting social behavior.* Englewood Cliffs, NJ: Prentice-Hall.

Akerlof, G. A., & Shiller, R. J. (2009). *Animal spirits: How human psychology drives the economy, and why it matters for global capitalism.* Princeton, NJ: Princeton University Press.

Alagna, F. J., Whitcher, S. J., & Fisher, J. D. (1979). Evaluative reactions to interpersonal touch in a counseling interview. *Journal of Counseling Psychology, 26,* 465–472.

Albarracin, D., Johnson, B. T., Fishbein, M., & Muellerleile, P. A. (2001). Theories of reasoned action and planned behavior as models of condom use: A meta-analysis. *Psychological Bulletin, 127,* 142–161.

Alicke, M. D., Vredenburg, D. S., Hiatt, M., & Govorun, O. (2001). The better than myself effect. *Motivation and Emotion, 25,* 7–22.

Allen, K. (2003). Are pets a healthy pleasure? The influence of pets on blood pressure. *Current Directions in Cognitive Science, 12,* 236–239.

Allen, K., Shykoff, B. E., & Izzo, J. L. (2001). Pet ownership, but not ACE inhibitor therapy, blunts home blood pressure responses to mental stress. *Hypertension, 38,* 815–820.

Allgeier, E. R., & Wiederman, M. W. (1994). How useful is evolutionary psychology for understanding contemporary human sexual behavior? *Annual Review of Sex Research, 5,* 218–256.

Allport, F. H. (1920). The influence of the group upon association and thought. *Journal of Experimental Psychology, 3,* 159–182.

Allport, F. H. (1924). *Social psychology.* New York: Dodd, Mead.

Allport, G. W. (1954). *The nature of prejudice.* Cambridge, MA: Addison-Wesley.

Amato, P. R. (1986). Emotional arousal and helping behavior in a real-life emergency. *Journal of Applied Social Psychology, 16,* 633–641.

American Psychiatric Association. (1994). *Diagnostic and statistical manual of mental disorders* (4th ed.). Washington, DC: American Psychiatric Association.

Ames, D. R., Flynn, F. J., & Weber, E. U. (2004). It's the thought that counts: On perceiving how helpers decide to lend a hand. *Personality and Social Psychology Bulletin, 30,* 461–474.

Ames, D. R., Kammrath, L. K., Suppes, A., & Bolger, N. (2010). Not so fast: The (not-quite-complete) dissociation between accuracy and confidence in thin-slice impressions. *Personality and Social Psychology Bulletin, 36,* 264–277.

Amichai-Hamburger, Y., Wainapel, G., & Fox, S. (2002). "On the Internet no one knows I'm an introvert:" Extroversion, neuroticism, and Internet interaction. *CyberPsychology and Behavior, 5,* 125–128.

Amiot, C. E., Terry, D. J., & Callan, V. J. (2007). Status, fairness, and social identification during an intergroup merger: A longitudinal study. *British Journal of Social Psychology, 46,* 557–577.

Anderson, C. A. (1989). Temperature and aggression: Effects on quarterly, yearly, and city rates of violent and nonviolent crime. *Journal of Personality and Social Psychology, 52,* 1161–1173.

Anderson, C. A. (1998). Does the gun pull the trigger?: Automatic priming effects of weapon pictures and weapon names. *Psychological Science, 9,* 308–314.

Anderson, C. A. (2004). The influence of media violence on youth. Paper presented at the annual convention of the Association for Psychological Science, Los Angeles, CA.

Anderson, C. A., & Anderson, K. B. (1996). Violent crime rate studies in philosophical context: A destructive testing approach to heat and Southern culture of violence effects. *Journal of Personality and Social Psychology, 70,* 740–756.

Anderson, C. A., & Bushman, B. J. (2001). Effects of violent video games on aggressive behavior, aggressive cognition, aggressive affect, physiological arousal, and prosocial behavior: A meta-analytic review of the scientific literature. *Psychological Science, 12,* 353–359.

Anderson, C. A., & Bushman, B. J. (2002). Human aggression. *Annual Review of Psychology, 53,* 27–51.

Anderson, C. A., Anderson, K. B., & Deuser, W. E. (1996). Examining an affective aggression framework: Weapon and temperature effects on aggressive thoughts, affect, and attitudes. *Personality and Social Psychology Bulletin, 22,* 366–376.

Anderson, C. A., Berkowitz, L., Donnerstein, E., Huesmann, L. R. Johnson, J., Linz, D., et al. (2003). The influence of media violence on youth. *Psychological Science in the Public Interest, 4,* 81–110.

Anderson, C. A., Berkowitz, L., Donnerstein, E., Huesmann, L. R., Johnson, J. D., Linz, D., Malamuth, N. M., & Wartella, E. (2004). The influence of media violence on youth. *Psychology in the Public Interest, 4,* 81–110.

Anderson, C. A., Bushman, B. J., & Groom, R. W. (1997). Hot years and serious and deadly assault: Empirical tests of the heat hypothesis. *Journal of Personality and Social Psychology, 73,* 1213–1223.

Anderson, C. A., Carnagey, N. L., & Eubanks, J. (2003). Exposure to violent media: The effects of songs with violent lyrics on aggressive thoughts and feelings. *Journal of Personality and Social Psychology, 84,* 960–971.

Anderson, C. A., Carnagey, N. L., Flanagan, M., Benjamin, A. J., Eubanks, J., & Valentine, J. C. (2004). Violent video games: Specific effects of violent content on aggressive thoughts and behavior. In M. Zanna (Ed.), *Advances in experimental social psychology* (Vol. 36). New York: Elsevier.

Anderson, C. A., Miller, R. S., Riger, A. L., Dill, J. C., & Sedikides, C. (1994). Behavioral and characterological attributional styles as predictors of depression and loneliness: Review, refinement, and test. *Journal of Personality and Social Psychology, 66,* 549–558.

Anderson, C. A., Shibuy, A., Uhori, N., Swing, E. I., Bushman, B. J., Sakomoto, A., et al. (2010). Violent video game effects on aggression, empathy, and prosocial behavior in Eastern and Western countries: A meta-analytic review. *Psychological Bulletin, 136,* 151–178.

Anderson, V. L. (1993). Gender differences in altruism among holocaust rescuers. *Journal of Social Behavior and Personality, 8,* 43–58.

Andreou, E. (2000). Bully/victim problems and their association with psychological constructs in 8- to 12-year-old Greek schoolchildren. *Aggressive Behavior, 26,* 49–58.

Apanovitch, A. M., McCarthy, D., & Salovey, P. (2003). Using message framing to motivate HIV testing among low-income, ethnic minority women. *Health Psychology, 22,* 60–67.

Aquino, K., Reed, A., Thau, S., & Freeman, D. (2006). A grotesque and dark beauty: How moral identity and mechanisms of moral disengagement influence cognitive and emotional reactions to war. *Journal of Experimental Social Psychology, 43,* 385–392.

Archibald, F. S., Bartholomew, K., & Marx, R. (1995). Loneliness in early adolescence: A test of the cognitive discrepancy model of loneliness. *Personality and Social Psychology Bulletin, 21,* 296–301.

Aristotle. (1932). *The rhetoric* (L. Cooper, Trans.). New York: Appleton-Century-Crofts. (Original work published c. 330 b.c.)

Arkes, H. R., & Tetlock, P. E. (2004). Attributions of implicit prejudice, or "Would Jesse Jackson 'Fail' the Implicit Association Test?" *Psychological Inquiry, 15,* 257–278.

Armor, D. A., & Taylor, S. E. (2002). When predictions fail: The dilemma of unrealistic optimism. In T. Gilovich, D. Griffin, & D. Kahneman (Eds.), *Heuristics and biases: The psychology of intuitive judgment* (pp. 334–347). New York: Cambridge University Press.

Arnes, D. R, Kammrath, L. K., Suppes, A., & Bolger, N. (2010). Not so fast: The (not-quite complete) dissociation between accuracy and confidence in thin-slice impressions. *Personality and Social Psychology Bulletin, 36,* 264–277.

Aron, A., & Westbay, L. (1996). Dimensions of the prototype of love. *Journal of Personality and Social Psychology, 70,* 535–551.

Aron, A., Aron, E. N., & Allen, J. (1998). Motivations for unreciprocated love. *Personality and Social Psychology Bulletin, 24,* 787–796.

Aron, A., Dutton, D. G., Aron, E. N., & Iverson, A. (1989). Experiences of falling in love. *Journal of Social and Personal Relationships, 6,* 243–257.

Aronoff, J., Woike, B. A., & Hyman, L. M. (1992). Which are the stimuli in facial displays of anger and happiness? Configurational bases of emotion recognition. *Journal of Personality and Social Psychology, 62,* 1050–1066.

Aronson, E., & Mills, J. S. (1959). The effect of severity of initiation on liking for a group. *Journal of Abnormal and Social Psychology, 59,* 177–181.

Aronson, J., Lustina, M. J., Good, C., Keough, K., Steele, C. M., & Brown, J. (1999). When white men can't do math: Necessary and sufficient factors in stereotype threat. *Journal of Experimental Social Psychology, 35,* 29–46.

Arriaga, X. B., Reed, J. T., Goodfriend, W., & Agnew, C. R. (2006). Relationship perceptions and persistence: Do fluctuations in perceived partner commitment undermine dating relationships? *Journal of Personality and Social Psychology, 91,* 1045–1065.

Asch, S. (1946). Forming impressions of personality. *Journal of Abnormal and Social Psychology, 41,* 258–290.

Asch, S. E. (1951). Effects of group pressure upon the modification and distortion of judgment. In H. Guetzkow (Ed.), *Groups, leadership, and men.* Pittsburgh: Carnegie.

Asch, S. E. (1955). Opinions and social pressure. *Scientific American, 193*(5), 31–35.

Asch, S. E. (1956). Studies of independence and conformity: A minority of one against unanimous majority. *Psychological Monographs, 70* (Whole No. 416).

Asch, S. E. (1959). A perspective on social psychology. In S. Koch (Ed.), *Psychology: A study of a science* (Vol. 3, pp. 363–383). New York: McGraw-Hill.

Asendorpf, J. B. (1992). A Brunswickean approach to trait continuity: Application to shyness. *Journal of Personality, 60,* 55–77.

Asher, S. R., & Paquette, J. A. (2003). Loneliness and peer relations in childhood. *Current Directions in Psychological Science, 12,* 75–78.

Ashforth, B. E., Harrison, S. H., & Corley, K. G. (2008). Identification in organizations: An examination of four fundamental questions. *Journal of Management, 34,* 325–374.

Ashmore, R. D., Solomon, M. R., & Longo, L. C. (1996). Thinking about fashion models' looks: A multidimensional approach to the structure of perceived physical attractiveness. *Personality and Social Psychology Bulletin, 22,* 1083–1104.

Avenanti, A., Sirigu, A., & Aglioti, S. M. (2010). Racial bias reduces empathic sensorimotor resonance with other-race pain. *Current Biology, 20,* 1018–1022.

Averill, J. R., & Boothroyd, P. (1977). On falling in love: Conformance with romantic ideal. *Motivation and Emotion, 1,* 235–247.

Azar, B. (1997, November). Defining the trait that makes us human. *APA Monitor, 1,* 15.

Azar, O. H. (2007). The social norm of tipping: A review. *Journal of Applied Social Psychology, 137,* 380–402.

Baas, M., De Dreu, C. K. W., Nijstad, B. A. (2008). A metaanalysis of 25 years of mood-creativity research: Hedonic tone, activation, or regulatory focus? *Psychological Bulletin, 134,* 779–806.

Back, M. D., Schmukle, S. C., & Egloff, B. (2010). Why area Narcissists so charming at first sight?: Decoding the Narcissism–popularity link at zero acquaintance. *Journal of Personality and Social Psychology, 98,* 132–145.

Back, M. J., Hopfer, J. M., Vazire, S., Gaddis, S., Schmukle, S. C., Egloff, B., & Gosling, S. D. (2010). Facebook profiles reflect actual personality, not self-idealization. *Psychological Science, 21,* 372–374.

Baddeley, A. D. (1990). *Human memory.* Boston: Allyn & Bacon.

Baker, N. V., Gregware, P. R., & Cassidy, M. A. (1999). Family killing fields: Honor rationales in the murder of women. *Violence Against Women, 5,* 164–184.

Baldwin, D. A. (2000). Interpersonal understanding fuels knowledge acquisition. *Current Directions in Psychological Science, 9,* 40–45.

Baldwin, M. W., Carrell, S. E., & Lopez, D. F. (1990). Priming relationship schemas: My advisor and the Pope are watching me from the back of my mind. *Journal of Experimental Social Psychology, 26,* 435–454.

Banaji, M., & Hardin, C. (1996). Automatic stereotyping. *Psychological Science, 7,* 136–141.

Bandura, A. (1986). Social foundations of thought and action: A social cognitive theory. Englewood Cliffs, NJ.; Prentice-Hall.

Bandura, A. (1990). Selective activation and disengagement of moral control. *Journal of Social Issues, 46,* 27–46.

Bandura, A. (1997). *Self-efficacy: The exercise of control.* New York: W. H. Freeman.

Bandura, A. (1999). Moral disengagement in the perpetration of inhumanities. *Personality and Social Psychology Review, 3,* 193–209.

Bandura, A., Ross, D., & Ross, S. (1963a). Imitation of filmmediated aggressive models. *Journal of Abnormal and Social Psychology, 66,* 3–11.

Bandura, A., Ross, D., & Ross, S. (1963b). Vicarious reinforcement and imitative learning. *Journal of Abnormal and Social Psychology, 67,* 601–607.

Bar-Tal, D. (2003). Collective memory of physical violence: Its contribution to the culture of violence. In E. Cairns & M. D. Roe (Eds.), *The role of memory in ethnic conflict* (pp. 77–93). New York: Palgrave Macmillan.

Barclay, L. J., Skarlicki, D. P., & Pugh, S. D. (2005). Exploring the role of emotions in injustice perceptions and retaliation. *Journal of Applied Psychology, 90,* 629–643.

Bargh, J. A., & Chartrand, T. L. (2000). Studying the mind in the middle: A practical guide to priming and automaticity research. In H. Reis & C. Judd (Eds.), *Handbook of research methods in social psychology* (pp. 253–285). New York: Cambridge University Press.

Bargh, J. A., Chen, M., & Burrows, L. (1996). Automaticity of social behavior: Direct effects of trait construct and stereotype activation on action. *Journal of Personality and Social Psychology, 71,* 230–234.

Bargh, J. A., Gollwitzer, P. M., Lee-Chai, A., Barndollar, K., & Trotschel, R. (2001). The automated will: Nonconscious activation and pursuit of behavioral goals. *Journal of Personality and Social Psychology, 18,* 1014–1027.

Bargh, J. A., McKenna, K. Y. A., & Fitzsimons, G. M. (2002). Can you see the real me?: Activation and expression of the "true self" on the Internet. *Journal of Social Issues, 58,* 22–48.

Barlow, F. K., Louis, W. R., & Terry, D. J. (2010). Minority report: Social identity, cognitions of rejection and intergroup anxiety predicting prejudice from one racially marginalized group towards another. *European Journal of Social Psychology, 40,* 805–818.

Baron, R. A. (1972). Aggression as a function of ambient temperature and prior anger arousal. *Journal of Personality and Social Psychology, 21,* 183–189.

Baron, R. A. (1986). Self-presentation in job interviews: When there can be "too much of a good thing." *Journal of Applied Social Psychology, 16,* 16–28.

Baron, R. A. (1990). Attributions and organizational conflict. In S. Graha & V. Folkes (Eds.), *Attribution theory: Applications to achievement, mental health, and interpersonal conflict* (pp. 185–204). Hillsdale, NJ: Erlbaum.

Baron, R. A. (1993a). Effects of interviewers' moods and applicant qualifications on ratings of job applicants. *Journal of Applied Social Psychology, 23,* 254–271.

Baron, R. A. (1993b). Reducing aggression and conflict: The incompatible response approach, or why people who feel good usually won't be bad. In G. C. Brannigan & M. R. Merrens (Eds.), *The undaunted psychologist* (pp. 203–218). Philadelphia: Temple University Press.

Baron, R. A. (1997). The sweet smell of helping: Effects of pleasant ambient fragrance on prosocial behavior in shopping malls. *Personality and Social Psychology Bulletin, 23,* 498–503.

Baron, R. A. (2008). The role of affect in the entrepreneurial process. *Academy of Management Review, 33,* 328–340.

Baron, R. A., & Richardson, D. R. (1994). *Human aggression* (2nd ed.). New York: Plenum.

Baron, R. A., & Thomley, J. (1994). A whiff of reality: Positive affect as a potential mediator of the effects of pleasant fragrances on task performance and helping. *Environment and Behavior, 26,* 766–784.

Baron, R. A., Russell, G. W., & Arms, R. L. (1985). Negative ions and behavior: Impact on mood, memory, and aggression among Type A and Type B persons. *Journal of Personality and Social Psychology, 48,* 746–754.

Baron, R. S. (1986). Distraction/conflict theory: Progress and problems. In L. Berkwoitz (Ed.), *Advances in experimental social psychology* (Vol. 19, pp. 1–40). Orlando: Academic Press.

Baron, R. S., Vandello, U. A., & Brunsman, B. (1996). The forgotten variable in conformity research: Impact of task importance on social influence. *Journal of Personality and Social Psychology, 71,* 915–927.

Baron, R.A., Hmieleski, K.M., & Henry, R.A. (In press). Entrepreneurs' dispositional positive affect: The Potential benefits—and potential costs—of being "up." *Journal of Business Venturing*

Baron, R.A., Hmieleski, K.M., & Tang, J. (In press). Entrepreneurs' dispositional positive affect and firm performance: When there can be "too much of a good thing." *Strategic Entrepreneurship Journal.*

Barreto, M., & Ellemers, N. (2005). The perils of political correctness: Responses of men and women to old-fashioned and modern sexist views. *Social Psychology Quarterly, 68,* 75–88.

Barrett, L. F., & Bliss-Moreau, E. (2009). She's emotional, he's having a bad day: Attributional explanations for emotion stereotypes. *Emotion, 9,* 649–658.

Barrick, M. R., Shaffer, J. A., & DeGrassi, S. W. (2009). What you see may not be what you get: Relationships among self-presentation tactics and ratings of interview and job performance. *Journal of Applied Psychology, 94,* 1394–1411.

Barsky, A., & Kaplan, S. A. (2007). If you feel bad, it's unfair: A quantitative synthesis of affect and organizational justice perceptions. *Journal of Applied Psychology, 92,* 286–295.

Bartholow, B. D., & Heinz, A. (2006). Alcohol and aggression without consumption: Alcohol cues, aggressive thoughts, and hostile perception bias. *Psychological Science, 17,* 30–37.

Bartholow, B. D., Bushman, B. J., & Sestir, M. A. (2006). Chronic violent video game exposure and desensitization to violence: Behavioral and event-related brain potential data. *Journal of Experimental Social Psychology, 42,* 532–539.

Bartholow, B. D., Dickter, C. L., & Sestir, M. A. (2006). Stereotype activation and control of race bias: Cognitive control of inhibition and its impairment by alcohol. *Journal of Personality and Social Psychology, 90,* 272–287.

Bartholow, B. D., Pearson, M. A., Gratton, G., & Fabiani, M. (2003). Effects of alcohol on person perception: A social cognitive neuroscience approach. *Journal of Personality and Social Psychology, 85,* 627–638.

Bassili, J. N. (2003). The minority slowness effect: Subtle inhibitions in the expression of views not shared by others. *Journal of Personality and Social Psychology, 84,* 261–276.

Batson, C. D., & Oleson, K. C. (1991). Current status of the empathy–altruism hypothesis. In M. S. Clark (Ed.), *Prosocial behavior* (pp. 62–85). Newbury Park, CA: Sage.

Batson, C. D., Ahmed, N., Yin, J., Bedell, S. J., Johnson, J. W., Templin, C. M., & Whiteside, A. (1999). Two threats to the common good: Self-interested egoism and empathy-induced altruism. *Personality and Social Psychology Bulletin, 25,* 3–16.

Batson, C. D., Batson, J. G., Todd, R. M., Brummett, B. H., Shaw, L. L., & Aldeguer, C. M. R. (1995). Empathy and the collective good: Caring for one of the others in a social dilemma. *Journal of Personality and Social Psychology, 68,* 619–631.

Batson, C. D., Duncan, B. D., Ackerman, P., Buckley, T., & Birch, K. (1981). Is empathic emotion a source of altruistic motivation? *Journal of Personality and Social Psychology, 40,* 290–302.

Batson, C. D., Early, S., & Salvarani, G. (1997). Perspective taking: Imagining how another feels versus imagining how you would feel. *Personality and Social Psychology Bulletin, 23,* 751–758.

Batson, C. D., Klein, T. R., Highberger, L., & Shaw, L. L. (1995). Immorality from empathy-induced altruism: When compassion and justice conflict. *Journal of Personality and Social Psychology, 68,* 1042–1054.

Batson, C. D., Kobrynowicz, D., Dinnerstein, J. L., Kampf, H.C., & Wilson, A. D. (1997). In a very different voice: Unmasking moral hypocrisy. *Journal of Personality and Social Psychology, 72,* 1335-1348.

Batson, C. D., Lishner, D. A., Carpenter, A., Dulin, L., Harjusola-Webb, S., Stocks, E. L., Gale, S., Hassan, O., & Sampat, B. (2003). ". . . As you would have them do unto you.": Does imagining yourself in the other's place stimulate moral action? *Personality and Social Psychology Bulletin, 29,* 1190–1201.

Batson, C.D., & Oleson, K.C. (1991). Current status of the empathy-altruism hypothesis. In M.S. Cark (Ed.), *Prosocial Behavior, 62–85.* Newbury Park, CA: Sage.

Baumeister, R. F. (1991). *Escaping the self.* New York: Basic Books.

Baumeister, R. F. (1998). The self. In D. T. Gilbert, S. T. Fiske, & G. Lindzey (Eds.), *Handbook of social psychology* (4th ed., Vol. 1, pp. 680–740). New York: McGraw-Hill.

Baumeister, R. F. (2005). *The cultural animal: Human nature, meaning, and social life.* New York: Oxford University Press.

Baumeister, R. F., & Leary, M. R. (1995). The need to belong: Desire for interpersonal attachments as a fundamental human motivation. *Psychological Bulletin, 117,* 497–529.

Baumeister, R. F., & Twenge, J. M. (2003). The social self. In T. Millon & M. J. Lerner (Eds.), *Handbook of psychology: Personality and social psychology.* (Vol. 5, pp. 327–352). New York: John Wiley.

Baumeister, R. F., & Masicampo, E. J. (2010). Conscious thought is for facilitating social and cultural interactions: How mental simulations serve the animal–culture interface. *Psychological Review, 117,* 945–971.

Baumeister, R. F., Bratslavsky, E., Finkenauer, C., & Vohs, K. D. (2001). Bad is stronger than good. *Review of General Psychology 5,* 323–370.

Baumeister, R. F., Campbell, D. J., Krueger, J. I., & Vohs, K. D. (2003). Does high self-esteem cause better performance, interpersonal success, happiness, or healthier lifestyles? *Psychological Science in the Public Interest, 4,* 1–44.

Baumeister, R. F., Campbell, J. D., Krueger, J. I., & Vohs, K. D. (2005). Exploding the self-esteem myth. *Scientific American, 292,* 84–92.

Baumeister, R. F., Heatherton, T. D., & Tice, D. M. (1994). *Losing control: How and why people fail at self-regulation.* San Diego, CA: Academic Press.

Baumeister, R. F., Twenge, J. M., & Nuss, C. K. (2002). Effects of social exclusion on cognitive processes: Anticipated aloneness reduces intelligent thought. *Journal of Personality and Social Psychology, 83,* 817–827.

Baumeister, R. F., Vohs, K. D., & Tice, D. M. (2007). The strength model of self-control. *Current Directions in Psychological Science, 16,* 351–355.

Baxter, L. A. (1990). Dialectical contradictions in relationship development. *Journal of Social and Personal Relationships, 7,* 69–88.

Becker, S. W., & Eagly, A. H. (2005). The heroism of women and men. *American Psychologist, 39,* 163–178.

Behm-Morawitz, E., & Mastro, D. (2009). The effects of the sexualization of female video game characters on gender stereotyping and female self-concept. *Sex Roles, 61,* 808–823.

Bell, B. (1993). Emotional loneliness and the perceived similarity of one's ideas and interests. *Journal of Social Behavior and Personality, 8,* 273–280.

Bell, P. A. (1992). In defense of the negative affect escape model of heat and aggression. *Psychological Bulletin, 111,* 342–346.

Bell, P. A., Greene, T. C., Fisher, J. D., & Baum, A. (2001). *Environmental psychology* (5th ed.). Belmont, CA: Wadsworth/Thomson Learning.

Ben-Porath, D. D. (2002). Stigmatization of individuals who receive psychotherapy: An interaction between help-seeking behavior and the presence of depression. *Journal of Social and Clinical Psychology, 21,* 400–413.

Benjamin, E. (1998, January 14). Storm brings out good, bad and greedy. Albany *Times Union,* pp. A1, A6.

Benoit, W. L. (1998). Forewarning and persuasion. In M. Allen & R. Priess (Eds.), *Persuasion: Advances through meta-analysis* (pp. 159–184). Cresskill, NJ: Hampton Press.

Berg, J. H., & McQuinn, R. D. (1989). Loneliness and aspects of social support networks. *Journal of Social and Personal Relationships, 6,* 359–372.

Berkowitz, L. (1989). Frustration-aggression hypothesis: Examination and reformulation. *Psychological Bulletin, 106,* 59–73.

Berkowitz, L. (1993). *Aggression: Its causes, consequences, and control.* New York: McGraw-Hill.

Berman, M., Gladue, & Taylor, S.P. (1993). The effects of hormones, Type A behavior pattern, and provocation oin aggression in men. *Motivation and Emotion, 17,* 125–138.

Bernieri, F. J., Gillis, J. S., Davis, J. M., & Grahe, J. E. (1996). Dyad rapport and the accuracy of its judgment across situations: A lens model analysis. *Journal of Personality and Social Psychology, 71,* 110–129.

Berry, D. S., & Hansen, J. S. (1996). Positive affect, negative affect, and social interaction. *Journal of Personality and Social Psychology, 71,* 796–809.

Berscheid, E., & Hatfield, E. (1974). A little bit about love. In T. L. Huston (Ed.), *Foundations of interpersonal attraction* (pp. 355–381). New York: Academic Press.

Bettencourt, B. A., & Miller, N. (1996). Gender differences in aggression as a function of provocation: A meta-analysis. *Psychological Bulletin, 119,* 422–447.

Bettencourt, B. A., Molix, L., Talley, A. E., & Sheldon, K. M. (2006). Psychological need satisfaction through social roles. In T. Postmes & J. Jetten (Eds.), *Individuality and the group: Advances in social identity* (pp. 196–214). London: Sage.

Biernat, M. (2005). *Standards and expectancies: Contrast and assimilation in judgments of self and others.* New York: Psychology Press.

Biernat, M., & Thompson, E. R. (2002). Shifting standards and contextual variation in stereotyping. *European Review of Social Psychology, 12,* 103–137.

Biernat, M., Collins, E. C., Katzarska-Miller, I., & Thompson, E. R. (2009). Race-based shifting standards and racial discrimination. *Personality and Social Psychology Bulletin, 35,* 16–28.

Biernat, M., Eidelman, S., & Fuegan, K. (2002). Judgment standards and the social self: A shifting standards perspective. In J. P. Forgas & K. D. Williams (Eds.), *The social self: Cognitive, interpersonal, and intergroup perspectives* (pp. 51–72). Philadelphia: Psychology Press.

Bies, R. J., Shapiro, D. L., & Cummings, L. L. (1988). Causal accounts and managing organizational conflict: Is it enough to say it's not my fault? *Communication Research, 15,* 381–399.

Biesanz, J.C., Human, L.J., Paquin, A.., Chan, M., Parisotto, K.L., Sarrachino, J., & Gillis, R.L. (2011). Do we klnow when our impressions of others are vlaid? Evidence for realistic accuracy awareness in first impressions of personality. *Social Psychological and Personality Science, in press.*

Bizer, G. Y., Tormala, Z. L., Rucker, D. D., & Petty, R. E. (2006). Memory-based versus on-line processing: Implications for attitude strength. *Journal of Experimental Social Psychology, 42,* 646–653.

Björkqvist, K., Österman, K., & Lagerspetz, K. M. J. (1994b). Sex differences in covert aggression among adults. *Aggressive Behavior, 20,* 27–33.

Björkqvist, K., Lagerspetz, K. M., & Kaukiainen, A. (1992). Do girls manipulate and boys fight? Developmental trends in regard to direct and indirect aggression. *Aggressive Behavior, 18,* 117–127.

Blagrove, E., & Watson, D. G. (2010). Visual marking and facial affect: Can an emotional face be ignored? *Emotion, 10,* 147–168.

Blair, I. V. (2002). The malleability of automatic stereotypes and prejudice. *Personality and Social Psychology Review, 6,* 242–261.

Blanchette, I., & Richards, A. (2010). The influence of affect on higher level cognition: A review of research on interpretation, judgement, decision making and reasoning. *Cognition and Emotion, 24,* 561–595.

Blankenship, K. L., & Wegener, D. T. (2008). Opening the mind to close it: Considering a message in light of important values increases message processing and later resistance to change. *Journal of Personality and Social Psychology, 94,* 196–213.

Blazer, D. G., Kessler, R. C., McGonagle, K. A., & Swartz, M. S. (1994). The prevalence and distribution of major depression in a national community sample: The National Comorbidity Survey. *American Journal of Psychiatry, 151,* 979–986.

Bobo, L. (1983). Whites' opposition to busing: Symbolic racism or realistic group conflict? *Journal of Personality and Social Psychology, 45,* 1196–1210.

Boden, M. T., & Berenbaum, H. (2010). The bidirectional relations between affect and belief. *Review of General Psychology, 14,* 227–239.

Bodenhausen, G. F. (1993). Emotion, arousal, and stereotypic judgment: A heuristic model of affect and stereotyping. In D. Mackie & D. Hamilton (Eds.), *Affect, cognition, and stereotyping: Intergroup processes in intergroup perception* (pp. 13–37). San Diego, CA: Academic Press.

Bodenhausen, G. V., & Hugenberg, K. (2009). Attention, perception, and social cognition. In F. Strack & J. Förster (Eds.), *Social cognition: The basis of human interaction* (pp. 1–22). Philadelphia: Psychology Press.

Boen, F., Vanbeselaere, N., & Wostyn, P. (2010). When the best become the rest: The interactive effect of premerger status and relative representation on postmerger identification and ingroup bias. *Group Processes and Intergroup Relations, 13,* 461–475.

Boer, F., Westenberg, M., McHale, S. M., Updegraff, K. A., & Stocker, C. M. (1997). The factorial structure of the Sibling Relationship Inventory (SRI) in American and Dutch samples. *Journal of Social and Personal Relationships, 14,* 851–859.

Bogard, M. (1990). Why we need gender to understand human violence. *Journal of Interpersonal Violence, 5,* 132–135.

Bolino, M. C., & Turnley, W. H. (1999). Measuring impression management in organizations: A scale development based on the Jones and Pittman taxonomy. *Organizational Research Methods, 2,* 187–206.

Bond, R., & Smith, P. B. (1996). Culture and conformity: A meta-analysis of studies using Asch's (1952b, 1956) line judgment task. *Psychological Bulletin, 119,* 111–137.

Borkenau, P., Mauer, N., Riemann, R., Spinath, F.M., & Angleitner, A. (2004). Thin slices of behavior as cues of personality and intelligence. *Journal of Personality and Social Psychology, 86,* 599–614.

Borman, W. C., Penner, L. A., Allen, T. D., & Motowidlo, S. J. (2001). Personality predictors of citizenship performance. *International Journal of Selection and Assessment, 9,* 52–69

Bornstein, R. F., & D'Agostino, P. R. (1992). Stimulus recognition and the mere exposure effect. *Journal of Personality and Social Psychology, 63,* 545–552.

Bossard, J. H. S. (1932). Residential propinquity as a factor in marriage selection. *American Journal of Sociology, 38,* 219–224.

Bosson, J. K., Haymovitz, E. L., & Pinel, E. C. (2004). When saying and doing diverge: The effects of stereotype threat on self-reported versus non-verbal anxiety. *Journal of Experimental Social Psychology, 40,* 247–255.

Bosson, J. K., Vandello, J. A., Burnaford, R., Weaver, J. R., & Wasti, S.A. (2009). Precarious manhood and displays of physical aggression. *Personality and Social Psychology Bulletin, 35,* 623–634.

Botha, M. (1990). Television exposure and aggression among adolescents: A follow-up study over 5 years. *Aggressive Behavior, 16,* 361–380.

Bothwell, R. K., Pigott, M. A., Foley, L. A., & McFatter, R. M. (2006). Racial bias in juridic judgment at private and public levels. *Journal of Applied Social Psychology, 36,* 2134–2149.

Bowlby, J. (1969). *Attachment and loss: Vol. 1. Attachment.* New York: Basic Books.

Bowlby, J. (1973). *Attachment and loss: Vol. 2. Separation.* New York: Basic Books.

Boyce, C. R., Brown, G. D. A., & Moore, S. C. (2010). Money and happiness: Rank of income income, affects life satisfaction. *Psychological Science, 21,* 471–475.

Brandon, D. P., & Hollingshead, A. B. (2007). Characterizing online groups. In A. N. Joinson, K. Y. A. McKenna, T. Postmes, & U.-D. Reips (Eds.), *The Oxford handbook of internet psychology* (pp. 105–119). New York: Oxford University Press.

Branscombe, N. R. (2004). A social psychological process perspective on collective guilt. In N. R. Branscombe & B. Doosje (Eds.), *Collective guilt: International perspectives* (pp. 320–334). New York: Cambridge University Press.

Branscombe, N. R., & Miron, A. M. (2004). Interpreting the ingroup's negative actions toward another group: Emotional reactions to appraised harm. In L. Z. Tiedens & C. W. Leach (Eds.), *The social life of emotions* (pp. 314–335). New York: Cambridge University Press.

Branscombe, N. R., & Wann, D. L. (1994). Collective self-esteem consequences of outgroup derogation when a valued social identity is on trial. *European Journal of Social Psychology, 24,* 641–657.

Branscombe, N. R., Owen, S., Garstka, T., & Coleman, J. (1996). Rape and accident counterfactuals: Who might have done otherwise and would it have changed the outcome? *Journal of Applied Social Psychology, 26,* 1042–1067.

Branscombe, N. R., Schmitt, M. T., & Harvey, R. D. (1999). Perceiving pervasive discrimination among African-Americans: Implications for group identification and well-being. *Journal of Personality and Social Psychology, 77,* 135–149.

Branscombe, N. R., Schmitt, M. T., & Schiffhauer, K. (2007). Racial attitudes in response to thoughts of White privilege. *European Journal of Social Psychology, 37,* 203–215.

Braza, P., Braza, F., Carreras, M. R., & Munoz, J. M. (1993). Measuring the social ability of preschool children. *Social Behavior and Personality, 21,* 145–158.

Breen, G. M., & Matusitz, J. (2009). Excitation transfer theory: an analysis of the Abu Ghrais prison abuse scandal. *Journal of Applied Security Research, 4,* 309–321.

Brehm, J. W. (1966). *A theory of psychological reactance.* New York: Academic Press.

Brewer, M. B., & Brown, R. (1998). Intergroup relations. In D. T. Gilbert, S. T. Fiske, & G. Lindzey (Eds.), *The handbook of social psychology* (4th ed., Vol. 2, pp. 554–594). New York: McGraw-Hill.

Brickner, M., Harkins, S., & Ostrom, T. (1986). Personal involvement: Thought provoking implications for social loafing. *Journal of Personality and Social Psychology, 51,* 763–769.

Bringle, R. G., & Winnick, T. A. (1992, October). *The nature of unrequited love.* Paper presented at the first Asian Conference in Psychology, Singapore.

Brinol, P., Rucker, D. D., Tormala, Z. L., & Petty, R. E. (2004). Individual differences in resistance to persuasion: The role of beliefs and meta-beliefs. In E. S. Knowles & J. A. Linn (Eds.), *Resistance to persuasion* (pp. 83–104). Mahwah, NJ: Lawrence Erlbaum.

Brodbeck, F. C., Kerschreiter, R., Mojzisch, A., Frey, D., & Schulz-Hardt, S. (2002). The dissemination of critical, unshared information in decision-making groups: The effects of pre-discussion dissent. *European Journal of Social Psychology, 32,* 35–56.

Broemer, P. (2004). Ease of imagination moderates reactions to differently framed health messages. *European Journal of Social Psychology, 34,* 103–119.

Brooks-Gunn, J., & Lewis, M. (1981). Infant social perception: Responses to pictures of parents and strangers. *Developmental Psychology, 17,* 647–649.

Brown, J. D. (1991). Staying fit and staying well: Physical fitness as a moderator of life stress. *Journal of Personality and Social Psychology, 60,* 555–561.

Brown, J. D., & Rogers, R. J. (1991). Self-serving attributions: The role of physiological arousal. *Personality and Social Psychology Bulletin, 17,* 501–506.

Brown, L. M. (1998). Ethnic stigma as a contextual experience: Possible selves perspective. *Personality and Social Psychology Bulletin, 24,* 165–172.

Brown, R. P., Charnsangavej, T., Keough, K. A., Newman, M. L., & Rentfrow, P. J. (2000). Putting the "affirm" into affirmative action: Preferential selection and academic performance. *Journal of Personality and Social Psychology, 79,* 736–747.

Brown, S. L., Nesse, R. M., Vinokur, A. D., & Smith, D. M. (2003). Providing social support may be more beneficial than receiving it. *Psychological Science, 14,* 320–327.

Bruckmüller, S., & Branscombe, N. R. (2010). The glass cliff: When and why women are selected as leaders in crisis contexts. *British Journal of Social Psychology, 49,* 433–451.

Bryan, J. H., & Test, M. A. (1967). Models and helping: Naturalistic studies in aiding behavior. *Journal of Personality and Social Psychology, 6,* 400–407.

Budson, A. E., & Price, B. H. (2005). Memory dysfunction. *New England Journal of Medicine, 352,* 692–699.

Buehler, R., & Griffin, D. (1994). Change-of-meaning effects in conformity and dissent: Observing construal processes over time. *Journal of Personality and Social Psychology, 67,* 984–996.

Buehler, R., Griffin, D., & MacDonald, H. (1997). The role of motivated reasoning in optimistic time predictions. *Personality and Social Psychology Bulletin, 23,* 238–247.

Buehler, R., Griffin, D., & Ross, M. (1994). Exploring the "planning fallacy": Why people underestimate their task completion times. *Journal of Personality and Social Psychology, 67,* 366–381.

Bureau of Justice Statistics. (2003, February). *Intimate partner violence 1993–2000.* Washington, DC: U.S. Department of Justice.

Bureau of Justice Statistics. (2007, December). *Intimate partner violence: Victim characteristics, 1976–2005.* Washington, DC: U.S. Department of Justice.

Burger, J. M. (1986). Increasing compliance by improving the deal: The that's-not-all technique. *Journal of Personality and Social Psychology, 51,* 277–283.

Burger, J. M. (1995). Individual differences in preference for solitude. *Journal of Research in Personality, 29,* 85–108.

Burger, J. M. (2009). Replicating Milgram: Would people still obey today? *American Psychologist, 64,* 1–11.

Burger, J. M., & Cornelius, T. (2003). Raising the price of agreement: Public commitment and the lowball compliance procedure. *Journal of Applied Social Psychology, 33,* 923–934.

Burger, J. M., Messian, N., Patel, S., del Pardo, A., & Anderson, C. (2004). What a coincidence! The effects of incidental similarity on compliance. *Personality and Social Psychology Bulletin, 30,* 35–43.

Burkley, E. (2008). The role of self-control in resistance to persuasion. *Personality and Social Psychology Bulletin, 34,* 419–431.

Burnstein, E. (1983). Persuasion as argument processing. In M. Brandstatter, J. H. Davis, & G. Stocker-Kriechgauer (Eds.), *Group decision processes.* London: Academic Press.

Burnstein, E., Crandall, C., & Kitayama, S. (1994). Some neo-Darwinian rules for altruism: Weighing cues for inclusive fitness as a function of the biological importance of the decision. *Journal of Personality and Social Psychology, 67,* 773–789.

Burris, E. R., Rodgers, M. S., Mannix, E. A., Hendron, M. G., & Oldroyd, J. B. (2009). Playing favorites: The influence of leaders' inner circle on group processes and performance. *Personality and Social Psychology Bulletin, 35,* 1244–1257.

Burriss, R.P., Roberts, S.C., Welling, L.L.M., Puts, D.A., & Little, A.C. (2011). Hetersexual romantic couples mate assortatively for facial symmetry, but not for masculinigy. *Personality and Social Psychology Bulletin, 37,* 601–613.

Burrus, J., & Roese, N. J. (2006). Long ago it was meant to be: The interplay between time, construal, and fate beliefs. *Personality and Social Psychology Bulletin, 32,* 1050–1058.

Burt, M. R. (1980). Cultural myths and supports for rape. *Journal of Personality and Social Psychology, 38,* 217–230.

Bushman, B. J. (1988). The effects of apparel on compliance: A field experiment with a female authority figure. *Personality and Social Psychology Bulletin, 14,* 459–467.

Bushman, B. J. (1998). Effects of television violence on memory for commercial messages. *Journal of Experimental Psychology: Applied, 4,* 1–17.

Bushman, B. J. (2001). Does venting anger feed or extinguish the flame? Catharsis, rumination, distraction, anger, and aggressive responding. Manuscript under review.

Bushman, B. J., & Anderson, C. A. (2002). Violent video games and hostile expectations: A test of the general aggression model. *Personality and Social Psychology Bulletin, 24,* 949–960 and *Social Psychology Bulletin, 28,* 1679–1686.

Bushman, B. J., & Baumeister, R. F. (1998). Threatened egotism, narcissism, self-esteem, and direct and displaced aggression: Does self-love or self-hate lead to violence? *Journal of Personality and Social Psychology, 75,* 219–229.

Bushman, B. J., & Cooper, H. M. (1990). Effects of alcohol on human aggression: An integrative research review. *Psychological Bulletin, 107,* 341–354.

Bushman, B. J., & Huesmann, L. R. (2001). Effects of televised violence on aggression. In D. Singer & J. Singer (Eds.), *Handbook of children and the media* (pp. 223–254). Thousands Oaks, CA: Sage.

Bushman, B. J., & Anderson, C. A. (2009). Comfortably numb: Desensitizing effects of violent media on helping others. *Psychological Science, 20,* 273–277.

Bushman, B. J., Baumeister, R. F., & Stack, A. D. (1999). Catharsis messages and anger-reducing activities. *Journal of Personality and Social Psychology, 76,* 367–376.

Buss, D. M. (1994). The strategies of human mating. *American Scientist, 82,* 238–249.

Buss, D. M. (2000). The dangerous passion: Why jealousy is as necessary as love and sex. New York: The Free Press.

Buss, D. M. (2004). *Evolutionary psychology: The new science of the mind.* (2nd ed.). Boston: Allyn and Bacon.

Buss, D. M., & Shackelford, T. K. (1997). From vigilance to violence: Mate retention tactics in married couples. *Journal of Personality and Social Psychology, 72,* 346–361.

Buss, D. M., Larsen, R. J., Westen, D., & Semmelroth, J. (1992). Sex differences in jealousy: Evolution, physiology, and psychology. *Psychological Science, 3,* 251–255.

Buss, D.M. (1999). *Evolutionary psychology: The new science of the mind.* Needham Heights, MA: Allyn & Bacon.

Buss, D.M. (2008). *Evolutionary psychology: The new science of the mind,* 3nd Edition. Boston: Allyn & Bacon.

Buunk, B. P., Dukstra, P., Fetchenhauer, D., & Kenrick, D. T. (2002). Age and gender differences in mate selection criteria for various involvement levels. *Personal Relationships, 9,* 271–278.

Byrne, D. (1961a). The influence of propinquity and opportunities for interaction on classroom relationships. *Human Relations, 14,* 63–69.

Byrne, D. (1961b). Interpersonal attraction and attitude similarity. *Journal of Abnormal and Social Psychology, 62,* 713–715.

Byrne, D. (1971). *The attraction paradigm.* New York: Academic Press.

Byrne, D. (1991). Perspectives on research classics: This ugly duckling has yet to become a swan. *Contemporary Social Psychology, 15,* 84–85.

Byrne, D. (1992). The transition from controlled laboratory experimentation to less controlled settings: Surprise!

Additional variables are operative. *Communication Monographs, 59*, 190–198.

Byrne, D. (1997a). An overview (and underview) of research and theory within the attraction paradigm. *Journal of Social and Personal Relationships, 14*, 417–431.

Byrne, D., & Blaylock, B. (1963). Similarity and assumed similarity of attitudes among husbands and wives. *Journal of Abnormal and Social Psychology, 67*, 636–640.

Byrne, D., & Nelson, D. (1965). Attraction as a linear function of proportion of positive reinforcements. *Journal of Personality and Social Psychology, 1*, 659–663.

Byrne, R. L. (2001, June 1). *Good safety advice.* Internet.

Cacioppo, J. T., Berntson, G. G., Long, T. S., Norris, C. J., Rickhett, E., & Nusbaum, H. (2003). Just because you're imaging the brain doesn't mean you can stop using your head: A primer and set of first principles. *Journal of Personality and Social Psychology, 85*, 650–661.

Cacioppo, J. T., Hawkley, L. C., Berntson, G. G., Ernst, J. M., Gibbs, A. C., Stickgold, R., & Hobson, J. A. (2002). Do lonely days invade the nights? Potential social modulation of sleep efficiency. *Psychological Science, 13*, 384–387.

Callan, M. J., Kay, A. C., Olson, J. M., Brar, N., & Whitefield, N. (2010). The effects of priming legal concepts on perceived trust and competitiveness, self-interested attitudes, and competitive behavior. *Journal of Experimental Social Psychology, 46*, 325–335

Campbell, D. T. (1958). Common fate, similarity, and other indices of the status of aggregates of persons as social entities. *Behavioral Science, 4*, 14–25.

Campbell, W. K. (1999). Narcissism and romantic attraction. *Journal of Personality and Social Psychology, 77*, 1254–1270.

Campbell, W. K., & Foster, C. A. (2002). Narcissism and commitment to romantic relationships: An investment model analysis. *Personality and Social Psychology Bulletin, 28*, 484–495.

Campos, B., Keltner, D., Beck, J. M., Gonzaga, G. C., & John, O. P. (2007). Culture and teasing: The relational benefits of reduced desire for positive self-differentiation. *Personality and Social Psychology Bulletin, 33*, 3–16.

Cann, A., Calhoun, L. G., & Banks, J. S. (1995). On the role of humor appreciation in interpersonal attraction: It's no joking matter. *Humor: International Journal of Humor Research.*

Caplan, S. E. (2005). A social skill account of problematic internet use. *Journal of Communication, 55*, 721–736.

Caprara, G. V., Barbaranelli, C., Pastorelli, C., Bandura, A., & Zimbardo, P. G. (2000). Prosocial foundations of children's academic achievement. *Psychological Science, 11*, 302–306.

Caputo, D., & Dunning, D. (2005). What you don't know: The role played by errors of omission in imperfect self-assessments. *Journal of Experimental Social Psychology, 41*, 488–505.

Carey, M. P., Morrison-Beedy, D., & Johnson, B. T. (1997). The HIV-Knowledge Questionnaire: Development and evaluation of a reliable, valid, and practical self-administered questionnaire. *AIDS and Behavior, 1*, 61–74.

Carlsmith, K. M., Darley, J. M., & Robinson, P. H. (2002). Why do we punish? Deterrence and just deserts as motives for punishment. *Journal of Personality and Social Psychology, 83*, 284–299.

Carney, D. R., Colvin, D. W., & Hall, J. A. (2007). A thin slice perspective on the accuracy of first impressions. *Journal of Research in Personality, 41*, 1054–1072.

Carre, J. M., McCormick, C. M., & Moundloch, C. J. (2009); Facial structure is a reliable cue of aggressive behavior. *Psychological Science, 10*, 1194–1198.

Carroll, J.M., & Russell, J.A. 1996). Do facial expressions signal specific emotions? Judging emotion from the face in context. *Journal of Personality and Social Psychology, 70*, 205–218.

Caruso, E. M. (2008). Use of experienced retrieval ease in self and social judgments. *Journal of Experimental Social Psychology, 44*, 148–155.

Carvallo, M., & Gabriel, S. (2006). No man is an island: The need to belong and dismissing avoidant attachment style. *Personality and Social Psychology Bulletin, 32*, 697–709.

Carver, C. S., & Glass, D. C. (1978). Coronary-prone behavior pattern and interpersonal aggression. *Journal of Personality and Social Psychology, 376*, 361–366.

Caspi, A., & Herbener, E. S. (1990). Continuity and change: Assortative marriage and the consistency of personality in adulthood. *Journal of Personality and Social Psychology, 58*, 250–258.

Caspi, A., Herbener, E. S., & Ozer, D. J. (1992). Shared experiences and the similarity of personalities: A longitudinal study of married couples. *Journal of Personality and Social Psychology, 62*, 281–291.

Castelli, L., Zogmaister, C., & Smith, E. R. (2004). On the automatic evaluation of social exemplars. *Journal of Personality and Social Psychology, 86*, 373–387.

Catalyst (2010). *2010 Catalyst census: Financial post 500 women senior officers and top earners.* Retrieved May 12, 2011 from http://www.catalyst.org

Center for American Women and Politics (2005). *Sex differences in voter turnout.* Retrieved June 28, 2007 from the Eagleton Institute of Politics, Rutgers University Web site: http://www.cawp.rutgers.edu/ Facts/Elections/Womensvote2004.html

Center for American Women and Politics (2010). *Can more women run? Reevaluating women's election to the state legislatures.* Retrieved September 10, 2010 from http://www.cawp.rutgers.edu/research

Cesario, J., Plaks, J. E., & Higgins, E. (2006). Automatic social behavior as motivated preparation to interact. *Journal of Personality and Social Psychology, 90*, 893–910.

Chaiken, S., & Trope, Y. (1999). *Dual-process theories in social psychology.* New York: Guilford Press.

Chaiken, S., Liberman, A., & Eagly, A. H. (1989). Heuristic and systematic processing within and beyond persuasion context. In J. S. Uleman & J. A. Bargh (Eds.), *Unintended thought* (pp. 212–252). New York: Guilford.

Chajut, E., & Algom, D. (2003). Selective attention improves under stress: Implications for theories of social cognition. *Journal of Personality and Social Psychology, 85,* 231–248.

Chambers, J. R., Epley, N., Savitsky, K., & Windschitl, P. D. (2008). Knowing too much: Using private knowledge to predict how one is viewed by others. *Psychological Science, 19,* 542–548.

Chaplin, W. F., Phillips, J. B., Brown, J. D., Clanton, N. R., & Stein, J. L. (2000). Handshaking, gender, personality, and first impressions. *Journal of Personality and Social Psychology, 79,* 110–117.

Chen, F. F., & Kenrick, D. T. (2002). Repulsion or attraction? Group membership and assumed attitude similarity. *Journal of Personality and Social Psychology, 83,* 11–125.

Chen, S. H., & Lee, K. P. (2008). The role of personality traits and perceived values in persuasion: An elaboration likelihood model perspective on online shopping. *Social Behavior and Personality, 36,* 1379–1400.

Chen, S., Chen, K., & Shaw, L. (2004). Self-verification motives at the collective level of self-definition. *Journal of Personality and Social Psychology, 86,* 77–94.

Cheung, M. Y., Luo, C., Sia, C. L., & Chen, H. (2009). Credibility of electronic word-of-mouth: Informational and normative determinants of on-line consumer recommendations. *International Journal of Electronic Commerce, 13,* 9–38.

Chin, J. L. (2010). Introduction to the special issue on diversity and leadership. *American Psychologist, 65,* 150–156.

Choi, I., Dalal, R., Kim-Prieto, C., & Park, H. (2003). Culture and judgment of causal relevance. *Journal of Personality and Social Psychology, 84,* 46–59.

Christy, P. R., Gelfand, D. M., & Hartmann, D. P. (1971). Effects of competition-induced frustration on two classes of modeled behavior. *Developmental Psychology, 5,* 104–111.

Cialdini, R. B. (1994). *Influence: Science and practice* (3rd ed.). New York: Harper Collins.

Cialdini, R. B. (2000). *Influence: Science and practice* (4th ed.). Boston: Allyn & Bacon.

Cialdini, R. B. (2006). *Influence: The psychology of persuasion.* New York: Collins

Cialdini, R. B. (2008). *Influence: Science and practice* (5th ed). Boston: Allyn & Bacon.

Cialdini, R. B., & Petty, R. (1979). Anticipatory opinion effects. In B. Petty, T. Ostrom, & T. Brock (Eds.), *Cognitive responses in persuasion.* Hillsdale, NJ: Erlbaum.

Cialdini, R. B., Baumann, D. J., & Kenrick, D. T. (1981). Insights from sadness: A three-step model of the development of altruism as hedonism. *Developmental Review, 1,* 207–223.

Cialdini, R. B., Cacioppo, J. T., Bassett, R., & Miller J. A. (1978). A low-ball procedure for producing compliance:

Commitment then cost. *Journal of Personality and Social Psychology, 36,* 463–476.

Cialdini, R. B., Kallgren, C. A., & Reno, R. R. (1991). A focus theory of normative conduct. *Advances in Experimental Social Psychology, 24,* 201–234.

Cialdini, R. B., Kenrick, D. T., & Baumann, D. J. (1982). Effects of mood on prosocial behavior in children and adults. In N. Eisenberg-Berg (Ed.), *Development of prosocial behavior.* New York: Academic Press.

Cialdini, R. B., Reno, R. R., & Kallgren, C. A. (1990). A focus theory of normative conduct : Recycling the concept of norms to reduce littering in public places. *Journal of Personality and Social Psychology, 91,* 105-1026.

Cialdini, R. B., Schaller, M., Houlainham, D., Arps, K., Fultz, J., & Beaman, A. L. (1987). Empathy-based helping: Is it selflessly or selfishly motivated? *Journal of Personality and Social Psychology, 52,* 749–758.

Cialdini, R. B., Vincent, J. E., Lewis, S. K., Catalan, J., Wheeler, D., & Darby, B. L. (1975). Reciprocal concessions procedure for inducing compliance: The door-in-the-face technique. *Journal of Personality and Social Psychology, 31,* 206–215.

Cialdini, R., Brown, S., Lewis, B., Luce, C., & Neuberg, S. (1997). Reinterpreting the empathy-altruism relationships: When one into one equals oneness. *Journal of Personality and Social Psychology, 67,* 773–789.

Cicero, L., Pierro, A., & van Knippenberg, D. (2007). Leader group prototypicality and job satisfaction: The moderating role of job stress and team identification. *Group Dynamics: Theory, Research, and Practice, 11,* 165–175.

Cikara, M., & Fiske, S. T. (2009). Warmth, competence, and ambivalent sexism: vertical assault and collateral damage. In M. Barreto, M. K. Ryan, & M. T. Schmitt (Eds.), *The glass ceiling in the 21st century* (pp. 73–96). Washington, DC: American Psychological Association.

Clark, L. A., Kochanska, G., & Ready, R. (2000). Mothers' personality and its interaction with child temperament as predictors of parenting behavior. *Journal of Personality and Social Psychology, 79,* 274–285.

Clark, M. S., Lemay, E. P., Graham, S. M., Pataki, S. P., & Finkel, E. J. (in press). Ways of giving and receiving benefits in marriage: Norm use and attachment related variability. *Psychological Science.*

Clarkson, J. J., Tormala, Z. L., DeSensi, D. L., & Wheeler, S. C. (2009). Does attitude certainty beget self-certainty? *Journal of Experimental Social Psychology, 45,* 436–439.

Clore, G. L., Schwarz, N., & Conway, M. (1993). Affective causes and consequences of social information processing. In R. S. Wyer & T. K. Srull (Eds.), *Handbook of social cognition* (2nd ed.). Hilldsale, NJ: Erlbaum.

Cohen, D., & Nisbett, R. E. (1994). Self-protection and the culture of honor: Explaining southern violence. *Personality and Social Psychology Bulletin, 20,* 551–567.

Cohen, D., & Nisbett, R. E. (1997). Field experiments examining the culture of honor: The role of institutions in perpetuating norms about violence. *Personality and Social Psychology Bulletin, 23,* 1188–1199.

Cohen, J. D. (2005). The vulcanization of the human brain: A neural perspective on interactions between cognition and emotion. *Journal of Economic Perspectives, 19,* 3–24.

Cohen, S., & Janicki-Deverts, D. (2009). Can we improve our physical health by altering our social networks? *Perspectives on Psychological Science, 4, 375–38.*

Cohen, S., Doyle, W. J., Turner, R. B., Alper, C. M., & Skoner, D. P. (2003). Emotional style and susceptibility to the common cold. *Psychosomatic Medicine, 65,* 652–657.

Cohen, S., Frank, E., Doyle, W. J., Skoner, D. P., Rabin, B. S., & Gwaltuey, J. M., Jr. (1998). Types of stressors that increasesusceptibility to the common cold in healthy adults. *Health Psychology, 17,* 214–223.

Cohen, S., Kaplan, J. R., Cunnick, J. E., Manuck, S. B., & Rabin, B. S. (1992). Chronic social stress, affiliation, and cellular immune response in non-human primates. *Psychological Science, 3,* 301–304.

Cohen, T. R., Montoya, R. M., & Insko, C. A. (2006). Group morality and intergroup relations: Cross-cultural and experimental evidence. *Personality and Social Psychology Bulletin, 32,* 1559–1572.

Cohn, E. G., & Rotton, J. (1997). Assault as a function of time and temperature: A moderator-variable time-series analysis. *Journal of Personality and Social Psychology, 72,* 1322–1334.

Collins, M. A., & Zebrowitz, L. A. (1995). The contributions of appearance to occupational outcomes in civilian and military settings. *Journal of Applied Social Psychology, 25,* 129–163.

Collins, N. L., & Feeney, B. C. (2000). A safe haven: An attachment theory perspective on support seeking and caregiving in intimate relationships. *Journal of Personality and Social Psychology, 78,* 1053–1073.

Condon, J. W., & Crano, W. D. (1988) Inferred evaluation and the relation between attitude similarity and interpersonal attraction. *Journal of Personality and Social Psychology, 54,* 789–797.

Coniff, R. (2004, January). Reading faces. *Smithsonian,* 44–50.

Correll, J., Urland, G. R., & Ito, T. A. (2006). Event-related potentials and the decision to shoot: The role of threat perception and cognitive control. *Journal of Experimental Social Psychology, 42,* 120–128.

Cottrell, C. A., & Neuberg, S. L. (2005). Different emotional reactions to different groups: A sociofunctional threat-based approach to "prejudice." *Journal of Personality and Social Psychology, 88,* 770–789.

Cottrell, C. A., Neuberg, S. L., & Li, N. P. (2007). What do people desire in others? A sociofunctional perspective on the importance of different valued characteristics. *Journal of Personality and Social Psychology, 92,* 208–231.

Cottrell, N. B., Wack, K. L., Sekerak, G. J., & Rittle, R. (1968). Social facilitation of dominant responses by the presence of an audience and the mere presence of others. *Journal of Personality and Social Psychology, 9,* 245–250.

Cramer, R. E., McMaster, M. R., Bartell, P. A., & Dragma, M. (1988). Subject competence and minimization of the bystander effect. *Journal of Applied Social Psychology, 18,* 1133–1148.

Crandall, C. C., & Martinez, R. (1996). Culture, ideology, and antifat attitudes. *Personality and Social Psychology Bulletin, 22,* 1165–1176.

Crandall, C. S. (1988). Social contagion of binge eating. *Journal of Personality and Social Psychology, 55,* 588–598.

Crandall, C. S., Eidelman, S., Skitka, L. J., & Morgan, G. S. (2009). Status quo framing increases support for torture. *Social Influence, 4,* 1–10.

Crandall, C. S., Eshleman, A., & O'Brien, L. T. (2002). Social norms and the expression and suppression of prejudice: The struggle for internalization. *Journal of Personality and Social Psychology, 82,* 359–378.

Crano, W. D. (1995). Attitude strength and vested interest. In R. E. Petty & J. A. Krosnick (Eds.), *Attitude strength: Antecedents and consequences* (Vol. 4, pp. 131–157). Hillsdale, NJ: Erlbaum.

Crites, S. L., & Cacioppo, J. T. (1996). Electrocortical differentiation of evaluative and nonevaluative categorizations. *Psychological Science, 7,* 318–321.

Crocker, J., & Major, B. (1989). Social stigma and self-esteem: The self-protective properties of stigma. *Psychological Review, 96,* 608–630.

Cropanzano, R. (Ed.). (1993). *Justice in the workplace* (pp. 79–103). Hillsdale, NJ: Erlbaum.

Crosby, F. J. (2004). *Affirmative action is dead: Long live affirmative action.* New Haven, CT: Yale University Press.

Cruse, D. F., and Leigh, B. C. "Adam's Rib" revisited: Legal and non-legal influences on the processing of trial testimony. *Social Behavior,* 1987, *2,* 221-230

Crutchfield, R. A. (1955). Conformity and character. *American Psychologist, 10,* 191–198.

Cunningham, M. R. (1979). Weather, mood, and helping behavior: Quasi-experiments with the sunshine Samaritan. *Journal of Personality and Social Psychology, 37,* 1947–1956.

Cunningham, M. R. (1986). Measuring the physical in physical attractiveness: Quasi-experiments on the sociobiology of female facial beauty. *Journal of Personality and Social Psychology, 50,* 925–935.

Cunningham, M. R., Roberts, A. R., Wu, C.-H., Barbee, A. P., & Druen, P. B. (1995). "Their ideas of beauty are, on the whole, the same as ours": Consistency and variability in the cross-cultural perception of female physical attractiveness. *Journal of Personality and Social Psychology, 68,* 261–279.

Cunningham, M. R., Shaffer, D. R., Barbee, A. P., Wolff, P. L., & Kelley, D. J. (1990). Separate processes in the relation of elation and depression to helping: Social versus personal concerns. *Journal of Experimental Social Psychology, 26,* 13–33.

Cunningham, W. A., Johnson, M. K., Gatenby, J. C., Gore, J. C., & Banaji, M. R. (2003). Neural components of social evaluation. *Journal of Personality and Social Psychology, 85,* 639–649.

Danaher, K., & Branscombe, N. R. (2010). Maintaining the system with tokenism: Bolstering individual mobility beliefs and identification with a discriminatory organization. *British Journal of Social Psychology, 49,* 343–362.

Dancygier, R. M., & Green, D. P. (2010). Hate crime. In J. F. Dovidio, M. Hewstone, P. Glick & V. M. Esses (Eds.), *Sage handbook of prejudice, stereotyping and discrimination* (pp. 294–311). London: Sage.

Darley, J. M. (1993). Research on morality: Possible approaches, actual approaches. *Psychological Science, 4,* 353–357.

Darley, J. M. (1995). Constructive and destructive obedience: A taxonomy of principal-agent relationships. *Journal of Social Issues, 125,* 125–154.

Darley, J. M., & Latané, B. (1968). Bystander intervention in emergencies: Diffusion of responsibility. *Journal of Personality and Social Psychology, 8,* 377–383.

Darley, J. M., Carlsmith, K. M., & Robinson, P. H. (2000). Incapacitation and just desserts as motives for punishment. *Law and Human Behavior, 24,* 659–684

Dasgupta, N., & Asgari, S. (2004). Seeing is believing: Exposure to counterstereotypical women leaders and its effect on the malleability of automatic gender stereotyping. *Journal of Experimental Social Psychology, 40,* 642–658.

Dasgupta, N., Banji, M. R., & Abelson, R. P. (1999). Group entiativity and group perception: Association between physical features and psychological judgment. *Journal of Personality and Social Psychology, 75,* 991–1005.

Davis, C. G., Lehman, D. R., Wortman, C. B., Silver, R. C., & Thompson, S. C. (1995). The undoing of tragic life events. *Personality and Social Psychology Bulletin, 21,* 109–124.

Davis, J. I., Senghas, A., Brandt, F., & Ochsner, K. N. (2010). The effects of BOTOX injections on emotional experience. *Emotion, 10,* 433–40.

De Hoog, N., Stroebe, W., & de Wit, J. B. F. (2007). The impact of vulnerability to and severity of a health risk on processing and acceptance of fear-arousing communications: A meta-analysis. *Review of General Psychology, 11,* 258–285.

Deaux, K., & LaFrance, M. (1998). Gender. In D. T. Gilbert, S. T. Fiske, & G. Lindzey (Eds.), *The handbook of social psychology* (4th ed., Vol. 1, pp. 788–827). New York: McGraw-Hill.

DeDreu, C. K. W. (2010). Conflict at work: Basic principles and applied issues. In S. Zedeck (Ed.), *Handbook of industrial and organizational psychology* (pp. 461–493). Washington, DC: American Psychological Association.

DeDreu, C. K. W., & Van Lange, P. A. M. (1995). Impact of social value orientation on negotiator cognition and behavior. *Personality and Social Psychology Bulletin, 21,* 1178–1188.

DeHart, T., & Pelham, B. W. (2007). Fluctuations in state implicit self-esteem in response to daily negative events. *Journal of Experimental Social Psychology, 43,* 157–165.

DeHart, T., Pelham, B. W., & Tennen, H. (2006). What lies beneath: Parenting style and implicit self-esteem. *Journal of Experimental Social Psychology, 42,* 1–17.

DeJong, W., & Musilli, L. (1982). External pressure to comply: Handicapped versus nonhandicapped requesters and the foot-in-the-door phenomenon. *Personality and Social Psychology Bulletin, 8,* 522–527.

DeLongis, A., Folkman, S., & Lazarus, R. S. (1988). The impact of daily stress on health and mood: Psychological and social resources as mediators. *Journal of Personality and Social Psychology, 54,* 486–595.

DePaulo, B. M. (2006). *Singled out: How singles are stereotyped, stigmatized, and ignored, and still live happily ever after.* New York: St. Martin's Press.

DePaulo, B. M., & Kashy, D. A. (1998). Everyday lies in close and casual relationships. *Journal of Personality and Social Psychology, 74,* 63–79.

DePaulo, B. M., & Morris, W. L. (2006). The unrecognized stereotyping and discrimination against singles. *Current Directions in Psychological Science, 15,* 251–254.

DePaulo, B. M., Brown, P. L., Ishii, S., & Fisher, J. D. (1981). Help that works: The effects of aid on subsequent task performance. *Journal of Personality and Social Psychology, 41,* 478–487.

DePaulo, B. M., Lindsay, J. J., Malone, B. E., Muhlenbruck, L., Chandler, K., & Cooper, H. (2003). Cues to deception. *Psychological Bulletin, 129,* 74–118.

DeSteno, D. (2004). *New perspectives on jealousy: An integrative view of the most social of social emotions.* Paper presented at the meeting of the American Psychological Society, Chicago, IL.

DeSteno, D., Dasgupta, N., Bartlett, M. Y., & Cajdric, A. (2004). Prejudice from thin air: The effect of emotion on automatic intergroup attitudes. *Psychological Science, 15,* 319–324.

DeSteno, D., Valdesolo, P., & Bartlett, M. Y. (2006). Jealousy and the threatened self: Getting to the heart of the green-eyed monster. *Journal of Personality and Social Psychology, 91,* 626–641.

Deutsch, M., & Gerard, H. B. (1955). A study of normative and informational social influences upon individual judgment. *Journal of Abnormal and Social Psychology, 51,* 629–636.

Devine, P. G., Plant, E. A., & Blair, I. V. (2001). Classic and contemporary analyses of racial prejudice. In R. Brown & S. Gaertner (Eds.), *Blackwell handbook of social psychology: Intergroup processes* (pp. 198–217). Oxford, UK: Blackwell.

DeVoe, S. E., & Pfeffer, J. (2010). The stingy hour: How accounting for time affects volunteering. *Personality and Social Psychology Bulletin, 36,* 470–483

DeWall, C. N., MacDonald, G., Webster, G. D., Masten, C. L., Baumeister, R. F., Powell, C., et al. (2010).

Acetaminophen reduces social pain: Behavioral and neural evidence. *Psychological Science, 21,* 931–937.

DeWall, C. N., Twenge, J. M., Gitter, S. A., & Baumeister, R. F. (20089). It's the thought that counts: The role of hostile cognition in shaping aggressive responses to social exclusion. *Journal of Personality and Social Psychology, 96,* 45–59.

Diener, E. (2000). Subjective well-being: The science of happiness, and a proposal for a national index. *American Psychologist, 55,* 34–43.

Diener, E., & Lucas, R. R. (1999). Personality and subjective well-being. In E. Kahneman, E. Diener, & N. Schwarz (Eds.), *Well-being: The foundations of hedonic psychology* (pp. 434–450). New York: Russell Stage Foundation.

Diener, E., & Oishi, S. (2005). The nonobvious social psychology of happiness. *Psychological Inquiry, 16,* 162–167.

Diener, E., Lucas, R., & Scollon, C. N. (2006). Beyond the hedonic treadmill: Revising the adaptation theory of well-being. *American Psychologist, 61,* 305–314.

Diener, E., Ng, W., Harter, J., & Arora, R. (2010). Wealth and happiness across the world: Material prosperity predicts life evaluation, whereas psychosocial prosperity predicts positive feelings. *Journal of Personality and Social Psychology, 99,* 52–61.

Diener, E., Suh, E. M., Lucas, R. E., & Smith, H. L. (1999). Subjective well-being: Three decades of progress. *Psychological Bulletin, 125,* 276–302.

Diener, E., Wolsic, B., & Fujita, F. (1995). Physical attractiveness and subjective well-being. *Journal of Personality and Social Psychology, 69,* 120–129.

Dietrich, D. M., & Berkowitz, L. (1997). Alleviation of dissonance by engaging in prosocial behavior or receiving ego-enhancing feedback. *Journal of Social Behavior and Personality, 12,* 557–566.

Dijksterhuis, A. (2004). I like myself but I don't know why: Enhancing implicit self-esteem by subliminal evaluative conditioning. *Journal of Personality and Social Psychology, 86,* 345–355.

Dijksterhuis, A., & Bargh, J. A. (2001). The perception-behavior expressway: Automatic effects of social perception and social behavior. In M. P. Zanna (Ed.), *Advances in experimental social psychology* (Vol. 33, pp. 1–40). San Diego: Academic Press.

Dijksterhuis, A., & Nordgren, L. F. (2007). A theory of unconscious thought. *Perspectives on Psychological Science.*

Dijksterhuis, A., & van Olden, Z. (2006). On the benefits of thinking unconsciously: Unconscious thought can increase post-choice satisfaction. *Journal of Experimental Social Psychology, 42,* 627–631.

Dill, K. E., & Thill, K. P. (2007). Video game characters and the socialization of gender roles: Young people's perceptions mirror sexist media depictions. *Sex Roles, 57,* 851–865.

Dill, K. E., Brown, B., & Collins, M. (2008). Effects of exposure to sex-stereotyped video game characters on tolerance of sexual harassment. *Journal of Experimental Social Psychology, 44,* 1402–1408.

Dion, K. K., Berscheid, E., & Hatfield (Walster), E. (1972). What is beautiful is good. *Journal of Personality and Social Psychology, 24,* 285–290.

Dollard, J., Doob, L., Miller, N., Mowerer, O. H., & Sears, R. R. (1939). *Frustration and aggression.* New Haven, CT: Yale University Press.

Dovidio, J. F., Brigham, J., Johnson, B., & Gaertner, S. (1996). Stereotyping, prejudice, and discrimination: Another look. In N. Macrae, C. Stangor, & M. Hwestone (Eds.), *Stereotypes and stereotyping* (pp. 1276–1319). New York: Guilford.

Dovidio, J. F., Evans, N., & Tyler, R. B. (1986). Racial stereotypes: The contents of their cognitive representations. *Journal of Experimental Social Psychology, 22,* 22–37.

Dovidio, J. F., Gaertner, S. L., & Validzic, A. (1998). Intergroup bias: Status differentiation and a common ingroup identity. *Journal of Personality and Social Psychology, 75,* 109–120.

Dovidio, J. F., Gaertner, S. L., & Kawakami, K. (2010). Racism. In J. F. Dovidio, M. Hewstone, P. Glick, & V.M. Esses (Eds.), *Sage handbook of prejudice, stereotyping and discrimination* (pp. 312–327). London: Sage.

Dovidio, J. F., Gaertner, S. L., Isen, A. M., & Lowrance, R. (1995). Group representations and intergroup bias: Positive affect, similarity, and group size. *Personality and Social Psychology Bulletin, 21,* 856–865.

Downs, A. C., & Lyons, P. M. (1991). Natural observations of the links between attractiveness and initial legal judgments. *Personality and Social Psychology Bulletin, 17,* 541–547.

Duan, C. (2000). Being empathic: The role of motivation to empathize and the nature of target emotions. *Motivation and Emotion, 24,* 29–49.

Duck, J. M., Hogg, M. A., & Terry, D. J. (1999). Social identity and perceptions of media persuasion: Are we always less influenced than others? *Journal of Applied Social Psychology, 29,* 1879–1899.

Duck, S., Pond, K., & Leatham, G. (1994). Loneliness and the evaluation of relational events. *Journal of Social and Personal Relationships, 11,* 253–276.

Duehr, E. E., & Bono, J. E. (2006). Men, women, and managers: Are stereotypes finally changing? *Personnel Psychology, 59,* 459–471.

Duggan, E. S., & Brennan, K. A. (1994). Social avoidance and its relation to Bartholomew's adult attachment typology. *Journal of Social and Personal Relationships, 11,* 147–153.

Dugosh, K. L., & Paulus, P. B. (2005). Cognitive and social comparison processes in brainstorming. *Journal of Experimental Social Psychology, 41,* 313–320.

Duncan, J., & Owen, A. W. (2000). Common regions of the human frontal lobe recruited by diverse cognitive demands. *Trends in Cognitive Science, 23,* 475–483.

Dunn, E. W., Arknin, L. B., & Norton, M. I. (2008). Spending money on others promotes happiness. *Science, 319,* 1687–1688.

Dunn, E. W., Biesanz, J. C., Human. L. J, & Finn, S. (2007). Misunderstanding the affective consequences of everyday social interactions: the hidden benefits of putting one's best face forward. *Journal of Personality and Social Psychology, 92,* 990–1003.

Dunn, E., & Ashton-James, C. (2008). On emotional innumeracy: Predicted and actual affective responses to grand-scale tragedies. *Journal of Experimental Social Psychology, 44,* 692–698.

Dunn, E., & Laham, S. A. (2006). A user's guide to emotional time travel: Progress on key issues in affective forecasting. In J. Forgas (Ed.), *Hearts and minds: Affective influences on social cognition and behavior* (pp. 177–193). New York: Psychology Press.

Dunn, J. (1992). Siblings and development. *Current Directions in Psychological Science, 1,* 6–11.

Durrheim, K., Dixon, J., Tredoux, C., Eaton, L., Quayle, M., & Clack, B. (2009). Predicting support for racial transformation policies: Intergroup threat, racial prejudice, sense of group entitlement and strength of identification. *European Journal of Social Psychology.*

Dutton, D. G., & Aron, A. P. (1974). Some evidence for heightened sexual attraction under conditions of high anxiety. *Journal of Personality and Social Psychology, 30,* 510–517.

Eagly, A. H. (1987). *Sex differences in social behavior: A social-role interpretation.* Hillsdale, NJ: Erlbaum.

Eagly, A. H. (2007). Female leadership advantage and disadvantage: Resolving the contradictions. *Psychology of Women Quarterly, 31,* 1–12.

Eagly, A. H., & Carli, L. (1981). Sex of researchers and sex-typed communications as determinants of sex differences in influence-ability: A meta-analysis of social influence studies. *Psychological Bulletin, 90,* 1–20.

Eagly, A. H., & Chaiken, S. (1993). *The psychology of attitudes.* Orlando, FL: Harcourt Brace Jovanovich.

Eagly, A. H., & Chaiken, S. (1998). Attitude structure and function. In G. Lindsey, S. T., Fiske, & D. T. Gilbert (Eds.), *Handbook of social psychology* (4th ed.). New York: Oxford University Press and McGraw-Hill.

Eagly, A. H., & Karau, S. J. (2002). Role congruity theory of prejudice toward female leaders. *Psychological Review, 109,* 573–598.

Eagly, A. H., & Mladinic, A. (1994). Are people prejudiced against women? Some answers from research on attitudes, gender stereotypes, and judgments of competence. In W. Sroebe & M. Hewstone (Eds.), *European review of social psychology* (Vol. 5, pp. 1–35). New York: Wiley.

Eagly, A. H., & Sczesny, S. (2009). Stereotypes about women, men, and leaders: Have times changed? In M. Barreto, M. K. Ryan, & M. T. Schmitt (Eds.), *The glass ceiling in the 21st century* (pp. 21–47). Washington, DC: American Psychological Association.

Eagly, A. H., & Wood, W. (2011). Gender roles in a biosocial world. In P. van Lange, A. Kruglanski, & E. T. Higgins (Eds.), *Handbook of theories in social psychology.* London: Sage.

Eagly, A. H., Chaiken, S., & Wood, W. (1981). An attributional analysis of persuasion. In J. H. Harvey, W. Ickes, & R. F. Kidd (Eds.), *New directions in attribution research* (pp. 37–62). Hillsdale, NJ: Lawrence Erlbaum.

Eagly, A. H., Chen, S., Chaiken, S., & Shaw-Barnes, K. (1999). The impact of attitudes on memory: An affair to remember. *Psychological Bulletin, 124,* 64–89.

Eagly, A. H., Eastwick, P. W., & Johannesen-Schmidt, M. (2009). Possible selves in marital roles: the impact of the anticipated vision of labor on the mate preferences of women and men. *Personality and Social Psychology Bulletin, 35* 403–413.

Eagly, A. H., Kulesa, P., Brannon, L. A., Shaw, K., & Hutson-Comeaux, S. (2000). Why counterattitudinal messages are as memorable as proattitudinal messages: The importance of active defense against attack. *Personality and Social Psychology Bulletin, 26,* 1392–1408.

Eagly, A. H., Makhijani, M. G., & Klonsky, B. G. (1992). Gender and the evaluation of leaders: A meta-analysis. *Psychological Bulletin, 111,* 3–22.

Eaton, A. A., Majka, E. A., & Visser, P. S. (2008). Emerging perspectives on the structure and function of attitude strength. *European Review of Social Psychology, 19,* 165–201.

Eaton, A. A., Visser, P. S., Kosnick, J. A., & Anand, S. (2009). Social power and attitude strength over the life course. *Personality and Social Psychology Bulletin, 35,* 1646–1660.

Effenbaum & Armady—in 12th edition reference list

Ehrenreich, B. (2009). *Bright-sided: How positive thinking is undermining America.* New York: Metropolitan Books.

Eibach, R. P., & Keegan, T. (2006). Free at last? Social dominance, loss aversion, and White and Black Americans' differing assessments of racial progress. *Journal of Personality and Social Psychology, 90,* 453–467.

Eich, E. (1995). Searching for mood dependent memory. *Psychological Science, 6,* 67–75.

Eid, M., & Diener, E. (2004). Global judgments of subjective well-being: Situational variability and long-term stability. *Social Indicators Research, 65,* 245–277.

Eidelman, S., Pattershall, J., & Crandall, C.S. (2010). Longer is better. *Journal of Experimental Social Psychology.*

Eisenberg, N. (2000). Emotion regulation and moral development. *Annual Review of Psychology, 51,* 665–697.

Eisenberg, N., Guthrie, I,K.,., Cumberland, A., Murphy, B.C., Shepard, S.A., Zhou, O., & Carlo, G. (2001). Prosocial development in early ajuthood: A longitudinal study. *Journal of Personality and Social Psychology, 82,* 993–1006.

Eisenman, R. (1985). Marijuana use and attraction: Support for Byrne's similarity-attraction concept. *Perceptual and Motor Skills, 61,* 582.

Eisenstadt, D., & Leippe, M. R. (1994). The self-comparison process and self-discrepant feedback: Consequences of learning you are what you thought you were not. *Journal of Personality and Social Psychology, 67,* 611–626.

Ekman, P. (2001). *Telling lies: Clues to deceit in the marketplace, politics, and marriage* (3rd ed.). New York: Norton.

Ekman, P. (2003). *Emotions revealed.* New York: Times Books.

Ekman, P., & Friesen, W. V. (1975). *Unmasking the face.* Englewood Cliffs, NJ: Prentice-Hall.

Ellemers, N., de Gilder, D., & Haslam, S. A. (2004). Motivating individuals and groups at work: A social identity perspective on leadership and group performance. *Academy of Management Review, 29,* 459–478.

Elliot, A. J., & Devine, P. G. (1994). On the motivational nature of cognitive dissonance: Dissonance as psychological discomfort. *Journal of Personality and Social Psychology, 67,* 382–394.

Elliot, A. J., & Niesta, D. (2008). Romantic red: red enhances men's attraction to women. *Journal of Personality and Social Psychology, 95,* 1150–1164.

Ellison, N. B., Steinfield, C., & Lampe, C. (2007). The benefits of Facebook "friends:" Social capital and college students' use of online social network sites. *Journal of Computer-Mediated Communication, 12,* 1143–1168.

Ellison, N., Heino, R., & Gibbs, J. (2006). Managing impressions online: Self-presentation processes in the online dating environment. *Journal of Computer-Mediated Communication, 11,* 415–441.

Ellsworth, P. C., & Carlsmith, J. M. (1973). Eye contact and gaze aversion in aggressive encounter. *Journal of Personality and Social Psychology, 33,* 117–122.

Englehart, J. M. (2006). Teacher perceptions of student behavior as a function of class size. *Social Psychology of Education, 9,* 245–272.

Englich, B., Mussweiler, T., & Strack, F. (2006). Playing dice with criminal sentences: The influence of irrelevant anchors on experts' judicial decision making. *Personality and Social Psychology Bulletin, 32,* 188–200.

Epley, N., & Gilovich, T. (2006). The anchoring-and-adjustment heuristic: Why the adjustments are insufficient. *Psychological Science, 17,* 311–318.

Epley, N., & Huff, C. (1998). Suspicion, affective response, and educational benefit as a result of deception in psychology research. *Personality and Social Psychology Bulletin, 24,* 759–768.

Epstude, K., & Mussweiler, T. (2009). What you feel is how you compare: How comparisons influence the social induction of affect. *Emotion, 9,* 1–14.

Erwin, P. G., & Letchford, J. (2003). Types of preschool experience and sociometric status in the primary school. *Social Behavior and Personalty, 31,* 129–132.

Escobedo, J. R., & Adolphs, R. (2010). Becoming a better person: Temporal remoteness biases autobiographical memories for moral events. *Emotion, 10,* 511–518.

Esses, V. M., Jackson, L. M., & Bennett-AbuAyyash, C. (2010). Intergroup competition. In J. F. Dovidio, M. Hewstone, P. Glick, & V. M. Esses (Eds.), *Sage handbook of prejudice, stereotyping and discrimination* (pp. 225–240). London: Sage.

Esses, V. M., Jackson, L. M., Nolan, J. M., & Armstrong, T. L. (1999). Economic threat and attitudes toward immigrants.

In S. Halli & L. Drieger (Eds.), *Immigrant Canada: Demographic, economic and social challenges* (pp. 212–229). Toronto: University of Toronto Press.

Estrada, C. A., Isen, A. M., & Young, M. J. (1995). Positive affect improves creative problem solving and influences reported source of practice satisfaction in physicians. *Motivation and Emotion, 18,* 285–300.

Etcoff, N. L., Ekman, P., Magee, J. J., & Frank, M. G. (2000). Lie detection and language comprehension. *Nature, 40,* 139.

European and World ValuesSurveys Integrated Data File, 1999–2002, Release I User Guide and Codebook Ronald Inglehart et al. *University of Michigan Institute for Social Research*Second ICPSR Version January 2005,

Exline, J. J., & Lobel, M. (1999). The perils of outperformance: Sensitivity about being the target of a threatening upward comparison. *Psychological Bulletin, 125,* 307–337.

Falomir-Pichastor, J. M., Munoz-Rojas, D., Invernizzi, F., & Mugny, G. (2004). Perceived in-group threat as a factor moderating the influence of in-group norms on discrimination against foreigners. *European Journal of Social Psychology, 34,* 135–153.

Fazio, R. H. (2000). Accessible attitudes as tools for object appraisal: The costs and benefits. In G. R. Maio & J. M. Olson (Eds.), *Why we evaluate: Functions of attitudes* (pp. 1–26). Mahwah, NJ: Erlbaum.

Fazio, R. H., & Hilden, L. E. (2001). Emotional reactions to a seemingly prejudiced response: The role of automatically activated racial attitudes and motivation to control prejudiced reactions. *Personality and Social Psychology Bulletin, 27,* 538–549.

Fazio, R. H., & Olson, M. A. (2003). Implicit measures in social cognition research: Their meaning and uses. *Annual Review of Psychology, 54,* 297–327.

Fazio, R. H., & Roskos-Ewoldsen, D. R. (1994). Acting as we feel: When and how attitudes guide behavior. In S. Shavitt & T. C. Brock (Eds.), *Persuasion* (pp. 71–93). Boston: Allyn and Bacon.

Fazio, R. H., Ledbetter, J. E., & Towles-Schwen, T. (2000). On the costs of accessible attitudes: Detecting that the attitude object has changed. *Journal of Personality and Social Psychology, 78,* 197–210.

Fazio, R.H. (1990). Multiple processes by which attitudes guide behavior: The MODE model as an integrative framework. In M.P. Zanna (Ed.), *Advances in experimental social psychology* (Vol. 23, pp. 75–109). San Diego, CA: Academic Press.

Feagin, J. R., & Vera, H. (1995). *White racism.* New York: Routledge.

Fehr, B. (2004). Intimacy expectations in same-sex friendships: A prototype interaction-pattern model. *Journal of Personality and Social Psychology, 86,* 265–284.

Fehr, B., & Broughton, R. (2001). Gender and personality differences in conceptions of love: An interpersonal theory analysis. *Personal Relationships, 8,* 115–136.

Feingold, A. (1992). Good-looking people are not what we think. *Psychological Bulletin, 111*, 304–341.

Feldman Barrett L, Robin L, Pietromonaco PR, Eyssell KM. Are women the "more emotional" sex? Evidence from emotional experiences in social context. *Cognition and Emotion.* 1998;12:555–578

Feldman, R. S., Forrest, J. A., & Happ, B. R. (2002). Self-presentation and verbal deception: Do self-presenters lie more? *Basic and Applied Social Psychology, 24*, 163–170.

Felmlee, D. H. (1995). Fatal attractions: Affection and disaffection in intimate relationships. *Journal of Social and Personal Relationships, 12*, 295–311.

Felmlee, D. H. (1998). "Be careful what you wish for . . .": A quantitative and qualitative investigation of "fatal attractions." *Personal Relationships, 5*, 235–253.

Ferris, G. R., Davidson, S. L., & Perrewe, P. L. (2006). *Political skill at work: Impact on work effectiveness.* New York: Davis-Black Publishing

Feshbach, S. (1984). The catharsis hypothesis, aggressive drive, and the reduction of aggression. *Aggressive Behavior, 10*, 91–101.

Festinger, L. (1954). A theory of social comparison processes. *Human Relations, 7*, 117–140.

Festinger, L., & Carlsmith, J. M. (1959). Cognitive consequences of forced compliance. *Journal of Abnormal and Social Psychology, 58*, 203–210.

Festinger, L., Schachter, S., & Back, K. (1950). *Social pressures in informal groups: A study of a housing community.* New York: Harper.

Fiedler, K., Messner, C., & Bluemke, M. (2006). Unresolved problems with the "I", the "A", and the "T": A logical and psychometric critique of the Implicit Association Test (IAT). *European Review of Social Psychology, 17*, 74–147.

Fielding, K. S., & Hogg, M. A. (1997). Social identity, self-categorization, and leadership: A field study of small interactive groups. *Group Dynamics: Theory, Research, and Practice, 1*, 39–51.

Fink, B., & Penton-Voak, I. (2002). Evolutionary psychology of facial attractiveness. *Current Directions in Psychological Science, 11*, 154–158.

Fischer, P., & Greitemeyer, T. (2006). Music and aggression: The impact of sexual-aggressive song lyrics on aggression-related thoughts, emotions, and behavior toward the same and the opposite sex. *Personality and Social Psychology Bulletin 32*, 1165–1176.

Fisher, R.P,. Milne, R., & Bull, R. (2011). Interviewing cooperative witnesses. *Current Perspectives on Psychological Science, 20*, 16–19

Fiske, S. T. (2009). Social cognition. In D. Sander & K. R. Scherer (Eds.), *Oxford companion to emotion and the affective sciences* (pp. 371–373). Oxford, UK: Oxford University Press.

Fiske, S. T., & Stevens, L. E. (1993). What's so special about sex? Gender stereotyping and discrimination. In S. Oskamp & M. Costanzo (Eds.), *Gender issues in contemporary society* (pp. 173–196). Newbury Park, CA: Sage.

Fiske, S. T., & Taylor, S. E. (2008). *Social cognition: From brains to culture.* New York: McGraw-Hill.

Fiske, S. T., Cuddy, A. J. C., Glick, P., & Xu, J. (2002). A model of (often mixed) stereotype content: Competence and warmth respectively follow from perceived status and competition. *Journal of Personality and Social Psychology, 82*, 878–902.

Fitzsimmons, G. M., & Bargh, J. A. (2003). Thinking of you: Nonconscious pursuit of interpersonal goals associated with relationships partners. *Journal of Personality and Social Psychology, 84*, 148–164.

Fitzsimons, G. M., & Kay, A. C. (2004). Language and interpersonal cognition: Causal effects of variations in pronoun usage on perceptions of closeness. *Personality and Social Psychology Bulletin, 30*, 547–557.

Fleming, M. A., & Petty, R. E. (2000). Identity and persuasion: An elaboration likelihood approach. In D. J. Terry & M. A. Hogg (Eds.), *Attitudes, behavior, and social context* (pp. 171–199). Mahwah, NJ: Erlbaum.

Fletcher, G. J. O., Simpson, J. A., & Boyes, A. D. (2006). Accuracy and bias in romantic relationships: An evolutionary and social psychological analysis. In M. Schaller, J. A. Simpson, & D. T. Kenrick (Eds.), *Evolution and social psychology* (pp. 1890–210). New York: Psychology Press.

Flynn, F. J., Reagans, R. E., Amanatullah, E. T., & Ames, D. R. (2006). Helping one's way to the top: Self-monitors achieve status by helping others and knowing who helps them. *Journal of Personality and Social Psychology, 91*, 1123–1137.

Folger, R., & Baron, R. A. (1996). Violence and hostility at work: A model of reactions to perceived injustice. In G. R. VandenBos and E. Q. Bulato (Eds.), *Violence on the job: Identifying risks and developing solutions* (pp. 51–85). Washington, DC: American Psychological Association.

Forgas, J. P. (Ed.). (2000). *Feeling and thinking: Affective influences on social cognition.* New York: Cambridge University Press.

Forgas, J. P., Baumeister, R. F., & Tice, D.N. (2009). *The psychology of self-regulation.* Sydney, Australia: Psychology Press.

Forgas, J. P., Vargas, P., & Laham, S. (2005). Mood effects on eyewitness memory: Affective influences on susceptibility to misinformation. *Journal of Experimental Social Psychology, 41*, 574–588.

Forrest, J. A., & Feldman, R. S. (2000). Detecting deception and judge's involvement; lower task involvement leads to better lit detection. *Personality and Social Psychology Bulletin, 26*, 118–125.

Fowers, B., Lyons, E., Montel, K., & Shaked, N. (2001). Positive illusions about marriage among married and single individuals. *Journal of Family Psychology*, 95–109.

Fox, J., & Bailenson, J. (2009). Virtual virgins and vamps: The effects of exposure to female characters' sexualized appearance and gaze in an immersive virtual environment. *Sex Roles, 61*, 147–157.

Frank, E., & Brandstatter, V. (2002). Approach versus avoidance: Different types of commitment to intimate relationships. *Journal of Personality and Social Psychology, 82,* 208–221.

Frank, T. (2004). What's the matter with Kansas?: How conservatives won the heart of America. *New York: Metropolitan Books.*

Fredrickson, B. L. (1995). Socioemotional behavior at the end of college life. *Journal of Social and Personal Relationships, 12,* 261–276.

Fredrickson, B. L. 2001. The role of positive emotions in positive psychology: The broaden-and-build theory of positive emotions. *American Psychologist 56,* 218–226.

Fredrickson, B. L., & Joiner, T. (2002). Positive emotions trigger upward spirals toward emotional well-being. *Psychological Science, 13,* 172–175.

Freedman, J. L., & Fraser, S. C. (1966). Compliance without pressure: The foot-in-the-door technique. *Journal of Personality and Social Psychology, 4,* 195–202.

Frenda, S.J., Nichols, R.M., & Loftus, E. (2011). Current issues s and advances in misinformation research. *Current Perspectives on Psychological Science, 20,* 20–23.

Fritzsche, B. A., Finkelstein, M. A., & Penner, L. A. (2000). To help or not to help: Capturing individuals' decision policies. *Social Behavior and Personality, 28,* 561–578.

Frye, G. D. J., & Lord, C. G. (2009). Effects of time frame on the relationship between source monitoring errors and attitude change. *Social Cognition, 27,* 867–882.

Fuegen, K., & Brehm, J. W. (2004). The intensity of affect and resistance to social influence. In E. S. Knowles & J. A. Linn (Eds.), *Resistance and persuasion* (pp. 39–63). Mahwah, NJ: Erlbaum.

Fujita, K., & Han, H. A. (2009). Moving beyond deliberative control of impulses: The effect of construal levels on evaluative associations in self-control conflicts. *Psychological Science, 20,* 799–804.

Fultz, J., Shaller, M., & Cialdini, R. B. (1988). Empathy, sadness, and distress: Three related but distant vicarious affective responses to another's suffering. *Personality and Social Psychology Bulletin, 14,* 312–325.

Funk, J. B., Bechtoldt-Baldacci, H., Pasold, T., & Baumgartner, J. (2004). Violence exposure in real-life, video games, television, movies, and the internet: Is there desensitization? *Journal of Adolescence, 27,* 23–39.

Furr, R. M., & Funder, D. C. (1998). A multimodal analysis of personal negativity. *Journal of Personality and Social Psychology, 74,* 1580–1591.

Gärling, T., Kirchler, E., Lewis, A., & van Raaij, F. (2009). Psychology, financial decision making, and financial crises. *Psychological Science in the Public Interest, 10,* 1–47.

Gabaix, X. & Laibson, L. (2006). Shrouded attributes, consumer myopia, and information suppression in competitive markets. *Quarterly Journal of Economics, 121.* 505–540.

Gaertner, S. L., Mann, J. A., Dovidio, J. F., Murrell, A. J., & Pomare, M. (1990). How does cooperation reduce intergroup bias? *Journal of Personality and Social Psychology, 59,* 692–704.

Gaertner, S. L., Mann, J., Murrell, A., & Dovidio, J. F. (1989). Reducing intergroup bias: The benefits of recategorization. *Journal of Personality and Social Psychology, 57,* 239–249.

Gaertner, S. L., Rust, M. C., Dovidio, J. F., Bachman, B. A., & Anastasio, P. A. (1994). The contact hypothesis: The role of common ingroup identity on reducing intergroup bias. *Small Group Research, 25,* 224–249.

Galdi, S., Arcuri, L., & Gawronski, B. (2008). Automatic mental associations predict future choices of undecided decision-makers. *Science, 321,* 1100–1102.

Galinsky, A. D., Magee, J. C., Gruenfeld, D. H., Whitson, J. A., & Liljenquist, K. A. (2008). Power reduces the press of the situation: Implications for creativity, conformity, and dissonance. *Journal of Personality and Social Psychology, 95,* 1450–1466.

Galinsky, A.D., Magee, J.C., Inesi, M.E., & Gruenfeld, D. (2006). Power and perspectives not taken. *Psychologial Science, 17,* 1068–1073.

Galton, F. (1952). *Hereditary genius: An inquiry into its laws and consequences.* New York: Horizon. (Original work published 1870.)

Gantner, A. B., & Taylor, S. P. (1992). Human physical aggression as a function of alcohol and threat of harm. *Aggressive Behavior, 18,* 29–36.

Garcia, D. M., Schmitt, M. T., Branscombe, N. R., & Ellemers, N. (2010). Women's reactions to ingroup members who protest discriminatory treatment: The importance of beliefs about inequality and response appropriateness. *European Journal of Social Psychology, 40,* 733–745.

Garcia, S. M., Weaver, K., Moskowitz, G. B., & Darley, J. M. (2002). Crowded minds: The implicit bystander effect. *Journal of Personality and Social Psychology, 83,* 843–853.

Garcia-Marques, T., Mackie, D. M., Claypool, H. M., & Garcia-Marques, L. (2004). Positivity can cue familiarity. *Personality and Social Psychology Bulletin, 30,* 585–593.

Gardner, R. M., & Tockerman, Y. R. (1994). A computer–TV methodology for investigating the influence of somatotype on perceived personality traits. *Journal of Social Behavior and Personality, 9,* 555–563.

Gawronski, B., LeBel, E. P., & Peters, K. R. (2007). What do implicit measures tell us? *Perspectives on Psychological Science, 2,* 181–193.

Gazzola, V., Aziz-Zadeh, L., & Keysers, C. (2006) Empathy and the somatotopic auditory mirror system in humans. *Current Biology, 16,* 1824–1829.

Geary, D. C., Vigil, J., & Byrd-Craven, J. (2004). Evolution of human mate choice. *Journal of Sex Research, 41,* 27–42.

Gentile, D. A. & Gentile, J. R. (2008). Violent video games as exemplary teachers: A conceptual analysis. *Journal of Youth and Adolescence, 9,* 127–141

Gentile, D. A., Anderson, C. A., Yukawa, S., Ihori, N., Saleem, M., Ming, L.K., et al. (2009). The effects of prosocial video games on prosocial behaviors: International evidence form correlational, longitudinal, and experimental studies. *Personality and Social Psychology Bulletin, 35,* 752–763.

Gentile, D.A., et al. (2009). The effects of prosocial video games on prosocial behaviors: International evidence from correlational, longitudinal, and experimental studies. *Personality and Social Psychology Bulletin, 35,* 741–763.

Gerard, H. B., Wilhelmy, R. A., & Conolley, E. S. (1968). Conformity and group size. *Journal of Personality and Social Psychology, 8,* 79–82.

Gibbons, D., & Olk, P. M. (2003). Individual and structural origins of friendship and social position among professionals. *Journal of Personality and Social Psychology, 84,* 340–351.

Gibbons, F. X., Eggleston, T. J., & Benthin, A. C. (1997). Cognitive reactions to smoking relapse: The reciprocal relation between dissonance and self-esteem. *Journal of Personality and Social Psychology, 72,* 184–195.

Giessner, S. R., & van Knippenberg, D. (2008). "License to fail": Goal definition, leader group prototypicality, and perceptions of leadership effectiveness after leader failure. *Organizational Behavior and Human Decision Processes, 105,* 14–35.

Gigone, D., & Hastie, R. (1997). The impact of information on small group choice. *Journal of Personality and Social Psychology, 72,* 132–140.

Gilbert, D. T. (2002). Inferential correction. In T. Gilovich, D. W. Griffin, & D. Kahneman (Eds.), *Heuristics and biases: The psychology of intuitive judgment* (pp. 167–184) New York: Cambridge University Press.

Gilbert, D. T. (2006). *Stumbling on happiness.* New York: Knopf.

Gilbert, D. T., & Malone, P. S. (1995). The correspondence bias. *Psychological Bulletin, 117,* 21–38.

Gilbert, D. T., & Wilson, T. D. (2000). Miswanting: Some problems in the forecasting of future affective states. In J. Forgas (Ed.), *Feeling and thinking: The role of affect in social cognition.* New York: Cambridge University Press.

Gillath, O., Shaver, P. R., Baek, J. M., & Chun, S. D. (2008). Genetic correlates of adult attachment style. *Personality and Social Psychology Bulletin, 34,* 1396–1405.

Gladue, B. A., & Delaney, H. J. (1990). Gender differences in perception of attractiveness of men and women in bars. *Personality and Social Psychology Bulletin, 16,* 378–391.

Gladwell, M. *Blink.* New York: Little, Brown.

Glass, D. C. (1977). *Behavior patterns, stress, and coronary disease.* Hillsdale, NJ: Erlbaum.

Gleason, K. A., Jensen-Campbell, L. A., & Ickes, W. (2009). The role of empathic accuracy in adolescents' peer relations and adjustment. *Personality and Social Psychology Bulletin, 35,* 997–1011.

Gleibs, I. H., Noack, P., & Mummendey, A. (2010). We are still better than them: A longitudinal field study of ingroup favouritism during a merger. *European Journal of Social Psychology, 40,* 819–836.

Glick, P. (2002). Sacrificial lambs dressed in wolves' clothing: Envious prejudice, ideology, and the scapegoating of Jews. In *Understanding genocide: The social psychology of the Holocaust* (pp. 113–142). New York: Oxford University Press.

Glick, P., & Rudman, L. A. (2010). Sexism. In J. F. Dovidio, M. Hewstone, P. Glick, & V. M. Esses (Eds.), *Sage handbook of prejudice, stereotyping and discrimination* (pp. 328–344). London: Sage.

Goel, S., Mason, W., Watts, & Watts, D.J. (2010). *Journal of Personality and Social Psychology, 99,* 611–621.

Goethals, G. R., & Darley, J. (1977). Social comparison theory: An attributional approach. In J. M. Suls & R. L. Miller (Eds.), *Social comparison processes: Theoretical and empirical perspectives* (pp. 259–278). Washington, DC: Hemisphere.

Goetz, J. L., Keltner, D., & Simon-Thomas, E. (2010). Compassion: An evolutionary analysis and empirical review. *Psychological Bulletin, 136,* 351–374.

Goff, P. A., Eberhardt, J. L., Williams, M. J., & Jackson, M. C. (2008). Not yet human: Implicit knowledge, historical dehumanization, and contemporary consequences. *Journal of Personality and Social Psychology, 94,* 292–306.

Goff, P. A., Steele, C. M., & Davies, P. G. (2008). The space between us: Stereotype threat and distance in interracial contexts. *Journal of Personality and Social Psychology, 94,* 91–107.

Goldenberg, J. L., Pyszczynski, T., Greenberg, J., McCoy, S. K., & Solomon, S. (1999). Death, sex, love, and neuroticism: Why is sex such a problem? *Journal of Personality and Social Psychology, 77,* 1173–1187.

Goldinger, S. D., Kleider, H. M., Azuma, T., & Beike, D. R. (2003). "Blaming the victim" under memory load. *Psychological Science, 14,* 81–85.

Gollwitzer, P. M. (1999). Implementation intentions: Strong effects of simple plans. *American Psychologist, 54,* 493–503.

Goodwin, R., Cook, O., & Yung, Y. (2001). Loneliness and life satisfaction among three cultural groups. *Personal Relationships, 8,* 225–230.

Gordon, R. A. (1996). Impact of ingratiation in judgments and evaluations: A meta-analytic investigation. *Journal of Personality and Social Psychology, 71,* 54–70.

Graham, S., & Folkes, V. (Eds.). (1990). *Attribution theory: Applications to achievement, mental health, and interpersonal conflict.* Hillsdale, NJ: Erlbaum.

Grant, A. M., & Gino, F. (2010). A little thanks goes a long way: Explaining why gratitude expressions motivate prosocial behavior. *Journal of Personality and Social Psychology, 98,* 946–955.

Graves, K. N. (2007). Not always sugar and spice: Expanding theoretical and functional explanations for why females aggress. *Aggression and Violent Behavior, 12,* 131–140.

Gray, H. M. (2008). To what extent and under what conditions are first impressions valid? In N. Ambady & J. Skowronski (Eds.), *First impressions* (pp. 106–128). New York: Guilford Press.

Green, M. C. (2007). Trust and social interaction on the internet. In A. N. Joinson, K. Y. A. McKenna, T. Postmes, & U.-D. Reips (Eds.), *The Oxford handbook of internet psychology* (pp. 43–51). New York: Oxford University Press.

Greenbaum, P., & Rosenfield, H. W. (1978). Patterns of avoidance in responses to interpersonal staring and proximity: Effects of bystanders on drivers at a traffic intersection. *Journal of Personality and Social Psychology, 36,* 575–587.

Greenberg, J. (1993). Justice and organizational citizenship: A commentary on the state of the science. *Employee Responsibilities and Rights Journal, 6,* 249-256.

Greenberg, J., Martens, A., Jonas, E., Eisenstadt, D., Pyszczynski, T., & Solomon, S. (2003). Psychological defense in anticipation of anxiety: Eliminating the potential for anxiety eliminates the effects of mortality salience on worldview defense. *Psychological Science, 14,* 516–519.

Greenberg, J., Pyszczynski, T., & Solomon, S. (1986). The causes and consequences of a need for self-esteem: A terror management theory. In R. F. Baumeister (Ed.), Public self and private self (p. 189–212). New York: Springer-Verlag.

Greene, E., & Bornstein, B.H. (2003). Determining damages: The opsychology of jury awards. Washington, D.C.: *The American Psychological Association. Bornstein.* Washington, D.C.: *The American Psychological Association,* 2003.

Greenwald, A. G. (2002). Constructs in student ratings of instructors. In H. I. Braun & D. N. Douglas (Eds.), *The role of constructs in psychological and educational measurement* (pp. 277–297). Mahwah, NJ: Erlbaum.

Greenwald, A. G., & Banaji, M. R. (1995). Implicit social cognition: Attitudes, self-esteem, and stereotypes. *Psychological Review, 102,* 4–27.

Greenwald, A. G., & Farnham, S. (2000). Using the Implicit Association Test to measure self- esteem and self-concept. *Journal of Personality and Social Psychology, 79,* 1022–1038.

Greenwald, A. G., & Nosek, B. A. (2008). Attitudinal dissociation: What does it mean? In R. E. Petty, R. H. Fazio & P. Brinol (Eds.), *Attitudes: Insights from the new implicit measures* (pp. 65–82). Hillsdale, NJ: Erlbaum.

Greenwald, A. G., Banaji, M. R., Rudman, L. A., Farnham, S. D., Nosek, B. A., & Mellott, D. S. (2002). A unified theory of implicit attitudes, stereotypes, self-esteem, and self-concept. *Psychological Review, 109,* 3–25.

Greenwald, A. G., McGhee, D. E., & Schwarz, J. L. K. (1998). Measuring individual differences in implicit cognition: The Implicit Association Test. *Journal of Personality and Social Psychology, 74,* 1464–1480.

Greenwald, A. G., Poehlman, T. A., Uhlmann, E. L., & Banaji, M. R. (2009). Understanding and using the Implicit Association Test: III. Meta-analysis of predictive validity. *Journal of Personality and Social Psychology, 97,* 17–41.

Greitmeyer, T., & Osswald, S. (2010). Effects of prosocial video games on prosocial behavior. *Journal of Personality and Social Psychology, 98,* 211–221.

Griskevicius, V., Goldstein, N. J., Mortensen, D. R., Cialdini, R. B., & Kenrick, D. T. (2006). Going along versus going alone: When fundamental motives facilitate strategic (non) conformity. *Journal of Personality and Social Psychology, 91,* 281–294.

Griskevicius, V., Tybur, J. M., Gangestad, S. W., Perea, E. F., Shapiro, J. R., & Kenrick, D. T. (2009). Aggress to impress: Hostility as an evolved context-dependent strategy. *Journal of Personality and Social Psychology 96,* 980–994.

Griskevicius, V., Tybus, J. M., Gangestad, S. W., Perea, E. F., Shapiro, J. R., & Kenrick, D. T. (in press). Aggress to impress: Hostility as an evolved context-dependent strategy. *Journal of Personality and Social Psychology.*

Guéguen. N. (in press). Color and Women Hitchhikers' Attractiveness: Gentlemen Drivers Prefer Red. *Color Research and Application.*

Gueguen, N. (2003). Fund-raising on the Web: The effect of an electronic door-in-the-face technique in compliance to a request. *CyberPsychlogy & Behavior, 2,* 189–193.

Guimond, S. (2000). Group socialization and prejudice: The social transmission of intergroup attitudes and beliefs. *European Journal of Social Psychology, 30,* 335–354.

Guimond, S., Branscombe, N. R., Brunot, S., Buunk, B. P., Chatard, A., Désert, M., et al. (2007). Culture, gender, and the self: Variations and impact of social comparison processes. *Journal of Personality and Social Psychology, 92,* 1118–1134.

Guinote, A., Judd, C. M., & Brauer, M. (2002). Effects of power on perceived and objective group variability: Evidence that more powerful groups are more variable. *Journal of Personality and Social Psychology, 82,* 708–721.

Gump, B. B., & Kulik, J. A. (1997). Stress, affiliation, and emotional contagion. *Journal of Personality and Social Psychology, 72,* 305–319.

Gustafson, R. (1990). Wine and male physical aggression. *Journal of Drug Issues, 20,* 75–86.

Gustafson, R. (1992). Alcohol and aggression: A replication study controlling for potential confounding variables. *Aggressive Behavior, 18,* 21–28.

Hackman, J. R., & Wageman, R. (2007). Asking the right questions about leadership. *American Psychologist, 62,* 43–47.

Hagger, M. S., Wood, C., Stiff, C., & Chatzisarantis, N. L. D. (2010). Ego depletion and the strength model of self-control: A meta analysis. *Psychological Bulletin, 136,* 495–525.

Halberstadt, J., & Rhodes, G. (2000). The attractiveness of nonface averages: Implications for an evolutionary explanation of the attractiveness of average faces. *Psychological Science, 11,* 285–289.

Hall-Elston, C., & Mullins, L. C. (1999). Social relationships, emotional closeness, and loneliness among older meal program participants. *Social Behavior and Personality, 27,* 503–518.

Hamilton, D. L., Levine, J. M., & Thurston, J. A. (2008). Perceiving continuity and change in groups. In F. Sani (Ed.), *Self continuity: Individual and collective perspectives* (pp. 117–130). New York: Psychology Press.

Hamilton, G. V. (1978). Obedience and responsibility: A jury simulation. *Journal of Personality and Social Psychology, 36,* 126–146.

Hanko, K., Master, S., & Sabini, J. (2004). Some evidence about character and mate selection. *Personality and Social Psychology Bulletin, 30,* 732–742.

Hansen, N., & Sassenberg, K. (2006). Does social identification harm or serve as a buffer? The impact of social identification on anger after experiencing social discrimination. *Personality and Social Psychology Bulletin, 32,* 983–996.

Hareli, S., & Weiner, B. (2000). Accounts for success as determinants of perceived arrogance and modesty. *Motivation and Emotion, 24,* 215–236.

Harmon-Jones, E. (2000). Cognitive dissonance and experienced negative affect: Evidence that dissonance increases experienced negative affect even in the absence of aversive consequences. *Personality and Social Psychology Bulletin, 26,* 1490–1501.

Harmon-Jones, E., & Allen, J. J. B. (2001). The role of affect in the mere exposure effect: Evidence from psychophysiological and individual differences approaches. *Personality and Social Psychology Bulletin, 27,* 889–898.

Harmon-Jones, E., Harmon-Jones, C., Fearn, M., Sigelman, J. D., & Johnson, P. (2008). Left frontal cortical activation and spreading of alternatives: Tests of the action-based model of dissonance. *Journal of Personality and Social Psychology, 94,* 1–15.

Harris, C. R. (2003). A review of sex differences in sexual jealousy, including self-report data, psychophysiological responses, interpersonal violence, and morbid jealousy. *Personality and Social Psychology Review, 7,* 102–128.

Harris, L. R., & Weiss, D. J. (1995). Judgments of consent in simulated rape cases. *Journal of Social Behavior and Personality, 10,* 79–90.

Harris, M. B. (1992). Sex, race, and experiences of aggression. *Aggressive Behavior, 18,* 201–217.

Harris, M. B. (1993). How provoking! What makes men and women angry? *Journal of Applied Social Psychology, 23,* 199–211.

Harris, M. B. (1994). Gender of subject and target as mediators of aggression. *Journal of Applied Social Psychology, 24,* 453–471.

Harrison, M. (2003). "What is love?" Personal communication.

Haslam, S. A. (2004). *Psychology in organizations: The social identity approach* (2nd ed.). London: Sage.

Haslam, S. A. (2004). *Psychology in organizations: The social identity approach* (2nd ed.). Thousand Oaks, CA: Sage.

Haslam, S. A., & Platow, M. J. (2001). The link between leadership and followership: How affirming social identity translates vision into action. *Personality and Social Psychology Bulletin, 27,* 1469–1479.

Haslam, S. A., & Reicher, S. D. (2006). Stressing the group: Social identity and the unfolding dynamics of responses to stress. *Journal of Applied Psychology, 91,* 1037–1052.

Haslam, S. A., & Wilson, A. (2000). In what sense are prejudicial beliefs personal? The importance of an in-group's shared stereotypes. *British Journal of Social Psychology, 39,* 45–63.

Haslam, S. A., Reicher, S., & Platow, M. J. (2010). *The new psychology of leadership: Identity, influence and power.* New York: Psychology Press.

Haslam, S. A., Ryan, M. K., Kulich, C., Trojanowski, G., & Atkins, C. (2010). Investing with prejudice: The relationship between women's presence on company boards and objective and subjective measures of company performance. *British Journal of Management, 21,* 484–497.

Haslam, S. A., Ryan, M. K., Postmes, T., Spears, R., Jetten, J., & Webley, P. (2006). Sticking to our guns: Social identity as a basis for the maintenance of commitment to faltering organizational projects. *Journal of Organizational Behavior, 27,* 607–628.

Hassin, R., & Trope, Y. (2000). Facing faces: Studies on the cognitive aspects of physiognomy. *Journal of Personality and Social Psychology, 78,* 837–852.

Hatfield, E., & Rapson, R. L. (1993). Historical and cross-cultural perspectives on passionate love and sexual desire. *Annual Review of Sex Research, 4,* 67–97.

Hatfield, E., & Sprecher, S. (1966b). Measuring passionate lives in intimate relations. *Journal of Adolescence, 9,* 383-410.

Hatfield, E., & Walster, G. W. (1981). *A new look at love.* Reading, MA: Addison-Wesley.

Hatfield, E., & Rapson, R. L. (2009). Love. In I. B. Weiner & W. E. Craighead (Eds.). Encyclopedia of Psychology, 4th Edition. Hoboken, NJ: John Wiley and Sons.

Hatfield, E., Cacioppo, J., & Rapson, R.L. (1994). *Emotional contagion. New York: Cambridge University Press.*

Haugtvedt, C. P., & Wegener, D. T. (1994). Message order effects in persuasion: An attitude strength perspective. *Journal of Consumer Research, 21,* 205–218.

Hawkey, L. C., Thisted, R. A., Masi, C. M., Cacioppo, J. T. (2010). Loneliness predicts increased blood pressure: 5-year cross-lagged analyses in middle-aged and older adults. *Psychology and Aging, 25,* 132–141.

Hawkley, L. C., Burleson, M. H., Berntson, G. G., & Cacioppo, J. T. (2003). Loneliness in everyday life: Cardiovascular activity, psychosocial context, and health behaviors. *Journal of Personality and Social Psychology, 85,* 105–120.

Hawkley, L. C., Thisted, R. A., Masi, C. M., & Cacioppo, J. T. (2010). Loneliness predicts increased blood pressure: Five-year cross-lagged analysis in middle-aged and older adults. *Psychology and Aging, 25,* 132–141.

Hawley, P. H., Card, N., & Little, T. D., (2007). The allure of a mean friend: Relationship quality and processes of aggressive adolescents with prosocial skills. *International Journal of Behavioral Development, 32,* 21–32.

Hawley, P. H., Little, T. D., & Rodin, P. C., (Eds). (2007). *Aggression and adaptation: The bright side of bad behavior.* Mahwah, NJ: Lawrence Erlbaum.

Hayden, S. R., Jackson, T. T., & Guydish, J. N. (1984). Helping behavior of females: Effects of stress and commonality of fate. *Journal of Psychology, 117,* 233–237.

Hebl, M. & Dovidio, J.F. (2005). Promoting the "social" in the examination of social stigmas. *Personality and Social Psychology Review, 9,* 156–182.

Heider, F. (1958). *The psychology of interpersonal relations.* New York: Wiley.

Heilman, M. E. (2001). Description and prescription: How gender stereotypes prevent women's ascent up the organizational ladder. *Journal of Social Issues, 57,* 657–674.

Herrera, N. C., Zajonc, R. B., Wieczorkowska, G., & Cichomski, B. (2003). Beliefs about birth rank and their reflection in reality. *Journal of Personality and Social Psychology, 85,* 142–150.

Hetherington, M. M., Anderson, A. S., Norton, G. N., & Newson, L. (2006). Situational effects on meal intake: A comparison of eating alone and eating with others. *Physiology and Behavior, 88,* 498–505.

Hewlin, P. F. (2009). Wearing the cloak: Antecedents and consequences of creating facades of conformtiy. *Journal of Applied Psychology, 94,* 727–741.

Hicks, J. A., Cicero, D. C., Trent, J., Burton, C. M., & King, L. A. (2010). Positive affect, intuition, and feelings of meaning. *Journal of Personality and Social Psychology, 98,* 967–979.

Higgins, E. T., & Kruglanski, A. W. (Eds.). (1996). *Social psychology: Handbook of basic principles.* New York: Guilford Press.

Higgins, N. C., & Shaw, J. K. (1999). Attributional style moderates the impact of causal controlability information on helping behavior. *Social Behavior and Personality, 27,* 221–236.

Higham, P. A., & Carment, W. D. (1992). The rise and fall of politicians: The judged heights of Broadbent, Mulroney and Turner before and after the 1988 Canadian federal election. *Canadian Journal of Behavioral Science, 24,* 404–409.

Hilton, N. Z., Harris, G. T., & Rice, M. E. (2000). The functions of aggression by male teenagers. *Journal of Personality and Social Psychology, 79,* 988–994.

Hinsz, V. B. (1995). Goal setting by groups performing an additive task: A comparison with individual goal setting. *Journal of Applied Social Psychology, 25,* 965–990.

Hmieleski, K. M., & Baron, R. A. (2009). Entrepreneurs' optimism and new venture performance: A social cognitive perspective. *Academy of Management Journal, 52,* 473–488.

Ho, S. S., Brossard, D., & Scheufele, D. A. (2008). Effects of value predispositions, mass media use, and knowledge on public attitudes toward embryonic stem cell research. *International Journal of Public Opinion Research, 20,* 171–192.

Hoaken, P. N. S., Giancola, P. R., & Pihl, R. O. (1998). Executive cognitive functions as mediators of alcohol-related aggression. *Alcohol and Alcoholism, 33,* 45–53.

Hochschild, A. R. (1983). *The managed heart: Commercialization of human feelings.* Berkeley: University of California Press.

Hodges, S. D., Kiel, K. J., Kramer, A. D. I., Veach, D., & Villaneuva, B. R. (2010). Giving birth to empathy: The effects of similar experience on empathic accuracy, empathic concern, and perceived empathy. *Personality and Social Psychology Bulletin, 36,* 398–409.

Hoffer, E. (1953). *The passionate state of mind and other aphorisms.* Cutchogue, NY: Buccaneer Books.

Hogg, M. A. (2001). A social identity theory of leadership. *Personality and Social Psychology Reviewer, 5,* 184–200.

Hogg, M. A. (2007). Organizational orthodoxy and corporate autocrats: Some nasty consequences of organizational identification in uncertain times. In C. Bartel, S. Blader & A. Wrzesniewski (Eds.), *Identity and the modern organization* (pp. 35–59). Mahwah, NJ: Erlbaum.

Holmes, T. H., & Rahe, R. H. (1967). The social readjustment rating scale. *Journal of Psychosomatic Research, 22,* 213–218.

Hope, D. A., Holt, C. S., & Heimberg, R. G. (1995). Social phobia. In T. R. Giles (Ed.), *Handbook of effective psychotherapy* (pp. 227–251). New York: Plenum.

Hornsey, M. J., & Imani, A. (2004). Criticizing groups from the inside and the outside: An identity perspective on the intergroup sensitivity effect. *Personality and Social Psychology Bulletin, 30,* 365–383.

Hornsey, M. J., de Bruijn, P., Creed, J., Allen, J., Ariyanto, A., & Svensson, A. (2005). Keeping it in-house: How audience affects responses to group criticism. *European Journal of Social Psychology, 35,* 291–312.

Hornsey, M. J., Jetten, J., McAuliffe, B. J., & Hogg, M. A. (2006). The impact of individualist and collectivist group norms on evaluations of dissenting group members. *Journal of Experimental Social Psychology, 42,* 57–68.

House, J. S., Landis, K. R., & Umberson, D. (1988). Social relationships and health. *Science, 241,* 540–545.

Hovland, C. I., & Weiss, W. (1951). The influence of source credibility on communication effectiveness. *Public Opinion Quarterly, 15,* 635–650.

Hovland, C. I., Janis, I. L., & Kelley, H. H. (1953). *Communication and persuasion: Psychological studies of opinion change.* New Haven, CT: Yale University Press.

Huesmann, L. R., & Eron, L. D. (1984). Cognitive processes and the persistence of aggressive behavior. *Aggressive Behavior, 10,* 243–251.

Huesmann, L. R., & Eron, L. D. (1986). *Television and the aggressive child: A cross-national comparison.* Hillsdale, NJ: Erlbaum.

Hugenberg, K., & Bodenhausen, G. V. (2003). Facing prejudice: Implicit prejudice and the perception of facial threat. *Psychological Science, 14,* 640–643.

Hummert, M. L., Crockett, W. H., & Kemper, S. (1990). Processing mechanisms underlying use of the balance scheme. *Journal of Personality and Social Psychology, 58,* 5–21.

Hunt, A. McC. (1935). A study of the relative value of certain ideals. *Journal of Abnormal and Social Psychology, 30,* 222–228.

Hunt, C. V., Kim, A., Borgida, E., & Chaiken, S. (2010). Revisiting the self-interest versus values debate: The role of temporal perspective. *Journal of Experimental Social Psychology, 46,* 1155–1158.

Imhoff, R., & Erb, H-P. (2009) What motivates nonconformity?: Uniqueness seeking blocks majority influence. *Personality and Social Psychology Bulletin, 33,* 309–320.

Insel, T. R. & Carter, C. S. (1995, August). The monogamous brain. *Natural History,* 12–14. Jones, Carpenter, & Quintana. (1985).

Insko, C. A. (1985). Balance theory, the Jordan paradigm, and the West tetrahedron. In L. Berkowitz (Ed.), *Advances in experimental social psychology.* New York: Academic Press.

Inzlicht, M., & Ben-Zeev, T. (2000). A threatening intellectual environment: Why females are susceptible to experiencing problem-solving deficits in the presence of males. *Psychological Science, 11,* 365–371.

Ireland, C. A., & Ireland, J. L. (2000). Descriptive analysis of the nature and extent of bullying behavior in a maximum security prison. *Aggressive Behavior, 26,* 213–222.

Ireland, J. L., & Archer, J. (2002). The perceived consequences of responding to bullying with aggression: A study of male and female adult prisoners. *Aggressive Behavior, 28,* 257–272.

Isen, A. M. (1984). Toward understanding the role of affect in cognition. In S. R. Wyer & T. K. Srull (Eds.), *Handbook of social cognition* (Vol. 3, pp. 179–236). Hillsdale, NJ: Erlbaum.

Isen, A. M. (2000). Positive affect and decision making. In M. Lewis & J. M. Haviland-Jones (Eds.), *Handbook of emotions* (2nd ed., pp. 417–435). New York: Guilford Press.

Isen, A. M., & Levin, P. A. (1972). Effect of feeling good on helping: Cookies and kindness. *Journal of Personality and Social Psychology, 21,* 384–388.

Isen, A.M. & Labroo, A.A. (2003). "Some Ways in Which Positive Affect Facilitates Decision Making and Judgment." In S. Schneider & J. Shanteau (Eds.) *Emerging Perspectives on Judgment and Decision Research.* NY, Cambridge: 365–393.

Isen, A.M. (1970). Success, failure, attention, and reaction to others: The warm glow of success. *Journal of Personality and Social Psychology, 15,* 294–301.

Istvan, J., Griffitt, W., & Weidner, G. (1983). Sexual arousal and the polarization of perceived sexual attractiveness. *Basic and Applied Social Psychology, 4,* 307–318.

Iyer, A., Jetten, J., & Tsivrikos, D. (2008). Torn between identities: Predictors of adjustment to identity change. In F. Sani (Ed.), *Self continuity: Individual and collective perspectives* (pp. 187–197). New York: Psychology Press.

Izard, C. (1991). *The psychology of emotions.* New York: Plenum.

Jackman, M. R. (1994). *The velvet glove: Paternalism and conflict in gender, class, and race relations.* Berkeley, CA: University of California Press.

Jackson, T., Soderlind, A., & Weiss, K. E. (2000). Personality traits and quality of relationships as predictors of future loneliness among American college students. *Social Behavior and Personality, 28,* 463–470.

James, W. (1894). Principles of psychology. London: Macmillan.

Janis, I. L. (1982). *Victims of groupthink* (2nd ed.). Boston: Houghton Mifflin.

Janis, I., & Feshbach, S. (1953). Effects of fear-arousing communications. *Journal of Abnormal and Social Psychology, 48,* 78–92.

Jetten, J., Branscombe, N. R., Schmitt, M. T., & Spears, R. (2001). Rebels with a cause: Group identification as a response to perceived discrimination from the mainstream. *Personality and Social Psychology Bulletin, 27,* 1204–1213.

Jetten, J., Haslam, C., & Haslam, S.A. (2011). *The social cure: Identity, health, and well-being.* Hove UK: Psychology Press.

Jetten, J., Haslam, C., Haslam, S. A., & Branscombe, N. R. (2009). The social cure. *Scientifi wAmerican, September–October,* 26–33.

Jetten, J., Haslam, C., Pugliesse, C., Tonks, J., & Haslam, S.A. (2010). Declining autobiographicsl memory and the loss of identity: effects on well-being. *Journal of Clinical Experimental Neuropsychology, 32,* 405–416.

Jetten, J., Hornsey, M. A., & Adarves-Yorno, I. (2006).When group members admit to being conformist: The role of relative intragroup status in conformity self-reports. *Personality and Social Psychology Bulletin, 32,* 162–173.

Jetten, J., Schmitt, M. T., Branscombe, N. R., Garza, A.A., & Mewse, A.J. (2011). Group commitment in the face of discrimination: The role of legitimacy appraisals. *European Journal of Social Psychology, 41,* 116–126.

Jetten, J., Spears, R., & Manstead, A. S. R. (1997). Strength of identification and intergroup differentiation: The influence of group norms. *European Journal of Social Psychology, 27,* 603–609.

Johnson, B. T. (1994). Effects of outcome-relevant involvement and prior information on persuasion. *Journal of Experimental Social Psychology, 30,* 556–579.

Johnson, J. C., Poteat, G. M., & Ironsmith, M. (1991). Structural vs. marginal effects: A note on the importance of structure in determining sociometric status. *Journal of Social Behavior and Personality, 6,* 489–508.

Johnson, J. D., Simmons, C., Trawalter, S., Ferguson, T., & Reed, W. (2003). Observer race and White anti-Black bias: Factors that influence and mediate attributions of "ambiguously racist" behavior. *Personality and Social Psychology Bulletin, 29,* 609–622.

Johnson, M. K., & Sherman, S. J. (1990). Constructing and reconstructing the past and the future in the present. In E. T. Higgins & R. M. Sorrentino (Eds.), *Handbook of motivation and social cognition: Foundations of social behavior* (pp. 482–526). New York: Guilford.

Johnston, V. S., & Oliver-Rodriguez, J. C. (1997). Facial beauty and the late positive component of event-related potentials. *Journal of Sex Research, 34,* 188–198.

Johnstone, B., Frame, C. L., & Bouman, D. (1992). Physical attractiveness and athletic and academic ability in controversial–aggressive and rejected–aggressive children. *Journal of Social and Clinical Psychology, 11,* 71–79.

Joinson, A. N. (2003). *Understanding the psychology of Internet behavior: Virtual worlds, real lives.* Palgrave, UK: Macmillan.

Joinson, A. N., McKenna, K. Y. A., Postmes, T., & Reips, U. D. (Eds.). (2007). *Oxford handbook of Internet psychology.* Oxford, UK: Oxford University Press.

Jones, E. E. (1964). *Ingratiation: A social psychology analysis.* New York: Appleton-Century-Crofts.

Jones, E. E. (1979). The rocky road from acts to dispositions. *American Psychologist, 34,* 107–117.

Jones, E. E., & Davis, K. E. (1965). From acts to disposition: The attribution process in person perception. In L. Berkowitz (Ed.), *Advances in experimental social psychology* (Vol. 2, pp. 219–266). New York: Academic Press.

Jones, E. E., & Harris, V. A. (1967). The attribution of attitudes. *Journal of Experimental Social Psychology, 3,* 1–24.

Jones, E. E., & McGillis, D. (1976). Corresponding inferences and attribution cube: A comparative reappraisal. In J. H. Har, W. J. Ickes, & R. F. Kidd (Eds.), *New directions in attribution research* (Vol. 1). Morristown, NJ: Erlbaum.

Jones, E. E., & Nisbett, R. E. (1971). *The actor and the observer: Divergent perceptions of the causes of behavior.* Morristown, NJ: General Learning Press.

Jones, W.H., Carpenter, R.N., &* Quintana, D. (1985). Personality and interpersonal predictors of loneliness in two cultures. *Journal of Personality and Social Psychology, 48,* 1053–1511.

Judge, T. A., & Cable, T. A. (2004). The effect of physical height on workplace success and income: Preliminary test of a theoretical model. *Journal of Applied Psychology, 89,* 428–441.

Junemann, E., & Lloyd, B. (2003). Consulting for virtual excellence: Virtual teamwork as a task for consultants. *Team Performance: An International Journal, 9,* 182–189.

Kahneman, D. & Tversky, A. (1982). Judgment under uncertainty: Heuristics and biases. In D. Kahneman P,. Slovic, & A. Tversky (Eds.). *Judgment under uncertainty: Heuristics and biases* (pp. 3–22). Cambridge, England: Cambridge Univeristy Press.

Kahneman, D., & Miller, D. T. (1986). Norm theory: Comparing reality to its alternatives. *Psychological Review, 93,* 136–153.

Kahneman, D., & Tversky, A. (1984). Choices, values, and frames. *American Psychologist, 39,* 341–350.

Kahneman, D., & Frederick, S. (2002). Representativeness revisited: Attribute substitution in intuitive judgment. In T. Gilovich, D. Griffin, & D. Kahneman (Eds.), *Heuristics and biases: the psychology of intuitive judgment* (pp. 41–81). New York: Cambridge University Press.

Kahneman, D., & Tversky, A. (1973). On the psychology of prediction. *Psychological Review, 80,* 237–251.

Kahneman, D., Diener, E., & Schwarz, N. (2003). (Eds.). *Well-being; the foundations of hedonic psychology.* New York: Russell Sage Foundation.

Kaighobadi F., Shackelford, T. K., & Goetz, A. T. (2009). From mate retention to murder: Evolutionary psychological perspectives on men's partner-directed violence. *Review of General Psychology, 13,* 327–334.

Kaighobadi, F., Shackelford, T.K., Popp, D., Moyer, R.M., Bates, V.M., & Liddle, J.R. (2008). Perceived riosk of female infidelity moderates the relationshiop between men's personality and partner-directed violence. *Journal of Research in Personality, 43,* 1033–1039.

Kaiser, C. R., & Miller, C. T. (2001). Stop complaining! The social costs of making attributions to discrimination. *Personality and Social Psychology Bulletin, 27,* 254–263.

Kaiser, C. R., Drury, B. J., Spalding, K. E., Cheryan, S., & O'Brien, L.T. (2009). The ironic consequences of Obama's election: Decreased support for social justice. *Journal of Experimental Social Psychology, 45,* 556–559.

Kallgren, C. A., Reno, R. R., & Cialdini, R. B. (2000). A focus theory of normative conduct: When norms do and do not affect behavior. *Personality and Social Psychology Bulletin, 26,* 1002–1012.

Kameda, T., & Sugimori, S. (1993). Psychological entrapment in group decision making: An assigned decision rule and a groupthink phenomenon. *Journal of Personality and Social Psychology, 65,* 282–292.

Kammarath, L. K., Mendoza-Denton, R., & Mischel, W. (2005). Incorporating if . . . then . . . personality signatures in person perception: Beyond the person-situation dichotomy. *Journal of Personality and Social Psychology, 88,* 605–618.

Karau, S. J., & Williams, K. D. (1993). Social loafing: A meta-analytic review and theoretical integration. *Journal of Personality and Social Psychology, 65,* 681–706.

Karraker, K. H., & Stern, M. (1990). Infant physical attractiveness and facial expression: Effects on adult perceptions. *Basic and Applied Social Psychology, 11,* 371–385.

Kashy, D. A., & DePaulo, B. M. (1996). Who lies? *Journal of Personality and Social Psychology, 70,* 1037–1051.

Katz, E., & Lazarsfeld, P. F. (1955). *Personal influence: The part played by people in the flow of mass communication.* Glencoe, IL: The Free Press.

Katzer, C., Fetchenhauier, D., & Belschak, F. (2009). Cyberbullying: Who are the vicdtims? *Journal of Media Psychology, 21,* 25–36.

Kawakami K., & Dovidio, J. F. (2001). The reliability of implicit stereotyping. *Personality and Social Psychology Bulletin, 27*, 212–225.

Kawakami K., Dovidio, J. F., Moll, J., Hermsen, S., & Russn, A. (2000). Just say no (to stereotyping): Effects of training in the negation of stereotypic associations on stereotype activation. *Journal and Personality and Social Psychology, 78*, 871–888.

Kelley, H. H. (1972). Attribution in social interaction. In E. E. Jones et al. (Eds.), *Attribution: Perceiving the causes of behavior*. Morristown, NJ: General Learning Press.

Kelley, H. H., & Michela, J. L. (1980). Attribution theory and research. *Annual Review of Psychology, 31*, 57–501.

Kelman, H. C. (1967). Human use of human subjects: The problem of deception in social psychological experiments. *Psychological Bulletin, 67*, 1–11.

Keltner, D., Gruenfeld, D. H., & Anderson, C. (2003). Power, approach, and inhibition. *Psychological Review, 110*, 265–284.

Kemeny, M. E. (2003). The psychobiology of stress. *Current Directions in Psychological Science, 12*, 124–129.

Kenealy, P., Gleeson, K., Frude, N., & Shaw, W. (1991). The importance of the individual in the 'causal' relationship between attractiveness and self-esteem. *Journal of Community and Applied Social Psychology, 1*, 45–56.

Kenrick, D. T., Neuberg, S. L., Zierk, K. L., & Krones, J. M. (1994). Evolution and social cognition: Contrast effects as a function of sex, dominance, and physical attractiveness. *Personality and Social Psychology Bulletin, 20*, 210–217.

Kenrick, D. T., Sundie, J. M., Nicastle, L. D., & Stone, G. O. (2001). Can one ever be too wealthy or too chaste? Searching for nonlinearities in mate judgement. *Journal of Personality and Social Psychology, 80*, 462–471.

Kenworthy, J. B., & Miller, N. (2001). Perceptual asymmetry in consensus estimates of majority and minority members. *Journal of Personality and Social Psychology, 80*, 597–612.

Kernis, M. H., Cornell, D. P., Sun, C. R., Berry, A. J., & Harlow, T. (1993). There's more to self-esteem than whether it is high or low: The importance of stability of self-esteem. *Journal of Personality and Social Psychology, 65*, 1190–1204.

Kiecolt-Glaser, J. K., Fisher, L., Ogrocki, P., Stout, J. C., Speicher, C. E., & Glaser, R. (1987). Marital quality, marital disruption, and immune function. *Psychosomatic Medicine, 49*, 13–34.

Kiecolt-Glaser, J. K., Kennedy, S., Malkoff, S., Fisher, L., Speicher, C. E., & Glaser, R. (1988). Marital discord and immunity in males. *Psychosomatic Medicine, 50*, 213–229.

Kilduff, M., & Day, D. V. (1994). Do chameleons get ahead? The effects of self-monitoring on managerial careers. *Academy of Management Journal, 37*, 1047–1060.

Kilham, W., & Mann, L. (1974). Level of destructive obedience as a function of transmitter and executant roles in the Milgram obedience paradigm. *Journal of Personality and Social Psychology, 29*, 696–702.

Killeya, L. A., & Johnson, B. T. (1998). Experimental induction of biased systematic processing: The directed through technique. *Personality and Social Psychology Bulletin, 24*, 17–33.

Kim, H., Park, K., & Schwarz, N. (2010). Will this trip really be exciting?: The role of incidental emotions in product evaluation. *Journal of Consumer Research, 36*, 983–991.

Kitzmann, K. M., Cohen, R., & Lockwood, R. L. (2002). Are only children missing out? Comparison of the peer-related social competence of only children and siblings. *Journal of Social and Personal Relationships, 19*, 299–316.

Klar, Y. (2002). Way beyond compare: The nonselective superiority and inferiority biases in judging randomly assigned group members relative to their peers. *Journal of Experimental Social Psychology, 38*, 331–351.

Kleinke, C. L. (1986). Gaze and eye contact: A research review. *Psychological Bulletin, 100*, 78–100.

Klohnen, E. C., & Bera, S. (1998). Behavioral and experiential patterns of avoidantly and securely attached women across adulthood: A 31-year longitudinal perspective. *Journal of Personality and Social Psychology, 74*, 211–223.

Klohnen, E. C., & Luo, S. (2003). Interpersonal attraction and personality: What is attractive—self similarity, ideal similarity, complementarity, or attachment security? *Journal of Personality and Social Psychology, 85*, 709–722.

Ko, S. J., Judd, C. M., & Blair, I. V. (2006). What the voice reveals: Within- and between-category stereotyping on the basis of voice. Personality and Social Psychology Bulletin, 32, 806–819. L.aird, J. D. (I 984). The real role of facial response in the experience of emotion: A reply to Tourangeau and Ellsworth, and others. Journal of Personality and Social Psychology, 47, 909–91

Kochanska, G., Friesenborg, A. F., Lange, L. A., & Martel, M. M. (2004). Parents' personality and infants' temperament as contributors to their emerging relationship. *Journal of Personality and Social Psychology, 86*, 744–759.

Kogan, N., & Wallach, M. A. (1964). *Risk-taking: A study in cognition and personality*. New York: Henry Holt.

Komorita, M., & Parks, G. (1994). Interpersonal relations: Mixed-motive interaction. *Annual Review of Psychology, 46*, 183–207.

Konrath, S.H., O'Brien, E.H, & Hsing, C. (2011). Changes in dispositional empathy in American college students over time: A met-analysis. *Personality and Social Psychology Review, 15*, 180–198.

Koo, M., Algoe, S. B., Wilson, T. D., & Gilbert, D. T. (2008). It's a wonderful life: Mentally subtracting positive events improves people's affective states, contrary to their affective forecasts. *Journal of Personality and Social Psychology, 95*, 1217–1224.

Koole, S. L., Greenberg, J., & Pyszczynski, T. (2006). Introducing science to the psychology of the soul: Experimental existential psychology. *Current Directions in Psychological Science, 15*, 211–216.

Korsgaard, M. A., Meglino, B. M., Lester, S. W., & Jeong, S. S. (2010). Paying you back or paying me forward: Understanding rewarded and unrewarded organizational citizenship behavior. *Journal of Applied Psychology, 95*, 277–290.

Kowalski, R. M. (1996). Complaints and complaining: Functions, antecedents, and consequences. *Psychological Bulletin, 119*, 179–196.

Kowalski, R. M. (2001). The aversive side of social interaction revisited. In R. M. Kowalski (Ed.), *Behaving badly: Aversive behaviors in interpersonal relationships* (pp. 297–309). Washington, DC: American Psychological Association.

Kozak, M. N., Marsh, A. A., & Wegner, D. M. (2006). What do I think you're doing? Action identification and mind attribution. *Journal of Personality and Social Psychology, 90*, 543–555.

Krahe, B., Moller, I., Huesmann, L.R., Kirwill, L., Felber, J., & Berger, A. (2011). Desensitization to media violence: Link with habitual media violence exposure, aggressive cognitions, and aggressive behavior, *Journal of Personality and Social Psychology*, 0100, 630–646.

Krahe, B., Mullerm, I., Huesamann, L.R., Kirwil, L., Felber, J., & Berger, A. (2011). Desensitization to media violence: Links with habitual media violence 3exposure, aggressive cognitions, and aggressive behavior. *Journal of Personality and Social Psychology, 100*, 630–646.

Krause, N. (2007). Longitudinal study of social support and meaning in life. *Psychology and Aging, 22*, 456–459.

Kray, L. J., Galinsky, A. D., & Wong, E. M. (2006). Thinking within the box: The relational processing style elicited by counterfactual mind-sets. *Journal of Personality and Social Psychology, 91*, 33–48.

Krosnick, J. A., Betz, A. L., Jussim, L. J., & Lynn, A. R. (1992). Subliminal conditioning of attitudes. *Personality and Social Psychology Bulletin, 18*, 152–162.

Kruger, J., & Burrus, J. (2004). Egocentrism and focalism in unrealistic optimism (and pessimism). *Journal of Experimental Social Psychology, 40*, 332–340.

Kruger, J., Epley, N., Parker, J., & Ng, Z. W. (2005). Egocentrism over e-mail: Can we communicate as well as we think? *Journal of Personality and Social Psychology, 89*, 925–936.

Kulik, J. A., Mahler, H. I. M., & Moore, P. J. (1996). Social comparison and affiliation under threat: Effects on recovery from major surgery. *Journal of Personality and Social Psychology, 71*, 967–979.

Kunda, Z. (1999). *Social cognition: Making sense of people.* Cambridge, MA: MIT Press.

Kunstman, J. W., & Plant, E. A. (2009). Racing to help: racial bias in high emergency helping situations. *Journal of Personality and Social Psychology, 95*, 1499–1510.

Kurzban, R., & Neuberg, S. L. (2005). Managing ingroup and outgroup relationships. In D. M. Buss (Ed.), *Handbook of evolutionary psychology*, (pp. 653–675). New York: John Wiley.

Kwan, L. A., (1998). *Attitudes and attraction: A new view of how to diagnose the moderating effects of personality.* Unpublished master's thesis, National Universsity of Singapore.

Lalonde, R. N., & Silverman, R. A. (1994). Behavioral preferences in response to social injustice: The effects of group permeability and social identity salience. *Journal of Personality and Social Psychology, 66*, 78–85.

Landau, M. J., Meier, B. P., & Keefer, L. A. (2010). A metaphor-enriched social cognition. *Psychological Bulletin, 136*, 1045–1067.

Landau, M. J., Solomon, S., Greenberg, J., Cohen, F., Pyszczynski, T., Arndt, J., et al. (2004). Deliver us from evil: The effects of mortality salience and reminders of 9/11 on support for President George W. Bush. *Personality and Social Psychology Bulletin, 30*, 1136–1150.

Landau, M. J., Sullivan, D., & Greenberg, J. (2009). Evidence that self-relevant motives and metaphoric framing interact to influence political and social attitudes. *Psychological Science, 20*, 1421–1427.

Langlois, J. H., & Roggman, L. A. (1990). Attractive faces are only average. *Psychological Science, 1*, 115–121.

Langlois, J. H., Roggman, L. A., & Musselman, L. (1994). What is average and what is not average about attractive faces? *Psychological Science, 5*, 214–220.

LaPiere, R. T. (1934). Attitude and actions. *Social Forces, 13*, 230–237.

Larrick, R.P., Timmerman, T.A., Carton, A.M., & Abrevaya, J. (2011). *Psychological Science, 22*, 423–428.

Larrick, R.P., Timmerman, T.A., Carton, A.M., & Abrevaya, J. (2011). Temper, temperature, and temptation: Heat-related retaliation in baseball. *Psychological Science, 11*, 423–428.

Larsen, J. T., & McKibbon, A. R. (2008). Is happiness having what you want, wanting what you have, or both? *Psychological Science, 19*, 371–377.

Larson, J. R., Jr., Foster-Fishman, P. G., & Franz, T. M. (1998). Leadership style and the discussion of shared and unshared information in decision-making groups. *Personality and Social Psychology Bulletin, 24*, 482–495.

Latané, B., & Darley, J. M. (1968). Group inhibition of bystander intervention in emergencies. *Journal of Personality and Social Psychology, 10*, 215–221.

Latané, B., & Darley, J. M. (1970). *The unresponsive bystander: Why doesn't he help?* New York: Appleton-Century-Crofts.

Latané, B., & L'Herrou, T. (1996). Spatial clustering in the conformity game: Dynamic social impact in electronic groups. *Journal of Personality and Social Psychology, 70*, 1218–1230.

Latané, B., Williams, K., & Harkins, S. (1979). Many hands make light the work: The causes and consequences of social loafing. *Journal of Personality and Social Psychology, 37*, 822–832.

Lau, S., & Gruen, G. E. (1992). The social stigma of loneliness: Effect of target person's and perceiver's sex. *Personality and Social Psychology Bulletin, 18*, 182–189.

Laurenceau, J.P., Barrett, L. F., & Pietromonaco, P. R. (1998). Intimacy as an interpersonal process: The importance of self-disclosure, partner disclosure, and perceived partner responsiveness in interpersonal exchanges. *Journal of Personality and Social Psychology, 74,* 1238–1251.

Lazarus R. A. & Folkman, S. (1984). *Stress appraisal and coping.* New York Springer.

Lazarus, R. S., Opton, E. M., Nomikos, M. S., & Rankin, N. O. (1985). The principle of short-circuiting of threat: Further evidence. *Journal of Personality, 33,* 622–635.

Leary, M. R., **Twenge, J. M.,** & Quinlivan. E. (2006). Interpersonal rejection as a determinant of anger and aggression. ***Personality and Social Psychology Review,** 10,* 111–132.

LeBoeuf, R. A., Shafir, E., & Bayuk, J. B. (2010). The conflicting choices of alternating selves. *Organizational Behavior and Human Decision Processes, 111,* 48–61.

LeBoeuf, R., & Shafir, E. (in press). Decision making. In K. Holyoak & R. Morrison (Eds.), *Cambridge handbook of thinking and reasoning.* New York: Cambridge University Press.

Lee, A. Y. (2001). The mere exposure effect: An uncertainty reduction explanation revisited. *Personality and Social Psychology Bulletin, 27,* 1255–1266.

Lee, M., & Youn, S. (2009). Electronic word-of-mouth (eWOM): How eWOM platforms influence consumer product judgement. *International Journal of Advertising, 28,* 473–499.

Lee, S., Rogge, R. D., & Reis, H. T. (2010). Assessing the seeds of relationships decay: Using implicit evaluations to detect the early signs of disillusionment. *Psychological Science.*

Lee, Y. T., & Seligman, M. E. P. (1997). Are Americans more optimistic than the Chinese? *Personality and Social Psychology Bulletin, 23,* 32–40.

Lehmiller, J. J. (2009). Secret romantic relationships: Consequences for personal and relationship well-being. *Personality and Social Psychology Bulletin, 35,* 1452–1466.

Leippe, M. R., & Eisenstadt, D. (1994). Generalization of dissonance reduction: Decreasing prejudice through induced compliance. *Journal of Personality and Social Psychology, 67,* 395–413.

Lemay, E. P., Clark, M. S., & Greenberg, A. (2010). What is beautiful is good because what is beautiful is desired: Physical attractiveness stereotyping as project of interpersonal goals. *Personality and Social Psychology Bulletin, 36,* 339–353.

Lemley, B. (2000, February). Isn't she lovely? *Discover,* 42–49.

Lemonick, M. D., & Dorfman, A. (2001, July 23). One giant step for mankind. *Time,* 54–61.

Levav, J., & Argo, J. J. (2010). Physical contact and financial risk taking. *Psychological Science, 21,* 804–810.

Levine, J. M., Moreland, R. L., & Hausmann, L. R. M. (2005). Managing group composition: Inclusive and exclusive role transitions. In D. Abrams, M. A. Hogg, & J. M. Marques (Eds.), *The social psychology of inclusion and exclusion* (pp. 139–160). New York: Psychology Press.

Levine, M., & Wallach, L. (2002). *Psychological problems, social issues, and the law.* Boston: Allyn & Bacon, Inc.

Levine, M., Prosser, A., Evans, D., & Reicher, S. (2005). Identiyt and emergency intervention: How wsocial group membership and inclusiveness of group boundaries shape helping behavior. *Personality and Social Psychology Bulletin, 31,* 443–453.

Levine, R. V., Martinez, T. S., Brase, G., & Sorenson, K. (1994). Helping in 36 U.S. cities. *Journal of Personality and Social Psychology, 67,* 69–82.

Levitan, L. C., & Visser, P. S. (2008). The impact of the social context on resistance to persuasion: Effortful versus effortless responses to counter-attitudinal information. *Journal of Experimental Social Psychology, 44,* 640–649.

Levitan, L. C., & Visser, P. S. (2009). Social network composition and attitude strength: Exploring the dynamics within newly formed social networks. *Journal of Experimental Social Psychology, 45,* 1057–1067.

Leyens, J.-P., Desert, M., Croizet, J.-C., & Darcis, C. (2000). Stereotype threat: Are lower status and history of stigmatization preconditions of stereotype threat? *Personality and Social Psychology Bulletin, 26,* 1189–1199.

Li, N. P., & Kenrick, D. T. (2006). Sex similarities and differences in preferences for short-term mates: What, whether, and why. *Journal of Personality and Social Psychology, 90,* 468–489.

Li, N. P., Bailey, J. M., Kenrick, D. T., & Linsenmeier, J. A. W. (2002). The necessities and luxuries of male preferences: Testing the tradeoffs. *Journal of Personality and Social Psychology, 82,* 947–955.

Li, N. P., Griskevicius, V., Durante, K. M., Jonason, P. K., Pasisz, D. J., & Aumer, K. (2009). An evolutionary perspective on humor: Sexual selection of interest indication? *Social Psychology Bulletin, 35,* 923–936.

Liberman, A., & Chaiken, S. (1992). Defensive processing of personally relevant health messages. *Personality and Social Psychology Bulletin, 18,* 669–679.

Lickel, B., Hamilton, D. L., & Sherman, S. J. (2001). Elements of a lay theory of groups: Types of groups, relational styles, and the perception of group entitativity. *Personality and Social Psychology Review, 5,* 129–140.

Lickel, B., Hamilton, D. L., Wieczorkowski, G., Lewis, A., Sherman, S. J., & Uhles, A. N. (2000). Varieties of groups and the perception of group entiativity. *Journal of Personality and Social Psychology, 78,* 223–246.

Lickel, B., Rutchick, A. M., Hamilton, D. L., & Sherman, S. J. (2006). Intuitive theories of group types and relational principles. *Journal of Experimental Social Psychology, 42,* 28–39.

Liden, R. C., & Mitchell, T. R. (1988). Ingratiatory behaviors in organizational settings. *Academy of Management Review, 13,* 572–587.

Lin, M.-C., & Haywood, J. (2003). Accommodation predictors of grandparent-grandchild relational solidarity in Taiwan. *Journal of Social and Personal Relationships, 20,* 537–563.

Linden, E. (1992). Chimpanzees with a difference: Bonobos. *National Geographic, 18*(3), 46–53.

Lindsey, E. W., Mize, J., & Pettit, G. S. (1997). Mutuality in parent–child play: Consequences for children's peer competence. *Journal of Social and Personal Relationships, 14,* 523–538.

Lockwood, P., & Kunda, Z. (1999). Increasing the salience of one's best selves can undermine inspiration by outstanding role models. *Journal of Personality and Social Psychology, 76,* 214–228.

Logel, C., Walton, G. M., Spencer, S. J., Iserman, E. C., von Hippel, W., & Bell, A. E. (2009). Interacting with sexist men triggers social identity threat among female engineers. *Journal of Personality and Social Psychology, 96,* 1089–1103.

Lonnqvist, J. E., Leikas, S., Paunonen, S., Nissinen, V., & Verkasalo, M. (2006). Conformism moderates the relations between values, anticipated regret, and behavior. *Personality and Social Psychology Bulletin, 32,* 1469–1481.

Lopez, F. G., Gover, M. R., Leskela, J., Sauer, E. M., Schirmer, L., & Wyssmann, J. (1997). Attachment styles, shame, guilt, and collaborative problem-solving orientations. *Personal Relationships, 4,* 187–199.

Lord, C. G., & Saenz, D. S. (1985). Memory deficits and memory surfeits: Differential cognitive consequences of tokenism for tokens and observers. *Journal of Personality and Social Psychology, 49,* 918–926.

Lorenz, K. (1966). *On aggression.* New York: Harcourt, Brace, & World.

Lorenz, K. (1974). *Civilized man's eight deadly sins.* New York: Harcourt, Brace, Jovanovich.

Lowery, B. S., Unzueta, M. M., Goff, P. A., & Knowles, E. D. (2006). Concern for the in-group and opposition to affirmative action. *Journal of Personality and Social Psychology, 90,* 961–974.

Lun, J., Oishi, S., Coan, J. A., Akimoto, S., & Miao, F. F. (2010). Cultural variations in motivational responses to felt misunderstanding. *Personality and Social Psychology Bulletin, 36,* 986–996.

Luo, S., & Snider, A. G. (2009). Accuracy and biases in newlyweds' perception ns of each others. *Psychological Science, 20,* 1332–1339.

Lykken, A. & Tellegan, D. (1996). Happiness is a stochastic phenomenon. *Psychological Science, 7,* 186–189.

Lyness, K. S., & Heilman, M. E. (2006). When fit is fundamental: Performance evaluations and promotions of upper-level female and male managers. *Journal of Applied Psychology, 91,* 777–785.

Lyubomirsky, S., King, L., & Diener, E. (2005). The benefits of frequent positive affect: Does happiness lead to success? *Psychological Bulletin, 131,* 803–855.

Lyubomirsky, S., King, L., Diener, E. 2005. Benefits of frequent positive affect. *Psychological Bulletin, 131,* 803–855.

Lyubomirsky, S., Sheldon, K. M., & Schkade, D. (2005). Pursuing happiness: The architecture of sustainable change. *Review of General Psychology, 9,* 111–131.

Ma, H. K., Shek, D. T. L., Cheung, P. C., & Tam, K. K. (2002). A longitudinal study of peer and teacher influences on prosocial and antisocial behavior of Hong Kong Chinese adolescents. *Social Behavior and Personality, 30,* 157–168.

Maass, A., & Clark, R. D. III (1984). Hidden impact of minorities: Fifteen years of minority influence research. *Psychological Bulletin, 95,* 233–243.

Maass, A., Cadinu, M., Guarnieri, G., & Grasselli, A. (2003). Sexual harassment under social identity threat: The computer harassment paradigm. *Journal of Personality and Social Psychology, 85,* 853–870.

MacDonald, T. K., Zanna, M. P., & Fong, G. T. (1995). Decision making in altered states: Effects of alcohol on attitudes toward drinking and driving. *Journal of Personality and Social Psychology, 68,* 973–985.

Mackie, D. M., & Smith, E. R. (2002). Beyond prejudice: Moving from positive and negative evaluations to differentiated reactions to social groups. In D. M. Mackie & E. R. Smith (Eds.), *From prejudice to intergroup emotions: Differentiated reactions to social groups* (pp. 1–12). New York: Psychology Press.

Mackie, D. M., & Worth, L. T. (1989). Cognitive deficits and the mediation of positive affect in persuasion. *Journal of Personality and Social Psychology, 57,* 27–40.

Mackie, D. M., Devos, T., & Smith, E. R. (2000). Intergroup emotions: Explaining offensive action tendencies in an intergroup context. *Journal of Personality and Social Psychology, 79,* 602–616.

Macrae, C. N., Bodenhausen, G. V., Milne, A. B., & Ford, R. (1997). On the regulation of recollection: The intentional forgetting of sterotypical memories. *Journal of Personality and Social Psychology, 72,* 709–719.

Macrae, C. N., Milne, A. B., & Bodenhausen, G. V. (1994). Stereotypes as energy-saving devices: A peek inside the cognitive toolbox. *Journal of Personality and Social Psychology, 66,* 37–47.

Maddux, W. W., Barden, J., Brewer, M. B., & Petty, R. E. (2005). Saying no to negativity: The effects of context and motivation to control prejudice on automatic evaluative responses. *Journal of Experimental Social Psychology, 41,* 19–35.

Maeda, E., & Ritchie, L. D. (2003). The concept of *shinyuu* in Japan: A replication of and comparison to Cole and Bradac's study on U.S. friendship. *Journal of Social and Personal Relationships, 20,* 579–598.

Maheswaran, D., & Chaiken, S. (1991). Promoting systematic processing in low-motivation settings: Effect of incongruent information on processing and judgment. *Journal of Personality and Social Psychology, 61,* 13–25.

Maio, G. R., & Thomas, G. (2007). The epistemic-teleologic model of deliberate self-persuasion. *Personality and Social Psychology Review, 11,* 46–67.

Maio, G. R., Esses, V. M., & Bell, D. W. (1994). The formation of attitudes toward new immigrant groups. *Journal of Applied Social Psychology, 24,* 1762–1776.

Maio, G. R., Fincham, F. D., & Lycett, E. J. (2000). Attitudinal ambivalence toward parents and attachment style. *Personality and Social Psychology Bulletin, 26*, 1451–1464.

Major, B. (1994). From social inequality to personal entitlement: The role of social comparisons, legitimacy appraisals, and group membership. In M. P. Zanna (Ed.), *Advances in experimental social psychology* (Vol. 26, pp. 293–348). San Diego, CA: Academic Press.

Major, B., Barr, L., Zubek, J., & Babey, S. H. (1999). Gender and self-esteem: A meta-analysis. In W. B. Swann, J. H. Langlois, & L. A. Gilbert (Eds.), *Sexism and stereotypes in modern society* (pp. 223–253). Washington, DC: American Psychological Association.

Malone, B.E., & DePaulo, B.M. (2001). Measuring sensitivity to deception. In J.A. Hall & F. Bernieri (Eds.), Interpersonal sensitivity: Theory, measurement, and application (pp. 103-124). NJ: Erlbaum.

Marcus, B., Machilek, F., & Schütz, A. (2006). Personality in cyberspace: Personal web sites as media for personality expressions and impressions. *Journal of Personality and Social Psychology, 90*, 1014–1031.

Marcus, D. K., & Miller, R. S. (2003). Sex differences in judgments of physical attractiveness: A social relations analysis. *Personality and Social Psychology Bulletin, 29*, 325–335.

Markey, P. M., Funder, D. C., & Ozer, D. J. (2003). Complementarity of interpersonal behaviors in dyadic interactions. *Personality and Social Psychology Bulletin, 29*, 1082–1090.

Markus, H., & Nurius, P. (1986). Possible selves. *American Psychologist, 41*, 954–969.

Marshall, M. A., & Brown, J. D. (2006). Trait aggressiveness and situational provocation: A test of the traits as situational sensitivities (TASS) model. *Personality and Social Psychology Bulletin, 32*, 1100–1113.

Martens, A., Johns, M., Greenberg, J., & Schimel, J. (2006). Combating stereotype threat: The effect of self-affirmation on women's intellectual performance. *Journal of Experimental Social Psychology, 42*, 236-243.

Martin, P. Y., Hamilton, V. E., McKimmie, B. M., Terry, D. J., & Martin, R. (2007). Effects of caffeine on persuasion and attitude change: The role of secondary tasks in manipulating systematic message processing. *European Journal of Social Psychology, 37*, 320–338.

Maruta, T., Colligan, R. C., Malinchoc, M., & Offord, K. P. (2000). Optimists vs. pessimists: Survival rate among medical patients over a 30-year period. *Mayo Clinic Proceedings, 75*, 140–143

Marx, D. M., Ko, S. J., & Friedman, R. A. (2009). The "Obama effect": How a salient role model reduces race-based performance differences. *Journal of Experimental Social Psychology, 45*, 953–956.

Matsumoto, D., & Willingham, B. (2006). The thrill of victory and the agony of defeat: Spontaneous expressions of medal winners of the 2004 Athens Olympic games. *Journal of Personality and Social Psychology, 91*, 568-581.

Matsushima, R., & Shiomi, K. (2002). Self-disclosure and friendship in junior high school students. *Social Behavior and Personality, 30*, 515–526.

Mauss, I. B., Evers, C., Wilhelm, F. H., & Gross, J. J. (2006). How to bite your tongue without blowing your top: Implicit evaluation of emotion regulation predicts affective responding to anger provocation. *Personality and Social Psychology Bulletin, 32*, 589–602.

May, J. L., & Hamilton, P. A. (1980). Effects of musically evoked affect on women's interpersonal attraction and perceptual judgments of physical attractiveness of men. *Motivation and Emotion, 4*, 217–228.

Mazzella, R., & Feingold, A. (1994). The effects of physical attractiveness, race, socioeconomic status, and gender of defendants and victims on judgments of mock jurors: A meta-analysis. *Journal of Applied Social Psychology, 24*, 1315–1344.

McCall, M. (1997). Physical attractiveness and access to alcohol: What is beautiful does not get carded. *Journal of Applied Social Psychology, 23*, 453–562.

McClure, S., Laibson, D Loewenstein, G., & Cohen, J. D. (2004). Separate neural systems value immediate and delayed monetary rewards, *Science 306*, October 15, 2004.

McConahay, J. B. (1986). Modern racism, ambivalence, and the Modern Racism Scale. In J. F. Dovidio & S. L. Gaertner (Eds.), *Prejudice, discrimination, and racism* (pp. 91–125). New York: Academic Press.

McCullough, M. E., Fincham, F. D., & Tsang, J. A. (2003). Forgiveness, forbearance, and time: The temporal unfolding of transgression-related interpersonal motivations. *Journal of Personality and Social Psychology, 84*, 540–557.

McCullough, **M. E.,** Kilpatrick, **S. D.,** Emmons, **R. A., &** Larson, **D. B.** (2001). Is gratitude a moral affect? *Psychological Bulletin, 127*, 249–266

McDonald, H. E., & Hirt, E. R. (1997). When expectancy meets desire: Motivational effects in reconstructive memory. *Journal of Personality and Social Psychology, 72*, 5–23.

McGonagle, K. A., Kessler, R. C., & Schilling, E. A. (1992). The frequency and determinants of marital disagreements in a community sample. *Journal of Social and Personal Relationships, 9*, 507–524.

McNulty, J. K. (2010). When positive processes hurt relationships. *Current Directions in Psychological Science, 19*, 161–171.

McNulty, J. K., & Karney, B. R. (2004). Positive expectations in the early years of marriage: Should couples expect the best or brace for the worst? *Journal of Personality and Social Psychology, 86*, 729–743.

Mead, G. H. (1934). *Mind, self, and society*. Chicago: University of Chicago Press.

Mead, N. L., Baumeister, R. F., Gino, F., Schweitzer, M. E., & Ariely, D. (2009). Too tired to tell the truth: Self-control resource depletion and dishonesty. *Journal of Experimental Social Psychology, 45,* 594–597.

Medvec, V. H., Madey, S. F., & Gilovich, T. (1995). When less is more: Counterfactual thinking and satisfaction among Olympic athletes. *Journal of Personality and Social Psychology, 69,* 603–610.

Mehl, M. R., Vazire, S., Holleran, S. E., & Clark, C. S. (2010). Eavesdropping on happiness: Wellbeing is related to having less small talk and more substantive conversations. *Psychological Science, 21,* 539–541.

Meier, B. P., Robinson, M. D., & Wilkowski, B. M. (2006). Turning the other cheek: Agreeableness and the regulation of aggression-related primes. *Psychological Science, 17,* 136–142.

Meleshko, K. G. A., & Alden, L. E. (1993). Anxiety and self-disclosure: Toward a motivational model. *Journal of Personality and Social Psychology, 64,* 1000–1009.

Mendoza-Denton, R., Ayduk, O., Mischel, W., Shoda, Y., & Testa, A. (2001). Person X situation interactionism in self-encoding (*I am . . . When . . .*): Implications for affect regulation and social information processing. *Journal of Personality and Social Psychology, 80,* 533–544.

Mesquita, B., & Leu, J. (2007). The cultural psychology of emotion. In S. Kitayama & D. Cohen (Eds.), *Handbook of cultural psychology* (pp. 734–759). New York: Guilford Press.

Meyers, S. A., & Berscheid, E. (1997). The language of love: The difference a preposition makes. *Personality and Social Psychology Bulletin, 23,* 347–362.

Mikulincer, M. (1998). Adult attachment style and individual differences in functional versus dysfunctional experiences of anger. *Journal of Personality and Social Psychology, 74,* 513–524.

Mikulincer, M., Gillath, O., Halevy, V., Avihou, N., Avidan, S., & Eshkoli, N. (2001). Attachment theory and reactions to others' needs: Evidence that activation of the sense of attachment security promotes empathic responses. *Journal of Personality and Social Psychology, 81,* 1205–1224.

Miles, S. M., & Carey, G. (1997). Genetic and environmental architecture of human aggression. *Journal of Personality and Social Psychology, 72,* 207–217.

Milgram, S. (1963). Behavior study of obedience. *Journal of Abnormal and Social Psychology, 67,* 371–378.

Milgram, S. (1965a). Liberating effects of group pressure. *Journal of Personality and Social Psychology, 1,* 127–134.

Milgram, S. (1965b). Some conditions of obedience and disobedience to authority. *Human Relations, 18,* 57–76.

Milgram, S. (1974). *Obedience to authority.* New York: Harper.

Miller, D. A., Cronin, T., Garcia, A. L., & Branscombe, N. R. (2009). The relative impact of anger and efficacy on collective action is affected by feelings of fear. *Group Processes and Intergroup Relations, 12,* 445–462.

Miller, D. A., Smith, E. R., & Mackie, D. M. (2004). Effects of intergroup contact and political predispositions on prejudice: Role of intergroup emotions. *Group Processes and Intergroup Relations, 7,* 221–237.

Miller, D. T., & McFarland, C. (1987). Pluralistic ignorance: When similarity is interpreted as dissimilarity. *Journal of Personality and Social Psychology, 53,* 298–305.

Miller, D. T., & Ross, M. (1975) Self-serving biases in the attribution of causality: Fact or fiction? *Psychological Bulletin, 82,* 213–225.

Miller, D. T., & Morrison, K. R. (2009). Expressing deviant opinions: Believing you are in the majority helps. *Journal of Experimental Social Psychology, 45,* 740–747.

Miller, L. (2010, February 17). R.I.P. on Facebook: The uses and abuses of virtual grief. *Newsweek.*

Miller, L. C., Putcha-Bhagavatula, A., & Pedersen, W. C. (2002, June). Men's and women's mating preferences: Distinct evolutionary mechanisms? *Current Directions in Psychological Science, 11,* 88–93.

Miller, P. J. E., & Rempel, J. K. (2004). Trust and partner-enhancing attributions in close relationships. *Personality and Social Psychology Bulletin, 30,* 695–705.

Miller, P. J. E., Caughlin, J. P., & Huston, T. L. (2003). Trait expressiveness and marital satisfaction: The role of idealization processes. *Journal of Marriage and Family, 65,* 978–995.

Miller, S. L., & Maner, J. K. (2010). Scent of a woman: Men's testosterone responses to olfactory ovulation cues. *Psychological Science, 21,* 276–283.

Miron, A. M., Branscombe, N. R., & Schmitt, M. T. (2006). Collective guilt as distress over illegitimate intergroup inequality. *Group Processes and Intergroup Relations, 9,* 163–180.

Miron, A. M., Warner, R. H., & Branscombe, N. R. (in press). Accounting for group differences in appraisals of social inequality: Differential injustice standards. *British Journal of Social Psychology.*

Mobbs, D., Hassabis, D., Seymour, B., Marechant, J. L., Weiskopf, N., Dolan, R. J., et al. (2009). Choking on the money: Reward-based performance decrements are associated with midbrain activity. *Psychological Science, 20,* 955–962.

Mojzisch, A., & Schulz-Hardt, S. (2010). Knowing others' preferences degrades the quality of group decisions. *Journal of Personality and Social Psychology, 98,* 794–808.

Mondloch, C. J., Lewis, T. L., Budreau, D. R., Maurer, D., Dannemiller, J. L., Stephens, B. R., et al. (1999). Face perception during early infancy. Psychological Science, 10, 419–422

Monin, B. (2003). The warm glow heuristic: When liking leads to familiarity. *Journal of Personality and Social Psychology, 85,* 1035–1048.

Monin, B., & Miller, D. T. (2001). Moral credentials and the expression of prejudice. *Journal of Personality and Social Psychology, 81,* 33–43.

Monteith, M. J., Ashburn-Nardo, L., Voils, C. I., & Czopp, A. M. (2002). Putting the brakes on prejudice: On the development and operation of cues for control. *Journal of Personality and Social Psychology, 83,* 1029–1050.

Monteith, M. J., Devine, P. G., & Zuwerink, J. R. (1993). Self-directed versus other-directed affect as a consequence of prejudice-related discrepancies. *Journal of Personality and Social Psychology, 64,* 198–210.

Montgomery, K. J., Seeherman, K. R., & Haxby, J. V. (2009). The well-tempered social brain. *Psychological Science, 20,* 1211–1213.

Moons, W. G., Mackie, D. M., & Garcia-Marques, T. (2009). The impact of repetition-induced familiarity on agreement with weak and strong arguments. *Journal of Personality and Social Psychology, 96,* 32–44.

Moreland, R. L., & Beach, S. R. (1992). Exposure effects in the classroom: The development of affinity among students. *Journal of Experimental Social Psychology, 28,* 255–276.

Moreland, R. L., & Levine, J. M. (2001). Socialization in organizations and work groups. In M. Turner (Ed.), *Groups at work: Theory and research* (pp. 69–112). Mahwah, NJ: Erlbaum.

Morewedge, C. K. (2009). Negativity bias in attribution of external agency. *Journal of Experimental Psychology, 138,* 535–545.

Morison, L. A., Cozzolino, P. J., & Orbell, S. (2010). Temporal perspective and parental intention to accept the human papilomavirus vaccination for their daughter. *British Journal of Health Psychology, 15,* 151–165.

Morris, M. L., Sinclair, S., & DePaulo, B. M. (2007). No shelter for singles: The perceived legitimacy of marital status discrimination. *Group Processes and Intergroup Relations, 10,* 457–470.

Morrison, E. W., & Bies, R. J. (1991). Impression management in the feedback-seeking process: A literature review and research agenda. *Academy of Management Review, 16,* 322–341.

Moscovici, S. (1985). Social influence and conformity. In G. Lindzey & E. Aronson (Eds.), *Handbook of social psychology* (3rd ed.). New York: Random House.

Mugny, G. (1975). Negotiations, image of the other and the process of minority influence. *European Journal of Social Psychology, 5,* 209–229.

Mulder, L. B., van Dijk, E., De Cremer, D., & Wilke, H. A. M. (2006). Undermining trust and cooperation: The paradox of sanctioning systems in social dilemmas. *Journal of Experimental Social Psychology, 42,* 147–162.

Mullen, B., & Cooper, C. (1994). The relation between group cohesiveness and performance: An integration. *Psychological Bulletin, 115,* 210–227.

Mullen, E., & Skitka, L.J. (2006). Exploring the psychological underpinnings of the moral mandate effect: Motivated reasoning, group differentiation, or anger? *Journal of Personality and Social Psychology, 90,* 629–643.

Munkes, J., & Diehl, M. (2003). Matching or competition? Performance comparison processes in an idea generation task. *Group Processes and Intergroup Relations, 6,* 305–320.

Murray, L., & Trevarthen, C. (1986). The infant's role in mother-infant communications. *Journal of Child Language, 13,* 15–29.

Murray, S. L., Griffin, D. W., Rose, P., and Bellavia, G. (2006). For better or worse? Self-esteem and the contingencies of acceptance in marriage. *Personality and Social Psychology Bulletin, 32,* 866-880.

Murray, S. L., Holmes, J. G., & Griffin, D. W. (2000). Self-esteem and the quest for felt security: How perceived regard regulates attachment processes. *Journal of Personality and Social Psychology, 78,* 478–498.

Murray, S. L., Holmes, J. G., & Griffin, D. W. (1996). The benefits of positive illusions: Idealization and the construction of satisfaction in close relationships. *Journal of Personality and Social Psychology, 70,* 79–98.

Murray, S. L., Holmes, J. G., Griffin, D. W., Bellavia, G., & Rose, P. (2001). The mismeasure of love: How self-doubt contaminates relationship beliefs. *Personality and Social Psychology Bulletin, 27,* 423–436.

Mynard, H., & Joseph, S. (1997). Bully victim problems and their association with Eysenck's personality dimensions in 8 to 13 year olds. *British Journal of Educational Psychology, 67,* 51–54.

Nadler, A., & Halabi, S. (2006). Intergroup helping as status relations: Effects of status stability, identification, and type of help on receptivity to high-status group's help. *Journal of Personality and Social Psychology, 91,* 97–110.

Nadler, A., Fisher, J. D., & Itzhak, S. B. (1983). With a little help from my friend: Effect of a single or multiple acts of aid as a function of donor and task characteristics. *Journal of Personality and Social Psychology, 44,* 310–321.

Nadler, A., Harpaz-Gorodeisky, & Ben-David, Y. (2009). Defensive helping: Threat to group identity, ingroup identification, status stability, and common group identity as determinants of intergroup help-giving. *Journal of Personality and Social Psychology, 97,* 823–834.

Naqvi, N., Shiv, B., & Bechara, A. (2006). The role of emotion in decision making: A cognitive neuroscience perspective. *Current Directions in Psychological Science, 15,* 260–264.

Nario-Redmond, M. R., & Branscombe, N. A. (1996). It could have better and it might have been worse: Implications for blame assignment in rape cases. *Basic and Applied Social Psychology, 18,* 347–366.

Naumann, L. P. Vazire, S., Rentfrow, P. J., & Gosling, S. D. (2009).Personality judgments based on physical appearance. *Personality and Social Psychology Bulletin, 35,* 1661–1671.

Nemeth, C. J., Personnaz, B., Personnaz, M., & Goncalo, J. A. (2004). The liberating role of conflict in group creativity: A study in two countries. *European Journal of Social Psychology, 34,* 365–374.

Neuman, J. S., & Baron, R. A. (in press). Social antecedents of bullying. In S. Einarsen, H. Hoel, D. Zapf, & C. L. Cooper (Eds.), *Workplace bullying: Development in theory, research and practice* (2nd ed). London: CRC Press.

Newby-Clark, I. R., & Ross, M. (2003). Conceiving the past and future. *Personality and Social Psychology Bulletin, 29,* 807–818.

Newcomb, T. M. (1956). The prediction of interpersonal attraction. *Psychological Review, 60,* 393–404.

Newcomb, T. M. (1961). *The acquaintance process.* New York: Holt, Rinehart and Winston.

Newman, R. S., & Murray, B. J. (2005). How students and teachers view the seriousness of peer harassment: When is it appropriate to seek help? *Journal of Educational Psychology, 97,* 345–365.

Neyer, F. J., & Lang, F. R. (2003). Blood is thicker than water: Kinship orientation across adulthood. *Journal of Personality and Social Psychology, 84,* 310–321.

Nida, S. A., & Koon, J. (1983). They get better looking at closing time around here, too. *Psychological Reports, 52,* 657–658.

Nisbett, R. E. (1990). Evolutionary psychology, biology, and cultural evolution. *Motivation and Emotion, 14,* 255–264.

Nisbett, R. E., & Wilson, T. D. (1977). Telling more than we can know: Verbal reports on mental processes. *Psychological Review, 84,* 231–259.

Nisbett, R. E., Caputo, C., Legbant, P., & Marecek, J. (1973). Behavior as seen by the actor and as seen by the observer. *Journal of Personality and Social Psychology, 27,* 154–164.

Noel, J. G., Wann, D. L., & Branscombe, N. R. (1995). Peripheral ingroup membership status and public negativity toward outgroups. *Journal of Personality and Social Psychology, 68,* 127–137.

Noel, J. G., Wann, D. L., & Branscombe, N. R. (1995). Peripheral ingroup membership status and public negativity toward outgroups. *Journal of Personality and Social Psychology, 68,* 127–137.

Norenzayan, A., & Hansen, G. (2006). Belief in supernatural agents in the face of death. *Personality and Social Psychology Bulletin, 32,* 174–187.

Norenzayan, A., & Lee, A. (2010). It was meant to happen: Explaining cultural variations in fate attributions. *Journal of Personality and Social Psychology, 98,* 702–720.

Norton, M. I., Frost, J. H., & Ariely, D. (2006). Less is more: The lure of ambiguity, or why familiarity breeds contempt. *Journal of Personality and Social Psychology, 92,* 97–105.

Norton, M. I., Sommers, S. R., Apfelbaum, E. P., Pura, N., & Ariely, D. (2006). Color blindness and interracial interaction: Playing the political correctness game. *Psychological Science, 17,* 949–953.

Nussbaum, S., Trope, Y., & Liberman, N. (2003). Creeping dispositionism: The temporal dynamics of behavior prediction. *Journal of Personality and Social Psychology 84,* 485–497.

Nyman, L. (1995). The identification of birth order personality attributes. *The Journal of Psychology, 129,* 51–59.

O'Brien, L. T., Crandall, C. S., Horstman-Reser, A., Warner, R., Alsbrooks, A., & Blodorn, A. (2010). But I'm no bigot: How prejudiced White Americans maintain unprejudiced self-images. *Journal of Applied Social Psychology, 40,* 917–946.

O'Connor, S. C., & Rosenblood, L. K. (1996). Affiliation motivation in everyday experience: A theoretical comparison. *Journal of Personality and Social Psychology, 70,* 513–522.

O'Leary, S. G. (1995). Parental discipline mistakes. *Current Directions in Psychological Science, 4,* 11–13.

O'Moore, M. N. (2000). Critical issues for teacher training to counter bullying and victimization in Ireland. *Aggressive Behavior, 26,* 99–112.

O'Sullivan, M. (2003). The fundamental attribution error in detecting deception: The boy-who-cried-wolf effect. *Personality and Social Psychology Bulletin, 29,* 1316–1327.

Oakes, P. J., & Reynolds, K. J. (1997). Asking the accuracy question: Is measurement the answer? In R. Spears, P. J. Oakes, N. Ellemers, & S. A. Haslam (Eds.), *The social psychology of stereotyping and group life* (pp. 51–71). Oxford: Blackwell.

Oakes, P. J., Haslam, S. A., & Turner, J. C. (1994). *Stereotyping and social reality.* Oxford: Blackwell.

Odgers, C. L., Moretti, M. M., Burnette, M. L., Chauhan, P.,Waite, D., & Reppucci, N. D. (2007). A latent variable modeling approach to identifying subtypes of serious and violent female juvenile offenders. *Aggressive Behavior, 33,* 339–352.

Oettingen, G. (1995). Explanatory style in the context of culture. In G. M. Buchanan & M. E. P. Seligman (Eds.), *Explanatory style.* Hillsdale, NJ: Erlbaum.

Oettingen, G., & Seligman, M. E. P. (1990). Pessimism and behavioral signs of depression in East versus West Berlin. *European Journal of Social Psychology, 201,* 207–220.

Oishi, S., Diener, E., & Lucas, R. E. (2007). The optimum level of well-being: Can people be too happy? *Perspectives on Psychological Science, 2,* 346–360.

Olson, M. A., & Fazio, R. H. (2001). Implicit attitude formation through classical conditioning. *Psychological Science, 12,* 413–417.

Olson, M. A., & Kendrick, R. V. (2008). Origins of attitudes. In W. D. Crano & R. Prislin (Eds.), *Attitudes and attitude change* (pp. 111–130). New York: Psychology Press.

Olweus, D. (1999). Sweden. In P. K. Smith, Y. Morita, J. Junger-Tas, D. Olweus, R. F. Catalano, & P. Slee (Eds.), *The nature of school bullying: A cross-national perspective* (pp. 7–27). New York: Routledge.

Orbell, S., Blair, C., Sherlock, K., & Conner, M. (2001). The theory of planned behavior and ecstasy use: Roles for habit and perceived control over taking versus obtaining substances. *Journal of Applied Social Psychology, 31,* 31–47.

Orth, U., Trzesniewski, K. H., & Robins, R. W. (2010). Self-esteem development from young adulthood to old age: A cohort-sequential longitudinal study. *Journal of Personality and Social Psychology, 98,* 645–658.

Osborne, J. W. (2001). Testing stereotype threat: Does anxiety explain race and sex differences in achievement? *Contemporary Educational Psychology, 26,* 291–310.

Oskamp, S., & Schultz, P.W. (2005). *Attitudes and Opinions (3rd ed.).* Mahwah, NJ: Lawrence Erlbaum.

Paik, H., & Comstock, G. (1994). The effects of television violence on antisocial behavior: A meta-analysis. *Communication Research, 21,* 516–546.

Palmer, J., & Byrne, D. (1970). Attraction toward dominant and submissive strangers: Similarity versus complementarity. Journal of Experimental Research in Personality, 4, 108–115.

Park, J., & Banaji, M. R. (2000). Mood and heuristics: The influence of happy and sad states on sensitivity and bias in stereotyping. Journal of Personality and Social Psychology, 78, 1005–1023.

Park, L. E., & Pelham, B. W. (2006). Self versus others' ratings of physical attractiveness. Unpublished raw data.

Pascoe, E. A., & Smart Richman, L. (2009). Perceived discrimination and health: A meta-analytic review. *Psychological Bulletin, 135,* 531–554.

Patrick, H., Neighbors, C., & Knee, C. R. (2004). Appearance-related social comparisons: The role of contingent self-esteem and self-perceptions of attractiveness. Personality and Social Psychology Bulletin, 30, 501–514.

Pavalko, E. K., Mossakowski, K. N., & Hamilton, V. J. (2003). Does perceived discrimination affect health? Longitudinal relationships between work discrimination and women's physical and emotional health. Journal of Health and Social Behavior, 43, 18–33.

Peale, N. V. (1952). *The power of positive thinking.* New York: Prentice-Hall.

Pelham, B. W., Mirenberg, M. C., & Jones, J. T. (2002). Why Susie sells seashells by the seashore: Implicit egotism and major life decisions. Journal of Personality and Social Psychology, 82, 469–487.

Pennebaker, J. W., Dyer, M. A., Caulkins, R. S., Litowicz, D. L., Ackerman, P. L., & Anderson, D. B. (1979). Don't the girls all get prettier at closing time: A country and western application to psychology. Personality and Social Psychology Bulletin, 5, 122–125.

Penner, L. A., Dovidio, J. F., Piliavin, J. A., & Schroeder, D. A. (2005). Prosocial behavior: Multilevel perspective. Annual Review of Psychology, 46, 365–392.

Pentony, J. F. (1995). The effect of negative campaigning on voting, semantic differential, and thought listing. Journal of Social Behavior and Personality, 10, 631–644.

Pereira, C., Vala, J., & Costa-Lopes, R. (2009). From prejudice to discrimination: The legitimizing role of perceived threat in discrimination against immigrants. *European Journal of Social Psychology,*

Petrocelli, J. V., & Sherman, S. J. (2010). Event detail and confidence in gambling: The role of counterfactual thought

reactions. *Journal of Experimental Social Psychology, 46,* 61–72.

Petrocelli, J. V., Clarkson, J. J., Tormala, Z. L., & Hendrix, K. S. (2010). Perceiving stability as a means to attitude certainty: The role of implicit theories. *Journal of Experimental Social Psychology, 46,* 874–883.

Petrocelli, J. V., Tormala, Z. L., & Rucker, D. D. (2007). Unpacking attitude certainty: Attitude clarity and attitude correctness. *Journal of Personality and Social Psychology, 92,* 30–41.

Pettigrew, T. F. (1981). Extending the stereotype concept. In D. L. Hamilton (Ed.), *Cognitive processes in stereotyping and intergroup behavior* (pp. 303–331). Hillsdale, NJ: Erlbaum.

Pettigrew, T. F. (1997). Generalized intergroup contact effects on prejudice. *Personality and Social Psychology Bulletin, 23,* 173–185.

Pettigrew, T. W. (2007). Still a long way to go: American Black-White relations today. In G. Adams, M. Biernat, N. R. Branscombe, C. S. Crandall, & L. S. Wrightsman (Eds.), *Commemorating Brown: The social psychology of racism and discrimination.* Washington, DC: American Psychological Association.

Pettijohn, T. E. F., II, & Jungeberg, B. J. (2004). Playboy playmate curves: Changes in facial and body feature preferences across social and economic conditions. *Personality and Social Psychology Bulletin, 30,* 1186–1197.

Petty, R. E., & Cacioppo, J. T. (1986). The elaboration likelihood model of persuasion. In L. Berkowitz (Ed.), *Advances in experimental social psychology* (Vol. 19, pp. 123–205). New York: Academic Press.

Petty, R. E., Wheeler, C., & Tormala, Z. L. (2003). Persuasion and attitude change. In T. Millon & M. J. Lerner (Eds.), *Handbook of psychology: Personality and social psychology* (Vol. 5, pp. 353–382). New York: Wiley.

Petty, R. J., & Krosnick, J. A. (Eds.). (1995). *Attitude strength: Antecedents and consequences* (Vol. 4). Hillsdale, NJ: Erlbaum.

Petty, R.E. (1995). Attitude change. In A. Tesser (Ed.), *Advanced social psychology* (pp. 195–255). New York: McGraw-Hill.

Petty, R.E., Cacioppo, J.T., Strathman, A.J., & Priester, J.R. (2005). To think or not to think: Exploring two routes to persuasion. In T.C. Brock & M.C. Green (Eds.), *Persuasion: Psychological insights and perspectives* (2nd ed., pp. 81–116). Thousand Oaks, CA: Sage.

Phelps, E. A., O'Connor, K. J., Gatenby, J. C., Gore, J. C., Grillon, C., & Davis, M. (2001). Activation of the left amygdala to a cognitive representation of fear. *Nature Neuroscience, 4,* 437–441.

Pines, A. (1997). Fatal attractions or wise unconscious choices: The relationship between causes for entering and breaking intimate relationships. *Personal Relationship Issues, 4,* 1–6.

Pinker, S. (1998). *How the mind works.* New York: Norton.

Pinquart, M., & Sorensen, S. (2000). Influences of socioeconomic status, social network, and competence on subjective well-being in later life: A meta-analysis. *Psychology and Aging, 15,* 187–224.

Pittman, T. S. (1993). Control motivation and attitude change. In G. Weary, F. Gleicher, & empirical review. *Psychological Bulletin, 130,* 435–468.

Plant, E. A., & Devine, P. G. (1998). Internal and external motivation to respond without prejudice. *Journal of Personality and Social Psychology, 75,* 811–832.

Polivy, J., & Herman, C. P. (2000). The false-hope syndrome: Unfulfilled expectations of self-change. *Current Directions in Psychological Science, 9,* 128–131.

Pollak, K. I., & Niemann, Y. F. (1998). Black and white tokens in academia: A difference in chronic versus acute distinctiveness. *Journal of Applied Social Psychology, 28,* 954–972.

Postmes, T., & Branscombe, N. R. (2002). Influence of long-term racial environmental composition on subjective well-being in African Americans. *Journal of Personality and Social Psychology, 83,* 735–751.

Postmes, T., & Spears, R. (1998). Deindividuation and antinormative behavior: A meta-analysis. *Psychological Bulletin, 123,* 238–259.

Poteat, V. P., & Spanierman, L. B. (2010). Do the ideological beliefs of peers predict the prejudiced attitudes of other individuals in the group? *Group Processes and Intergroup Relations, 13,* 495–514.

Powers, S., Pietromonaco, P. R., Gunlicks, M., & Sayer, A. (2008). Dating couples' attachment styles and patterns of cortisol reactivity and recover in response to a relationship conflict. *Journal of Personality and Social Psychology, 90,* 613–628.

Pozzulo, J. D., & Lindsay, R. C. L. (1999). Elimination lineups: An improved identification for child eyewitnesses. *Journal of Applied Psychology, 84,* 167–176.

Pozzulo, J., D., & Demopsey, J. (2006). Biased lineup instructions: Examining the effect of pressure on children's andadultas' eyewitness identification accuracy. *Journal of Applied Social Psychology, 36,* 1381–1394.

Prentice, D. A., & Miller, D. T. (1992). When small effects are impressive. *Psychological Bulletin, 112,* 160–164.

Prentice, D. A., Miller, D. T., & Lightdale, J. R. (1994). Asymmetries in attachments to groups and to their members: Distinguishing between common-identity and common-bond groups. *Personality and Social Psychology Bulletin, 20,* 484–493.

Price, K. H., Harrison, D. A., & Gavin, J. H. (2006). Withholding inputs in team contexts: Member composition, interaction processes, evaluation structure, and social loafing. *Journal of Applied Psychology, 91,* 1375–1384.

Pronin, E., & Ross, L. (2006). Temporal differences in trait self-ascription: When the self is seen as an other. *Journal of Personality and Social Psychology, 90,* 197–209.

Pronin, E., & Kruger, M. B. (2007). Valuing thoughts, ignoring behavior: The introspection illusion as a source of bias blind spot. *Journal of Experimental Social Psychology, 43,* 565–578.

Pronin, E., Berger, J., & Molouki, S. (2007). Alone in a crowd of sheep: Asymmetric perceptions of conformity and their roots in an introspection illusion. *Journal of Personality and Social Psychology, 92,* 585–595.

Pronin, E., Kruger, J., Savitsky, K., & Ross, L. (2001). You don't know me, but I know you: The illusion of asymmetric insight. *Journal of Personality and Social Psychology, 81,* 639–656.

Pronin, E., Steele, C. M., & Ross, L. (2004). Identity bifurcation in response to stereotype threat: Women and mathematics. *Journal of Experimental Social Psychology, 40,* 152–168.

Pruitt, D. G., & Carnevale, P. J. (1993). *Negotiation in social conflict.* Pacific Grove, CA: Brooks/Cole.

Pryor, J. B., Reeder, G. D., Yeadon, C., & Hesson-McInnis, M. (2004). A dual-process model of reactions to perceived stigma. *Journal of Personality and Social Psychology, 87,* 436–452.

Przybylski, A. K. Ryan, R. M., & Rigby, G. S. (2009). The motivating role of violence in video games. *Personality and Social Psychology Bulletin, 35,* 241–259.

Puente, S., & Cohen, D. (2003). Jealousy and the meaning (or nonmeaning) of violence. *Personality and Social Psychology Bulletin, 29,* 449–460.

Putnam, R. (2000). *Bowling alone.* New York: Simon & Schuster.

Queller, S., & Smith, E. R. (2002). Subtyping versus bookkeeping in stereotype learning and change: Connectionist simulations and empirical findings. *Journal of Personality and Social Psychology, 82,* 300–313.

Quigley, B. M., Johnson, A. B., & Byrne, D. (1995, June). *Mock jury sentencing decisions: A meta-analysis of the attractiveness–leniency effect.* Paper presented at the meeting of the American Psychological Society, New York.

Quinn, J. M., & Wood, W. (2004). Forewarnings of influence appeals: Inducing resistance and acceptance. In E. S. Knowles & J. A. Linn (Eds.), *Resistance and persuasion* (pp. 193–213). Mahwah, NJ: Erlbaum.

Quoidbach, J., Dunn, E. W., Petrides, K. V., & Mikolajczak, M. (2010). Money giveth, money taken away: The dual effect of wealth on happiness. *Psychological Science, 21,* 759–763.

Ranganath, K. A., Smith, C. T., & Nosek, B. A. (2008). Distinguishing automatic and controlled components of attitudes from direct and indirect measurement. *Journal of Experimental Social Psychology, 44,* 386–396.

Ray, G. E., Cohen, R., Secrist, M. E., & Duncan, M. K. (1997). Relating aggressive victimization behaviors to children's sociometric status and friendships. *Journal of Social and Personal Relationships, 14,* 95–108.

Read, S. J., & Miller, L. C. (1998). *Connectionist and PDP models of social reasoning and social behavior.* Mahwah, NJ: Erlbaum.

Redersdorff, S., Martinot, D., & Branscombe, N. R. (2004). The impact of thinking about group-based disadvantages or advantages on women's well-being: An experimental test of the rejection-identification model. *Current Psychology of Cognition, 22,* 203–222.

Reicher, S., & Haslam, S. A. (2006). Rethinking the psychology of tyranny: The BBC prison study. *British Journal of Social Psychology, 45,* 1–40.

Reisenzein, R., Bordgen, S., Holtbernd, T., & Matz, D. (2006). Evidence for strong dissociation between emotion and facial displays: The case of surprise. *Journal of Personality and Social Psychology, 91,* 295–315.

Reiss, A. J., & Roth, J. A. (Eds.). (1993). *Understanding and preventing violence.* Washington, DC: National Academy Press.

Reno, R. R., Cialdini, R. B., & Kallgren, C. A. (1993). The transsituational influence of social norms. *Journal of Personality and Social Psychology, 64,* 104–112.

Reno, R. R., Cialdini, R. B., & Kallgren, C. A. (1993). The transsituational influence of social norms. *Journal of Personality and Social Psychology, 64,* 104–112.

Rensberger, B. (1993, November 9). Certain chemistry between vole pairs. *Albany Times Union,* pp. C-1, C-3.

Reskin, B., & Padavic, I. (1994). *Women and men at work.* Thousand Oaks, CA: Pine Forge Press.

Reynolds, K. J., Turner, J. C., Branscombe, N. R., Mavor, K. I., Bizumic, B., & Subasic, E. (2010). Interactionism in personality and social psychology: An integrated approach to understanding the mind and behavior. *European Journal of Personality, 24,* 458–482.

Rhodes, G., & Tremewan, T. (1996). Averageness, exaggeration, and facial attractiveness. *Psychological Science, 7,* 105–110.

Richard, F. D., Bond, C. F., Jr., & Stokes-Zoota, J. J. (2001). "That's completely obvious . . . and important." Lay judgments of social psychological findings. *Personality and Social Psychology Bulletin, 27,* 497–505.

Richard, N. T., & Wright, S. C. (2010). Advantaged group members' reactions to tokenism. *Group Processes and Intergroup Relations, 13,* 559–569.

Richards, Z., & Hewstone, M. (2001). Subtyping and subgrouping: Processes for the prevention and promotion of stereotype change. *Personality and Social Psychology Review, 5,* 52–73.

Richardson, D. S., & Hammock, G. (2007). Social context of human aggression: Are we paying too much attention to gender? *Aggression and Violent Behavior, 12,* 417–426

Rickenberg, R., & Reeves, B. (2000). The effects of animated characters on anxiety, task performance, and evaluations of user interfaces. In *Proceedings of CHI 2000* (pp. 49–56). New York: ACM Press.

Riegelsberger, J., Sasse, M. A., & McCarthy, J. D. (2007). Trust in mediated communications. In A. N. Joinson, K. Y. A. McKenna, T. Postmes, & U.-D. Reips (Eds.), *The Oxford handbook of internet psychology* (pp. 53–60). New York: Oxford University Press.

Riek, B. M., Mania, E. W., Gaertner, S. L., McDonald, S. A., & Lamoreaux, M. J. (2010). Does a common ingroup identity reduce intergroup threat? *Group Processes and Intergroup Relations, 13,* 403–423.

Righetti, F., & Finkenauer, C. (2011). If you are able to control yourself, I will trust you: The role of perceived self-control in interpersonal trust. Journal of Personality and Social Psychology, 100, 874-886.

Risen, J. L., & Gilovich, T. (2007). Another look at why people are reluctant to exchange lottery tickets. *Journal of Personality and Social Psychology, 93,* 12–22.

Ritzer, G. (2011). *The Mcdonalization of society* (6th ed.). New York: Pine Forge Press.

Robbins, T. L., & DeNisi, A. S. (1994). A closer look at interpersonal affect as a distinct influence on cognitive processing in performance evaluations. *Journal of Applied Psychology, 79,* 341–353.

Robins, R. W., Hendin, H. M., & Trzesniewski, K. H. (2001). *Personality and Social Psychology Bulletin, 27,* 151–161.

Robins, R. W., Spranca, M. D., & Mendelsohn, G. A. (1996). The actor–observer effect revisited: Effects of individual differences and repeated social interactions on actor and observer attribution. *Journal of Personality and Social Psychology, 71,* 375–389.

Robinson, L. A., Berman, J. S., & Neimeyer, R. A. (1990). Psychotherapy for the treatment of depression: A comprehensive review of controlled outcome research. *Psychological Bulletin, 108,* 30–49.

Roccas, S. (2003). Identification and status revisited: The moderating role of self-enhancement and self-transcendence values. *Personality and Social Psychology Bulletin, 29,* 726–736.

Rochat, F., & Modigliani, A. (1995). The ordinary quality of resistance: From Milgram's laboratory to the village of Le Chambon. *Journal of Social Issues, 5,* 195–210.

Rodrigo, M. F., & Ato, M. (2002). Testing the group polarization hypothesis by using logit models. *European Journal of Social Psychology, 32,* 3–18.

Rogers, R. W. (1980). *Subjects' reactions to experimental deception.* Unpublished manuscript, University of Alabama, Tuscaloosa.

Rogers, R. W., & Ketcher, C. M. (1979). Effects of anonymity and arousal on aggression. *Journal of Psychology, 102,* 13–19.

Rokach, A., & Neto, F. (2000). Coping with loneliness in adolescence: A cross-cultural study. *Social Behavior and Personality, 28,* 329–342.

Roland, E. (2002). Aggression, depression, and bullying others. *Aggressive Behavior, 28,* 198–206.

Rosenbaum, M. E. (1986). The repulsion hypothesis: On the nondevelopment of relationships. *Journal of Personality and Social Psychology, 51,* 1156–1166.

Rosenberg, M. (1965). *Society and the adolescent self-image.* Princeton, NJ: Princeton University Press.

Rosenhan, D. L., Salovey, P., & Hargis, K. (1981). The joys of helping: Focus of attention mediates the impact of positive affect on altruism. *Journal of Personality and Social Psychology, 40,* 899–905.

Ross, L. (1977). The intuitive scientist and his shortcoming. In L. Berkowitz (Ed.), *Advances in experimental social psychology* (Vol. 10, pp. 174–221). New York: Academic Press.

Ross, M., & Wilson, A. E. (2003). Autobiographical memory and conceptions of self: Getting better all the time. *Current Directions in Psychological Science, 12,* 66–69.

Rotenberg, K. J., & Kmill, J. (1992). Perception of lonely and non-lonely persons as a function of individual differences in loneliness. *Journal of Social and Personal Relationships, 9,* 325–330.

Rothman, A. J., & Hardin, C. D. (1997). Differential use of the availability heuristic in social judgment. *Personality and Social Psychology Bulletin, 23,* 123–138.

Rotton, J., & Cohn, E. G. (2000). Violence is a curvilinear function of temperature in Dallas: A replication. *Journal of Personality and Social Psychology, 78,* 1074–1081.

Rotton, J., & Kelley, I. W. (1985). Much ado about the full moon: A meta-analysis of lunar-lunacy research. *Psychological Bulletin, 97,* 286–306.

Rowe, P. M. (1996, September). On the neurobiological basis of affiliation. *APS Observer,* 17–18.

Rozin, P., & Nemeroff, C. (1990). The laws of sympathetic magic: A psychological analysis of similarity and contagion. In W. Stigler, R. A. Shweder, & G. Herdt (Eds.), *Cultural psychology: Essays in comparative human development* (pp. 205–232). Cambridge, England: Cambridge University Press.

Rozin, P., Lowery, L., & Ebert, R. (1994). Varieties of disgust faces and the structure of disgust. *Journal of Personality and Social Psychology, 66,* 870–881.

Rubin, J. Z. (1985). Deceiving ourselves about deception: Comment on Smith and Richardson's "Amelioration of deception and harm in psychological research." *Journal of Personality and Social Psychology, 48,* 252–253.

Ruder, M., & Bless, H. (2003). Mood and the reliance on the ease of retrieval heuristic. *Journal of Personality and Social Psychology, 85,* 20–32.

Rudman, L. A., & Fairchild, K. (2004). Reactions to counterstereotypic behavior: The role of backlash in cultural stereotype maintenance. *Journal of Personality and Social Psychology, 87,* 157–176.

Rusbult, C. E., & Van Lange, P. A. M. (2003). Interdependence, interaction, and relationships. *Annual Review of Psychology, 54,* 351–375.

Russell, J. A. (1994). Is there universal recognition of emotion from facial expressions? A review of cross-cultural studies. *Psychological Bulletin, 115,* 102–141.

Rutkowski, G. K., Gruder, C. L., & Romer, D. (1983). Group cohesiveness, social norms, and bystander intervention. *Journal of Personality and Social Psychology, 44,* 542–552.

Ryan, M. K., & Haslam, S. A. (2005). The glass cliff: Evidence that women are over-represented in precarious leadership positions. *British Journal of Management, 16,* 81–90.

Ryan, M. K., & Haslam, S. A. (2007). The glass cliff: Exploring the dynamics surrounding women's appointment to precarious leadership positions. *Academy of Management Review, 32,* 549–572.

Ryan, M. K., David, B., & Reynolds, K. J. (2004). Who cares? The effect of gender and context on the self and moral reasoning. *Psychology of Women Quarterly, 28,* 246–255.

Ryan, M. K., Haslam, S. A., Hersby, M. D., Kulich, C., & Wilson-Kovacs, M. D. (2009). The stress of working on the edge: Implications of glass cliffs for both women and organizations. In M. Barreto, M. K. Ryan, & M. T. Schmitt (Eds.), *The glass it ceiling in the 21st century* (pp. 153–169). Washington, DC: American Psychological Association.

Ryan, R. M., & Deci, E. L. (2000). Self-determination theory and the facilitation of intrinsic motivation, social development, and well-being. *American Psychologist, 55,* 68–78.

Ryan, R. M., & Deci, E. L. (2007). Active human nature: Self-determination theory and the promotion and maintenance of sport, exercise, and health. In M. S. Hagger & N. L. D. Chatzisarantis (Eds.)., *Self-determination in sport and exercise* (pp. 1–19). New York: Human Kinetics.

Sadler, P., & Woody, E. (2003). Is who you are who you're talking to? Interpersonal style and complementarity in mixed-sex interactions. *Journal of Personality and Social Psychology, 84,* 80–96.

Sahdra, B., & Ross, M. (2007). Group identification and historical memory. *Personality and Social Psychology Bulletin, 33,* 384–395.

Sanderson, C. A., & Cantor, N. (1999). A life task perspective on personality coherence: Stability versus change in tasks, goals, strategies, and outcomes. In D. Cervone & Y.

Sanfey, A. G. Rilling, J. K., Aronson, J. A., Nystrom L. E. & Cohen, J. D. (2003). The neural basis of economic decision making in the ultimatum game. *Science, 300,* 1755–1757.

Sangrador, J. L., & Yela, C. (2000). 'What is beautiful is loved': Physical attractiveness in love relationships in a representative sample. *Social Behavior and Personality, 28,* 207–218.

Sani, F. (2005). When subgroups secede: Extending and refining the social psychological model of schism in groups. *Personality and Social Psychology Bulletin, 31,* 1074–1086.

Sani, F. (2009). When groups fall apart: A social psychological model of the schismatic process. In F. Butera & J. M. Levine

(Eds.), *Coping with minority status: Responses to exclusion and inclusion* (pp. 243–266). New York: Cambridge University Press.

Sanitioso, R. B., & Wlodarski, R. (2004). In search of information that confirms a desired self-perception: Motivated processing of social feedback and choice of social interactions. *Personality and Social Psychology Bulletin, 30*, 412–422.

Sanna, L. J. (1997). Self-efficacy and counterfactual thinking: Up a creek with and without a paddle. *Personality and Social Psychology Bulletin, 23*, 654–666.

Sassenberg, K., Jonas, K. J., Shah, J. Y., & Brazy, P. C. (2007). Why some groups just feel better: The regulatory fit of group power. *Journal of Personality and Social Psychology, 92*, 249–267.

Saucier, D. A. (2002). Self-reports of racist attitudes for oneself and others. *Psychological Belgica, 42*, 99–105.

Schachter, S. (1951). Deviation, rejection, and communication. *Journal of Abnormal and Social Psychology, 46*, 190–207.

Schachter, S. (1959). *The psychology of affiliation*. Stanford, CA: Stanford University Press.

Schachter, S. (1964). The interaction of cognitive and physiological determinants of emotional state. In L. Berkowitz (Ed.), *Advances in experimental social psychology* (Vol. 1, pp. 48–81). New York: Academic Press.

Schein, V. E. (2001). A global look at psychological barriers to women's progress in management. *Journal of Social Issues, 57*, 675–688.

Scheithauer, H., & Hayer, T. (2007). Psychologische Aggressionstheorien [Psychological theories of aggression]. In M. Gollwitzer, J. Pfetsch, V. Schneider, A. Schulz, T. Steffke, & C. Ulrich (Eds.), *Prevention of violence for children and juveniles: Volume 1. Basics of aggression and violence in childhood and adolescence* (pp. 15–37). Göttingen: Hogrefe.

Schmader, T. (2010). Stereotype threat deconstructed. Current *Directions in Psychological Science, 19*, 14–18.

Schmitt, D. P. (2004). Patterns and universals of mate poaching across 53 nations: The effects of sex, culture, and personality on romantically attracting another person's partner. *Journal of Personality and Social Psychology, 86*, 560–584.

Schmitt, D. P., & Buss, D. M. (2001). Human mate poaching: Tactics and temptations for infiltrating existing mateships. *Journal of Personality and Social Psychology, 80*, 894–917.

Schmitt, M. T., Branscombe, N. R., & Postmes, T. (2003). Women's emotional responses to the pervasiveness of gender discrimination. *European Journal of Social Psychology, 33*, 297–312.

Schmitt, M. T., Ellemers, N., & Branscombe, N. R. (2003). Perceiving and responding to gender discrimination at work. In S. A. Haslam, D. van Knippenberg, M. Platow, & N. Ellemers (Eds.), *Social identity at work: Developing theory for organizational practice* (pp. 277–292). Philadelphia, PA: Psychology Press.

Schmitt, M. T., Lehmiller, J. J., & Walsh, A. L. (2007). The role of heterosexual identity threat in differential support for same-sex "civil unions" versus "marriages." *Group Processes and Intergroup Relations, 10*, 443–455.

Schmitt, M. T., Silvia, P. J., & Branscombe, N. R. (2000). The intersection of self-evaluation maintenance and social identity theories: Intragroup judgment in interpersonal and intergroup contexts. *Personality and Social Psychology Bulletin, 26*, 1598–1606.

Schnall, S., Roper, J., & Fessler, D.M.T. (2010). Elevation leads to altruistic behavior. *Psychological Science, 21*, 315–320.

Schul, Y., & Vinokur, A. D. (2000). Projection in person perception among spouses as a function of the similarity in their shared experiences. *Personality and Social Psychology Bulletin, 26*, 987–1001.

Schulz-Hardt, S., Brodbeck, F. C., Mojzisch, A., Kerschreiter, R., & Frey, D. (2009). Group decision making in hidden profile situations: Dissent as a facilitator for decision quality. *Journal of Personality and Social Psychology, 91*, 1080–1093.

Schutte, J. W., & Hosch, H. M. (1997). Gender differences in sexual assault verdicts: A meta-analysis. *Journal of Social Behavior and Personality, 12*, 759–772.

Schwartz, B. (2004). *The paradox of choice: Why more is less*. New York: HarperPerennial.

Schwarz, N., & Bohner, G. (2001). The construction of attitudes. In A. Tesser & N. Schwarz (Eds.), *Blackwell handbook of social psychology: Intrapersonal processes* (pp. 436–457). Oxford, UK: Blackwell.

Schwarz, N., & Clore, G. L. (1983). Mood, misattribution, and judgments of well-being: Informative and directive functions of affective states. *Journal of Personality and Social Psychology, 45*, 513–523.

Schwarz, N., & Clore, G. L. (2007). Feelings and phenomenal experiences. In A. W. Kruglanski & E. T. Higgins (Eds.), *Social psychology: Handbook of basic principles* (pp. 385–407). New York: Guilford Press.

Schwarz, N., Bless, H., Strack, F., Klumpp, G., Rittenauer-Schatka, G., & Simons, A. (1991). Ease of retrieval as information: Another look at the availability heuristic. *Journal of Personality and Social Psychology, 61*, 195–202.

Schwarzer, R. (1994). Optimism, vulnerability, and self-beliefs as health-related cognitions: A sytematic overview. *Psychology and Health, 9*, 161–180.

Scutt, D., Manning, J. T., Whitehouse, G. H., Leinster, S. J., & Massey, C. P. (1997). The relationship between breast symmetry, breast size and occurrence of breast cancer. *British Journal of Radiology, 70*, 1017–1021.

Sears, D. O. (2007).. The Americn color line fifty years after Brown v. Board: Many "Peoples of color" or Black exceptionalism? In G. Adams, M. Biernat, N. R. Branscombe, C. S. Crandall, & L. S. Wrightsman (Eds.), *Commemorating Brown: The social psychology of racism and discrimination*. Washington, DC: American Psychological Association.

Sedikides, C., & Anderson, C. A. (1994). Causal perception of intertrait relations: The glue that holds person types together. *Personality and Social Psychology Bulletin, 21,* 294–302.

Sedikides, C., & Gregg, A. P. (2003). Portraits of the self. In M. A. Hogg & J. Cooper (Eds.), *The Sage handbook of social psychology* (pp. 110–138). Thousand Oaks, CA: Sage.

Sedikides, C., Wildschut, T., Arndt, J., & Routledge, C. (2008). Nostalgia: Past, present, and future. *Current Directions in Psychological Science, 17,* 304–307.

Seery, M. D., Blascovich, J., Weisbuch, M., & Vick, B. (2004). The relationship between self-esteem level, self-esteem stability, and cardiovascular reactions to performance feedback. *Journal of Personality and Social Psychology, 87,* 133–145.

Segal, M. M. (1974). Alphabet and attraction: An unobtrusive measure of the effect of propinquity in a field setting. *Journal of Personality and Social Psychology, 30,* 654–657.

Selfhout, M., Denissen, J., Branje, S., & Meeus, W. (2009). In the eye of the beholder: Perceived, actual, ad peer-rated similarity in personality, communication, and friendship intensity during the acquaintanceship process. *Journal of Personality and Social Psychology, 96,* 1152–1165.

Seligman, M.E.P., Steen, T.A., Park, N., & Peterson, C. (2005). Positive psychology progress: empirical validation of interventions. *American Psychologist, 60,* 410–421.

Seta, C. E., Hayes, N. S., & Seta, J. J. (1994). Mood, memory, and vigilance: The influence of distraction on recall and impression formation. *Personality and Social Psychology Bulletin, 20,* 170–177.

Setter, J.S., Brownless, G.M., & Sanders, M. (2011). Persuasion by wah of example: Does including gratuity guidelines on customers' checks affect restaurant tipping behavior? *Journal of Applied Social Psychology, 41,* 150–159.

Shah, A. K., & Oppenheimer, D. M. (2009). The path of least resistance: Using easy-to-access information. *Current Directions in Psychological Science, 18,* 232–236.

Shah, J. (2003). Automatic for the people; How representations of significant others implicitly affect goal pursuit. *Journal of Personality and Social Psychology, 84,* 661–681.

Shaked-Schroer, M. A., & Costanzo, M. (2008). Reducing racial bias in the penalty phase ofcapital trials. *Behavioral Science and the Law, 26,* 603–617.

Shams, M. (2001). Social support, loneliness and friendship preference among British Asian and non-Asian adolescents. *Social Behavior and Personality, 29,* 399–404.

Shanab, M. E., & Yahya, K. A. (1977). A behavioral study of obedience in children. *Journal of Personality and Social Psychology, 35,* 530–536.

Sharp, D., Adair, J. G., & Roese, N. J. (1992). Twenty years of deception research: A decline in subjects' trust? *Personality and Social Psychology Bulletin, 18,* 585–590.

Sharp, M. J., & Getz, J. G. (1996). Substance use as impression management. *Personality and Social Psychology Bulletin, 22,* 60–67.

Shaver, P. R., & Brennan, K. A. (1992). Attachment styles and the "big five" personality traits: Their connections with each other and with romantic relationship outcomes. *Personality and Social Psychology Bulletin, 18,* 536–545.

Shaver, P. R., Morgan, H. J., & Wu, S. (1996). Is love a "basic" emotion? *Personal Relationships, 3,* 81–96.

Shaver, P. R., Murdaya, U., & Fraley, R. C. (2001). The structure of the Indonesian emotion lexicon. *Asian Journal of Social Psychology, 4,* 201–224.

Shaw, J. I., Borough, H. W., & Fink, M. I. (1994). Perceived sexual orientation and helping behavior by males and females: The wrong number technique. *Journal of Psychology and Human Sexuality, 6,* 73–81.

Sheeks, M. S., & Birchmeier, Z. P. (2007). Shyness, sociability, and the use of computer-mediated communication in relationship development. *CyberPsychology and Behavior, 10,* 7, 64–70.

Sheldon, K.M., Abad, N., & Hinsch, C. (2011). A two-process view of facebook use and relatedness need-satisfaction: Disconnection drives use, and connection rewards it. *Journal of Personality and Social Psychology, 100,* 766–775.

Shelton, J. N., Richeson, J. A., & Vorauer, J. D. (2006). Threatened identities and interethnic interactions. *European Review of Social Psychology, 17,* 321–358.

Shepperd, J. A., & Taylor, K. M. (1999). Social loafing and expectancy-value theory. *Personality and Social Psychology Bulletin, 25,* 1147–1158.

Shepperd, J. A., Carroll, P. J., & Sweeny, K. (2008). A functional approach to explaining fluctuations in future outlooks: From self-enhancement to self-criticism. In E. Chang (Ed.), *Self-criticism and self-enhancement: Theory, research and clinical implications* (pp. 161–180). Washington, DC: American Psychological Association.

Sherif, M. A. (1937). An experimental approach to the study of attitudes. *Sociometry, 1,* 90–98.

Sherif, M., Harvey, D. J., White, B. J., Hood, W. R, & Sherif, C. W. (1961). *The Robbers' cave experiment.* Norman, OK: Institute of Group Relations.

Sherman, J. W., Gawronski, B., Gonsalkorale, K., Hugenberg, K., Allen, T. J., & Groom, C. J. (2008). The self-regulation of automatic associations and behavioral impulses. *Psychological Review, 115,* 314–335.

Sherman, M. D., & Thelen, M. H. (1996). Fear of intimacy scale: Validation and extension with adolescents. *Journal of Social and Personal Relationships, 13,* 507–521.

Sherman, S. S. (1980). On the self-erasing nature of errors of prediction. *Journal of Personality and Social Psychology, 16,* 388–403.

Shoda (Eds.), The coherence of personality: Social-cognitive bases of consistency, variability, and organization (pp. 372–392). New York: Guilford Press.

Sidanius, J., & Pratto, F. (1999). *Social dominance.* New York: Cambridge University Press.

Sigall, H. (1997). Ethical considerations in social psychological research: Is the bogus pipeline a special case? *Journal of Applied Social Psychology, 27*, 574–581.

Sillars, A. L., Folwell, A. L., Hill, K. C., Maki, B. K., Hurst, A. P., & Casano, R. A. (1994). *Journal of Social and Personal Relationships, 11*, 611–617.

Simon, B. (2004). *Identity in modern society: A social psychological perspective*. Oxford: Blackwell.

Simon, B., & Klandermans, B. (2001). Politicized collective identity: A social psychological analysis. *American Psychologist, 56*, 319–331.

Simon, L., Greenberg, J., & Brehm, J. (1995). Trivialization: The forgotten mode of dissonance reduction. *Journal of Personality and Social Psychology, 68*, 247–260.

Simons, G & Parkinson, B. (2009). Time-dependent observational and diary methodologies for assessing social referencing and interpersonal emotion regulation. *21st Century Society, 4*, 175–186

Simonton, D. K. (2009). Historiometry in personality and social psychology. *Review of General Psychology, 13*, 315–326.

Sinclair, S., Dunn, E., & Lowery, B. S. (2005). The relationship between parental racial attitudes and children's implicit prejudice. *Journal of Experimental Social Psychology, 41*, 283–289.

Singh, R., & Ho, S. Y. (2000). Attitudes and attraction: A new test of the attraction, repulsion and similarity–dissimilarity asymmetry hypotheses. *British Journal of Social Psychology, 39*, 197–211.

Sistrunk, F., & McDavid, J. W. (1971). Sex variable in conforming behavior. *Journal of Personality and Social Psychology, 17*, 200–207.

Sivacek, J., & Crano, W.D. (1982). Vested interest as a moderator of attitude-behavior consistency. *Journal of Personality and Social Psychology, 43*, 210–221.

Slotter, E. B., Gardner, W. L., & Finkel, E. J. (2010). Who am I without you?: The influence of romantic breakup on the self-concept. *Personality and Social Psychology Bulletin, 36*, 147–160.

Smeaton, G., Byrne, D., & Murnen, S. K. (1989). The repulsion hypothesis revisited: Similarity irrelevance or dissimilarity bias? *Journal of Personality and Social Psychology, 56*, 54–59.

Smith, K. D., Keating, J. P., & Stotland, E. (1989). Altruism reconsidered: The effect of denying feedback on a victim's status to empathetic witnesses. *Journal of Personality and Social Psychology, 57*, 641–650.

Smith, S. S., & Richardson, D. (1985). On deceiving ourselves about deception: Reply to Rubin. *Journal of Personality and Social Psychology, 48*, 254–255.

Smorti, A., & Ciucci, E. (2000). Narrative strategies in bullies and victims in Italian schoolchildren. *Aggressive Behavior, 26*, 33–48.

Sniffen, M.J, (1999, November 22) . Serious crime declines sharply. *Associated Press.*

Snyder, C.R., & Fromkin, H.L. (1980). *Uniqueness, the human pursuit of difference.* New York : Plenum Press, c1980

Sparrow, B., & Wegner, D. M. (2006). Unpriming: The deactivation of thoughts through expression. *Journal of Personality and Social Psychology, 9*, 1009–1019.

Sparrowe, R. T., Soetjipto, B. W., & Kraimer, M. L. (2006). Do leaders' influence tactics relate to members' helping behavior? It depends on the quality of the relationships. *Academy of Management Journal, 49*, 1194–1208.

Spencer, S. J., Steele, C. M., & Quinn, D. M. (1999). Stereotype threat and women's math performance. *Journal of Experimental Social Psychology, 35*, 4–28.

Spencer-Rodgers, J., Hamilton, D. L., & Sherman, S. J. (2007). The central role of entitativity in stereotypes of social categories and task groups. *Journal of Personality and Social Psychology, 92*, 369–388.

Spielmann, S. S., MacDonald, G., & Wilson, A. E. (2009). On the rebound: Focusing on someone new helps anxiously attached individuals let go of ex-partners. *Personality and Social Psychology Bulletin, 35*, 1382–1394.

Spina, R. R., Ji, L.-J., Guo, T., Zhang, Z., Li, Y., & Fabrigar, L. (2010). Cultural differences in the representativeness heuristic: Expecting a correspondence in magnitude between cause and effect. *Personality and Social Psychology Bulletin, 36*, 583–597.

Sprecher, S., Zimmerman, C., & Abrahams, A. M. (2010). Choosing compassionate strategies to end a relationship. *Social Psychology, 41*, 66–73.

Stürmer, S., & Snyder, M. (2010). Helping "us" versus "them": Towards a group-level theory of helping and altruism within and across group boundaries. In S. Stürmer & M. Snyder (Eds.), *The psy-chology of prosocial behavior: Group processes, intergroup relations, and helping* (pp. 33–58). Ox-ford: Wiley & Blackwell.

Stürmer, S., Snyder, M., Kropp, A., & Siem, B. (2006). Empathy-motivated helping: The moderating role of group membership. *Personality and Social Psychology Bulletin, 32*, 943–956.

Stahl, C., Unkelbach, C., & Corneille, O. (2009). On the respective contributions of awareness of unconditioned stimulus valence and unconditioned stimulus identity in attitude formation through evaluative conditioning. *Journal of Personality and Social Psychology, 97*, 404–420.

Stangor, C., & McMillan, D. (1992). Memory for expectancy-congruent and expectancy-incongruent information: A review of the social and social developmental literatures. *Psychological Bulletin, 111*, 42–61.

Stangor, C., Sechrist, G. B., & Jost, T. J. (2001). Changing racial beliefs by providing consensus information. *Personality and Social Psychology Bulletin, 27*, 486–496.

Starratt, V. G., Shackelford, T. K., Goetz, A. T., & McKiddin, W. F. (2007). Male mate retention behaviors vary with risk of female infidelity and sperm competition. *Acta Psychologica Sinica, 39*, 523–527.

Stasser, G. (1992). Pooling of unshared information during group discussion. In S. Worchel, W. Wood, & J. H. Simpson (Eds.), *Group process and productivity* (pp. 48–67). Newbury Park, CA: Sage.

Staub, E. (1989). *The roots of evil.* New York: Cambridge University Press.

Steblay, N. M., Dysart, J., Fulero, S., & Lindsay, R. C. L. (2001). Eyewitness accuracy rates in sequential and simultaneous lineup presentations: A met-analytic comparison. *Law and Human Behavior, 25,* 459–473.

Steele, C. M. (1988). The psychology of self-affirmation: Sustaining the integrity of the self. In L. Berkowitz (Ed.), *Advances in experimental social psychology* (pp. 261–302). Hillsdale, NJ: Erlbaum.

Steele, C. M. (1997). A threat in the air: How stereotypes shape the intellectual identities and performance of women and African-Americans. *American Psychologist, 52,* 613–629.

Steele, C. M., & Aronson, J. (1995). Stereotype threat and the intellectual test performance of African Americans. *Journal of Personality and Social Psychology, 69,* 797–811.

Steele, C. M., & Lui, T. J. (1983). Dissonance processes as self-affirmation. *Journal of Personality and Social Psychology, 45,* 5–19.

Steele, C. M., Spencer, S. J., & Aronson, J. (2002). Contending with group image: The psychology of stereotype and social identity threat. *Advances in Experimental Social Psychology, 34,* 379–439.

Steele, C. M., Spencer, S. J., & Lynch, M. (1993). Self-image resilience and dissonance: The role of affirmational resources. *Journal of Personality and Social Psychology, 64,* 885–896.

Steele, C. M., Spencer, S. J., & Aronson, J. (2002). Contending with group image: The psychology of stereotype and social identity threat. In M. P. Zanna (Ed.), *Advances in experimental social psychology* (Vol. 34, pp. 379–440). San Diego, CA: Academic Press.

Stephan, W. G., Boniecki, K. A., Ybarra, O., Bettencourt, A., Ervin, K. S., Jackson, L. A., et al. (2002). The role of threats in the racial attitudes of Blacks and Whites. *Personality and Social Psychology Bulletin, 28,* 1242–1254.

Stephan, W. G., Renfro, C. L., Esses, V. M., Stephan, C. W., & Martin, T. (2005). The effects of feeling threatened on attitudes toward immigrants. *International Journal of Intercultural Relations, 29,* 1–19.

Sternberg, R. J. (1986). A triangular theory of love. *Psychological Review, 93,* 119–135.

Stevens, C. K., & Kristof, A. L. (1995). Making the right impression: A field study of applicant impression management during job interviews. *Journal of Applied Psychology, 80,* 587–606.

Stewart, T. L., Latu, I. M., Branscombe, N. R., & Denney, H. D. (2010). Yes we can! Prejudice reduction through seeing (inequality) and believing (in social change). *Psychological Science, 21,* 1557–1562.

Stewart, T. L., Latu, I. M., Kawakami, K., & Myers, A. C. (2010). Consider the situation: Reducing automatic stereotyping through situational attributional training. *Journal of Experimental Social Psychology, 46,* 221–225.

Stewart, T. L., Vassar, P. M., Sanchez, D. T., & David, S. E. (2000). Attitudes toward women's societal roles moderates the effect of gender cues on target individuation. *Journal of Personality and Social Psychology, 79,* 143–157.

Stocks, E.L., Lishner, D.A., Waits, B.L., & Dlownum, E.M. (2011). I'm embarrassed for you: the effect of valuing and perspective taking on empathic embarrassment and empathic concern. *Journal of Applied Social Psychology, 2011, 41,* 1–26.

Stone, J., Lynch, C. I., Sjomeling, M., & Darley, J. M. (1999). Stereotype threat effects on Black and White athletic performance. *Journal of Personality and Social Psychology, 77,* 1213–1227.

Stone, J., Wiegand, A. W., Cooper, J., & Aronson, E. (1997). When exemplification fails: Hypocrisy and the motives for self-integrity. *Journal of Personality and Social Psychology, 72,* 54–65.

Stott, C. J., Hutchison, P., & Drury, J. (2001). 'Hooligans' abroad? Inter-group dynamics, social identity and participation in collective 'disorder' at the 1998 World Cup Finals. *British Journal of Social Psychology, 40,* 359–384.

Stroebe, W., Diehl, M., & Abakoumkin, G. (1992). The illusion of group effectivity. *Personality and Social Psychology Bulletin, 18,* 643–650.

Stroh, L. K., Langlands, C. L., & Simpson, P. A. (2004). Shattering the glass ceiling in the new millenium. In M. S. Stockdale and F. J. Crosby (Eds.), *The psychology and management of workplace diversity* (pp. 147–167). Malden, MA: Blackwell.

Strube, M. J. (1989). Evidence for the Type in Type A behavior: A taxonometric analysis. *Journal of Personality and Social Psychology, 56,* 972–987.

Strube, M., Turner, C. W., Cerro, D., Stevens, J., & Hinchey, F. (1984). Interpersonal aggression and the Type A coronary-prone behavior pattern: A theoretical distinction and practical implications. *Journal of Personality and Social Psychology, 47,* 839–847.

Stuermer, S., Snyder, M., Kropp, A., & Siem, B. (2006). Empathy-motivated helping: The moderating role of group membership. *Personality and Social Psychology Bulletin, 32,* 943–956.

Suls, J., & Rosnow, J. (1988). Concerns about artifacts in behavioral research. In M. Morawski (Ed.), *The rise of experimentation in American psychology* (pp. 163–187). New Haven, CT: Yale University Press.

Sundie, J.M., Kenrick, D.T., Griskevicius, V., Tybur, J.M., Vohs, K.D., & Beal, D.J. (in press). "Peacocks, Porsches, and Thorstein Veblen: Conspicuous Consumption as a Sexual Signaling System," *Journal of Personality and Social Psychology.*

Swami, V., Frederick, D.A., Aavik, T., Alcalay, L., Ailik, J., Anderson, D., Andrianto, S. . (2010). The attractive female body weight and female body dissatisfaction in 26 countries across 10 world regions: Results of the international body project I. *Personality and Social Psychology Bulletin, 36,* 309–325.

Swann, W. B. (2005). The self and identity negotiation. *Interaction Studies: Social Behavior and Communication in Biological and Artificial Systems, 6,* 69–83.

Swann, W. B., & Bosson, J. K. (2010). Self and identity. In S. T. Fiske, D. T. Gilbert, & G. Lindzey (Eds.), *Handbook of social psychology* (5th ed., pp. 589–628). New York: McGraw-Hill.

Swann, W. B., Chang-Schneider, C., & McClarty, K. L. (2007). Do people's self-views matter? Self-concept and self-esteem in everyday life. *American Psychologist, 62,* 84–94.

Swann, W. B., Gómez, Á., Dovidio, J. F., Hart, S., & Jetten, J. (2010). Dying and killing for one's group: Identity fusion moderates responses to intergroup versions of the trolley problem. *Psychological Science, 21,* 1176–1183.

Swann, W. B., Jr., & Gill, M. J. (1997). Confidence and accuracy in person perception: Do we know what we think we know about our relationship partners? *Journal of Personality and Social Psychology, 73,* 747–757.

Swann, W. B., Jr., Rentfrow, P. J., & Gosling, S. D. (2003). The precarious couple effect: verbally inhibited men + critical, disinhibited women = bad chemistry. *Journal of Personality and Social Psychology, 85,* 1095–1106.

Swap, W. C. (1977). Interpersonal attraction and repeated exposure to rewarders and punishers. *Personality and Social Psychology Bulletin, 3,* 248–251.

Sweeny, K., & Shepperd, J. A. (2010). The costs of optimism and the benefits of pessimism. *Emotion, 10,* 750–753.

Sweldens, S., van Osselaer, S. M. J., & Janiszewski, C. (2010). Evaluative conditioning procedures and the resilience of conditioned brand attitudes. *Journal of Consumer Research, 37,* 473–489.

Swim, J. K., & Campbell, B. (2001). Sexism: Attitudes, beliefs, and behaviors. In R. Brown & S. Gaertner (Eds.), *Blackwell handbook of social psychology: Intergroup processes* (pp. 218–237). Oxford, UK: Blackwell.

Swim, J. K., Aikin, K. J., Hall, W. S., & Hunter, B. A. (1995). Sexism and racism: Old-fashioned and modern prejudices. *Journal of Personality and Social Psychology, 68,* 199–214.

Tajfel, H. (1978). *The social psychology of the minority.* New York: Minority Rights Group.

Tajfel, H. (1981). Social stereotypes and social groups. In J. C. Turner & H. Giles (Eds.), *Intergroup behavior* (pp. 144–167). Chicago, IL: University of Chicago Press.

Tajfel, H. (1982). *Social identity and intergroup relations.* Cambridge, England: Cambridge University Press.

Tajfel, H., & Turner, J. C. (1986). The social identity theory of intergroup behavior. In S. Worchel & W. G. Austin (Eds.), *The social psychology of intergroup relations* (2nd ed., pp. 7–24). Monterey, CA: Brooks-Cole.

Tajfel, H., Billig, M., Bundy, R., & Flament, C. (1971). Social categorization and intergroup behaviour. *European Journal of Social Psychology, 1,* 149–178.

Talaska, C. A., Fiske, S. T., & Chaiken, S. (2008). Legitimating racial discrimination: A meta-analysis of the racial attitude–behavior literature shows that emotions, not beliefs, best predict discrimination. *Social Justice Research, 21,* 263–296.

Tan, D. T. Y., & Singh, R. (1995). Attitudes and attraction: A developmental study of the similarity– attraction and dissimilarity–repulsion hypotheses. *Personality and Social Psychology Bulletin, 21* 975–986.

Tausch, N., Hewstone, M., Kenworthy, J. B., & Cairns, E. (2007). Cross-community contact, perceived status differences and intergroup attitudes in Northern Ireland: the mediating role of individual-level vs. group-level threats and the moderating role of social identification. *Political Psychology, 28,* 53–68.

Taylor, K. M., & Shepperd, J. A. (1998). Bracing for the worst: Severity, testing, and feedback timing as moderators of the optimistic bias. *Personality and Social Psychology Bulletin, 24,* 915–926.

Taylor, S. E. (1989). *Positive illusions: Creative self-deception and the healthy mind.* New York: Basic Books.

Taylor, S. E. (2002). *Health psychology* (5th ed.). New York: McGraw-Hill.

Taylor, S. E., & Brown, J. D. (1988). Illusion and well-being: A social psychological perspective on mental health. *Psychological Bulletin, 103,* 193–210.

Taylor, S. E., Helgeson, V. S., Reed, G. M., & Skokan, L. A. (1991). Self-generated feelings of control and adjustment to physical illness. *Journal of Social Issues, 47,* 91–109.

Taylor, S. E., Lerner, J. S., Sherman, D. K., Sage, R. M., & McDowell, N. K. (2003). Are self-enhancing cognitions associated with healthy or unhealthy biological profiles? *Journal of Personality and Social Psychology, 85,* 605–615.

Taylor, S. E., Seeman, T. E., Eisenberger, N. I., Kozanian,, T. I., Moore, A. N., & Moons, W. G. (2010). Effects of a supportive or an unsupportive audience on biological and psychological responses to stress. *Journal of Personality and Social Psychology, 98,* 47–56.

'Taylor, S. E. (2007). Social support. In H. S. Friedman & R. C. Silver (Eds.), *Foundations of health psychology* (pp. 145–171). New York: Oxford University Press.

Tellegen, A., Lykken, D. T., Bouchard, T. J., Wilcox, K. J., Segal, N. L., & Rich, S. (1988) similarity in twins reared together and apart *Journal of Personality and Social Psy???,* 1031–1039.

Terman, L. M., & Buttenwieser, P. (1935a). Personality factors in marital compatibility: I. *Journal of Social Psychology, 6,* 143–171.

Terman, L. M., & Buttenwieser, P. (1935b). Personality factors in marital compatibility: II. *Journal of Social Psychology, 6,* 267–289.

Terry, D. J., & Hogg, M. A. (1996). Group norms and the attitude-behavior relationship: A role for group identification. *Personality and Social Psychology Bulletin, 22,* 776–793.

Terry, D. J., Hogg, M. A., & Duck, J. M. (1999). Group membership, social identity, and attitudes. In D. Abrams & M. A. Hogg (Eds.), *Social identity and social cognition* (pp. 280–314). Oxford: Blackwell.

Tesser, A. (1988). Toward a self-evaluation maintenance model of social behavior. *Advances in Experimental Social Psychology, 21,* 181–227.

Tesser, A., & Martin, L. (1996). The psychology of evaluation. In E. T. Higgins & A. W. Kruglanski (Eds.), *Social psychology: Handbook of basic principles* (pp. 400–423). New York: Guilford Press.

Tesser, A., Martin, L. L., & Cornell, D. P. (1996). On the substitutability of the self-protecting mechanisms. In P. Gollwitzer & J. Bargh (Eds.), *The psychology of action* (pp. 48–68). New York: Guilford.

Tetlock, P. E., Peterson, R. S., McGuire, C., Change, S., & Feld, P. (1992). Assessing political group dynamics: A test of the groupthink model. *Journal of Personality and Social Psychology, 63,* 403–425.

Thaler, R. H., & Sunstein, C. R. (2008). *Nudge: Improving decisions about health, wealth, and happiness.* New Haven, CT: Yale University Press.

Thomaes, S., Bushman, B. J., de Castro, B. O., Cohen, G. L., & Denissen, J. J. A. (2009). Reducing narcissistic aggression by buttressing self-esteem. *Psychological Science, 21,* 1536–1541.

Thomaes, S., Bushman, B. J., Stegge, H., & Olthof, T. (2008). Trumping shame by blasts of noise: Narcissism, self-esteem, shame, and aggression in young adolescents. *Child Development, 79,* 1792–1801.

Thomaes, S., Stegge, H., Bushman, B. J., Olthof, T., & Denissen, J. (2008). Development and validation of the Childhood Narcissism Scale. *Journal of Personality Assessment, 90,* 382–391.

Thompson, L. (1998). *The mind and heart of the negotiator.* Upper Saddle River, NJ: Prentice-Hall.

Thomson, J. W., Patel, S., Platek, S. M., & Shackelford, T. K. (2007). Sex differences in implicit association and attentional demands for information about infidelity. *Evolutionary Psychology, 5,* 569–583.

Tice, D. M., Bratslavsky, E., & Baumeister, R. F. (2000). Emotional distress regulation takes precedence over impulse control: If you feel bad, do it! *Journal of Personality and Social Psychology, 80,* 53–67.

Tice, D. M., Butler, J. L., Muraven, M. B., & Stillwell, A. M. (1995). When modesty prevails: Differential favorability of self-presentation to friends and strangers. *Journal of Personality and Social Psychology, 69,* 1120–1138.

Tidwell, M.-C. O., Reis, H. T., & Shaver, P. R. (1996). Attachment, attractiveness, and social interaction: A diary study. *Journal of Personality and Social Psychology, 71,* 729–745.

Tiedens, L. Z., & Fragale, A. R. (2003). Power moves: Complementarity in dominant and submissive nonverbal behavior. *Journal of Personality and Social Psychology, 84,* 558–568.

Timmerman, T. A. (2007). "It was a thought pitch": Personal, situational, and target influences on hit-by-pitch events across time. *Journal of Applied Psychology, 92,* 876-884.

Tomaskovic-Devey, D., Zimmer, C., Strainback, K., Robinson, C., Taylor, T., & McTague, T. (2006). Documenting desegregation: Segregation in American workplaces by race, ethnicity, and sex, 1966–2003. *American Sociological Review, 71,* 565–588.

Tormala, Z. L., & Rucker, D. D. (2007). Attitude certainty: A review of past findings and emerging perspectives. *Social and Personality Psychology Compass, 1,* 469–492.

Tormala, Z. L., Petty, R. E., & Brinol, P (2002). Ease of retrieval effects in persuasion: A self-validation analysis. *Personality and Social Psychology Bulletin, 28,* 1700–1712.

Towles-Schwen, T., & Fazio, R. H. (2001). On the origins of racial attitudes: Correlates of childhood experiences. *Personality and Social Psychology Bulletin, 27,* 162–175.

Trafimow, D., Silverman, E., Fan, R., & Law, J. (1997). The effects of language and priming on the relative accessibility of the private self and collective self. *Journal of Cross-Cultural Psychology, 28,* 107–123.

Tremblay, P. F., & Belchevski, M. (2004). Did the instigator intend to provoke? A key moderator in the relation between trait aggression and aggressive behaviour. *Aggressive Behavior, 30,* 409–424.

Trevarthen, C. (1993). The function of emotions in early infant communication and development. In J. Nadel & L. Camaioni (Eds.), *New perspectives in early communication development* (pp. 48–81). London: Routledge.

Trobst, K. K., Collins, R. L., & Embree, J. M. (1994). The role of emotion in social support provision: Gender, empathy, and expressions of distress. *Journal of Social and Personal Relationships, 11,* 45–62.

Trope, Y., & Liberman, N. (2003). Temporal construal. *Psychological Review, 110,* 401–421.

Tsao, D. Y., & Livingstone, M. S. (2008). Mechanisms of face perception. *Annual Review of Neuroscience, 31,* 411–437.

Turan, B., & Horowitz, L. M. (2007). Can I count on you to be there for me?: Individual differences in a knowledge structure. *Journal of Personality and Social Psychology, 93,* 447–465.

Turan, B., & Vicary, A. M. (2010). Who recognizes and chooses behaviors that are best for a relationships?: The separate roles of knowledge, attachment, and motivation. *Personality and Social Psychology Bulletin, 36,* 119–131.

Turner, J. C. (1991). *Social influence.* Pacific Grove, CA: Brooks/Cole.

Turner, J. C. (2005). Explaining the nature of power: A three-process theory. *European Journal of Social Psychology, 35,* 1–22.

Turner, J. C. (2006). Tyranny, freedom and social structure: Escaping our theoretical prisons. *British Journal of Social Psychology, 45,* 41–46.

Turner, J. C., & Onorato, R. S. (1999). Social identity, personality, and the self-concept: A self-categorization perspective. In T. R. Tyler, R. M. Kramer & O. P. John (Eds.), *The psychology of the social self* (pp. 11–46). Mahwah, NJ: Erlbaum.

Turner, J. C., Hogg, M. A., Oakes, P. J., Reicher, S. D., & Wetherell, M. S. (1987). *Rediscovering the social group: A self-categorization theory.* Oxford, UK: Blackwell.

Twenge, J. M., & Manis, M. M. (1998). First-name desirability and adjustment: Self-satisfaction, others' ratings, and family background. *Journal of Applied Social Psychology, 24,* 41–51.

Twenge, J. M., & Campbell, W. K. (2008). Increases in positive self-views among high school students. *Psychological Science, 19,* 1082–1086.

Twenge, J. M., Abebe, E. M., & Campbell, W. K. (2010). Fitting in or standing out: Trends in American parents' choices for children's names, 1880–2007. *Social Psychological and Personality Science, 1,* 19–25.

Twenge, J. M., Baumeister, R. F., DeWall, C. N., Ciarocco, N. J., & Bartels, J. M. (2007). Social exclusion decreases prosocial behavior. *Journal of Personality and Social Psychology, 92,* 56–66.

Twenge, J. M., Konrath, S., Foster, J. D., Campbell, W. K., & Bushman, B. J. (2008). Egos inflating over time: A cross-temporal meta-analysis of the Narcissistic Personality Inventory. *Journal of Personality, 76,* 875–901.

Tybout, A. M., Sternthal, B., Malaviya, P., Bakamitsos, G. A., & Park, S. (2005). Information accessibility as a moderator of judgments: The role of content versus retrieval ease. *Journal of Consumer Research, 32,* 76–85.

Tykocinski, O. E. (2001). I never had a chance: Using hindsight tactics to mitigate disappointments. *Personality and Social Psychology Bulletin, 27,* 376–382.

Tykocinski, O. E. (2008). Insurance, risk, and magical thinking. *Personality and Social Psychology Bulletin, 34,* 1346–1356.

Tyler, Feldman, & Reichert, 2006—in 12th edition reference list.

Tyler, J. M., & Feldman R. S. (2004). Cognitive demand and self-presentation efforts: The influence of situational importance and interactions goal. *Self and Identity, 3,* 364–377.

Tyler, J. M., & Rosier, J. G. (2009). Examining self-presentation as a motivational explanation for comparative optimism. *Journal of Personality and Social Psychology, 97,* 716–727.

Tyler, T. R., & Blader, S. (2000). *Cooperation in groups: Procedural justice, social identity and behavioral engagement.* Philadelphia, PA: Psychology Press.

Tyler, T. R., & Blader, S. L. (2003). The group engagement model: Procedural justice, social identity, and cooperative behavior. *Personality and Social Psychology Review, 7,* 349–361.

Tyler, T. R., Boeckmann, R. J., Smith, H. J., & Huo, Y. J. (1997). *Social justice in a diverse society.* Boulder, CO: Westview.

U.S. Bureau of Labor Statistics. (2006). *Women in the labor force: A databook.* Report 996. Retrieved May 21, 2007, from www.bls.gov/news.release/pdf/atus.pdf.

U.S. Census Bureau. (2007). *Statistical abstract of the United States: 2007.* Retrieved October 14, 2010, from http://www.census.gov/prod/www/statistical-abstract.html.

U.S. Department of Justice. (2003). *Sourcebook of criminal justice statistics.* Washington, DC: U.S. Government Printing Office.

U.S.Bureau of Labor Statistics. (2007). *Volunteering in the United States, 2006.* Washington DC: Bureau of Labor Statistics.

Uchida, Y., Townsend, S. S. M, Markus, H. R., & Bergsieker, H. B. (2009). Emotions as within or between people? Lay theory of emotion expression and emotion inference across cultures. *Personality and Social Psychology Bulletin, 35,* 1427–1439.

Urbanski, L. (1992, May 21). Study uncovers traits people seek in friends. *The Evangelist,* 4.

Valkenburg, P. M., Schouten, A. P., & Peter, J. (2005). Adolescents' identity experiments on the Internet. *New Media and Society, 7,* 383–402.

Vallone, R.P., Griffin, D.W., Lin, S., & Ross, L. (1990). Overconfident prediction of future actions and outcomes by self and others. *Journal of Personality and Social Psychology, 58,* 582–592.

Van Berkum, J. J. A., Hollmean, B., Nieuwaland, M., Otten, M., & Murre, J. (2009). Right or wrong?: The brain's fast response to morally objectionable statements. *Psychological Science, 20,* 1092–1099.

Van den Bos, K. (2009). Making sense of life: The existential self trying to deal with personal uncertainty. *Psychological Inquiry, 20,* 197–217.

Van den Bos, K., & Lind, E. W. (2001). Uncertainty management by means of fairness judgments. In M. P. Zanna (Ed.), *Advances in experimental social psychology* (Vol. 34, pp. 1–60). San Diego, CA: Academic Press.

Van Dick, R., Wagner, U., Pettigrew, T.F., Christ, O., Wolf, C., et al. (2004). Role of perceived importance in intergroup contact. *Journal of Personality and Social Psychology, 87,* 211–227.

Van Lange, P. A. M., & Joireman, J. A. (2010). Social and temporal orientations in social dilemmas. In R. M. Kramer, A. E. Tenbrunsel, & M. H. Bazerman (Eds.), *Social decision making: Social dilemmas, social values, and ethical judgments* (pp. 71–94). New York: Routledge.

Van Overwalle, F. (1998). Causal explanation as constraint satisfaction: A critique and a feedforward connectionist alternative. *Journal of Personality and Social Psychology, 74,* 312–328.

Van Prooijen, J. W., van den Bos, K., Lind, E. A., & Wilke, H. A. M. (2006). How do people react to negative procedures?

On the moderating role of authority's biased attitudes. *Journal of Experimental Social Psychology, 42,* 632–645.

Van Straaten, I., Engels, R. G., Finkenauer, C., & Holland, R. W. (2009). Meeting your match: How attractiveness similarity affects approach behavior in mixed-sex dyads. *Personality and Social Psychology Bulletin, 35,* 685–697.

Vandello, J. A., & Cohen, D. (2003). Male honor and female fidelity: Implicit cultural scripts that perpetuate domestic violence. *Journal of Personality and Social Psychology, 84,* 997–1010.

Vanderbilt, A. (1957). *Amy Vanderbilt's complete book of etiquette.* Garden City, NY: Doubleday.

Vasquez, M. J. T. (2001). Leveling the playing field—Toward the emancipation of women. *Psychology of Women Quarterly, 25,* 89–97.

Vazire, S. (2010). Who knows what about a person?: The self–other knowledge asymmetry (SOKA) model. *Journal of Personality and Social Psychology, 98,* 281–300.

Vazire, S., & Mehl, M. R. (2008). Knowing me, knowing you: the accuracy and unique predictive validity of self-ratings and other-ratings of daily behavior. *Journal of Personality and Social Psychology, 95,* 1202–1216.

Vertue, F. M. (2003). From adaptive emotion to dysfunction: An attachment perspective on social anxiety disorder. *Personality and Social Psychology Review, 7,* 170–191.

Vignovic, J. A., & Thompson, L. F. (2010) Computer-mediated cross-cultural collaboration: Attribution communication errors to the person versus the situation. *Journal of Applied Psychology, 95,* 265–276.

Vinokur, A. D., & Schul, Y. (2000). Projection in person perception among spouses as a function of the similarity in their shared experiences. *Personality and Social Psychology Bulletin, 26,* 987–1001.

Vinokur, A., & Burnstein, E. (1974). Effects of partially shared persuasive arguments on group-induced shifts: A group problem-solving approach. *Journal of Personality and Social Psychology, 29,* 305–315.

Visser, P. S., Bizer, G. Y., & Krosnick, J. A. (2006). Exploring the latent structure of strength-related attitude attributes. *Advances in Experimental Social Psychology, 38,* 1–67.

Visser, P. S., Krosnick, J. A., & Simmons, J. P. (2003). Distinguishing the cognitive and behavioral consequences of attitude and certainty: A new approach to testing the common-factor hypothesis. *Journal of Experimental Social Psychology, 39,* 118–141.

Vogel, T., Kutzner, F., Fiedler, K., & Freytag, P. (2010). Exploiting attractiveness in persuasion: Senders' implicit theories about receivers' processing motivation. *Personality and Social Psychology Bulletin, 36,* 830–842.

Vohs, K. D., & Heatherton, T. F. (2000). Self-regulatory failure: A resource-depletion approach. *Psychological Science, 11,* 249–254.

Vohs, K. D., Baumeister, R. F., Schmeichel, B. J., Twenge, J. M., Nelson, N. M., & Tice, D. M. (2008). Making choices impairs subsequent self-control: A limited-resource account of decision making, self-regulation, and active initiative. *Journal of Personality and Social Psychology, 94,* 883–898.

Vonk, R. (1998). The slime effect: Suspicion and dislike of likeable behavior toward superiors. *Journal of Personality and Social Psychology, 74,* 849–864.

Vonk, R. (1999). Differential evaluations of likeable and dislikeable behaviours enacted towards superiors and subordinates. *European Journal of Social Psychology, 29,* 139–146.

Vonk, R. (2002). Self-serving interpretations of flattery: Why ingratiation works. *Journal of Personality and Social Psychology, 82,* 515–526.

Vonofakou, C., Hewstone, M., & Voci, A. (2007). Contact with out-group friends as a predictor of meta-attitudinal strength and accessibility of attitudes toward gay men. *Journal of Personality and Social Psychology, 92,* 804–820.

Vorauer, J. D. (2003). Dominant group members in intergroup interaction: Safety or vulnerability in numbers? *Personality and Social Psychology Bulletin, 29,* 498–511.

Vorauer, J. D., Hunter, A. J., Main, K. J., & Roy, S. A. (2000). Meta-stereotype activation: Evidence from indirect measures for specific evaluative concerns experienced by members of dominant groups in intergroup interaction. *Journal of Personality and Social Psychology, 78,* 690–707.

Vorauer, J.D. (2006). An information search model of evaluative concerns in intergroup interaction. *Psychological Review, 113,* 862–886.

Wadden, T. A., Brownell, K. D., & Foster, G. D. (2002). Obesity: Responding to the global epidemic. *Journal of Counseling and Clinical Psychology, 70,* 510–525.

Walker, I., & Smith, H. J. (Eds.). (2002). *Relative deprivation: Specification, development and integration.* Cambridge, UK: Cambridge University Press.

Walker, S., Richardson, D. S., & Green, L. R. (2000). Aggression among older adults: The relationship of interaction networks and gender role to direct and indirect responses. *Aggressive Behavior, 26,* 145–154.

Walster, E., & Festinger, L. (1962). The effectiveness of "overheard" persuasive communication. *Journal of Abnormal and Social Psychology, 65,* 395–402.

Walster, E., Walster, G. W., Piliavin, J., & Schmidt, L. (1973). "Playing hard-to-get": Understanding an elusive phenomenon. *Journal of Personality and Social Psychology, 26,* 113–121.

Wang, J., Novemsky, N., Dhar, R., & Baumeister, R. F. (2010). Trade-offs and depletion in choice. *Journal of Marketing Research, 47,* 910–919.

Wann, D. L., & Branscombe, N. R. (1993). Sports fans: Measuring degree of identification with their team. *International Journal of Sport Psychology, 24,* 1–17.

Waters, H. F., Block, D., Friday, C., & Gordon, J. (1993, July 12). Networks under the gun. *Newsweek,* 64–66.

Watts, B. L. (1982). Individual differences in circadian activity rhythms and their effects on roommate relationships. *Journal of Personality, 50,* 374–384.

Wayne, S. J., & Ferris, G. R. (1990). Influence tactics, and exchange quality in supervisor–subordinate interactions: A laboratory experiment and field study. *Journal of Applied Psychology, 75,* 487–499.

Wayne, S. J., & Liden, R. C. (1995). Effects of impression management on performance ratings: A longitudinal study. *Academy of Management Journal, 38,* 232–260.

Wayne, S. J., Liden, R. C., Graf, I. K., & Ferris, G. R. (1997). The role of upward influence tactics in human resource decisions. *Personnel Psychology, 50,* 979–1006.

Webb, T. L., & Sheeran, P. (2007). *How do implementation intentions promote goal attainment? A test of component processes. Journal of Experimental Social Psychology, 43,* 295-302.

Wegener, D. T., & Carlston, D. E. (2005). Cognitive processes in attitude formation and change. In D. Albarracin, B. T. Johnson, & M. P. Zanna (Eds.), *The handbook of attitudes* (pp. 493–542). Mahwah, NJ: Lawrence Erlbaum.

Wegener, D. T., Petty, R. E., Smoak, N. D., & Fabrigar, L. R. (2004). Multiple routes to resisting attitude change. In E. S. Knowles & J. A. Linn (Eds.), *Resistance and persuasion* (pp. 13–38). Mahwah, NJ: Erlbaum.

Wegner, D. T., & Petty, R. E. (1994). Mood management across affective states: The hedonic contingency hypothesis. *Journal of Personality and Social Psychology, 66,* 1034–1048.

Weick, M., & Guinote, A. (2010). How long will it take?: Power biases time predictions. *Journal of Experimental Social Psychology, 46,* 595–604.

Weiner, B. (1980). A cognitive (attribution) emotion–action model of motivated behavior: An analysis of judgments of help-giving. *Journal of Personality and Social Psychology, 39,* 186–200.

Weiner, B. (1985). An attributional theory of achievement motivation and emotion. *Psychological Review, 92,* 548–573.

Weiner, B. (1993). On sin versus sickness: A theory of perceived responsibility and social motivation. *American Psychologist, 48,* 957–965.

Weiner, B. (1995). *Judgments of responsibility: A foundation for a theory of social conduct.* New York: Guilford.

Weiner, B., Osborne, D., & Rudolph, U. (2011). An attributional analysis of reactions to poverty: The political ideology of the giver and the perceived morality of the receiver. *Personaltiy and Social Psychology Review, 1,* 199–213.

Weinstein, N., & Ryan, R. M. (2010). When helping help: Autonomous motivation for prosocial behavior and its influence on well-being for the helper and recipient. *Journal of Personality and Social Psychology, 98,* 222–244.

Weiss, A., Bates, T. C., & Luciano, M. (2008). Happiness is a personal(ity) thing: The genetic of personality and well-being in a representative sample. *Psychological Science, 19,* 205–210.

Weldon, E., & Mustari, L. (1988). Felt dispensability in groups of coactors: The effects of shared responsibility and explicit anonymity on cognitive effort. *Organizational Behavior and Human Decision Processes, 41,* 330–351.

Wheeler, L., & Kim, Y. (1997). What is beautiful is culturally good: The physical attractiveness stereotype has different content in collectivistic cultures. *Personality and Social Psychology Bulletin, 23,* 795–800.

Wheeler, S. C., Brinol, P., & Hermann, A. D. (2007). Resistance to persuasion as self-regulation: Ego-depletion and its effects on attitude change processes. *Journal of Experimental Social Psychology, 43,* 150–156.

Whiffen, V. E., Aube, J. A., Thompson, J. M., & Campbell, T. L. (2000). Attachment beliefs and interpersonal contexts associated with dependency and self-criticism. *Journal of Social and Clinical Psychology, 19,* 184–205.

Wiederman, M. W., & Allgeier, E. R. (1996). Expectations and attributions regarding extramarital sex among young married individuals. *Journal of Psychology & Human Sexuality, 8,* 21–35.

Wilkins, A. C. (2008). "Happier than non-Christians": Collective emotions and symbolic boundaries among Evangelical Christians. *Social Psychology Quarterly, 71,* 281–301.

Williams, J. E., & Best, D. L. (1990). *Sex and psyche: Gender and self viewed cross-culturally.* Newbury Park, CA: Sage.

Williams, K. B., Radefeld, P. A., Binning, J. F., & Suadk, J. R. (1993). When job candidates are "hard-" versus "easy-to-get": Effects of candidate availability on employment decisions. *Journal of Applied Social Psychology, 23,* 169–198.

Williams, K. D. (2001). *Ostracism: The power of silence.* New York: Guilford Press.

Williams, K. D., & Karau, S. J. (1991). Social loafing and social compensation: The effects of expectations of co-worker performance. *Journal of Personality and Social Psychology, 61,* 570–581.

Williams, K. D., Harkins, S., & Latané, B. (1981). Identifiability as a deterrent to social loafing: Two cheering experiments. *Journal of Personality and Social Psychology, 40,* 303–311.

Williams, M. J., Paluck, E. L., & Spencer-Rodgers, J. (2010). The masculinity of money: Automatic stereotypes predict gender differences in estimated salaries. *Psychology of Women Quarterly, 34,* 7–20.

Willingham, D. T., & Dunn, E. W. (2003). What neuroimaging and brain localization can do, cannot, and should not do for social psychology. *Journal of Personality and Social Psychology, 85,* 662–671.

Willis, J., & Todorov, A. (2006). First impression: Making up your mind after a 100-ms. exposure to a face. *Psychological Science, 17,* 592–598.

Wilson, A. E., & Ross, M. (2001). From chump to champ: People's appraisals of their earlier and present selves. *Journal of Personality and Social Psychology, 80,* 572-584.

Wilson, D. W. (1981). Is helping a laughing matter? *Psychology, 18,* 6–9.

Wilson, J. P., & Petruska, R. (1984). Motivation, model attributes, and prosocial behavior. *Journal of Personality and Social Psychology, 46,* 458–468.

Wilson, T. D., & Kraft, D. (1993). Why do I love thee?: Effects of repeated introspections about a dating relationship on attitudes toward the relationship. *Personality and Social Psychology Bulletin, 19,* 409–418.

Wilson, T. D., & Dunn, E. W. (2004). Self-knowledge: Its limits, value, and potential for improvement. *Annual Review of Psychology, 55,* 493–518.

Winograd, E., Goldstein, F. C., Monarch, E. S., Peluso, J. P., & Goldman, W. P. (1999). The mere exposure effect in patients with Alzheimer's disease. *Neuropsychology, 13,* 41–46.

Wisman, A., & Koole, S. L. (2003). Hiding in the crowd: Can mortality salience promote affiliation with others who oppose one's world view? *Journal of Personality and Social Psychology, 84,* 511–526.

Witt, L. A., & Ferris, G. B. (2003). Social skill as moderator of the conscientiousness-performance relationship: Convergent results across four studies. *Journal of Applied Psychology, 88,* 808–820.

Wohl, M. J. A., & Branscombe, N. R. (2005). Forgiveness and collective guilt assignment to historical perpetrator groups depend on level of social category inclusiveness. *Journal of Personality and Social Psychology, 88,* 288–303.

Wohl, M. J. A., Branscombe, N. R., & Reysen, S. (2010). Perceiving your group's future to be in jeopardy: Extinction threat induces collective angst and the desire to strengthen the ingroup. *Personality and Social Psychology Bulletin, 36,* 898–910.

Wohl, M. J. A., Giguère, B., Branscombe, N. R., & McVicar, D. N. (2011). One day we might be no more: Collective angst and protective action from potential distinctiveness loss. *European Journal of Social Psychology, 41,* 289–300.

Wolf, S. (2010). Counterfactual thinking in the jury room. *Small Group Research, 41,* 474–494.

Wood, G. S. (2004, April 12 & 19). Pursuits of happiness. *The New Republic,* 38–42.

Wood, J. V. (1989). Theory and research concerning social comparisons of personal attributes. *Psychological Bulletin, 106,* 231–248.

Wood, J. V., & Wilson, A. E. (2003). How important is social comparison? In M. R. Leary & J. P. Tangney (Eds.), *Handbook of self and identity* (pp. 344–366). New York: Guilford Press.

Wood, J. V., Perunovic, W. Q. E., & Lee, J. W. (2009). Positive self-statements: Power for some, peril for others. *Psychological Science, 20,* 860–866.

Wood, W., & Quinn, J. M. (2003). Forewarned and forearmed? Two meta-analytic syntheses of forewarning of influence appeals. *Psychological Bulletin, 129,* 119–138.

Wood, W., Quinn, J. M., & Kashy, D. A. (2002). Habits in everyday life: Thought, emotion, and action. *Journal of Personality and Social Psychology, 83,* 1281–1297.

Wright, S. C. (2001). Strategic collective action: Social psychology and social change. In R. Brown & S. Gaertner (Eds.), *Blackwell handbook of social psychology: Intergroup processes* (pp. 409–430). Oxford: Blackwell.

Wright, S. C., Aron, A., McLaughlin-Volpe, T., & Ropp, S. A. (1997). The extended contact effect: Knowledge of cross-group friendships and prejudice. *Journal of Personality and Social Psychology, 73,* 73–90.

Wright, S. C., Taylor, D. M., & Moghaddam, F. M. (1990). Responding to membership in a disadvantaged group: From acceptance to collective protest. *Journal of Personality and Social Psychology, 58,* 994–1003.

Wuensch, K. L., Castellow, W. A., & Moore, C. H. (1991). Effects of defendant attractiveness and type of crime on juridic judgment. *Journal of Social Behavior and Personality, 6,* 713–724.

Wyer, R. S., Jr., & Srull, T. K. (Eds.). (1994). *Handbook of social cognition* (2nd ed., Vol. 1). Hillsdale, NJ: Erlbaum.

Xu, J., & Robert, R. E. (2010). The power of positive emotions: It's a matter of life or death—subjective well-being and longevity over 28 years in a general population. *Health Psychology, 29,* 9–19.

Yoder, J. D., & Berendsen, L. L. (2001). "Outsider within" the firehouse: African American and white women firefighters. *Psychology of Women Quarterly, 25,* 27–36.

Yukl, G. A. (1998). *Leadership in organizations* (4th ed.). Englewood Cliffs, NJ: Prentice-Hall.

Yukl, G. A. (2006). *Leadership in organizations* (6th ed.). Upper Saddle River, NJ: Prentice-Hall.

Yukl, G., & Falbe, C. M. (1991). Importance of different power sources in downward and lateral relations. *Journal of Applied Psychology, 76,* 416–423.

Yzerbyt, V. Y., & Demoulin, S. (2010). Intergroup relations. In S. T. Fiske, D. T. Gilbert, & G. Lindzey (Eds.), *Handbook of social psychology* (5th ed., Vol. 2, pp. 1023–1083). Hoboken, NJ: Wiley.

Yzerbyt, V. Y., Corneille, O., & Estrada, C. (2001). The interplay of subjective essentialism and entitativity in the formation of stereotypes. *Personality and Social Psychology Review, 5,* 141–155.

Yzerbyt, V., Rocher, S., & Schradron, G. (1997). Stereotypes as explanations: A subjective essentialist view of group perception. In R. Spears, P. J. Oakes, N. Ellemers, & S. A. Haslam (Eds.), *The social psychology of stereotyping and group life* (pp. 20–50). Oxford: Blackwell.

Zaccaro, S. J. (2007). Trait-based perspective on leadership. *American Psychologist, 62,* 6–16.

Zadro, L., Boland, C., & Richardson, R. (2006). How long does it last? The persistence of the effects of ostracism in the socially anxious. *Journal of Experimental Social Psychology, 42,* 692–697.

Zajonc, R. B. (1965). Social facilitation. *Science, 149,* 269–274.

Zajonc, R. B. (2001). Mere exposure: A gateway to the subliminal. *Current Directions in Psychological Science, 10,* 224–228.

Zajonc, R. B., Heingartner, A., & Herman, E. M. (1969). Social enhancement and impairment of performance in the cockroach. *Journal of Personality and Social Psychology, 13,* 83–92.

Zaslow, J. (2010, May 5). Surviving the age of humiliation. *Wall Street Journal,* pp. D1, D3.

Zebrowitz, L. A., Collins, M. A., & Dutta, R. (1998). The relationship between appearance and personality across the life span. *Personality and Social Psychology Bulletin, 24,* 736–749.

Zebrowitz, L. A., Kikuchi, M., & Fellous, J. M. (2007). Are effects of emotion expression on trait Impressions mediated by babyfaceness?: Evidence from connectionist modeling. *Personality and Social Psychology Bulletin, 33,* 648–662.

Zebrowitz, L. A., Kikuchi, M., & Fellous, J. M.. (in press). Facial resemblance toe: Group differences, impression effects, and race stereotypes. *Journal of Personality and Social Psychology.*

Zhang, F., & Parmely, M. (2011). What youre best friend sees that I don't see: Comparing female close friends and casual acquaintances on the perception of emotional facial expressions of varying intensities. *Personality and Social Psychology Bulletin, 37,* 38–39.

Zhang, S., Schmader, T., & Forbes, C. (2009). The effects of gender stereotypes on women's career choice: Opening the glass door. In M. Barreto, M. K. Ryan, & M. T. Schmitt (Eds.), *The glass ceiling in the 21st century* (pp. 125–150). Washington, DC: American Psychological Association.

Zhong, C-B., Bohns, V. K., & Gino, F. (2010). Good lamps are the best police: Darkness increase dishonesty and self-interested behavior. *Psychological Science, 21,* 311–314.

Zhu, F., & Zhang, X. (2010). Impact of online consumer reviews on sales: The moderating role of product and consumer characteristics. *Journal of Marketing, 74,* 133–148.

Zillmann, D. (1979). *Hostility and aggression.* Hillsdale, NJ: Erlbaum.

Zillmann, D. (1983). Transfer of excitation in emotional behavior. In J. T. Cacioppo & R. E. Petty (Eds.), *Social psychophysiology: A sourcebook* (pp. 215–240). New York: Guilford Press.

Zillmann, D. (1988). Cognition–excitation interdependencies in aggressive behavior. *Aggressive Behavior, 14,* 51–64.

Zillmann, D. (1994). Cognition–excitation interdependencies in the escalation of anger and angry aggression. In M. Potegal & J. F. Knutson (Eds.), *The dynamics of aggression.* Hillsdale, NJ: Erlbaum.

Zillmann, D., Baron, R. A., & Tamborini, R. (1981). The social costs of smoking: Effects of tobacco smoke on hostile behavior. *Journal of Applied Social Psychology, 11,* 548–561.

Zimbardo, P. G. (2007). *The Lucifer effect: How good people turn evil.* New York: Random House.

Zimbardo, P.G. (1970). The human choice: Individuation, reason, and order versus deindividuation, impulse, and chaos. In W.J. Arnold & D. Levine (Eds.), *Nebraska Symposium on Motivation* (Vol. 17, pp. 237–307). Lincoln, NE: University of Nebraska Press.

Zuckerman, M., & O'Loughlin, R. E. (2006). Self-enhancement by social comparison: A prospective analysis. *Personality and Social Psychology Bulletin, 32,* 751–760.

Zywica, J., & Danowski, J. (2005). The *faces of facebookers:* Investigating social enhancement and social compensation hypotheses; predicting Facebook and offline popularity from sociability and self-esteem, and mapping the meanings of popularity with semantic networks. *Journal of Computer-Mediated Communication, 14,* 1–34.

Photo **Credits**

CHAPTER 1

Pages 2, 3: Fancy/Alamy; 4: Pixar Animation Studios/Walt Disney Pictures/Newscom; 6 (top left): Viki2win/Dreamstime; 6 (top center): Sergey Mironov/Shutterstock; 8 (bottom left): AF archive/Alamy; 8 (bottom center): Bonnie Kamin/PhotoEdit; 11 (top right): Fancy/Alamy; 11 (bottom center): Exactostock/SuperStock; 11 (bottom right): EPA/Raminder Pal Singh/Landov; 14: Uniquely India/Age Fotostock; 18: Photofusion Picture Library/Alamy; 21: Bill Aron/PhotoEdit; 24: David Young-Wolff/PhotoEdit; 30: Marty Heitner/The Image Works.

CHAPTER 2

Pages 34, 35: Aurora Photos/Alamy; 36: Monika Graff/UPI/Landov; 37: Adam Zyglis/Cagle Cartoons; 39: Pascal Parrot/Sygma/Corbis; 44 (top left): Aurora Photos/Alamy; 44 (center left): Ghislain & Marie David de Lossy/cultura/Corbis; 54: Jerry King; 55: Corbis Bridge/Alamy; 58: Dave King/DK Images; 62 (bottom left): U.S. Army/AP Images; 62 (bottom right): U.S. Army, Pvt. Terri Rorke/AP Images; 64 (top center): Andresr/Shutterstock; 64 (top right): Ersler Dmitry/Shutterstock.

CHAPTER 3

Pages 68, 69: Vitelle/Shutterstock; 70: Richard Cline/The New Yorker Collection/Cartoonbank; 71: Courtesy of Robert A. Baron; 74: Photo's courtesy of Robert A. Baron; 77: Felicia Martinez/PhotoEdit; 80 (top left): Xinhua News Agency/eyevine/Redux; 80 (top right): Valdrin Xhemaj/epa/Corbis; 88 (top left): soleilc1/Fotolia; 88 (top right): Amy Walters/Fotolia; 91: Vitelle/Shutterstock; 97 (center right): Stewart Cohen/Index Stock Imagery/PhotoLibrary; 97 (bottom right): Glow Images SuperStock; 99 (center left): Poznyakov/Shutterstock; 99 (center right): Michael Mahovlich/Masterfile.

CHAPTER 4

Pages 102, 103: Aaron Paden/KU University Relations; 104: Cardow/The Ottawa Citizen; 105: Cartoon by Peter Steiner/Cartoonbank; 110: Edward Koren/The New Yorker Collection/Cartoonbank; 111: David Young-Wolff/PhotoEdit; 119: Ocean/Corbis; 120: Aaron Paden/KU University Relations; 123 (top left): Sychugina/Shutterstock; 123 (top right): George Doyle/Stockbyte/Thinkstock; 124: Bonnie Kamin/PhotoEdit; 126: Peter Glass/Alamy; 132: Mark Lennihan/AP Images.

CHAPTER 5

Pages 138, 139: DenisNata/Shutterstock; 140: Brooks Kraft/Corbis; 141: Joe Heller/Cagle Cartoons; 142: Jeff Greenberg/Alamy; 143 (center): Allstar Picture Library/Alamy; 143 (top right): Ian Langsdon/epa/Corbis; 145 (top right): Mark Peterson/Redux; 145 (bottom right): Advertising Archives; 147: Tom Cheney/The New Yorker Collection/Cartoonbank; 154 (bottom left): DenisNata/Shutterstock; 154 (bottom right): Haveseen/Shutterstock; 157: Chris Ryan/Alamy; 158 (bottom left): Susan Van Etten/PhotoEdit; 158 (bottom right): Susan Van Ette/PhotoEdit; 159 (center): Advertising Archives; 159 (center right): Advertising Archives; 160 (center left): Shaun Best/Reuters/Landov; 160 (bottom left): Anja Niedringhaus/AP Images; 163: Fancy/Alamy; 164: David J. Green/Alamy; 172: Susan Van Etten/PhotoEdit.

CHAPTER 6

Pages 176, 177: Bob Daemmrich/The Image Works; 178 (bottom left): Karimala/Dreamstime; 178 (bottom right): Fabiano/SIPA/Newscom; 180 (bottom left): Michael J. Doolittle/The Image Works; 180 (bottom right): Jean-Yves Rabeuf/The Image Works; 185: Warren Miller/The New Yorker Collection/Cartoonbank; 187 (center left): Andreas Meyer/Shutterstock; 187 (center right): United States Senate; 189 (top left): Christophe Karaba/epa/Corbis; 189 (top center): Harry E. Walker/MCT/Landov; 191 (top left): Image Source/Alamy; 191 (top center): Rebecca Cook/Reuters/Landov; 193: Photo's courtesy of Nyla R. Branscombe; 193 (bottom right): Corbis/SuperStock; 199 (bottom left): Nir Alon/Alamy; 199 (bottom right): Kord/Age Fotostock/Robert Harding; 200 (bottom left): akg-images/Newscom; 200 (bottom center): akg-images/Newscom; 206 (top left): Bob Daemmrich/The Image Works; 211: Reprinted from *Journal of Experimental Social Psychology*, vol. 46, no. 1, Tracie L. Stewart, Ioana M. Latu, Kerry Kawakami, and Ashley C. Myers, "Consider the situation: Reducing automatic sterotyping through Situational Attribution Training," pages 221–225, Copyright 2010, with permission from Elsevier.

CHAPTER 7

Pages 214, 215: Jeff Greenberg/PhotoEdit; 217 (top left): Jeff Greenberg/PhotoEdit; 217 (top right): zimmytws/Shutterstock; 218: Lonely Planet/SuperStock; 220 (bottom left): Pete Souza/Rapport Press/Newscom; 220 (bottom right): The Granger Collection; 224: Miramax Films/Courtesy Everett Collection; 225 (bottom left): Armando Gallo/Retna Ltd./Corbis; 225 (bottom center): World Entertainment News Network/Newscom; 226: Courtesy of Dr. Judith H. Langlois, Charles and Sarah Seay Regents Professor, Department of Psychology, University of Texas, Austin; 227 (top center): SuperStock/SuperStock; 227 (top right): Image Source/Alamy; 229 (bottom left): RD/Kirkland/Retna Digital/Retna Ltd./Corbis; 229 (bottom center): Stephen Flint/Alamy; 235: Tom Cheney/The New Yorker Collection/Cartoonbank; 238: Courtesy of Robert A. Baron; 239 (top left): Fancy Collection/SuperStock; 239 (top right): Kevin Dodge/Corbis; 241: Mary Evans/Ronald Grant/Everett Collection; 248: Eddie Mejia/Splash/Newscom.

CHAPTER 8

Pages 252, 253: Spencer Grant/Art Directors & TRIP/Alamy; 254 (top right): Stan Fellerman/Alamy; 254 (center right): Ralf-Finn Hestoft/Corbis; 254 (bottom right): NetPhotos/Alamy; 256: Insadco/Age Fotostock; 260 (bottom left): Spencer Grant/Art Directors & TRIP/Alamy; 260 (bottom right): Andrew Hetherington/Redux; 262 (top left): Don Mason/Blend Images/Age Fotostock; 262 (top right): Andrey Armyagov/Shutterstock; 266: Bill Clark/Roll Call Photos/Newscom; 268 (bottom left): Michael Newman/PhotoEdit; 268 (bottom right): Image Source/Alamy; 270 (top left): Spencer Grant/PhotoEdit; 270 (top right): Hill Street Studios/Blend Images/Corbis; 272: Ints Kalnins/Reuters/Landov; 273: Peter C. Vey/The New Yorker Collection/Cartoonbank; 278: NetPhotos/Alamy; 282: Courtesy Alexandra Milgram.

CHAPTER 9

Pages 288, 289: Con Tanasiuk/PhotoLibrary; 290 (bottom left): Con Tanasiuk/PhotoLibrary; 290 (bottom right): LWA-Sharie Kennedy/Corbis; 294: Sue Ogrocki/AP Images; 298 (top left): Tony Dejak/AP Images; 298 (center left): KRT/Newscom; 298 (bottom left): Images-USA/Alamy; 300: Edgar Romero/AP Images; 303 (bottom left): T.M.O. Pictures/Alamy; 303 (bottom right): Chris Smith/PhotoEdit; 305 (bottom right): Datacraft Co. Ltd./PhotoLibrary; 308: Norbert Schaefer/Corbis; 309: Katarina Stoltz/Reuters/Corbis; 311: Toronto Star/Age Fotostock; 312: Leo Cullum/The New Yorker Collection/Cartoonbank; 313: Abby Gray; 314: Mike Twohy/The New Yorker Collection/Cartoonbank.

CHAPTER 10

Pages 320, 321: Ace Stock Limited/Alamy; 322: AF archive/Alamy; 324: Bob Daemmrich/Alamy; 327: Mike Fiala/AFP/Newscom; 332: Martin Novak/Shutterstock; 333 (top right): Everett Collection; 333 (bottom left): Courtesy Albert Bandura; 334: Tony Freeman/PhotoEdit; 340: Frank Muckenheim/Westend61 GmbH/Alamy; 340: F1 Online/SuperStock; 343: akg-images/Newscom; 345: Sarah Hadley/Alamy; 348 (bottom left): Ace Stock Limited/Alamy; 348 (bottom right): Radius/SuperStock; 351: Laura Ashley/Alamy; 354: age fotostock/SuperStock.

CHAPTER 11

Pages 358, 359: GlowImages/Alamy; 360 (top left): 2009 Marilyn Humphries/Newscom; 360 (top right): Gerald Herbert/AP Images; 361 (bottom left): GlowImages/Alamy; 361 (bottom right): Moodboard/Alamy; 362 (bottom left): Exactostock/SuperStock; 362 (bottom right): Michael Weber/imagebroker/Alamy; 366 (bottom left): Matthias Schrader/dpa/Landov; 366 (bottom right): Jessica Rinaldi/Reuters/Landov; 368: Peter Steiner/The New Yorker Collection/Cartoonbank; 371: Lee Foster/Alamy; 372: Matthew Polak/Sygma/Corbis; 374: Courtesy of Zach Rothschild; 376: Vladimir Wrangel/Used under license from Shutterstock; 378 (bottom left): Jack Guez/AFP/Getty Images/Newscom; 378 (bottom right): o44/ZUMA Press/Newscom; 380 (center left): Edward Bock/Corbis Flirt/Alamy; 380 (center right): Digital Vision/Thinkstock; 393: Charles Dharapak/AP Images.

CHAPTER 12

Pages 396, 397: Corbis Flirt/Alamy; 399: Corbis Cusp/Alamy; 402 (top left): DPA/The Image Works; 402 (center left): Bill Bachmann/Alamy; 407: Thinkstock/Comstock/Jupiter Images; 408: Photos.com/Jupiterimages; 411 (top left): Eric Nathan/Alamy; 411 (top right): Corbis Flirt/Alamy; 411 (bottom right): Mike Segar/Reuters /Landov; 412: David Young-Wolff/PhotoEdit; 415: Courtesy of Robert A. Baron; 416: Maxx images/SuperStock; 418 (top left): Jonathan Alcorn/ZUMA Press/Newscom; 418 (bottom left): Detroit news/SIPA/Newscom; 421 (bottom left): Corbis Flirt/Alamy; 421 (bottom right): Vojtch Vlk/Allphoto/Age Fotostock; 424 (top left): Max Earey/Shutterstock; 424 (center left): Morgan David de Lossy/Corbis; 424: Blend Images/SuperStock.

Name **Index**

Subject **Index**